Land and Tax Planning

Patrick C Soares, LLB, LLM, FTII
Barrister

Longman

ISBN 085121 4541

Published by

Longman Professional and Business Communications Division
Longman Group UK Limited
21–27 Lamb's Conduit Street, London WC1N 3NJ
Tel: 01–242–2548

Associated Offices

Australia Longman Cheshire Pty Ltd, Longman House, Kings Gardens, 91–97 Coventry Street, South Melbourne, Victoria 3205

Hong Kong Longman Group (Far East) Limited
Cornwall House, 18th Floor, Taikoo Trading Estate,
Tong Chong Street, Quarry Bay

Malaysia Longman Malaysia Sdn Bhd
No 3 Jalan Kilang A, Off Jalan Penchala
Petaling Jaya, Selangor, Malaysia

Singapore Longman Singapore Publishers (Pte) Ltd
25 First Lok Yang Road, Singapore 2262

USA Longman Group (USA) Inc
500 North Dearborn Street, Chicago, Illinois 60610

A CIP catalogue record for this book is available from the British Library.

Printed and bound in Great Britain by
Biddles Ltd, Guildford and King's Lynn

PREFACE

There are a large number of taxes which apply to land and I have attempted to deal here with all of the relevant taxes.

In examining complex land transactions it is necessary to be able to tick off the taxes which do not apply and concentrate on those which do.

I hope that this book will give an overall picture with regard to the taxes which apply to land so that when the adviser is analysing a particular tax in detail he can see it in its overall context. I have tried to concentrate on those areas which have importance in practice and I have dealt with the tax planning aspects of transactions. Needless to say, tax advisers must always refer to original sources — legislation, statutory instruments, case law and Revenue statements, booklets, concessions and practice notes.

Advisers must always be familiar with the actual wording of the legislation. To summarise the same can be dangerous: the legislation must be taken 'head-on'.

Behind every chapter in the book there is virtually an encyclopaedia, each the length of this book, dealing with the particular taxes. These books must also be referred to.

There are also several Revenue booklets dealing with a large number of the taxes covered in the book and some of these are very well and clearly written.

In practice there is an increasing tendency to obtain the views of the Inland Revenue or the Customs and Excise, as appropriate, on particular points and act according to those views in order to avoid any future dispute, even though the particular body may not be taking an approach which appears to be strictly in line with the legislation.

It must be emphasised that many areas of this book represent my view of the law and these may be contrary to views held by others, including the Revenue.

The law is stated as at 1 October 1988.

Patrick C Soares

October 1988

CONTENTS

TABLE OF STATUTES

TABLE OF STATUTORY INSTRUMENTS

Double Taxation Relief (Taxes on Income) (Guernsey) Order 1952 (SI No 1215)—
  art 3(2) 11.2.2
Double Taxation Relief (Taxes on Income) (Jersey) Order 1952 (SI No 1216) 26.7.1
VAT (Do-it-Yourself Builders) (Relief) Regulations 1975 (SI No 649) 15.4.6
Income Tax (Sub-Contractors in the Construction Industry) Regulations 1975 (SI No 1960) 14.1
Income Tax (Sub-Contractors in the Construction Industry) Regulations 1980 (SI No 1135) 14.1
Town and Country Planning General Development (Amendment) Order 1981 (SI No 245) 8.6.5
Income Tax (Sub-Contractors in the Construction Industry) Regulations 1985 (SI No 351) ... 14.1
VAT General Regulations 1985 (SI No 886) 12.10, 12.33
  reg 26 .... 12.7.1
  reg 30(1)(*a*) 12.6.2
    (*b*) 12.6.2, 12.35
    (*c*) 12.6.2
    (*d*) 12.6.3
  reg 34 .... 12.6.5
    (1)(*b*) 12.35
  reg 35 .... 12.6.5
Stamp Duty (Exempt Instrument) Regulations 1985 (SI No 1688) 13.21.1, 13.26.3
Stamp Duty (Exempt Instrument) Regulations 1987 (SI No 516) .. 13.38
Town and Country Planning (Use Classes) Order 1987 (SI 1987 No 764) ... 8.6.5
VAT (General) Amendment (No 2) Regulations 1987 (SI No 510) 13.6.1
Inland Revenue 'Benefits in kind: living accommodation' 18 August 1988 (1988 SI No 670) 15.9.1

TABLE OF CASES

1 LAND LAW AND TAXATION

This chapter looks at those land law and conveyancing principles which are essential to an understanding of the taxation rules which apply to land and which the practitioner will come across most often in practice when dealing with land tax situations. It deals mainly with English and Welsh land law, but there are references to Scottish land law. The chapter also deals briefly with the various tax entities which may be involved in land transactions and with the approach of the Courts to land transactions which are carried out to avoid or minimise tax.

1.1 THE BASIC APPROACH

Any analysis of a land tax problem involves the following features:

Facts and general legal position
Land transactions can take many forms and can sometimes be very complicated. The facts must be clearly established. In many cases one must distinguish between facts which can be evidenced and proved and those which may be difficult to prove, especially in the case of land trading transactions. A correct analysis in land law terms must be made of the relevant documents and transactions. Is a so called licence in reality a lease? Have equitable interests been created? Has there been a delivery in escrow? Is a sale coupled with an option really a mortgage?

Tax status of entity
The general tax status of the client should be ascertained. Is the client a pension fund, a charity, an investment company or a dealing company? Different tax rules may apply to different entities.

Particular tax position of entity
The particular tax position of the client should be ascertained. Is group relief available under TA 1988, 402? Are losses available from earlier years against profits from the same trade? Is it relevant to carry out a transaction within a particular accounting period of a company?

Application of relevant taxes
Once the above have been ascertained, it is necessary to apply the relevant

taxes to the particular transaction and there are a considerable number of taxes to consider.

Interaction of taxes
It is important to ensure that the various taxes properly interact so that there is no double charge to tax.

1.2 PRINCIPLES OF LAND LAW AND CONVEYANCING

One generally thinks of 'land' as a plot of visible soil and the earth beneath it. In law it would include corporeal hereditaments and incorporeal hereditaments. Corporeal hereditaments are physical objects such as land, buildings and fixtures. Incorporeal hereditaments are rights over land, eg, a private right of way. 'Hereditament' refers to property which went to the heir on intestacy under the rules operating before 1926, ie, it refers basically to real property, such as land, rather than personal property, such as chattels.

1.2.1 Legal and equitable rights

There is a fundamental distinction in land law between legal and equitable interests in land. The broad distinction is that legal rights are good against all the world whilst equitable rights are good against all persons except the bona fide purchaser of a legal estate for value without notice of the equitable rights.

Example 1A Legal and equitable rights

If X has the freehold he will have a legal estate in the land. If he contracts to sell it to Y, then Y will have an equitable interest in the Land. X will have the legal estate until he completes the contract when he will by deed of conveyance or transfer vest the legal estate in Y. If, before he completed the sale to Y, X sold the legal estate in the land (ie, by deed of conveyance or transfer) to a bona fide purchaser for value (Z) who had no notice of Y's interest, Z would have the legal estate and equitable interest and Y's only remedy would be to sue X for breach of contract. In order to give the whole world notice of his equitable interest, however, Y may have registered his contract as a Class C estate contract under the Land Charges Act 1925, in which case Z will be deemed to have had notice of his equitable interest and Z would take subject to it.

Only two kinds of legal estates can exist: these are the fee simple absolute in possession (the freehold) and a term of years absolute (leasehold): LPA 1925, s 1(1). Certain interests in land such as easements (eg, rights of way) can exist as legal interests: LPA 1925, s 1(2). All other interests in land are equitable: LPA 1925, s 1(3).

1.2.2 Freehold

The most ample estate which can exist in land is the freehold. It is, effectively, absolute ownership of the land. The freehold is in fact a type of feudal tenure with the Sovereign remaining the lord paramount of all the land within the realm (*A-G of Ontario* v *Mercer* [1883], 8 AC 767 at 772). The title 'tenant in fee simple' is still technically the correct title for the freeholder. For practical purposes, however, the freeholder is the absolute owner of the land.

1.2.3 Leasehold

Nature of a lease

A leasehold is an estate or interest in land for a fixed period, usually granted in consideration of a payment of rent. It is also called a 'term of years'. There are also tenancies which are not granted for fixed periods but they are nevertheless part of the subject of leases. In the Law of Property Act 1925, 'lease' includes any tenancy (ss 154, 205(1)(xxiii)). This may be of relevance with regard to VAT where a 'major interest' is defined to include a tenancy for a term certain exceeding 21 years (VATA 1983, s 48(1)).

It should be noted that a lease expressed to commence at a date prior to the instrument is a lease starting only on the date of the instrument. The lease cannot be backdated (*Shaw* v *Kay* (1847) 1 Ex 412; *Cadogan (Earl)* v *Guinness* [1936] 1 Ch 515; *Colton* v *Becouda Property Investments Ltd* [1950] 1 KB 216; and *Brikom Investments Ltd* v *Seaford* [1981] 1 WLR 863).

A leasehold is an estate in land, that is, a proprietary interest which will bind not only the grantor of the leasehold interest but also the rest of the world. This position is contrasted with that of a mere licensee who has contractual personal rights but no proprietary interest in the land. The distinction between the two is often critical. Where exclusive possession of the land is given this is likely to indicate the existence of a lease rather than a licence (see *Taylor* v *Caldwell* (1863) 3 B & S 826; see also *Somma* v *Hazlehurst* [1978] 2 All ER 1011, *O'Malley* v *Seymour* (1979) 250 EG 1083 and *Street* v *Mountford* [1985] 2 All ER 289).

The difference between a lease and a licence can be very important for the purposes of lease and tack duty which only applies to leases (Stamp Act 1891, Sched 1) and agreements for a lease (Stamp Act 1891, s 75 as amended by FA 1984, s 111.)

Types of lease

Leases may be of varying types–they may be for a fixed term, eg, X grants Y a lease of 21 years, or they may be periodic tenancies, eg, from week to week or month to month, until determined by a proper notice.

A lease may be granted for the life of a person. By LPA 1925, s 149(6), however, a lease at a rent or fine for life or lives or for any term of years determinable with life or lives or on the marriage of the lessee is converted into a term of 90 years. On the death or marriage of the original lessee either party may determine the lease by serving on the other at least one month's written notice to expire on one of the quarter days applicable to the tenancy or, if no special quarter days are applicable, one of the usual quarter days (the usual quarter days are Lady Day (25 March) Midsummer Day (24 June), Michaelmas (29 September) and Christmas (25 December).

The length of the term of a lease and in some cases the likely length of the term of a lease can be very important for the purposes of virtually all the taxes and duties which apply to land (see 2 PLB 46 and Chapter 24 hereof).

Statutory provisions
The following are statutory provisions in connection with leases which should be borne in mind

(*a*) *Rent Act 1977 and Housing Act 1980*
These Acts (as amended) control rent and provide security of tenure for residential tenants.

(*b*) *Landlord & Tenant Act 1954, Pt 11*
This Act (as amended) broadly, provides security of tenure for premises wholly or partly used for business purposes.

On the termination of a tenancy the tenant can ask the Court for a new tenancy not exceeding 14 years (s 33).

A new lease granted under the Act has been held not to amount to a continuation of the original lease for the purposes of time apportioning a capital gain for capital gains tax purposes (*Bayley* v *Rogers* [1980] STC 544).

(*c*) *Agricultural Holdings Act 1986*
This act provides security of tenure for agricultural tenants and regulates the rent and other aspects of any agricultural tenancy.

A tenant who quits the holding in consequence of a notice to quit given by the landlord is entitled to compensation for disturbance.

It was held in *Davis* v *Powell* [1977] STC 32 that the compensation payable under AHA 1948 s 34(1) (the predecessor of the 1986 Act) did not derive from a chargeable asset for CGT purposes—it derived from a statutory provision. It was therefore not chargeable to capital gains tax.

(*d*) *The Leasehold Reform Act 1967*
This Act (as amended) is basically designed to enable tenants of long leases (leases originally granted for more than 21 years) at low rents (ie, an annual rental of less than two-thirds of the rateable value) to buy the freehold from the landlord or demand that the lease be extended for a further period of 50 years from the date of its expiry. This is known as enfranchisement.

1.2.4 Fixtures

The general rule is that whatever is attached to the soil becomes part of it. Thus, if a building is erected on a site, the building and all objects permanently attached to it become land. They become the property of the landowner unless there is a contrary intention.

The law does not provide a single and wholly comprehensive definition of 'fixtures' whether for tax or land law purposes.

If a chattel is fixed to land or a building merely to facilitate its use or enjoyment then it is doubtful whether it is a fixture. On the other hand, if the real reason for fixing the chattel to the land or building is for the permanent or substantial improvement of the land or building then the asset is likely to be a fixture. Thus, in the case of an industrial building, the building is a fixture together with the central heating, lighting and ventilation equipment installed to improve the use of the building. Operating plant and machinery used for the purposes of the particular trade in the building such as manufacturing machinery may not amount to fixtures.

It should be noted that a conveyance of land, in the absence of an express exclusion, passes fixtures without there having to be a special provision to that effect (LPA 1925, s 62(1)).

1.2.5 Strict settlement and trust for sale

A trust of land can take one of two forms—a trust for sale or a strict settlement.

Trust for sale
This is where trustees hold property upon an 'immediate binding trust for sale' (LPA 1925, s 205(1)(xxix)). For there to be a trust for sale the trustees must actually be bound by trust to sell the property; thus, a conveyance to trustees on a trust for persons in succession giving the trustees a power of sale only creates a strict settlement, as there would be no trust for sale.

Where the trustees do hold the property on trust for sale the law implies that they have the power to postpone the date of sale (LPA 1925, s 24(1)).

Land held upon a trust for sale comes within the equitable doctrine of 'conversion'. This is because equity 'looks upon that as done which ought to be done'. Thus, from the commencement of the conveyance on trust for sale, whether there is an actual sale or not, the land, in equity, is regarded as if it were the cash proceeds which would be realised from the sale. This is a strange legal fiction.

A trust for sale may arise expressly (by expressly giving the trustees the duty to sell the land) or by operation of statute. For example, if two or more persons are entitled to land as joint tenants or tenants in common, a trust for sale is imposed by LPA 1925.

When examining land transactions it is important to take into account the existence of these trusts for sale.

Example 1B Trusts for sale and industrial building allowances

X Ltd may hold a parcel of land (freehold) and it may construct an industrial building thereon. Under CAA 1968, s 11(1) the freehold would be the 'relevant interest' for industrial building allowances purposes. If the land is sold to five people it would be held on a trust for sale, with the legal estate being vested in the first four named persons under LPA 1925, s 34(2). As the five purchasers only have interests under the trust for sale they cannot, in strict law, obtain the allowances as they would not have acquired the 'relevant interest'. It is understood that the Revenue do not take this point. If they were to take this point the taxpayer would have to argue that the trust for sale is no more than conveyancing mechanics and should be ignored for tax purposes.

Settled Land Act settlements (strict settlements)
Where it is desired that an actual parcel of land itself (as opposed to the proceeds of sale) shall be held in succession the object can be partly achieved by creating a strict settlement under the Settled Land Act 1925.

A strict settlement is created, broadly, where land is held in trust for persons in succession, eg, A for life and then to B absolutely, and not upon trust for sale (Settled Land Act 1925, s 1(7) amended by Law of Property Act (Amendment) Act 1926, s 7.

The legal estate is vested in the person who for the time being is beneficially entitled to possession of the settled land. He is the 'estate owner'. He is generally the tenant for life. Sometimes the legal estate may be vested in a 'statutory owner' if, for instance, the tenant for life is an infant.

He (the estate owner) alone makes title to the land when it is sold but he holds the estate as trustee for all the persons interested under the settlement. If he sells the property the capital sum received must be paid to the trustees of the settlement or into Court. The trustee will usually be the person named in the Deed of Settlement (see Settled Land Act 1925, s 30).

Strict settlements are not often found nowadays, although they may be created inadvertently if land is held in succession without a trust for sale having been created. They may also be useful if a testator wants to leave his widow a life interest in a particular property after his death.

1.2.6 Co-ownership

The principal methods of co-ownership are joint tenancy and tenancy-in-common. The references to 'tenancy' mean, simply, 'ownership', and have nothing to do with leases. Where land is held in co-ownership the legal estate must be held in joint tenancy although the beneficial interest can be held in tenancy-in-common or in joint tenancy.

Joint tenancy
If land is held by two or more persons beneficially as joint tenants the right of survivorship (*jus accrescendi*) will apply. This means that on the death of one joint tenant his interest in the land passes to the other joint tenants (LPA 1925, s 36(2)). This right of survivorship takes precedence over any disposition made by a joint tenant's will or under the rules of intestacy.

A joint tenant can sever the joint tenancy, thus turning it into a tenancy-in-common (LPA 1925, s 36(2)). He cannot, however, sever it in his will.

Tenancy-in-common
If property is held by tenants-in-common there is no right of survivorship. Thus, when a tenant-in-common dies his interest passes under his will or intestacy as he is free to dispose of his interest as he wishes (LPA 1925, s 34).

1.2.7 Mortgage

Legal mortgages
There are two forms of legal mortgage (LPA 1925, s 85(1)):

(*a*) a demise for a term of years absolute, subject to a provision for cesser on redemption; and

(*b*) a charge by deed expressed by way of legal mortgage.

A legal mortgage, therefore, can only be created by Deed.

Under the first type of legal mortgage A, a fee simple owner of a parcel of land, may wish to borrow from B. A grants B by deed a legal term of years, eg, a lease for 3,000 years, with a proviso that if the principal loan and interest are repaid by a certain date, usually 6 months from the loan, the term of years shall cease to have effect. A further covenants in the lease to repay the loan and interest upon the agreed date.

The legal charge, the second type of legal mortgage, is a statutory form of legal mortgage which is shorter and simpler than the first form described above. The deed merely states that the property has been charged with the debt by way of legal mortgage. There is no conveyance of any estate to the mortgagee (the lender). The effect of such a charge is that the mortgagee gets the same protection rights and powers as if he had a term of 3,000 years.

Once the period fixed for the repayment of the loan has passed (normally

6 months from the date of the loan) on the face of the documentation it may appear that the mortgagee has an indefeasible title to the lease or to the property. However, the Courts of equity disregard the terms of the contract and give the mortgagor (the borrower) a right to redeem the mortgage at any time until any sale or foreclosure by the mortgagee. This right in the mortgagor is known as the 'equity of redemption'. The mortgagor can only exercise this right if he repays the loan and any interest. The Courts further insist that there must be no restrictions on this right to redeem the mortgage; there must be 'no clog on the equity'.

Equitable mortgages
If X agrees to grant Y a legal mortgage but fails to do so Y may have an equitable mortgage if the agreement is evidenced in writing or there is a sufficient act of part performance (see p 9).

An equitable mortgage also arises where title deeds are merely deposited with someone, other than the owner, as security for a debt without any formal mortgage document.

Mortgage is not a disposal
A mortgage does not result in a disposal of the owner's interest in the land. The owner (mortgagor) is still the freeholder or leaseholder, as the case may be. He can sell the land but, if properly registered and protected, the purchaser will buy the land subject to the mortgage (unless it is discharged before the sale). The mortgage is only a method of providing security to raise money.

This fact is recognised by tax legislation. Thus, the creation of a mortgage is not a disposal for CGT purposes, even if there is a demise for a term of years absolute (CGTA 1979, s 23).

Example 1C   Mortgages and CGT

X Ltd has £1 million worth of land. If the land were sold the CGT would be, say, £0.35 million. If it is mortgaged to receive a loan of £1 million there will be no CGT payable.

1.2.8 Conveyancing

The normal conveyancing procedure involves the parties entering into contracts to dispose of the property with completion of the deed of conveyance or the transfer taking place, normally, 4 weeks after exchange of contracts. Before exchange of contracts and in certain cases before completion, the purchaser will make various searches with the local authority, the Land Charges Registry and HM Land Registry if the land is registered land.

Importance of contracts
Contracts will normally precede the formal deed of conveyance or transfer.

LPA 1925, s 40, replacing in part s 4 of the Statute of Frauds 1677, provides that:

> . . . no action may be brought upon any contract for the sale or other disposition of land or any interest in land, unless the agreement upon which such action is brought, or some memorandum or note thereof, is in writing, and signed by the party to be charged or by some other person thereunto by him lawfully authorised.

Thus, the general rule is that contracts for the sale of land must be in writing. However, if s 40 is not complied with, eg, the parties enter into an oral agreement to sell the land, the purchaser may still be able to enforce the agreement if he has carried out acts of part performance in connection with the land, such as taking possession with the vendor's consent or carrying out expensive alterations or improvements to the property (*Rawlinson* v *Ames* [1925] Ch 96).

The date of contract is very important for tax purposes. If the contract is unconditional it could give rise to a deemed disposal date for CGT purposes. If the contract is conditional the deemed disposal date can only arrive when the condition is satisfied (see 9.2.3).

After completion takes place, ie, the deed of conveyance or the transfer comes into effect, there may be a charge to stamp duty. Particulars have to be produced to the Inland Revenue under what is known as the Particulars Delivered (or PD) procedure. The following instruments have to be produced to the Inland Revenue under the PD procedure (FA 1931, s 28):

(*a*) any transfer on sale of the fee simple of the land;

(*b*) the grant of any lease of land for a term of 7 years or more; and

(*c*) any transfer on sale of any such leases.

Under FA 1985, s 89(1) it is provided that FA 1931, s 28 is not to apply in relation to instruments prescribed by regulations made by statutory instruments.

1.2.9 Note on Scottish land law

The Scottish property laws and conveyancing procedures are different from those which apply in England (and Wales and Northern Ireland):

(*a*) References to Scottish *heritable* property are to (1) land and buildings and fixtures and (2) interests in land and buildings and fixtures including leases.

(*b*) References to the *Dominium Utile* can generally be taken to denote a reference to the equivalent to the freehold in England.

(*c*) References to *leases* in both countries are more or less references to the same thing.

(*d*) References to contracts to dispose of land can generally be taken to be a reference to *missives* in Scotland.

However, whereas a contract to sell land may create an equitable interest (which is clearly an interest in land) in England no such interest is created in Scotland; the missives (contracts) create a personal right and if, for instance, the vendor wanted to sell the land and only missives had been entered into in favour of the proposed purchaser, the proposed purchaser could not prevent the sale of the land by the vendor to a third party. The proposed purchaser merely has a *jus crediti,* (see *Gibson and Hunter Home Designs Ltd* [1976] SC 23 SLT 96, SC 27.). This could be relevant, for instance, in ascertaining whether under CGTA 1979, s 27 a disposal of the land can be deemed to have taken place at the time of the exchange of contracts.

Completion of a land transaction in Scotland takes the form of the delivery of the deed known as the *disposition* which is more or less equivalent to the delivery of the transfer or conveyance in the case of land in England. The registration of deeds in Scotland is in a public register known as the Register of Sasines and a simplified system of registration of title (as opposed to the recording of deeds) is gradually being introduced throughout Scotland under the Land Registration (Scotland) Act 1979.

An understanding by English (and Welsh and Northern Irish) practitioners of Scottish law is particularly important with respect to certain decisions on stamp duty and value added tax.

It is also important when interpreting legislation to see how that legislation seeks to deal with the equivalent types of land structures in Scotland. The Courts in each jurisdiction (England and Wales, Northern Ireland and Scotland) will seek to follow the decisions of each other although there is no binding precedent. The House of Lords binds all the Courts of the realm.

1.3 TAXABLE ENTITIES

Once one has ascertained the factual and legal position it is necessary to examine the tax status of the entity which has carried out the transaction.

1.3.1 Individuals

Individuals, trading alone or in partnership, could be liable to tax at a maximum rate of 40% for 1988/89, depending on the amount of the trading profit; the profits are added to the individual's income for the tax year (year ended 5 April) and will normally be treated as earned income. The basic rate of tax for 1988/89 is 25%. It is chargeable on taxable income up to £19,300. The 40% rate is chargeable when income exceeds £19,300.

Apart from the commencing years and the closing years of a sole tradership or partnership trading profits are assessed on a preceding year basis, which means that whilst profits of the partnership are going up the individual or individuals will be in a favourable tax position (TA 1988, s 60).

If individuals receive investment income (including deemed income gains as a result of TA 1988, s 776 assessments) they can be liable for income tax at up to 40% (the rates are now the same as the earned income rates as the 15% investment income surcharge was abolished by the Finance Act 1984).

The annual CGT exemption for an individual is £5,000 for 1988/89 (with the taxable gain being taxed at the same rate as if it comprised part of the individual's income for the year). The tax year is the year ended 5 April. There are also allowances for inflation (FA 1982, ss 80, 86 and 87), as well as the exceptionally generous 're-basing relief' (if the taxpayer held the land or other asset on 31 March 1982 the market value of the asset at that date can be his capital gains tax base cost; see FA 1988, s 96).

1.3.2 Companies

UK resident companies and certain non-UK resident companies who trade in the UK through a branch or agency are liable to corporation tax (and not income tax) on trading profits and investment income. For the financial year beginning on 1 April 1988 the full rate of corporation tax is 35%. The rate of corporation tax for companies with small profits is 25%. The profits of the company are small for these purposes if the taxable profits are less than £100,000; for profits which exceed £100,000 but do not exceed £500,000 a marginal rate relief is available. The effective marginal rate of tax is 37.5%.

Close companies may have part of their estate and other income 'short-falled', ie, the Revenue can effectively compel the payment of a dividend, or at least levy tax as if a dividend had been paid (TA 1988, s 423 and Sched 19). Estate income is income taxable under:

(*a*) Schedule A (rents);

(*b*) Schedule B (woodlands managed commercially); and

(*c*) Schedule D (income, excluding interest, arising from the ownership or occupation of land) (TA 1988, Sched 19, para 5(2)).

Any income treated as trading income cannot be estate income. Trading income, ie, income which would be earned income in the hands of an individual (eg, land trading profits), of a trading company cannot be shortfalled (TA 1988, Sched 19, para 2(2)).

Companies are liable to corporation tax on chargeable gains (and not CGT as such) at the full 35% without relief for small gains. Capital gains cannot be shortfalled and they can be sheltered (unlike in the case of the individual) by industrial building or Enterprise Zone allowances under CAA 1968.

The profits of a company are computed by reference to the amount of the profits arising in any accounting period of the company (TA 1988, s 70(1)). Cases arise in practice where accounts may be made up over, say, 3 years, and the profits apportioned equally between the 3 accounting periods. It appears that the correct approach is to see what transactions actually took place in the particular accounting periods and tax them accordingly, where at least land trading is concerned (TA 1988, s 72(1) and *Marshall Hus & Partners Ltd* v *Bolton* [1981] STC 18).

The timing of land disposals by a company (whether land trading disposals or land investment disposals) will be determined by reference to a company's accounting period and not by reference to 5 April in any year.

1.3.3 Family trusts

Generally, trusts are only liable to the basic rate of tax on their income. This is presently 25% (1988/89). Discretionary and accumulation trusts, on the other hand, may additionally be liable to a further 10% charge (TA 1988 s 686 and s 832(1) 'additional rate').

Subject to an annual exemption of £2,500 (in some cases £5,000) for 1988/89 (which may be reduced if multiple trusts are set up by the same settlor) the trust will be liable to CGT at 25% or 35% in the case of an accumulation and maintenance settlement (FA 1988 s 98(1) and s 100(1)).

If the settlor has an interest in the trust the gain of the trust can, in certain cases, be taxed as if they were the gain of the settlor (FA 1988 Sched 10).

There are no special distinctions as far as trusts are concerned between investment income and trading income; the tax borne by the trust will either be 25% or 35% as the case may be. This is assuming they are not caught by the anti-avoidance provisions in TA 1988, Pt XV where the settlor or his spouse has retained an interest in the assets settled.

1.3.4 Charitable trusts and companies

Charitable trusts are generally exempt from CGT and income tax on their investment income (CGTA 1979, s 145 and TA s 505). They are chargeable to tax on any trading income.

Charitable companies (normally companies limited by guarantee) are exempt from corporation tax on chargeable gains and investment income. They are liable for corporation tax on trading income.

Apart from limited reliefs (see, eg, VATA 1983, Sched 5, Groups 14 and 16) charities bear VAT in the normal way. Charities are, in general, exempt from stamp duty (see FA 1982, s 129). Charities are not exempt from tax under TA 1988, s 776.

1.3.5 Pension schemes

Pension schemes which are exempt approved retirement benefit schemes, ie, are Revenue approved under TA 1988 Part XIV, Chapter 1 (Retirement Benefit Schemes), are generally exempt from CGT and income tax on investment income. They are not exempt from tax on land trading profits, (see TA 1988, s 592).

No particular stamp duty reliefs for land transactions are available to pension funds.

1.4 THE COURTS' APPROACH TO TAX AVOIDANCE AND TAX PLANNING

When carrying out any arrangements to mitigate taxation applicable to land transactions it is very important to appreciate what the attitude of the Courts is likely to be.

It seems that there are three essential elements in trying to predict how the Courts will view a particular tax planning transaction. There is a solid bedrock of case law under which the Courts have looked to the strict form of transactions giving narrow interpretations to tax legislation. Then there is also what may be termed the *Sargaison* v *Roberts* principle under which the Courts, in looking at land transactions, have tended to ignore technical land law concepts in order to apply tax law in a practical, sensible way. Finally there is the newly evolved '*Ramsay* doctrine' under which the Courts will, in a variety of circumstances, look to the substance of transactions and ignore the technical legal form in which they were carried out. The Revenue 'see through' (see 1.4.7) approach may well have derived from Ramsay thinking.

1.4.1 The bedrock

There have been a substantial number of cases in which the Courts have looked at the technical legal way in which transactions have been carried out in order to ascertain the correct tax position, even where tax avoidance schemes have been involved. The leading case is *IRC* v *Duke of Westminster* [1935] All ER 259.

Under this doctrine the taxpayer is free to enter into tax avoidance schemes which, provided they fall out of the particular taxing legislation, will be held to avoid the particular tax charge. If a particular arrangement is not caught by the *Ramsay* doctrine then the strict rules of interpretation will apply in the usual way, even though a tax avoidance scheme may clearly be in point.

1.4.2 The *Sargaison* v *Roberts* principle

The tax Courts may often ignore technical land law points and concepts in tax cases and look to the substance of transactions. In *IRC* v *The Land Securities Investment Trust Ltd* [1969] 2 All ER 430, the House of Lords, in a unanimous judgment delivered by Lord Donovan, decided that rent charges were in reality payments for the purchase of a capital asset and so were not deductible from the taxpayer's profits.

In *Sargaison* v *Roberts* [1969] 3 All ER 1076, at 1077, Megarry J, who had to consider whether a taxpayer had disposed of the whole of his interest when he entered into a gift and leaseback arrangement, stated:

> I appreciate that what I have to do is to construe the words used, and not to insert words which are not there, or to resort to a so-called 'equitable construction' of a taxing statute. But even when I have given full weight to this consideration, I think that I am entitled to distinguish between the substance of a transaction and the machinery used to carry it through. Processes such as that of making reservations, on the one hand, and that of grant and regrant, on the other hand (and I have in mind the chequered history of easements), seem to me to be matters of machinery which may differ from one system to another. In speaking of cases where 'the whole of his interest in the land in question . . . is transferred . . . to some other person', I think Parliament is referring to a process whereby the whole of the interest of A is transferred to B, and stays transferred for more than an imaginary moment in time, and not to a process whereby, in the twinkling of an eye, A's interest in the land is merely reduced from a fee simple to a term of years, and B acquires no more than the fee simple subject to the term. 'Substance' and 'form' are words which must no doubt be applied with caution in the field of statutory construction. Nevertheless, where the technicalities of English conveyancing and land law are brought into juxtaposition with a United Kingdom taxing statute, I am encouraged to look at the realities at the expense of the technicalities. The taxpayer's interest has, *uno ictu*, been merely reduced from ownership of the freehold to ownership of a lease: the whole of his interest in the land has therefore not been transferred to another; and that is the end of the case. I respectfully agree with the commonsense approach of the General Commissioners, and merely add that commonsense is not a quality wholly to be abjured in the construction even of a taxing statute.

This extract from the judgment of Megarry J is very important: it will be seen that when technical land law concepts prevent tax reliefs being available the taxpayer may be able to use this judgment to overcome the problem. Another useful case to similar effect is *Kidson* v *Macdonald* 49 TC 503.

The *Sargaison* v *Roberts* principle, however, has to be used by taxpayers with a certain degree of care. In *Stokes* v *Costain Property Investments Ltd*

[1983] STC 405 (In the High Court) the taxpayers, before Harman J, sought to argue that where plant and machinery was owned by a freeholder and used by a tenant that in economic terms, because of the length of the lease, the machinery in reality (economic reality) belonged to the tenant. Therefore the tenant, it was claimed, was entitled to capital allowances. Harman J referred to the decision of *Sargaison* v *Robertson* being illuminating and helpful but the case did not closely compare with the case he had to deal with. In *Sargaison* v *Roberts* he said: 'Points *slightly against* too much regard being paid to the niceties of real property law or to the accurate use of language by Parliamentary draftsmen.' It was held that the plant and machinery belonged to the landlord and not the tenant and that the doctrine could not aid the particular taxpayer (see p 411H.)

1.4.5 The *Ramsay* doctrine and *Furniss* v *Dawson*

The House of Lords in *W T Ramsay Ltd* v *IRC* and *Eilbeck* v *Rawling* [1981] STC 174 formulated the *Ramsay* doctrine under which the Court will look at all the various transactions entered into where there is a scheme to mitigate tax and ascertain what in substance occurred. When they have done that they will tax the matter according to that substance and not according to the technical legal arrangements which may have been entered into. The doctrine was reaffirmed in the House of Lords decision of *IRC* v *Burmah Oil Co Ltd* [1982] STC 30. The House of Lords decision of *Furniss* v *Dawson* [1984] STC 153 greatly extended the *Ramsay* doctrine. Subsequent decisions seem to be aimed at interpreting the words of the doctrine as expounded in *Furniss* v *Dawson*. It is as if a new anti-tax avoidance section had been enacted by the House of Lords.

The author feels that this section (the *Furniss* section) effectively reads as set out below:

(1) The *Furniss* principle only applies if the taxpayer has entered into a transaction or transactions to avoid tax (which includes the deferment of the payment of tax).

(2) The Furniss principle can only apply provided the following conditions are satisfied:

(*a*) there must be a pre-ordained series of transactions (it may be that the taxpayer can set up a scheme to, say, save capital gains tax on the sale of his land without any particular purchaser in mind: if he ultimately finds a purchaser and sells the land the doctrine may not apply because of the lack of pre-ordination: see *Craven* v *White, IRC* v *Bowater* and *Baylis* v *Gregory* [1988] STC 476, and

(*b*) there must be steps which have no commercial (business) purpose apart from the avoidance of liability to tax.

(3) If the above conditions are satisfied, the inserted steps which have no

commercial (business) purpose apart from the avoidance of liability to tax are disregarded for the purposes of taxation and the court must apply the tax rules by looking at the end result. Precisely how the end result will be taxed will depend on the terms of the taxing statute sought to be applied. It may be that some schemes cannot be sensibly adjusted to counter-act the tax avoidance and these schemes may be unaffected by the doctrine. It is clear that the end result cannot be ignored under the doctrine.

(4) The non-commercial steps referred to above may be steps which are required to be contractually carried out as arranged or where there is an arrangement which falls short of a binding contract under which the steps will be carried out.

(5) If the courts ignore various steps and just look at the end result in order to apply the taxation rules, they would seek to ensure that there is no double charge to taxation.

(6) For the transactions to be preordained it is not sufficient that they were merely contemplated or planned; it is necessary that they are so indissolubly linked together, both in fact and intention, as to be properly and realistically viewed as a composite whole (*Craven* v *White* at 503.)

(7) As to whether the doctrine applies is essentially a question of fact for the Commissioners of Income Tax to decide.

(8) For the avoidance of doubt 'taxation' includes stamp duty (*Ingrams* v *IRC* [1985] STC 835) and (it appears) value added tax (see 12.12.1).

1.4.6 Revenue 'see through' problems and warnings

Land and development transactions can take many forms, and by and large, the taxpayer can choose the way in which he implements and documents his particular transaction.

However, taxpayers must be warned of the possible Revenue 'see through' approach to transactions and there are set out below some of the areas where this may be relevant.

This Revenue 'see through' approach may well have had its origin in the *Ramsay* doctrine (*Ramsay* v *IRC* [1981] STC 174) although it is not limited to tax avoidance schemes.

1.4.7 What is the Revenue 'see through' approach?

The author has heard of and come across cases where the Revenue have sought to 'see through' the labels attached to transactions, and have tried to tax situations based on what they considered to be the substance of the transactions.

The following are some of the areas where this 'see through' approach may be relevant:

1.4.8 Sub-contractors

Under the sub-contractor provisions contained in TA 1988, s 559 *et seq*, payments made by contractors to sub-contractors may require that tax at 25% be deducted at source by the contractor and paid over to the Inland Revenue.

These provisions only apply if the contractor requires the sub-contractor to carry out construction operations. Construction operations are widely defined. They include the construction, alteration, repair, extension, demolition or dismantling of any buildings or structures, whether permanent or not.

A contractor is broadly a person for whom construction operations are carried out by a sub-contractor.

A person can also be a contractor if he carries on a business at any time if:

(*a*) his average annual expenditure on construction operations in the period of three years, ending with the end of the last period to which he makes up his accounts, before that time exceeds £250,000; or

(*b*) where he was not carrying on the business at the beginning of that period of three years, one-third of his total expenditure on the construction operations for the part of that period during which he has been carrying on his business exceeds £250,000.

A party to a contract relating to construction operations is a sub-contractor if, under the contract:

(*a*) he is under a duty to the contractor to carry out the operations or to furnish his own labour (that is to say, in the case of a company, the labour of employees or officers of the company) or the labour of others in the carrying out of operations, or to arrange for the labour of others to be furnished in the carrying out of the operations; or

(*b*) he is answerable to the contractor for the carrying out of the operations by others, whether under a contract or under other arrangements made or to be made by him.

This definition is very wide, and if a contractor were to employ in certain cases a project manager or a developer, these provisions might be relevant.

There will, however, be no requirement to deduct tax at 25% if the sub-contractor can produce a sub-contractor's certificate stating that no tax is to be deducted. These sub-contractors' certificates can be obtained from the Inland Revenue. These are extremely important provisions to watch out for.

The Revenue may apply their 'see through' approach where, for instance, a large fund which carries out substantial building operations lends money to a developer with a view to the developer selling the land to the fund at the end of the day; the sale will be in consideration of the extinction of the loan made to the developer in the first instance. If the developer cannot produce a sub-contractor's certificate, the Revenue may seek to argue that in substance the loan was really a payment under a contract for construction operations or they may simply argue that the contract relates to construction operations and seek to charge the fund for the 25% tax which it failed to deduct at source (see 14.6.2).

1.4.9 Plant and machinery allowances

Plant and machinery allowances are available where a person carrying on a trade incurs capital expenditure on the provision of machinery or plant for the purposes of the trade, and in consequence of his incurring the expenditure, the machinery or plant belongs to him at some time during the chargeable period related to the incurring of the expenditure (FA 1971, s 41(1)).

The taxpayer may, for instance, arrange for an office to be constructed on his land and pay the builder for bricks and mortar (on which no allowances are available) and additionally pay him to provide for machinery or plant in the building. Monies may have to be paid to the architect by the taxpayer to advise in connection with the installation of the machinery or plant. If the taxpayer paid the architect's fees, in spite of certain dicta in the case of *Ben-Odeco Ltd* v *Powlson* [1978] STC 111 (Ch D), [1978] STC 360 (HL), no machinery or plant allowances may be available on such expenditure.

The parties may then seek to arrange for the architect to provide services to the builder. The builder would then charge on the services by increasing the fee charged for the provision of the machinery or plant.

The Revenue may seek to see through the transaction and not permit the taxpayer to obtain plant and machinery allowances on the part of the expenditure referrable to the architect fees paid by the builder. Where the Revenue *did* make such a contention in a particular case of which the author is aware, in the particular circumstances of that case, the Revenue did not pursue the matter. It may be the Revenue accepted that architect fees would qualify for allowances anyhow if paid direct although their practice in this field varies from inspector to inspector.

Also in connection with plant and machinery allowances, in the High Court in *Stokes* v *Costain* [1983] STC 405 (no point in this matter being taken to the Court of Appeal), money was lent by a bank to the developer. The obligation to repay was to be satisfied by the grant of a head lease to the lending institution. It was contended by the Revenue that this amounted to some form of 'subsidy' within CAA 1968, s 84, so that the taxpayer did not incur the expenditure. This was an attempted 'see through' by the Revenue. The judge, however, held that there was a real obligation to repay and that the commercial risk of the development going wrong with the overrun of costs, etc, would fall upon the taxpayer, and the fact of the obligation to pay which might be set off against the premiums payable on the grant of the lease, did not change the nature of the relationship between the parties. The monies were loans and were not payments to meet the taxpayer's expenditure in any relevant sense.

1.4.10 Enterprise Zone Allowances

Under CAA 1968, s 1, an initial allowance is available where a person incurs capital expenditure on the construction of a building or structure which is to be a commercial building or structure occupied for the purposes of a trade carried on either by that person or by his lessee or licensee.

If a developer agrees to construct a commercial building on an investor's land with the developer, for instance, agreeing to pay the investor's stamp duty or other costs and expenses which may not qualify for allowances, and then charging an additional amount for the construction of the building to cover those expenses, the Revenue may well apply a 'see through' argument and restrict the allowances with respect to those outlays.

1.4.11 VAT and development agreements

A developer may agree to construct a new building on the investor's land, charging an additional development fee should the developer find a tenant within the period of twelve months from the completion of the construction of the building.

The developer may agree to guarantee the rent on the premises for, say, two years.

The basic charge made by the developer should be zero-rated (VATA 1983, Sched 5, Group 8, item 2 as amended).

The additional fee, although described as a development fee or an enhanced development fee, may (the Customs may contend) be chargeable to VAT as being a service which relates to the finding of a tenant by the developer. This service may be chargeable at 15%. Also, with regard to the rental guarantee, it may be argued that this is a service chargeable at 15%, or, more likely, an exempt supply of finance, within VATA 1983, Sched 6, Group 8.

The Customs & Excise appear to have a variable practice in connection with transactions such as this. What is clear, however, is that where discernible figures are attributable to those items, it is more likely that the Customs will seek to apply some sort of 'see through' approach and charge VAT accordingly. However, for the Customs & Excise to apply a 'see through' approach, they have to overcome the Court of Appeal decision of *BRB* v *The Commissioners* [1977] STC 221 in which the Court said, broadly, that to ascertain the nature of a VAT supply you look to what in essence has been supplied without necessarily having to dissect the supply into its various components. This is known as the 'composite supply doctrine' (see 12.32).

1.4.12 Conclusions

The Revenue 'see through' concept as mentioned is probably part of the general approach in Revenue matters to look at the substance of transactions and ignore labels. If the Revenue were to pursue this approach, it would no doubt take a number of cases to see where the law will finally end.

In the case, for instance, of a builder charging for the construction of an Enterprise Zone commercial building where amounts referrable to the purchaser's stamp duty and legal fees are included (ie instead of the purchaser bearing these direct, the builder bears them and charges them on as part of the building cost) it is possible that the courts will hold that such items do not qualify for allowances. This is because the courts will hold that they are the types of expenses which a purchaser would normally bear, and which the courts would reasonably expect them to bear. Other items, however, such as the builder's agency fees, etc. effectively charged to the purchaser as part of the builder's costs, would, the author feels, qualify within the allowances legislation, so enabling the investor to obtain allowances on the same.

2 RENT: THE PASSIVE INCOME

2.1 INTRODUCTION

This chapter deals with the taxation of rent. From the taxation point of view, rent is not normally an attractive type of income to receive; it is investment income. In the hands of an individual it can be liable to tax at the highest rate of 40% and in the case of close companies the rent may even be shortfalled, effectively causing a company to pay a dividend. Individuals and small companies may thus want to carry out some tax planning to create deductions to offset against the rental income.

There is also an unexpectedly large number of tax traps in an area where one would expect the taxation treatment to be fairly straightforward. Expenditure on maintenance and repair is not always deductible from rent. In general, the mere entitlement of a landlord to receive rent renders him liable to tax whether or not he finally receives it; the basic tax maxim of 'receivability without receipt is nothing' has no application here (*Leigh* v *IRC* [1928] KB 73, *Dewar* v *IRC* [1935] 2 KB 351 and *Whitworth Park Coal Ltd* v *IRC* [1961] AC 31). Expenditure which exceeds rent in connection with a letting can only be used against rents from certain other properties. The area calls for a thorough appreciation of the rules and very careful tax planning.

2.1.1 General principles

Annual profits or gains arising in respect of any rents under leases of land in the UK are charged to tax as income under TA 1988, s 15 (Sched A).

However, in the case of furnished lettings where the landlord does not carry on a trade, the payments for the use of the furniture may be taxable under Case VI of Schedule D. The landlord in this case will be taxed under Case VI with regard to the rent also, unless he elects for the rent to be separately charged under Schedule A (TA 1988, s 15(1), (4)). Special rules apply if the landlord is carrying on a trade assessable under Case 1 of Schedule D (the entire rents and profits may be assessed under Case 1). It is extremely difficult (if not impossible) to establish that a trade is being carried on in the case of lettings. There may be a business or an undertaking but that is not sufficient to come within Case 1 of Schedule D. There must be a trade (see *American Leaf Blending Co* v *DG of IR* [1978] STC 561).

These Schedule D provisions are not dealt with further in this chapter (for a discussion of Case 1 see Chapter 4 and of Case VI see Chapter 10).

As well as rental profits the following annual profits or gains are chargeable to tax under Schedule A:

(*a*) rent charges, ground annuals and feu duties and any other annual payments arising out of land (TA 1988 s 15(1)1(*b*); and

(*b*) other receipts arising from the ownership of land in the UK (TA 1988, s 15(1)(*c*).

The following are expressly stated (see TA 1988, s 15(1)3 and FA 1988 Sched 6 para 6) not to be taxable under Schedule A:

(*a*) yearly interest;

(*b*) profits or gains arising from a person's occupation of any woodlands which are managed on a commercial basis and with a view to the realisation of profits;

(*c*) profits or gains arising from mines, quarries and other concerns taxable under Schedule D; and

(*d*) mining etc rents and royalties charged under TA 1988, ss 119 or 120.

2.1.2 Meaning of rent

Rent ordinarily means periodical payments in respect of land where the relationship of landlord and tenant exists. The meaning of the term is extended for Schedule A tax purposes to include a payment made by a tenant to defray the cost of works of maintenance and repairs to the premises, not being works required by the lease to be carried out by the tenant (TA 1988, s 24(6)(*b*)).

2.2 DEDUCTIONS FROM RENT

2.2.1 Specific deductions

In order to ascertain the profit chargeable to tax one takes the gross rentals and deducts therefrom the permitted deductions (s 25(1)). The following are the permitted deductions:

Maintenance and repair (s 25(2)(a))
Maintenance and repairs must be distinguished from improvements and alterations. There is a substantial amount of case law on the subject borrowed from other areas of the law—see, for instance, *Lurcott* v *Wakeley & Wheeler* [1911] 1 KB 905, *O'Grady* v *Bullcroft Main Collieries Ltd* (1932) 17 TC 93, *Margrett* v *Lowestoft Water & Gas Co* (1935) 19 TC 481, and *Smedley* v *Chumley and Hawke Ltd* (1982) 126 SJ 33—where maintenance and repair has generally been taken to mean the restoration by renewal or the replacement of subsidiary parts of a whole (see 5.4).

Improvements and additions are normally capital but by extra-statutory concession B4 (see *Inland Revenue Practices and Concessions*, Longman), where maintenance and repairs of property are obviated by improvements which do not amount to the reconstruction of the property, so much of the outlay as is equal to the estimated cost of the maintenance and repairs is generally allowed as a deduction.

Insurance (s 25(2)(a))
This refers to premiums for a policy of insurance in respect of the building. It has been held that premiums payable on a leasehold redemptions policy are not deductible (*Pearce* v *Doulton* (1947) 27 TC 405).

Management (s 25(2)(a))
This would include the usual expenses for managing property, eg, the cost of finding tenants (*Southern* v *Aldwych Property Trust Ltd* [1940] 2 KB 266).

Services (s 25(2)(b))
This would include such services as cleaning the building and the provision of a gardener.

Rates and other charges (s 25(2)(c))
Rates would include general rates and water rates.

Rents, rent charges and similar payments (s 25(2)(d))
The landlord may not be the freeholder, in which case he can deduct the rents he has to pay for the premises to his landlord. Also, if the landlord has to pay a rent charge he can deduct that.

Example 2A: Expenses deductible from rent

		£
Rent received by X		10,000
His deductible expenses are:		
	£	
Maintenance and repair	2,000	
Improvements (£1,000)		
Rates	100	
Head rents	2,200	4,100
Taxable income (Schedule A)		5,900

NB The £5,900 is added to X's other income to ascertain the rate of tax applicable thereto. The improvement expenditure (£1,000) is not deductible from the rent but may form part of the CGT base on a disposal of the property.

2.2.2 Special cases

Special rules apply to properties managed as one estate (TA 1988, s 26), sporting rights (TA 1988, s 29), expenditure on making sea walls (TA 1988, s 30) and agricultural land (TA 1988, s 33).

2.2.3 General rules concerning deductions

Amounts must be paid
The expenses (listed above) are not deductible until they are actually paid by the taxpayer (s 25(2)). Thus, simply setting aside funds to replace a central heating system in years to come does not give rise to a deduction from rents. It often happens that it is the landlord's responsibility to replace the system and the tenant has to pay extra rent to the landlord to create a replacement fund. Payments into that fund by the landlord are unlikely to be deductible amounts.

Made in respect of the premises
In order to be deductible from the rent the payments listed above must be made in respect of the premises comprised in the lease (s 25(3)(*a*)). There are cases, however, where expenses in respect of premises can be offset against rent from other premises owned by the same lessor (see below).

The periods to which the expenses relate

(1) General rules

In the case of a payment for maintenance and repair the expenses will only be allowed if they were incurred by reason of a dilapidation attributable to a period falling within 'the currency of the lease'. In the case of all other expenses it is only necessary for these to have been incurred in respect of such a period (s 25(3)(*b*)).

For the commercial investor in properties the restrictions on the length of the currency of the lease, etc, in (2) and (3) below will not normally have any relevance as there should not be any lettings at an undervalue nor any periods of owner-occupation.

(2) *Expenditure during currency of lease*

The 'currency of the lease' means the term of the lease in existence, provided that where the taxpayer became the landlord during the term of the lease in existence, the reference to 'currency of the lease' does not include any time before he became landlord (s 25(4)).

Example 2B: Currency of lease

L Ltd buys Blackacre subject to a 50 year lease of which 10 years have expired. The currency of the lease is 40 years.

However, it is provided by s 25(5) that where a lease is at a full rent the 'currency of the lease' shall be extended to include a previous qualifying period which means:

(*a*) the duration of any previous lease at a full rent during which the chargeable person was the landlord; and

(*b*) any void periods beginning either (i) with the termination of an earlier lease at a full rent of the premises or (ii) with the acquisition by the person chargeable of an interest in the premises giving him the right to possession thereof.

Example 2C: A previous qualifying period

L Ltd buys Blackacre. It lets it to T Ltd for 10 years at a full rent. After the 10 years it grants a lease to A Ltd for 20 years at a full rent. The currency of the lease is 20 years plus 10 years (the 10 years is 'a previously qualifying period').

However, a period shall not be a 'previous qualifying period' if it preceded a period ending before the beginning of the lease which was not itself a previous qualifying period. There must therefore not be any disqualifying gaps in the letting.

It is clear from the above that the currency of the lease cannot be extended backwards beyond (i) any period when the chargeable person occupies the demised premises (s 25(2) 'void period'), as this would not be a void period, or (ii) any period when the demised premises are let otherwise than at a full rent (s 25(5)).

Where rent is payable under a lease at a full rent (whether or not it is a tenant's repairing lease) and the rent is insufficient to absorb the expenditure incurred during the currency of the lease, the excess may be offset against rent arising from another lease at a full rent which is not a 'tenant's repairing lease'. This restriction must be carefully borne in mind. Any excess can be carried forward against the income from the particular lease and against income from other leases which are not tenant's repairing leases.

Extra-statutory concession A23 (see *Inland Revenue Practices and Concessions*, Longman) provides that expenditure incurred on maintenance and repairs by reason of dilapidations attributable to a period before the person chargeable became the landlord may be deducted from rents for the purposes of Schedule A where the immediately preceding landlord was the husband or wife (or the trustee for the husband or wife) of the person chargeable or of the person for whom the person chargeable acts as trustee.

A rent is a 'full rent' if it is sufficient, taking one year with another, to defray the cost to the lessor of fulfilling his obligations under the lease and of meeting his obligations to maintain and repair etc (s 24(7)).

A 'tenant's repairing lease' means a lease where the lessee is obliged to maintain and repair the whole, or substantially the whole, of the premises (s 24(6)(*c*)).

(3) *Void periods*

Expenditure incurred during the currency of the lease during a void period after a lease at a full rent expires may be offset against income from other properties which are not tenant's repairing leases or carried forward and offset against current income from leases which are not tenant's repairing leases or income from the same property. The property when subsequently let must be at a full rent and must not be owner-occupied, otherwise the right to carry forward the expenditure will be restricted.

If a property is void immediately after acquisition and expenditure is incurred during the currency of the lease it may be set off against rent from other leases which are not tenant's repairing leases or carried forward and set off against future income from the same property or other properties where the leases are not tenant's repairing leases. The property when let must be at a full rent (whether or not it is a tenant's repairing lease) and it must not be occupied by the owner, otherwise no relief will be allowed for the expenditure.

'Void period' means the period during which the chargeable person was not in occupation of the premises but was entitled to possession of the premises (TA 1988, s 25(2) 'void period').

Example 2D: The period to which expenses relate

X purchases Blackacre on 1 May 1975 and lets it at a full rent until 1 May 1978. It is void (unoccupied) from 2 May 1978 to 1 May 1980. It is then let at a full rent from 2 May 1980 to 1 May 1981. The currency of the lease is the entire period from 1 May 1975 to 1 May 1981.

The Law Shipping rule
As well as the specific restrictions in s 25 it was held in *Law Shipping Co Ltd* v *IRC* (1924) 12 TC 621 (as modified by the decision in *Odeon Associated Theatres Ltd* v *Jones* 49 ATC 315) that where property is purchased in a dilapidated state the expenditure incurred in making it good may be capital and thus cannot be allowed as a deduction against income.

Interest relief
It is to be noted that under the interest relief provisions in TA 1988, s 354(2)(*a*), a loan which is taken out to cover expenditure on maintenance or repair work related to a period prior to the acquisition of the premises may qualify for interest relief, but not otherwise. The interest is not a Schedule A expense as such. It is deductible from rents as a 'charge of income' if the conditions of s 354 are satisfied.

Restricted availability of losses
Apart from the restricted cases mentioned above (where excess expenditure may be offset against rents from certain other premises), a loss

under Schedule A cannot be offset against income assessable under any other schedule, nor can it be offset against any charge to CGT. If, however, expenditure is disallowed as being capital expenditure under the *Law Shipping* principle, it should be deductible under any future CGT computation on the disposal of the property in question.

2.2.4 Interest relief and Schedule A

This part brings together various points concerning interest and Schedule A.

(*a*) If a taxpayer receives interest this is taxable under Schedule D not Schedule A (s 15(1)3(*a*)) specifically states that yearly interest does not come within Schedule A).

(*b*) Interest (whether yearly or otherwise) is not one of the 'permitted deductions' under Schedule A (TA 1988, s 25(2)). If the taxpayer is to obtain relief he must look elsewhere in the taxing code:
(i) Under s 74 as a trading deduction
(ii) Under s 354 as a charge on income (available to individuals, most trustees and non-resident companies which do not pay corporation tax)
(iii) Under, exceptionally, s 75 as an investment company management expense and
(iv) Under s 338 as a company charge on income.

2.3 ASSESSMENT

Tax under Schedule A for individuals is assessed on the basis of the annual profits or gains arising in the particular year ended 5 April (TA 1988, s 22). Thus, tax for the year of assessment 1984/85 is based on the annual profits or gains arising in the year ended 5 April 1985.

The tax will normally be payable on 1 January in the year for which it is charged. Since the full facts of the taxpayer's Schedule A liability will not be known until the end of the tax year (5 April) the 1 January payment is made on a provisional basis; assuming that all the sources of income are the same, it is based on the receipts and expenses of the last preceding tax year. After the end of the year, appropriate adjustments will be made.

2.3.1 Rent is chargeable whether or not received

All assessments under Schedule A shall be charged on and paid by the person receiving or entitled to the profits or gains (s 21). Thus, there will be a liability even if the landlord does not receive his rent from the tenant.

TA 1988, s 41 allows a person to claim relief, where he has not received the rent to which he is entitled, in two cases:

(*a*) where he has taken all reasonable steps available to him to enforce payment (s 41(1)(*b*)); and

(*b*) where he has waived payment without consideration and it was reasonable for him to do this in order to avoid hardship (s 41(1)(*c*)).

If rent is reduced (prior to a waiver) rather than waived the situation is different. The Revenue have written as follows:

> Taxes Act 1970, section 87 (TA 1988, s 41) is a relieving section which comes into play where a sum has become chargeable to tax under Schedule A by virtue of Taxes Act 1970, section 67(1)2 (TA 1988, s 15(1)2). That charge is on the rents that the landlord is entitled to demand on rent days falling in the chargeable period. If there is a prior agreement to reduce the rent, the entitlement is consequently reduced when the rent day arrives. If there is any consideration for the reduction a charge might arise under Taxes Act 1970, section 80(4) (TA 1988, s 34(5)) (22 January 1979, Inland Revenue letter, 'Waiver of Rent (Taxes Act 1970, section 87)').

2.3.2 Disposal of future rent rights

There is nothing in principle to prevent a landlord from disposing of, say, 10 years of future rental income. In the author's view, for Schedule A purposes he will have effectively disposed of the income so that he would not continue to be taxable on the rent as it arises. The future rent was in fact disposed of in the leading case of *Vestey* v *IRC* (1949) 31 TC 1. Under general law the same can be done with respect to dividends and interest from securities (*Paget* v *IRC* (1938) 21 TC 677) although in that case special anti-avoidance provisions now apply (TA 1988, s 730).

2.3.3 Joint landlords

It may be that a number of individuals will purchase property for investment. If they are strangers they are likely to hold the property as tenants-in-common. The rules concerning deductions and rents will apply, with appropriate apportionments being made among the individuals.

For convenience they may arrange for the legal estate to be held by a company as nominee for them.

Under Partnership Act 1890, s 2(1) a joint holding of land does not of itself create a partnership as to the land, even if the owners share the rents. This is important because if the individuals are found to be partners or are found to carry on a trade jointly they can be liable for each other's income tax, debts and torts (TA 1988, s 111, and Partnership Act 1890, ss 9, 10 and 12).

2.3.4 Close companies

The estate income (rents etc) of close companies may, in part, be apportioned amongst shareholders under TA 1988, Sched 19.

2.3.5 Rent received by land dealers

See 16.2.1.

2.4 COLLECTION

Payment of rent to non-residents

Where a tenant pays rent direct to a landlord whose usual place of abode is outside the UK, he must deduct tax at the basic rate and pay it over to the Inland Revenue. This would cover the situation where the rent is credited to the landlord's UK bank account.

If the payment is made to the landlord's UK resident agent, the tenant can pay it without deducting tax. The agent in this case must deduct tax when accounting to the landlord (TA 1988, s 43). The following Revenue Practice (FRP5/B22) should be noted:

> **Schedule A: deduction of tax from rents**
>
> Clarification is sought regarding the position of a lessee who pays rent into his landlord's bank account without deduction of tax in ignorance of the fact that the landlord has moved and that his usual place of abode is consequently outside the UK. The landlord may be unwilling to authorise the lessee to deduct the accrued liability from future payments of rent. It is assumed that no attempt would be made to hold the lessee liable for not having deducted tax at source whilst he was unaware of his landlord's change of abode but confirmation is sought that this is the case. The Revenue could still assess the non-resident landlord, with the property as security.
>
> The Revenue confirmed that the lessee would not be held liable for not deducting tax at source if unaware of his landlord's change of abode.

2.4.1 Collection from lessees and agents

There are provisions to enable the Revenue to collect tax from lessees and agents of the lessor, if the lessor defaults in the payment of the tax (TA 1988, s 23).

2.5 CAPITAL ALLOWANCES

Capital allowances are available under the provisions of TA 1988, s 32 for expenditure on machinery and plant used in estate management. This would include a computer dealing with the recording of rent as well as machinery to be used to repair and maintain the property.

2.6 TAX PLANNING

(*a*) Rents receivable by an individual can be taxed at rates as high as 40%. Consideration should be given to seeing whether the land can be transferred or rents assigned so that the rents can arise in a company or a trust in order to reduce the tax charge. A company may sell its property to its own self-administered pension fund and take a lease back. The rents will be deductible and they will be tax-free in the hands of the pension fund if it is an Exempt Approved Pension Fund.

(*b*) It may be necessary to purchase plant and machinery to obtain allowances to offset against the charge on the rents. It may also be possible to have deductible interest payments (see Chapter 7), and losses on certain leases can be offset against profits on others (see 2.2.3).

(*c*) When buying premises the state of repair is important as certain expenditure incurred subsequent to the purchase may be non-deductible against the rent (see p 26).

(*d*) Rent cannot simply be waived. If a tenant is defaulting, steps must be taken and be seen to be taken to obtain the rent, or the tenant must make out a case of hardship.

(*e*) If land is owned by an overseas company with no branch or agency in the UK, only the basic rate of tax (under general principles and assuming no anti-avoidance provisions such as TA 1988, s 739 apply) can be chargeable on the rents (the charge will be under Schedule A or if appropriate Case VI of Schedule D). If the owner is an overseas individual the rents could be liable to the highest rate of IT (40%). The appropriate double taxation treaty may relieve this charge in whole or in part, but this is unlikely.

(*f*) The restrictions on the rights to offset expenditure against future rents and rents arising from other premises must be fully appreciated. In particular, expenditure on a lease cannot be offset against rents arising from another lease which is a tenant's repairing lease.

(*g*) The obligation to deduct tax from rental payments made to overseas persons must not be overlooked. It is possible for an overseas investor to borrow money from a bank carrying on business in the UK to purchase the property and obtain tax relief for the interest (TA 1988, s 354). In this event there will be no taxable income in the UK if the interest covers the rent so that consequently (because no rent will be paid to the landlord) there will be no liability to deduct tax at source. It may also be possible for the borrowing in the UK to be backed with an overseas deposit so that effectively the income arises abroad without tax being deducted at source.

3 LEASE PREMIUM PROVISIONS: CONVERSION OF CAPITAL INTO INCOME

3.1 INTRODUCTION

There are provisions in TA 1988, ss 34–38 generally known as the 'lease premium provisions' which attempt to tax certain capital amounts arising from land transactions as if they were income.

These provisions are anti-avoidance provisions and can apply to a wide variety of transactions ranging from leases and sub-leases to assignments and variations of leases.

The provisions must be watched carefully. A taxpayer expecting to pay perhaps 40% capital gains tax with the benefit of the 1982 rebasing, indexation and the £5,000 annual exemption on a capital receipt may find that because of these provisions he is paying income tax on the receipt.

Since the Finance Act 1988, which charges capital gains as if they comprised (for rates purposes) part of the taxpayer's income, these provisions do not have the great significance they once had when the rates were widely different (at one time the capital gain was taxed at 30% and income at 98%). The provisions have lost their 'former glory'. They may wither on the vine.

3.2 GRANT OF A LEASE

The major provision is TA 1988, s 34. This provides that where the payment of any premium is required under a lease, or otherwise under the terms subject to which a lease is granted, and the duration of the lease does not exceed 50 years, the landlord shall be treated for the purposes of the Tax Acts as becoming entitled when the lease is granted to an amount by way of rent (in addition to any actual rent) equal to the amount of the premium reduced by one-fiftieth of that amount for each complete period of 12 months (other than the first) comprised in the duration of the lease.

Example 3A: Grant of lease

L Ltd a property investment company grants a 26 year lease to T Ltd at a premium of £100,000. £50,000 will be taxed as rent under these provisions

$(\frac{26-1}{50} \times £100{,}000)$ and the remaining £50,000 will be liable to corporation tax as a chargeable gain (for the detailed interaction provisions see CGTA 1979, Sched 3, para 5).

Thus, the provision only applies to the grant of a lease where a premium (actual or deemed) is received and where the duration of the lease does not exceed 50 years.

It is clear that a premium is taxable in full if the lease is for less than two years. If the lease is for two years or more but less than three years 98% is to be taxed and if say a lease is for 30 years, 42% of the premium will be taxed. Premiums for leases longer than 50 years are not liable to tax under these provisions.

The aim of the provision is to catch situations where a landlord might reduce the amount of the rent (which he would otherwise take) and charge a large premium, thereby avoiding the IT (or CT in the case of a company) which would otherwise have been paid on the rent.

A 'lease' includes an agreement for a lease and any tenancy, but does not include a mortgage or heritable security and 'lessee', 'lessor' and 'letting' shall be construed accordingly (TA 1988, s 41).

Even so it may be argued that the provisions do not cover agreements for lease as an agreement for lease is incapable of being 'granted' as such. In the case of *City Permanent Building Society* v *Miller* [1952] 1 Ch 840, Jenkins LJ at p 853 stated:

> In my judgement the word 'granted' necessarily imports the actual creation of a term, and that excludes, by force of the context, the case of a mere agreement for lease, having no more than a contractual effect.

3.2.1 Premiums

Actual premium A premium is stated in TA 1988, s 24(1) to include any like sum, whether payable to the immediate or a superior landlord or to a person connected within the meaning of TA 1988, s 839 with the immediate or a superior landlord. It is also stated in s 24(2) that any sum other than rent paid on or in connection with the granting of a tenancy shall be presumed to have been paid by way of premium except insofar as other sufficient consideration for the payment is shown to have been given. Paying a sum to the landlord to cover the landlord's solicitor's costs may amount to a premium, and the Revenue have been known to take that point.

Deemed premiums

(1) *Tenant's improvements*

If the landlord grants a lease to a tenant and the lease imposes on the tenant an obligation to carry out certain works on the premises, the landlord is deemed under TA 1988, s 34(2) to receive a premium of an amount equal to:

(*a*) the amount by which the value of the landlord's interest immediately after the commencement of the lease exceeds

(*b*) what its then value would have been if the said obligation had not been imposed on the tenant.

That restriction on the amount chargeable is very important as in the great majority of cases where the parties are at arm's length and a rack rent charged, no deemed premium is likely to arise. The charge is not based on the cost of the works carried out by the tenant. There can be no charge unless there is a benefit to the landlord's reversion. This is a question of valuation.

The type of situation which would seem to be envisaged by s 34(2) is where L lets property to T. In order to avoid income tax on the rent L agrees with T to allow T to use the property rent free for 5 years provided T builds a property thereon and T's lease expires at the end of the 5 years so that L has the building and the freehold unencumbered by any lease. In this case L will have effectively received a premium because he would have the building, constructed by T, at the end of the 5 years. The amount of that premium is equal to the amount of which the value of L's estate or interest immediately after the commencement of the lease exceeds what its then value would have been if the terms of the lease had not imposed the obligation on T to carry out the building work.

Example 3B: Tenant's improvements

Landlord Ltd grants Tenant Ltd a lease of an office for 21 years. Tenant Ltd is under an obligation to carry out structural alterations. Any increase in the value of the landlord's reversion as a result of that obligation would amount to a deemed premium. Tenant Ltd, however, may have ensured that the terms of the lease are such that Landlord Ltd's reversion does not benefit significantly from Tenant Ltd's works but it is essentially a question of valuation.

There can also be no charge if the obligations imposed on the tenant require the tenant to carry out works which, had the landlord carried out the works instead of the tenant, would have given rise to income tax deductible payments (under TA 1988, ss 25–30) by the landlord.

Example 3C: Tenant's repairs

Landlord Ltd grants a 21-year lease to Tenant Ltd imposing an obligation upon the tenant to carry out repair, maintenance and decoration works. There is no deemed premium, provided that if Landlord Ltd had carried out the works it would have been entitled to deductions against its income if it had actually borne the tenant's expenditure.

(2) *Payments in lieu of rent, surrenders, waivers or variations of leases (s 34(4) and (5))*

Payments in lieu of rent Where, under the terms subject to which a lease is granted, a tenant pays a sum in lieu of the whole or a part of the rent for any period there shall be a deemed premium of the amount of that sum payable in the year it becomes payable by the tenant. The premium is discounted on the basis that the duration of the lease excludes any period other than that in relation to which the sum is payable.

Payments for surrender Where, under the terms subject to which a lease is granted, a sum becomes payable by the tenant as consideration for the surrender of the lease, that sum is a deemed premium in the year it becomes payable by the tenant. The premium is discounted on the basis that the duration of the lease extends from its commencement to its surrender.

Variation Where, as consideration for the variation of any of the terms of a lease, a sum becomes payable by the tenant otherwise than by way of rent, the lease shall be deemed for the purposes of these provisions to have required a premium to be due to the landlord and it shall be deemed to have been required when the contract providing for the variation is entered into.

A general payment to avoid proceedings for breach of the terms of a lease and its forfeiture is regarded as a payment for the variation of a lease (*Banning* v *Wright* 48 TC 421). The premium is discounted on the basis that the duration of the lease is the period during which the variation is to have effect.

Waiver Where, as consideration for the waiver of any of the terms of a lease, a sum becomes payable by the tenant otherwise than by way of rent, the lease shall be deemed for the purposes of these provisions to have required the payment of a premium to the landlord and it shall be deemed to have been required when the contract providing for the waiver is entered into. The premium is discounted on the basis that the duration of the lease is the period during which the waiver is to have effect.

Example 3D: Consideration for waiver

A 60-year lease is granted by X to Y. After 15 years they contract to reduce the rent for a 10-year period, ie, the landlord will waive the rent. Any payment for that waiver is treated as a premium under a 10-year lease (TA 1988, s 34(5)).

3.2.2 Duration of leases (s 38)

The following provisions shall apply in determining the duration of a lease:

(*a*) if the term of a lease, for example, in respect of forfeiture, or other circumstances, render it unlikely that the lease will run beyond a date before the expiry of the term provided in the lease, and the premium is not greater than the amount that would be required for such a shorter lease, the term is taken as ending not later than on that date (s 38(1)(*a*));

(*b*) if the term of the lease can be extended by the tenant, one may take account of circumstances whereby it is likely that he would extend the lease (s 38(1)(*b*)); and

(*c*) if the tenant, or any person connected with him, is or may become entitled to the grant of a further lease of the same premises or part of them, the lease may be treated as continuing until the expiry of that further lease (s 38(1)(*c*)).

These provisions shall be applied by reference to the facts which were known or ascertainable at the time of the grant of the lease. It is assumed that the landlord and tenant are acting at arm's length, and anti-avoidance provisions are included if any benefits etc are given to secure a tax advantage (s 38(2)–(4)).

3.2.3 Calculating the tax liability

Permitted discount
It is necessary first to calculate the permitted discount, ie, a reduction of one-fiftieth for each year of the term of the lease other than the first year. Only whole years are taken into account. Thus, a lease of 10½ years gives rise to a deduction of nine-fiftieths. In the same way a lease granted for 1 year and 11 months is taxable in full (s 34(1)).

Example 3E: Calculation of permitted discount

X grants a lease for 12 years at a premium of £50,000. He is liable on a proportion thereof under Schedule A as follows:

		£
Premium		50,000
Less term of lease	12	
Less	1	
	11	
$\frac{11}{50} \times £50{,}000 =$		11,000
Taxable as rental income		39,000

£11,000 is the permitted discount

3.2.4 Premiums payable by instalments

Where an amount by reference to which a person is chargeable to tax by virtue of the lease premium provisions is payable by instalments, the tax chargeable by reference to that amount may, if he satisfies the Revenue that he would otherwise suffer undue hardship, be paid at his option by such instalments as the Revenue may allow over a period not exceeding 8 years and ending not later than the time at which the last of the first-mentioned instalments is payable (TA 1988, s 34(8)).

3.2.5 Position of trader-lessee and 'mirror premium relief'

Where a lessee pays a premium in respect of property used in connection with a trade carried on by him, and part of that premium is assessed on the landlord under these provisions (or would be assessed but for some tax exemption) the tenant trader is allowed a special deduction (commonly referred to as 'mirror premium relief') in computing the profits of his trade (TA 1988, s 87 (Taxable Premiums etc)). The proportion assessed on the landlord is spread over the relevant period and the tenant trader may deduct the appropriate proportion each year.

This 'mirror premium relief' is available to a tenant even though the tax charge arises on the landlord under s 34(2) because the tenant has carried out works on the premises.

If a tenant is obliged to carry out such works, however, and he is able to obtain capital allowances in respect thereto he is not able to obtain tax relief twice, ie, he can claim his capital allowances but he will not be able to get any income tax relief in respect of the expenditure on the plant and machinery under the provisions of TA 1988, s 87 (see s 87(8)).

In order to avoid these lease premium provisions, the parties could ensure that no obligation is imposed upon the tenant to carry out these works, although the overall tax effect of this move must be carefully considered.

Example 3F: Expenditure on plant

L grants a 21-year lease of a building to T. T is under an obligation to put plant and machinery into the building under which capital allowances are available to T under FA 1971, s 41. T will obtain his capital allowances but he cannot claim 'mirror premium relief' also under TA 1988, s 87.

The fact that the landlord is a land dealer (so that the whole of the premium will be chargeable as income) will not prevent the tenant obtaining relief under this provision.

This mirror premium relief is also available even where the grantor of the lease at a premium did not in fact bear tax on the same, for example, because the grantor is a charity which is exempt from tax or because the liability is reduced or eliminated by the deduction of expenses (see IR 27, para 89).

Trading tenants would prefer to take grants of leases rather than purchase leases as there will be no immediate CT on income (or income tax) deduction in the latter case. Rollover relief for CGT, however, may be appropriate.

Example 3G: Effect on tenant trader

Selling Ltd has a lease for 15 years which it is willing to surrender to Landlord Ltd for £100,000. Landlord Ltd wishes to grant a new lease to Purchasing Ltd for 15 years. That new lease will be granted at £100,000. If Selling Ltd were simply to sell its interest to Purchasing Ltd, Purchasing Ltd would get no corporation tax on income relief. Selling Ltd may be liable to corporation tax on chargeable gains. However, if Selling Ltd surrendered its interest and Landlord Ltd granted a lease to Purchasing Ltd then Purchasing Ltd would get some tax relief from corporation tax on income on the premium paid of £100,000. However, Landlord Ltd would suffer tax on the premium as if it were, substantially, income. If Landlord Ltd has losses available there should be no difficulty in the negotiations but otherwise it will be a question of who was in the stronger commercial position. Landlord Ltd could find the situation unattractive because it might pay tax on the receipt as if it were in part income and must find additional monies in order to pay the £100,000 to Selling Ltd.

If the tenant is not a trader he may still obtain relief for the premium he pays under TA 1988, s 37(3).

3.2.6 The so-called 'Lease premium trap' for traders

A land trader may purchase a lease for say 12 years for £400,000. He may grant a sub-lease of the same for 11 years for a premium £500,000.

One fifth of the premium (£100,000) would come into the Schedule D, Case I trading computation. The remaining four-fifths (£400,000) would come into a Schedule A computation.

The amounts brought into the Schedule A computation cannot be brought into the trading computation in *Salisbury House Estate Limited* v *Fry* 15 TC 266. Lord Atkin at p 318 stated that Schedule A income is not to be brought into account for the purposes of Schedule D. The Schedule A monies cannot form an item in the computation of liability to tax under Schedule D.

Some difficult points then arise as to how the trading computation is to be calculated (see *IRC* v *Emery* 20 TC 213, *Utting* v *Hughes* 23 TC 174, *McMillan* v *IRC* 24 TC 417, and *Heather* v *Redfern* 26 TC 119). It may be that following such a computation through the cost figure of £400,000 is available effectively for offset against the part of the premium charged as a Case I, Schedule D receipt with the lower of cost or market value of the reversion coming into the computation at the end of the period of account. The balance can then be offset against general income under TA 1988, s 380. What is clear is that no part of the £400,000 (cost) can be offset against the £400,000 as such which is chargeable under Schedule A, by virtue of the lease premium provisions as it does not comprise a Schedule A deduction.

The sums taxable under the lease premium provisions are deemed to be rent without the legislation expressly making the point that the sums are income (see *IRC* v *Land Securities Investment Trust* (1969) 45 TC 495 and *Littlewoods Mail Order Stores Ltd* v *McGregor* (1969) 45 TC 519). This may be relevant if the taxpayer was not trading and the transaction was a capital gains tax transaction. However, where the taxpayer is trading the monies are deemed to be rent so being brought within Schedule A, but they still retain their character as income. Thus it seems clear that capital allowances which are available for instance by way of discharge or repayment of tax which can be offset against the taxpayer's general income could be used to shelter all the taxpayer's income including the taxable part of the premium so effectively avoiding tax on the entire premium.

The part which escapes tax could not be chargeable to capital gains tax because the receipt is a revenue receipt within CGTA 1979, s 31; it is taken into account as a receipt in computing income or profits or gains or losses of the taxpayer even though no tax is ultimately payable on it.

The taxpayer may be tempted to arrange for a charity to purchase the 12 year lease with the charity then granting a lease at the premium. The charity is exempt from tax under Schedule A, so the lease premium provisions will be of no taxable consequence (TA 1988, s 505 and see also IR 27 '*Notes on the Taxation of Income from Real Property*', para 89). If the computations, however, throw up a trading profit in the hands of the charity this profit will not be protected by virtue of the charitable status of the charity.

If the taxpayer had sold the property interest, ie, the 12 year lease, to an exempt pension fund the author is of the view that the exempt pension fund would not be relieved from any of the Schedule A, or Case I, Schedule D, tax charges on the premium (TA 1988, s 592(2) only provides exemption from income tax in respect of income derived from investments or deposits if or to such an extent as the Board are satisfied that it is income from investments or deposits held for the purposes of the scheme).

3.3 GRANT OF A SUB-LEASE

In general the grant of a sub-lease for 50 years or less will be taxed in the same way as the grant of a head lease.

However, certain special rules apply where a lessor grants a sub-lease (the second charge) and the lessor is deemed to have paid a premium for the lease out of which the sub-lease is granted (the first charge). In this type of case a reduction is made in the second charge which reflects the amount chargeable under the first charge (TA 1988, s 37).

Example 3H: Grant of sub-lease

L owns the freehold of land. The tenant is T. T has a 5 year lease. L wants to buy the lease of T for say £500,000 and then let the same to X. If L simply buys that lease the position will be that T will be chargeable to capital gains tax on the disposal and L will not obtain any income tax relief for the £500,000 which he pays.

In this situation L may contemplate taking a sub-lease from T paying T a premium of £500,000 with L in his capacity as sub-lessee then granting a further lease to the new proposed occupational tenant (X).

In this event T will be chargeable under the lease premium provisions but L in his capacity as sub-tenant will be entitled to a measure of income tax relief under the mirror premium provisions, namely TA 1988 s 37. CGTA 1979 s 25(4) (value shifting) should not normally be relevant.

3.4 ASSIGNMENT OF A LEASE

Where a lease is sold for a capital sum there will generally be no charge to IT on that sum unless, for instance, the vendor is a trader or TA 1988, s 776 applies. Where the original lease was granted at an undervalue there could be a charge to IT under the lease premium provisions when the lease is subsequently assigned.

TA 1988, s 35 states that where the original lease was for a period not exceeding 50 years and the lessor could have required an additional sum by way of premium (referred to as the 'amount forgone') there could be a charge on the assignment of the lease for a consideration under Case VI of Schedule D.

These provisions were designed to catch the situation where A wished to grant B a lease at a premium but would be taxable under s 34. That provision (s 34) only applies to the grant of a lease and not to an assignment, so A could grant the lease at an undervalue (so that there would be an 'amount forgone') to a connected company which would assign it to B at a premium equal to the 'amount forgone'. That premium is taxable under these provisions.

Example 31: Assignment of lease

A grants B a 21-year lease at a premium of £100,000 when he could have demanded a premium of £150,000. £50,000 is the amount forgone. If B assigns the lease to C for £130,000, B is chargeable on £30,000 and if C assigns the lease there could be a further charge on his profit, up to £20,000 (the amount left of the original amount forgone (£50,000)).

In computing the amount chargeable on B and C the period of the lease is taken as the original 21-year lease even though at the times B and C assign the lease some of the years of the lease may have expired. In the final analysis, the chargeable amount should be the same as if the lease had been granted for 21 years at a premium of £150,000. Thus,

If chargeable on £150,000

				Permitted discount £
£150,000	×	$\frac{(21 - 1)}{50}$	=	60,000
This is the same as: (A's lease)				
£100,000	×	$\frac{(21 - 1)}{50}$	=	40,000
Plus (B's assignment)				
£30,000	×	$\frac{(21 - 1)}{50}$	=	12,000
Plus (if C assigns at a profit) of at least £20,000)				
£20,000	×	$\frac{(21 - 1)}{50}$	=	8,000
				60,000

3.5 SALE WITH A RIGHT OF RECONVEYANCE OR TO A LEASEBACK

TA 1988, s 36 is essentially a self-contained charging provision which charges profits as if they were income profits where land is sold with a right of reconveyance or land is sold with a right to take a leaseback.

3.5.1 Sale and reconveyance

Section 36(1) can be divided into three parts. Part I sets out the provisions which must be satisfied before this section can apply. Part II sets out the head under which the charges take place and Part III deals with the computation of the chargeable profit.

Part I: Requirements to be satisfied before a charge can arise
The section applies where the terms subject to which an estate of interest is sold provide that it shall be, or may be required to be, conveyed at a future date to the vendor or a person who is connected with the vendor within the terms of TA 1988 s 839.

Part II: The head of charge
If the section applies the vendor shall be chargeable to tax under Schedule D, Case VI.

Part III: Computation of chargeable amount
The tax chargeable under Case VI of Schedule D shall be on any amount by which the price at which the estate or interest is sold exceeds the price at which it is to be reconveyed, or, if the earliest date at which in accordance with those terms it would fall to be reconveyed is the date two years or more after the sale, on that excess reduced by one fiftieth thereof for each complete year (other than the first) in the period between the sale and that date.

Special provisions apply if the date of the reconveyance is not fixed.

There has never been a case on s 36 and there are some difficult points of interpretation.

The author is of the view that the reference to 'sold' and 'price' in s 36(1) means that the section can only apply where the vendor sells his estate or interest in land for cash or a cash equivalent (banker's draft, cheque etc). Thus the transfer of a freehold in return for another interest in land would not in the author's opinion cause this provision to apply (see *Littlewood's Mail Order Stores Ltd* v *IRC* [1963] AC 135). It is not felt that s 24(4) changes that analysis.

Also the reference to 'sold' in the author's opinion means the date of completion rather than the date of contract. A contract is merely an agreement to sell. The sale would be the completion.

The author is not aware of the Revenue's view on those two points, ie, whether there can be a sale without cash and whether the sale takes place at the time of completion or contracts.

Example 3J: Sale and reconveyance

X sells its freehold to Y for £1m. It has a right to take a reconveyance of the freehold for £0.8m in 7 years' time. Effectively it may be said that Y has had a lease of the premises for £0.2m. The £0.2m reduced by one fiftieth thereof for each complete year other than the first in the period between the sale and the reconveyance (ie 7 years minus 1 year).

3.5.2 Sale and leaseback

The taxpayer may seek to overcome the tax charge under the sale and reconveyance provisions mentioned above by requiring a leaseback instead of a reconveyance. Section 36(3) seeks to close any such loophole. The provision is engrafted onto the main charging provision, namely s 36(1). It can thus be split into three parts.

Part I: Requirements for a charge to arise
This section applies where the terms subject to which an estate or interest in land is sold provide for the grant of a lease directly or indirectly out of the estate or interest so sold to the vendor or a person who is connected with him.

If that is the case then the grant of the lease is to be treated as the reconveyance of the estate or interest which was sold by the vendor to the purchaser.

Part II: The head of charge
The head of charge is Schedule D, Case VI; thus the gain is taxed as income.

Part III: Computation
The tax charge under Case VI of Schedule D shall be imposed on the difference between the price at which the estate or interest was sold by the vendor to the purchaser and the sum of:

(*a*) the amount of the premium if any paid for the lease by the vendor and

(*b*) the value at the date of the sale of the right to receive a conveyance of the reversion immediately after the lease begins to run.

It is also provided that the special leaseback provisions do not apply if the lease is granted and begins to run within one month after the sale.

It is arguable that the reference to the grant of the lease requires there to be formal grant as opposed to an agreement for a lease. This is in spite of the fact that s 24 provides that a lease includes an agreement for lease. It may be that the use of the word 'grant' demonstrates that the context requires there to be a formal lease.

Also it is noted that s 24(4) states that a sum should include the value of any consideration and a reference to a sum paid or payable or to the payment of a sum shall be construed accordingly.

It may be that the reference to 'sum' in s 36(3) is not intended to come within that definition because it is used in an entirely different sense. Nevertheless in many transactions not much would turn on that particular point.

Example 3K: Sale and leaseback

X sells his freehold to Y for £1m subject to a right to take a leaseback of the same 7 years later at a premium of £0.8m. Y would retain the reversion. The leaseback is for 999 years at an annual rent of 1p. The value of that reversion at the time when the leaseback comes into effect (ie 7 years along the line) is minimal. Thus applying the above provisions dealing with the computation of a gain X would receive £0.2m reduced by one fiftieth thereof for each complete year (other than the first) in the period between the sale and the leaseback.

Example 3L: Sale and leaseback within one month

X sells his freehold to Y for £1m and takes an immediate leaseback at a full rent. Section 36 would not apply because the lease is granted and begins to run within one month after the sale.

Example 3M: Sale and leaseback after one month

X sells his freehold to Y for £1m and the full rental leaseback is granted and begins to run 2 months after the sale. These provisions would therefore apply but one may expect very little taxable profit to be produced. The sale consideration is £1m. One can offset against that the amount of any premium paid (nil) plus the value at the date of the sale of the right to receive a conveyance of the reversion immediately after the lease begins to run. The reversion would be worth £1m. In this case no gain would be thrown up. It may be that in certain circumstances the value of the reversion (with the benefit of a lease of course) is worth less than £1m but (hopefully) that should be exceptional in an arm's length deal. Thus, in a classical sale of leaseback transaction even if this provision is offended because the one month period is overrun the author would not expect any significant or relevant tax charge to arise.

Example 3N: Sale and leaseback and city centre development

X is doing a major city centre property development and as part of the structuring transfers its freehold worth £1m to Y, taking a 999 year leaseback at a peppercorn rent. The lease in the hands of X is worth £1m. If the sale and leaseback come within the one month period limitation then no problems at all arise (TA 1988, s 36(3) (proviso).

If that period of one month in the example immediately above is exceeded it may be argued that the freehold was sold in return for the leasehold thus the first part of the computation shows £1m worth of sales proceeds. The author actually feels that that would be wrong because *sale denotes a disposal for cash.* Assume however that '*sold*' is interpreted to mean a disposal in return for something of value (see *Nichols* v *IRC* [1975] STC 278, *Sargaison* v *Roberts* and *Littlewood's Mail Order Stores* v *IRC* [1963] AC 513). If one looks at the deductible items one finds that the value of the reversion immediately after the lease begins to run is minimal and it is quite clear that no premium has been paid for the leaseback. It is very difficult to argue that the transfer of the freehold was the premium for the leaseback; the freehold must have first been obtained by Y and there is thereafter a leaseback. Thus, if taxpayers do not wish to rely on the 'sold' argument (a sale only takes place if cash, cheques etc are received) then they should ensure that the leaseback takes place within one month after the sale. Often such transactions are complicated by virtue of the fact that X may transfer £1m worth of land to the local authority and take a lease of that land plus other land comprised in the project. The arguments, however, will be the same; there is no sale because there is no cash and additionally one should ensure that the lease is granted and begins to run within one month after the sale. With respect to the new land, there may be taxable land exchanges for capital gains tax purposes.

A further argument that the reference to the 'grant' of a lease means a formal lease is that it is likely that in very many cases where property is sold with a right to take a formal lease in 7 years' time that that right comprises an agreement for lease. If that is the case then the provision becomes somewhat anomalous unless lease in this context means a formal grant.

3.6 PAYMENT OF PREMIUMS ETC TO NON-RESIDENTS

The deduction-at-source provisions which relate to rent paid to non-residents also apply where a premium or similar payment taxable under the Schedule A lease premium provisions is paid to a person whose usual place of abode is abroad (TA 1988, s 43). The payer need only deduct tax from the income-taxable portion of the sum paid to the non-resident (see IR27 *Notes on the Taxation of Income from Real Property,* para 59). This is an important provision and must not be overlooked.

3.7 TAX PLANNING

(*a*) Trading tenants should try to pay premiums on grants of leases rather than taking assignments of leases. This will enable them to obtain some IT relief or CT on income relief, as the case may be, on part of the premium.

(*b*) If it is intended to grant leases for over 50 years the documents should be carefully checked to make sure that they are not deemed to be leases for shorter periods under these lease premium provisions. If they are deemed to be for shorter periods then adverse tax consequences can flow.

(*c*) Payments of premiums and other sums taxable under these provisions to non-resident lessors or vendors may require tax to be deducted at source from part of the premium under TA 1988, s 43 and this requirement must not be overlooked.

(*d*) Payment of a sum by a tenant to the landlord to cover the landlord's solicitor's costs may be a premium under these provisions and the tenant may be able to claim tax relief under TA 1988, s 87 (Taxable premiums etc).

(*e*) A person proposing to take an assignment of a lease may have to make enquiries to ensure that it was not granted at an undervalue, so that TA 1988, s 35 has application. He may be able to obtain an appropriate clearance from his Inspector of Taxes (TA 1988, s 35).

(*f*) The taxing of capital gains at the same rates as income will mean that in many cases these provisions will not have great relevance. In view of this, the Chancellor may be tempted in years to come to abolish these provisions.

4 DEALERS AND DEVELOPERS WHO DEAL IN LAND

4.1 INTRODUCTION

In examining land transactions it is nearly always necessary to bear in mind the provisions relating to land trading. This chapter deals with the land trading provisions and, in particular, the various badges of trade.

A trading transaction is usually one where the taxpayer has acquired property in order to sell it at a profit, whether after developing it or not, and carries out the transaction accordingly.

A trade is statutorily defined in TA 1988, s 832(1) to include 'every trade, manufacture, adventure or concern in the nature of trade'.

That is not a very helpful definition and it is necessary to look at a substantial body of case law to discover whether a particular land transaction amounts to a trade. A study of these cases may be necessary when planning land transactions. Virtually any act or omission in connection with a land transaction can have a bearing on whether it is a trading transaction or not.

As to whether a trade exists is a mixed question of fact and law (*Edwards* v *Bairstow and Harrison* [1956] AC 14). The General or Special Commissioners will make findings of fact and decide whether there was a trade or not. Their conclusion may be upset on appeal if no person acting judicially and properly instructed as to the relevant law could have come to the decision arrived at. It is clear that if the Commissioners decide against the taxpayer the chances of a successful appeal are not likely to be high.

It is not possible for an asset to be both trading stock and a permanent investment at the same time (*Simmons* v *IRC* [1980] STC 350, *per* Lord Wilberforce at p 352H). However, it is perfectly possible for a taxpayer to buy property as an investment and subsequently, perhaps after many years, appropriate the land to trading stock and then dispose of the same. Megarry J expressly stated this in *Taylor* v *Good* 49 TC 277 at p 288. 'Quite apart from authority I would hold that property acquired with no thought of trade may afterwards become the subject of a trade.' It seems clear that one must bring that property into the trading account at its value not when acquired but when appropriated to stock (see p 290D).

4.2 TAX RATES

If a transaction in land is found to be a trading transaction then the profit will be subject to tax under Case I of Schedule D (TA 1988 s 18(3)).

Individuals will pay tax on the profits according to the normal rates of IT (basic rate of 25% or 40%). Profits will normally be taxed on the preceding year basis.

Companies pay CT on such profits as if they were income profits: top rate of tax, 35%. The small profits relief can reduce the rate to as low as 25% (FA 1988 s 27).

4.3 BADGES OF TRADE

Some of the factors which have a bearing on whether a trade exists or not will now be examined. There are a large number of such factors.

The Master of the Rolls in *Erichsen* v *Last* (1881) 8 QBD 414 stated at p 416:

> There is not, I think, any principle of law which lays down what carrying on a trade is. There are a multitude of things which together make up the carrying on of a trade, but I know no one distinguishing incident, for it is a compound fact made up of a variety of things.

4.3.1 Has the taxpayer carried out a similar transaction before?

If the taxpayer has carried out similar land transactions before he is more likely to be found to be a trader than had he not carried out those transactions. In *J Bolson & Son, Ltd* v *Farrelly* 34 TC 161, X ran a passenger service but bought and sold a number of boats in a short time, after having modified them. Harman J held that X had traded. He said at p 167:

> A deal done once is probably not [an activity in the nature of a trade], though it may be. Done three or four times it usually is. Each case must depend on its own facts.

In *Page* v *Pogson* (1954) 35 TC 545 the taxpayer successfully built and sold two bungalows. He had built them himself and had lived in them. The Court held that he had traded with regard to the second bungalow but not the first.

If the taxpayer carries out a transaction the Commissioners are entitled to take into consideration any subsequent transactions which throw light upon the nature of the original transaction.

In *Leach* v *Pogson* 40 TC 585 the taxpayer set up a driving school and subsequently disposed of the same for cash and shares. He set up the school in early 1954 and disposed of it in December 1955. By 1959 the taxpayer had carried out 29 similar transactions, ie, disposing of driving schools. The initial driving school was disposed of, the taxpayer claimed, in order to enable him to raise money to buy subsequent driving schools which he could then turn over at a profit. Ungoed-Thomas J at p 594 stated:

> . . . the Commissioners were clearly entitled to take into consideration the subsequent 29 transactions to throw light upon the nature of the original transaction of sale . . . and to come to the conclusion that, at the time the appellant sold . . . he had intended to embark—and was in fact embarking—upon a course of trade consisting of selling schools of motoring.

In that particular case it appears that the taxpayer did not *buy* the original school with a view to trading but no arguments were raised about the appropriation to stock (of the original driving school) and whether the gain up to appropriation should be free of income tax. When it was sold the original driving school was clearly stock.

However, it is possible for one isolated transaction to be a trading transaction (*Martin* v *Lowry* [1927] AC 312, and *Rutledge* v *IRC* (1929) 14 TC 490). This will depend on the property in question. If some derelict non-income-producing land is bought and sold in an isolated transaction this is more likely to be a trading transaction than if rent-producing houses are purchased and resold.

Even if property is purchased with the intention of selling it at a future date this does not of necessity mean that there is a trading transaction, because this is the expectation of most, if not all, people who make investments (*IRC* v *Reinhold* (1953) 34 TC 389). The sale of an ordinary investment at an enhanced price is not a trading transaction (*Californian Copper Syndicate Ltd* v *Harris* (1905) 5 TC 159).

4.3.2 Has the taxpayer been involved in other types of operation involving land?

Where a person is closely associated with land transactions (such as a builder, developer, etc) there is a presumption, although this is a rebuttable presumption, that the person's land transactions are dealing transactions and taxable under Case I of Schedule D.

In *Harvey* v *Caulcott* (1952) 33 TC 159, a builder sold shops which he had let and a house which had been built for his foreman to live in. His contention that these were realisations of investments was accepted by the High Court. Donovan J, as he was then, stated at p 165:

> Such a case as the present is always coloured by the fact that the man is a builder. That no doubt puts a particular onus on him to show that profit from the sale of some property is profit from an investment, or profit

> from something which is not trading stock. That onus is not incapable of discharge.

4.3.3 What did the taxpayer intend when he purchased the property?

If the taxpayer intended to hold land as an investment when he purchased it or to hold it for his own use and enjoyment this would indicate that the land was not trading stock.

In *Taylor* v *Good* [1974] STC 148, the taxpayer carried on the business of a grocer and newsagent. He and his wife lived in a council flat above the grocer's shop. In July 1959 he noticed that a house with about 9½ acres of ground was advertised for sale by auction. The taxpayer's parents had once worked at the house and he had known it as a boy. He attended the auction and made a bid. He did not expect to be successful in his bid but in the event he was successful and purchased the house for £5,100. The taxpayer had in mind that he and his wife would live in the house but it soon became apparent to them that this was impractical. In September 1959 the taxpayer consulted a planning consultant and ultimately obtained planning permission for the erection of 90 dwellings on the property.

The taxpayer finally sold the property in August 1963 for £54,000. The taxpayer was assessed on his gain under Schedule D, Case I. The Court held that the taxpayer was not chargeable as the gain was not a trading gain. This was because the taxpayer had not purchased the property with a view to resale. The fact that he subsequently took steps to enhance the value of the property in order to get a better price on the sale was not sufficient to make the transaction a trading transaction. After quoting a number of cases the judge said 'all these cases, it seems to me, point strongly against the theory of law that a man who owns or buys without a present intention to sell land is engaged in trade if he subsequently, not being himself a developer, merely takes steps to enhance the value of the property in the eyes of a developer who might wish to buy for development' (p 154J).

In *Simmons* v *IRC* [1980] STC 350 a group of companies acquired various properties for development and retention, but it could foresee that it was possible that it would not be able to hold on to all the properties and that its intention may change so that the properties would be disposed of. Additionally, adverse circumstances arose: there was the passing of the Rent Act 1965, FA 1965 introduced CGT and the economic climate was unfavourable. The decision was taken to liquidate the group and dispose of the properties. The Revenue contended that the land gains on the disposal of the properties were of a trading nature. The taxpayer contended that the land gains were of an investment nature and the House of Lords accepted this.

Lord Wilberforce stated(at p 355):

> Frustration of a plan for investment, which compels realisation, even if foreseen as a possibility, surely cannot give rise to an intention to trade.

Thus, taxpayers who for instance borrow money to purchase properties with a view to obtaining sufficient rentals to cover the interest and capital repayments will not be found to be traders if they intended to hold the property as an investment but it turns out that the rents are not sufficient to cover the outgoings and the properties have to be disposed of. This is so even though the taxpayer may have foreseen the possibility of not being able to get sufficient rent from the outset.

4.3.4 Has the taxpayer personally used and enjoyed the land?

If the taxpayer buys a house and uses it as his residence this would indicate that the land is not trading stock. The same principle applies if a company (or other trader) buys land from which it carries out its trade, eg, if a manufacturing company buys a factory from which it carries out its manufacturing activities.

4.3.5 Is the land income-producing?

If the rents from the land exceed the outgoings it is more likely to be an investment than if the opposite were the case.

In *Cooke* v *Haddock* (1960) 39 TC 64, the rents from the land in question were less than the interest on the mortgage the taxpayer raised in order to buy the land. This was a factor which indicated that the transaction—the purchase and sale of the land at a profit—was a trading transaction. The taxpayer in that case was a solicitor and the case is notable for the large number of the badges of trade which existed. Pennycuick J stated at p 71:

> (i) The land was ripe for building subject to the necessary licences being obtained; (ii) the land was unsuitable for occupation by the Appellant or for retention as an income producing investment by the Appellant; (iii) the Appellant obtained planning permission for development of the estate (although this was to safeguard himself against the threat of compulsory purchase and not with a view to developing the estate himself); (iv) the Appellant sold parts of the land piecemeal; and (v) the Appellant has been concerned in companies and a partnership firm engaged in dealings in land.

It may be that nowadays the importance of achieving a rental profit is not so great. In the case of *Marson* v *Morton* [1986] STC 463 (Chancery Division, Sir Nicholas Browne-Wilkinson V-C) the taxpayers, wholesale potato merchants, disposed of non-income producing land within a few months and the gain was held not to be a trading gain. At p 472 the Vice-Chancellor stated:

> ... in my judgment it (the fact that income is produced) plainly is a relevant factor. But in my judgment in 1986 it is not any longer self-evident that unless land is producing income it cannot be an investment. The legal principle of course cannot change with the passage of time: but life does. Since the arrival of inflation and high rates of tax on income new approaches to investment have emerged putting the emphasis in investment on the

> making of capital profit at the expense of income yield. For example, the purchase of short-dated stocks giving a capital yield on redemption but no income has become commonplace. Similarly, split-level investment trusts have been invented which produce capital profits on one type of share and income on another. Again, institutions now purchase works of art by way of investment. In my judgment those are plainly not trading deals; yet no income is produced from them. I can see no reason why land should be any different and the mere fact that land is not income-producing should not be decisive or even virtually decisive on the question whether it was bought as an investment.

4.3.6 Did the taxpayer acquire the property by gift or inheritance?

Property acquired by way of gift or inheritance would tend not to be trading land as it would be difficult for the Revenue to show that the land was acquired with a view to resale (*McClelland* v *Taxation Commissioner of Commonwealth of Australia* [1971] 1 All ER 969).

However, they may be able to establish that an intention to trade was formed some time after the land was acquired in which case the asset would be brought into trading stock at its value at that time. In *Pilkington* v *Randall* (1966) 42 TC 662, a taxpayer purchased land from his sister (which she had inherited) with a view to making a trading profit and it was found as a fact that he appropriated his own property, which he had also inherited, to trading stock at the same time.

With regard to land trading transactions, it is certainly possible for the taxpayer to change his intentions with regard to property (so that land which was originally an investment becomes stock) after he has acquired it (*Mitchell* v *Tomlinson* [1957] TC 224) but nevertheless the courts will presume that he has retained the original intention unless it can be demonstrated otherwise (*Dunn Trust Ltd* v *Williams* [1950] 31 TC 447, also in *Simmons* v *IRC* [1980] 2 All ER 798).

4.3.7 How long has the land been held?

If the land has been held for a short period it is more likely to be trading stock. In *Burrell and Others* v *Davis* (1948) 38 TC 307 land was sold within 6 months of its purchase and was held to be within Case I of Schedule D.

In *Turner* v *Last* (1965) 42 TC 517 a farmer purchased land and very shortly thereafter sold one part. His financial position indicated that he needed to sell in order to reimburse himself for the acquisition cost.

Quick resales are an indication of trading. Cross J at p 522 stated:

> A man may buy something, whether it be land or a chattel, for his own use and enjoyment with no idea of a quick resale, and then, quite unexpectedly, he may receive an offer to buy which is too tempting to refuse. That is a perfectly possible state of facts; but the fact that there was a quick resale

> naturally leads one to scrutinise the evidence that it was not envisaged from the first very carefully.

He also continued at p 523:

> Of course, the mere fact that when you buy property, as well as intending to use and enjoy it, you have also in your mind the possibility that it will appreciate in value, and that a time may come when you want to sell it and make a profit on it, does not of itself make you a trader; but if the position is that you intended to sell it as soon as you can to recover the cost of the purchase, the position is obviously very different . . .

4.3.8 Would the taxpayer find it difficult to retain the land long term?

If the taxpayer would find it difficult to retain the property long term the transaction is more likely to amount to a trading transaction than if this were not the case. In *Johnson* v *Heath* [1970] 3 All ER 915, a building company employee bought land and resold it immediately. The purchase price was £15,000 and the sale price was £25,000. The taxpayer's only capital was £2,250. It was held that the gain was a trading gain because he had no intention of holding the property as an investment and his means were insufficient to service the loan required to hold the property as an investment. The land itself was not income-producing.

4.3.9 Is there too much land for the taxpayer's use?

If the taxpayer buys more land than is required for his use the surplus land may come within Case I of Schedule D.

In *Iswera* v *Ceylon Commissioners of Inland Revenue* (1965) 44 ATC 157, the taxpayer wanted to be near his children who were at a school. He bought the only available land near the school on which to build a house. The land he purchased was too big for his house and he sold the surplus land for building sites. The gains on the sales were taxable under Case I of Schedule D.

4.3.10 Has the taxpayer carried out work on the land?

If the taxpayer carried out work on the land which is of the type which a property developer or trader would carry out this would indicate trading. The important thing is the amount of work and type of work on the asset. In *IRC* v *Livingston* (1926) 11 TC 538, three persons purchased a cargo vessel, converted it into a steam-drifter and sold it at a gain. They had never been involved in this type of business before. They were held to have carried out what was characteristic of that carried out by professional ship repairers. They were traders. Lord Sands stated at p 544 as follows:

> The subject matter of the purchase and sale may be so treated in the interval as to bring the transaction within the category of carrying on a trade.

> I do not think that putting the article in question in a suitable condition for a favourable sale would necessarily have this effect, as, for example, having a picture cleaned or a ship's boilers cleaned and the hull repainted. But I am disposed to think that it would introduce the element of carrying on a trade if the purchaser were . . . to carry through a manufacturing process which changed the character of the article. An illustration might be the purchasing of a quantity of pig-iron and having it manufactured into steel, or of gold bearing ore and having the gold extracted by milling the ore.

In the property world, if a person buys land and constructs new buildings thereon or extensively improves the buildings already thereon and then sells the same, this is more likely to be a trading transaction than if he had simply bought income-producing land and sold it. In *IRC* v *Toll Property Co Ltd* (1952) 34 TC 13 the taxpayer company held property and part of the building thereon was demolished while the remainder was altered and repaired. The site was generally tidied up. This was the type of operation which a property developer would undertake and the taxpayer company was held to have traded even though this was the only transaction it had carried out.

There is clearly a line to be drawn between trading situations and where the taxpayer is merely carrying out work to his property which is an investment property in order to get the best price on a sale. Thus if an investment property is repainted in order to get the best price on the sale of the investment this would not indicate trading.

If the taxpayer holds land as an investment he may clear the land and construct roads and sell off parts, ploughing the proceeds of sales back into the lands to develop the same. In this case the question is whether the taxpayer has gone beyond the stage of merely realising an investment and has actually traded. The taxpayer may be said to have traded in part of his land in order to enable the proceeds to be ploughed back into the remaining part which may be an investment property. The cases can go either way. In *C H Rand* v *Alberni Land Company Ltd* (1920) 7 TC 629 a company held land as an investment. It cleared the land and constructed roads. It sold parts of it and kept some of the money and re-invested in the land. It gave a share of the capital to certain people who were instrumental in bringing a railroad to the land. The fact that they had carried out some development and set up machinery to deal with the disposal of parcels had not caused the transactions to amount to trading transactions.

In the *Hudson's Bay Co Ltd* v *Stevens* (1905) 5 TC 425 the Court of Appeal stated clearly that if the landowner holds a property as an investment or for the purposes of carrying out his trade therefrom (for instance if a landowner owns land for farming) and he sells part of the land for building purposes that would not cause him to be a trader.

Further, Farwell L J stated at p 437:

> Again, a landowner may lay out part of his estate with roads and sewers and sell it in lots for building, but he does this as owner, not as a land speculator. It would be different if a landowner . . . entered into the business of buying

> and developing and selling land; but the case of the owner, whether of land, or pictures, or jewels, selling his own land, although he may have expended money on them in getting them up for sale, is entirely different; he sells as owner not as trader.

That case was distinguished in *Alabama Coal Co Ltd* v *Mylam* (1926) 11 TC 232 where Rowlatt J at p 253 said that even a person in the position of a landowner can use his existing land as an article of trade if that is the true view of what he has done with it.

4.3.11 Has the taxpayer applied for planning permission to develop the land?

If the taxpayer has obtained or applied for planning permission to increase his profit on the sale of the land, this is likely to indicate trading (*Turner* v *Last* (1965) 42 TC 517) although if the taxpayer acquired the land without any intention of reselling it the mere obtaining of planning permission will not cause the transaction to be a trading transaction (*Taylor* v *Good* [1974] 1 All ER 1137).

4.3.12 Has the taxpayer improved the nature of his interest in the land?

If the taxpayer has a leasehold interest as an investment and goes through a surrender and regrant to obtain a more valuable interest to sell on then this would indicate trading.

Example 4A: Enlargement of interest

X Ltd has a 70 year lease from a local authority. It is a valuable lease and it wishes to sell the same to a fund and take a lease back. If it were to simply sell the property and take the lease back the disposal proceeds would amount to a capital disposal giving rise to a charge to corporation tax on the chargeable gain. However, the fund may require a lease of over 70 years. Thus X Ltd may pay a sum to the local authority in order to take a lease for 125 years and then dispose of the new 125 year lease to the fund taking a lease back. In this case it may well be argued that the sale proceeds are chargeable to corporation tax on income. It is very likely that the gain up to the surrender of the 70 year lease and the grant of the 125 year lease is of a capital nature with the land then being appropriated to stock and any further gain being a gain of an income nature. Thus the overall tax consequences may not be too serious except that if the premises were used for the purposes of carrying out X Ltd's trade then roll-over relief may not be available under the provisions of CGTA 1979, s 115 because of the appropriation to stock prior to the disposal to the fund of the 125 year lease.

4.3.13 Has the land been acquired for tax avoidance purposes?

In *Coates* v *Arndale* [1984] STC 124 (CA), [1984] STC 637 (HL) property was transferred between members of a group of companies in order to obtain tax advantages by virtue of *inter alia* TA 1970 s 274(1). In order to obtain the tax advantages it was essential that the relevant company acquired the land as trading stock. The Court of Appeal held that because the transaction was entered into to obtain a tax benefit the land could not amount to trading stock. Lawton J stated at p 129F:

> In my judgment if the acquisition of an asset lacks a commercial character it cannot be said to have been acquired as trading stock: but if it has the character the reason why the acquisition was made, in the absence of other factors, ought not to deprive it of that character.

That line of reasoning was adopted in the Lords ([1984] STC 637 at p 641F).

4.3.14 Why was the land sold?

If land was sold because of supervening events occurring after acquisition, this may not indicate trading. In *West* v *Phillips* (1958) 38 TC 203, a builder held land as trading stock and other land for investment purposes. The builder sold the investment land for reasons unconnected with his land trade (relating to rent control, the rising cost of repairs and increased taxation) and it was held that the sales did not give rise to trading gains.

4.3.15 Is the taxpayer an investment company?

The professed objects of a company are relevant to the determination of whether a transaction is a trading transaction (*Balgowrie Land Trust Ltd* v *IRC* (1929) 14 TC 684). However, if a company makes a profit by trading, that profit is assessable even if the company is described as an investment company (*IRC* v *Hyndland Investment Co Ltd* (1929) 14 TC 694).

4.3.16 Does the taxpayer understand what is going on?

In the case of *Marson* v *Morton* [1986] STC 463 the taxpayers were wholesale potato merchants. On the advice of an estate agent they decided to invest a trading surplus in land. They bought the land in June 1977 intending to hold the same as an investment for 1 to 2 years. The land had the benefit of planning permission but produced no income. In September 1977, acting again on the advice of the estate agent, the taxpayer sold the land making a profit. It was held that the transaction was not a trading transaction. Some emphasis was laid on the fact (p 472F) that the taxpayers did

> carry through an extraordinary transaction *without knowing or understanding what was going on.* It may be they were doing so as dealers trying to turn a quick profit. It may equally be that they were doing it with a view to investing money.

The taxpayers borrowed money in order to buy the property as well as putting some of their own money in but

> *they did not know they were borrowing as such;* they knew they were

not good enough for the whole purchase money but until they signed the document they did not know of the borrowing.

It seems therefore in appropriate cases lack of knowledge of what was going on may assist in defeating a trade claim. Of course the taxpayer who is generally involved in the property industry is unlikely to be able to make use of this defence.

4.3.17 Is the taxpayer dead?

The burden of discharging the assessment in placed upon the taxpayer. If the taxpayer has died, the personal representatives should bear in mind the fact that the chances of discharging an assessment are reduced, in some cases substantially reduced. The taxpayer could not give oral evidence of his intentions and in appropriate cases the burden may not be capable of being overturned.

4.4 WHEN PROFITS ARE TAXABLE

Tax under Case I of Schedule D is payable on the trading profits, being the difference between actual or deemed trading income less allowable expenses.

4.4.1 Buying land as stock

When a trading company buys land as trading stock, it will obtain a deduction for the monies laid out to acquire that trading stock but the computation will normally require that the lower of cost or market value of that stock be brought into the trading computation. For instance, in the accounting period ended 31 December 1985 X Ltd may have sold land for £100,000. It may have purchased that property during 1984 for £10,000 and as at 1 January 1985, £10,000 was the lower of cost and market value of that land. During 1985 it may have purchased another parcel of land (greenacre) for £20,000 which land has increased in value since the date of acquisition. The trading computation will require that the £100,000 sale proceeds be added to £20,000 which is the lower of cost and market value of greenacre. That gives a figure of £120,000. One can deduct therefrom the value of the stock held by the company on 1 January 1985 being the lower of market value and cost which is £10,000. One can also deduct £20,000 being the monies laid out to purchase greenacre. That gives a figure of £30,000. That £30,000 is deducted from £120,000 leaving £90,000 which is the taxable profit.

4.4.2 Obligations to pay the trader

A receipt is a proper credit item in the accounting year in which the obligations to pay the trader arose, although payment is to be made at some time in the future. However, a debt owed to the trader but which is not payable until a future date and which does not carry appropriate interest may be discounted when it is brought into the trading account.

In *Absalom* v *Talbot* [1944] AC 204, part of the sale price of a house was left outstanding for a long period, secured by a second mortgage with a purchaser with little financial means. It was held that the second mortgage should be valued (if possible) and only that value brought into account.

If the taxpayer is not able to show that the value of the monies owing to him is less than the face value of the consideration, then the full amount of the consideration must be brought into account at the time of the sale. In *Lock* v *Jones* (1941) 23 TC 749, a builder sold land to a company at £12,500 more than the price which he paid for it. The builder had agreed with the company that the £12,500 would be left outstanding until the company disposed of the property. The builder was held to be immediately taxable on the £12,500.

In *Harrison* v *John Cronk & Sons Ltd* [1937] AC 185; 20 TC 612 part of the sale price of land was deposited with a building society which the builder would get if the purchaser paid a number of instalments to the building society. It was held that the builder's interest in the sum deposited must be brought in at a value, if it was possible to ascertain one, and if it could not be valued it was not to be brought in until the builder was entitled to the money.

In the later case of *Chibbett* v *Harold Brookfield & Son Ltd* (1952) 33 TC 467, no value was placed on the deposit when it was made. Later the building society intimated that it was willing to repay it but did not in fact repay it until the builder had ceased trading. It was held that the deposit should be brought into account when the society was willing to repay it.

In the case of a normal contract to buy and sell land the date of the contract will be the relevant purchase and sale date and this date may be specially planned to come within the appropriate taxing period of the individual or company. It may be, however, that for a particular taxpayer the Revenue will accept that, with regard to its trade, completion date is the relevant time for ascertaining the date of purchase or sale.

4.4.3 Conditions to be fulfilled

The above principles only apply if all the conditions necessary to earn the monies have been fulfilled by the trader. In *Johnson* v *W S Try Ltd* (1946) 27 TC 176, a company trading in land was refused consent to develop on its land in one year and some years later the land was sold and a sum was received in compensation for the earlier refusal of the consent. It was held that all the necessary conditions to entitle the company to compensation were not fulfilled until the agreement for sale was made. Accordingly, the compensation only became part of the company's profit at that time.

4.4.4 Land traders and options

X Ltd may have an option to acquire the land of Mr Y for £100,000. At the time when the option is exercised the land may be worth £300,000. 3 years later X Ltd may sell the land for £500,000.

When the option is exercised it will not give rise to a trading profit in the hands of X Ltd. The option is not deemed to be disposed of in consideration of the acquisition of the land (*Varty* v *British South Africa Co* 42 TC 406). When the land is ultimately sold, however, there will have been a trading profit on the difference between the original £100,000 paid on the exercise of the option (plus any amounts paid to acquire the option) and the disposal of proceeds £500,000.

The position, however, may be different if the option is not exercised but is exchanged for another asset or another option; in this case there may be a disposal of the original option in consideration of the market value of new option or new asset.

This may be relevant if, for instance, Mr A has 'agreed' to sell to B Ltd his land over three years, the parties having entered into put and call options. Assume that the land had grown considerably in value and Mr A decides to cancel the put option with B Ltd agreeing to terminate the call option in consideration of the grant of a new call option. B Ltd may realise trading profits from the disposal of the old call option in consideration of the new call option in the year in which the termination and new grant takes place.

4.4.5 Developer's fee in the form of land

If a developer, as part of his development fee, is given a land interest, the value of that land interest must be brought into charge to corporation tax on income or income tax as the case may be. This is the case even if the developer takes the land interest as an investment.

Development schemes should be carefully scrutinised with this point in mind and the client is forewarned.

It is clear from *Gold Coast Selection Trust Ltd* v *Humphrey* 30 TC 209 that the market value of the asset (in this case the land interest) which represents the consideration for services provided by the developer, can be brought into the trading computation of the developer.

Where it is not possible to value the assets they will be brought into account when they can be valued (*Harrison* v *Cronk & Sons* [1937] AC 185).

Example 4B: Developer's fee in form of land

A pension fund may own a parcel of land. It may agree with D Limited (the Developer) for D Limited to arrange for a building to be constructed on the land

and for D Limited to take a lease. D Limited will then grant an occupational lease (see Figure **4.1** below). Let us say of the £1 rent paid by the tenants to D Limited, D Limited has to pay £0.7 rent to the fund. Thus D Limited takes its developer's profit in the form of a land interest. It is assumed that D Limited decides to hold onto the land as an investment.

It appears that the Revenue argue that the value of D Limited's land interest must come in as effectively a fee paid by the pension fund to D Limited for carrying out development works.

The author is aware of cases where the Revenue have taken this point even though D Limited was given an agreement for lease by the fund at the commencement of the works. If that is the case it follows that D Limited will have made a supply for VAT though the author is not aware of any situation where the Customs and Excise have taken a point such as this.

Figure 4.1: Developer's fee in the form of land

A Pension fund

Agreement and lease

D Ltd

Sub lease

O Occupational tenant

4.4.6 Disposals otherwise than in the course of trade

Where a trader disposes of trading stock otherwise than in the course of trade, eg, if he gives it away or takes it for his own personal use, the market value of the stock will be credited as a receipt in his trading accounts (*Sharkey* v *Wernher* [1956] AC 58).

Example 4C: Taking property out of stock

Mr X is a dealer in land. He gives a parcel of land, held by him as trading stock, to his wife. He paid £1,000 for it. Its market value at the date of the gift was £5,000. He is deemed to have received £5,000 as Case I Sched D trading consideration.

4.4.7 Reverse *Sharkey* v *Wernher*

It is clear that if there is a transfer by, for instance, one member of a trading group of companies to another member of trading stock at an undervalue the Revenue may be able to bring in market value as the disposal consideration as far as the transferor company is concerned (see *Petrotim Securities Ltd* v *Ayres* (1963) 41 TC 389 and *Skinner* v *Berry Head Lands Ltd* (1970) 46 TC 377; compare *Julius Bendit* v *IRC* (1945) 27 TC 44,

Craddock v *Zevo Finance Ltd* (1946) 27 TC 267 and *Jacgilden (Weston Hall) Ltd* v *Castle* (1969) 45 TC 685). In this case if the transferee company has underpaid for the land there is a good argument that its (the transferee company's) acquisition cost of the trading stock (the land) should also be market value (see *Petrotim Securities Ltd* v *Ayres* [1963] 41 TC 389 at p 407 and also at p 409).

In the case of *Petrotim Securities Ltd* v *Ayres* 41 TC 389, X Ltd sold shares worth £835,000 for £205,000 to Y Ltd an associated company. Lord Denning MR held that where there was a sale at such a gross undervalue, this could not have been carried out in the course of the trade of X Ltd. This being the case, market value was to be substituted for the actual sale price of £205,000 in carrying out the Case I of Schedule D trading computation. Lord Denning (at page 407) said that the doctrine applies:

> . . . to any case where a trader may, for no reason, choose to give things away or throw them into the sea. So when he put securities through his books at a derisory price, the figures are to be regarded as struck out for tax purposes; and in there place you must put in the market realisable value at the time.

4.4.8 Avoiding *Sharkey* v *Wernher*

In *Jacgilen (Western Hall) Ltd* v *Castle* (1969) 45 TC 685 Mr X contracted to acquire land. When it came to completion he arranged for his company to complete the acquisition and pay £72,000 and a few months later the company disposed of the land for £155,000. The Revenue argued the application of *Sharkey* v *Wernher* 36 TC 275 and claimed that the taxpayer had made a gift of value to the company. The Special Commissioners found that was not the case and Plowman J in the High Court agreed. At p 700C he stated:

> There is no question of the contracts for the sale and purchase of the hotel at £72,000 having been an elusory or colourable or fraudulent transaction; it was a perfectly straightforward and honest bargain between Mr Rowe (the taxpayer) and the vendors. It is, in my judgment, therefore, clear that, subject to the question of gift, the proper figure to be debted in respect of the hotel is its cost, £72,000. The Special Commissioners have found that the acquisition was a commercial acquisition and inferentially, if not explicitly, that the transaction was not one of gift. The question which I have to decide therefore comes down simply to this; is that a conclusion which the Special Commissioners were entitled to reach on the evidence.
>
> In my judgement, it was. It seems to me that they were entitled to conclude, as a matter of business common sense and notwithstanding any element of gift there may have been, the transaction with which they were concerned was not a gift or a sale by Mr Rowe to the company at an undervalue, but a purchase by the company of trading stock at a price which had been fairly negotiated between Mr Rowe and the vendors. The *Sharkey* v *Wernher* line of authority has never, so far as I am aware, been applied to a case where the price at which the property passed had been negotiated as a fair and proper price, and because it is an exceptional line of authority I think that the court should be slow to extend it. I therefore dismiss the appeal.

The author feels that in general there must be a fairly significant difference between the sale price and the market value of the property before the Revenue can apply *Sharkey* v *Wernher*.

4.4.9 TA 1988, s 770 (Sales at undervalue/overvalue)

TA 1988, s 770 is designed to prevent the avoidance of tax by the disposal of assets at an undervalue between associated persons. The provision applies, broadly, where any property is sold and:

(*a*) the buyer is a body of persons over whom the seller has control or the seller is a body of persons over whom the buyer has control or both the seller and the buyer are bodies of persons and some other person has control over both of them; and
(*b*) the property is sold at a price less than the price which it might have been expected to fetch if the parties to the transaction had been independent persons dealing at arm's length.

If a sale falls within this provision the Revenue can adjust the seller's tax computation, substituting market value for the actual sale price. The provision does not apply if the purchaser is a UK resident trading company and the property is brought into its trading computation (s 485(1), proviso). The provision may also have application to certain sales at overvalue (s 485(2)).

Even if a case falls outside the provision the Revenue may use the *Sharkey* v *Wernher* [1956] AC 58 principle to substitute market value on a disposal. In *Skinner* v *Berry Head Lands Ltd* [1971] 1 All ER 222, W Co purchased the whole of the issued share capital of T Co, a land-dealing company. On the same day T Co sold certain land to W Co for £4,175 which had a market value of £40,000. Following *Sharkey* v *Wernher,* it was held that T Co should be taxable on the basis of the market value of the land, £40,000.

4.4.10 Trading companies: special accounting period rules

A company pays tax on the full amount of the profits arising in any accounting period of the company (TA 1988, s 12). If profits arise over a period, say 3 years, and then accounts are made up (3 accounts), these are generally apportioned over the period (3-year) on a time basis under TA 1988, s 72(1). Special rules, however, apply to land companies. In *Marshall Hus & Partners Ltd* v *Bolton* [1981] STC 18, the taxpayer was a property-trading company which made various sales over the years but only submitted one set of accounts for six full accounting periods. The taxpayer contended that it was necessary and lawful to apportion the profits on a time basis under TA 1988, s 72(1). Goulding J in the Chancery Division held that the profits should be chargeable by reference to the relevant transactions in the appropriate accounting periods.

This takes away some of the flexibility of using extended accounting periods to mitigate tax, at least as far as property-trading companies are concerned.

4.4.11 Appropriation to capital

If property is taken out of a taxpayer's trading account and put into capital account, an income tax or corporation tax on income charge can arise. The taxpayer has 'traded' with himself.

CGTA 1979, s 122(2) provides that if at any time an asset forming part of the trading stock of a person's trade is appropriated by him for any other purpose, or is retained by him on ceasing to carry on a trade, it shall be treated as having been acquired at that time for a consideration equal to the amount brought into the accounts of the trade in respect of it for tax purposes on the appropriation, or on the trader's ceasing to carry on the trade, as the case may be.

The growth in the value of the land after appropriation until sale will be capital growth (and only be chargeable to CGT or corporation tax on chargeable gains).

Example 4D: Appropriation to capital—Capital Allowances

X Ltd may hold twelve parcels of land as trading stock. It may decide to develop six of the parcels as Enterprise Zone commercial buildings and sell them on to purchasers. It may, however, decide to keep the remaining six parcels as an investment and obtain capital allowances. It should bear in mind that on taking the property out of trading stock and putting it into capital account, there will be a deemed disposal at market value (under *Sharkey* v *Wernher* [1956] AC 58) as at the time the property is taken out of the trading account, and so a charge to tax may arise in respect thereof (see Figure **4.2** below). This is a point the Revenue do take.

Figure 4.2

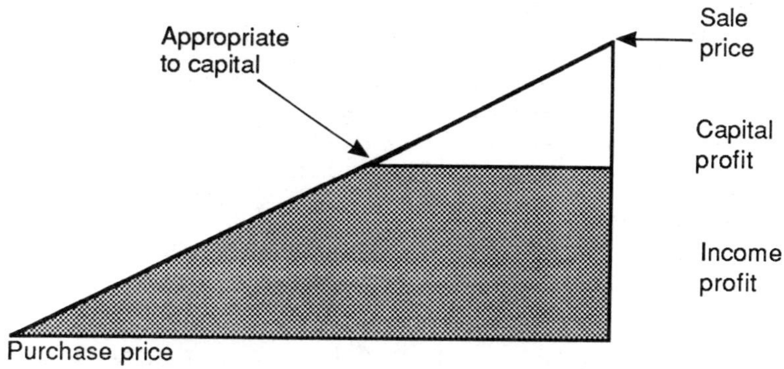

4.4.12 Appropriation to stock

A company may hold property on capital account and then appropriate it to trading stock. In this case a charge to CGT arises under CGT 1979, s 122, although this charge can be, effectively, 'rolled over' under s 122(3) if an appropriate election is made.

Figure 4.3

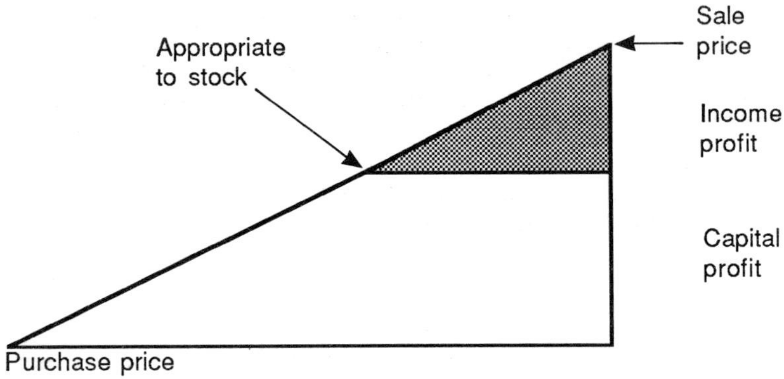

A roll over election may not always prove attractive. If the gain is not rolled over, the growth up to appropriation is capital and the growth after appropriation is income growth (see Fig **4.3** above). If the gain is rolled over this will convert the pre-appropriation growth (but note the 'generous' words of s 122(3)) into income which will be relevant generally when the property is ultimately sold.

4.4.13 Discontinuance of a trade

When a trade is discontinued, the stock is deemed to have been disposed of at market value (TA 1988, s 100(1)(*b*)). The actual disposal proceeds, however, are brought into account if the stock is sold on discontinuance to another trader who takes it into his stock (TA 1988, s 100(1)(*a*)).

In *Moore* v *R J Mackenzie and Sons* (1972) 48 TC 196, the taxpayer company, which dealt in property, owned in 1958, as its sole asset, properties (flats) having a book value of £27,686 but a market value of £95,000. If the taxpayer company had sold the flats to an outside purchaser, it could not have avoided bringing the sale price of £95,000 into its accounts. Thus a scheme was devised whereby the two shareholders of the taxpayer company sold their shares to S for £87,250, and later on the same day a directors' meeting of the taxpayer company was held at which it was resolved that the company should sell its trading stock to S for £27,686 and that simultaneously its trading activities should be discontinued. S then sold the properties to the outside purchaser for £95,000. The taxpayer company claimed that s 137(1)(*a*) (now s 100(1)(*a*)) applied, since the properties were 'trading stock belonging to the trade at the discontinuance', and that therefore only £27,686 had to be brought into its final profit and loss account. The Revenue claimed that the sale to S took place before the discontinuance, that therefore s 100(1)(*a*) could not apply, and that the principle of *Sharkey* v *Wernher* applied, requiring the taxpayer company to bring the properties into its final accounts at market value. Megarry J found in favour of the taxpayer company, holding that the s 100(1) 'relief' was available even though the stock was sold at the same moment that the trade discontinued (p 208). He went on to suggest, however, that it might have been argued by the Revenue that the 'value of the consideration given for the transfer', which is to be brought into account under s 100(1)(*a*), was £27,686 plus the excess of the price paid by S for the shares (S paid £87,250 for the shares) over their true value (£27,686).

It is not usually difficult to say when a particular trading activity has started although sometimes it may be difficult to say when preparation for the beginning of a trade merges into the trade itself (*Cannop Coal Co Ltd* v *IRC* (1918) 12 TC 31 and *Birmingham District Cattle By-Products Co Ltd* v *IRC* (1919) 12 TC 92).

It can be difficult to ascertain when a trade has ceased. This is especially the case where the cessation is only temporary and the activities are later recommenced because in that case the trade will not usually be regarded as having been permanently discontinued. Lord Summner in *South Behar Railway Co* v *IRC* [1925] AC 476 at p 488; 12 TC 657 at p 712 stated that business is not confined to being busy; in many businesses long intervals of inactivity occur.

This applies in particular to land development and realisation transactions with the consequence that it is not always easy to say when a trade of this nature has been discontinued (*Gladstone Development Co Ltd* v *Strick* (1948) 30 TC 131; *Goff* v *Osborn Co Ltd* (Scheifield) (1953) 34 TC 411; *Forest Side Properties (Chingford) Ltd* v *Pearce* (1961) 39 TC 665; cf *Bradshaw* v *Blunden* (1956) 36 TC 397).

The real point in issue in these cases relates to the carry forward of losses. If a trade has ceased and a new one commenced it will not be possible to carry forward the losses.

In *Kirk and Randall Limited* v *Dunn* [1924] 8 TC 663 a company acquired the business of a firm of contractors and until the outbreak of war in 1914 it was engaged in completing contracts into which the firm had entered but it obtained no fresh contracts. From that time, persistent efforts were made to obtain new contracts, but all such efforts were unsuccessful until early in 1920 when additional capital was put into the company, a different business policy adopted and fresh plant acquired. The company had retained its registered office and held the prescribed annual meetings; the directors' fees and the secretary's salary were paid; substantial payments were made for expenses, including those incurred by the directors in endeavouring to obtain contracts. The Special Commissioners held that there had been no trade between 1914 and 1920 and that a new trade was set up and commenced in the latter year; but their decision was reversed by the courts on the grounds that the evidence did not go so far as to show that the changes which were made in 1920 resulted in the establishment of the new business. Reliance was placed on the fact that the field of business was the same after 1920 as before. It was also held that the question was one of law.

A taxpayer may, however, want to cease its building trade on a particular date. This is a question of fact and merely resolving that the trade has ceased would not be sufficient. What is fatal is for the taxpayer to decide that a trade has ceased on a particular date and change his mind then revert back to the earlier date as the credibility of the resolution is thrown into question.

A similar thing happened in the case of *Gladstone Development Co Ltd* v *Strick* (1948) 30 TC 130 where the taxpayer company carried on the trade of builders, estate developers etc. The company claimed that it ceased trading on a particular date and then became a property investment company. The Special Commissioners found that the company had not ceased trading and the indecision on the part of the taxpayer in deciding on a date and then changing its mind was a material point. Atkinson J at p 146 stated:

> What had the Commissioners here before them? They had before them this up and down policy of the previous five years, the company saying: 'we stopped business permanently in 1939', and then soon after withdrawing, saying they were treating themselves as still carrying a business, until that ceased to be a beneficial line for them to take, and then they switched over again to the claim that, even on that original date they had permanently discontinued the business. I should have thought, in view of all that, that the Commissioners were well entitled to say: 'it is for us to judge of the quality of this resolution. It binds nobody to anything. They could change their minds the next day. In view of past history, in our view it is merely a colourable resolution to enable them to get out of paying any tax for which they may be liable. It binds them to nothing.'

Disposal consideration (shares)

It is important to identify the real consideration received on a disposal as the following example shows.

In *Californian Copper Syndicate Ltd* v *Harris* 5 TC 159 land held as trading stock was transferred to a company with the purchase price being satisfied by fully paid shares in the company (ie the company which took the land). The Commissioners held that the transferor company was assessable under Case I, Schedule D, on the difference between the original purchase price and the value of the shares received on the sale. This decision was upheld on appeal.

Example 4E: Transfer of stock to company

Mr X has land worth £1m. He sets up a new company putting in £½m by way of share capital and he owns all the shares therein. He sells the land to the company for £½m. If the land was held as trading stock his disposal consideration for Case I Schedule D purposes, in the author's opinion, would be £½m cash plus the £½m increase in the value of the shares in the shares in the company.

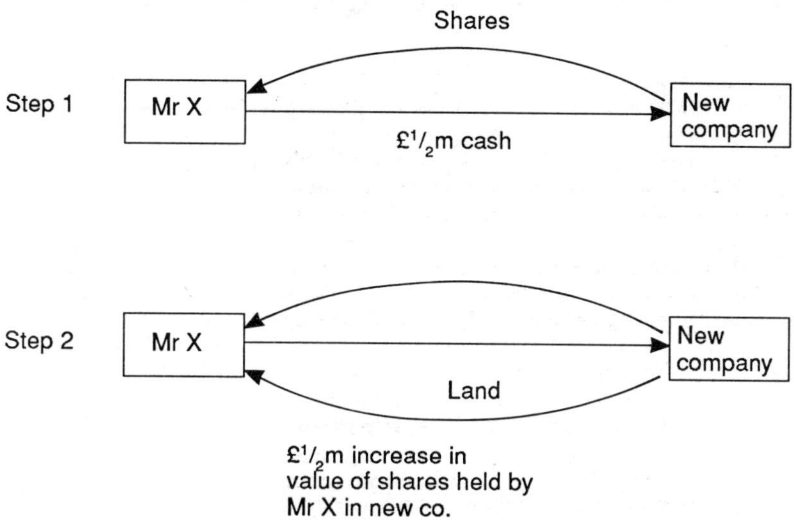

4.4.14 Constructive trading

An individual can only be taxed as a trader if he actually carries out the trade himself or if the trade is carried out through his agent or nominee (*Del Pol* v *Cunningham* (1974) 49 TC 445; *Smart* v *Lowndes* [1948] STC 607).

Where an individual is involved in the organising of a profit by his family companies or trust he cannot be taxable on the trading profit which arises to the company or trust (*Ransom* v *Higgs* [1974] 3 All ER 949).

The Revenue sought in *Ransom* v *Higgs* to argue that an individual taxpayer (which Lord Wilberforce said the Revenue were attempting to liken to Napoleon (p 90f) who had arranged or procured for a trading gain to be made by various companies and trusts could not be said to be the trader himself. Lord Wilberforce at p 90 stated:

> How can a man who procures others to do acts which amount to trading by them with their own assets be said to trade within any conception, however wide, one may have of trading? None of the characteristics of trading are present—the implications of so wide and vague an extension are alarming. If procuring persons to trade were itself to be a trade, it is obvious that the Commissioners of Income Tax would be faced with a multitude of cases where there is some sort of relation between the trade and the persons sought to be

> taxed and with the necessity of deciding whether the former was procured by the latter. Since 'procurement' has no statutory warrant, or, this case apart, basis in authority, this would open a new and completely unchartered field, placing the taxpayer at the mercy of findings of fact which he could not challenge. In particular, this doctrine would lead inevitably to claims being made, over a wide range, resulting in individuals being assessed in respect of the profits of companies.

Different rules may apply to companies. In the case of *Associated London Properties Ltd* v *Henriksen* X Limited managed, developed and dealt in real property. In 1935 Y Limited a private development company was set up and was owned 50% by X Limited and 50% by an individual Mr Y. X Limited advanced monies to the company and X Limited sold a site to Y Limited for Y Limited to erect a building on the site. It had been agreed that when the building had been erected either of the parties might acquire the shares of the other and X Limited accordingly disposed of its shares in Y Limited to Mr Y at a profit. X Limited's accounts referred to the profit being from sales in connection with land. The General Commissioners found that the profit had been made in the ordinary course of X Limited's property dealing trade and accordingly the profits were liable to income tax. That decision was upheld on appeal. In the case of *Fundfarms Developments Ltd* v *Parsons* 45 TC 707, A Limited carried on the trade of buying land, developing it and selling it off in plots. The labour and materials were provided by P Limited an associated company and A Limited did the marketing. It was held that the acquisition of the shares in G Limited (a property company) by A Limited was not an acquisition forming part of A Limited's trade as property dealers and developers even though when G Limited was acquired it owned the property which was to be developed by P Limited. The directors of A Limited looked upon the acquisition of the G Limited shares as being an operation equivalent to the purchase of land for development.

Buckley J found that the shares never comprised part of the trading stock of A Limited. At p 71 he stated

> I cannot, I think, ignore the fact that the land never became the property of (A Limited). I cannot ignore the fact, I think, that (A Limited) never took any part in the development of the land or in the sale of the land. The fact of the matter is that the advantage that (A Limited) derived from this transaction was an advantage resulting from exploiting the value in the shares of G Limited, not, I think, an advantage derived from exploiting the site . . . To regard it in the latter sense is to ignore the independent existence of G Limited and to look behind the reality of the transaction, searching for what I think is not really a true appreciation of the nature of this business but a picture which the facts are really inappropriate to support . . . I think the case is distinguishable from the Henriksen case because there the subject matter of the whole transaction was land which formed part of the stock in trade, so to call it, of (X Limited). Here (A Limited) never acquired anything but shares in another company, which proved a profitable investment.

The distinction between the two cases is quite fine but it is clear that it is likely to be very difficult for a property development company to successfully get shares in subsidiaries treated as part of its property trading stock.

4.4.15 One trade or two

It is often essential to ascertain whether a property company is carrying on 1 or 2 separate trades. This can be important for the purposes of carrying forward trading losses. In *Spiers and Son Ltd* v *Ogden* (1932) 17 TC 117 it was held that the property building and contracting work carried out by a company did not comprise a separate trade from that comprising the acquisition of land, the construction of buildings thereon and the sale of the same. These points, however, are difficult questions of fact. In *Bolson* v *Farrelly* 34 TC 161, the Court of Appeal did not upset a finding that a company which carried out a passenger boat service trade was carrying out a separate trade as ship builders and repairers at a ship yard where it built ships for the passenger boat service trade.

4.4.16 When a land trader grants a lease

Difficult problems can arise when a trader receives rent or grants leases (whether or not at a premium) and then makes a disposal of his reversion.

It appears that if the trader makes a total disposal of his interest, eg he disposes of his freehold or of his leasehold interest, then in calculating the Schedule D, Case I position of the trader one may have to bring in not only the cash proceeds but also the capitalised value of any 'ground annuals'. A ground annual in Scotland is an obligation created so that the land becomes subject to what in England may be called a rent charge so that the purchaser becomes liable to make annual payments. It is not a personal obligation on the purchaser. It is a real burden upon the land. The benefits of such ground annuals can be freely sold. They can be valued and are a marketable security in the sense of something which can be realised at anytime by going to the market. In *John Emery & Sons* v *IRC* (1936) 20 TC 213, a trader sold the total interest in his properties for cash plus ground annuals. Lord Atkin in the House of Lords at p 226 stated:

> In those circumstances the case appears to me to be as plain as can be. It is a case where people have sold in the course of business part of their stock for money plus monies' worth, namely, the equivalent of a marketable security. The position in respect of ground annuals appears to me to be precisely the same as though they had sold the land for money plus an annuity or plus a bond conditioned for the payment of these particular sums, or for debentures under which those monies were payable annually; it could be put in a great many different ways. However you put it, the result is not that they exchange part of their stock for a different kind of stock, but that they dispose of the whole of their stock for money plus monies' worth. In those circumstances it seems to me on the plainest principles that the value of that marketable security has to be brought into account for the purpose of assessing the profits which they made in the particular years of trade.

The taxpayer's contention that the capitalised value of the ground annuals should only be brought into account when the traders sold the same was rejected.

In the subsequent case of *Utting & Co Ltd* v *Hughes* (1940) 23 TC 174, that case was distinguished. The taxpayer in *Utting* was a dealer and he granted long leases at premiums. It was held that the taxpayer had not made a total disposal of his trading stock. He had merely made a part disposal on the grant of leasehold interests. He had retained the reversionary estate. If he would sell the reversion it would then come into the trading accounts but only when sold. There was no question of capitalising the right to receive the reversionary rents at the time when the leases were granted.

The case of *Emery* was distinguished because in *Emery* the total land interest of the taxpayer had been disposed on in consideration of ground annuals whereas in the case of the grant of a lease the freeholder still retained the freehold. Ground annuals were equated with rent charges in England.

It was also held that if a premium was taxable under Schedule A, it could not form an item in the computation of liability to tax under Schedule D (see p 187).

In *Broadbridge* v *Beattie* (1944) 26 TC 63 (a case involving the sale of houses) a claim that the principle in *Utting* applied did not succeed before the Special Commissioners, because the sales of the houses were for chief rents with no estate in the land being reserved to the vendor. The Special Commissioners considered that the case was governed by the decision in *Emery.* This question was not argued in the appeal to the High Court.

In *McMillan* v *IRC* (1942) 24 TC 417, the builder disposed of property in return for cash payments plus a feu duty payable to himself as immediate superior. It was agreed that the feu duty was not akin to ground annuals. Thus the case of *Utting* was applicable. This being the case it was necessary to ascertain how much of the cost could properly be said to be referable to the sales of the houses which were made burdened with the feu duty. To calculate this it appears that one takes the total deductible costs (£100,000 say) and multiplies that by the sale proceeds of the houses subject to the feu duties (say £200,000) over the estimated capital value of the feu duty (say £50,000) plus the sale proceeds of the houses, subject to the feu duties.

The formula is thus: £100,000 multiplied by £200,000 over £50,000 plus £200,000.

In *Heather* v *Redfern* (1944) 26 TC 119 Macnaughten J made the point that if there is a grant of lease at a premium with a ground rent being retained then

> the ground rent must be included as a trading receipt in the account at cost or market value, whichever is lower.

4.5 TAX PLANNING

(*a*) The badges of trade must be very carefully considered. Important intentions and decisions should be carefully recorded if the Revenue are likely to argue that a trade exists and this is to be refuted.

(*b*) In some cases it will be advantageous to argue that a trade exists, eg, if trading losses are to be used up.

(*c*) There is no clearance procedure for trading transactions.

(*d*) if a person is to carry out trading and investment activities it may be better to carry these out through separate companies so that the investment activities will be 'tainted' to the least degree by the trading activities.

(*e*) Where it is likely to be difficult to argue that a transaction is not a trading transaction—for example, where a person is to buy land but it is clear from his finances that he cannot hold onto it long—the taxpayer could admit to trading and try to mitigate the tax in other ways, eg, seeing whether a family trading trust can make the gains so possibly paying tax at lower rates. The Revenue should not normally succeed in taxing the trading gains of the trust upon the person who procured that the trust carried out the trade (*Ransom* v *Higgs*) although the provisions of TA 1988, s 776 must be carefully avoided by making certain that no capital gain is realised by the trustees or the beneficiaries on the disposal of trust interests.

(*f*) The situations where market value can be substituted in transactions must be watched carefully (*Sharkey* v *Wernher,* TA 1988, s 770 and s 100(1)(*b*). Stock acquired at less than market value may come into the purchaser's computation at market value under a 'reverse *Sharkey* v *Wernher*' (*Petrotim Securities Ltd* v *Ayres* (1964) 41 TC 389 at p 407).

(*g*) There are no company inter-group transfer reliefs for trading stock as there are for corporation tax on chargeable gains. Thus if property is to be transferred inter-group and the trading gain, if any, 'rolled over', TA 1988, s 100 must be satisfied and the transferor's trade must be discontinued. It is vital that practitioners distinguish clearly between land in a group which is held as an investment and land which is held as stock—entirely separate tax codes apply.

(*h*) There are exceptional cases where even if land is disposed of at less than market value, market value cannot be substituted under *Sharkey* v *Wernher* (see *Jacgilden (Weston Hall) Ltd* v *Castle* (1969) 45 TC 685).

(*i*) If X Ltd (a developer which develops the land of other companies) has a number of development agreements and one is cancelled, the compensation is likely to be a trading receipt. If there are a number of companies each with one development agreement and one agreement is cancelled, the compensation may amount to a capital (not trading) receipt (*Van den Berghs Ltd* v *Clark* 19 TC 390 (HL)).

5 TAX DEDUCTIBLE EXPENDITURE ON PROPERTY

5.1 INTRODUCTION

Chapter 4 dealt with the situation where property is held as trading stock and disposed of with a view to making a profit. This chapter deals with the situation where a manufacturer or shopkeeper, for instance, purchases property, eg, a factory, or office premises or a shop, to enable him to carry out his trade, profession or vocation therefrom, and he incurs expenditure on the property.

The business profits will be taxable under Schedule D, Case I or II and the question will arise whether the expenditure in purchasing that asset or in improving or repairing it can be deducted from the trading profits of the manufacturer or shopkeeper, etc.

Tax is charged under this head on the annual profits or gains from the trade, profession or vocation (TA 1988, s 18(3)). The reference to 'annual' is unfortunate because it is clear that even one transaction can be caught as a trading transaction under Schedule D, Case I (*Martin* v *Lowry* [1926] 1 KB 550).

Generally, before a sum can be deducted from trading or professional or vocational income it must be:

(*a*) revenue expenditure as opposed to capital expenditure (TA 1988, s 74(*f*) and (*g*));

(*b*) incurred wholly and exclusively for the purposes of the trade, profession or vocation (TA 1988, s 74(*a*)); and

(*c*) it must not be disallowed under any of the other specific heads in TA 1988, s 74.

5.2 REVENUE EXPENDITURE

If the expenditure is laid out in order to bring into existence an asset or advantage for the enduring benefit of the trade, the expenditure will normally be capital expenditure and therefore not deductible in computing trading profits (see also *British Insulated and Helsby Cables Ltd* v *Atherton* [1926] AC 205 at p 214).

Additionally, any capital employed in improvements to premises occupied for the purposes of the trade, profession or vocation is specifically disallowed as a deduction in computing profits (TA 1988, s 74(*g*)).

Example 6A: Capital expenditure

X Ltd, a manufacturing company, buys a freehold factory from which it is to carry out its trade. That expenditure will be capital expenditure and therefore will not be deductible in computing profits. It builds a substantial extension to the building; that expenditure also will not be tax-deductible in computing the trading profits of the company because it will be capital employed in improving the premises (TA 1988, s 74(*g*)).

A deduction is available to the taxpayer, however, for expenditure on repairs to the business premises but not if the expenditure exceeds the sum properly applied for the repairs (TA 1988, s 74(*d*)).

There is a considerable number of cases concerning the distinction between capital and revenue expenditure (see for instance *Regent Oil Co Ltd* v *Strick* [1966] AC 295; *Rolfe* v *Wimpey Waste Management Ltd* [1988] STC 329). In *Tucker* v *Granada Motorway Services Ltd* [1979] STC 393 a trading tenant had approximately 40 years left to run under the lease of its premises from which it carried on its trade. It paid to the landlord £122,220 effectively to secure a reduction in the rent payable over the term of the lease. The tenant claimed that the payment was deductible in computing trading profits. The House of Lords held (Lord Salmon dissenting) that the payment was not deductible but was a 'once and for all' payment on a capital asset designed to make it more advantageous. It was, therefore, disallowed under TA 1970, s 130(*f*) (now TA 1988, s 74(*f*)).

If the taxpayer laid out monies in order to acquire an asset from which he can obtain his raw material—as where a dealer in sand and gravel buys unworked gravel deposits—he is likely to have laid out expenditure on a capital asset which would not be tax-deductible, although capital allowances in appropriate cases may be available under the mines and minerals provisions (see *Stow Bardoph Gravel Co Ltd* v *Poole* (39 TC 459); *H J Rorke Ltd* v *IRC* (1960) 39 TC 194; *Southern* v *Borax Consolidated Ltd* [1941] 1 KB 111; *Mallet* v *Staveley Co and Iron Co Ltd* [1928] 2 KB 405; and *Strick* v *Regent Oil Co Ltd* [1966] AC 295).

Expenditure, even though it may be labelled 'rent', for instance, can amount to capital expenditure. In *Littlewoods Mail Order Stores Ltd* v *MacGregor* (1969) 45 TC 519, a company leased premises at a rent of approximately £23,500. A subsidiary acquired the freehold and the lease was surrendered. A new lease was granted by the subsidiary at £42,500. The excess (£19,000) was not tax-deductible because it represented the price of acquiring a capital asset even though the taxpayers had labelled the sum 'rent'.

The payment of a premium on a lease will nearly always be capital expenditure and therefore not tax-deductible. However, where the recipient is chargeable or could be chargeable but for an exemption to IT on the premium under the lease premium provisions the tenant will be entitled to some relief under TA 1988, s 87 (see 3.2.5).

If the outlay relates to a capital item, even a rent charge may be non-deductible as being of a capital nature. In *IRC* v *Land Securities Investment Trust Ltd* [1969] 2 All ER 430, a property-investment company effectively purchased land interests in consideration for rent charges payable for fixed periods. The House of Lords held that the rent charges were not deductible in computing the profits of the company for profit tax purposes since the legal effect of the arrangement was to purchase capital assets. It is possible for a capital asset to be purchased by income payments and if a perpetual rent charge had been created, for instance, the payments may have been deductible. The same principles would apply if the company had been a normal trading company (eg, a manufacturer) and not a property-investment company.

If expenditure is found to be capital expenditure it is not possible to get a deduction in computing Schedule D, Case I or Case II profits under general principles. The taxpayer must then look to the capital allowances provisions to see whether he may still obtain a deduction from profits under those provisions (see Chapter 8).

If the expenditure is held not to be capital then the taxpayer cannot get any capital allowances, but he must then see whether he can get the amounts allowable as expenses on satisfying the requirements now to be dealt with.

5.3 PURPOSE OF THE EXPENDITURE

In order to obtain a deduction for the revenue item, it is necessary that it involved expenditure which was laid out wholly and exclusively for the purposes of the trade, profession or vocation (TA 1988, s 74(*a*)).

Rent paid for the use of the business premises would be deductible (*Russell* v *Aberdeen Town & County Bank* (1888) 2 TC 321). Rental payments which effectively relate to capital items may be disallowed under the cases of *Littlewoods Mail Order Stores Ltd* and *Land Securities Investment Trust Ltd* mentioned above.

If the premises are partly used for business purposes and partly for non-business purposes, the amount deductible will be apportioned according to the respective users (TA 1988, s 74(*c*)).

Expenditure laid out in connection with the private residence or other property which is not connected with the trade of the taxpayer shall not be deducted from the trading profits (TA 1988, s 74(*b*)).

Rent paid for unoccupied premises no longer required for business purposes may be allowed as a deduction in computing profits (see *IRC* v *Falkirk Iron Co Ltd* (1933) 17 TC 625 and *Hyett* v *Lennard* (1940) 23 TC 346).

A rent which varies with the profits of the business will also be deductible (*Union Cold Storage Co Ltd* v *Adamson* (1930–31) 16 TC 293).

5.4 REPAIRS AND IMPROVEMENTS TO A BUILDING—THE ACID TEST

The taxpayer may have owned a building for many years from which he carries out his trade or profession. If he carries out works to the building, what tests are to be applied to ascertain whether the expenditure is of a capital or income nature? The relevant cases on this issue are: *Highland Railway Co* v *Balderston Ex (S)* (1889) 2 TC 485, *Fitzgerald* v *IRC* 1 ITC 100, *O'Grady* v *Bullcroft Main Collieries Ltd* 17 TC 93, *Margrett* v *The Lowestoft Water and Gas Co* 19 TC 481; *Lawrie* v *IRC* 34 TC 20, *Wilson* v *Emmerson* 39 TC 360, *Curtin* v *M Ltd* 3 ITC 227, *Jones (Samuel) & Co (Devondale) Ltd* v *IRC* 32 TC 513, *Hodgkins* v *Plunder & Pollak (Ireland) Ltd* 3 ITC 135, *Conn* v *Robins Bros Ltd* 43 TC 266, *Brown* v *Burnley Football and Athletic Co Ltd* 53 TC 357 and *Lurcott* v *Wakely & Wheeler* [1911] 1 KB 905.

The true test is to be found in the case of *Lurcott* v *Wakely & Wheeler.* At p 924 Buckley L J states:

> Repair is restoration by renewal or replacement of subsidiary parts of a whole. Renewal, as distinguished from repair, is restoration of the entirety, meaning by the entirety not necessarily the whole but substantially the whole subject-matter under discussion.

Thus, one must find the entirety. If one replaces a subsidiary part of that entirety then one has carried out a repair. If of course the work on the subsidiary part goes beyond the mere replacement of the same then the works may amount to an extension or improvement and thus be disallowed.

Thus the tests are:

(*a*) Find the entirety.

(*b*) When one has found the entirety one must decide whether the entirety has been replaced; if so expenditure will be disallowed as not comprising a repair.

(*c*) If one has found the entirety and one replaces a subsidiary part of the entirety the expenditure will be allowed.

(*d*) If one finds the entirety and one does more than replace a subsidiary part of it but extends and improves the same then the expenditure will be disallowed.

The cases of *Hodgkins* v *Plunder & Pollack* and *Jones (Samuel) & Co (Devonvale) Ltd* v *IRC* indicated that in order to find the entirety one should discover whether there was a single industrial profit making undertaking. If so, that is the entirety. However, Vinelott J in the *Burnley Football Club* case at p 370 stated that those judgments

> should not be taken as laying down a principle that the renewal of part of what can be seen as physically, commercially and functionally a profit earning whole is *prima facie* a repair.

He said that the judges' remarks should be restricted to the particular facts of those cases and the author feels that Vinelott J is correct. Otherwise one could have a situation where buildings are separated from each other by great distances and still argue that they are all one entirety and thus the replacement of one of the buildings is a replacement of a subsidiary part of the entirety.

If a chimney which consists of part of a factory is replaced the expenditure is likely to amount to repair expenditure (*Samuel Jones & Co (Devonvale) Ltd* v *IRC* [1951] 32 TC 513). If on the other hand the chimney could be looked upon as a unit on its own then the replacement of the same would not amount to a tax deductible repair (*O'Grady* v *Bullcroft Main Collieries* [1932] 17 TC 93). Also if the essential part of a structure has been replaced even though it may comprise part of a larger structure nevertheless the expenditure may still amount to capital expenditure (see *Wynne-Jones* v *Bedale Auction Ltd* [1977] STC 50; 51 TC 426 and also *Brown* v *Burnley Football and Athletic Co Ltd* [1980] 53 TC 357).

Expenditure on newly acquired assets to improve the building beyond the state in which it was acquired will normally be capital expenditure. In *Jackson* v *Laskers Home Furnishers Limited* [1956] 3 All ER 891 a company took on premises paying a very low rent because the premises were in a poor state of repair. The company covenanted to repair the same. It was held that the expenditure was capital. This is the position even though had the landlord carried out the works and charged rent the rent would have been tax deductible.

That basic principle is modified if the purchase price was not reduced as a result of the state of repair and the asset was capable of profitable use upon acquisition (see *Odeon Associated Theatres Ltd* v *Jones* [1973] CH 288).

It is clear that if a taxpayer replaces a roof which is in a poor state of repair with another roof in an identical form the expenditure will be tax deductible as being revenue expenditure. In the case of *Lawrie* v *IRC* 34 TC 20 the taxpayer carried on the trade of manufacturing concrete slabs and blocks. The roof was in a state of disrepair. The taxpayer however, instead of simply repairing the roof, took the opportunity to reconstruct the premises involving the lengthening and heightening of the building and the construction of a new roof.

It was held that because the taxpayer had decided to reconstruct the building rather than just simply carrying out the repairs the expenditure was not allowable. The taxpayer sought to argue that an amount equal to what would have been spent on repairs should be tax deductible. The Court of Session was quite clear in holding that one could not deduct such a hypothetical figure.

Lord Carmont stated at p 26:

> In the present case, the Appellants, having made up their minds to deal with their premises on the basis of renewal, are not entitled to treat any part of that outlay as income expenditure. They are not entitled to say that if they had treated the premises by repairing them they would in that event have spent X pounds and to suggest that they are entitled to separate that sum estimated as repairs from the cost actually spent for renewal and to debit it against income.

Thus it is clear that taxpayers should give much thought as to what works they propose to carry out. In particular they should see whether capital allowances may be available or whether by concession the Revenue may allow some of the expenditure. However as a matter of strict law if the taxpayer does decide to substantially improve or reconstruct rather than simply repair then he must face the problem that the expenditure will in total be disallowed.

The following Concession B4 may, however, be relevant:

5.4.1 Maintenance and repairs of property obviated by alterations etc: Schedule A assessments

Where maintenance and repairs of property are obviated by improvements, additions and alterations, so much of the outlay as is equal to the estimated cost of the maintenance and repairs is allowed as a deduction in computing liability in respect of rents under Schedule A. This concession does not apply where:

(*a*) the alterations, etc are so extensive as to amount to the reconstruction of the property, or

(*b*) there is a change in the use of the property which would have made such maintenance or repairs unnecessary.

5.4.2 Cost of unsuccessful planning application

In *ECC Quarries Ltd* v *Watkis* (Ch D 1975) 51 TC 153; [1975] STC 578; [1977] 1 WLR 1386, a company made an unsuccessful claim for planning permission to extract sand and gravel from certain sites, which, if successful, would have enabled it to pursue its activities at the sites until well after the year 2000. The cost of the unsuccessful application was held to be capital.

The expenditure had been charged to revenue in the accounts, but the accountancy evidence did not persuade the Court that it was revenue for tax purposes.

5.5 OTHER HEADS OF TA 1988, s 74

If expenditure is not excluded from deductibility under (*a*) or (*b*) in para 5.1 above, it is important to check to make certain that it is not disallowed under any of the other heads of TA 1988, s 74. Interest on monies borrowed to purchase a property to be used for the carrying out of the business or for capital expenditure will normally be tax-deductible because it will not be capital expenditure and will have been laid out wholly and exclusively for the purposes of the trade, profession or vocation. However, any interest paid to a person not resident in the UK, insofar as it is interest at more than a reasonable commercial rate, is not deductible as a trading expense under Case I or Case II of Schedule D (TA 1988, s 74(*n*)).

Also, any rent, royalty or other payment paid in connection with mining operations which is declared to be subject to the deduction of tax is not allowable as a Case I or Case II of Schedule D trading expense (TA 1988, s 74(*q*)).

Interest paid generally to a person who is not resident in the UK has to satisfy the provisions of TA 1988, s 82(1)–(5) before relief is available.

Example 6B: Allowable trading expenses

A trader (a manufacturer) may borrow money to purchase a factory and a separate office block (which are not in an Enterprise Zone) from which he is to carry out his trade. The outlay on the purchase of the factory will be capital expenditure and so will not be deductible under the general rules of Schedule D. He may, however, obtain industrial buildings allowances on the factory (see 8.1).

The outlay on the office block will be capital expenditure and also non-allowable under the general Schedule D provisions. No capital allowances will be available in connection with the bricks and mortar although plant and machinery allowances may be available and the same also applies to any plant and machinery in the industrial building (see 8.14.1).

Tax relief under general Schedule D principles should be available on the interest paid to the lender. Subject to the interaction with the capital allowances provisions (see 8.4.2), the capital expenditure will be expenditure available to reduce any charge to CGT which may arise on the disposal of the industrial building or the office, although that charge may be postponed if the expenditure is used within the appropriate period to purchase other qualifying assets (ie, rollover relief, or heldover relief, is available—see p 162).

6 PROPERTY INVESTMENT COMPANIES: RELIEF FOR MANAGEMENT EXPENSES

6.1 INTRODUCTION

A property investment company will receive rents from the letting of property.

It will often be critical for that company to obtain relief from corporation tax for management expenses.

The relevant legislation is TA 1988, s 75. This legislation permits an investment company resident in the United Kingdom to deduct sums disbursed as 'expenses of management (including commissions)'.

There is expressly excluded from such deductible expenditure monies laid out in computing income for the purposes of Schedule A.

'Investment Company' is defined in s 130. It means any company whose business consists wholly or mainly in the making of investments and the principal part of whose income is derived therefrom.

6.2 MANAGEMENT EXPENSES: THE RELEVANT CASES

The Courts have provided guidance over the years on the meaning of the term 'expenses of management (including commissions)'.

From the author's reading of the relevant cases the following points are established:

6.2.1 No definition

The term 'expenses of management' is not defined and has been held to be 'insusceptible of precise definition' (Viscount Simonds in *Sun Life Assurance Society* v *Davidson* and *Phoenix Assurance Co Ltd* v *Logan* 37 TC 330 at p 354).

6.2.2 Not limited to 'Higher' Management

Expenses of management are not restricted to management type expenses in the sense of board and managerial decisions at the higher levels as compared with expenditure related to the actual carrying out by executives and employees of the particular decisions. Putting it at its simplest the fees paid to directors and managers as opposed to those paid to executives and employees (who may have to actually carry out the particular decisions) are not to be treated differently (*Capital and National Trust* v *Golder* 31 TC 265 sought to draw such a distinction but this was rejected by the Lords in the *Sun Life* case—Lord Somervell at p 362).

6.2.3 Management of the business

Expenses of management are concerned with the managing of the investment business carried on by the company. Expenses related to the managing of a particular property will be deducted under Schedule A; such expenses may, however, also on the face of it, in certain cases amount to expenses of management within TA 1988, s 75; hence the express provision stating that expenses deductible from income under Schedule A cannot also be deductible as expenses of management within TA 1988, s 75 (see TA 1988, s 75(1)).

6.2.4 Specific exclusions

All the expenses, however, laid out in running the company's business will not amount to management expenses; hence all management expenses are expenses in carrying on the business but not all the expenses in carrying on the business are management expenses. The following types of *expenses* would be excluded:

(*a*) direct expenditure (including necessary costs) on the purchase and sale of investments (see below);

(*b*) expenditure allowable under Schedule A (see above);

(*c*) other expenditure which may amount to an 'expense' but not to an 'expense of management' (this head is critical and is discussed below).

6.2.5 Purchase of an investment

Monies laid out on the purchase of an investment is not a management expense. The precise reason for this is not entirely clear from the judgments especially as Counsel agreed ex concessis in the *Sun Life* case that the expenses were not management expenses. The reason is probably that contained in the Commissioner's decision which was effectively repeated and accepted by Tucker L J in the Court of Appeal in *Capital and National Trusts Ltd* v *Golder* 31 TC 265 at p 272:

> In our view, in the case of the appellant company, *expenses of management are mainly concerned with matters up to the time when the actual purchase or sale of an investment is effected.* These matters include the payment for the services of those whose duty it is to maintain as far as possible the income yield from the investments, to keep a constant watch on those investments and to decide when and what changes are advisable. *Once a decision about a change in the investments has been arrived at* we are unable to say that the charges for brokerage and stamp duty necessarily incurred in a purchase or sale constitute expenses of management within the meaning of the said section. (The emphasis is the author's.)

Perhaps the simple answer is that monies laid out to buy an investment are not expenses of management, they are monies laid out to buy an asset pursuant to a decision of management; the management function ends when the decision to purchase is finally made. The subsequent transactions are formal or substantially formal.

6.2.6 Incidental purchase expenses

The House of Lords in *Sun Life* felt that expenses which were

> so closely linked with the transaction of purchase that they may naturally be considered as items in the total cost of a purchase which has already been resolved upon by the management of the company

are not expenses of management. Hence stamp duty on the purchase of property would not be allowable and although Lord Reid dissented on the brokerage point in *Sun Life* the majority of the House of Lords agreed that brokerage expenditure was so closely related to the purchase that it was part of the expense of purchase.

6.2.7 Material for management consideration

The case of *Sun Life* clearly tells one what (in certain cases) is not a management expense—purchase price, stampage and brokerage—but it does not tell us what is a management expense. The Court of Appeal in *Hoechst Finance* v *Gumbrell* [1983] STC 150 had to decide whether a 'commission' which had to be paid in order to obtain a guarantee with respect to the raising of finance was a management expense. Dillon L J summarised the judgments of the House of Lords in *Sun Life* and held that the 'commission' could not be severed from the cost of acquisition. Once the decision by the management had been taken to take the loan then the 'commission' had to be paid. It was part and parcel of the acquisition of the asset (the loan). It was a 'mechanical' or formal payment which necessarily followed once the board decided to take the loan; that was not an expense of management; it was an expense in carrying out a decision of management which necessarily followed from the taking of the loan.

The Court of Appeal did not feel that the judgments of the House of Lords could properly be divided into those judges who took a wide interpretation and those who took a narrow interpretation of the expression expenses of management. The judgment of Lord Reid, although he dissented on the question of brokerage, does seem to be the one which provides the best guidance on the meaning of management expenses. He stated at p 360:

> But looking to the purpose and content of the Section it appears to me that the phrase has a fairly wide meaning, so that, for example, expenses of investigation and consideration whether to pay out money either in settlement of a claim or in acquisition of an investment must be held to be expenses of management. And the collocation of the words '(including commissions)' shows that a sum can be an expense of management whether the work in question is done by the company's staff or done by someone else on a commission basis, and it must follow that if a work of an appropriate kind is done for a fixed fee that the fee may also be an expense of management.
>
> Admittedly the price paid for an investment is not an expense of management, and Counsel for the appellants did not and could not reasonably withhold the admission that a sum spent on enhancing the value of a trading asset is not an expense of management. I do not think that it is practicable or reasonable to draw a rigid line between payments which enhance the value of an asset and payments which do not. For example, if a call is made in respect of shares not fully paid, paying the sum necessary would not be an expense of management, although there have been cases where shares remained of no value after becoming fully paid. It seems to be more reasonable to ask, with regard to a payment whether it should be regarded as part of the cost of acquisition on the one hand or, on the other hand, something severable from the cost of acquisition which can properly be regarded as an expense of management.

6.2.8 Capital or income

The British Tax Encyclopaedia at 17-02 states that *capital expenditure cannot be an expense of management* referring to the cases of *Bennett* v *Underground Electric Railway* 8 TC 475 and *London County Freehold and Leasehold Properties* v *Sweet* 14 TC 412. The taxpayers lost in all the cases on expenses of management and the Courts have never had to make a critical finding on the point; the taxpayers failed because the particular expenses were not expenses of management; the Courts did not have to decide whether the particular expenses were capital or not. Croom-Johnson J in *Capital and National Trust Ltd* v *Golder* 31 TC 264 at p 270 (whose judgment was approved of in the Court of Appeal) held that he did not have to decide whether the outlay in question was revenue or capital because it (the particular expenditure) did not amount to an expense of management for other reasons. He nevertheless stated that he found the distinction between capital and income *'rather attractive'*. One then has the subsequent High Court decision of *London County Freehold and Leasehold Properties Limited* v *Sweet* 24 TC 412 (a mere High Court decision by Macnaghten, J) where the judge stated that the nature of the expense (as to whether it is capital or income) was immaterial. He did not, however, refer to the earlier judgments in *Golder's* case in the High

Court as approved in the Court of Appeal. One then has the subsequent decision of *Sun Life* where the question of capital *versus* income was left open although there are indications that they (the Lords) did not consider the distinction especially important (*Sun Life* pp 355 and 356). The author would make the following points:

(*a*) There is no express provision in the legislation stating that management expenses must be of a revenue nature.

(*b*) Certainly the Revenue have a case that the distinction can be drawn between capital and income especially as the High Court and Court of Appeal did find the distinction 'rather attractive' in the *Golder* case.

(*c*) Parts of the judgments in *Sun Life* seem to indicate that the House of Lords was not concerned with the question of whether the payments were of an income or capital nature.

It will generally be the case that expenses of a revenue nature will tend to exhibit the features of a management expense whilst capital expenses will tend to the opposite, but the author is of the view that an expense may be a management expense even though it may be of a capital nature.

6.2.9 Abortive expenditure

Viscount Simonds in *Sun Life* at p 355 stated:

> Counsel for the Society, though they contended that the expenses of management were the same as the expenses of conducting, carrying on or running its business, yet conceded that some qualification must be introduced and, quite illogically as it appeared to me, admitted that there could not be included in such expenses the cost of purchase of the investments themselves. I do not know why not, the acquisition of the necessary stock-in-trade would appear to be a first expense of carrying on a business. *A further refinement was indeed introduced and it was said that such an expense could only be excluded if, and to the extent to which, it was represented by an asset of the business. I do not follow and cannot give effect to this argument.* The concession is nevertheless of value, for, if the expense of purchasing an asset is not an expense of management, I can see no valid ground of distinction between the price of the stock which is purchased and the stamp duty paid upon contract of transfer and the brokerage paid to the broker. (The author's emphasis.)

This is a curious passage in the judgment. It is dealing with the cost of purchase. The taxpayer admitted that the cost of purchase was not deductible. The taxpayer sought to draw a distinction between that case and the case where there is presumably a cost but there is no asset in the business. Perhaps this would cover a case where a deposit is paid to purchase property and the deposit is lost because completion does not take place due to the default of the purchaser. Viscount Simonds indicated that he would not consider that such a payment would be a management expense. The point does not help the taxpayer but is obiter and the only firm point decided was that if an asset was acquired then the expenditure on acquisition and the expenditure directly related to that acquisition would not comprise management expenses.

6.3 CONCLUSIONS ON TA 1988, s 75 AND CASE LAW

Outlays on the actual purchase of property investments including stamp duty and 'brokerage' will not be tax deductible as expenses of management.

Expenses related to the investigation and consideration whether to acquire investments by management (at whatever level) should amount to expenses of management whether the deal goes abortive or not.

The question whether abortive acquisition expenditure (not falling within the paragraph above) qualifies as a management expense is an open matter. All the cases were concerned with situations where outlays were actually made to acquire assets and expenditure such as stamp duty was paid with respect to the same. None of the cases concerned abortive transactions although Viscount Simonds in *Sun Life* did not seem to attach much significance to the distinction; nevertheless the matter is open and arguable although the author does not feel especially optimistic on the point as far as the taxpayer is concerned.

7 INTEREST RELIEF

7.1 INTRODUCTION

This chapter deals with the relief for interest which is available to individuals who borrow money to purchase or improve land and buildings. These provisions can be extremely important and the legislation, which is of a very technical nature, has to be very carefully checked.

7.1.1 Trading expenses—interest is deductible

If an individual carries on a trade, profession or vocation he will be able to obtain tax relief for any interest paid whether it is annual interest or not and whether it derives from a loan or an overdraft, provided it is a proper expense of the trade, profession or vocation under the provisions of Cases I or II of Schedule D.

Example 7A: Trading expense—stock

Mr X is a land dealer. He borrows to buy trading stock. The interest on the borrowing should amount to a trading expense.

Example 7B: Trading expense—premises

X, Y and Z are solicitors in partnership. They borrow to buy their premises from which to carry out their profession. The interest will be a trading expense within TA 1988, s 74.

7.1.2 Companies

In the case of companies interest may be deductible, even if it is not a trading expense, under the provisions of TA 1988, s 338, if it is a charge on income.

Example 7C: Charge on income

X Ltd, a trading company, buys for £250,000 a house for Mr Y, one of its directors, to live in. X Ltd will obtain relief for the interest it pays on the £250,000 loan as a charge on income under TA 1988, s 338. The interest may amount to a trading expense, but this is unlikely. In a case the author was concerned with the Revenue claimed the outlay was not a trading expense. There should be no relevant income apportionment problems (shortfall) under TA 1988, ss 423 and 424 (under those sections interest paid by a company can be apportioned to participators in the company in certain circumstances).

When companies pay yearly interest the general rule is that they must deduct tax at 25 per cent at source. This requirement is contained in TA 1988, s 348. However, there is no requirement to deduct tax with respect to interest payable in the United Kingdom on an advance from a bank carrying on a bona fide banking business in the United Kingdom. Thus a UK property company which pays interest to an overseas bank need not deduct tax at source provided the overseas bank is carrying on a bona fide banking business in the United Kingdom.

In *Hafton Properties Ltd* v *McHugh* [1987] STC 16 Hafton Properties Ltd, a property company resident in the United Kingdom, paid interest on a loan facility from an overseas bank. It was held on the facts that the overseas bank was not carrying on a bona fide banking business in the United Kingdom and therefore Hafton Properties Ltd was liable for the tax which it had omitted to deduct at source.

In borderline cases it may be prudent for property companies to ask the bank to provide them with a letter from the relevant Inspector of Taxes confirming that in the view of the Revenue the particular bank is carrying on a bona fide banking business in the United Kingdom. It is clear that if the loan from the overseas bank is secured on UK located property owned by the UK property company (the borrower) that would not in itself mean that the overseas bank was carrying on a bona fide banking business in the United Kingdom.

7.1.3 Individuals who are not traders

In the case of an individual, unless the expenditure is allowable as a deduction under Case I or Case II of Schedule D, the interest will not comprise a charge or deduction against total income within the meaning of TA 1988, s 835 (see *IRC* v *Frere* 42 TC 125).

There is, however, specific legislation which permits interest to be deducted, in restricted cases, where loans are taken out to purchase land or to improve land. The legislation is to be found in TA 1988, s 354.

The Revenue has issued a booklet on these provisions entitled 'Tax Treatment of Interest Paid' (IR 11 (1985)—see *Inland Revenue Official Tax Guides*, Longman).

This chapter only deals with interest relief on loans for the purchase or improvement of land taken out by an individual who has not taken out the loan for the purposes of his trade. It, therefore, deals with the position of individuals who borrow to invest in land to produce income and individuals who borrow to buy a house or other property to live in.

7.2 THE REQUIREMENTS

Tax relief is only available to a person who pays in any year of assessment:

(*a*) annual interest chargeable to tax under Case III of Schedule D (this would cover all annual interest payment unless the obligation to pay the interest arises from a foreign source); or

(*b*) interest payable in the UK on an advance from a bank carrying on a bona fide banking business in the UK or from a person carrying on a bona fide business as a member of the Stock Exchange in the UK or bona fide carrying on the business of a discount house in the UK (TA 1988, s 353).

7.2.1 Loans and overdrafts

Relief will not be given in respect of interest on a debt incurred on an overdraft or by the debiting of the account of any person as the holder of a credit card or under any similar arrangement. It is necessary, therefore, for there to be a loan before any relief can be available (TA 1988, s 353(3)(*a*) and see *Potts* v *IRC* (1951) AC 443 at 455).

7.2.2 Commercial rate of interest

Where the interest is paid at a rate in excess of a reasonable commercial rate relief shall not be given in respect of so much of the interest as represents the excess over the reasonable commercial rate (TA 1988, s 353(3)(*b*)).

7.2.3 Qualifying purpose

Interest is only eligible for relief if it is paid by a person for the time being owning an estate or interest in land in the UK or the Republic of Ireland on a loan to defray money applied:

(*a*) in purchasing the estate or interest, or one absorbed into or given up to obtain the estate or interest; or

(*b*) improving or developing the land, or buildings on the land. (Note that by virtue of FA 1988, s 43 relief is now not available on loans taken out to improve or develop the only or main residence of the borrower, otherwise than in the case where a new building is erected on the land which is not part of an existing building and where immediately before the improvement or development began there was no building on the land; the new rules apply generally to loans made on or after 6 April 1988); or

(*c*) in paying off another loan where the claimant could have claimed relief under the provisions for interest on that other loan if it had not been paid off (and, if free of interest, assuming it carried interest).

The provisions do not apply to loans taken out to purchase property, etc, outside the UK or Ireland; separate provisions apply in that case and the general rule is that tax relief will not be available for the interest (see Schedule D, Case V and *Ockenden* v *Mackley* [1982] STC 513; TCA 65); in cases such as this it may be appropriate for a company to buy the property and obtain tax relief on the interest as a charge on income.

The expression 'a loan to defray money applied' is a curious one. It seems to indicate that the taxpayer must first lay out monies for the qualifying purpose and then take out a loan to cover the outlay. The Revenue accepts, however, that if the loan is applied direct for the qualifying purpose, it will qualify (IR 11, para 8). Taxpayers, however, who carry out tax avoidance arrangements concerning interest would do well to bear the strict position in mind.

7.2.4 Loan must be connected with qualifying application of monies

The relief above does not apply to a loan unless made in connection with the qualifying application of the money and either on the occasion of its qualifying application or within what is in the circumstances a reasonable time from the qualifying application of the money.

What is a reasonable time-lapse between the application of the monies for the qualifying purpose and the taking out of a loan must depend on the facts of the case. The legislation gives no guidance. The Revenue has indicated that it will always accept a 6-month interval as reasonable (IR 11, para 7).

Example 7D: Time-lapse before loan taken out: 6 months

X completes the purchase of a property for letting on 1 January 1987 using his own money. He borrows money at the end of June 1987 to reimburse himself for the outlay on 1 January 1987. He should get interest relief on the loan.

Example 7E: Time-lapse before loan taken out: longer than 6 months

C completes the purchase of property on 1 January 1987 using his own money. He borrows money at the end of March 1988 to reimburse himself for the outlay in January 1987. He may also get interest relief if he can show that in the circumstances a 15-month delay is reasonable, eg, he had unexpected problems borrowing the money.

Loan first applied for non-qualifying purpose
Relief is not available if the monies borrowed are applied for some other non-qualifying purpose before being used for a qualifying purpose.

The Revenue is likely to accept that if the money is temporarily placed on deposit pending the completion of the purchase etc the relief will not be lost (IR 11, para 19).

7.2.5 Mortgages, rent charges, etc

Interest on loans to purchase rent charges, mortgages or charges does not qualify for tax relief (TA 1988, s 354(4)).

Example 7F: Purchase of mortgage

Mr X lends £100,000 to Mr Y. Mr Y's property is mortgaged. Mr Z borrows £100,000 and buys the loan from Mr X with the benefit of the mortgage. Mr Z cannot obtain interest relief for any interest he pays on the loan to him (Mr Z) of £100,000 under these provisions.

7.2.6 Pre-acquisition dilapidation

Money applied in 'improving' land or buildings covers payments in respect of maintenance or repairs incurred by reason of dilapidations attributable to a period before the estate or interest was acquired but otherwise does not include references to payments in respect of maintenance or repairs, or any of the other payments mentioned in TA 1988, s 25(1) (payments deductible from rent) (TA 1988, s 354(2)).

Example 7G: Pre-acquisition dilapidation

Mr X buys Greenoaks as an investment in a dilapidated state from Mr Y. He borrows £100,000 to make good the pre-acquisition dilapidations. Income tax relief is available on the interest paid on the loan.

7.2.7 Unpaid purchase price

Where part of the purchase price of property remains unpaid and the purchaser pays interest to the vendor, or interest becomes payable before the contractual date for completion because the purchaser has been allowed to occupy the property, the interest is treated as interest on a loan (TA 1988, s 367(3) and IR 11 para 30).

Similarly, if a plot of land is bought from a builder who is to build a house on it for the purchaser and the builder allows part of the cost of the building of the house to remain unpaid on condition that interest is paid on it, the Revenue seems to accept that the interest constitutes interest on a loan.

Unpaid purchase price is not generally in law considered to be a 'loan' (*Ramsden* v *IRC* (1957) 37 TC 619).

7.2.8. Relief restricted to 'interest'

Relief is only available for payments of interest. Thus, the repayment of the capital borrowed will not enable interest relief to be claimed.

If X borrows money and the interest qualifies, Y who has guaranteed the loan will not get tax relief if he has to discharge the interest which has accrued on X's loan (see *Hendy* v *Hadley* [1980] STC 292 and *IRC* v *Holder* 16 TC 540, cf *Westminster Bank Exors and Trustee Co (CI) Ltd* v *National Bank of Greece* SA 46 TC 472, especially 494 G).

'Interest' is the just recompense to a creditor for being deprived of the use of his money (*Schulze* v *Bensted* (1915) 7 TC 30—see also *Cairns* v *MacDairmid* [1982] STC 226).

7.2.9 *Euro hotel* 'interest' payments

'Interest' figures in many development agreements are not likely to be interest properly so called according to the *Euro Hotel* case.

In *Re Euro Hotel (Belgravia) Ltd* [1975] STC 682, L granted a building lease to T who sold it to a bank for £1.5m and received funding from the bank to do the development. The bank charged interest on 'the Current Total Investment' (ie the bank's development cost outlay). It was held that there was no interest properly so called. This is an important case which practitioners must refer to in appropriate situations, where they are drafting development agreements containing 'interest provisions'.

Megarry J at pp 691–692 stated thus:

> It seems to me that running through the cases there is the concept that as a general rule two requirements must be satisfied for a payment to amount to interest, and *a fortiori* to amount to 'interest of money'. First, there must be a sum of money by reference to which the payment which is said to be interest is to be ascertained. Plainly, there are sums of 'money' in the present case. Second, those sums of money must be sums that are due to the person entitled to the alleged interest; and it is this latter requirement that is mainly in issue before me. I do not, of course, say that in every case these two requirements are exhaustive, or that they are inescapable. Thus I do not see why payments should not be 'interest of money' if A lends money to B and stipulates that the interest should be paid not to him but to X; yet for the ordinary case I think that they suffice.
>
> Now in the case before me there is no question of any loan. True, the petitioning creditor (the 'lender') has paid money to the company (the developer who 'borrowed' the money) but that money has been paid not as a loan but as an out-and-out payment to the company for carrying out the development

and giving the petitioning creditor property rights in the development, and so on. The provision for payment of 'interest' on the Current Total Investment when it reaches the maximum amount was doubtless intended to act as a spur to the company to complete the development economically in order to obtain the underlease, and to get the agreement for the sub-underlease made in order to increase the maximum amount. Once the Current Total Investment had reached £2,135,000, 'interest' on it became payable by the company to the petitioning creditor under cl 5(1)(*b*) of the sub-building agreement, unless the company had increased the 'maximum amount' under the agreement to £2,303,000, which the company could do by entering into the agreement for the sub-underlease of part of the premises in a satisfactory form: and if 'interest' became payable under this head, it continued until the 'maximum amount' was duly increased. Further, when the Current Total Investment reached £2,303,000, 'interest' on it was to become payable by the company to the petitioning creditor under cl 5(1)(*a*) until the underlease was granted to the company by the petitioning creditor: and this would not be done until the development was completed. The general import of the provision for 'interest' seems to be to provide an incentive to the company to hasten on both with making the agreement for the sub-underlease and with completing the development.

Such payments do not seem to me to be 'interest', and certainly not 'interest of money', within the statute. There are indeed sums of money from which the 'interest' will be ascertained, but I cannot see that those sums of money are anything more than units of calculation. What the company has to do is to make certain payments, the amount of which has to be calculated from the sums of money in question: but the payments do not seem to me to be 'interest' on those sums in any true sense of the word. The sums of money have been paid to the company once and for all, and are not due to the petitioning creditor in any way. They are not debts or obligations of the company, and they are not sums which belong to the petitioning creditor in even the most colloquial sense. The payments to be made are not payments made for the use of the money of another, but payments made because the company has not proceeded fast enough with its obligations to complete the development and enter into an agreement for the grant of the sub-underlease. The payments are not compensation for delay in payment but for delay in performance of other obligations: and the payments are not payments by time for the use of money but payments by time for non-performance of those obligations. It is not easy to think of a suitably comparable case, but there seems to be a possible analogy if a landowner were to sell part of his land, covenanting to erect a dividing wall within three months of completion, and also, if the wall was not then complete, to pay 'interest' on the purchase money paid by the purchaser until the wall was completed. Such payments do not seem to me to wear any of the guise of 'interest of money'.

Reference should also be made to the case of *Chevron Petroleum (UK) Ltd & Others* v *BP Petroleum Dev Ltd & Others* 57 TC 137.

7.2.10 Anti-avoidance

Relief is not available on a loan taken out to *purchase* an estate or interest in land (heading (*a*) above, at 7.2.3) where:

(*a*) the purchaser and seller are husband and wife and either sells to the other; or (*b*) the purchaser or the wife or husband of the purchaser has since 15 April 1969 disposed of the estate or interest of the land in question and it appears that the main purpose of the disposal and purchase was to obtain relief in respect of interest on the loan; or

(*c*) the purchasers are trustees of a settlement and the seller is a settlor or the wife or husband of the settlor and it appears that the main purpose of the purchase is to obtain relief in respect of interest on the loan; or

(*d*) the purchaser is directly or indirectly purchasing from a person who is, within the terms of TA 1988, s 839, connected with him, and the price exceeds the value of what is acquired (TA 1988, s 355(5)).

Relief is not available under heading (*b*) above (see 7.2.3), ie, *improving or developing* land etc, where the person spending the money is, within the terms of TA 1988, s 836, connected with the person who, directly or indirectly, receives the money, and the money so paid exceeds the value of the work done.

As well as the above general requirements which must be satisfied, the expenditure must also fall within either of the following two headings to be allowable:

(*a*) expenditure on main residence (TA 1988, s 355(1)(*a*)); or

(*b*) expenditure on let property (TA 1988, s 355(1)(*b*)).

7.2.11 Main residence

The basic requirements
The loan must be taken to purchase the residence or to construct a new residence (see below) and at the time the interest is paid the property must be used as the only or main residence of the person by whom it is paid (the borrower) or, if the interest is paid less than 12 months after the date on which the loan is made, is so used within 12 months after that date (TA 1988, s 355(1)(*a*)).

The Revenue has a discretion to extend the 12-month period (TA 1988, s 355(2)).

In *Frost* v *Feltham* [1981] STC 115, the taxpayer was the tenant and licensee of a public house in Essex. His tenancy rights could be terminated by the landlord on giving 12 months' notice. The taxpayer purchased a house in Wales in the joint names of himself and his wife with the assistance of a mortgage. It was held by Nourse J in the Chancery Division that relief was available for the mortgage interest under FA 1974, Sched 1, para 4(1)(*a*) (now TA 1988, s 355(1)(*a*)) as the house was the only or main residence of the taxpayer. 'Main residence' meant the principal or most important residence. Just because the taxpayer spent most of his time at the public house did not mean that the house in Wales was prevented from being his principal or most important residence. The house in Wales was fully furnished and equipped as a home and the taxpayer and his wife visited the property and spent some time there each month. The tenancy of the public house could be terminated at any time by the brewers giving 12 months' notice and this was a real power of determination not restricted under the Rent Acts. Some weight was also given to the fact that the taxpayer considered the house in Wales to be his only or main residence.

The £30,000 ceiling (1988/89) (FA 1988 s 41).
The relief is restricted to that of a loan of £30,000 (1988/89) (plus £1,000 of interest which may have been added to capital). If the borrowing exceeds that figure the interest is proportionately reduced.

In respect of loans taken out before 1 August 1988 to purchase the borrower's main residence, the interest relief ceiling applies to each borrower (although a single limit applies to a husband and wife who are not separated) (TA 1988, s 357). However, where such loans are taken out after 31 July 1988 the limit applies to the residence rather than to the borrower (FA 1988, s 42).

Personal representatives and trustees
Special provisions deal with the case of interest paid by persons as a personal representative of a deceased person or as trustees of a settlement made by will (TA 1988, s 358).

Bridging loans
There are special provisions contained in TA 1988, s 354(5) and (6) to cover bridging loans in cases where interest is payable before the land etc is used as a residence (see also *Hughes* v *Viner* [1985] STC 235).

Temporary absences from mortgaged property
The Revenue has issued an extra-statutory concession, A27 (see *Inland Revenue Practices and Concessions,* Longman) which provides *inter alia*:

> . . . where a person is required by his employment to move from his home to another place, either in the United Kingdom or abroad, for a period not expected to exceed four years, any property being purchased with the aid of a mortgage which was being used as his only or main residence before he went away, will still be treated as his only or main residence, provided it can reasonably be expected to be so used again on his return.

Home improvements
No interest relief is available on a loan made after 5 April 1988 for the making of home improvements. Such a loan is known as a 'home improvement loan' and is defined to mean 'a loan to defray money applied in improving or developing land or buildings on land, otherwise by the erection of a new building (which is not part of an existing residence) on land which immediately before the improvement or development began had no building on it' (FA 1988, s 43(1)).

7.2.12 Buying superior land interests

It appears that if X owns the freehold of property and Y is the tenant that if Y borrows to buy the freehold then interest relief will be available with respect to the borrowing provided the property is used as Y's (ie the tenant's) residential accommodation. Similarly it appears if A has let to B who has let to C that if C is using the land as his residence that if he borrows to buy the interest of A (leaving B's intermediate interest subsisting) interest relief will be available under the private residence provisions.

7.2.13 Let property

Where relief is not available under the main residence provisions, interest is eligible for relief if the land is in any period of 52 weeks comprising the time at which the interest is payable and falling wholly or partly within the year of assessment, let at a commercial rent for more than 26 weeks and when not so let either is available for letting at such a rent or is used as a residence (within the main residence provisions discussed above) or is prevented from being so available or used by any works of construction or repair (TA 1988, s 355(1)(*b*)).

Relief unlimited in amount
There is no limit to the amount of interest which can qualify for relief under this heading, ie, the £30,000 limitation does not apply.

Relief available against rents only
Relief, however, is only available against income from the letting of the particular property or from the letting of any other land, caravan or houseboat. If the income is insufficient in a particular year of assessment to cover the amount of interest, relief is given against such rental income the following year and so on provided that the letting which gives rise to the surplus carry-forward of interest continues to satisfy the requirements set out above, ie, the property is let at a commercial rent for more than 26 weeks etc (TA 1988, s 355(4)).

There is no provision requiring the other let property to satisfy the requirements of TA 1988, s 355(1)(*b*) before the interest can be offset against the rents of such property.

Example 7H: Interest relief available against rents

X lets Blackacre which satisfies the requirements of TA 1988, s 355(1)(*b*). The interest on borrowings with respect to the purchase of Blackacre exceeds the rent derived from Blackacre. He has also let Redacre which does not satisfy the requirements of TA 1988, s 355(1)(*b*). The excess interest can nevertheless be offset against the rents from Redacre.

Interest relief is not available against the borrower's general income, such as emoluments, dividend income, trading income etc.

Note also that the relief is available on a loan to improve or develop the property; the restrictions on loan interest with respect to a 'home improvement loan' only apply if the taxpayer is seeking to get relief because the property is to be used as his residence (as opposed to being let by him).

7.3 INTEREST PAID TO NON-RESIDENTS

Special provisions apply where annual interest is paid to an overseas person by companies and individuals. Tax may have to be deducted at source (see TA 1988, ss 74, 338, 339, 340 and 349, and TMA 1970, s 83(2) and extra-statutory concession B13—see *Inland Revenue Practices and Concessions,* Longman).

7.4 ANTI-AVOIDANCE PROVISIONS

Apart from the specific provisions mentioned previously (see pp 89 and 90), TA 1988, s 787 prevents tax relief being available if a scheme has been effected or arrangements have been made such that the sole or main benefit that might be expected to accrue to the claimant from the transaction under which the interest is paid was the obtaining of a reduction in tax liability by means of such relief.

It is not felt that this provision could apply to the normal case where the taxpayer borrows money to buy a property to let (rather than use his own money) even though he borrowed with a view to getting the tax relief.

7.5 DEDUCTIONS AT SOURCE

With respect to interest payable on certain loans after 31 March 1983 the provisions of TA 1988, s 369 *et seq* entitles borrowers to deduct and retain the basic rate of tax from each payment. This is the MIRAS Scheme, ie Mortgage Interest Relief At Source. The purpose of the new scheme is to provide a more efficient method of granting relief and it does not affect the net income tax liability of individuals.

7.6 TAX PLANNING

(*a*) These interest provisions can be very important because of the substantial amount of tax which can be saved for many years if interest qualifies for relief.

(*b*) The provisions are very technical and any proposed purchase of land should be carefully examined to ensure that, if at all possible, the interest will qualify for relief.

(*c*) Even if the taxpayer has used his own money to purchase an investment property, for instance, he can still obtain relief on a loan if he subsequently, within a reasonable period, uses the loan monies to defray his initial outlay.

(*d*) If the taxpayer has enough money of his own to acquire an asset which qualifies for interest relief (eg, investment property) he should if appropriate borrow to acquire that asset and use his own money to acquire a non-qualifying asset (eg, a private yacht).

(*e*) If the taxpayer has a non-qualifying loan, as to part, on his house, he should consider selling the house to his company which may get relief for its borrowings as a charge on income (TA 1988, s 338).

(*d*) Relief for interest on borrowings to buy investment property can only be offset against income from the letting of property (TA 1988, s 355(4)). This is not the same as income chargeable under Sched A (TA 1988, s 15). In some Enterprise Zone schemes individuals may receive 'rent' guarantee payments from people who may not have an interest in the land. They cannot offset the interest against such receipts.

8 TAX RELIEF THROUGH CAPITAL ALLOWANCES

Valuable allowances are available for capital expenditure incurred in connection with:

(*a*) industrial buildings and structures;

(*b*) commercial buildings and structures in Enterprise Zones; and

(*c*) machinery or plant.

Capital allowances are a very important tax relief. The principal legislation is contained in CAA 1968 (industrial buildings and structures) FA 1980 (Enterprise Zones) and FA 1971 (machinery or plant).

PART I INDUSTRIAL BUILDINGS AND STRUCTURES

8.1 INTRODUCTION

This Part deals with the tax allowances available to companies, individuals and other taxable entities for capital expenditure incurred on the construction, repair and purchase of industrial buildings or structures used for the purposes of a trade. These allowances are valuable. They enable tax deductions to be claimed for IT and CT purposes, even though the expenditure is of a capital nature. If the building or structure falls within an Enterprise Zone the valuable 100% initial allowance is available and reference should be made to Part II below (p 117).

When considering these allowances it would normally be necessary also to consider the position with regard to plant and machinery allowances. The rules applying to plant and machinery allowances, however, are different and it is vital that they are considered and dealt with. A transaction which may have no adverse consequences as far as industrial building allowances are concerned may give rise to adverse tax consequences with regard to plant and machinery allowances.

Prior to the Finance Act 1984 there was a 75% initial allowance and an annual 4% allowance on the construction expenditure.

Under the FA 1984 the initial allowance was gradually abolished as follows:

(*a*) it was 50% in respect of expenditure incurred on or after 14 March 1984;

(*b*) it was 25% in respect of expenditure incurred on or after 1 April 1985;

(*c*) it is nil in respect of expenditure incurred on or after 1 April 1986.

Thus there are no initial allowances available with respect to industrial buildings and structures unless they are in an Enterprise Zone (see p 117). There is only the 4% annual writing down allowance.

How the allowances can be used

The writing down allowances which fall to be made to a trading entity can be treated as a deduction from IT profits or CT profits as the case may be. If no trade is being carried on then relief would be given by way of discharge or repayment of tax which the individual or company will otherwise have been liable for. Exactly what uses will be made of the allowances will depend upon the tax position of the company or individual or partnership in question.

Not only can they be offset against the taxable income in the year in which the allowance becomes due, these allowances also have uses that range from being surrendered to obtain group relief within a group of companies to being carried back in certain cases against income in the three previous years of assessment in the case of an individual who trades.

It is important that the particular income which is to be relieved by the allowances in question is identified and relieved from tax as far as possible.

Example 8A: Entitlement to writing allowance

X Ltd is a manufacturing company which has accounting periods ending on 31 March. In the accounting period ended 31 March 1988 it buys a new factory from a builder. Exluding the value of the land, the factory cost £100,000. X Ltd will be entitled to allowance in that accounting period of £4,000. It will be treated as an allowable trading expense and X Ltd can offset that £4,000 against its CT liability.

8.2 THE ALLOWANCE (WRITING-DOWN ALLOWANCES)

Conditions to be satisfied

The following conditions must be satisfied before a person may obtain the writing-down allowances:

(*a*) the person must be entitled to an interest in an industrial building or structure at the end of the chargeable period or its basis period;

(*b*) at the end of the said chargeable period or basis period the building or structure must be an industrial building or structure; and

(*c*) the interest held by that person must be the 'relevant interest' in relation to the capital expenditure incurred on the construction of that building or structure.

If a building falls into temporary disuse as an industrial building, s 12 enables condition (*b*) above to continue to be satisfied. This is done by deeming the building to be used for industrial purposes during such a temporary period. Special balancing charges and allowance provisions apply where there has been a cessation of industrial use or use for non-qualifying purposes (FA 1981, ss 74 and 75).

The meaning of 'relevant interest' is discussed later in this chapter as also is the position where the relevant interest is disposed of.

The amount of the writing-down allowance
The writing-down allowance shall be equal to 4% of the expenditure incurred on the construction of the building or structure except that for any chargeable period of less than a year the amounts of the annual allowances shall be proportionately reduced.

When the allowances are available
The writing-down allowance is available if at the end of a chargeable period or its basis period the claimant has the relevant interest in the building or structure which is at that time used as an industrial building or structure.

Where the relevant interest is sold the provisions with regard to writing-down allowances are modified. These modifications are dealt with below.

8.3 BALANCING ALLOWANCES AND BALANCING CHARGES

A balancing charge or a balancing allowance may arise if any of the following events occur while the building or structure is in use as an industrial building or structure, or (subject to certain transitional provisions in FA 1981, s 74(6)) after it has ceased to be one, that is to say:

(*a*) the relevant interest in the building or structure is sold; or

(*b*) the interest, being an interest depending on the duration of a foreign concession, comes to an end; or

(*c*) the interest, being a leasehold interest, comes to an end otherwise than on the person entitled thereto acquiring the interest which is reversionary thereon; or

(*d*) the building or structure is demolished or destroyed, or, without being demolished or destroyed, ceases altogether to be used.

See s 3(1), as amended by FA 1981, s 74.)

The most common event will be a sale of the building or structure. As far as the nature of the case allows, the other three events mentioned above will give rise to similar consequences as a sale with any insurance, salvage or compensation monies being, broadly, treated as if they were sale proceeds (s 3).

In a simple case, if the sale proceeds of the industrial building or structure exceed the written down value (ie the original qualifying expenditure less any initial and annual allowances actually given) the excess is subject to a balancing charge. If the tax written-down value exceeds the proceeds of sale the taxpayer is given an additional allowance equal to the excess. That is the balancing allowance.

The amount of a balancing charge on any person cannot exceed the amount of the allowances previously made to him in respect of the building (s 3(6)). Also, adjustments may have to be made if there have been periods when writing-down allowances were not due as the building was not occupied for a qualifying purpose at the end of the chargeable period (s 4).

No balancing allowance or charge shall be made by reason of any event occuring more than 25 years (or, if the expenditure was incurred before 6 November 1962, 50 years) after the building was first used and where two or more events occur during a period when the building or structure is not an industrial building or structure, no balancing allowance or balancing charge shall be made on the occurrence of any of those events except the first.

Example 8B: Application of balancing charge

X Ltd has obtained allowances on an industrial building or structure of £75,000. If it holds on to the building it will over the years obtain a further £25,000 of allowances. Instead it sells the building for £90,000. It will suffer a balancing charge on the sale of £65,000, ie the difference between the sale proceeds (£90,000) and the written-down value of the building (£25,000).

Example 8C: Application of balancing allowance

Y Ltd has obtained £75,000 worth of written-down allowances and is entitled, if it continues to hold the relevant interest, to a further £25,000 worth of allowances. Instead of holding on to the relevant interest it sells the same for £10,000. It would be entitled to a balancing allowance of £15,000, being the amount by which the written-down value—£25,000—exceeds the proceeds of sale, namely the £10,000.

For sales (or any event which may give rise to a balancing adjustment) taking place after 17 December 1980, special rules contained in FA 1981, ss 74 and 75 apply to reflect fully in the balancing adjustments periods of non-industrial user of the building.

For the purposes of industrial building allowances, any transfer of the relevant interest in a building or structure otherwise than by way of sale shall be treated as a sale of the interest for a price other than that which it would have fetched if sold on the open market. The provisions of CAA 1968, Sched 7 then apply and the transfer is treated as though it were a sale at open market value but subject to the existing right of the transferor and transferee in certain cases to make a joint election that the building be treated as having been transferred at tax written-down value. This provision applies to transfers after 10 March 1981 which were not contracted for on or before that date. The insertion of market value (unless an election to take at written-down value is made) enables appropriate balancing adjustments to be made. Additionally, FA 1981, s 76 has widened the scope of CAA 1968, Sched 7 (see p 116) so that it covers sales between connected persons and sales with a view to obtaining a greater allowance or deduction under Part I or Part II of the Act or the avoidance or reduction of a tax charge.

8.4 AVOIDING THE BALANCING CHARGE BY DEATH AND INTERACTION WITH CGT

8.4.1 Death and the balancing charge

It appears (although the point is arguable) to be the case that if the taxpayer who has attained industrial building allowances dies there can be no balancing charge. Death is not one of the listed events which can occasion a balancing charge within CAA 1968, s 3(1).

A sale can, of course, be an occasion for a balancing charge (CAA 1968, s 3(1)(*a*)). Certain sales at an undervalue and gifts may also be occasions for a balancing charge as they may be deemed to be sales at market value (CAA 1968, Sched 7 and FA 1981, s 76).

If there is simply a gift then only FA 1981, s 76 would be in point and under that provision market value can be substituted; it applies with respect to any transfer of the relevant interest in the building or structure otherwise than by way of sale; on the transfer the property is deemed to be sold at market value for capital allowances purposes.

It appears to be the case that if Mr X dies there will be no 'transfer' by the deceased to his personal representatives as 'transfer' if the word is to be given its ordinary meaning means a transfer from one person to another and this implies that there must be both a transferor and transferee (see *Moodie* v *W & J Shepherd Ltd* [1949] 2 All ER 1044 at p 1053). Thus there would be no occasion of charge if the property were vested in the personal representatives. The author is also of the view that when the personal representatives transfer the property to the beneficiary there will be no charge. This is because although in that case there will be a transfer within the meaning of FA 1981, s 76 the personal representatives will not have obtained allowances themselves and CAA 1968, s 3(6) states that in no case shall the amount on which a balancing charge is made on a person in respect of any expenditure on the construction of a building or structure exceed the amount of the allowances which he obtained.

Ramsay (and suitable clients) permitting, there may be some scope for death bed income tax washing arrangements.

8.4.2 Double relief

A taxpayer may be able to obtain a capital allowance and subsequently dispose of the property without any further charge to tax.

The position may arise where Mr X is granted a long lease of an industrial building paying a ground rent and obtaining a capital allowance. Assume the property is in an enterprise zone so that he obtains 100% allowance on the premium referable to the acquisition of the building.

Provided the acquisition is for purposes of an investment if Mr X subsequently grants a sub lease at a premium there should not normally be any charge to capital gains tax because the premium which Mr X paid assuming all the leases are long leases within the capital gains tax legislation would comprise capital gains tax expenditure and the fact that he obtained capital allowances on that premium would not prevent that expenditure coming in as part of his base cost.

This is because although CGTA 1979, s 33 generally disallows any expenditure which is allowable 'as a deduction in computing any other income or profits or gains or losses for purposes of the income tax acts' it does not apply to capital allowance expenditure because of CGTA 1979, s 34(1).

However it is not possible for Mr X to get icing on top of the icing on the cake by claiming that he has made a loss because CGTA 1979, s 34(2) states:

> there shall be excluded from the sums allowable as a deduction any expenditure to the extent to which a capital allowance . . . has been or may have been made in respect of it.

8.5 PURCHASER OF A USED INDUSTRIAL BUILDING

The capital allowances available to a purchaser will partly depend on the position of the vendor. It is essential that the purchaser buys the relevant interest and satisfies the other requirements for obtaining writing-down allowances.

The purchaser must ascertain the 'new residue'. This is ascertained by looking at the position of the person from whom he purchased the building. One ascertains how much expenditure on the construction of the building was not used (by way of tax relief for the allowances) by the vendor. This will leave the residue of expenditure still unallowed. One adds to that figure any balancing charge if this has been suffered by the vendor, or, if the vendor is entitled to a balancing allowance, one subtracts from that figure the amount of the balancing allowance. That leaves the 'new residue'. The purchaser's writing-down allowances are fixed at such an amount as will result in the 'new residue' being evenly written off by the end of a 25-year period after the building was first used.

Special adjustments may have to be made if for any reason the building did not qualify for a writing-down allowance in some years while it did in others.

Example 8D: Calculation of new residue

A building constructed for industrial use has been used for 10 years. The expenditure available for allowances is £100,000. £40,000 worth of allowances have been claimed leaving a residue of unused expenditure of £60,000. The building is sold for £90,000

The new residue will be £60,000 plus the balancing charge of £30,000, ie, £90,000. That figure is divided by 15 (25 years–10 years) in order to find what the annual allowance would be. This gives an annual allowance of £6,000.

By concession (B20), the allowances are available where a let and occupied building is purchased from the builder; even though the builder would not have incurred any 'capital expenditure' on the construction of the building, (he would have laid out revenue expenditure being a trader).

8.6 MEANING OF KEY TERMS

8.6.1 Incur

The general rule is that expenditure is incurred on the date the obligation to pay the amount becomes unconditional (see the detailed rules in FA 1985, s 56).

If the taxpayer buys a completed Enterprise Zone building from a builder and immediately pays over the purchase monies he is deemed to have incurred, on the date when the purchase price became payable, expenditure on the construction of the building equal to the amount of the purchase price less than the part attributable to any land value. The timing of the allowances are governed by the provisions of s 5(1) and not by the provisions of FA 1985 s 56.

The provisions in FA 1985, s 56 cannot affect the timing of that expenditure. This is for two reasons:

(*a*) When CAA 1968, s 82(3) (now repealed) was extant the position was abundantly clear because the general rule as to timing (then set out in s 82(3)) was made expressly subject to any other relevant provisions of CAA 1968. Thus the date the purchase price became payable would clearly be the date when the expenditure was incurred as CAA 1968, s 5(1) specifically stated and states so. However, CAA 1968, s 82(3) was replaced by FA 1985, s 56 without those rules being subject to any specific provisions in CAA 1968. On the face of it therefore the relevant part of CAA 1968, s 5 may have been abrogated by FA 1985, s 56 (*'Leges posteriores priores contrarias abrogant'*: *Paise* v *Slater* (1883) 11 QBD 120). Nevertheless, the author feels that one can apply the maxim of *'generalia specialibus non derogant'*, ie, general provisions will not abrogate special provisions (*Gloucester (Bishop)* v *Cunnington* [1943] KB 101).

(*b*) It is not felt that FA 1985, s 56 can alter the date on which monies were actually paid.

There are anti-avoidance provisions to prevent taxpayers in certain cases obtaining allowances early by paying 'up-front' (see FA 1984, Sched 12) but these do not apply to Enterprise Zone properties (see FA 1984, s 58(4)).

8.6.2 Contributing to another's expenditure

A person shall not be treated as having incurred any expenditure insofar as it has been or is to be *met* directly or indirectly by another person (s 84(1)).

In the case of *Cyril Lord Carpets Ltd* v *Schofield* 42 TC 637 the taxpayer company incurred expenditure on plant or machinery. Subsequently the company received a discretionary grant from the government of Northern Ireland. The Revenue contended that because of this grant the taxpayer was not entitled to an allowance because CAA 1968, s 84(1) deems expenditure to have been incurred by the person giving the grant so that the taxpayer could not have incurred the expenditure. The Court of Appeal in Northern Ireland agreed with the Revenue contention. If it could be said that the government of Northern Ireland had 'met' the expenditure within s 84 then the taxpayer could not claim allowances. Lord MacDermott CJ at 648 stated 'In common parlance a liability which has been discharged may be "met" by a payment no less than a liability which has not been discharged. In its natural signification the word connotes something set against or opposed to something else, and in pecuniary transactions it is, I think, as aptly used of a payment to be set against the cost of a debt discharged as it is of the payment made in actually discharging the debt. A, for example, flies to London from Belfast to give a lecture at the request of B. A pays for his ticket as he gets it and has therefore both incurred and paid for that expenditure. Later, B insists on paying A the amount of his expenditure. In doing so B has surely met the expenditure incurred as plainly as would have been the case if A had travelled on credit and B had paid the fare to the carrier.'

However, another person (X Ltd) shall not be treated as having met the expenditure which has been incurred by Y Ltd merely because X Ltd pays out insurance or compensation monies in respect of any asset of Y Ltd which has been demolished, destroyed or put out of use. Y Ltd will also not be treated as having met the expenditure incurred by Y Ltd where X Ltd cannot claim an allowance as a contributor under s 85.

Section 85 states that where a person, for the purpose of a trade carried on or to be carried on by him or by a tenant of land in which he has an interest, *contributes* a capital sum to expenditure on the provision of an asset (being expenditure which would be regarded as wholly incurred by another person apart from this provision and in respect of which that other person would obtain industrial building allowances) such allowances attributable to the capital sum shall be made to the contributor.

This provision does not apply if the person making the contribution and the person receiving it are connected persons within TA 1988, s 839.

The provisions of Capital Allowances Act 1968, ss 84and 85 apply to Industrial Building allowances and Enterprise Zone allowances. They also apply to the plant and machinery allowances with some minor adaptations (see FA 1971, Sched 8, para 15(5) and (6)). It is provided in FA 1985, s 59(8) that CAA 1968, s 85 (allowances in respect of contributions of a capital nature) shall not be affected by FA 1985, s 59 and Sched 17.

Harman J in *Stokes* v *Costain Property Investments Ltd* [1984] 57 TC 688 at p 700C–E indicated that CAA 1968, s 84 was concerned only with situations where X by way of *bounty* directly or indirectly met expenditure incurred by Y; in that case Y will not *generally* be entitled to any capital allowances.

That may be a point for argument in another case. However, if one assumes that Harman J was correct in his interpretation of the section, the following interpretation *may* be applied to the provisions of ss 84 and 85:

Crown etc (bounty)
If a body such as the Crown or any governmental or public or local authority whether in the United Kingdom or elsewhere directly or indirectly meets the expenditure which has been incurred by the taxpayer then the taxpayer will not be entitled to an allowance with respect to that expenditure so met.

Example 8E: Crown contribution

X Ltd incurs £100,000 on installing new machinery in its building. The expenditure is met by a local authority contribution. X will not obtain any capital allowances (CAA 1968, s 84(1)).

Not the Crown (bounty)
If a person *other than* the Crown or a governmental body or public or local authority *bounteously* meets the expenditure incurred by the taxpayer then, unless the person who meets the expenditure (Y) can claim an allowance under s 85, the bounteous contribution will be ignored and X (the person who incurred the expenditure in the first instance) will be entitled to the allowances.

Example 8F: Non-crown contribution

Y is the landlord. Y is not the Crown or a government body or public or local authority. X is the tenant. X incurs expenditure on plant and machinery in the sum of £100,000. Y contributes £100,000 towards that expenditure. The contribution is bounteous and because, for instance, the two parties are connected Y cannot claim an allowance under CAA 1968, s 85. In this case X will be entitled to the allowances.

No bounty, s 85 applies
If the landlord makes a non-bounteous contribution towards the tenant's expenditure then the landlord (and not the tenant) may be entitled to the allowances under CAA 1968, s 85. This may be the case even though the tenant may be the Crown or a public or local authority in the UK (see s 85(2A)).

No bounty, s 85 does not apply
If the landlord makes a non-bounteous contribution towards the expenditure incurred by the tenant but s 85 is not applicable because, for instance, the parties are connected then it appears:

(*a*) Section 84 is still not relevant as it only applies to bounteous contributions and

(*b*) The Revenue are left with the argument that the landlord cannot obtain the allowances because s 84 is not relevant and nor can the tenant obtain the allowances because he did not incur the expenditure. There are certain indications in *Stokes* v *Costain* that the Revenue have an arguable case in that respect but the author feels that the taxpayer also has a very good case; the tenant clearly incurred the expenditure; the fact that it may be borne by somebody else is technically not relevant; hence the special provisions in s 84 and s 85 which show that if somebody else does bear the expenditure then the person who incurred it may not get the allowances; if those provisions are not relevant it indicates that even though another person may have borne the expenditure the allowances are still available to the person which incurred the expenditure in the first place. The case of *Cyril Lord Carpets Ltd* v *Schofield* 42 TC 637 is also helpful to the taxpayer in that respect.

8.6.3 Capital expenditure

Capital expenditure and capital sum in relation to the person incurring the expenditure or paying the sums do not include any expenditure or sum which is allowed to be deducted in computing, for the purposes of tax, the profits or gains of a trade, profession, office, employment or vocation carried on or held by him (Capital Allowances Act 1968, s 82(1)(*a*)).

Example 8G: Non-capital expenditure

The purchase of a freehold (£1m) by an investor, the laying out of expenditure by the investor on the construction of industrial buildings thereon by the investor

(£10m) and the immediate grant of a 999 year lease at peppercorn rent for an £11m premium is not likely to have given rise to an outlay of *capital* expenditure by the investor so the investor gets no allowances.

Some guidance as to the meaning of capital can be obtained from the decision of *Atherton* v *British Insulated and Helsby Cables Ltd,* 10 TC 155 where a lump sum was contributed by a company to a pension fund for the benefit of clerical and technical staff of the company. The expenditure was disallowed in the computations of the company because it amounted to a capital contribution. Viscount Cave LC at p 912 stated:

> But when an expenditure is made, not only once and for all, but with a view to bringing into existence an asset or an advantage for the enduring benefit of a trade, I think that there is very good reason (in the absence of special circumstances leading to an opposite conclusion) for treating such an expenditure as properly attributable not to revenue but to capital.

8.6.4 Construction

The allowances are only available if there has been a construction of an industrial building. References in the legislation to expenditure incurred on the construction of a building or structure do not include any expenditure incurred on the acquisition of, or rights in or over, the land (s 17(1)).

A person who has incurred expenditure on the construction of a building or structure shall be deemed to have the interest in the land which he has when he completes the construction (s 17(3)). This gets over the problem which arises where the building construction period takes some time and the land interests of the person incurring the expenditure differ from time to time. This provision fixes the interest—which is important for the purpose of ascertaining the 'relevant interest' in land and writing-down allowances—at the time of completion of the building.

Expenditure on repairs to buildings which are industrial buildings is deemed to be construction expenditure provided it is not already allowable as a trading expense (s 8).

Property purchased unused from a builder/developer
Where an industrial building or structure satisfying the provisions of CAA 1968, s 5(2) is bought unused from a builder or developer the purchase price thereof is deemed to be incurred on the construction of the building for the purposes of enabling the purchaser to obtain the allowances. The allowances will be based on the purchase price of the building.

There is an argument that allowances will also be available for the part of the price attributable to the land because s 5(2) refers to expenditure on the 'relevant interest' which would include the land. However, s 17(1) is aimed at preventing allowances on expenditure on the land and the word 'therein' in s 5(2) may be construed as referring to the building or structure rather than the relevant interest. CAA 1978, s 11(1) is also in point. The author does not consider that allowances can be obtained for the expenditure on the land.

Builders may be able to create ground leases so that buyers will effectively be buying the building with only a small part (if any) of the price being referable to the land.

Property purchased unused from a non-builder/developer
If a purchaser acquires the structure unused from someone other than the builder/developer special rules apply and these may restrict the allowances (see s 5(1)). Broadly, in a simple case, the purchaser's allowances are restricted to the amount which the vendor paid to have the building constructed in the first place.

8.6.5 Industrial building or structure

'Industrial' building or structure refers not so much to the physical structure of the building as to the use to which it is put. It is not enough to have a building or structure; it must be an industrial building or structure. This means (s 7(1)) a building or structure in use:

(*a*) for the purposes of a trade carried on in a mill, factory or other similar premises; or

(*b*) for the purposes of a transport, dock, inland navigation, water, electricity or hydraulic power undertaking; or

(*c*) for the purposes of a tunnel undertaking; or

(*d*) for the purposes of a bridge undertaking; or

(*e*) for the purposes of a trade which consists in the manufacture of goods or materials or the subjection of goods or materials to any process (this is an important head—see *Kilmarnock Equitable Co-operative Society Ltd* v *IRC* (1966) 42 TC 675; and *Bourne* v *Norwich Crematorium Ltd* (1967) 44 TC 164); or

(*f*) for the purposes of a trade which consists in the storage:
(i) of goods or materials which are to be used in the manufacture of other goods or materials; or
(ii) of goods or materials which are to be subjected, in the course of a trade, to any process; or
(iii) of goods or materials which, having been manufactured or produced or subjected, in the course of a trade, to any process, have not yet been delivered to any purchaser; or
(iv) of goods or materials on their arrival by sea or air into any part of the UK ((*f*) is another important head (especially (iii) above—see *Dale* v *Johnson Bros* (1951) 32 TC 487; *Saxone Lilley & Skinner (Holdings) Ltd* v *IRC* (1967) 44 TC 122)); or

(*g*) for the purposes of a trade which consists in the working of any mine, oil well or other source of mineral deposits, or of a foreign plantation; or

(*h*) for the purposes of a trade consisting in all or any of the following activities, that is to say, ploughing or cultivating land (other than land in the occupation of the person carrying on the trade) or doing any other agricultural operation on such land, or threshing the crops of another person; or

(*i*) for the purposes of a trade which consists in the catching or taking of fish or shellfish.

There is excluded from any allowance any building or structure in use as, or as part of, a dwelling-house, retail shop, showroom, hotel or office or for any purpose ancillary to the purpose of a dwelling-house, retail shop, etc (s 7(3)). However, where 25% or less of the cost of the whole building or structure is attributable to the cost of such premises, the whole building or structure is treated as industrial. This would include a small office built as part of the factory.

Subject to that a building may have to be apportioned between qualifying industrial use and other use which does not qualify for allowances. But a sports pavilion occupied by the person carrying on a trade and used as a sports pavilion for the welfare of all or any of the workers employed in that trade is treated as an industrial building (s 10).

Although 25% non-industrial use may be ignored in the building (s 7(4)) this will not be the case if the non-industrial use is in a separate building. If it is a separate building no allowances will be available on it. In *Abbot Laboratories Ltd* v *Carmody* (1968) 44 TC 569, the fact that an administrative building was connected by a covered passage to the industrial building did not make it part of the industrial building. Thus no allowances could be obtained in respect of the expenditure on the administrative building.

It should be noted that the 'industrial building or structure' definition is established by reference to s 7 of the Act. It is not dependent on any Town and Country Planning legislation or use classes so that if there are any alterations in the planning use classes—there are 16 'use classes' listed in the Town and Country Planning (Use Classes) Order 1987 (SI 1987 No 764)—this will not affect the definition for industrial buildings allowances purposes. Also, lettings where the landlord wishes to obtain allowances should restrict the tenant's user to CAA 1968, s 7 and need not refer to any planning legislation.

8.6.6 Wide definition

In *Buckingham* v *Securities Properties Ltd [1980] STC 166, an area of a building was used for the storage of coins and notes, for breaking down bulk coins and notes into individual wage packets, as a service to customers and as a communications centre. Slade J in the Chancery Division held that the coins and notes were not goods or materials within CAA 1968, s 7(1)(e).* Thus, the area in question was not an industrial building or structure entitled to capital allowances.

He gave some useful guidance on the width of the words 'subjection of goods to any process'. He stated at p 173:

> The 1968 Act contains no definition of the words 'use' or 'process'. Counsel for the Crown submitted that, even if the subject-matter of the wage packeting operations carried out by Group 4 constituted 'goods' within the meaning of section 7(1)(*e*), the operations did not constitute 'the subjection of goods to any process', within the meaning of the sub-section, because nothing was done to the notes and coins to enhance their value or make them more marketable, or alter their substance.
>
> Counsel for the taxpayer company however relied on, *inter alia,* what was said by Lord Cameron in *Kilmarnock Equitable Co-operative Society Ltd* v *Inland Revenue Commissioners* (1966) 42 TC 675 which was a decision of the Court of Session concerning section 271(1)(*c*) of the Income Tax Act 1952, a forerunner of section 7(1)(*e*) of the 1968 Act.
>
> Lord Cameron said:
>
> > 'The word "process" in its ordinary connotation seems to me to mean no more than the application of a method of manufacture or adaptation of goods or materials towards a particular use, purpose or end, while "to subject" means no more than to treat in some manner or other.'
>
> Counsel for the taxpayer company also referred me to one of the definitions of the word 'process' which is to be found in the Shorter Oxford Dictionary, 3rd edition. It reads as follows:
>
> > 'a continuous and regular action or succession of actions taking place or carried on in a definite manner; a continuous (natural or artificial) operation or series of operations'.
>
> One of the definitions of the word 'subject' to be found in the same dictionary is:
>
> > 'to bring under the operation of an agency or process: to submit to certain treatment; to cause to undergo or experience something'.
>
> I would be inclined to accept Counsel's submission for the taxpayer company that, if the subject-matter of Group 4's activities in the wage packeting area constituted 'goods', then such activities constituted a subjection of such goods to a process, within the meaning of the sub-section. As he pointed out, the coins and notes came into the security area in bulk form and left it reduced to individual wage packets, after being dealt with through the activities of a staff, requiring numeracy and accuracy, who had to take care that each wage packet contained the right amount and selection of notes and coins, broken down according to the employer's specifications. I am inclined to think that these activities did involve the subjection of the coins and notes to a 'process' within the ordinary meaning of the words and within the meaning of the sub-section, even though it could not be said that their texture, substance or value was

> altered by such activities. I derive some support from the *Kilmarnock* case, where the Lord President (Clyde) specifically said that in his view alteration of the material in question (in that case, coal) was not essential to involve subjecting it to a process.

Warehouses for imported goods
Under CAA 1968, s 7(1)(*f*)(iv), capital allowances are available for a building in use for the purposes of a trade which consists in the storage of goods and materials on their arrival by sea or air into any part of the UK (the allowances are available whether the goods are purchased from an overseas manufacturer or a dealer). To qualify under this head the warehouse must reasonably serve the particular port at which the goods arrived, and must be a transit warehouse (ie, not the warehouse of the ultimate consignee). On this point, see the case of *Copol* v *Hindmarch* [1982] STC 421 (Ch D) and [1984] STC 33 (CA).

If goods are manufactured overseas and imported direct from the manufacturer into the UK and held in a warehouse, the UK importer may be able to obtain allowances under CAA 1968, s 7(1)(*f*)(iii) if he obtains the goods not as a purchaser but as an agent for the overseas manufacturer (see *Dale* v *Johnson Bros* (1951) 32 TC 487 which is not affected on this point by the case of *Crusabridge* mentioned below).

If the UK importer is, say, the subsidiary of the overseas manufacturer, the parties should consider arranging their contractual relationship so that the requirements above can be satisfied.

Storage before sending to manufacturers
In the case of *Crusabridge Investments Ltd* v *Casings International Ltd* [1979] TC Leaflet No 2799), Casings (the taxpayer) stored used tyres which it later sent to various manufacturers to be subjected to a process (they were remoulded). It was held that this was a qualifying industrial use; it was not necessary for Casings itself to subject the tyres to any process.

The above was not a tax case but the Inland Revenue issued a Press Release on 8 March 1982 stating that it would accept the case. The Revenue stated that in broad terms allowances would be available for buildings used for warehousing and storage by traders and wholesalers, where the goods involved are to be used for an industrial process (Inland Revenue, 26 March 1982 'Industrial Buildings Allowance and the Small Workshop Scheme', para 13 (see FRPI/IS, *IR Practices and Concessions,* Longman)).

A loophole in the legislation which was first brought to light in the case of *Saxone Lilley & Skinner (Holdings) Ltd* v *IRC* (1967) 44 TC 122 and which was referred to in the *Crusabridge* case, is that if a warehouse is used entirely for a trade part of which (say, one-third) qualifies as an industrial use and part does not (the remaining two-thirds), the entire building will qualify as an industrial bulding, because although the Act does deal with a case where one part of a building is used for one purpose and another part is used for a different purpose it contains no machinery for dealing with the dual use of the same part (see CAA 1968, s 7(2)).

Repair and maintenance of goods
In *Vibroplant Ltd* v *Holland* [1982] STC 164, it was held that a building used by a plant hire operator to clean, service and if necessary repair plant was not an industrial building.

FA 1982 has amended the law. The amendment, however, does not appear to help taxpayers in the situation of *Vibroplant.* FA 1982, s 75 provides that the maintaining or repairing of any goods or materials shall be an industrial use. However, this extension of the industrial use class shall not apply to the maintenance or repair by any person (X Ltd) of goods or materials employed by that person (X Ltd) in any trade or undertaking unless that trade or undertaking carried on by X Ltd itself falls within one of the industrial use classes.

Additionally, if the maintenance or repair activities are carried out in a retail shop, allowances are not available.

Mr Ridley in Standing Committee A, 8 June 1982, House of Commons, gave the following example.

> . . . the cobbler who sells shoes and mends them in the back of his shop would not qualify, but the cobbler who sells shoes and sets up a special plant or building to repair shoes would qualify in respect of that part.

The allowances with regard to the repair plant would not be restricted because although the cobbler also sells shoes the repaired shoes are not employed in his non-industrial shoe sale trade.

If X Ltd hires out television sets and builds a warehouse to maintain and repair the television sets which are to be hired out, capital allowances will not be available. However, it appears that if X Ltd creates a new subsidiary which is to carry out the maintenance and repair works and which is to carry out a separate trade in respect thereof (even though it exclusively does the maintenance and repair work required by X Ltd) capital allowances would be available.

Motor car repair workshops
The Revenue practice (which is still extant) with regard to car repair workshops, which form part of a retail car sales business, is that allowances are available where:

(*a*) the repair workshop is completely isolated from the rest of the motor dealer's premises:

(*b*) it does not include the reception area for cars; and

(*c*) access to it by the public is discouraged.

8.6.7 Drawing office qualifies

In *IRC* v *Lambhill Iron Works* 31 TC 393 the taxpayer carried on a business as structural engineers in a building (that clearly qualifed as an industrial building) and the ground floor of a separate building was used as a general office dealing with orders from clients and the upper storey housed the drawing office. No allowances could be available with respect to the general offices (CAA 1968, s 7(3)). The question was raised as to whether allowances would be available with respect to the drawing office. No significance was to be attached to the fact that it was to be referred to as a drawing office any more than one would say that a machine shop was a shop (p 399). The Court of Session found that the drawing office had been used predominantly for the making up of drawings for clients who had already placed work to be executed in the factory. It was therefore part of the factory user and therefore qualified for the allowances. The fact that part of the use related to clerical or managerial work not related to the work to be carried out in the factory (ie, the preparation of drawings in respect of work which had been enquired about by prospective customers but for which the order for the work had not been then given to the company) was held not to be important as one had to look to the predominant use. Also the fact that some such work was so carried out in the drawing office did not mean that the drawing office became *ancillary* to the general office within CAA 1968, s 7(3).

Thus allowances were available in full with respect to the drawing office.

The term 'office' in general would tend to indicate a building in which clerical or paper work is carried out (see *Minister of Labour* v *Morgan* 1967 2 ALL ER 732 per Lord Parker, CJ at 735 dealing with the Offices, Shops and Railway Premises Act 1963, s 1).

8.6.8 Roads

The word structure clearly has a wider meaning than the word building.

The Shorter Oxford Dictionary defines a structure as, 'a building or edifice of any kind especially one of considerable size and imposing appearance'.

A road may or may not amount to a structure. Some guidance on this was given in the case of *IRC* v *Smyth* [1914] 3 KB 406 at 421 where Scrutton J stated as follows:

> In my view it is a question of fact in each case; a gravel path though from repeated gravellings it is harder than the surrounding soil would not in my opinion be a structure, while the roads one is familiar with in Switzerland, the Tyrol, and Italy, in parts built up on mountain sides, in parts cut out of solid rock, would I think clearly be structures, as would the elaborate compositions of concrete, wood blocks, and tarmac used for heavy motor traffic at the present day. Between the two there is every variety of degree of solidity and permanence . . . I think a structure is something artificially

> erected, constructed, put together, of a certain degree of size and permanence, which is still maintained as an artificial erection, or which, though not so maintained, has not become indistinguishable in bounds from the natural earth surroundings. What degree of size and permanence will do is a question of fact in each case.

That case was dealing with the provisions of an old Finance Act which was not concerned with capital allowances but nevertheless the guidance is very useful with respect to capital allowances.

Under Statutory Concession B3 where the owner of an industrial trading estate has incurred capital expenditure on the provision on the estate of private roads which remain in his occupation, and he is not himself carrying on a trade which would qualify him for industrial building allowances in respect of the expenditure, he is treated in practice as if he were carrying on a qualifying trade and so entitled to the allowances if the premises on the industrial estate are occupied wholly or mainly by leasees who are themselves carrying on qualifying trades.

8.6.9 Use for trade

It is essential that the industrial building is used for trading purposes (CAA 1968, s 7(1) and (5) ('undertaking')). There have been numerous cases before the Courts to determine whether an activity is or is not a trade (see Chapter 4).

8.6.10 Relevant interest

Only the person who has the 'relevant interest' in the industrial building can claim a writing-down allowance (s 2(1)(*c*)). The relevant interest is the interest in the building which was held by the person who incurred the initial expenditure (s 11(1)).

An interest shall not cease to be the relevant interest for the purposes of the allowances by reason of the creation of any lease or other interest to which the interest is subject (s 11(3)).

Example 8H: Relevant interest in an industrial building

X Ltd has a 99-year lease. It expends capital monies on the construction of an industrial building and lets the same to a trading company. The letting is for 90 years. X Ltd will have retained the relevant interest (*Woods* v *R M Mallen (Engineering) Ltd* (1969) 45 TC 619). It makes no difference that X Ltd may have obtained a capital premium on the grant of the lease. It should be noted, however, that if X Ltd buys a freehold building for £1 million and grants a lease for 999 years at a peppercorn rent for a premium of £1 million with a view to retaining the relevant interest and obtaining writing-down allowances, the author is of the view that, in strict law, the expenditure on acquiring the building may not amount to 'capital expenditure'.

Special provisions apply where leases are extinguished by reason of the surrender of a lease or by reason of the person entitled to the lease acquiring the interest which is reversionary thereon; in these cases the interest into which the leasehold interest merges will become the relevant interest (s 11(3) and (4)).

If the taxpayer, for instance, has a leasehold interest and he pays his sub-tenant monies to purchase the sub-tenant's interest and the sub-tenant's interest is the relevant interest and the two interests merge then the superior leasehold interest will be the relevant interest.

Example 8I: Surrender not assignment

A (the freeholder) lets property to B for 99 years. B is a builder within CAA 1968, s 5(2). B constructs an industrial building thereon. An overriding lease of 100 years is granted to C an investor. B surrenders its interest by operation of law and it merges with the leasehold interest (for 100 years) of C. C will take the relevant interest because of CAA 1968, s 11(3) and the transaction, *Ramsay* permitting, will have resulted in the mitigation of Stamp Duty because the surrender would have been by operation of law; this contrasts with the situation if B had sold the leasehold interest to C: in that case it would have been a conveyance on sale carried out under seal and ad valorem duty will have been payable.

There are certain other cases where the relevant interest in a lease is deemed to continue although the lease has come to an end. These cases are as follows:

(*a*) where, with the consent of the lessor, a lessee of any building or structure remains in possession thereof after the termination of the lease without a new lease being granted to him (s 13(2));

(*b*) where on the termination of a lease a new lease is granted to the lessee in pursuance of an option available to him under the terms of the first lease (s 13(3));

(*c*) where, on the termination of a lease, the lessor pays any sum to the lessee in respect of a building or structure comprised in the lease (s 13(4)); and

(*d*) where, on the termination of a lease, another lease is granted to a different lessee and, in connection with the transaction, the lessee pays a sum to the person who was the lessee under the first lease (s 13(5)).

Except in those situations, where a lease comes to an end the relevant interest is lost and no further writing-down allowances are available. This would be the case if, for instance, the lease expires by effluxion of time or is brought to an end by forfeiture and the leasee leaves the premises.

Construction works carried out before completion

These relevant-interest provisions can give rise to problems. X Ltd may contract to buy the freehold of certain land from Y Ltd and simultaneously enter into an agreement to grant a lease to Z Ltd when the building is completed. Immediately before the grant of the lease, when the building is completed, X Ltd would four weeks later complete the purchase of the freehold. Where is the relevant interest in this situation? The interest of X Ltd when it constructed the building was the contract to purchase the freehold and not the freehold itself. X Ltd would have no right to the freehold as it would have to rely upon the discretionary remedy of specific performance to obtain this. If the contract is the relevant interest what happens to that interest after the freehold is obtained; is it extinguished, does it survive in the freehold or does the freehold become the relevant interest? In the author's view the contract should be treated as surviving in the freehold so that if X Ltd contracts to sell the freehold it will have disposed of the relevant interest. This could be important if X Ltd allows that subsequent sale to rest on contracts. The author understands that the Revenue takes the view that after completion the freehold will be the relevant interest. Prior to that the contractual interest will be the relevant interest.

Interests under trusts for sale
A similar point can arise where the landowner disposes of land to a number of persons. X Ltd, a builder, may construct a building and sell it unused to five investors. The builder will have had the absolute freehold interest in possession. There will be no trust for sale. In fact, no trust will have been created at all. When he disposes of the land to five investors, however, they will be acquiring interests under the trust for sale. The property will vest in the name of the first four investors as trustees for the five investors. That interest is different from the interest of the builder. It is understood that the Revenue does not take this point. If it were to take the point the author feels that it can be successfully argued that the trust for sale is no more than a conveyancing mechanism and should be ignored for the purposes of tax (see *Sargaison* v *Roberts* (1969) 45 TC 612).

Special provisions contained in FA 1978 apply to long leases granted at premiums. These provisions are dealt with subsequently in this chapter.

8.6.11 Lessee, lessor and lease

CAA 1968, s 87(1) states that 'lease' includes an agreement for a lease where the term to be covered by the lease has begun, and any tenancy, but it does not include a mortgage, and 'lessee', 'lessor' and 'leasehold interest' shall be construed accordingly.

8.6.12 Time of sale

For the purposes of ascertaining when a balancing charge may arise or when a balancing allowance may be given (s 3) it is important to know the time when a sale takes place—is it exchange of contracts or completion? Section 87(6) provides that any reference in the Act to the time of any sale shall be construed as a reference to the time of completion or the time when possession is given, whichever is the earlier.

8.7 INTERACTION WITH PLANT AND MACHINERY ALLOWANCES

No allowances can be made under the industrial building and structure provisions if an allowance can also be made under the plant and machinery provisions (or indeed under any of the other capital allowances provisions, such as those relating to mines, oil wells, etc) (s 14(1) and (2)).

Special provisions apply to expenditure on the preparation of sites for the installation of machinery or plant (see s 9).

8.8 SPECIAL CASES

8.8.1 Long leases

Where expenditure has been incurred on the construction of a building or structure and a long lease is granted out of the relevant interest, the following shall apply if the lessor and lessee so elect:

(a) the grant of the lease shall be treated as if it were a sale of the relevant interest by the lessor to the lessee at the time when the lease takes effect;

(*b*) any capital sum paid by the lessee in consideration for the grant of the lease shall be treated as the purchase price of the relevant interest which is sold; and

(*c*) the interest out of which the lease is granted shall be treated as having ceased and the interest granted by the lease shall be treated as if it had become the relevant interest in relation to the capital expenditure (FA 1978, s 37(1)).

This provision can be important. In effect it enables a lessor to surrender allowances to a lessee whilst at the same time enabling the lessor to keep what would otherwise be the relevant interest.

8.8.2 Two possible traps, connected persons etc and long leases

It should be noted that the ability to surrender the relevant interest under s 37 of the Finance Act 1978 will not be available if the lessor and lessee are connected persons within Taxes Act 1988, s 839, or it appears that the sole or main benefit that may be expected to accrue to the lessor from the grant of the lease and the making of an election is the obtaining of a balancing allowance under Capital Allowances Act 1968, s 3.

Example 8J: No election if connected

X Ltd grants a lease of 100 years to its 100% subsidiary Y Ltd. The parties are connected so that no election can be made.

However, where the lessor is a body discharging statutory functions and the lessee is a company under its control the fact that they are connected would not prevent the surrender of the relevant interest being made if an election is made.

Another possible trap is the requirement that the lease is a long lease. This means a lease the duration of which ascertained in accordance with Taxes Act 1988, s 38 exceeds 50 years. Any question whether a lease is a long lease shall be determined without reference to Capital Allowances Act 1968, s 13(3) (options for renewal).

Example 8K: Option to buy freehold

X Limited constructs an industrial building on Blackacre. It grants a lease of 99 years to Y Limited with an election being made to enable the relevant interest to be surrendered by X Limited to Y Limited. However before entering into the deal Y Limited was granted an option which became effective when the deal was entered into to enable Y Limited at the end of 25 years to buy the freehold. It is very likely under these circumstances that the election to surrender the relevant interest under FA 1978 s 37 will not be available because the lease will only last for 25 years.

8.9 ANTI-AVOIDANCE PROVISIONS: CHECK LIST

8.9.1 Sales between associated persons

If, *inter alia,* the vendor and purchaser of a building are under common control as defined in s 87(1), or if the one has control of the other, special rules apply for computing the capital allowances when the sale price is not at market value (s 78 and Sched 7). The provisions have been widened in scope by FA 1981, s 76 and must be carefully examined especially if tax avoidance schemes are proposed or complicated manoeuvres are entered into to obtain allowances.

8.9.2 Sole or main benefit is the obtaining of allowances

Where it appears with respect to a sale, or with respect to transactions of which the sale is one, that the sole or main benefit that might be expected to accrue to the parties from the transaction or transactions was the obtaining of an allowance or deduction, the obtaining of a greater allowance or deduction or the avoidance or reduction of a charge, then the sale should be treated as if it had been made at open market value so that for capital allowances purposes the amount of the sale proceeds of the vendor and the capital expenditure incurred by the purchaser will be adjusted to open market value (see Sched 7, para 1(1)(*b*) and FA 1981, s 76(3)(*b*)).

Unless it can be shown that a sale and leaseback falls within this head or the preceding head, the sale proceeds would be used as the basis of calculating the balancing allowance or balancing charge on the sale. The sale and leaseback would normally be caught by anti-avoidance provisions insofar as plant and machinery allowances are concerned (FA 1971, Sched 8, para 3, and FA 1972, s 68(1)(*b*)).

8.9.3 Apportionment of sale proceeds

Where there is a composite sale of land, buildings, plant, work in progress etc, the Revenue may apportion the proceeds so as to attribute a fair amount to the industrial building allowances. The Revenue does not have to accept the figures put on the various items by the parties involved (s 77). In the case of *Fitton* v *Guilders and Heaton* 36 TC 233 the taxpayer sold a lease and goodwill and equipment. The final figures in the document differed from those in the original draft document (the amount attributable to the equipment was higher in the draft than in the final document). This was done in order to enable the purchaser to obtain an advance from his bank. Wynn-Parry J held that the General Commisioners were entitled to go behind the terms of the agreement and decide on a just and reasonable basis what amounts were properly referable to the equipment and the other items.

8.9.4 Restriction of balancing allowances

Prior to FA 1972 a common scheme to expedite balancing allowances involved the granting of a lease inter-group with a subsequent disposal of the relevant interest at the then market value which, because of the grant of the lease, would be very small. Consequently, an immediate balancing allowance was obtained. It was essential to grant a lease in order not to dispose of the relevant interest.

Schemes such as that to obtain balancing allowances were stopped by FA 1972, s 69

8.9.5 Restriction of set off against general income

If there have been transactions involving partners, connected persons or transfers at under values the provisions of FA 1976, s 45(6) should be considered.

PART II ENTERPRISE ZONE ALLOWANCES

The above provisions deal with capital allowances and industrial buildings and structures.

That body of law also applies to capital expenditure on industrial and commercial buildings and structures and qualifying hotels in Enterprise Zones (FA 1980, s 74(2)) except that:

(*a*) an initial allowance of 100% is available,

(*b*) if the owner of the relevant interest wishes, he can take only a part of the initial allowance, in which case the balance will be written off at 25% of the cost a year on a straight line basis (this is the allowance). Thus if he elects for a 60% initial allowance the writing down allowances will be 25% and 15%. Balancing adjustments are made if the building is sold within 25 years (see p 98).

Many individuals and companies will be interested in investing in Enterprise Zone buildings and structures to obtain the 100% allowance. The investors will normally let the property to commercial users. Outside the Enterprise Zones the allowance for expenditure on industrial buildings and structures is only 4% per year so that only actual industrialists using the properties themselves are likely to be interested in those allowances.

8.10 WHAT USES QUALIFY

Industrial buildings and structures will qualify. Hotels within FA 1978, s.38 will qualify. Commercial buildings or structures will qualify.

FA 1980, s 74 states that a commercial building or structure means a building or structure (other than an industrial building or structure or a qualifying hotel: which are specifically stated to qualify elsewhere) which is used for the purposes of a trade, profession or vocation or, whether or not for such a purpose, as an office or offices but it does not include any building in use as, or as part of, a dwelling house.

Normally there should be little difficulty in ascertaining whether a particular use qualifies for the allowance.

The author feels that lettings of structures to commercial car parking operators should qualify for relief with the aid, in appropriate cases, of TA 1988, s 53(3) (deemed trade).

8.10.1 Enterprise Zone structures

Structuring deals to enable investors to obtain the 100% Enterprise Zone allowance tend to require the deals to fall into one of three patterns each of which require four conditions to be satisfied (or to be deemed to be satisfied).

Requirements
- Incur capital expenditure
- Construction
- Qualifying building
- Used by payer or his tenant or licensee

8.11 ENTERPRISE ZONE ALLOWANCES—FOUR CONDITIONS

Before a commercial user or an investor can obtain allowances he must satisfy or be deemed to have satisfied the four conditions set out in the Capital Allowances Act 1968, s 1(1). This will entitle the investor to the initial allowance.

In order to obtain the initial allowances a person must:

(*a*) incur (see 8.6.1) capital expenditure (see 8.6.3)

(*b*) on the construction of

(*c*) a building or structure which is to be a commercial building or structure (or indeed a qualifying hotel or an industrial building or structure)

(*d*) occupied for the purposes of a trade carried on either by that person or by a lessee (or even a licensee; see below).

(CAA 1968, s 1(1) and FA 1980, Sched 13, para 1).

8.11.1 Three out of four not enough

It is necessary to satisfy all the requirements of (*a*)–(*d*).

Example 8L: Four requirements

X Ltd is a land dealer. It buys Blackacre and constructs a factory thereon which is let to a qualifying tenant. No allowances are available to X Ltd as it holds the land as stock—the expenditure is not capital expenditure.

8.11.2 Sub-lessees OK

A sub-lessee of the person who incurred the expenditure, if a commercial user (the sub-lessee), is sufficient to enable the allowances to be available.

In support of the argument that it is not necessary for a person claiming the allowance to have an interest which is immediately reversionary on the interest occupied by the qualifying tenant, one can refer to TA 1988, s 30(3)(*b*).

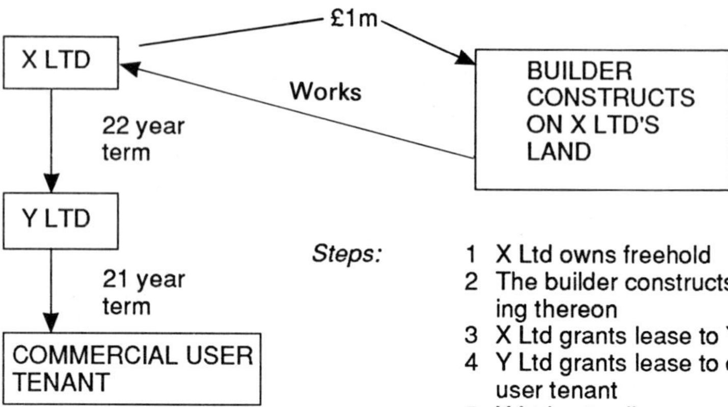

Steps:

1 X Ltd owns freehold
2 The builder constructs a building thereon
3 X Ltd grants lease to Y Ltd
4 Y Ltd grants lease to commercial user tenant
5 X Ltd gets allowances on £1m

That provision deals with sea walls and uses the words 'the owner of the interest in immediate reversion of the lease'. It may be argued, on those words, that where the taxing statutes mean 'immediate reversion' they say so. The word 'immediate', if it does not expressly appear, is not to be imported into the legislation. Similar provisions apply with respect to expenditure on agricultural land and buildings: in CAA 1968, ss 68(5) and (6) there are references made to the 'immediate' reversion.

8.12 ACCEPTABLE ENTERPRISE ZONE PROPERTY INVESTMENT STRUCTURES

Property deals which are structured to give investors the 100% Enterprise Zone allowance generally fall into three basic patterns or combinations of patterns.

8.12.1 Employ builder/developer route

Investor has interest in land (he takes a lease or buys the freehold) and pays builder/developer to construct buildings
An investor may take a long lease of bare land, for instance, from a Local Authority and then employ a developer/builder to construct a commercial building on his land with the investor then granting a lease to a commercial tenant. The investor will obtain the 100% allowance under CAA 1968, s 1(1) on the amount paid to the developer/builder.

Premiums and Ground Rents
If the investor has paid a premium to the Local Authority for the lease of the bare land (which he then has developed and lets on) he will not get any allowances for the premium (Capital Allowances Act 1968, s 17(1)) although if he pays a ground rent he will be able to offset that against the tax payable on the rents he receives from the commercial tenant.

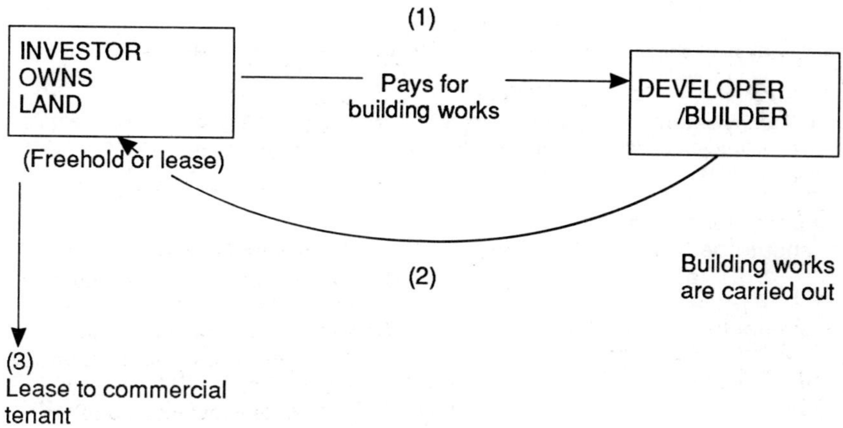

8.12.2 Buy building from builder/developer route

Investor buys the relevant interest from a builder/developer
The investor may obtain his allowances by buying the relevant interest (ie, the land interest which the builder/developer had when he constructed the building thereon prior to the sale to the investor) from the builder/developer (CAA 1968, s 1(1) and s 5(2)).

Example 8M: Builder sells interest to developer

X, the builder constructs a commercial building on its own freehold land. X then sells (contracts and then completes) the building to Mr Y, an investor. Mr Y will obtain industrial building allowances with regard to the purchase price referable to the building.

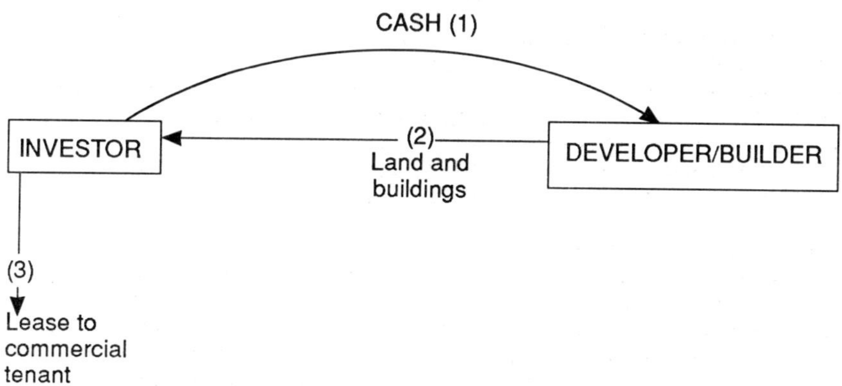

Example 8N: Investor obtains lease

If X had taken a leasehold interest from a Local Authority at a full ground rent and then constructed the building thereon and then sold the leasehold interest, with the obligation to pay the ground rents, to Y, it may be that Y will obtain allowances on his total outlay because the ground rents may have effectively taken away the value of the bare land on which allowances cannot be available. The relevant documentation must be carefully drafted (CAA 1968, s 17(1)).

Building must be unused
It should be noted that the investor must buy the property unused from X in order to obtain the 100% allowance. There are no problems if the property has already been let by X prior to Y purchasing the interest but the tenants must not have used the property.

The words used in CAA 1968, s 5(1) are 'is used'. The fact that the building may be available for use or may be waiting to be used does not mean that the building is used. In a capital allowances case concerning plant and machinery the relevant wording was 'is in use'. Megarry J in *Schapira* v *Kirby* 46 TC 320 at 325 stated:

> The words of the Statute are, of course, 'is in use'. The section does not include words such as 'waiting to be used' or 'available for use': nothing short of being in use suffices. I cannot see how it can be said that a car reposing peacefully in a garage for the entire basis period can be said to be 'in use for the purposes of a doctor's practice'.
>
> In the particular case the doctor sought (but failed) to obtain capital allowances for the car while garaged.

8.12.3 Take long lease from builder/developer route:

Investor is granted a long lease at a premium
The developer may have, say, the freehold of the land. It may employ a builder to construct a building thereon and then grant a long lease (lease exceeding 50 years) at a peppercorn rent taking a premium. The investor will take the lease and pay the premium which will equate to the 'purchase price' of the building and he will obtain an appropriate allowance (FA 1978, s 37; CAA1968, s 1(1) and 5(1)).

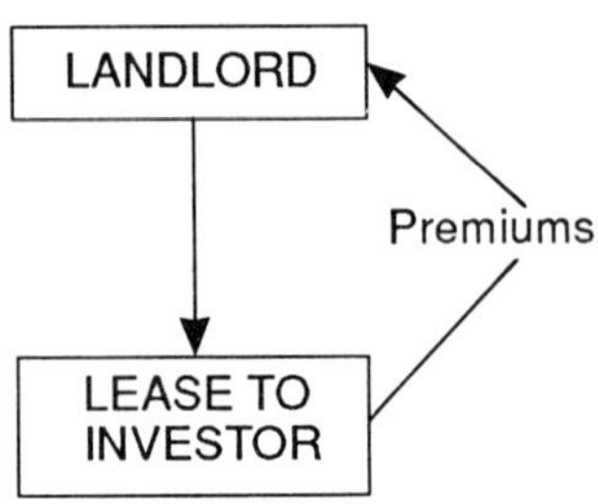

No Allowances on Land
The investor cannot obtain allowances in the example just mentioned on the entire premium he pays because some will relate to the land.

8.12.4 Combinations of routes:

An investor may obtain allowances by a combination of one or more of the above routes

Example 80: Combination of routes

A builder may own the freehold of the land and may have half constructed the building thereon. He may grant a lease at a premium to the inventor so with respect to that premium or part thereof the investor would obtain allowances under FA 1978, s 37. To complete the balance of the works the investor may employ the builder paying the appropriate building fees under a building agreement. In this case, for the balance of the building, the investor will obtain allowances simply under CAA 1968, s 1(1).

8.13 ENTERPRISE ZONE STRUCTURES—PURCHASE FROM BUILDER

When an investor buys a newly constructed Enterprise Zone building he should inquire whether the vendor is a builder or a developer who satisfies the conditions of CAA1968, s 5(2).

Where expenditure is incurred on the construction of a building or structure by a person carrying on a trade which consists, as to the whole or part thereof, in the construction of buildings or structures with a view to their sale, then a purchaser can obtain allowances based on the purchase price of the buildings or structure. The investor must ensure he is buying from a 's 5(2)' builder/developer.

The builder must dispose of the relevant interest (CAA 1968, s 5(2)).

Are you buying from a section 5(2) builder/developer?
If the investor buys from a s 5(2) person he will get allowances on £800,000. They will not be restricted to £600,000 under CAA 1968, s 5(1).

Tax Planning
Investors should obtain warranties in respect of the CAA 1968, s 5(2) requirements.

Multiple sales of relevant interest

Property sold unused. Purchaser II is the investor. Purchaser II gets allowances on £0.5m. Purchaser I gets no allowances (s 5(1))as amended by s 5(2))(*b*)).

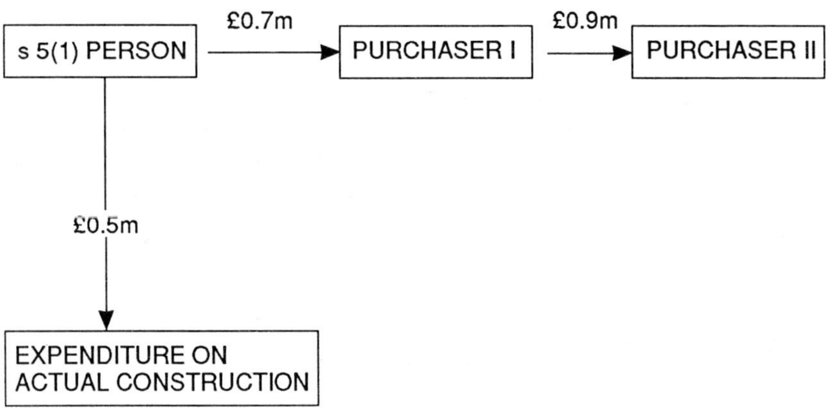

Property sold unused. Purchaser II is the investor. Purchaser II gets allowances on £0.5m (s 5(1) proviso).

8.13.1 Concession for plant or machinery in Enterprise Zones

On 6 January 1987 the Inland Revenue published an Extra Statutory Concession concerning fixed plant or machinery in buildings within Enterprise Zones. The effect of the concession is that certain expenditure on such machinery or plant can qualify for a 100% initial allowance instead of the normal 25% annual allowance.

The full text of the concession is as follows:

> The rate of capital allowances on expenditure on machinery or plant, whether the assets are chattels or fixtures (including parts of a building), is normally 25% of the reducing balance. This is a higher rate than that due on expenditure on the construction of an industrial building (4 per cent straight line) whilst in general no allowances at all are due on the construction of a commercial building. Exceptionally a 100% initial allowance is due on expenditure on the construction of an industrial building or a commercial building in an Enterprise Zone.
>
> Such expenditure does not, however, include expenditure on the provision of machinery or plant, which becomes an integral part of such a building; expenditure on such machinery or plant only qualifies for a 25% writing down allowance. By concession, where a taxpayer is entitled to a 100% initial allowance in respect of expenditure on the construction of an industrial or commercial building in an Enterprise Zone, he may elect to treat as part of the said expenditure, expenditure on the provision of machinery or plant which is to be an integral part of such a building.

PART III PLANT AND MACHINERY

8.14 INTRODUCTION

Valuable writing down allowances are available for capital expenditure incurred on the acquisition of plant and machinery which is used for the purposes of a trade, profession or vocation or office or employment or is deemed to be so used.

The obtaining of these allowances is often a critical factor in determining how property deals are to be structured.

At one time there used to be first year allowances at 100% of the capital expenditure but all first year allowances were abolished in respect of capital expenditure incurred after 31 March 1986 (see FA 1984, Sched 12, para 12(1)).

The writing down allowance is an annual allowance of 25% of the expenditure on the machinery left after taking off capital allowances already given (FA 1971, s 44(2)(*a*)(i)).

8.14.1 Obtaining the writing down allowance

The writing down allowances can only be claimed if the following conditions are satisfied or are deemed to be satisfied:

(*a*) a person must carry on a *trade*;

(*b*) that person must have *incurred expenditure*;

(*c*) the expenditure must be *capital* expenditure;

(*d*) the expenditure must be on the provision of *machinery or plant* for the purposes of the trade; and

(*e*) in consequence of that person incurring the expenditure, the machinery or plant must belong, or must have belonged to him.

Requirements —
- Trade
- Incur expenditure
- Capital
- Machinery or plant
- Belongs

8.14.2 Balancing allowances and balancing charges

If the taxpayer has obtained capital allowances with respect to the plant and machinery and then, for instance, he sells the machinery he may suffer a balancing charge or obtain a balancing allowance (FA 1971, s 44(5) and (6)). Thus if the plant is disposed of at a price exceeding the written down value of the plant, taking the pool of machinery or plant as a whole, then a balancing charge may arise or, alternatively, if the disposal value is less than the written down value, a capital allowance will be available.

The disposal value to be brought into account depends on the event by reason of which it falls to be taken into account. In the usual case of a disposal by sale this value will be the amount of net proceeds of sale. If the event is the sale of the plant or machinery at a price lower than that which it would have fetched if sold in the open market and otherwise under circumstances such that the buyer's expenditure on the acquisition of the plant or machinery can be taken into account in making allowances to him, the disposal value shall be equal to the price which the plant or machinery would have fetched if sold in the open market (FA 1971, s 44(6)(*b*)(i)).

There is an overriding restriction that the disposal value of any machinery or plant shall in no case exceed the capital expenditure incurred by the person in question on the provision of the machinery or plant for the purposes of the trade (FA 1971, s 44(6) proviso). Special provisions, however, apply where there have been transactions between connected persons within the meaning of TA 1988 s 839 (FA 1971, s 44(7)).

8.14.3 Plant or machinery on lease

As mentioned the above five requirements must be actually or be deemed to be satisfied before the taxpayer can obtain a capital allowance.

If L Ltd is the freeholder and he instals a lift in the building then all the above requirements should be satisfied when the freeholder grants a lease to a tenant except that it is very unlikely that the taxpayer (the freeholder) is carrying on a trade. The other conditions should be satisfied because L Ltd would have *incurred capital expenditure* on the provision of *plant and machinery* (the lift) and the machinery would *belong* to him (*Stokes* v *Costain Property Investments Ltd* [1984] STC 204).

Finance Act 1971, s 46(1), however, provides that where machinery or plant is first let by any person otherwise than in the course of a trade then whether or not it is used for the purposes of a trade carried on by the lessee the capital expenditure incurred by the lessor in providing the machinery or plant shall be treated for the purposes of the plant and machinery legislation as having been incurred in providing it for the purposes of a trade begun to be carried on by him separately from any other trade which he may carry on at the commencement of the letting.

Thus L Ltd would be entitled to its allowances; it would actually satisfy all the above requirements except that of trading and it will be deemed to have satisfied the trading requirement by virtue of FA 1971, s 46(1).

It should be noted that FA 1971, s 50(4) states that for the purposes of these allowances any expenditure incurred for the purposes of a trade by a person about to carry it on shall be treated as if it had been incurred by him on the first day on which he does carry it on. Therefore it is felt that one must look to the *letting* as being the relevant day with respect to the obtaining of the allowances. There is nothing to indicate that a letting includes an agreement to let. Strictly, therefore, there must be a formal letting although the Revenue may take a more generous view.

8.15 ENTITLEMENT FOR ALLOWANCES FOR MACHINERY AND PLANT WHICH ARE FIXTURES

It was held in *Stokes* v *Costain Property Investments Ltd* that if, for instance, a tenant installed lifts and ventilating equipment in a building and paid for the same the tenant would not be entitled to allowances because the machinery would belong to the freeholder. Thus the belonging requirement in the legislation would *not* be satisfied.

The position may well be different if the fixtures were *tenant's* fixtures. In that case one may not have to concern oneself with any 'deemed belonging' provisions (in FA 1985). In *Stokes* v *Costain* in the High Court the judge stated at 698B (57 TC 628):

> I say nothing about plant or machinery installed by a tenant in such a way that it remains a tenant's fixture. A machine tool which is fixed down for the better use of it as a machine tool, and not as an improvement to the premises, which machine tool could be removed by the tenant at the expiry of his term and then disposed of by him, may well be said to 'belong' to that tenant. The point does not arise before me and I make no decision on it.

There are provisions contained in FA 1985, s 59 and Sched 17 which are designed to ensure that in appropriate cases tenants can obtain capital allowances. The provisions in FA 1985 generally apply to cases where the expenditure is incurred after 11 July 1984 although there are certain transitional provisions (FA 1985, s 59(2)).

These provisions in FA 1985 are concerned with deeming the 'belonging' requirement to be satisfied.

For example, if L lets property to T and T lets it to OT and T instals a lift in the building then the likelihood is that the lift will *belong* to L so that T will not be entitled to any allowances. Finance Act 1985, s 59 and Sched 17 are designed to remedy that problem.

8.15.1 Situation one: Lessee incurs expenditure

Schedule 2(1) provides in any case where:

(*a*) a person incurs capital expenditure on the provision of machinery or plant either for the purposes of a trade carried on by him or for leasing otherwise than in the course of the trade and

(*b*) the machinery or plant becomes a fixture and

(*c*) at the time when the machinery or plant becomes a fixture that person *has an interest* in the relevant land (relevant land means the building or other description of land which the fixture becomes part of),

then the fixture is treated as belonging to the person who incurred that expenditure.

It will be noted that this provision is simply concerned to ensure that the belonging requirement is satisfied.

Example 8P: Lessee incurs expenditure

L grants a lease to T who grants a lease to OT. T incurs expenditure on plant and machinery. The expenditure is capital expenditure. He incurs it for the purposes of a trade carried on by him or for leasing otherwise than in the ordinary course of trade and the machinery has become a fixture. He has an interest in the land in which the fixture is incorporated and thus the machinery is treated as belonging to him. He then needs to refer back to FA 1971, s 44 to see that the other requirements are satisfied. He certainly incurred capital expenditure so that that requirement is satisfied. It is on the provision of plant and machinery wholly and exclusively for the purpose of a trade so that that requirement is satisfied. He does not actually carry on a trade but FA 1971, s 46 *deems him to be carrying on a trade* so that the trade requirement is satisfied.

Special provisions apply if in respect of the same fixture there are two or more persons with the different interests in the relevant land (FA 1985, Sched 17, para 2(2)).

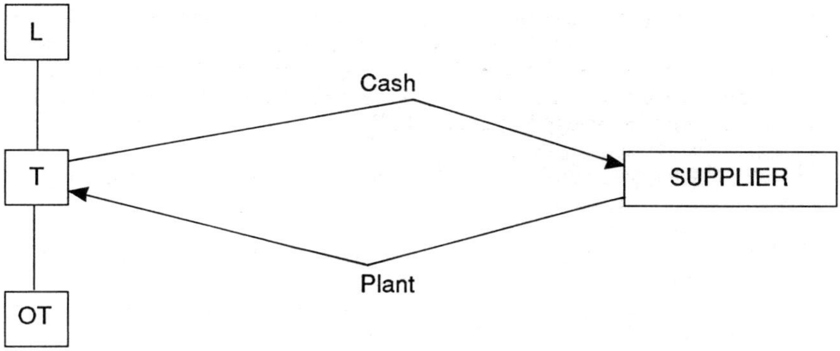

8.15.2 Situation two: Expenditure incurred by equipment lessor

It may be that X carries out the trade of letting plant and machinery. He may let plant and machinery to Y who instals this in his building (Y's building) so that it becomes a fixture. As a result of that X cannot claim that the machinery belongs to him. In that case X would not be entitled to any capital allowances as the belonging requirement would not be satisfied.

Schedule 17, para 3 states in any case where:

(1) a person (the equipment lessor) incurs capital expenditure on a provision of machinery or plant for leasing and

(2) an agreement is entered into for the lease directly or indirectly from the equipment lessor, of the machinery or plant (otherwise than as part of the relevant land) to another person (the equipment lessee) for the purposes of a trade carried on by the equipment lessee or for leasing otherwise than in the course of a trade, and

(3) the machinery or plant becomes a fixture, and

(4) if the expenditure incurred under (1) above had been incurred by the equipment lessee, the fixture would have been treated for material purposes (for the purposes of the capital allowances legislation on plant and machinery) as belonging to him in consequence of his incurring the expenditure and

(5) the equipment lessor and the equipment lessee elect that the paragraph shall apply.

then the equipment lessor shall be deemed to have satisfied the belonging requirement. As he would satisfy all the other requirements, ie, he has incurred capital expenditure on the provision of plant and machinery for the purposes of a trade, he will obtain the allowances.

Example 8Q: Equipment lessor

L lets property to T, Z leases machinery to T which he uses for the purposes of his trade. The consequence is the plant and machinery become a fixture when it is installed in the building. *Prima facie* Z would obtain no allowances because the machinery no longer belongs to him. Nevertheless Sched 17, para 3 deems the machinery and plant to belong to Z and he (Z) can claim the allowances.

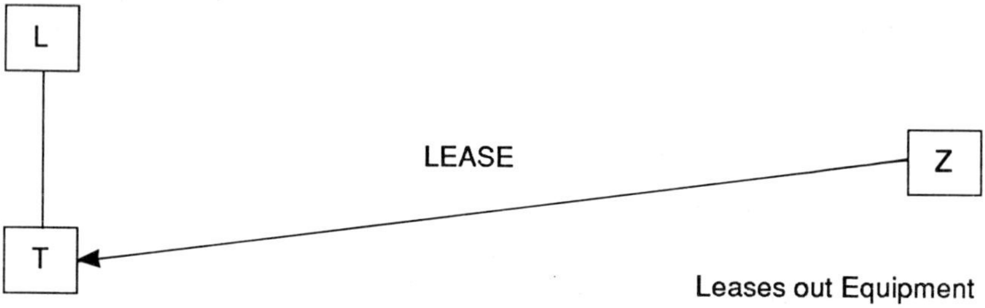

Strictly it may be argued that if Z had leased the machinery to L the freeholder that Sched 17, para 3(1)(*d*) would not be satisfied because the fixture would not by virtue of Sched 17, para 2 have been treated as belonging to L in consequence of his incurring the expenditure; a freeholder would not need to rely on para 2 because he would own the machinery and it would actually belong to him. He would not have to look at Sched 17, para 2. Nevertheless, probably the better construction is that para 2 still applies to deem the machinery to belong to L even though it belongs to him under general principles.

These equipment lessor provisions could be relevant in cases where two taxpayers own several parcels of land but wish to enter a *joint venture* with one taxpayer effectively putting plant and machinery into the other taxpayer's building.

8.15.3 Situation three: The sale of lease

Where a tenant has put machinery in a building so that it becomes a fixture he will in general have obtained allowances under Sched 17, para 2. Paragraph 4 of Sched 17 deals with the situation where the tenant sells his interest to a purchaser. In this case the purchaser can obtain allowances on the part of the purchase price which refers to the plant and machinery provided that at the time of the purchaser's acquisition of the tenant's lease either no person has previously become entitled to an allowance in respect of any capital expenditure incurred on the provision of the fixture or if any person has become so entitled, that person has been or is required to bring the disposal value of the fixture into account under FA 1971, s 44.

If those conditions are satisfied then the purchaser of the lease is deemed to satisfy the belonging requirement and the other requirements would also be satisfied (the other requirements being those in FA 1971, s 44(1)).

Example 8R: Sale of lease

L Ltd grants a lease to T Ltd who grants a lease to OT Ltd. T Ltd expends money on plant and machinery such as the lift and central heating system. T Ltd is a trader and cannot obtain any capital allowances. Nobody else is entitled to allowances with respect to that expenditure as they have not incurred any of the expenditure on putting the machinery into the building. T Ltd assigns his lease to X. The sale price is £10m. Two million pounds of that is referable to plant and machinery. X can obtain allowances on £2m. Note that if T had actually incurred expenditure and obtained allowances then he might have suffered a balancing charge on the disposal to X and X's ability to claim allowances may be restricted (see FA 1985, Sched 17, para 9(10)).

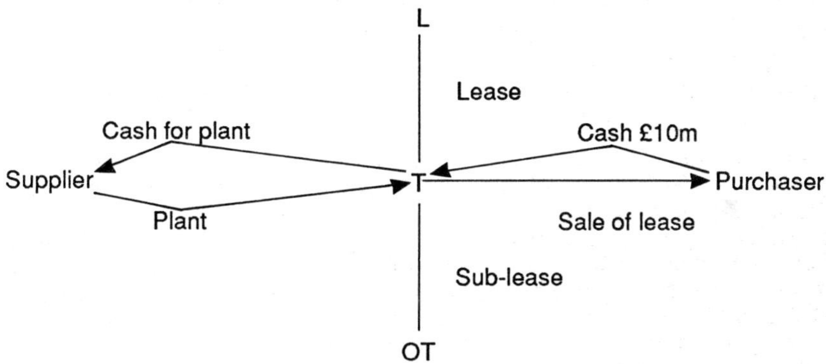

8.15.4 Situation four: Surrender of allowances to tenant

Finance At 1985, Sched 17, para 5 states that in any case where:

(1) after any machinery or plant has become a fixture a person (the lessor) who has an interest in the land and the buildings in which the machinery is installed grants a lease and

(2) the lessor would be entitled to an allowance in respect of the expenditure incurred on the provision of the fixture and

(3) the consideration which the lessee gives for the lease is or includes a capital sum which in whole or part falls to be treated for material purposes (ie for the purpose of the capital allowances legislation on plant and machinery) as expenditure on the provision of the fixture and

(4) the lessor and lessee make an election for the relief to apply,

then on or after the grant of the lease the fixture shall be deemed to belong to the lessee.

Under general principles of course in a situation such as that the lessee would not be entitled to allowances because following *Stokes* v *Costain* the machinery would belong to the freeholder. This provision, provided an election is made, enables the belonging requirement to be satisfied. The other requirements should also be satisfied; the lessee would have paid out capital expenditure on the provision of plant and machinery and he will either use it for the purposes of his own trade or let the property and therefore be deemed to be carrying out a trade by virtue of FA 1971, s 46.

An election cannot be made if the lessor and lessee are connected with each other within TA 1988, s 839 or it appears that the sole or main benefit which may be expected to accrue to the lessor from the grant of the lease and the making of the election is the obtaining of an allowance or deduction or a greater allowance or deduction or the avoidance or reduction of a charge under FA 1971, (Chapter 1 of Part III).

Example 8S: Surrendering the allowance

L owns the freehold. He has spent 1 million pounds in installing plant and machinery in the building. He grants a lease to T and T pays a capital sum and part of that sum relates to the expenditure on the provision of the fixture. An election is made under Sched 17, para 5(1)(*d*) so that he is able to obtain allowances. The relief is only available assuming that L and T are not connected within TA 1988, s 839 and that there is no tax avoidance arrangement within FA 1985, Sched 17, para 5(4)(7)(*b*).

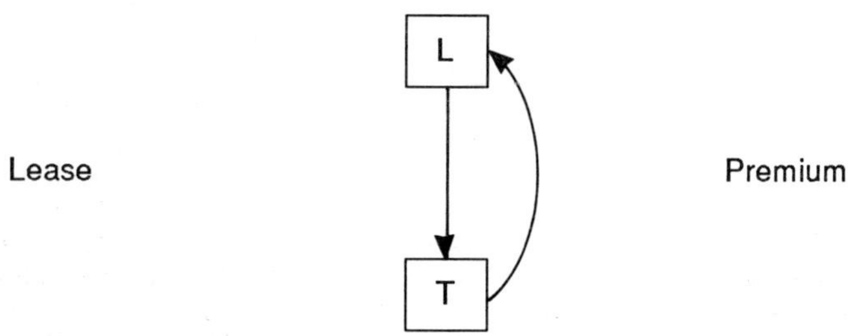

8.15.5 Situation five: Lessor not entitled to any allowances

The situation may arise where X is the freeholder and is a property dealer. He may install fixtures in the building and grant a lease to T for a capital sum. Schedule 17, para 6 states that provided at the time of the grant of the lease no person had previously become entitled to an allowance in respect of any capital expenditure incurred on the provision of a fixture and the fixture had not before that time been used for the purposes of a trade by the lessor or any person connected with him within TA 1988, s 839 the machinery shall be deemed to belong to the lessee.

That (the belonging requirement) is the only requirement which the lessee would not otherwise satisfy. All the other requirements of FA 1971, s 44 would be satisfied, ie the lessee incurs capital expenditure on the provision of machinery or plant and the building is used for the purposes of his own trade or he lets the same (in which case there is a deemed trade within FA 1971, s 46(1)).

Example 8T: Lessor not entitled to allowances

Z plc is a property trader. It constructs a new building and puts machinery therein. It grants a lease to Y plc. Y plc pays a capital sum (premium). If Z plc had not previously used nor had a person connected with it previously used the fixture for the purposes of a trade the tenant would be entitled to the allowances. No election is necessary.

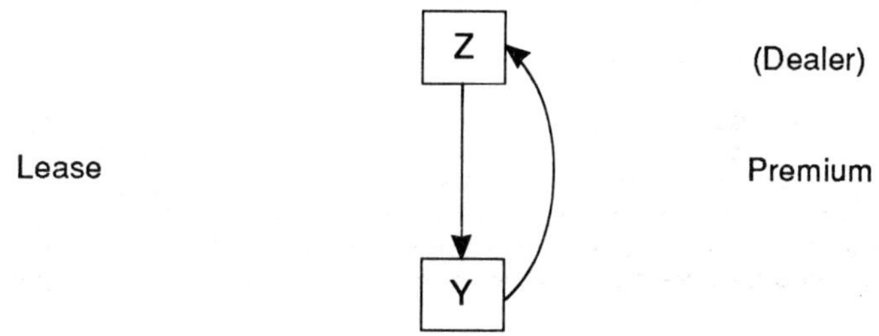

If a taxpayer has obtained an allowance because, for instance, he is a lessee who has incurred capital expenditure on the machinery (Sched 17, para 2), or he has purchased an interest such as a lease and there is plant and machinery in the building (Sched 17, para 4) or he is a lessee who has paid a premium in the form of a capital sum to the lessor and the allowances are made available to the lessee under Sched 17, paras 5 and 6, then a balancing charge may arise if the taxpayer (who is entitled to the allowance) ceases to hold the land interest which gave him the allowance in the first place. He may cease to hold the interest because of the 'transfer, surrender, expiry of the interest or otherwise' (FA 1985, Sched 17, para 7). If the taxpayer ceases to have the interest then the fixture will cease to belong to him at that time and there will then be a balancing charge or a balancing allowance imposed or allowed as the case may be (FA 1971, s 44(5)s 44(5) (*c*)(i) and FA 1985, Sched 17, para 7(2)).

There are certain circumstances where although the taxpayer's land interest may cease to be held by him or shall cease to exist he can nevertheless keep the allowances. These circumstances are set out in Sched 17, para 7.

If the interest ceases to exist by reason of the merger of the interest which is acquired in another interest held by the taxpayer then the interest will be treated as existing in the other interest. For example, L may own the freehold. He may have granted a lease to T and T may have installed machinery therein. T would obtain capital allowances under Sched 17, para 2 and when he sells his lease or surrenders his lease to L L would expect to get allowances under Sched 17, para 4. He should in fact obtain allowances in such a case except that on the face of it the lease may merge into the freehold so that L would not have the interest in the relevant land; the interest would have disappeared. Sched 17, para 4(*a*) is designed to ensure that the freehold is treated as the same interest as the leasehold interest for these purposes. Thus L can take the allowances. Similarly the relieving provisions apply on the termination of leases in certain circumstances and the termination of licences in certain circumstances.

There may also be a balancing charge where the machinery is severed from the building and on being severed it does not in fact belong to the person who severed the same (Sched 17 para 7(7)).

For example, L may have let property to T who may have granted a sub-lease to OT. T may have put machinery in the building. The machinery may have become a fixture so that T may have obtained allowances by virtue of Sched 17, para 2, ie, the machinery is deemed to belong to him. The machinery may then be severed from the building so that it then belongs to L. In this case there may be a balancing charge depending on how much T receives for the machinery, etc. However, if on the severance the machinery actually belongs to T then there is no balancing charge.

There are special provisions to ensure that there is a balancing charge if an equipment lessor (who has leased property to a tenant) sells the equipment for capital monies. In this case the equipment lessor can suffer a balancing charge (see Sched 17, para 8).

Schedule 17, para 9 deals with the situation where very broadly the machinery ceases to belong to the person to whom it was deemed to belong under Sched 17 and that person receives disposal proceeds. One has to calculate the amount of the balancing charge and in certain cases market value is substituted for the actual disposal proceeds.

8.16 MANNER OF MAKING ALLOWANCES AND CHARGES

Any allowance or charge made to any person under these provisions is allowed as an expense in the trade where the allowance is obtained by the person actually carrying on a trade (FA 1971, s 48(1)).

Where the allowance is obtained by virtue of the plant and machinery being let (under FA 1971, s 46) the allowance is available by way of discharge or repayment of tax and is primarily available against income from the letting of the machinery or plant (FA 1971, s 48(2)).

Use may be made of these allowances (subject to any anti-avoidance provisions) in similar ways to those available in connection with industrial building allowances (reference should be made to the provisions of TA 1988 ss 393 and 394).

8.17 MEANING OF KEY TERMS

8.17.1 Trade

Allowances can only be claimed for plant and machinery used for the purposes of a trade, if there is no actual trade carried on there must be a deemed trade carried on. The fact that the taxpayer is a trader or a deemed trader does not of itself entitle him to an allowance; the machinery must actually be used in the trade. Thus, in *Mason* v *Tyson* [1980] STC 284, the taxpayer expended monies on furniture in a flat for staying overnight when he worked outside his normal hours. It was held that although the furniture may have been machinery or plant no allowances were available as it formed no part of his profit-making apparatus with regard to trading activities.

8.17.2 Capital expenditure

This is, broadly, expenditure of an enduring nature. The provisions governing the meaning of capital expenditure for industrial buildings contained in CAA 1968, s 82(1) are made to apply to the plant and machinery provisions by FA 1971, s 50(1).

8.17.3 Plant and machinery

There has been a great number of cases dealing with the meaning of the term 'machinery or plant'.

The right to receive the benefit of the allowances is not limited in the statute to manufacturing industries in relation to which the use of the word 'plant' is familiar and normal. Whatever meaning is to be attached to the wording, FA 1971 makes it applicable to the widest variety of industrial and commercial undertakings as also to the exercise of a profession (FA 1971, s 57(1)).

The functional test
In determining whether an item is plant, one test commonly applied is a functional test; that is to say, does the item perform a function in the actual carrying out of the trade? in *Yarmouth* v *France* (1887) 19 QBD 647 at p 658, Lindley LJ put the matter as follows:

> There is no definition of plant in the Act: but in its ordinary sense, it includes whatever apparatus is used by a business man for carrying on his business,—not his stock-in-trade which he buys or makes for sale; but all goods and chattels, fixed or movable, live or dead, which he keeps for permanent employment in his business,

Light fittings (see also pages 140 and 141 below)
In *J Lyons & Co Ltd* v *Attorney-General* [1944] 1 Ch 281 Uthwatt J had to consider whether electric light fittings were plant; he held that they were not, since they were not part of the apparatus used for carrying on the taxpayer's business. In the course of his judgment he cited Lindley LJ's interpretation or explanation of the meaning of the word 'plant' and said, by way of *obiter dictum,* that plant does not include the place in which the business is carried on. In *Hinton* v *Maden & Ireland Ltd* [1959] 1 WLR 875; 38 TC 391 Lord Reid, at p 417, after remarking that 'plant' is an ordinary English word and that it is not altogether easy to construe and that it may have a more or less extensive meaning according to its context, cited Lindley LJ's formulation and also Uthwatt J's observations, with approval.

Movable partitions
In *Jarrold* v *John Good & Sons Ltd* [1963] 1 WLR 214; 40 TC 681 movable partitions used for dividing up the space in an office building so that the plan of the office accommodation within the building could be varied from time to time as circumstances required, were held to be plant. Pennycuick J, who heard the case in the Chancery Division, indicated, at p 688, that it seemed to him that the setting in which a business is carried on and the apparatus used for carrying on a business are not always necessarily mutually exclusive, but in the case before him it seemed to him to be impossible to deny that fixtures possessing the character of the movable partitions merited the title of apparatus used by the company for carrying on its business, and accordingly he held such partitions to be 'plant' within the meaning of the Act. Ormrod LJ, in the Court of Appeal, who thought the case was one which was very near to the dividing line, cited *Yarmouth* v *France* and *J Lyons & Co Ltd* v *Attorney-General* and said that in his judgment, the partitions should be regarded as something more than a mere setting for the carrying out of the trade, in other words as coming within the definition of 'plant'. Donovan LJ at p 694, said that he agreed with Pennycuick J that 'setting' and 'plant' were not mutually exclusive conceptions; but at p 695 he said that the definition given to plant by Lindley LJ in *Yarmouth* v *France* clearly embraced the partitions. He said:

> I would agree, however, that there may be cases, like *J Lyons & Co Ltd* v *Attorney-General,* where an asset or some article can be excluded from the definition because it is more a part of the setting than part of the apparatus for carrying on the trade. In the present case, however, the contrary is found. These partitions *are* required by the nature of the Respondent's trade, as the lamps in the case of *J Lyons & Co Ltd* v *Attorney-General* were *not.*

Pearson LJ, at the foot of p 695, 40 TC 681 said that plant was something to be distinguished from the premises in which the business is carried on. At p 696 he said:

> There can be no doubt, therefore, as to the main principles to be applied, and the short question in this case is whether the partitioning is part of the premises in which the business is carried on, or part of the plant with which the business is carried on.

He also agreed with the view taken by Pennycuick J.

Dry dock

In *IRC* v *Barclay, Curle & Co Ltd* [1969] 1 WLR 675; [1969] SC(HL) 30, 45 TC 221 the House of Lords had to decide whether a dry dock constituted plant. The provision of the dry dock had involved considerable excavation in the first place, and then the installation of some massive concrete works. Lord Reid, at the foot of page 238, said:

> As the Commissioners observed, buildings or structures and machinery and plant are not mutually exclusive, and that was recognised in *Good's* case. Undoubtedly this concrete dry dock is a structure, but is it also plant? The only reason why a structure should also be plant which has been suggested or which has occurred to me is that it fulfils the function of plant in the trader's operations. And, if that is so, no test has been suggested to distinguish one structure which fulfils such a function from another. I do not say that every structure which fulfils the function of plant must be regarded as plant, but I think that one would have to find some good reason for excluding such a structure, and I do not think that mere size is sufficient.

A few lines further down he says:

> It seems to me that every part of this dry dock plays an essential part in getting large vessels into a position where work on the outside of the hull can begin, and that it is wrong to regard either the concrete or any other part of the dock as a mere setting or part of the premises in which this operation takes place. The whole dock is, I think, the means by which, or plant with which, the operation is performed.

Lord Guest, at p 244, after referring to *Yarmouth* v *France* 19 QBD 647, says: 'The emphasis is on 'an apparatus used for carrying on business', and a few lines lower down he says:' In order to decide whether a particular subject is an 'apparatus' it seems obvious that an inquiry has to be made as to what operation it performs. The functional test is therefore essential, at any rate as a preliminary.' At p 25 he said: 'As Pearson LJ said'—and he is referring to *Jarrold* v *John Good & Sons, Ltd.*—'The subject is part of the plant with which the business is carried on as distinct from the premises in which the business is carried on.' Lord Donovan, the third of the members of the House of Lords who in that case constituted the majority, said, at p 250:

> At the end of the day I find the functional test propounded by Lindley LJ and by Pearson LJ to be as good as any, though, as was said in *Jarrold* v *John Good & Sons Ltd,* some plant may perform its function passively and not actively. But in the present case this dry dock, looked upon as a unit, accommodates ships, separates them from their element, and thus exposes them for repair, holds them in position while repairs are effected, and when this is done returns them to the water. Thus the dry dock is, despite its size, in the nature of a tool of the Respondents' trade, and therefore, in my view, 'plant'.

All three members of the majority in that case relied upon the way in which the dock was used.

Swimming pool

In *Cooke* v *Beach Station Caravans Ltd* [1974] 1 WLR 1398; 49 TC 514 Megarry J had to consider whether a swimming pool and a paddling pool provided at a caravan park, which were structures attached to the soil, were or were not plant, and he held that they were. At p 522 he said:

> First, the two pools should be considered as a unit, with all the attendant apparatus for purifying and heating the water and so on; for it is as a unit that they were constructed and as a unit that they are run. Second, the pools should be considered not on their own but in relation to the business carried on by the Company, namely, running its caravan park.

He then discussed the nature of the use of the pools, then at p 523 he said:

> . . . the pools are . . . part of the apparatus used by the Company for carrying on its business as caravan park operators. The pools are part of the means whereby trade is carried on and not merely the place at which it is carried on: see *per* Pearson LJ in *Jarrold's* case 40 TC 681 . . .

Laboratory and gymnasium

On the other hand, in *St John's School* v *Ward* 49 TC 524 a laboratory and a gymnasium, each consisting of a structure which was not attached to the soil at a school, were held not to constitute plant. Templeman J referred, at p 533, to the remark of Pearson LJ that:

> there can be no doubt, therefore, as to the main principles to be applied, and the short question in this case is whether the partitioning (the subject matter in dispute in Jarrold's case) is part of the premises in which the business is carried on, or part of the plant with which the business is carried on,

and then he went on in his judgment to say:

> If one asks the same question here—namely, whether the chemistry laboratory and the gymnasium are the premises in which the business is carried on or are part of the plant with which the business is carried on—the answer must be the former. Education is not carried on with these particular buildings but in these particular buildings; by contrast the climbing ropes seem to me to be part of the educative machinery.

At p 534 he said:

> In the present case neither the laboratory nor the gymnasium has any function to perform other than to shelter the persons who are being educated inside. The gymnasium was also used to attach ropes and apparatus and was strengthened for that purpose, but the building did not function. The building was only the structure within which the function of educating the boys was carried on.

His view was upheld in the Court of Appeal: see p 536 of the same report.

Grain silos

In *Schofield* v *R & H Hall Ltd* (1974) 49 TC 538 the Court of Appeal in Northern Ireland had to decide whether certain silos erected by a company carrying on the business of importing grain for sale to millers and to manufacturers of animal feeding stuffs were or were not plant. The company found itself obliged to equip itself for bulk unloading of grain and for that purpose it built silos on the dockside from which grain could be delivered with convenient ease to customers who came to collect what they had ordered. The grain was sucked up from the ship into the silos and from there it was released as required and from which it descended by gravity, or by gravity assisted by machinery, into the customer's lorry. Those silos were in that case held to constitute plant.

Petrol filling station canopy
In *Dixon* v *Fitch's Garage Ltd* [1976] 1 WLR 215; 50 TC 509 Brightman J had to consider whether a canopy erected over a petrol filling station constituted plant. It was a canopy covering the whole of the service area, its object being to provide adequate lighting and protection from the weather for the pumps, the employees and the customers of the company. At the foot of p 514 Brightman J said:

> The proper test is whether the canopy had a functional purpose to enable the company to perform the activity of supplying petrol to motor vehicles. I ask myself, 'Does the canopy help to supply petrol, or is it merely part of the setting where petrol is supplied?' To use the words of Lord Reid, which I have already read, is the canopy part of the means by which the operation of supplying petrol is performed? In my judgment this question admits only of a negative answer.

A little lower down he says:

> Further, there is a clear thread running through recent cases, including two Australian cases referred to in the silo case, showing that a structure is not plant if its only purpose is to provide shelter and if it plays no part in what may be termed 'the commercial process'. That conclusion is, I think, an inevitable result of the application of the functional test.

Floating restaurants
It was held in *Benson* v *Yard Arm Club Ltd* [1978] STC 408 that a floating restaurant does not amount to plant or machinery.

Football stand
In *Brown* v *Burnley Football and Athletic Co Ltd* [1980] STC 424, it was held that expenditure on replacing a football stand was not a repair and nor was it expenditure on plant. It was thus not tax-deductible.

*False ceiling*s
In *Hampton* v *Fortes Auto Grill Ltd* [1980] STC 80, the taxpayer company installed false ceilings in the premises from which it carried on the trade of caterers to the general public. The ceilings were a permanent installation providing cladding and support for services used by the company for carrying on its trade. The services included pipes for hot and cold water, beer and coca cola, electrical conduits, ventilation trunking and light apparatus. Fox J in the Chancery Division held that the functional test had to be applied, ie, did the item in question perform a function in the actual carrying on of the trade? He held that the ceilings were not necessary for the functioning of any apparatus used for the purposes of the company's trade and were not part of the means by which the trade was carried

on. Accordingly, capital allowances under FA 1971, s 41(1) were not available.

Decor
In *IRC* v *Scottish & Newcastle Breweries Ltd* [1982] STC 296, TCA 40, the taxpayer company carried on the business of a hotelier and operator of licensed premises. It expended monies on electric light fittings, décor and murals in their hotels and licensed premises in order to enhance the setting and thereby to create the right sort of atmosphere, ie, an atmosphere conducive to the comfort and well-being of the customers. The décor and murals included wall plaques, tapestries, murals, pictures and sculptures. The House of Lords held that the creation of atmosphere was an important function of the particular trade and was a means to an end in the carrying on of such a trade. The expenditure therefore qualified as plant. Although the various items may be said to be part of the setting they were nevertheless intended to go further and offer the customers something to resort to and enjoy. They had an additional function therefore, ie, a function as plant (Lord Wilberforce at p 299E).

However, it was held by Hoffman J in the High Court in *Wimpy International Ltd* v *Warland* that major changes in 'fast food' restaurants comprising the installation of, *inter alia,* shop fronts, light fittings and wiring, raised floors, tiles, wall panels and mirrors, suspended ceilings, balustrading, cold water piping and water tanks, decorative brickwork, murals, built-in storage units and dispensers did not (apart from the expenditure on light fittings) give rise to expenditure on plant. The judge indicated that in order to establish whether or not an item constituted plant, three essential questions had to be posed:

(1) Did the item in question form the premises or part of the premises or place in or upon which the business was conducted.

(2) If the answer to (1) was 'no' was the item used for the purpose of the particular trade in question

(3) If the answer to (2) was 'yes', was the item part of the business' stock in trade.

If the answer to (3) was 'no', the item was plant (see (1988) STC 149).

Electrical installation
In *Cole Brothers Ltd* v *Philips* [1982] STC 307, TCA 46, the taxpayer carried on the trade of a department store. The installation comprised, *inter alia,* the following groups of items:

(*a*) transformers to reduce the voltage at which electric current was supplied by the Electricity Board to a usable level, switchgear between the Electricity Board's switchgear and the transformers, and the main switchboard through which the converted current from the transformers passed to the electrical installation;

(*b*) specially designed and other lighting fittings and cables to those lighting fittings; and

(*c*) wiring to a number of specific items such as fire alarms, clocks, heating and ventilation systems, stand-by supply systems etc.

The taxpayer company claimed that the expenditure on the entire electrical installation was capital expenditure on the provision of machinery and plant within FA 1971, s 41. The Revenue conceded that the items in group (*c*) qualified as plant, but rejected the taxpayer company's claim in respect of items in groups (*a*) and (*b*). The Special Commissioners had rejected the taxpayer company's claim that the installation should be regarded as a single item of plant and determined that the transformers, but not the main switchboard or the specially designed and other light fittings, were plant.

The House of Lords refused to upset the findings of the Special Commissioners. It is open to the Commissioners to find that one could not look at the entire system as a single entity in order to ascertain whether or not it was plant (although Lord Hailsham stated that he might well have come to a different conclusion on the facts had he been a Commissioner (p 312J)). Also, the individual findings of the Commissioners with regard to the transformers, etc would not be upset by the House of Lords.

Finance
In the case of *Ben-Odeco Limited* v *Powlson* [1978] STC 460 it was held that monies expended by a company on interest and commitment fees in order to raise cash to buy plant and machinery did not qualify as expenditure on the provision of plant. It was expenditure on the acquisition of money which was to be used for the acquisition of plant as distinct from money expended in order to pay for the plant.

However, Lord Russell of Killowen did state at page 472(d):

> I would add that I do not seek to confine qualifying expenditure to the price paid to the supplier of the plant. I should have thought, for example, that if the cost of transport from the supplier to the place of user is directly borne by the taxpayer it will be expenditure on the provision of plant for the purposes of the taxpayer's trade. There may well be other examples of expenditure, additional to the price paid to the supplier, which would qualify on similar grounds. But such matters are not for decision on this appeal.

Those words in the judgment have given rise to a considerable number of cases where taxpayers have claimed capital allowances from the Revenue on, for instance, architects' fees, lawyers' fees, etc.

The following 2 points may also be said to have been established in the case of *Ben-Odeco:*

(1) If the Company which provided the machinery had borrowed to finance the construction of the rig and increased the sale price the

purchaser will have obtained allowances on the full purchase price including the amount referable to the interest charge. Lord Hailsham of St Marylebone stated 'It was agreed in argument that if the constructing company borrowed money in order to finance the construction of the rig and added the interest and commitment fees into the price charged to the purchaser, the total price would rank for first year allowance.' Lord Russell at p 481 also stated:

> The point was made for the appellant that if the provider of the plant borrowed working capital and incurred as a result liability for interest and perhaps a commitment fee in respect of such borrowing, these liabilities would be reflected in the price paid, the whole of which would qualify as relevant capital expenditure by the company buying the plant. That is so.

(2) Lord Salmon at p 479H referred to the fact that if taxpayers try to increase the disposal proceeds of plant by artificial means involving perhaps connected companies then the courts may treat that as 'a mere colourable device' for increasing the available allowances.

In the case of *Van Arkadie* v *Sterling Coated Materials Ltd*[1983] STC 95 it was held that an exchange loss on repayment of a loan linked with the purchase of plant involved the payment of additional sums directly connected with the expenditure on the plant and therefore allowances were available with respect to the payments. The case of *Ben-Odeco* was distinguished because the interest and commitment fees were held to be too remote from the expenditure on the purchase of the plant.

8.17.4 Special case of greenhouses

There is an argument that a modern 'high-tech' greenhouse comprises plant (*Wangoratta Woollen Mills Ltd* v *The C of T of the C of Australia* (1969) ALJR) without possibly giving rise to problems (ie a reduced 4% agricultural buildings allowance) because it may also comprise a building (agricultural building). See FA 1986, s 56(5) and compare that with CAA 1968, s 50(2).

8.17.5 Alterations to building

It is expressly provided in FA 1971, Sched 8, para 3(1) that expenditure on alterations to an existing building incidental to the installation of machinery or plant for the purposes of the trade is capital expenditure on the provision of the machinery or plant.

8.17.6 Belong

It will have been seen that it is necessary, before a first year or a writing-down allowance can be obtained that the machinery must belong to the person claiming the allowance (see 8.14.1). Alternatively, it must be deemed to belong to that person (FA 1985, s 46(2) and FA 1985 Sched 17).

8.17.7 Incur

Meaning
(see 8.6.1).

Landlord contributions and government tenants
The situation may arise where 'X' Ltd is a property investment company. It may have let an office to a government department. The Government Department may spend say £100,000 in putting plant machinery into the building which plant machinery comprises landlord's fixtures. The landlord may contribute £50,000 towards the expenditure. It would appear the landlord could obtain a capital allowance, with regard to that £50,000 contribution. This is if the following is satisfied. First the landlord must be deemed to be carrying on a trade under s 46(1) of FA 1971. There should be no problem in that respect. Secondly, the machinery must belong to it. On the face of it because the tenant—the government department—cannot claim an allowance no allowances will be available to 'X' Ltd (see CAA 1968, s 85(1) and *Bridge House (Reigate Hill) Limited* v *Hinder* 47 TC 182 especially Denning M R 180 e–g). However, an amendment to s 85(1) by Finance Act 1970 Sch 4, para 7 which inserted a new sub-section 2(A) in s 85 of CAA 1968 states that the requirement that the tenant must be a person who could have obtained an allowance (but for the contribution) does not apply in relation to any contribution made after 5 April 1970 to expenditure incurred after that date by the Crown, or by any public or local authority in the United Kingdom. That contribution provision (s 85) basically deems expenditure to be incurred by the contributor although it was incurred by somebody else and there are also provisions which deem the machinery to belong to the contributor in appropriate circumstances (CAA 1968 s 85(1)(2) and 2(A) and FA 1981 Sched 8, para 15(6)) (see also 8.6.1). The allowances should thus be available to X Ltd up to £50,000.

8.17.8 Provision

In order to obtain the allowances the taxpayer must have incurred the capital expenditure on the *provision* of machinery or plant. In *IRC* v *George Guthrie and Sons* TC 327 the respondent paid £1,144 7s 4d in December 1948, to a motor dealing company as the purchase price of a motor car to be used for business purposes. He subsequently discovered that in September 1948 the company had sold the same car to another customer, to whom it was delivered in January 1949. The motor dealing company went into liquidation in May 1949 and the respondent was unable to recover any part of his payment. On appeal before the Special Commissioners against an assessment to income tax under Schedule D for the year 1949/50 the respondent contended that he was entitled to an initial allowance for the expenditure incurred with the object of acquiring the car, although it had not been delivered to him. The Commissioners allowed the appeal. The Court of Session held that the Commissioners' decision was correct.

Clearly the word 'provision' has a very wide meaning. However, the requirement that the machinery must belong or be deemed to belong to the taxpayer (a requirement added to the legislation subsequent to the *Guthrie* decision) means that in practice such a wide meaning given to the word 'provision' will not have great importance.

8.17.9 Plant allowances and local authorities

Local authorities benefit from very wide tax exemptions under TA 1988 s 519.

If a local authority pays for the construction of an office block for its own use, it would not be able to make use of any plant or machinery allowances in connection with lifts, etc, installed in the building.

The local authority may be the freeholder of the land and building built thereon. It could grant a lease of, say, 21 years to a tax paying company which company would then install the necessary plant and machinery in the building and lease back the entire property (including the plant and machinery) to the local authority.

The taxpayer company should be able to obtain allowances under FA 1971 and FA 1985 Sched 17.

The amount of the rental payments would appropriately reflect the tax reliefs obtained with the local authority overall obtaining a better deal.

8.18 SUCCESSIONS TO TRADES BETWEEN CONNECTED PERSONS

Where a person (the successor) succeeds to the trade which was until that time carried on by another person (the predecessor) and the two persons are connected with each other within TA 1988, s 839, the parties may make an election so that the successor stands in the shoes of the successor as far as plant allowances are concerned, if the conditions in FA 1971 Sched 8 para 13, as inserted by FA 1988 s 92 are satisfied. If satisfied:

(*a*) the machinery or plant shall (notwithstanding any actual sale or transfer) be treated as sold by the predecessor to the successor at a price which does not give rise to a balancing allowance or a balancing charge; and

(*b*) allowances and charges shall be made to or on the successor as if everything done to or by the predecessor had been done by the successor.

8.19 ANTI-AVOIDANCE PROVISIONS

There are anti-avoidance provisions contained in FA 1971, Sched 8, and FA 1972, s 68 to deal with situations where transactions are carried out between connected persons or where there is a sale and leaseback of machinery or in situations where it appears with respect to a sale that the sole or main benefit which might be expected to accrue to the parties or any of them is the obtaining of an allowance.

Where a purchaser acquires plant from a connected person who incurred the capital expenditure on plant before 27 October 1970 the purchaser's capital allowances are governed by the rules of the old capital allowances provisions notwithstanding the fact that he incurs his expenditure on or after 27 October 1970. Similar rules apply where the purchaser, although not connected with the vendor, leases the plant back to him so that he continues to use it for the purposes of his trade (FA 1971, s 40(2), as amended by FA 1972, s 68(1)(*b*)).

For further anti-avoidance provisions concerning partnerships and let plant see FA 1976, s 41, FA 1980 s 64 et seq and FA 1982 s 70.

Some of the provisions are only of historical interest now that it is only possible to claim writing down allowances rather than first year allowances which were at one time 100% of the expenditure.

8.20 TAX PLANNING

(*a*) The capital allowances benefits available to investors who acquire machinery or plant and let the same have been substantially restricted by FA 1976, FA 1980, FA 1982 and FA 1984.

(*b*) If the taxpayer has to decide whether to buy the shares of a company or the property held by a company he should see what allowances may be available in connection with the acquisition of the property; industrial building allowances or machinery or plant allowances. No capital allowances are available on the acquisition of shares.

(*c*) For property-investment companies, which have very few allowances available, plant and machinery allowances are very important as apart from maintenance and repair expenditure and management charge expenditure capital allowances provide one of the few tax deductions available. Such property-investment companies may wish to acquire industrial buildings or commercial buildings in an Enterprise Zone to let in order to obtain allowances for offset against rental income.

9 CAPITAL GAINS TAX

9.1 INTRODUCTION

This is an extremely important tax and of very wide application. It is a tax for which there is a substantial number of reliefs and exemptions available and it is important that the taxpayer is able to identify these and make use of them. It is chargeable at the top rate of 40% in the case of individuals, and 35% in the case of companies and applies to the disposal of virtually all types of assets including land. It does not apply, however, to trading gains or other gains which come into charge to income tax. Companies pay corporation tax on these chargeable gains.

Reference to legislation in this chapter, unless otherwise stated, are to the Capital Gains Tax Act 1979.

9.1.1 Basic features

A charge to CGT may arise on the disposal or part disposal of assets. A disposal may occur where the asset is sold, exchanged or given away or if the legislation deems the same to be disposed of. An asset for the purposes of this tax will include land and interests in land whether legal or equitable (s 19(1)).

The gain which is chargeable to CGT is calculated by ascertaining the consideration received or deemed to be received on the disposal of the asset and deducting therefrom all allowable deductions. If a lease is granted at a full rent and without a premium there will be a disposal for the purposes of this tax but no consideration will be brought into charge; one does not capitalise the rental income (s 31(3) not having application).

Section 32(1) lists the various items which can be deducted in making a capital gains computation, eg, one deducts expenditure wholly and exclusively incurred in acquiring the asset and in establishing, preserving or defending title to that asset (this would include, for instance, the costs incurred in fighting a compulsory purchase order).

It is especially provided in s 32(2) that any payment of interest shall not be allowed as a deduction in calculating any CGT liability. However, certain building companies may be able to obtain relief under TA 1988, s 345 where interest is charged to capital.

Expenditure on initial repairs to a property (including expenditure on decorations) undertaken in order to put it into a fit state for letting and which is not allowable for the purposes of Schedule A, is regarded as allowable expenditure for CGT purposes under s 32(1) (CCAB June 1969: see FRP5/B14 in *Inland Revenue Practices and Concessions*).

Under the FA 1988 the base date for CGT computation purposes is 31 March 1982. This means, broadly, that only gains accrued since that date will be brought into charge to tax. Indexation relief is also available for gains accruing from 31 March 1982 and there is a small annual exemption available to individuals (£5000 for 1988/89) and trusts (£2500 and in some cases £5000 for 1988/89) but not to companies.

9.2 DISPOSALS

9.2.1 Part disposals

On a part disposal of land the following formula applies to determine the cost deductible in respect of the part disposed of:

$$\frac{A}{A + B} \times \text{Deductible expenditure}$$

where A is the gross consideration for the part disposal of and B is the market value of what remains.

It may be possible on a practical basis to agree an apportionment of part of the deductible expenditure with the Revenue, so avoiding the need to apply the strict formula above.

Incidental costs of disposal are not apportioned. They are deducted from the sale proceeds of the part disposed of (ss 32(1)(*c*) and s 35(1)).

Deductible expenses do not come within the apportionment provisions at all if they relate solely to the part retained or solely to the part disposed of (s 35(4)).

Small part disposals
Special provisions apply to disposals where the amount or value of the consideration for disposal is small compared with the market value of the landholding which subsisted immediately before the transfer (s 107(1)(*a*)). In these cases the consideration received is offset against the allowable cost of the land, ie, the base cost will be reduced for the future. The Revenue takes 'small' to mean 5% or less of the value of the land (s 107).

These small part disposal provisions do not apply:

(*a*) if the amount or value of the consideration for the transfer exceeds £20,000; or

(*b*) where in the year of assessment in which the transfer is made the transferor made other disposals of land, and the total amount or value of the consideration for all disposals of land made by the transferor in that year exceeds £20,000.

Small part disposals to an authority under compulsory purchase are ignored with regard to the £20,000 limit (s 107(4)).

Wasting assets cannot be the subject of a claim (s 107(7)).

The transfer must not be one between husband and wife or between group companies (s 107(1)(*b*)).

If the consideration received on the part disposal exceeds the allowable cost of the entire land the excess will be chargeable to tax (s 109).

The Revenue has issued a statement (22 April 1971) in connection with these part disposal provisions (see/1971 in *Inland Revenue Practices and Concessions,* Oyez Longman).

It is important not to overlook these provisions where there is a small part disposal of land.

Grant of a lease
Where the payment of a premium is required under a lease of land, or otherwise under the terms subject to which the lease is granted, there is deemed to be a part disposal of the interest out of which the lease is granted (Sched 3, para 2).

In applying the part disposal formula in s 35 of the Act the property which remains undisposed of includes a right to any rent or other payments, other than a premium, payable under the lease, and that right shall be valued as at the time of the part disposal (Sched 3, para 2(2)).

The word 'premium' is not defined in the Act. It is by Sched 3, para 10(2) expressed to include 'any like sum, whether payable to the intermediate or a superior landlord, and for the purpose of this Schedule any sum (other than rent) paid on or in connection with the granting of a tenancy shall be presumed to have been paid by way of premium except insofar as (the) other sufficient consideration for the payment is shown to have been given' (the word 'the' in that paragraph appears to be an error).

In *Clarke* v *United Real (Moorgate) Ltd* [1988] STC 273, the taxpayer company owned a site which was redeveloped under an agreement for a lease dated May 1979. The tenant agreed to reimburse the landlord the cost of redeveloping the site and the landlord agreed to grant the tenant a

99-year lease. The lease was granted in June 1981 when the rent was fixed under a formula which took into account the amount which the tenant had reimbursed the landlord. It was held that the amounts reimbursed by the tenant constituted a premium or like sum for capital gains tax purposes (CGTA 1979, Sched 13, paras 2 and 10).

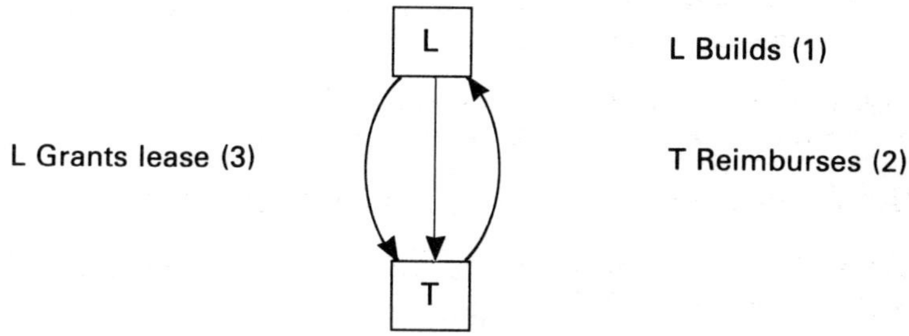

In certain cases, premiums are deemed to be paid, such as where a lease is granted and a sum becomes payable under the terms thereof in lieu of the whole or part of any rent (see Sched 3, para 3).

Where a landowner grants a building lease to a builder the author is of the view that this will not normally give rise to a charge to CGT, even though the tenant is obliged to carry out building operations.

Where there is a grant of a sub-lease out of a lease which is a short lease (under 50 years), special provisions apply to restrict the amount of the deductible base cost of the lease which can be offset against the disposal proceeds arising on the grant of the sub-lease (Sched 3, para 4).

Where a premium on a lease is chargeable to IT under TA 1988, s 34 there are interaction provisions in Sched 3, para 5 to prevent a double charge to tax.

There are special provisions contained in Sched 3, para 8 which may deem a lease to be of a shorter duration than that set out in the document as being the term of the lease or indeed in certain cases the lease may be deemed to be for a longer term than that set out in the document. For example, if the tenant has a right to call for a further lease.

9.2.2 Time of disposal and acquisition

Where an asset is disposed of and acquired under a contract the time at which the disposal and acquisition is made is the time the contract is made (and not, if different, the time when the asset is conveyed or transferred) (s 27).

If the contract is conditional (and in particular if it is conditional on the exercise of an option) the time at which the disposal and acquisition is made is the time when the condition is satisfied.

In order to be sure of creating a conditional contract there should normally be a condition which is outside the control of the parties and it should be a condition precedent to the contract coming into existence.

Example 9A: Disposal under conditional contracts

C Ltd contracts to sell land on 1 January subject to a condition precedent that he obtains planning permission to erect a building thereon. Planning permission is obtained on 1 February and completion takes place on 1 March. The disposal date is when the planning permission is obtained, ie, 1 February.

Grant of lease conditional on construction of building
If a building is to be erected and A enters into an agreement to grant B a lease when that building is put up, the date of disposal would be the date when the agreements are entered into and not when the building has been erected or the lease granted. The obligation to put the building up is a term or condition of the contract; it does not make the contract conditional on the construction of the building (*Eastham* v *Leigh London & Provincial Properties Ltd* (1971) 46 TC 687).

9.2.3 Contracts themselves do not result in a disposal

There is an extremely impressive argument that when taxpayers enter into unconditional contracts that that does not comprise the disposal of the relevant property.

It can be argued that if X unconditionally contracts to sell freehold land to Y that that does not result in a disposal of the property if completion does not take place.

It can be argued that CGTA 1979, s 27 is merely a timing section. If a disposal takes place and it was preceded by unconditional contracts then the disposal is deemed to relate back to the time of the contracts.

If the transaction is never completed then there is never a disposal and there is nothing to relate back. One is able to derive a certain degree of support for that contention from the recent cases of *Chaney* v *Watkis* [1986] STC 89 and *Magnavox* v *IRC* [1986] STC 561; see also *Whiteman & Wheatcroft* on Capital Gains Tax, pp 6–65 (2nd edition) and *IRC* v *Mobil North Sea Oil Ltd* [1986] STC 45 where at 63 Harman J expressed the view that 'in pursuance of' can mean 'under'.

The Revenue apparently accept the above analysis.

Tax Planning (The Option Scheme)
It can also be argued that if X wishes to sell land to Y and he gives Y an option to purchase the land with the option to be exercised in 3 years'

time with Y paying the full purchase price at the time when the option is granted that when completion takes place pursuant to the option which is exercised at, say, the time of completion that, although X has the use of the money for 3 years, a disposal only takes place when the option is exercised.

9.2.4 The *Thompson* v *Salah* Trap

Taxpayers should take special care when seeking to ascertain the date of disposal for the purposes of CGT. The case of *Thompson* v *Salah* 47 TC 559 represents a trap in this area.

The general rule for CGT is that if a disposal takes place the time of the disposals is deemed to be the time when unconditional contracts are entered into (CGTA 1979, s 27).

That section does not refer to unconditional *binding* contracts. It only refers to the time when the unconditional contracts were entered into.

In the case of *Thompson* v *Salah* there was (modifying the facts somewhat) an oral agreement by Y to sell a parcel of land to Z.

The contract was not enforceable because it was unwritten. This case was concerned with short-term capital gains tax (now abolished) but the wording of the relevant legislation is, for all relevant purposes, the same as that in the CGTA 1979, s 27.

The taxpayer argued that because the contract was unenforceable there was no contract for the purposes of that tax.

Megarry J at 563 stated:

> It is true that there was no written contract, but of course that does not mean that there was no contract; even if the contract was supported by neither writing nor part performance, it remains a contract despite being unenforceable by action.

It should be noted that under the Law of Property Act 1925, s 40 an oral contract to dispose of land is unenforceable unless there has been an act of what is known as part performance, ie the purchaser has carried out acts in connection with the land, such as bulding a house on it, based on the oral contract (see page 9).

This point can of course be very relevant if the taxpayer is seeking to dispose of land and wishes to postpone the disposal date until after the end of the particular tax year so that he has virtually a full year extra before he has to pay his CGT or he is seeking to emigrate and wants to ensure that the disposal takes place in a year during which he is neither resident nor ordinarily resident in the UK (in the latter case he should ensure that he breaks his residence and ordinary residence status and that s 12 of CGTA 1979 is not applicable).

The case is important because if the parties have agreed the arrangement in all its material particulars before the end of the first tax year and they merely sign the relevant contracts on 6 or 7 April in the second tax year the Revenue may seek to see whether in fact the disposal took place at the time when the oral contracts were entered into (in the first tax year).

Tax planning (Anti-Salah Contract)
If throughout 5 April (of the first tax year) and before there was a substantial aspect of the proposed land sale which had not been agreed between the parties, such as the price, or the precise parcels of land to be included in the sale, then there can be no question of this case having relevance; there will have been no contract at all let alone a binding contract.

This is a point which the Revenue do take.

9.3 SPECIAL CASES

9.3.1 Capital sum derived from land

There is a disposal of land for CGT purposes where capital sums are derived from land notwithstanding that no asset is acquired by the person paying the capital sums. The provisions apply in particular to:

(*a*) capital sums received by way of compensation for any kind of damage or injury to assets or for the loss, destruction or dissipation of assets or for any depreciation or risk of depreciation of an asset;

(*b*) capital sums received under a policy of insurance of the risk of any kind of damage or injury to, or the loss or depreciation of, assets;

(*c*) capital sums received in return for forfeiture or surrender of rights or for refraining from exercising rights (eg, the release of a restrictive covenant affecting land); and

(*d*) capital sums received as consideration for use or exploitation of assets.

In the case of the above, the time of disposal shall be taken to be when the capital sum is received (s 20(2) and 27(1)). *This overrides the general rules concerning the time of disposals.* This is an important point not to overlook. It can be a tax trap.

Special rollover relief provisions apply if the capital sums received are used in restoring the asset which may have been lost or destroyed (see s 21). These rollover provisions can be very important and must be carefully examined to see if they are appropriate. See also ESC, DI.

If the capital sum is small (ie, less than 5%) when compared with the value of the interest in land before disposal, the disposal may be ignored and the sum deducted from the allowable expenditure on a future disposal (see s 21(1)(*a*) and (2)).

9.3.2 Tax free payments to tenants

Certain sums paid to tenants can be CGT free in their hands because they derive from statute, despite the general rule that such payments are taxable.

As a general rule, if a tenant of business premises sells or surrenders his lease he can be liable to CGT (or corporation tax on chargeable gains) on the money he receives.

Example 9C: Payment to tenant

X Ltd has a 21-year lease of premises from which it carries out its trade. It sells that lease to Y Ltd. X Ltd may be chargeable to corporation tax on chargeable gains on the monies received from Y Ltd.

Business tenancy—Statutory compensation is tax free
In *Drummond* v *Austin Brown* [1983] STC 506, ChD; [1984] STC 321 CA, a business tenant was obliged to give up his lease under the Landlord and Tenant Act 1954, Pt II because the landlord wished to occupy it for the purposes of its own business. Under s 37 of the Act the tenant was entitled to compensation of approximatley £30,000.

It was held that this money derived from statute and was a sum roughly estimated to cover the expenditure which the tenant would have to lay out in establishing his business elsewhere. Such payments could not give rise to any charge to CGT.

It seems also that had the sum been taxable the base cost for CGT purposes would be the value of the right to receive the sum so that there would have still been no charge to CGT (see p 514 and 515 and *Davenport* v *Chilver* [1983] STC 426).

Agricultural compensation
In the earlier case of *Davis* v *Powell* [1977] STC 32, which was approved in *Drummond* v *Austin Brown,* Templeman J. as he was then, held in the High Court that a landlord who paid the sum of approximately £600 by way of compensation for disturbance to a tenant under the Agricultural Holdings Act 1948, s 34(1) was paying a sum which, in the hands of the tenant, was tax free. This was because the sum derived from statute.

9.3.3 CGT free reverse premiums (assignment of lease)

In the writer's opinion, reverse premiums are CGT free.

A reverse premium arises where X Ltd has an onerous lease. It transfers that lease to Y Ltd and X Ltd pays Y Ltd, say, £100,000 in order that Y Ltd will take on the onerous lease. That £100,000 is a reverse premium and in the author's opinion is capital gains tax free (or more precisely, corporation tax on chargeable gains tax free) in the hands of Y Ltd (see figure below).

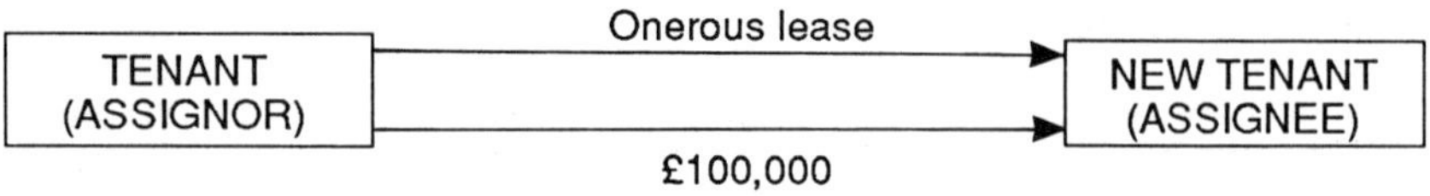

The author feels that the sum is free of CGT because it does not derive from the disposal of an asset by Y Ltd. It is paid because Y Ltd agrees to take over a liability (see CGTA 1979, ss 1, 19 and 20). (Note if T pays L monies so T can surrender his lease to L, CGT will be payable by L).

9.3.4 Reverse premiums and other taxes

The reverse premium mentioned above is not within the lease premium provisions contained in TA 1988, s 34 *et seq*.

The transfer document under which the lease is transferred is not chargeable to *ad valorem* stamp duty as it is difficult to see how it can be conveyance on sale under Stamp Act 1891.

The reverse premium is chargeable to VAT. The Revenue have been known to seek to charge the premium under Schedule D, Case I and VI.

9.3.5 Destruction of a building

If a building or structure is destroyed, the building or structure and its site (including any land acquired for purposes ancillary to the use of the building) are deemed to have been disposed of and immediately reacquired for CGT purposes for a consideration equal to market value (see s 22). This is normally useful insofar as it can give rise to a capital loss.

If compensation is received a charge to CGT may arise with respect thereto.

If, however, a capital sum is received by way of compensation for the loss or destruction or under a policy of insurance and the monies are applied in replacing the building (not necessarily on the same site) a special rollover relief is possible (s 21(4)).

See also the ESC, D19 entitled 'Replacement of Buildings Destroyed'.

9.3.6 Land for shares

Difficult taxation situations can arise where Mr X decides to transfer land to X Ltd in return for shares. Problems may arise with regard to capital gains tax or income tax (if the land comprises trading stock).

Example 9B: Land for shares

Mr X transfers Blackacre to X Ltd, Blackacre having a market value of £1m, in return for the issue of 500,000 shares of £1 each. The issue price of each such share for the purpose of satisfying the consideration for the acquisition of the land is £2. If X Ltd subsequently sells the lands and assuming the transaction is bona fide what will be the taxation consequences? If the land is trading stock in the hands of X Ltd, it would appear from the case of *Craddock* v *Zevo Finance Co Ltd* [1944] 1 All ER 566, 27 TC 267 that the base cost for trading purposes will be £1m regardless of what the value of the shares in X Ltd were at the time of the transaction. Similarly, if X Ltd makes a capital gain on the disposal of Blackacre its CGT base cost would be £1m (see *Stanton* v *Drayton* [1982] STC 585 which was dealing with the transaction where the parties were not connected and there was no suggestion by the Revenue that the documentation was colourable or other than *bona fide* and genuine; CGTA 1979, s 29(*a*)).

Any argument that when a company issues shares under general principles in consideration of the acquisition of an asset that it has in fact given no consideration for the asset whatsoever, has long been discredited. Such an analysis would be a failure to fully appreciate the true nature of the issue of shares (see Lord Greene MR in *Osborne* v *Steel Barrel Co Ltd* [1942] 1 All ER 634, at 637 and 638 and 24 TC 293 at 306 and 307).

9.3.7 Wasting assets and the vanishing base cost

A wasting asset is defined as an asset with a predictable life not exceeding 50 years but excluding freehold property (ss 155(1) and 37(1)(*a*)).

Plant and machinery is in every case regarded as having a predictable life of less than 50 years so that year by year part of the acquisition cost is written off so that it cannot be used as a deduction in any CGT computation when the plant and machinery is disposed of. Special rules apply, however, where capital allowances have been or could have been claimed for the plant and machinery (s 39).

Where there is a lease which has less than 50 years to run it will also be treated as a wasting asset. The allowable cost is written off over the term of the lease on a curved-line basis so that the amount of the cost which is disallowed as a deduction accelerates near the end of the term of the lease. The deduction from the cost is by reference to the table in Sched 3. The provisions have application to the situation where a lease of less than 50 years is sold.

The situation may occur where a local authority agrees to grant to a taxpayer a long lease of 999 years at the premium of say £1m. The property let may comprise bare land which the lessee intends to develop. On completion of the development it may be intended that the lessee will acquire the freehold interest for a nominal figure. In order to insure this at the time of the parties entering into the agreement to grant the long lease the lessee may be given an option by the council (the lessor) to call for the freehold on completion of the development.

The lessee may be carrying out the development or arranging for the development to be carried out so that it can hold onto the property as a long-term investment.

There is a danger, however, that the duration of the lease may be deemed to be for a very short period, ie, for the period from the date of the agreement for the lease and the date when the option can be exercised.

This being the case it may be necessary to apply the provisions of Sched 3, para 1 in order to reduce the base cost of the lease to potentially a nil or at least a nominal figure.

This comprises a tax trap although it is not clear whether the Revenue would seek to take a technical point such as this.

In order to avoid the problem entirely the freehold could be purchased at inception from the local authority without there being any leases granted but if it is not possible the problem may be overcome by the lessee ensuring that the freehold and the leasehold are not merged.

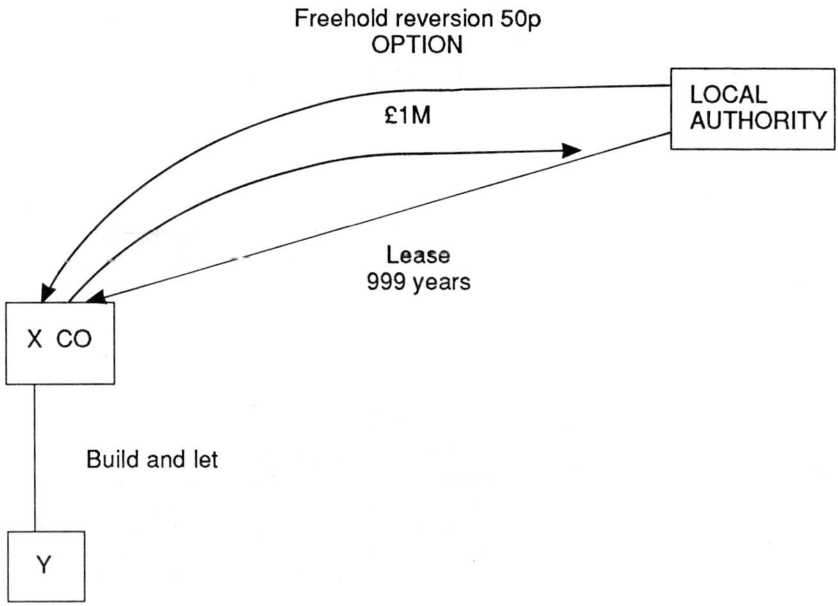

9.3.8 Compulsory acquisition

Special provisions apply if land or an interest in land is disposed of and it was acquired, or could have been acquired, under compulsory purchase powers (ss 108–111, and FA 1982, s 83, which provides for a rollover relief on certain compulsory acquisitions).

9.4 EXEMPTIONS AND RELIEFS

9.4.1 Annual exemption

If an individual disposes of capital property, he could be liable to CGT on the amount of his gain under CGTA 1979, s 1, although he will have available an annual exemption which, for 1988/89 (year ended 5 April 1989), is £5000.

An individual may seek to make disposals over a number of tax years in order to increase the number of annual exemptions available to him.

Companies pay corporation tax on their chargeable gains and there are no small exemptions available. A company should consider sheltering the chargeable gain by purchasing an unused commercial building in an Enterprise Zone.

9.4.2 Indexation

The CGT indexation allowance is applicable to certain disposals and is, essentially, aimed at reducing the amount brought into charge to CGT because of inflation (see FA 1982 and FA 1985).

9.4.3 Instalment relief

If the consideration for the disposal of the land is payable over a peiod exceeding 18 months from the disposal, the Revenue, if it feels the taxpayer would suffer undue hardship (see Hansard 22 June 1972) can allow the tax to be paid by instalments over a period not exceeding 8 years and ending not later than when the last instalment is due (s 40(1)).

Example 9D: Payment by instalments

Mr X sells Blackacre to Y Ltd for £100,000 payable in 10 equal instalments commencing 1 year from the date of the unconditional contract (legal completion of the sale having taken place 4 weeks after the unconditional contracts were entered into). *Prima facie* CGT is payable on the full £100,000 usually on or before 1 December following the end of the year of assessment in which the disposal took place. The tax may be paid by X by such instalments as the Revenue may allow (not exceeding 8 years) if undue hardship would be suffered by X. No instalment relief will be available on the first £10,000 paid as that is payable within 18 months from the contract.

9.4.4 Deferred consideration

In computing the amount of CGT payable no account shall be taken of the fact that the consideration is payable by instalments, ie, there is no discount for postponement of the right to receive any of the consideration (s 40(2)).

In the first instance no regard shall be paid to the fact that there is a risk that future consideration may be irrecoverable or that it is payable on a contingency. If, however, it is subsequently shown by the taxpayer that it is irrecoverable or is not payable the tax liability can be subsequently adjusted (s 40(2)).

In *Randall* v *Plumb* (1974) 50 TC 392 Mr X granted Y Ltd an option in consideration of an immediate deposit of £25,000 to purchase the fee simple of certain land for £100,000 including the £25,000 already paid. Under the option if Y Ltd did not obtain a relevant planning permission within 10 years the £25,000 was to be repaid to Y Ltd by Mr X.

Walton J in the High Court held that Mr X was to be charged to Capital Gains Tax on the value he received under the terms of the grant of the option, namely £25,000 less the value of the obligation to repay the monies in the event the planning permission was not obtained.

At p 198 Walton J stated:

> . . . it appears to me that the exercise which now falls to be carried out is that the value of what the taxpayer obtained for the grant of the option under the agreement falls to be ascertained; that is to say, the right to an immediate deposit of £25,000 with the incident that it may fall to be repaid (under certain provisions in the contract).

Special rules will apply if the option monies subject to the repayment obligations could not be valued. In this case one would have to value the option (the value of the option would be be the deemed disposal consideration) and this may (but it is unlikely) to give rise to a deemed disposal consideration which is less than the value of the option repayment rights.

Example 9E: 'Plumb' deals

Mr X grants Y Ltd an option to purchase his land exercisable within 2 years. Y Ltd pays Mr X £500,000 which sum is repayable at the end of the 2 years if the option is not exercised. It turns out that the option is not exercised. The Revenue will argue that the value of the £500,000 subject to the repayment obligation is the disposal consideration for the grant of the option. The Revenue will probably look to current rates of interest, but perhaps accepting the current statutory rates applicable to Schedule E benefits on loans. The taxpayer may seek to argue that if the benefit is determined by such interest rates then it should be calculated net of tax. The taxpayer may also argue that the consideration (the receipt of the monies plus the obligations to repay) cannot be valued and therefore one must value the option itself. This may give a lower valuation. The taxpayer will rely on the statement of Walton J, where he stated at p 198 and p 199:

> It has however, occurred to me that the valuation exercise may be one which those skilled in the art or mystery of valuation will say cannot be effected.

In the author's opinion it is possible to value such consideration so that the taxpayer would have some difficulty in trying to establish that the correct consideration is an amount equal to the market value of the option.

In *Marren* v *Ingles* [1980] STC 500 (HL), the taxpayer sold in 1970/71 shares for £750 per share plus a right to receive a further sum if the company, which was sold, was floated.

The further sum could only be quantified when the flotation occurred. There was thus 'a conditional and unquantified amount payable at an unascertained future date' (p 501).

In 1972/73 that further sum became payable because of the flotation. The House of Lords held that CGT was payable in 1970/71 on the cash paid of £750 per share plus the value of the right to receive the contingent figure in the future. When the contingent figure was paid in 1972/73 this was chargeable to CGT in that year (1972/73) as being a capital sum derived from an asset—a chose in action—within FA 1975, s 22(3) (now CGTA 1979, s 20(1)).

In *Marson* v *Marriage* [1980] STC 177, the taxpayer on 31 March 1965 sold 47 acres of land for £47,000 plus further amounts if the land should be compulsorily acquired in the future. Further monies could also be payable if planning permission was obtained. In January 1976 £348,250 was paid to the taxpayer in satisfaction of any rights to further sums it may have had under the agreement. It was held that if CGT had been in force on 31 March 1965 the proper amount to be brought into account would have been the cash payment of £47,000 plus the value of the rights to receive the possible unascertainable amounts subsequently. When the £348,250 was paid that was a disposal of a chose in action chargeable under FA 1965, s 22(3) (now CGTA 1979, s 20(1)). It was argued by the taxpayer that if the right to receive the future unascertainable amounts could be brought into charge on day one, the subsequent charge on the £348,250 caused a double incidence of tax to arise. Fox J disagreed. He said (at p 190(G)):

> There is no double taxation; there is simply the taxation of a new gain. I take an example . . . Suppose that on 1st January 1970 land is sold by X for £47,000 plus a chattel worth £10,000. The consideration on which capital gains tax is assessed is £57,000.
>
> If in 1975 X sells the chattel for £15,000 he will be charged on a capital gain of £5,000 in respect of the sale of the chattel.
>
> Similarly, in this case, there would (on the assumption that the statute had been in force on 31st March 1965) have been a charge to tax at that date on the basis of £47,000 plus the value of the relevant rights as at 31st March 1965. When, in 1976, s 22(3) (now CGTA 1979, s 20(1)) operated to produce a disposal of the incorporeal rights, tax was chargeable on £348,250 less the value of the relevant rights on 31st March 1965.

The tax treatment of the subsequent disposal of the incorporeal rights is unclear but the way the author sees the matter can be illustrated in the following example.

Example 9E: Subsequent disposal of incorporeal rights

X in 1986/87 sells Blackacre which he acquired in 1983 for £10,000 to Y for £100,000 plus 50% of any monies he receives from a resale of the land within two years. Those rights are worth £20,000. In 1987/88 the land is resold and X receives a further £90,000. The rate of CGT in the relevant years is 30%. X's tax liability, ignoring any exemptions and incidental costs, is as follows:

		£
1986/87 cash receipt	100,000	
Add value of incorporeal rights	20,000	
Total disposal proceeds	120,000	
Less (base cost)	10,000	
	110,000	× 30% = 33,000
1987/88 disposal proceeds (cash)	90,000	
Less (base cost)	20,000	
	70,000	× 30% = 21,000
Total CGT		54,000
This is the same as:		
Total cash receipts	190,000	
Less original base cost	10,000	
	180,000	× 30% = 54,000

Where the subsequent consideration is, at the outset, quantified but only payable on the happening of a contingency, the CGT rules are different and are governed by s 40(2). For a Revenue concession in this area where shares or securities are disposed of see IRC *Earn-out: New Revenue Concession* 26 April 1988 [1988] STI 365.

These provisions are only relevant to CGT. They do not apply, for instance, to land trading gains or for ascertaining when the beneficial interest in property passes for stamp duty or when there is a sale for the purpose of balancing allowances or balancing charges under CAA 1968 or FA 1971. Each tax must be examined separately to ascertain the relevant disposal dates.

9.4.5 Adjustments for contingent liabilities

In the first instance no allowance is available in a CGT computation for the following:

(*a*) in the case of the assignment of a lease of land or other property, for any liabilities remaining with, or assumed by, the assignor which is contingent on any default by the assignee of any obligations under the lease; or

(*b*) for any contingent liability of the person making the disposal in respect of any covenant for quiet enjoyment or other obligation assumed as vendor of land, or of any estate or interest in land, or as a lessor; or

(*c*) for any contingent liability in respect of a warranty or representation made on a disposal by way of sale or lease of any property other than land (s 41(1)).

If any such contingent liability shall become enforceable and is being or has been enforced the Inspector of Taxes shall make appropriate adjustments to the tax liability (s 41(2)).

9.4.6 Relief for gifts

There are rollover reliefs for gifts, provided appropriate elections are made, by individuals to other individuals and trusts and when transfers are made by trusteees to beneficiaries and other trustees (FA 1980, s 79, FA 1981, s 78 and FA 1982, s 82).

Restrictions apply if the recipient is or becomes non-resident or non-ordinary resident in the UK (see FA 1980, s 79(1) and FA 1981, s 79).

Roll-over relief may also be available on gifts of business assets by individuals to companies under CGTA 1979 s 126.

These gift provisions can be important where parties wish to carry out tax planning exercises.

9.4.7 Avoiding double CGT

It is still the case that if a company owns a capital asset a potential double charge to CGT can arise.

If a company owns a capital asset there can be two charges to CGT; one on the company when it disposes of the asset (strictly it is not a charge to CGT but a charge to CT on chargeable gains) and one on the shareholders when the shares are disposed of. The company could pay tax on the gain at 35% with the individual paying tax on the disposal of the shares on say, a liquidation, at 40%. The total tax charge on a gain made by the company could end up at 61% $(100 \times \frac{35}{100}) + (65 \times \frac{40}{100})$.

A shareholder will usually (but not always) want to sell his shares in a company because he may save this double charge to CGT. The purchaser will normally prefer to buy the assets from the company direct.

9.4.8 Land as a business asset

Trading stock
If land is held not as trading stock and it is then appropriated to trading stock there is a deemed disposal for the purposes of CGT at market value at the time when the appropriation takes place (s 122(1)).

However, the taxpayer can elect that instead of the asset being brought into the trade at market value it shall be brought in at its CGT allowable base figure (s 122(3)). In this event there is no CGT deemed disposal although the ultimate trading profit may be increased.

Appropriation from trading stock
If land is held as trading stock and it is then appropriated by the taxpayer for any other purposes its base CGT base cost on a future disposal is equal to the amount brought into the accounts of the trade (s 122(2)). This will normally be market value (see 4.4.6).

Retirement relief
Broadly, if an individual over 60 years disposes of his business or part thereof or shares in a family company retirement relief under FA 1985 s 69 *et seq* and Sched 20 may be available. Farmers disposing of part of their farmland must take special care in this area if they want to qualify for relief (see *McGregor* v *Adcock* [1977] STC 206 and *Mannion* v *Johnston* [1988] STI 582).

Replacement of business assets
If a person carrying on a trade disposes of an asset (the old asset) used, and used only, for the purposes of a trade throughout its period of ownership and employs the proceeds of sale to acquire another asset (the new asset) to be used for the purposes of the trade, any charge to CGT may be postponed until the sale of the new asset (s 155(1)).

This relief, known as roll-over relief, can only apply if the acquisition of, or the interest in, the new asset takes place in the period beginning 12 months before and ending 3 years after the disposal of the old asset. The may be postponed until the sale of the new asset (s 115(1)).

The provision applies in relation to a person who, either successively or at the same time, carries on two or more trades as if both or all of them were a single trade. It is thus possible to rollover into different trades (s 115(7)).

The relief applies to any building or part of a building and any permanent or semi-permanent structure in the nature of a building occupied (as well as used) only for the purposes of the trade. It also applies to any land occupied (as well as used) only for the purposes of the trade and any fixed plant or machinery which does not form part of a building or of a permanent or semi-permanent structure in the nature of a building.

Where the trade is one of dealing in or developing land, however, the relief will only be available if the property to be the subject of the relief is not held as stock of the trade (s 119(3))

References above to the building and land being 'occupied (as well as used), are important. In *Anderton* v *Lamb* (1981) STC 43, houses were occupied by active members of a farming partnership and this, because of their proximity to the farm, helped to double the farm production. Goulding J held that the properties were not 'occupied (as well as used)' for the purposes of the farming trade.

In *Temperley* v *Visibell Ltd* (1973) 49 TC 129 a company purchased a site with a view to building a factory for its special printing activities. Visits were made to the site and planning permission applied for and obtained. Following negotiations for the erection of the building it was decided not to go ahead with the development and the site was sold. It was held that rollover relief was not available as the site had not been occupied (as well as used) for the purposes of the trade.

It is notable that only 'fixed plant or machinery' qualifies. From the context, this refers to fixed plant and fixed machinery and not fixed plant and fixed or unfixed machinery (*Williams* v *Evans* [1982] STC 498, TCA 73, before Nourse J).

Where an individual holds the asset in question but it is used by a family company for trading purposes rollover relief may still be available under s 120. However, if the family company is purely a holding company and its trading subsidiaries use the property the Revenue has been known to argue that the relief is not available.

As well as 'trades' the relief is also available *inter alia* to professions, vocations, offices and employment, (s 121(1)(*d*)).

Special rules apply if only part of the consideration received from the disposal of assets is so used to purchase new assets (s 116).

Special provisions also apply if the proceeds from the disposal of an asset are 'rolled into' a depreciating asset. A depreciating asset is one which is, or will within 10 years of acquisition become, a wasting asset, ie, one with a predictable life not exceeding 50 years. The gain is, broadly, 'held over' until the expiration of a period of 10 years beginning with the acquisition of the second asset (the wasting asset). There may also be a charge if before the 10 years the claimant disposes of the asset (the wasting asset) or if he ceases to use the wasting asset for the purposes of a trade carried on by him (s 117(2)). This type of rollover relief is commonly referred to as 'held over' relief.

If, however, before the 10 years or before the second asset ceases to be used for the trade the second asset is disposed of and a non-wasting asset is acquired the gain will be effectively rolled over without any time limit.

Thus, for example, if a 75-year lease is disposed of (assuming that this 75 year lease was not the subject matter of a rollover claim itself with respect to the sale of another asset, it does not appear to be relevant to this example whether the first asset is a wasting asset or not) and the proceeds within the normal rollover relief claim periods (12 months and 3 years) are used to purchase a 21-year lease for the purposes of the continuing trade of the taxpayer and before the expiration of 10 years beginning with the acquisition of the 21-year lease the taxpayer purchases a freehold—say, 3 months before the disposal of the 21-year leasehold interest—the gain on the disposal of the 75-year lease may be rolled over into the freehold non-wasting asset.

9.4.9 Roll-over into investment property

If X sells property which he has used for his trade, eg, his factory premises, and uses the proceeds to buy other factory premises, subsequently finding out that matters do not work out and so he lets the same, relief is still available under CGTA 1979, s 115. Thus the gain: on the sale of the first factory is rolled-over although when the second factory is sold the ability to roll-over the proceeds of that sale will be restricted.

9.4.10 Rolling into roll-over relief

It may be that the taxpayer can make a gift to the donee who ultimately disposes of the property which has been given to him with the tax being mitigated.

Mr X may give property to his son Y (rolling over under FA 1980, s 79 any gain). From the time of the gift Y may use the same for the purposes of his trade. For instance, he may be a farmer. Two years later, Y may sell the property. It may be that the conditions of CGTA 1979, s 115 are satisfied so that when Y applies the proceeds of sale or a sum equal thereto to purchase another business asset any charge to capital gains tax can be rolled over.

The statute
CGTA 1979, s 115(1) states that if the consideration which a person carrying on a trade obtains for the disposal of, or of his interest in, assets *used and used only for the purposes of the trade throughout the period of ownership* is applied by him in acquiring other assets, or an interest in other assets which on the acquisition are taken into use and used only for the purposes of the trade then roll-over relief may be available.

9.4.11 Badly apportioned consideration

Disposal consideration in a capital gains tax computation can take the form of cash or kind. If the consideration relates to more than one asset, an apportionment may be made, notwithstanding that no such apportionment is agreed between the parties.

CGTA 1979, s 43(4) states that for the purposes of computing a gain:

> any necessary apportionment shall be made of any consideration or of any expenditure and the method of apportionment adopted shall, subject to the express provisions of this Chapter, be such method as appears to the inspector or on appeal the commissioners concerned to be just and reasonable.

However, where consideration is apportioned under any contract or transfer by the parties the position is different. In *Booth* v *Buckwell* [1980] STC 578 the parties had apportioned monies between shares and loan stock in an unfortunate way which was disadvantageous to the vendor Browne-Wilkinson J held that the parties could not adjust the figures.

He stated as p 584a:

> In my judgment, where parties to a composite transaction have, as a result of negotiations between themselves, provided that part of the consideration is to be paid for one part of the transaction and part for another, they cannot subsequently seek to reallocate the consideration for tax purposes. They have chosen to carry through the transaction in a particular manner, and the taxation consequences flow from the manner adopted. The Crown's position may well be different in certain cases. After all, the Crown was not a party to the transaction.

9.4.12 Super roll-over relief

Under the provisions of CGTA 1979, s 123 it is possible for an individual or other taxpayer other than a company to transfer a business as a going concern to a company in return for shares without any charge to CGT arising.

This roll-over relief, which is also available to trustees of a settlement, as well as individuals, is attractive. In particular, the following should be noted:

(*a*) It is only necessary for the taxpayer to transfer a business as a going concern. It is not necessary for a trade to be transferred. 'Business' is a much wider concept than trade. The letting of a number of properties may well amount to a business for the purposes of this relief although the Revenue may well try to put this point to the test (see *Walker* v *CCE* [1976] VATTR 10; *Williamson (RW & AAW)* v *CCE* [1978] 90; *American Leaf Blending Co* v *Director-General of Inland Revenue* [1978] STC 561 and *CCE* v *Fisher (Lord)* [1981] STC 238).
Note that estate income received by the company in the future may be shortfalled in part (TA 1988, Sched 19).

(*b*) It is not necessary for the company which issues shares to be resident in the UK.

(*c*) The base cost of the assets received by the company in return for the shares is equal to the market value of those assets as at the date of the roll-in. It is not necessary to get a Revenue clearance for this roll-over relief although if it is done exclusively for CGT purposes in order to increase the base cost of the assets rolled into the company then the decision of *Ramsay* v *IRC* [1981] STC 174 must be considered.

This super roll-over relief may prove useful in a number of circumstances. For instance, a non-United Kingdom domiciled (but United Kingdom resident) person may own a UK located business, eg, a farm. He could roll that business into a foreign company in return for shares, thus ending up, without having to pay CGT, with an overseas located asset for IHT purposes. He will have thus put himself out of the IHT regime.

9.4.13 The violent clashing, amalgamation and destruction of land interests—creating a 'Land Pot'

Taxpayers who own separate parcels of land and seek to bring them together for development purposes must carefully consider the capital gains tax situation.

Where separate land parcels are amalgamated so that the parties become tenants in common or they dispose of their interests in return for interests in other parcels of land there will under general principles be charges to CGT.

The following are the types of situations, or the main types of situations, where these major CGT problems (or corporation tax on chargeable gains problems) may be relieved:

Compulsory purchase

(*a*) There may be relief under CGTA 1979, s 111A (roll-over relief on compulsory acquisition) where land is disposed of by a person to an authority exercising or having compulsory powers and the landowner did not take steps by advertising or otherwise to dispose of that land or make his willingness to dispose of it known to the authority and the consideration for the disposal is applied by the taxpayer in acquiring other land (not being a property to be used as his private residence—CGTA 1979, s 111B).

Dividing land

(*b*) Extra Statutory Concession D26 grants relief for exchanges of joint interests where interests in land which are in the joint beneficial ownership of two or more persons are exchanged after 19 December 1984 and either the holdings of land were held jointly and as a result of the exchange each joint owner becomes sole owner of part of the land formerly owned jointly or a number of separate holdings of land are held jointly and as a result of the exchange each joint owner becomes sole owner of one or more holdings.

Exempt

(*c*) The disposal may be an exempt disposal for the purposes of capital gains tax, eg, the taxpayer may be disposing of his principal residence.

Sale and leaseback practice

(*d*) The transaction may amount to a sale and leaseback of the same parcel in which case, by way of Revenue practice, no charge to tax arises assuming the landowner does not receive cash on the disposal of his property in return for the leaseback.

Rollover under s 115

(*e*) If the taxpayer disposes of property used for the purposes of carrying on his trade (CGTA 1979, s 115) in return for other property and uses an amount equal to the disposal proceeds to purchase another property to be used for the purposes of his trade then roll-over relief will be available under the said s 115.

Variation of leases

(*f*) If a taxpayer owns a lease and the length of the term, by agreement with the landlord, is extended or there is a surrender of the lease and a new one granted without cash changing hands the Revenue, under current practice, do not seem to argue that there is a disposal for capital gains tax purposes but the base cost and expenditure is at risk.

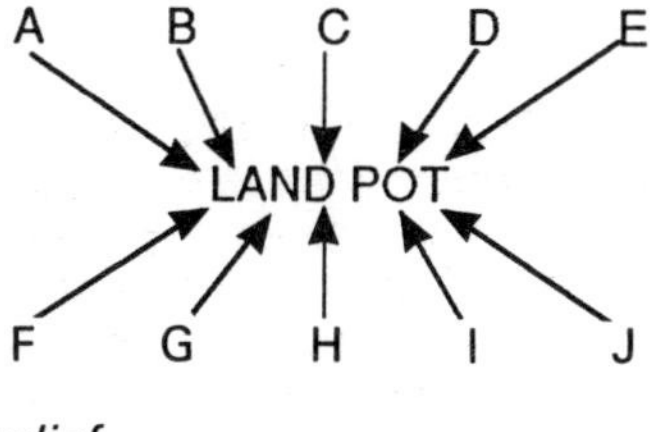

Small part disposals relief

(*g*) If the taxpayer makes a small part disposal (not exceeding one fifth of the market value of his land holding) the charge can be rolled over (CGTA 1979, s 107).

Part disposal to authority with compulsory powers

(*h*) If the taxpayer sells a small part of his holding to an authority exercising or having compulsory powers the charge may be rolled over under CGTA 1979, s 108.

9.5 TAX PLANNING

(*a*) CGT is a relatively straightforward tax which contains no wide anti-avoidance provisions such as provisions to catch associated operations which apply to IHT. The legislation, like all tax legislation, is normally interpretated literally and loopholes periodically come to light. However, where artificial tax schemes are involved it is clear from the House of Lords cases referred to at 1.4.5 and others that the Courts will take an overall view of the situation and perhaps cause such schemes to fail.

(*b*) When land is disposed of it may be disposed of over a number of years by individuals and trusts although most of these have a restricted annual exemption in order to obtain a number of annual exemptions.

(*c*) Although gifts of assets are chargeable to CGT there are a number of reliefs available to enable the tax charge to be rolled over; these reliefs often require elections to be made within certain time limits and these must be carefully considered.

(*d*) The special reliefs for small disposals of land interests and the roll-over provisions where sums are received in compensation for damage to property must be carefully considered (s 21 and ss 107– 109).

(*e*) Individuals can give assets to members of the family, rolling over the charge to CGT under FA 1980, s 79 so that the recipients can then sell the assets at appropriate intervals making use of any losses they may have available or any exemptions which may be available (such as the principal private residence exemption if they lie in the gifted property).

10 ANNUAL PROFITS OR GAINS (GENERAL CASE VI)

General Provisions

10.1 INTRODUCTION

Case VI of Schedule D is a residual charging provision. After the taxpayer has ensured that his profit is not taxable as income under any of the other heads of the tax legislation he should then look to make sure that he is not caught by this residual provision which can tax annual profits or gains derived from land, or indeed any other assets or activities.

10.1.1 Basic charging provisions

The provision, which taxes annual profits or gains, is on the face of it very widely worded. Tax under Case VI is to be charged on 'any annual profits or gains not falling under any other Case of Schedule D and not charged by virtue of Schedules A, B, C or E' (TA 1988, s 18(3) and s 833(1)).

It might be supposed that all profits not otherwise chargeable would be brought within this Case. However, the apparent scope of the provision has been limited by Courts.

10.1.2 Limitations

There are the following restrictions on the provision:

(*a*) *Income gains:* Only income gains can be chargeable under Case VI. The Lord President in *The Scottish Provident Institution* v *Farmer* [1912] 6 TC 34 at p 38 stated:

> . . . the expression 'annual profits and gains' . . . is there for the purpose of showing that this is a tax upon income, or in other words, annual profits and not upon capital.

Thus capital gains cannot be taxed under this provision.

Again in *Rayall* v *Hoare* 8 TC 521 Rowlatt J stated at p 525:

> In the first place, it is quite clear that anything in the nature of a capital accretion is outside the words 'profits or gains', as used in these Acts; that, of course, follows from the scope of the Acts, and it is sanctified by the usage of over a century. That rules out, of course, the well known case of a casual profit made upon an isolated buying and selling of some articles; that is a capital acretion, and unless it is merged with other similar transactions in the carrying on of a trade, and the trade is taxed, no tax is exigible in respect of a transaction of that kind. 'Profits or gains' means something which is in the nature of interest or fruit, as opposed to principal or tree.

(*b*) *Ejusdem generis:* an income gain can only be chargeable if it resembles a receipt which, but for some special feature, would come within one of the other Cases of Schedule D. Thus, the profits or gains must be *ejusdem generis* with the profits or gains specified under the other Cases of Schedule D. Thus, although Case VI unlike the other Cases and Schedules does not require a specific source—such as a trade (Case I of Sched D) or land (Sched A)—there must be profits or gains and the ejusdem generis rule must be satisfied (see *A-G* v *Black* ITC 52).

10.1.3 Case VI and 'Sweeteners'

In *Dickinson* v *Abel* 45 TC 352, the trustees of the taxpayer's wife's family trust owned land. A prospective purchaser offered the taxpayer £10,000 for the land but the taxpayer informed the prospective purchaser that he had no interest in the land and should get in touch with the trustees. The taxpayer informed the trustees that the purchaser was after the land. It was found as a fact that the taxpayer had not agreed to render any services on behalf of the purchaser and there was no contractual agreement between him and the purchaser. The purchaser nevertheless paid the taxpayer the £10,000. It was held that no liability under case VI of Sched D arose with respect to the payment as the payment was a gift.

10.1.4 Loans and guarantees and payments in kind

In *Wilson* v *Mannooch* 21 TC 178 a solicitor agreed to lend or arrange for a loan to a building company. The consideration for the same was agreed to be a share of the profits made by the company on the resale of the property. It was held that the profits the solicitor made were assessable under Schedule D. It often happens in property deals that X, the developer, does not have sufficient monies to buy and develop land and enters into a joint venture with Y. Y will lend the appropriate monies to buy the land and develop the same. When the land is sold Y may take a share of the profits. It can be important to ascertain exactly how Y's share should be taxed and under what schedule, not only for the purposes of the relevant income apportionment provisions in TA 1988, s 423 and Sched 19 but also for ascertaining whether tax should be deducted at source and for VAT purposes (a share of profits may in certain circumstances be zero rated whereas a payment of interest will be an exempt supply of finance).

The Court left open the question whether the payment made to the solicitor was chargeable under Case III of Schedule D or Case VI. Lawrence J simply said that the payments to the respondent was for the finding of money and the payments had the character of income and not capital and were therefore chargeable under Schedule D (see p 185).

Again in *Ruskin Investments Ltd* v *Copeman* [1943] 25 TC 187, X lent money to a building company to finance the erection of buildings. The repayments were to be made by the transfer to X of the ground rents created by the building company on the sale of the houses. The value of the ground rents they received was in excess of the amount of the loan. It was held that the amount of the excess was either interest assessable under Case III of Schedule D or profits assessable under Case VI.

In *Trenchard* v *Bennet* 17 TC 420, X agreed to guarantee unconditionally the payment of dividends on Y company's shares in consideration of an allotment to X of fully paid deferred shares in Y company. It was held that the value of the shares received was not in the nature of income assessable under Case VI of Schedule D. The undertaking with respect to the guarantee of the dividends was simply a method of payment for the acquisition of the shares. This type of analysis seems to turn the income tax code on its head but Finlay J was clear on the point. At p 430 he stated:

> I apprehend if they had purchased the shares for cash there would have been no room for argument. If they had purchased them for payment on a deferred date there would have been no room for argument. Can it be that, because the method of payment of the shares which they acquired was their undertaking to pay a dividend, that transforms these shares acquired, otherwise clearly as a capital asset, into an income receipt? I cannot convince myself that that is right . . .

A situation may arise where X owns land. Y may agree to act as consultant with respect to a development, and to pay him X may give Y an entitlement to a share of the land profits when the development is completed and the land sold. Can it be argued that on day one, Y must bring in to his Case I or Case II Schedule D computation the market value of the land rights?

The *Trenchard* case seems to indicate that far from obtaining an income, Y has merely purchased an asset in consideration of an agreement to carry out services rather than buying a share in the arrangement for cash etc. In that respect that case is very useful. Even if the contrary argument were to be upheld by the courts in the future it may well be that the market value of the interest in the development which Y obtains in consideration of agreeing to act as consultant will be so small that the tax charge is not significant. Alternatively it may be argued that the proper time to bring the profit into account is when Y has performed all the services required of him and this will be when the completed development is ultimately sold.

The decision in *Trenchard* turned on the particular facts of that case. It seems to be quite clear that if a taxpayer agrees to provide a guarantee and receives consideration for that in the form of cash or shares, the Case VI charge would arise. The judge pointed out however that this was a transaction where the parties were seeking to acquire control over the particular company which issued shares and they decided to acquire control by means of the purchase of shares. It was in the line of their business to acquire control. They needed to acquire control in order to prevent the particular company becoming a competitor. They paid for their shares by the provision of the guarantee. In situations such as that it would not be correct to bring in the value of the shares as Case VI income. That is perhaps analogous to the situation of the consultant in the above case. He has agreed to provide services as part of his business and needs to acquire a property interest in order to obtain a proper remuneration for the same. That may be contrasted with a case where the consultant may have agreed to provide services to X and X pays him up front in cash; that would clearly be taxable. If additionally it is part of the deal and the project with which the consultant is involved that X transfers an asset to the consultant as a fee, an income tax charge could arise probably under Case II of Schedule D or even Case I or Case VI.

10.1.5 Developer's libel (pinch of salt)?

CGTA 1979, s 19(5) provides:

> It is hereby declared that sums obtained by way of compensation or damages for any wrong or injury suffered by an individual in his person or in his profession or vocation are not chargeable gains.

Thus, if X has a derelict plot of land which he wishes to sell to D the developer and in the course of heated discussions X is libelled by D it may be that he (X) can get some tax free compensation from D (as well as possibly selling the land to D with capital gains tax being payable on the proceeds of the sale of the land). It is not thought that Case VI of Schedule D will be relevant.

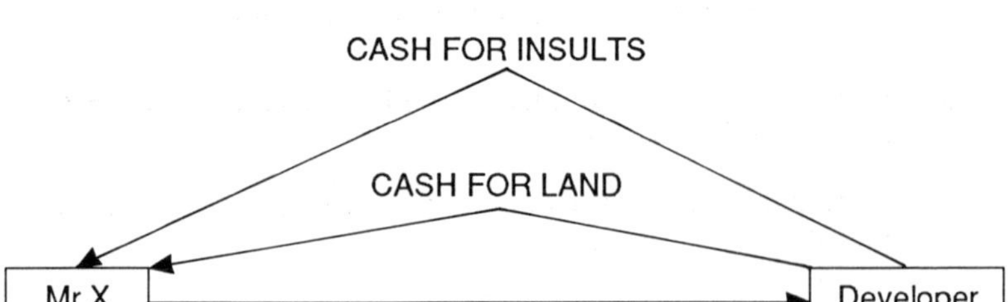

10.1.6 Furnished lettings

In *Griffiths* v *Jackson* [1983] STC184 furnished property was let mainly to students. The lessors were chartered accountants and upwards of 180 rooms were let. They supervised the lettings themselves and some services were provided. Vinelott J held that the income derived from the exercise of proprietory rights in land and therefore the profits were assessable under Case VI of Schedule D by virtue of TA 1988 s 18(1). Therefore the profits were not chargeable as trading profits under Schedule D, Case I.

In *Gittos* v *Barclay* [1982] STC 390 the taxpayer was a tenant of 2 holiday villas in a holiday village. The lease contained clauses restricting the use of the villas for any purpose other than holiday accommodation and requiring the villas to be closed from November to February. The villas were sub-let furnished during the period from March to October each year. The taxpayer's wife arranged the lettings by advertising, making bookings and arranging for cleaning and maintenance. Apart from times spent at the villas for necessary work they had not been occupied by the taxpayer or his wife. Goulding J held that the taxpayer was obtaining income from the letting of property. This was the exploitation of the landed property and it was a question of fact and degree as to whether this exploitation could amount to a trade. A hotelier for instance was undoubtedly carrying on a trade but the amount of activity required when letting holiday accommodation was not so nearly as much as that required when running a hotel. The judge held that the commissioners who found that the profits were taxable under Case VI of Schedule D had not misdirected themselves in law and he upheld their decision. The profits therefore could not be taxed under Case I.

As a result of these 2 decisions there was great pressure upon the government to change the law and changes finally came in the FA 1984, s 50, Sched 11 (now also see TA 1988, ss 503 and 504).

Special Income Tax, Corporation Tax and CGT reliefs are available for the commercial letting of furnished holiday accommodation in the United Kingdom.

A letting is a commercial letting if it is on a commercial basis and with a view to the realisation of profits. A letting is a letting of furnished accommodation if the tenant is entitled to the use of furniture.

Accommodation shall not be treated as holiday accommodation for the purposes of this relief unless:

(*a*) it is available for commercial letting to the public generally as holiday accommodation.

(*b*) the periods for which it is so available amount, in the aggregate, to not less than 140 days.

(*c*) the periods for which it is so let amount, in the aggregate, to at least 70 days; and

(*d*) for a period of at least seven months (which need not be continuous but includes the period referred to in (*c*) above) it is not normally in the same occupation for a continuous period exceeding 31 days.

If the above requirements are fulfilled any profits or gains arising to an individual in respect of any commercial letting of holiday or furnished holiday accommodation which is chargeable to tax under Schedule A or Case VI of Schedule D shall be treated for all purposes as earned income and furthermore rollover relief on the replacement of assets under CGTA 1979, ss 115–120 shall apply in relation to the commercial letting of furnished holiday accommodation as the relief applies in relation to a trade and also retirement relief may be available under FA 1985 Sched 20 CGTA 1979, s 124.

For further details and the list of other special reliefs from tax which are available see TA 1988, s 503(1) and the other supplementary provisions in s 504.

10.1.7 Allowable expenditure

If the taxpayer has let furnished premises under Case VI the question is often raised as to what expenditure is allowable against the rent and on what principles the allowability is to be based.

Case VI of Schedule D is notorious for giving no guidance as to what can be deducted in any computation. TA 1988, s 18 Case VI charges tax in respect of 'any annual profits or gains.' Section 69 of that Act refers to a tax charge under that Case on the 'full amount of the profits or gains', and that is to be contrasted with, for instance, s 65 which refers to the 'full amount of the income' arising, which tends to denote a gross receipt being charged to tax as opposed to a net receipt which is implied by the term 'profits or gains'.

Clearly the taxpayer can make deductions in a Case VI computation for such matters as rates, cleaning and agency, provided these relate to the property (see *Wylie* v *Eccott* 6 TC 128 at pp 130 and 131).

The author feels that one must generally look to commercial principles to decide what can be deducted (*Curtis Brown Ltd* v *Jarvis* 14 TC 744 at p 752, *Lowry* v *Consolidated African Selection Trust Ltd* 23 TC 259 at p 315 and *Coltness Iron Co* v *Black* 1 TC 287 at p 319), although the most succinct statement on the position is to be found in *Gresham Life Assurance Society* v *Styles* 3 TC 185 at p 195 where Lord Herschell stated:

> The expression, 'balance of the profits or gains' is not a happy one, but the meaning obviously is the balance arrived at by setting against the receipts the expenditure necessary to earn them.

That being the case, the most promising guidance to be obtained on the question of what is deductible is to be found in TA 1988, s 74, which refers to the computation of the amount of 'profits or gains' as amended by statutory exceptions and additions. Thus one must try and ascertain what is meant by 'profits or gains' within s 74 making due allowance for any specific statutory provisions which affect the meaning of that expression.

It is felt that the express exclusions in s 74 do throw light on the intended meaning of 'profits or gains' (although they do not actually apply to Case VI as such) and also the express exclusions from non-deductability under Cases I and II in other parts of the legislation such as in TA 1988, s 401 (relief for pre-trading expenditure) throw light on the expression.

It is felt the Courts would hold that expenditure of a *revenue character* would be allowed (as opposed to capital expenditure) provided the expenditure related to the particular property or properties as the case may be.

10.1.8 TA 1988, s 776

Certain gains are specifically brought within Case VI. Gains arising from artificial land transactions which fall within the provisions of TA 1988, s 776 are an example of this (see Chapter 11).

10.2 DISADVANTAGES

Restriction on losses

One of the main disadvantages of a transaction falling within Case VI is that losses may only be used against profits or gains arising from transactions for which the taxpayer is assessed under Case VI. Losses cannot be set off against other types of income.

Investment income

Income chargeable under Case VI may be taxed as investment income (since the abolition of the 15% investment income surcharge by FA 1984 s 17(2), this point is of minor significance).

10.3 TAX PLANNING

(*a*) The taxpayer should try to avoid assessments under Case VI. He can do this by making certain that the transactions carried out amount to trading transactions coming within Case I of Schedule D. This will enable the losses if they should arise to be more freely available for offset against other income. It will also ensure that any profit is not taxed as investment income. 'Trading' transactions designed to create artificial trading losses have to be carefully watched as they may only create restricted Case VI losses.

(*b*) If the taxpayer has made Case VI profits—from a land deal assessed under TA 1988, s 776 for instance—he may be able to accept that losses on, say, commodity deals, are Case VI losses. This is because the losses can be offset against the profit as they are both within Case VI. The tax years in which the losses are made can also be important and must be watched.

(*c*) To avoid assessments under Case VI the taxpayer must argue that:

(i) the gain is of a capital nature; or

(ii) it does not resemble charging situations under any of the other Cases under Schedule D; or

(iii) if appropriate, it is an isolated purchase and sale, and therefore comes within *Jones* v *Leeming* 15 TC 333: it is virtually impossible for a one–off land transaction to be caught by general Case VI.

11 ARTIFICIAL TRANSACTIONS IN LAND (SECTION 776)

11.1 INTRODUCTION

This chapter deals with the provisions of TA 1988, ss 776, 777 and 778 which were enacted to 'prevent the avoidance of tax by persons concerned with land or the development of land, (s 776(1)). The provisions are important, especially if schemes have been entered into to avoid or mitigate taxation on land profits; such schemes may stir the Revenue to use s 776 where otherwise they may have left it dormant.

Section 776 taxes capital gains derived from land, or land development, as if they were income gains of an investment nature. Thus, an individual could pay income tax under s 776 on a gain at a rate as high as 40% whilst companies could pay CT on such a gain at a rate as high as 35% for the financial year 1988.

The profit would also not be trading profit for the purposes of the close company shortfall provisions.

All statutory references in this chapter, unless otherwise stated, are to TA 1988.

11.2 THE FOUR CONDITIONS

In order for there to be a liability to tax under s 776, three or (just possibly but very unlikely) four conditions must be satisfied:

(*a*) there may have to be an element of tax avoidance; this is very unlikely following the Court of Appeal decision in *Page* v *Lowther* [1983] STC 799.

(*b*) the transactions must fall within one of the three situations set out in s 776(2)

(*c*) there must be a disposal of land; and

(*d*) a gain of a capital nature must be realised.

- s 776
  - Tax avoidance (?)
  - S 776(2) situations
    - Purchase for resale
    - Trading stock
    - Land for development
  - Disposal
  - Capital gain

The four conditions are now examined in turn.

11.2.1 An element of tax avoidance

It appeared at one stage that there had to be an element of tax avoidance before s 776 could apply (Court of Appeal in *Yuill* v *Wilson* [1979], STC 486 at pp 491 and 499). By this the Court seemed to indicate that there must be an intention on the part of the taxpayer to avoid tax (*Yuill* v *Wilson* [1979], STC 486 at p 491d).

Buckley LJ in *Yuill* v *Wilson* at p 419 stated:

> If the transaction is one in which there is no element of tax avoidance, the section may well not be applicable on account of [s 776(1)]. The section will, in my judgment, apply in any case falling within the language of [s 776(2)] where there is an element of tax avoidance . . . There is no specific finding in clear terms in the case to the effect that any of the transactions were carried out with a view to tax avoidance . . . It is, I think, manifest . . . that the Commissioners formed the view that the transactions were not straightforward commercial transactions, but that they were entered into for an ulterior motive, namely, tax avoidance.

In the case of *Yuill* v *Wilson* the taxpayer entered into various land transactions which effectively enabled capital gains to be realised by Jersey companies rather than being realised by English companies which gains would have been chargeable to UK tax. Because of this attempt to avoid UK tax a sufficient tax avoidance motive was established. The Court of Appeal did not elaborate on what UK tax would have been payable on the transaction—whether this was a capital or trading income tax or, in fact, a charge to tax under s 776 itself (note also the definition of 'tax' which does not include CGT—TA 1988, s 832(1)).

The author finds it difficult to see that the provisions of s 776 are satisfied if a person carried out a scheme to avoid a charge under s 776 itself. The section envisages transactions intended to avoid other tax charges—CGT, or a trading gain charge—with s 776 applying to tax the gain which would otherwise have avoided tax. However, the position is not entirely clear and the House of Lords did not appear to expressly deal with the requirement of a tax avoidance motive.

In *Winterton* v *Edwards* [1980] STC 206 the question of a tax avoidance motive was not dealt with in detail by Slade J. The taxpayers were successfully assessed under s 776. In that case there was an intention to avoid CGT which was manifested by the principal landowner entering into an artificial CGT avoidance scheme.

Vinelott J in *Chilcott* v *IRC* [1982] STC 1, especially at 23h took the view, referring to the decision in *Yuill* v *Wilson,* that a tax avoidance purpose was not necessary before the section could apply. Warner J in the Chancery Division in *Page* v *Lowther* [1983] STC 61 dealt with the question of a tax avoidance and it was not considered necessary to make a reference to the decision of *Yuill* v *Wilson.* The case was heard on 11 November 1982.

Warner J at p 69 stated as follows:

> What constitutes tax avoidance is, as was pointed out by Lord Wilberforce in *Mangin* v *IRC* [1971] AC 735 at 739 in a passage cited by Vinelott J in *Chilcott* v *IRC* [1982] STC 1 at 24, very much a matter of opinion, and it would, in my judgment, be dangerous in the extreme for a Judge to take it upon himself to modify the meaning of the words of sub-section (2), or in any subsequent provision that was relevant to the case before him, according to his own conception of what does and does not constitute tax avoidance.
>
> It seems to me, moreover, that the view is tenable that the transactions entered into by the trustees in this case may have resulted in the avoidance of tax by them, albeit perhaps unwittingly.

The judge then indicated at p 696 that by doing the transaction in the way carried out in *Page* v *Lowther* perhaps the trustees were obtaining or intending to obtain capital sums perhaps paying tax at only capital gains tax rates rather than being taxable on the gains under Case 1 of Schedule D (trading gains). The Court of Appeal in *Page* v *Lowther* affirmed the decision of Warner J and clearly took the view that a tax avoidance purpose was not a prerequisite to the section applying (see Slade LJ at p 805h).

11.2.2 The three chargeable situations (s 776(2))

The section applies wherever:

Purchase for resale

(*a*) land, or any property deriving its value from land (such as shares in a company), is acquired with the sole or main object of realising a gain from disposing of the land; or

Example 11A: Purchase for resale

Mr X buys land with the sole object of selling it at a gain and does so accordingly.

The Revenue is unable to establish that he has traded but it could assess him under s 776.

Trading Stock

(*b*) land is held as trading stock; or

Example 11B: Trading stock

Mr X controls X Ltd which holds land as trading stock. When Mr X sells X Ltd s 776 will be in point unless the relief in s 776(10) mentioned below is applicable.

Land for development

(*c*) land is developed with the sole or main object of realising a gain from disposing of the land when developed.

Example 11C: Land for development

X buys land for capital purposes. Subsequently, he decides to, and does, develop the same with the sole or main object of disposing of the same when developed. Section 776 will be in point.

Any one of the above three situations could bring the section into effect.

For the purposes of this section, land includes buildings and any estate in land or buildings (s 776(13)(*a*)). The term 'property deriving its value from land' is defined to include any shareholding in a company, partnership interest, or any interest in settled property, whether directly or indirectly deriving its value from land.

The section applies to all persons whether resident in the UK or not if all or any part of the land in question is situated in the UK. Relevant double tax treaties will have to be referred to but these will often not prevent a tax charge arising.

Example 11D: Application to non-UK residents

X, a UK resident, provides a Guernsey resident company, which he owns, with an opportunity of making a profit from a land transaction in the UK. There may be no 'permanent establishment' in the UK, so the Guernsey company may argue that under Article 3(2) of the Guernsey double tax treaty of 24 June 1952 (SI 1952 No 1215) no UK tax under s 776 or otherwise can be chargeable on the gain. The Revenue could probably argue successfully that under s 776 they are assessing X who is a UK resident, and he is not protected by the treaty, although the Guernsey company may be protected.

11.2.3 There must be a 'disposal'

There cannot be a tax charge under s 776 unless there is a disposal of land (s 776(2)). The term 'disposal' is not defined for s 776 purposes. Examples of disposals are, however, given in ss 776 and 777. A disposal would include a disposal of shares or an interest in a company, partnership or trust on its winding-up or dissolution (s 777(3)(*d*)).

Section 776(4) provides that the land shall be treated as disposed of if, by virtue of any arrangements whether concerning the land or property deriving its value from land, the property in the land or the control of the land is 'effectually' disposed of. Thus, the entry into put and call options to postpone the date of disposal for CGT purposes under CGTA 1979, s 27 (*Ramsay* permitting) until either of the options is exercised may not be effective for s 776 purposes; the date of entry into the options may be the disposal date (s 776(4)).

Complex schemes which indirectly but effectively dispose of the land will not prevent a disposal taking place. If the taxpayer has a part interest in equity in the land—as the taxpayer had in *Winterton* v *Edwards* (see below)—he would clearly come within this provision if the land is sold. However, if a taxpayer disposes of a non-controlling interest in a company which owns the land one could argue that there was no disposal for the purposes of this provision because the disposer did not have any property in the land—the company had this—and did not have control of the land because he was only a minority shareholder (s 776). The author has come across a case where the Revenue has argued that the provision applies where a number of minority shareholders sell at the same time so that adding all the shareholdings together control had passed even though no particular shareholder had control. If land is let this could amount to a disposal but there would be no charge to tax under s 776 if only rent is received; this is because no capital sum would be obtained from the disposal unless, exceptionally, the rent is not of an income nature in the hands of the recipient; the fact that it is a capital payment as far as the payer is concerned is not enough, it must be capital in the hands of the recipient before s 776 can apply (*Ainsley* v *Eden* 19 TC 303, *IRC* v *The Land Securities Investment Trust Ltd* [1969] 2 All ER 430, and *IRC* v *Church Commissioners for England* 50 TC 516).

11.2.4 Gain of a capital nature

This section only applies if a gain of a capital nature is obtained from the disposal of land. A gain is of a capital nature if 'it does not fall to be included in any computation of income for the purposes of the Tax Acts' (s 777(13)). If it falls into such a computation it may still be taxable because losses are available or possibly because it is protected from charge under a Double Tax Treaty. The definition in s 777(13) is exhaustive (*Sugarwhite* v *Budd* [1988] STC 533 at 537j) and the onus is on the taxpayer to show that the sum is not a 'capital' sum.

Rent

If land is let this could amount to a disposal but there would be no charge to tax under s 776 if only rent, chargeable, for instance, under Schedule A, is received; this is because no capital sum would be obtained from the disposal. TA 1988, s 777(13) states that for the purposes of s 776 'capital amount' means any amount, in money or money's worth, which, apart from the principal sections (this includes s 776) does not fall to be included in any computation of income for the purposes of the Tax Acts, and other expressions including the word 'capital' (which is used in s 776(2)) shall be construed accordingly.

Overseas element
This could well mean that if a trading gain is made overseas by an overseas trust or a company that this could still amount to a gain of a capital nature for these purposes because the gain, although a trading gain, would not be included in any computation of income for the purposes of the Tax Acts. This could be serious if a UK resident, for instance, directly or indirectly transmits the opportunity of making a gain within s 776(5)(*a*) to an overseas trust or company with the overseas entity making a trading gain by rapidly acquiring and disposing of the land.

Note that such a gain may of course (depending on the facts) be brought into a UK trading computation if it is found to have derived from the UK (see *Grainger & Son* v *Gough* (1896) AC 325, *The Calcutta Jute Mills Company Ltd* v *Nicholson* ITC 97 at pp 98 and 101, and the like) or to have been made through a branch or agency in the UK (see *Sugarwhite* v *Budd* [1988] STC 533 at 538c). In which case it may not be a 'capital sum' for s 776 purposes. This may be the case even if the gain is protected from charge under a Double Tax Treaty. If this is the case and there is no capital sum s 776 cannot apply.

11.2.5 Meaning of arrangement or scheme

It is clear from the case of *Page* v *Lowther* [1983] STC 799 that the word arrangement is to be given a very wide meaning. In that case it was submitted by Counsel for the taxpayer that the term scheme of arrangement should be construed as denoting only a scheme or arrangement of an artificial nature ie one in the nature of a self seeking contrivance; this would mean that to amount to a scheme or arrangement the transaction must be carried out in an unnatural way with a view to avoiding tax. In support of that submission, Counsel for the taxpayer relied on the juxtaposition of the word arrangement with the word scheme which latter word had an element of somewhat sinister import. Slade LJ rejected that attempt to restrict the meaning of the expression. Without defining the same he held that a lease under which the trustees of a settlement would obtain increased premiums depending on the success of a development to be carried out by the sublessee was an arrangement.

Thus the section has a very wide meaning. Not only is it not necessary for there to be a tax avoidance purpose before the section can apply but additionally if there is a scheme or arrangement and trading stock is disposed of with the taxpayer obtaining a capital sum (for instance if the taxpayer sells a company which holds trading stock) there is no clearance procedure available (see TA 1988, s 776(2)(*b*) and (10) and (11)).

11.3 THE CHARGEABLE PERSON

11.3.1 Person who realises the gain

Where s 776 applies the capital gain is taxable under Case VI of Schedule D. A charge is made for the chargeable period in which the gain is realised and is made on the person by whom the gain is realised (s 776(3)).

The chargeable gain must be realised ('or obtained'; the terms seem to be used interchangeably in s 776):

(*a*) by the person acquiring, holding or developing the land or by any connected person; or

(*b*) where any arrangement or scheme is effected as respects the land which enabled a gain to be realised by any indirect method, or by any series of transactions, by any person who is a party to, or concerned in, the arrangement or scheme.

Where under s 776(2)(*c*) any person is charged to tax on the realisation of a gain and the computation of the gain proceeded on the footing that the land or some other property was appropriated at any time as trading stock, that land or other property shall be treated on that footing also for the purposes of CGTA 1979, s 122 (s 777(11)).

This section also applies whether any such person obtains the gain for himself or for any other person.

In *Winteron* v *Edwards* [1980] STC 206, L acquired land with the object of realising a gain from the disposal of it and W and B were given small shares of 4½% and 5% respectively in any of the sale proceeds. W and B felt that they were entitled to these proceeds by virtue of their general business relationships with L. When L sold the land, s 776 assessments *inter alia* were made on W and B and these were upheld by Slade J in the High Court because although W and B were not parties to L's various transactions in connection with the land they were 'concerned in' the transactions by virtue of their interests in the proceeds of sale. This case is important as it tends to indicate that if one person has an intention of realising a gain within s 488 then other persons who may not have that intention may also be caught if they are concerned in any arrangement or scheme under which the land is disposed of.

The provisions can apply where a vendor of land retains a share in the ultimate development profits.

In *Page* v *Lowther* the trustees of a settlement held land which they had not acquired with a view to reselling at a gain. Additionally, the land was not held as trading stock.

The trustees granted a long lease of the land to developers (Trafalgar House

Developments Limited). The developers carried out the development and obtained premiums from the grant of underleases. A predetermined proportion of the premiums were paid to the trustees of the settlement.

The Court of Appeal held that although the trustees of the settlement did not themselves carry out the development, nevertheless there was an arrangement or scheme in existence with respect to the land which enabled a gain to be realised and the trustees were a party to that scheme. They could thus be taxed under s 776 on their receipts (s 776(2)(ii) and [1983] STC 799 at pp 805g and 807a).

It is clear from this case that if a vendor sells land for a gain of a capital nature to a developer the vendor could be liable for tax under s 776 if he retains a share in the ultimate development profits.

The author is of the view that if land is sold by the taxpayer subject to planning permission and (assuming the situation does not come within s 776(2)(*a*) or (*b*)) planning permission is subsequently obtained with the sale price then becoming payable, this would not bring the situation within s 776(2)(*c*). The taxpayer, in the author's view, will not be a party to the arrangement or scheme under which the land is ultimately developed and disposed of within s 776(2)(ii).

11.3.2 Premature sale or otherwise s 776(5)(*a*)

It is provided in s 776(5)(*a*) that where there is a sale prematurely or otherwise and a person (Mr A) directly or indirectly transmits the opportunity of making a gain to another person (Mr B) that person's gain (Mr B's gain) is deemed to be that of the first mentioned person (Mr A). Mr A will therefore be the taxable person.

This provision would apply to a case where a UK resident sells a piece of land to a non-resident trust at its market value prior to the grant of planning permission. If the trust sold the land and realised a gain a substantial profit may accrue. It may not be possible for the Revenue to collect the tax from the trust. This section would enable the Revenue to tax the gain upon the UK resident because he provided the opportunity to the overseas trust to realise the gain. This provision (s 776(5)(*a*)) is similar to s 776(8).

11.3.3 Provision of opportunity

Section 776(8) provides that where one person (A) provides directly or indirectly another person (B) with the opportunity of realising a gain the section shall apply to the gain as if A had made the gain.

There is clearly difficulty with regard to the provisions of s 776 with respect to ascertaining which persons can actually be liable for tax under s 776 (see TA 1988, s 776(2), 3(*b*) and (8) and also (5)).

Clearly if A owns the land and sells it to B, A is the person who realises the gain and can be charged under s 776 (s 776(3)(*b*)). If A provides land to C or presents C with the opportunity of realising a gain then when C disposes of the land to B, although C in fact realises a gain A is deemed to realise the gain, and can be liable under s 776 (TA 1988, s 776(*a*)).

Example 11E: Provision of opportunity

A has the opportunity of taking up a valuable land contract. Realising that he would pay tax on it, he arranges for his overseas trust to take up a contract. The trust takes up the contract and makes a large gain. A under s 776(8) is treated as the person who realises the gain and therefore can be brought into charge to tax (TA 1988, s 776(3)).

A may see an opportunity of making a gain from land. He buys the land for a £1,000 and sells it to a non-resident trust which he created for the members of his family. He sells it at £1,000. Planning permission is obtained and the trust sells the land making a capital gain of £100,000. The trust may well be found to have acquired the land with the sole or main object of realising a gain from disposing of the land within TA 1988, s 776(2)(*a*). It may well have made a gain of a capital nature and it will have obtained that gain from the disposal of the land. It will have obtained the gain for itself and will not have obtained the gain for any other person. Thus on the face of it only the Trustees can be assessed. However, TA 1988, s 776(8) states that if all or any part of the gain accruing to any person (the Trustees) is derived from an opportunity provided by some other person (the UK taxpayer) the provisions which deem the capital gain to be the income of a taxpayer shall apply as if the UK taxpayer had realised the gain. Thus the UK taxpayer can be chargeable under s 776.

It is difficult to know from the provision just how much legal or other rights A must have in the land before he can be said to have transferred or provided those rights or opportunities to other persons so that A could be chargeable upon the other person's gains. An interesting light has, however, been thrown on these provisions by Buckley LJ in the Court of Appeal in *Yuill* v *Wilson* [1979] STC 486 at p 494. He stated:

> If A has the legal capacity to transfer an opportunity to make a gain and in exercise of that capacity does transfer that opportunity to B by his own act, he does so directly. If in the exercise of his own capacity to do so he transfers or transmits the opportunity to B with the knowledge or assurance or expectation that the opportunity will consequently pass from B to C without any further act on A's part, he may be said to provide C with the opportunity indirectly. If he lacks the legal capacity to transfer the opportunity by his own act to anyone, but is in a position by persuasion to procure B, who has the opportunity, to transfer it to C, can A properly be said in this way to provide C with that opportunity indirectly?
>
> Bearing in mind the purpose of s 488 (now s 776) as stated in sub-section (1), I think that this question should be answered affirmatively. The possession of the legal capacity to transfer the opportunity is not, it seems to me, essential for the fulfilment of sub-section (8).

In *Yuill* v *Wilson* the taxpayer and his family trust held a controlling interest in Y Ltd. Y Ltd sold two parcels of land to two separate UK companies connected with the taxpayer. The taxpayer set up a trust in Guernsey which set up, in turn, C Ltd and M Ltd (two Guernsey companies), the shares in which were wholly owned by the trustees. These two Guernsey companies purchased the two parcels of land from the English companies at prices which fully reflected the undeveloped market value of the land. A year later the Guernsey trustees sold the two companies—C Ltd and M Ltd—to V Ltd, another Guernsey company which was owned by an unconnected overseas trust. There was uncontradicted evidence that the trust which owned all the shares in V Ltd was set up by an overseas settlor for overseas beneficiaries and the taxpayer and his family were not included in the class of beneficiaries.

Shortly after the sale planning permission to develop the land was obtained and Y Ltd purchased both parcels of land from C Ltd and M Ltd for a substantial sum but on contingently deferred terms. The taxpayer was assessed under s 776 on the gains made by C Ltd and M Ltd. The House of Lords held that by virtue of his powers over the companies and the family trust the taxpayer had provided C Ltd and M Ltd with the opportunity of making the gains within s 776(8).

The House of Lords held that the two Guernsey companies—C Ltd and M Ltd—were clearly within s 776 but because they were outside the jurisdiction no tax could be obtained from them. It was therefore important if the Revenue was to obtain any tax that it had to be able to show, *inter alia,* that the taxpayer gave the overseas companies the opportunity of making a gain; this it succeeded in doing (see figure below).

11.3.4 The *Yuill* v *Wilson* Plan

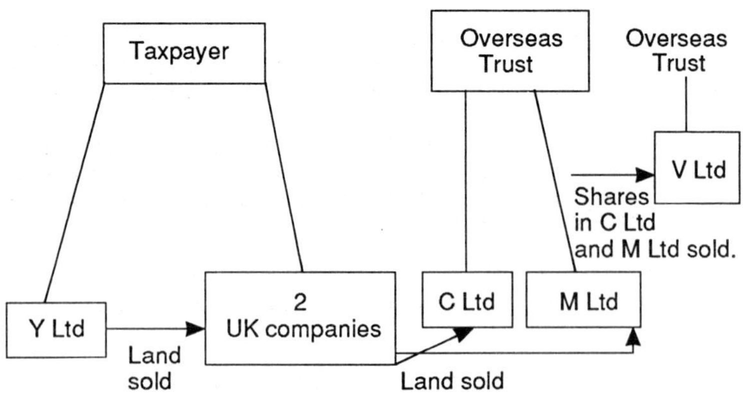

11.3.5 Sale by non-residents

If it appears to the Revenue that any person entitled to any consideration or other amount taxable under s 776 is not resident in the UK the Revenue may direct that s 349(1) shall apply to any payment forming part of the amount as if it were an annual payment chargeable to tax under Case III of Schedule D but this is without prejudice to any final determination of the liability of any person under s 776 (s 777(9)).

Thus, if a UK purchaser receives a direction from the Revenue to deduct tax at 25% from the proceeds of sale, under s 777(9), he must so deduct tax. There is no obligation to deduct tax if he does not receive a direction. The position is therefore 'no direction, no deduction'. The diagram below shows deduction at source.

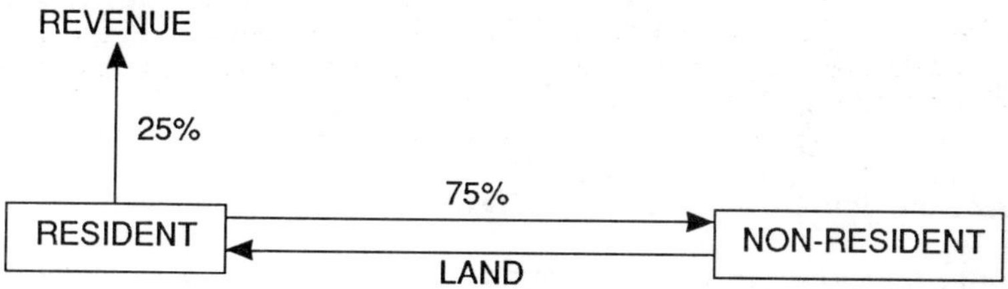

11.3.6 Sugarwhite deals

Taxpayers who dispose of land to overseas companies so those companies can make the profits must take note of the *Sugarwhite* v *Budd* case.

In the case of *Sugarwhite* v *Budd* [1987] STC 491(ChD); STC 533(CA) X purchased property with the intention of disposing of the same at a profit. He sold the same at an undervalue to a Bahamian company which subsequently sold the same onto the ultimate purchaser at a profit, with the profit being split between that Bahamian company and two other Bahamian companies and X who took a small share of the profit.

The Court of Appeal, affirming the decision of Vinelott J and substantially agreeing with the reasons he gave for his decision, held that Mr X was properly assessed under s 776. The position was analysed as follows:

(*a*) Mr X was a party to the arrangements for the disposal of the property. He had full knowledge of the arrangements. He had full knowledge of those arrangements before he made the disposal of the property to the first Bahamian company.

(*b*) The land was acquired by the three overseas companies with the sole or main object of disposing of it. Section 776(2)(*a*) was therefore satisfied.

(*c*) Gains were in fact derived from the disposal of the land by those three companies. In the absence of evidence to the contrary (which it is for the taxpayer to adduce and which he did not adduce) those gains must be assumed to be of a capital nature in accordance with the definition contained in s 776(13).

(*d*) Accordingly, the three overseas companies, having been parties to the arrangement or scheme which enabled the gains to be made by them within s 776(2)(ii), were chargeable under s 776(3)(*b*).

(*e*) Finally, under s 776(8) the taxpayer, being the person who directly or indirectly provided the opportunity of realising the gains to the overseas companies, was to be substituted as the taxable person for the three companies.

Note that it is very difficult for the Revenue to tax X under Case I of Schedule D on a gain made by Y if X presented Y with the opportunity of making the gain (*Ransom* v *Higgs* 50 TC 1). Hence the Revenue must seek to apply s 776 in cases such as that.

11.3.7 Section 776 and recovery of tax from non-residents

Where a person is assessed to tax under s 776 in respect of consideration receivable by another person:

(*a*) he is entitled to recover from that other person any part of the tax which he has paid, and

(*b*) if any part of that tax remains unpaid at the expiration of six months from the date when it became due and payable, it shall be recoverable from that other person as though he were the person assessed, but without prejudice to the right to recover it from the person actually assessed.

In the case of *Sugarwhite* v *Budd* the taxpayer in the UK effectively arranged for profits from a land transaction to accrue to three overseas Bahamian companies and he was assessed on the profits they received under s 776. Vinelott J at 501c referred to the right to recover the tax as follows:

> I should mention for completeness that the taxpayer is entitled to recover from the Bahamian companies the amount of the tax payable on the monies received by them (see s 777(8)). How far that right will be enforceable in the Bahamas I do not know.

11.4 REALISATION OF GAIN

In order to be assessed under s 776 it is essential to discover when a gain is realised (see s 776(3)). Section 777(13) states that any amount in money or money's worth shall not be regarded as having been receivable by a person until that person can effectively enjoy or dispose of it. Unless money is actually received one has to ascertain whether the rights to future sums can be valued and treated as part of the disposal proceeds. In *Yuill* v *Wilson* the monies to be received by the two Guernsey companies for the sale of the parcels of land to the UK company were subject to contingencies and deferments under the terms of the contracts such that the House of Lords held that apart from the actual cash paid over (which was small) no significant gain had been realised. The tax was therefore avoided at stage 1. If the future contingent sums could have been valued then that value would have been brought into charge to tax.

Yuill revisited
In the case of *Yuill* v *Wilson* as mentioned above it was held that the taxpayer could not be substantially assessed under the TA 1988, s 776 (artificial transactions in land) because the consideration he received from the disposal of land was contingent and unquantifiable. Some years later the various contingencies occurred and the monies became quantifiable and were payable to the taxpayer. The taxpayer argued in *Yuill* v *Fletcher* ([1984] STC 401 (CA)) ([1983] STC 598 (Ch D)), however, that the Revenue could only assess the taxpayer on day 1 when the disposal took place and it could not now assess the subsequent profit which had fallen in. Mr. Justice Walton in the High Court ([1984] STC 598) and the Court of Appeal, held that the argument could not be sustained.

In *Winterton* v *Edwards* the taxpayers were entitled to 4½% and 5% in the proceeds of sale of the property under the terms of declarations of trusts, which had certain odd and unexplained features. However, Slade J held that under the terms of the document the taxpayers could demand immediate payment of their shares in the proceeds so that the year in which the gain was made was the year in which they were taxable under s 488 and not when they actually received the sums of money which was, in the case of some of the payments, later than the year of the disposal of the land.

11.5 GIFTS TO OVERSEAS STRUCTURE

The taxpayer may give property to his overseas trust with a view to the trust ultimately selling on. The question is whether the gain made by the transferee would be caught under s 776. Its acquisition cost will be nil because it will have paid nothing for the land.

The author feels that the Revenue would have some difficulty in applying s 776 to the trust. In *McClelland* v *Commissioner of Taxation of the Commonwealth of Australia* [1971] 1 All ER 868, X inherited property and one of the questions was whether she fell within a provision which seemed to be similar to s 776 of the Taxes Act (s 26(*a*) of the Income Tax and Social Services Contribution Act 1936–1963). The decision of the Privy Council is not entirely clear but the key question was whether X had acquired property for the purpose of profit making by sale. Lord Donovan stated at p 973c:

> . . . it is not inaccurate to describe (X) as acquiring the land though the bounty of the testator. On that footing it would be quite inappropriate to say of X that she acquired land through the bounty of the testator 'for the purpose of profit-making by sale'.

Equally it may be inappropriate to say that X through the bounty of the testator 'acquired "land" with the sole or main object of realising a gain from disposing of the land' (TA 1988, s 776(2)(*a*)).

In the case of *McClelland* the land was acquired under a will. Equally the author feels that if land is transferred by D to his trust through the bounty of D the Revenue would have some difficulty in saying that the transaction falls within TA 1988, s 776(2)(*a*) as far as the trust is concerned.

In fact it would appear that neither the donor nor the trust can be chargeable under s 776 in a situation such as that stated above. Even if it may be said that the transactions which involve the donor and trust amounted to an arrangement or scheme it is still necessary, following the decision of *Page* v *Lowther* [1983] STC 799, to find what may be termed the operative disposal or the relevant disposal (see pp 803f and 806b). It is felt that because neither the donor nor the trust acquired the land with the sole or main object of realising a gain from disposing of the land (although the ultimate developer may have done so). The operative disposal which gives rise to the capital gain must be made by the person who acquired the land with the sole or main object of realising a gain from disposing of the land. Neither the donor nor the trust would fall within that category so that it is not felt that TA 1988, s 776 would apply. There are some points which can be raised with respect to s 776(2)(*b*), but in general these do not alter the author's conclusion mentioned above.

The author understands that there has been a case where a taxpayer has transferred property to a spouse who had then sold the property on to obtain an extra tax exemption with the taxpayer successfully arguing that the *Ramsay* doctrine could not apply to dismiss the transaction to the spouse because the transaction was carried out as part of an estate planning exercise. The donee spouse kept the sale proceeds. It is understood that this case was before the Special Commissioners.

11.6 COMPUTATION OF GAIN

11.6.1 The just and reasonable test

Section 776(6) states that such method of computing the gain shall be adopted as is just and reasonable in the circumstances taking into account the value of what is obtained when disposing of the land and allowing only such expenses as are attributable to the land disposed of. Special provisions apply to cases where a freehold is acquired and the reversion is retained on a disposal and where there have been certain premiums paid on the leases s 776(*a*) and (*b*).

11.6.2 Intention to develop

Figure 11.1 When was the intention to develop formed?

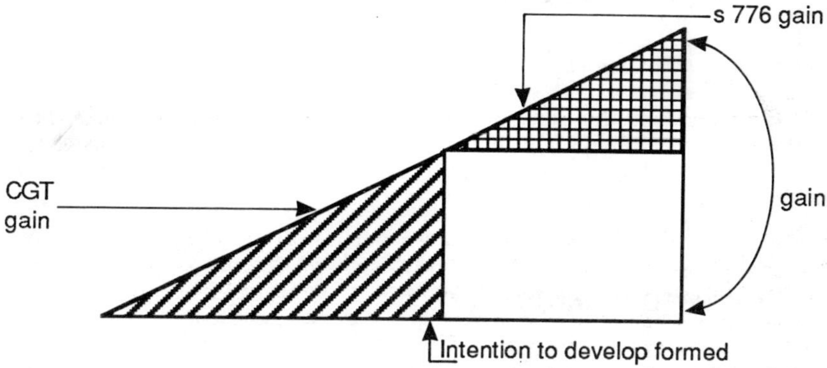

Sub-section (7) states that where sub-section (2)(*c*) applies so much of the gain that is fairly attributable to the period before the intention to develop was formed shall not be chargeable under s 776. This provision can give rise to difficult problems.

Example 11F: Intention to develop

A company may have a warehouse which is clearly held as an investment or for some business purpose. It may go for planning permission to demolish the same and build offices, construct the offices and then dispose of the land. The question is: what value is fairly attributable to the period before the intention to develop arises? Is it the current use value of the warehouse, the value with the hope of getting planning permission or the value with the planning permission? The answer is that one must look to when the actual intention to develop for sale was formed. It may well be that the landowner intended to get planning permission and sell the land without there being any intention to develop. Alternatively, when the planning application was made there may have been an intention to develop the land for sale formed at that time. If this is the case effectively hope value will be taken into account and not be chargeable under s 776. Appropriate company minutes can be important.

In *Winterton* v *Edwards* the taxpayers had spent a mere £2,500 with respect to building costs on a parcel of land which had then been disposed of. Counsel for the taxpayer pointed out that the sum spent on the development was small indicating that perhaps there had to be a substantial amount of expenditure on development work before s 776(2)(*c*) could apply. Slade J at p 217 said that s 776(2)(*c*) did not require the development to be substantial.

11.6.3 Shortfall and s 776

If a company makes a gain under section 776 it should consider the shortfall problems which may arise.

Example 11G: Shortfall and s 776

A company which is a close company for the purposes of TA 1988, s 423 and Sched 19 disposes of land and realises a capital gain. The circumstances of the sale are such that s 776 is applicable and the gain is treated as income chargeable under Schedule D, Case VI.

The Revenue take the view that the income under s 776 is not trading income for the purposes of Sched 19. It is regarded as estate income where the gain on the disposal of land accrues to and is chargeable under s 776 on the company which directly owned the land. In other circumstances, it is investment income.

11.7 EXEMPTIONS AND RELIEFS

11.7.1 Sale of shares in certain companies

Where there is a disposal of shares in a company which holds land as trading stock (or a company which owns directly or indirectly 90% or more of the ordinary share capital of another company which holds land as trading stock) and all the land so held is disposed of in the normal course of its trade by the company which held it, so as to ensure that the opportunity of profit in respect of the land arises to that company, s 776 does not apply to any gain accruing to the holder of shares as being a gain on property deriving value from the land (s 776(10)).

Mr X owns 100% of X Ltd which is a land trading company. He sells the shares to Y Ltd for £1 million. Can s 776 apply? The transaction comes within the wording of TA 1988, s 776(2), ie land is held as trading stock by the company and a gain of a capital nature is obtained by Mr X from the disposal of the land (indirectly through the disposal of the company) and the gain is obtained by a person connected with the person holding the land (ie Mr X is connected with the company).

The taxpayer must then see whether he is protected by TA 1988, s 776(10). He will be protected if the company holds land as trading stock and:

(*a*) all the land so held is disposed of in the normal course of its trade by the company which held it, and

(*b*) all opportunity of profit in respect of the land arises to that company.

This exemption only applies to a person within s 776(2)(i), that is, a person acquiring, holding or developing the land or any connected person and not a person within s 776(2)(ii), that is, a person who is involved in an arrangement or scheme with respect to the land.

In *Chilcott* v *IRC* [1982] STC 1, K Ltd disposed of land in the ordinary course of its trade, with the shareholders of K Ltd, then disposing of their entire shareholding in K Ltd. Vinelott J held that s 776 was inapplicable because of the exemption in s 776(10). The judge also held that the disposal was not allied with any artificial arrangement or scheme within s 776(2)(iii).

The judge said that s 776(10):

> makes it clear that [s 776] is not to apply to a simple sale of shares of a company holding land as trading stock if the land is sold in the ordinary course of trade at full value so that it falls to be brought into the company's computation of gains, and if the sale of the shares is not allied to some artificial arrangement or scheme of the kind described in [s 776(2)(ii)].

The author also feels that the case of *Chilcott* v *IRC* is authority for the proposition that if individuals own a property dealing company and the property is disposed of in the normal course of trade with the cash filled company then being liquidated, s 776 should not apply. At the time of liquidation the company only held cash, and if the Revenue were to find that there was an arrangement or scheme the only consequence of that would be the company may be 'treated' as owning land at the time of liquidation, and that land is disposed of in the normal course of trade which would bring the transaction back within s 776(10). The author takes the view that a disposal on liquidation is a disposal for the purposes of s 776(10).

It seems from the *Chilcott* decision that even if there is a scheme or arrangement in existence, provided the property is disposed of in the normal course of trade, whether before or after the sale of the company, or is disposed of prior to liquidation or in the liquidation, the Revenue may have some difficulty in making s 776 apply.

11.7.2 Principal private residence exemption

The section does not apply to a gain which has accrued to an individual which by virtue of the CGT exemption in respect of principal private residences (CGTA 1979, ss 101–105) is exempt from CGT or which would be exempt but for the provisions of CGTA 1979, s 103(3) (where the residence is acquired partly with a view to making a gain) (s 776(9)).

This exemption is, therefore, more favourable than the CGT exemption in that an individual's dwellinghouse acquired wholly or partly for the purpose of realising a gain is exempt from the charge under s 776, although such a gain is not exempt from CGT.

11.7.3 Gifts

There is no provision deeming consideration to arise with respect to s 776.

Example 11H: Gifts, Sales at Undervalue and s 776

If Mr X gives Blackacre to his wife, s 776 cannot apply. Also if land worth £1m is sold by X to his son Y for £¼m s 776 can only be in point with respect to the £¼m. Market value cannot be substituted.

Example 11I: Increases in value of shares and s 776

Mr X gives Blackacre worth £1m to a company. He owns all the shares in the company. It is arguable that the increase in the value of the shares as a result of the gift to the company is consideration received by Mr X.

11.7.4 Husband and wife

It should be noted that there is no particular relief available from a charge under 776 with regard to transactions between a husband and wife.

Example 11J: Husband and wife and s 776

Mr H acquires land with a view to selling it off at a profit and he sells the same to his wife at a profit. TA 1988, s 776 could apply to that profit.

11.7.5 No double charge

The Revenue often assesses taxpayers to capital gains tax and also under s 776 in the alternative. It is clear that if the taxpayer is liable to and has paid capital gains tax that if it is then established he is liable to tax under s 776 he would be entitled to a repayment of the capital gains tax (Vinelott J in *Chilcott* v *IRC* [1982] STC 1 at p 22D referring to FA 1965, Sched 6, para 2(1) now CGTA 1979, s 9).

11.7.6 Clearances

There is a clearance procedure provided under s 488(11). Application must be made to the Inspector of Taxes dealing with the affairs of the applicant. Thus, one applies to the local Inspector of Taxes for clearance and not to the Board of Inland Revenue at Somerset House.

The limitations on the clearance procedure under s 776 should be appreciated.

(*a*) It is possible to get a clearance in situations where sub-section (2)(*a*) may apply, ie, land or any property deriving its value from land is acquired for the sole or main object of realising a gain from disposing of a land.

(*b*) It is possible to obtain a clearance from sub-section (2)(*c*) ie where land is developed with the sole or main object of realising a gain from disposing of the land when developed.

(*c*) It is not possible to obtain a clearance for situations where the taxpayer obtains a gain of a capital nature as a result of the disposal of land held as trading stock (sub-section (2)(*b*)). However, if a company is disposed of within s 776(10) and the company holds trading stock then the section will not apply if the land so held by the company is disposed of in the normal course of its trade and in such a way as to procure that all opportunity of profit in respect of the land arises to that company. Both those conditions must be satisfied, ie, the normal course of trade condition plus the opportunity of profit condition. If that is the case then s 776 cannot apply provided that the gain of a capital nature obtained from the indirect disposal of the land is obtained by the person acquiring, holding, or developing the land or by any connected person and (*d*) below is not applicable.

(*d*) There is no clearance procedure available and the section will apply if there is such a disposal of shares in a trading company as mentioned above and a scheme or arrangement is effected as respects the land which enables a gain to be realised by any indirect method, or by any series of transactions, by any person who is a party, or concerned in, the arrangement or scheme.

(*e*) It is clear that the Revenue will not give clearances and the section may thus apply where the taxpayer has entered into arrangements or schemes to try and effectively convert an income profit into a capital gain.

11.8 PROVISION OF INFORMATION

The Board or an Inspector may by notice in writing require any person to furnish them within such time as the Board or the Inspector may direct (not being less than 30 days) with such particulars as the Board or Inspector may think necessary for the purposes of making an assessment under s 776 (s 778).

The powers conferred on the Inland Revenue Commissioners to obtain information for s 776 purposes are sufficiently wide to authorise enquiries not related to specific transactions or arrangements. Revenue 'fishing operations' are therefore possible (*Essex and Others* v *IRC* [1980] STC 378).

11.9 TAX PLANNING

(1) Consideration should be given to applying for clearances under s 776(11) in appropriate cases.

(2) Where a gain is to be made from the development of land the taxpayer should argue as high a value as possible for the land prior to when the intention to develop for sale was formed (s 776(7)). It may be helpful to have written evidence available to substantiate the time when the intention to develop for sale was formed.

(3) In appropriate cases the taxpayer should try to establish himself as a trader in order to avoid a s 776 assessment.

(4) On the sale of a landowning company the vendor should get a covenant from the purchaser that the company will sell the land in the normal course of its trade (s 776(10)). The vendor may apply for clearance under s 776(11) but note its limitations.

(5) If the land surrounding the principal private residence exceeds 1 acre the taxpayer should argue that it is required for the reasonable enjoyment of the residence (see s 776(9)).

(6) An overseas vendor may want to complete any sale as soon as possible in case the purchaser receives a direction from the Inland Revenue to deduct tax.

(7) Careful consideration should be given to any schemes designed to avoid capital gains tax on land disposals; the schemes may be successful in avoiding CGT but the taxpayer may end up paying tax under s 776. *This is particularly important because the capital gains tax scheme will have evidenced a tax avoidance motive.* It is as well to remember the words of Walton J in *Irving* v *Tesco Stores Limited* [1982] STC 881 at 905g: 'It may be that at the end of the day they have scraped home on this point by the skin of their teeth, but if they had not I do not see in the slightest why they should not have been left to gnash them in vain.'

(8) The House of Lords in *Yuill* v *Wilson* pointed to the weakness in the section; there can be no charge until the gain can be effectively enjoyed or disposed of; the gain may not be able to be effectively enjoyed or disposed of if the trusts and companies are involved in making it upon special *'Yuill* v *Wilson'* type terms. Ultimately, however, the Revenue

may have the last word (*Yuill* v *Fletcher* ChD [1983], STC 598, CA [1984], STC 401).

(9) It should be noted that if it is impossible for a company to avoid a charge under s 776 (because, for instance, it wishes to take an equity slice in the development), it should see whether it can shelter the s 776 gain by buying, for instance, an Enterprise Zone Property.

Example 11K: Section 776 shelter

X Ltd makes a s 776 gain in its accounting period ending 31 December 1987. It buys an unused Enterprise Zone building during that period or during the accounting period ending 31 December 1988, and offsets the allowances against the s 776 gain (Capital Allowances Act 1968, ss 1(1), 6 and 74(3)).

(10) Taxpayers must have a general awareness of this provision. It can catch charities and may also apply to certain business expansion schemes.

12 VALUE ADDED TAX AND PROPERTY TRANSACTIONS

PART I INTRODUCTION

Value Added Tax, which is administered by the Commissioners of Customs and Excise, is a tax on the final consumption of goods and services. It came into operation on 1 April 1973, and the main provisions appear in the Value Added Tax Act 1983, regulations made thereunder and EEC Directives.

All statutory references in this chapter, unless otherwise stated, are to the Value Added Tax Act 1983. The principal statutory instrument governing VAT is the Value Added Tax (General) Regulations 1985. The principal EEC directive is the Sixth Council Directive of 17 May 1977 (77/388/EEC).

12.1 BASIC FEATURES

VAT is generally chargeable on the supply of goods and services at the standard rate of 15 per cent. The supply must be a taxable supply made by a taxable person in the course or furtherance of any business carried on by him (s 2(1)).

12.1.1 Taxable person

A person is a taxable person where he is required to register, ie where his taxable supplies, broadly, exceed £22,100 pa (Sched 1, as amended).

12.1.2 Supply

All supplies are taxable supplies unless exempt, that is, exempt from any charge to VAT (s 2(2)). Most land transactions will be exempt. Some supplies are simply disregarded for all VAT purposes.

12.1.3 Business ('No business, no VAT')

Only goods and services supplied in the course or furtherance of a business can give rise to a charge to VAT (s 2(1)). 'Business' includes any trade, profession or vocation (s 47(1)). This is not a definition of the term. Section 47(1) merely sets out a list of activities included or deemed to be included in the term. The existence of a 'business' has been examined by the courts on many occasions. The taxation cases indicate that the expression 'business' tends to denote that one is dealing with (1) an *activity* (*IRC V Marine Steam Turbine* (1920) 12 TC 174 at 179) although there may be periods where not much is going on (*IRC* v *The Westleigh Estates Co Ltd* 12 TC 657 at 712) which is (2) generally related to the commercial sphere (*D A Chandler* v *The Commissioners* LON/73/89, *R A Archer* v *The Commissioners* (1974) VATTR 1 but see *The Commissioners* v *Morrison's Academy of Boarding Houses Association* [1978] STC 1)(3) which exhibits a degree of *continuity* (*Marine Steam Turbine* aforesaid and *Morrison's Academy* aforesaid) and which (4) may create an *entity* which is distinct from its separate parts (*McGregor* v *Adcock* [1977] STC 206 at 209; assets are 'bought to life' by being used in a business); in addition some element of (5) *organisation,* as in the case of a trade, may be necessary (*Ransom* v *Higgs* [1974] STC 539 at 554). The letting of three semi-detached houses may amount to a business even though the rent is investment income in the hands of the taxpayer (*Walker* v *CCE* [1976] VATTR 10). The same applies to the letting of sixty to seventy garages by two taxpayers jointly (*Williamson (R W and A A W)* v *CCE* [1978] VATTR 90).

In the *Williamson* case the taxpayers were actively concerned in the management of the garages and letting them out to tenants for rent and not merely receiving rents therefrom. At p 100 of the decision it is stated:

> ... such activity is essentially a business activity of a very normal and usual kind: it is regular, conducted on sound and recognised business principles, with a structure which can be recognised as providing a familiar constitutional mechanism for carrying on a commercial undertaking and it has as its purpose the provision, for a consideration, of services which are of a type provided in the course of everyday life and commerce. In all these respects it competes in the market with other persons and concerns offering precisely similar services to the public at large.

Both the above cases, however, involved the taxpayers carrying out some degree of control and management over what the tenants did, which went beyond the concept of mere investment. In *Chandler (E A)* v *CCE* (LON/73/89) the appellant built a house on his land in which he intended to live. He intended to find another piece of land and sell the first house and perhaps carry through the same procedure again. It was held that he could not be registered for VAT because he was not carrying on a business.

In *Archer (R A)* v *CCE* [1974] VATTR 1, the appellant (an Associate of the Royal Institution of Chartered Surveyors and employed as the Projects Officer of Essex University) was going to build a house on land which he owned for his own occupation. His application to be registered for VAT was turned down. The Tribunal held that a degree of commercial activity was essential to the concept of carrying on a business.

12.1.4 Inputs and outputs

Each quarter the taxpayer usually has to render a return to the Commissioners of all his output tax, ie tax on supplies he has made. The taxpayer is entitled to a credit in calculating his final tax bill for his input tax for the period, ie tax on goods and services supplied to him. No distinction is made at present between capital or revenue supplies.

12.1.5 Zero-rated and exempt supplies

Some supplies may be zero-rated or exempt. If a person makes only exempt supplies he cannot reclaim his input tax. Where his supplies are zero-rated the trader calculates his output tax at zero and can claim back in full his input tax. A person who makes taxable and exempt supplies will be a partly exempt person so that he can only claim back part of his input tax.

12.1.6 Goods and services

Supplies are either of goods or of services. The provision of any form of power, heat, refrigeration or ventilation is a supply of goods. The granting, assignment or surrender of a major interest in land is a supply of goods. The sale or grant of a short lease or licence is a supply of services. The significance of the distinction is that a supply of services for no consideration is not taxable whereas a supply of goods could be taxable. The factors determining the time of supply are also different.

12.1.7 Time of supply

Where services or services together with goods are supplied in the course of the construction, alteration, demolition, repair or maintenance of a building or of any civil engineering work under a contract which provides for payments for such works to be made periodically or from time to time, a supply shall be treated as taking place at the earlier of the following times:

(*a*) when a payment is received by a supplier where the consideration for the contract is wholly in money; or

(*b*) when the supplier issues a tax invoice (VAT (General) Regulations 1985, reg 26)

Where the contract does not provide for payments for such services to be made periodically or from time to time the general rules concerning the time of supply contained in s 4 (time when goods delivered or services performed) and s 5 (if earlier, when invoice issued or payment made) apply.

When money is paid to the supplier by cheque it is likely to be 'received' for VAT purposes when the monies are credited to the account of the payee (see *Parkside Leasing Ltd* v *Smith* [1985] STC 63 at 69d; *Rampling* v *The Commissioners* (MAN/85/267).

The following is an extract from correspondence with Customs and Excise setting out their practice.

> It is currently the policy of Customs and Excise to accept that when payment is made by a cheque which is honoured, the payee is deemed to have received payment for VAT purposes on the date when the cheque was received, provided the cheque was presented for payment within the normal timescale for the particular business (ie presentation was not withheld, for example until after a particular job had been completed). If a cheque is post-dated, the payee is deemed to have received payment on the date of the cheque. If the cheque is dishonoured no payment is deemed to have been received.

See also C & E 700 Notice, Part V (Time of Supply (Tax Point)).

12.2 VAT—DID THOSE UP-FRONT PAYMENT SCHEMES WORK?

Prior to the introduction of VAT at 15 per cent on alteration works on and from 1 June 1984 taxpayers sought to pay their monies to builders and developers in advance—ie up-front—in order to ensure zero rating. Did those schemes ever work? The cases are now coming through. It seems clear that some arrangements did work whilst others did not.

12.2.1 VAT tribunal decisions

In the case of *Faith Construction Ltd* v *The Commissioners* (LON/85/522) the client borrowed money from a bank and paid this to the contractor before 1 June 1984 with the contractor then lending the money back to the client who used it to repay the initial borrowing by the client. Over the term of the building programme the client then borrowed again to repay the loan made by the builder. It was held that the transaction was effective and that VAT was not chargeable. The Customs raised arguments based on the *Ramsay* decision ([1981] STC 174) but that doctrine was held on the facts not to apply. A similar but less provocative arrangement was also held to be successful in the case of *Dolomite Double Glazing Ltd v The Commissioners* [1985] VATTR 184.

In *Goodyer* v *The Commissioners* (MAN/85/316) the client paid over the monies special terms to builder and obtained a bank guarantee from the builder's bank. Under the terms of the arrangement, however, the monies paid over to the builder prior to 1 June 1984 could only be released in stages over the term of the building period depending on the issue of the architect's certificates. It was held in this case that although the client had paid the money the builder had not received the same (until after 31 May 1984) and the scheme was therefore not effective in avoiding the 15 per cent VAT charge.

In *Double Shield Window Co Ltd* v *The Commissioners* (MAN/84/227), payments were made to a solicitor before 1 June 1984 who held the monies as a stakeholder. It was held that payments had only been received by the contractor after 1 June 1984 (so that VAT at 15 per cent was chargeable) as and when the solicitor received certificates of satisfaction and released the monies to the contractor. See also *Dann* v *Roden* (MAN/85/247).

Figure 12.1 VAT up-front payments (Double Shield's case)

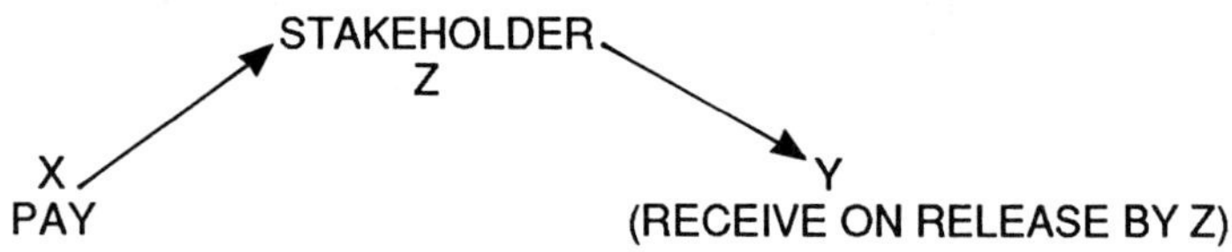

12.2.2 The High Court and the 1984 schemes

It seems that the High Court is taking a very favourable attitude, as far as taxpayers are concerned, with respect to the 1984 pre-payment schemes. The arrangements under which monies were effectively lent to the client who then used them to pay the builder up front (the monies being effectively lent by the builder) have not been struck down by the High Court and nor have the Customs been able to effectively apply the *Ramsay* doctrine to the same (see *The Commissioners* v *West Yorkshire Independent Hospital* (1988) STI 296 and *The Commissioners* v *Faith Construction Ltd* [1988] STC 35). Schemes under which monies are paid up front but subject to restrictions are also likely to achieve their objectives (*Dormers Builders (London) Ltd* v *The Commissioners* (1988) STI 339). These cases may be appealed.

Such decisions are critical for practitioners who are seeking to find an appropriate method of paying builders or developers 'up-front' before supplies of construction services relating to new non-domestic buildings become vatable after 31 March 1989 (see 12.38.4).

12.2.3 Terminology

The terminology in VAT is very confusing: your inputs are what you pay out and your outputs are what you get in and you do not bear VAT if you charge at the standard rate but you bear it fully if you are exempt.

One must identify and list the various supplies (for VAT purposes) which are being made and then identify the nature of those supplies (whether zero-rated etc). A project must be literally broken up into its various VAT components—leases, sales, licences, professional fees, finance, developers' profits, estate agent's fees, etc. Finally, one may be able to do some tax planning. Can an exempt supply be made zero-rated for instance and if so, what are the consequences?

12.3 FORGETTING TO CHARGE VAT CAN BE EXPENSIVE

If a taxpayer makes a supply and forgets to charge VAT or is not in a position to charge VAT over and above the charge he makes then he is deemed to have charged VAT and the amount of VAT is included in the charge he makes.

Thus if the taxpayer makes a supply for £100 of services one multiplies the £100 by 3/23 which equals £13. The amount of VAT payable is £13 and the value of the supply is £87.

Forgetting to charge VAT

$$£100 \times 3/23 = £13$$

A landlord may under the terms of his lease require a tenant to pay him an amount which covers the VAT on supplies of services *to* the landlord. However, that may not be good enough if the landlord is required to pay VAT on the services which he in turn makes to the tenant. Thus if a landlord who is not in a position to reclaim any VAT has repair services supplied to him of £100 plus £15 VAT he will have to bear the full cost. If under the terms of the lease he is entitled to a repayment of the £115 because it is effectively a service by the landlord to the tenant then the landlord must be in a position to charge VAT of £115 plus 15 per cent thereon (a total charge of £132.25) otherwise he will not have been effectively reimbursed for his outlay. See, however, **12.6** below.

12.4 THE IMPORTANT GROUP 8

Most land supplies will be exempt (Sched 6 Group 1 Item 1) although some are specifically made vatable at 15 per cent (Sched 6 Group 1 Item 1(*a*)–(*h*) and the EEC Sixth Directive, Article 13B(*b*)).

Schedule 5, Group 8 sets out details of the supplies which are zero-rated. This is a critically important Group. It comprises:

Item 1

The granting by a person constructing a building of a major interest in, or in any part of, the building or its site.

Item 2

The supply, in the course of the construction or demolition of any building or of any civil engineering work, of any services other than the services of any architect, surveyor or any person acting as a consultant or in a supervisory capacity.

Item 3

The supply by a person supplying services within Item 2 above and in connection with those services of materials or of other builders' hardware, sanitary ware or other articles of a kind ordinarily installed by builders as fixtures. A supply of the goods described includes any undivided share of the property or possession of the goods, and must be made by the person supplying the services within Item 2.

Special rules apply to listed buildings and are explained in 12.21.2.

12.5 APPROACH TO VAT

When seeking to resolve VAT problems practitioners should refer to UK legislation and statutory instruments, EEC Directives when necessary, Customs' Notices and Practice Statements and case law. The Customs have also agreed to a 'self imposed estoppel' ie they will not go back retrospectively on decisions or directions which they have unambiguously given in writing to tax payers (see Practice Note [1978] VATTR 278).

12.6 PROPERTY COMPANIES AND THE VAT PARTIAL EXEMPTION RULES

12.6.1 Partially exempt property companies have to get to grips with the new 1987 VAT regulations

The VAT (General) Amendment (No 2) Regulations 1987 (1987/510) amended the Value Added Tax (General) Regulations of 1985 (SI No 510). Useful guidance on the position can also be obtained from the Customs and Excise Notice 706 (April 1987) *'VAT: Partial Exemption'.*

12.6.2 Wholly referable supplies

Under the new rules a property company must identify the supplies which are made to it (reg 30(1)(*a*)), eg the supply of legal services by a solicitor to the property company. If the supplies made to the company are to be *wholly* used or are wholly used by that company in making taxable supplies then the input tax can be reclaimed (reg 30(1)(*b*)). However, if the supplies are to be wholly used or are wholly used by the taxpayer in making exempt supplies or in carrying on any activity other than the making of a taxable supply then the tax cannot be reclaimed (reg 30(1)(*c*)).

Example 12A: Wholly referable supplies

X Ltd is a property development company. It buys a parcel of land (parcel A) and incurs legal fees, planning costs, agents' fees, and fees in connection with securing vacant possession. VAT (input tax) is charged on those fees. Parcel A is sold without X Ltd having carried out any works to the same. The supply is an exempt supply by X Ltd. The VAT on the various fees cannot be reclaimed. X Ltd also bought parcel B. It incurred similar fees with VAT being charged thereon. However, in this case, X Ltd constructed a new building on the land and sold the same. Such a supply is a zero rated supply (VATA 1983, Sched 5, Group 8, Item 1) and the VAT on the fees can be reclaimed.

12.6.3 Overheads etc

Difficulties arise where VAT has been incurred on, say, legal fees and other matters and the supply made to the company is *not to be wholly used* or is not wholly used in making a taxable supply by the company. In this case reg 30(1)(*d*) requires the supplies made to the taxpayer, to the extent that they are used or are to be used by him in making taxable supplies, are to be ascertained and expressed as a proportion of the whole use made or to be made by him of such supplies. Thus an apportionment is necessary.

Example 12B: Overheads etc

A property company in its accounting year makes £100,000 worth of exempt supplies and £200,000 worth of zero rated supplies. It has overhead and other expenditure which does not wholly relate to either of those two supplies exclusively but relates to both of them. The company must seek to apportion those supplies made to it to the supplies made by it and it can claim an appropriate amount of input tax back. Thus if the overheads were £100 and the VAT £15 then it is *likely* that £10 of VAT can be reclaimed.

Example 12C: Short lease followed by sale

Y is a property company. It constructs a new building on its land and is capable of making a zero rated supply by the sale thereof (VATA 1983, Sched 5, Group 8). In its first year it reclaims all the VAT because it intends to make such a zero rated supply. In fact it lets the property on a short lease (lease not exceeding 21 years) and receives a rental of say £100,000 in total. In the fourth year it sells the freehold (a zero rated supply) for £900,000. The amount of input tax which it initially reclaimed was say £1,000. This was reclaimed on the assumption that it was going to make a zero rated supply. In fact an exempt supply, to the extent of £100,000 was made therefore it is possible the Customs would require Y Ltd to repay £100 of the £1,000 initially reclaimed (if not the full £1000).

12.6.4 Special schemes

The Customs and Excise have very wide powers to agree special schemes (see Customs and Excise Notice 706, paras 14, 15 and 16). They have generally agreed that with respect to VAT chargeable on overheads and the like the taxpayer can claim back a proportion of the input tax. The proportion is assessed 'using the ratio that the *input tax* directly attributable [to the taxpayer's] taxable supplied bears to [the taxpayer's] *total input tax'* (para 14 of the Notice). The Customs and Excise may also agree with the schemes which determine the amount of VAT (referable to overheads and the like) that can be reclaimed according to the supplies made by the taxpayer property company (rather than by the supplies made to it).

12.6.5 Adjustments within six years

As mentioned, if a taxpayer intends to make a zero rated supply he should be able to reclaim his VAT. If it subsequently turns out that he makes an exempt supply (for instance, instead of selling the freehold building which he had constructed he grants a lease not exceeding 21 years at a premium) then there are rules under which the taxpayer must repay the tax (or part thereof) which the Customs repaid to him. There is, however, a six year cut off period for this (see reg 34).

The converse can also arise. The taxpayer may think he is going to make an exempt supply and thus not reclaim his input tax. It may end up that he makes a zero rated supply in which case he can reclaim the VAT. Provided this is done within the six year period then there should be no difficulty with respect to the reclaim (see reg 35).

12.7 CONCLUSIONS

Taxpayers should see whether it is advisable to agree special schemes with Customs and Excise if this is likely to produce a more favourable tax result than if the general partial exemption rules were to be applied.

12.8 THE NEUVALE FACTOR

The cases of *Neuvale Limited* (LON/87/187) and *Frambeck Limited* (LON/87/188) (decision 2534) may have major repercussions for taxpayers who entered into tax planning arrangements prior to the introduction of the new partial exemption regulations in 1987.

In *Neuvale* the taxpayer carried out the taxable business of providing management services and the non-taxable business of letting properties (the supplies were exempt). Although in the particular tax year when input tax relating to the letting business was incurred there were only taxable outputs made by the company—provision of the management services—the Commissioners contended, following the decision of the House of Lords in *The Commissioners* v *Apple and Pear Development Council* [1986] STC 192, that one could not reclaim input tax referable to a proposed exempt supply even though the supply may amount to a business. VAT was concerned with taxable businesses.

Lord Grantchester accepted the Commissioners' contentions and held that the VAT referable to the letting business was not reclaimable. The point was also made that he did not see the taxpayers in the future making a vatable supply with respect to the letting business (p 16). It will be recollected that in the *Apple and Pear Development* case it was held that input tax is not deductable except in so far as the goods or services on which the tax had been levied were obtained for the purposes of the taxpayer's taxable transactions.

It may be that the *Neuvale* factor only applies where separate activities are being carried on—management services and letting for example. In a case where only one activity is carried on, possibly letting and building works may comprise one activity, it may be that the decision can be distinguished (*Spiers* v *Ogden* 17 TC 117).

12.8.1 HM Customs & Excise Statement on Neuvale (2/88)

Recent VAT Tribunal Cases (*Neuvale Ltd* and *Frambeck Ltd*) have called into question the extent to which, in cases prior to 1987, companies can claim input tax in relation to future exempt supplies. The Commissioners of Customs and Excise have given notice that, except where they think taxable supplies were made solely in order to recover input tax related to exempt supplies, they will not disallow claims for input tax (ie those based on *bona fide* supplies made for the purposes of the claimant's business).

It is a basic concept of VAT that the tax incurred on purchases of goods and services is recoverable as input tax only to the extent that those purchases are used, or are to be used, for the purpose of making taxable supplies. This concept is clear in the EEC Sixth Directive which provides the harmonised framework for the tax: and it was always the intention of UK law also. However, the way in which UK law was worded prior to FA 1987 led to the devising of various tax avoidance schemes which have succeeded in allowing businesses to deduct input tax in circumstances not envisaged or intended when the VAT law was originally enacted.

One of the intentions of the changes in the partial exemption rules introduced under FA 1987 was to restrict claims to input tax incurred in respect of exempt supplies made in a subsequent tax period, and it could therefore be inferred that such claims were allowable before 1 April 1987 when the changes took effect. The Commissioners of Customs and Excise do not dispute that such an inference can reasonably be drawn from their published guidance in force prior to the changes and indeed from the consultation document which preceded them. They do not seek to resile from what was said in these publications in those instances—the vast majority—where the taxable supplies on which the claim to input tax was based were *bona fide* supplies made for the purposes of the claimant's business. However, pending any further appeal by either *Neuvale Ltd* or *Frambeck Ltd,* they will not feel bound by what they have said in past publications in cases prior to the 1987 changes where the taxable supplies involved were, in their opinion, artificial and made solely as a device to obtain recovery of input tax related to exempt supplies.

In such cases they will feel free to deploy again the arguments they used in the cases of *Neuvale* and *Frambeck,* based on the judgments of the Court of Appeal and the House of Lords in the case of the *Apple and Pear Development Council* [see STI 190; (1986) STI]. In that case, Fox LJ in the Court of Appeal, made it clear that 'a person who conducts an activity in which he neither makes nor intends to make taxable supplies cannot claim credits for inputs in respect of that activity'.

12.9 THE EUROPEAN COURT OF JUSTICE HAS SPOKEN—VAT ON INDUSTRIAL AND COMMERCIAL BUILDINGS

In *Commission of the European Communities* v *United Kingdom* (Case 416/85) (*Times,* 22 June 1988 and [1988] STC 456) the European Court of Justice held that the UK government must introduce legislation requiring VAT to be charged by builders and developers on the construction of new commercial and industrial buildings and civil engineering works. VAT, however, will not be charged with respect to the construction of buildings intended for housing. *The legislation implementing these new rules will not apply to payments made before 1 April 1989.* The proposed position is dealt with in detail at 12.37 contained in statements in Parliament and in a consultative document.

12.10 CAPITAL GOODS—INPUT TAX DEDUCTION

As well as the new legislation to incorporate the European Court decision into UK statutory law the Customs issued some time ago a Consultation Document (News Release No 9/88) dealing with situations where companies acquire capital goods. Capital goods would exclude trading stock and repair works done to capital goods. The European Court of Justice has ruled that capital goods are goods used for the purposes of some business activity and distinguishable by their durable nature and their value and such that the acquisition costs are not normally treated as current expenditure, but are written off over several years.

The investment properties of a property investment company are liable to comprise capital goods. Such a company may buy an investment property and use it to make taxable supplies and then some years later make exempt supplies. The question is: how much input tax on the acquisition should be reclaimable? The Customs propose that the initial VAT reclaim portion should be adjusted by reference to transactions carried out with respect to the property within five years (or possibly ten years) from (broadly) acquisition. It seems to the author that the 1985 Regulations (as amended) and the proposed changes consequent on the European Court decision could largely cover any 'abuses' by taxpayers in this area. Nevertheless, the 1985 Regulations (as amended) are not easily applied where capital property is let or owner–occupied and subsequently sold, so that perhaps new legislation would be useful in clarifying the position. The following example taken from para 16 of the Consultation Document shows how the proposed new rules—if they reach the statute book—will apply to the disposal after it has been owner–occupied of a property assuming a five year adjustment period is chosen.

12.10.1 Exempt sale or transfer during the period of adjustment

Some supplies of capital goods may be exempt supplies (eg certain supplies of buildings). When such capital goods are disposed of during the adjustment period by way of exempt supply, no output tax is chargeable but the seller will make an adjustment to his input tax. The whole period of adjustment still to be covered will be regarded as if the goods had been applied in the business to fully exempt use.

For example, if an item which on acquisition cost £40,000 plus £6,000 VAT is put to fully taxable use in the first three years and then sold (exempt supply), the position would be as follows:

(*a*) £6,000 recovery of input tax on acquisition (100 per cent taxable use).

(*b*) No adjustments required for years two and three (no change of use).

(*c*) Final input tax adjustment on sale: £2,400 due to Customs.

(*d*) $\left(\frac{6,000}{5} \times 100 \text{ per cent} \times 2\right)$.

(*e*) Exempt supply—no output tax due.

Note that capital goods acquired before 1 April 1989 will not be affected by the new rules. It is not envisaged that the new rules will be implemented before 1 April 1989. The Customs would like any representations with respect to the new rules to reach them by 31 August 1988.

12.11 'SELF IMPOSED' ESTOPPEL

The Customs have agreed to a self imposed estoppel, ie they will not go back retrospectively on decisions or directions which they have unambiguously given in writing to taxpayers or if they have misled a trader (see Practice Note 1978 (VATTR 278)).

The Customs have agreed the following:

PRACTICE NOTE

Assessment contrary to previous ruling by Commissioners

The following is the text of a written question and answer in the House of Commons (*Hansard,* vol 161, 21 July 1978, col 426):

Mr Peter Rees asked the Chancellor of the Exchequer whether it is the policy of the Commissioners of Her Majesty's Customs and Excise to assess a registered person to value added tax contrary to advice previously given by them.

Mr Robert Sheldon: When it is established that an officer of Customs and Excise, with the full facts before him, has given a clear and unequivocal ruling on VAT in writing; or it is established that an officer knowing the full facts has misled a trader to his detriment, the Commissioners of Customs and Excise would only raise an assessment based on the correct ruling from the date the error was brought to the attention of the registered person concerned.

12.12 FURNISS V DAWSON AND VAT

The *Furniss* v *Dawson* doctrine is an anti–tax avoidance rule of interpretation created by the House of Lords in *Ramsay* v *IRC* [1981] STC 174. It reached, perhaps, its most articulated exposition in the decision of *Furniss* v *Dawson* [1983] STC 153. See 1.4.5.

12.12.1 Applicability of the doctrine to VAT

National Coal Board v *CCE*
It was thought at one time that the doctrine might not apply to VAT. In *National Coal Board* v *CCE* [1982] STC 863, Woolf J at 865 stated:

> There is no suggestion in this case that, although their motive was a desire to avoid payment of tax, the alterations which were made to the mineworkers' scheme were not genuine or that since they were made the scheme, as amended, has not reflected the reality of how the scheme was operated and, in the circumstances of this case, it was wrong for the tribunal to have taken into account this alleged motive of the Board in coming to its decision. In these circumstances, the question of whether or not VAT is payable must be judged objectively having regard to the terms of the schemes and the activities performed by the Board.

Spigot Lodge Ltd v *CCE*
This case was followed in the VAT Tribunal case of *Spigot Lodge Ltd* v *CCE* [1983] VATTR 221, where the Tribunal stated at p 225 that they accepted the submission of the counsel for the taxpayer 'that the objective test must be applied and that the motive to reduce (the taxpayer's) liability to tax should be ignored'.

In the High Court (*Spigot Lodge Ltd* v *CCE* [1985] STC 255) Hodgson J at 259 stated: 'The motive (for the relevant tax avoidance transaction) it is accepted, is irrelevant'.

However, in the High Court decision of *CCE* v *Faith Construction Ltd* [1988] STC 36 it was not argued that the doctrine could not apply to VAT although it was held on the facts of the particular case not to apply. One may therefore assume that the doctrine will apply to VAT planning arrangements but note the West Yorkshire Hospital case at 454d.

Part II Property Transactions Vatable at 15 Per Cent

12.13 INTRODUCTION

Section 1 of VATA 1983 states:

> A tax, to be known as value added tax, shall be charged in accordance with the provisions of this Act on the supply of goods and services in the United Kingdom (including anything treated as such a supply) and on the importation of goods into the United Kingdom.

That is the critical charging section.

Supplies which do not fall within the definitions of zero-rated or exempt supplies and which are not expressly disregarded for VAT purposes will be chargeable to VAT at 15 per cent. In addition, the following are specifically excluded from exemption in Schedule 6 Group 1 and it is very unlikely that any of these can be brought within the zero-rated item in Schedule 5. They are important vatable heads and should not be overlooked.

Hotels etc

(*a*) The provision of accommodation in an hotel, inn, boarding house or similar establishment of sleeping accommodation in rooms which are provided in conjunction therewith or for the purpose of a supply of catering;

Holiday accommodation

(*a*)(*a*) The provision in a house, flat, caravan or houseboat, of holiday accommodation.

Caravans and tents

(*b*) The granting of facilities for camping in tents or caravans.

Car parks

(*c*) The granting of facilities for parking a vehicle.

Fishing and game

(*d*) The granting of any right to take game or fish.

Timber

(*e*) The granting of any right to fell and remove standing timber.

Mooring

(*f*) The granting of facilities for housing, or storage of, an aircraft or for mooring and storage of a ship, boat or vessel.

Exhibition stands

(*g*) The provision to an exhibitor of a site or space at any exhibition or similar event, organised wholly or mainly for the display or advertisement of goods or services (to be abolished: see below).

Sports facilities

(*h*) The granting of facilities for playing any sport or participating in any physical recreation.

The basis of the above vatable heads is to be found in the EEC Sixth Directive, Article 13B(*b*). Heads (*a*), (aa), and (*b*) implement Article 13B(*b*)(1). Head (*c*) implements Article 13B(*b*)(2) which provides that 'the letting of premises and sites for parking vehicles' is vatable at 15 per cent. It may be that the granting of car parking facilities which do not amount to a letting or leasing of immovable property do not and cannot fall within this vatable head (so that the supply should be exempt unless the Article 13C option can be exercised).

Note also that under Article 13B the UK *can* (it is optional) add other heads to those four heads listed in Article 13B(*b*) and the heads (*c*) to (*h*) above have been so added. Note also that under Article 13B(*b*)(3) and (4) lettings of permanently installed equipment and machinery and the hire of safes comprise vatable (15 per cent) supplies. It is clear that Article 13B(*b*) is not well drafted; it relates only to the leasing or letting of immovable property but it excludes from its ambit the *hire* (which may be different from leasing and letting) of safes (which are unlikely to be immovable property unless the word is to have a very wide meaning).

Finally it is *proposed* in the Consultative Document of 22/7/88 see page 263 that (*g*) above will be deleted so that VAT at 15 per cent need not be charged.

Exhibition organisers will be able to use the option facility (the Article 13C option) (see p 261) if they wish to tax their supplies of space and stands to exhibitors. Otherwise the above heads are not affected by any proposed changes in the next Finance Act.

12.14 VAT AND CAR PARKING FACILITIES

Taxpayers must remember to charge VAT in leases where 'Parking Facilities' are provided. An omission to have a VAT charging clause in a long lease in cases where VAT is chargeable can be an unmitigated catastrophe.

12.14.1 Law and practice

A landlord must charge VAT where he grants facilities for parking a vehicle. VATA 1983, Sched 6, Item 1(*c*) states just that. A supply of parking facilities is made, the Customs accept, only if there is a specific and distinguishable grant and the sole or essential purpose of the grant is the provision of car parking facilities.

Landlords should ensure that they have the power to charge VAT if needs be.

Practitioners must refer to Customs leaflet No 701/24/84 for the current view of the Customs.

12.14.2 Charge VAT

(*a*) A landlord must charge VAT if he lets parking spaces or lock-garages, unless he lets them in conjunction with the letting of domestic accommodation.

(*b*) A landlord must charge VAT if he grants the right to a tenant to park a vehicle in a commercial car park or garage or, for example, in the grounds of a factory or office block, whether or not a specific site is allocated.

(*c*) The landlord must charge VAT if he lets a building or land where the lease stipulates that it must be used solely for vehicle parking unless exceptionally it is actually let to a car park operator in which case the car park operator would charge VAT to the users and the landlord would not charge VAT.

12.14.3 Do not charge VAT

(*d*) VAT need not be charged if the landlord lets land and buildings for commercial use where the lease stipulates that vehicle parking is just one of two or more uses to which the landlord's buildings are to be put.

(*e*) VAT need not be charged if the landlord lets a garage in conjunction with the letting of a house or flat; the letting can be covered by a single agreement or by separate agreements and can provide for a combined or separate rent; however, the house or flat and the garage must be in reasonable proximity to each other and the lettings must be by the same landlord to the same tenant.

(*f*) VAT need not be charged if the landlord lets land or buildings not primarily intended for vehicle parking and where the lease makes no reference to this use but the lessor takes advantage of land covered by the lease for vehicle parking—for example, the forecourt of an office block.

12.15 VAT ON CONTRIBUTIONS BY LANDLORDS (GLENEAGLES)

If a landlord is proposing to make contributions towards improvement or repair or indeed new construction expenditure to be laid out by an incoming tenant then the VAT implications following the recent case of *Gleneagles Hotel Plc* v *The Commissioners of Customs and Excise* (LON/85/473—report no 2152) must be considered although it is likely to be the tenant who will bear the brunt of the VAT problems.

In the *Gleneagles Hotel* case, L granted a lease to T and there was an agreement that T would carry out various works to the property including repair and re-equipment works and L would contribute £1.4m towards the expenditure (anticipated to be £7.5m). (See fig overleaf).

There were no provisions in the documentation for VAT so that if VAT was chargeable the payment of £1.4m would be deemed to be VAT inclusive.

12.15.1 The arguments

The Customs argued that VAT was payable as T provided the service to L of taking on the underlease with all its benefits and burdens. The analysis was akin to that of a reverse premium payment which is generally accepted by tax practitioners as being chargeable to VAT. Certainly the Customs take the view that reverse premiums are vatable.

The taxpayer argued that there was no provision of services by T, the tenant; the developer carried out the works on the property for T and L provided some of the money, but in no real sense could one say that T did anything for which he received consideration.

12.15.2 The decision

Lord Grantchester, the Tribunal Chairman, was impressed by neither argument and held that although one could not precisely identify the same, effectively T agreed to provide more beneficial terms in the lease to L because of the contribution of £1.4m by L. It was unrealistic to consider otherwise because this was a commercial arrangement with neither party intending to make gifts to the other. If the contribution had not been made then the benefits provided by T to L would have been lower. Lord Grantchester stated (at p 12):

> . . . I take the view that the £1.4m was a consideration provided by the landlord for the tenant agreeing to provide more valuable benefits under the contract and the underlease (as varied by the letter) than it otherwise would have done.

12.15.3 Consequences

The agreements providing those more valuable benefits was a provision of a service by T to L for which consideration was received by T, therefore VAT was chargeable.

Because there was no clause in the underlease or agreement enabling the tenant to charge VAT on top of the contribution, the contribution was deemed to be VAT inclusive (VATA 1983, s 10(2)) and therefore the tenant would have to bear the VAT and must account for the same to the Customs and Excise.

If L could not claim the VAT back this would result in a real loss in VAT terms.

12.15.4 Warning

Clearly parties entering into arrangements where the landlord is to contribute towards the tenant's expenditure must appreciate the VAT penalty which may arise in consequence of this case.

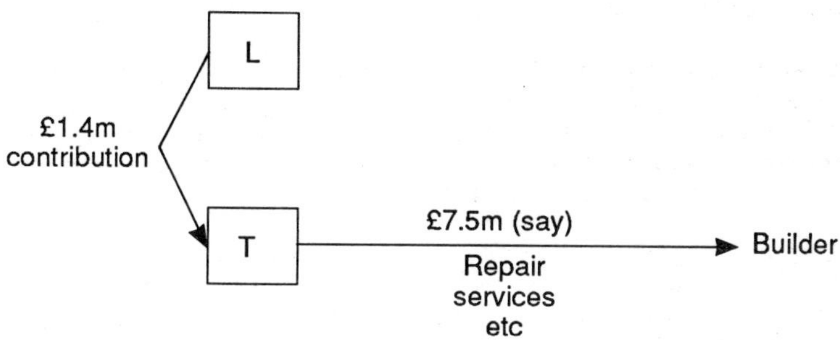

Note:

(*a*) The £1.4m was vatable. The payment was VAT inclusive.

(*b*) The decision would have been the same whether or not VAT was chargeable on the £7.5m supply by the builder.

(*c*) The future changes in the law are unlikely to alter the effects of this decision.

12.16 VAT ON CONTRIBUTIONS BY LANDLORD (NEVILLE RUSSELL)

If a landlord makes any sort of payment to an incoming tenant it is important that the parties carefully take into account the value added tax position following the recent case of *Neville Russell* v *The Commissioners* (LON/86/708).

In the above case the landlord, the Norwich Union Life Insurance Company, made payments to Neville Russell, a firm of Chartered Accountants. Norwich Union also gave them a period of rent reduction, in connection with Neville Russell's agreement to take a lease from the Norwich Union of 266 Bishopsgate.

The facts of the case were quite complicated because two properties were involved and there were some difficult conclusions on the facts but on the author's understanding of the decision the following general principles can be extracted.

12.16.1 Agreeing to undertake works (vatable)

If a landlord makes a payment to an incoming tenant, in consideration of the tenant undertaking to ensure that necessary refurbishment and other works are carried out to the premises, then the payment is vatable.

Example 12D: payment to cover refurbishment expenditure

L is the freeholder of 'green' building. £100,000 of refurbishment works need to be carried out to the building. T agrees to take a lease of the same. T agrees to carry out the refurbishment works (or employ a builder or developer to do the same) in consideration of L paying T £100,000. That £10,000 is vatable.

12.16.2 Inducement payments (vatable)

If a landlord pays monies to a potential tenant (T) in order to persuade T to accept a lease of 'yellow' building then the payment will be vatable.

Example 12E: inducement payment

L wishes to let premises to T. T is concerned that he is liable to pay the rents and his business in the future may not be prosperous enough to afford the rents. In order to induce T to take the lease L pays T £200,000. That sum will be vatable. Lord Grantchester in the *Neville Russell* case at p 18 stated:

> I am left with the question of whether a payment of a sum of money by a tenant in consideration of the acceptance by him of the lease to him of the demised premises is a supply of services for tax purposes . . . In my opinion the acceptance by a tenant of the lease of the demised premises involves the execution of the counterpart lease and the acceptance of the grant. In my opinion, this is something done. Further, in my view where a sum of money is paid for that to be done as in the present case, it is the supply of services for a consideration for tax purposes. I express this opinion solely in relation to an acceptance of a lease for a monetary consideration attributed or attributable to such acceptance.

12.16.3 Rent free period or rent reduction period (not vatable)

If a landlord seeks to induce a tenant to take a lease of premises by giving the tenant a rent free period or a period where the rent is reduced to half that of the market rent or what the parties consider the market rent to be then that reduction will *not* give rise to a vatable supply.

Example 12F: rent reduced period

L wishes to induce T to take a lease of 'blue' building. T is reluctant but L agrees to charge half the full rent for the first year of the lease. As a result of that T takes the lease. No VAT is charged on that rent reduction (see fig 12.2 below).

Lord Grantchester in the *Neville Russell* case held that the rent reduction could not be vatable, following the case of *National Coal Board* v *The Commissioners* [1982] STC 863.

Figure 12.2 Payments to Tenant

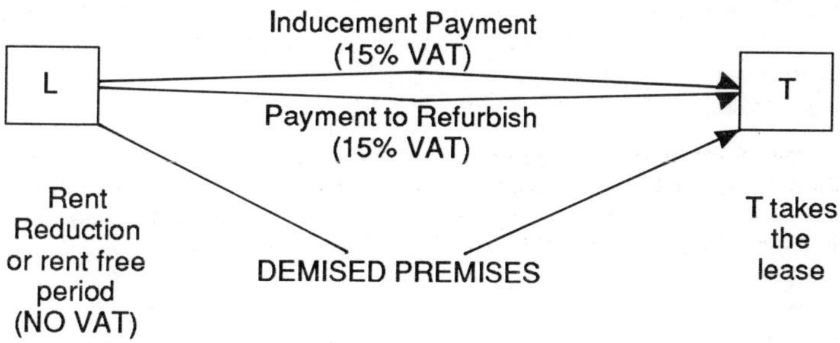

It must be noted that the above examples assume that any payments received by the tenant would result from services carried out in the course or furtherance of the business of the tenant and that the payments exceed the registration limits. Also note that the decision may be appealed against. Also note that the future changes in the law (see 12.37) are unlikely to affect this decision.

12.17 ENSURING THE LANDLORD DOES NOT LOSE

A landlord may consider it prudent to ensure that if VAT is charged on any supplies made by him to the tenant that he will be able to charge VAT over and above the charge which he would otherwise make.

It may be prudent to ensure that any clause enabling VAT to be charged refers to all the supplies which are made by the landlord to the tenant including rent, service charges, reimbursements of landlord's costs paid to solicitor for agreeing to assignments or variations etc. In this case should a particular service be found to be vatable or should VAT be imposed on those services in the future the landlord will have safeguarded his position expressly.

The type of clause could be similar to that set out below:

> **Value Added Tax**
>
> 1 In the event that Value Added Tax shall be chargeable on the Landlord in respect of any supplies made to the Tenant the Tenant shall in addition to any amounts otherwise payable pay to the Landlord the amount of the Value Added Tax so chargeable.

If there is no such clause VATA 1983, s 42 may assist in many cases. It provides that where, after the making of a contract for the supply of goods or services and before the goods or services are supplies, there is a change in the tax charged on the supply, then, unless the contract otherwise provides, there shall be added to or deducted from the consideration for the supply an amount equal to the change. References in this section to a change in the tax charged on a supply include references to a change to or from no tax being charged on the supply; this prevents the taxpayer arguing that if the tax charge is reduced from 15 per cent to nil in a particular case that the provision does not apply because there is no 'change'; there is an 'elimination' not a change.

12.18 PREMIUMS AND VAT

The present VAT position with regard to lease premiums is set out below. It should be noted that regardless of the nature of a premium a person will not be liable for VAT if his vatable supplies do not exceed the registration limits. Nor will a person be liable to VAT if he does not carry on a business. The likely future position with respect to premiums is contained in 12.37.

(*a*) A grants a lease at a premium of property and he did not construct the building on the property. The premium will be exempt.

(*b*) B constructed the building on the land and grants lease of over 21 years. The premium or rents will be zero rated.

(*e*) D is a freeholder. It pays E, its tenant, £100,000 in consideration of E surrendering its 99 year lease to D. That would be an exempt supply of land by E even though E may have been the person who constructed the building because the Customs would contend that a surrender does not amount to the grant of a major interest within VATA 1983, Sched 5, Group 8. In that case E may want to assign the lease for consideration to say a subsidiary of D in order to ensure that E obtains zero rated monies.

(*f*) F who is a tenant of land assigns his onerous lease to G and pays G £100,000 to take over the onerous lease. That payment would have been made as consideration for the acceptance of the assignment by the assignee (G) and the Customs take the view, probably correctly, that that would be a vatable supply; thus VAT at 15 per cent must be charged.

(*g*) G has granted H a 15 year lease. G subsequently agrees with H that he will pay H £10,000 if H agrees to the insertion of a new rent review clause in the lease. H so agrees and is so paid. The supply, in the author's opinion, is exempt. H has granted an interest *in his lease* to the landlord.

For the position with respect to possible future changes see 12.37.

12.19 SALE AND LEASEBACK

The position as to whether a sale and leaseback comprises a total disposal in the first instance with a subsequent disposal by the purchaser (X) back to the vendor (Y) or whether in fact there is only a part disposal by the vendor (Y) is not entirely free from doubt. In *Nichols* v *IRC* [1975] STC 278 the Court of Appeal held that where X transfers a free hold to Y by way of gift and there is a condition in the gift that Y grants a leaseback to X there is a total gift with a transfer back rather than a part disposal (see Goff J at 285a and also see the cases referred to at pages 282, 283 and 284 of the judgment).

On the other hand the case of *Sargaison* v *Roberts* (1969) 45 TC 612 (a case dealing with agricultural capital allowances) indicates that a gift or sale with a leaseback could amount to a part disposal.

If the taxpayer constructed the building and sold the freehold for a capital sum taking a leaseback, then that capital sum should give rise to a zero-rated supply. Thereafter, as a matter of strict law it may be argued that any rents from sub-lettings by the taxpayer would be exempt. It appears, however, that the CCE may permit the rents to be zero-rated provided the sale and leaseback takes place on the same day under the terms of an all embracing agreement.

Example 12G: Sale and leaseback and VAT

X constructs a building on its freehold land. The supplies to X would be zero-rated by the builder. When X sells the freehold to Y, a pension fund, that will be a zero-rated supply. The leaseback by Y (the pension fund) would be an exempt supply because Y had not constructed the building. Any sublease by X may be treated by the Customs and Excise if the sublease (and not just an agreement for sublease) is a major interest, as giving rise to zero-rated supplies.

If the taxpayer had not constructed the building then the sale to the pension fund would amount to an exempt supply, the leaseback would be an exempt supply and any sublettings regardless of the length of the term or terms would be exempt.

With respect to the proposed changes see 12.37.

12.20 DAMAGES (DAMAGES PAID TO LANDLORD FOR BREACH OF COVENANT)

The payment of damages can give rise to charges to VAT. X may supply furniture to Y for £100,000 plus VAT. Y may refuse to pay and X may sue for damages. VAT would be chargeable on the damages. If that were not the case there would be a coach and horses through the legislation.

12.20.1 Damages—settlements in general

Customs have reviewed their policy on the VAT treatment of payments made under out-of-court settlements of disputes, after proceedings have been commenced by service of originating process (or appointment of an arbitrator) (News Release No 82/87).

They now take the view that, where such payments are in essence compensatory and do not relate directly to supplies of goods or services, they are outside the scope of VAT. This will be so even if the settlement is expressed in terms that the payment is consideration for the plaintiff's agreement to abandon his rights to bring legal proceedings. But payments will remain taxable if, and to the extent that, they are the consideration for specific taxable supplies by the plaintiff, eg where the dispute concerns payment for an earlier supply, or where the plaintiff grants future rights to exploit copyright material under the settlement.

These changes of policy will be applied from 19 November 1987.

Customs had previously taken the view that all payments under out-of-court settlements were generally taxable. The revised VAT liability brings the VAT treatment of out-of-court settlements into line with the VAT treatment of payments under court orders.

12.20.2 Damages paid to landlord for breach of covenant

In *Elite Investments Ltd* v *TI Bainbridge Silencers Ltd (No 2)* (1987) STI 722, the plaintiffs claimed a sum in respect of value added tax at 15 per cent of the amount awarded in an earlier action (*Elite Investments Ltd* v *TI Bainbridge Silencers Ltd* [1986] 2 EGLR 43) representing the cost of repairs to premises which the defendant had failed to carry out as tenants of those premises. The plaintiff company was not registered for value added tax and would not have been able to recover the tax incurred if it undertook the repairs directly. That company was the assignee of the claim of the original landlord entitled to the benefit of the tenant's covenants. The original company was not registered for value added tax as it had been ordered to be wound up in 1985.

In the earlier case of *Drummond* v *S & U Stores Ltd* (1980) 258 EG 1293) Glidewell J decided that an individual landlord was entitled to recover, in addition to the cost of repairs, an amount equal to the value added tax, if any of the options open to the landlord involved incurring such tax in circumstances in which it could not be recovered.

The defendant argued that the landlord, although not registered for value added tax, could, for example, require the repairs to be carried out by a new tenant who was registered and could therefore recover the tax incurred.

Judge Paul Baker QC held that an amount could be claimed in respect of value added tax if, looking at the evidence as a whole, there was some realistic option open to the landlord for repairing the premises which would throw the burden of the value added tax in respect of the cost of those repairs onto the landlord. The option which gave this result need not be the landlord's only or probable choice; the court would not assess the likelihood of the burden falling on the landlord and discount the amount to allow for the possibility of the tax being recovered. However, in the present case, several months had elapsed since the compensation had been paid and no repairs had been carried out. In the absence of evidence as to the plaintiff's intentions, the carrying out of the repairs by the plaintiff directly was not apparently being considered as a realistic option. Accordingly this was not a case where a further amount in respect of value added tax could be added to the amount claimed.

Thus to summarise. If it can be shown that a landlord who is suing a tenant for breach of a repairing covenant will be imposing, or is likely to be imposing, the obligation to do the works on a new tenant (by, for instance, giving an appropriate rent reduction) and that new tenant can claim back any VAT charged by the repairer, the landlord may not be able to add a sum equal to the VAT to his compensation entitlement. If it is the case that the landlord will be bearing, or is likely to be bearing, the repair expenditure and he cannot reclaim the VAT charged thereon by the repairer then a sum equal to the VAT may be added to the compensation figure. The above cases give the critical guidance as to what side of the line any particular case is likely to fall.

Part III Zero Rating

12.21 CONSTRUCTION OF NEW BUILDINGS

12.21.1 Construction of new buildings and zero rated supplies

The relevant legislation *as it presently stands* is contained in Schedule 5, Group 8. Item 1 of the group provides that the granting by a person constructing a building of a major interest in or in any part of the building or its site will be a zero rated supply. Items 2 and 3 provide that the supply in the course of the construction or demolition of any building of any services and appropriate materials will be zero rated.

However, the references in Items 2 and 3 above to the supply in the course of the construction or demolition of any building do not include an alteration or enlargement of any existing building and the reference in Item 1 above to a person constructing a building shall be construed accordingly (Note 1A). Note also that Schedule 5, Group 8, Notes (1A)(*b*), provides that any extension or annexation to an existing building which provides for internal access to the existing building or of which the separate use, letting or disposal is prevented by the terms of any covenant, statutory planning consent or similar permission will not result in the construction of a new building. Supplies in connection with such works will therefore be vatable.

Thus, with respect to Item 1, if X Ltd constructs a building on its freehold land, X Ltd will not be able to make a zero rated supply if that new building results from the conversion, reconstruction, alteration or enlargement of any existing building; there are thus two tests to be satisfied. The first is a positive one and the second is a negative one: there must be a new building created (the first test) and that new building must not result from the conversion, reconstruction, alteration or enlargement of any existing building (the second test). Schedule 5, Group 8, Noted (1A)(*b*) must also not be offended.

Similarly, with regard to Items 2 and 3, it is necessary for X Ltd to construct or demolish a building and the reference to construction does not include a situation where a new building results from the conversion, reconstruction, alteration or enlargement of any existing building.

Under the *proposed changes* (see 12.37) Item 2, of Group 8, Schedule 5, will be amended to remove from zero-rating services in the course of:

(*a*) the construction of a non-domestic building;

(*b*) the construction or demolition of a civil engineering work; and

(*c*) the demolition of any building.

The Customs have asked for comments on how domestic and non-domestic buildings should be defined (see p 100).

Thus it is clear that the provision in Group 8, Item 2 (and 3) will remain intact with respect to new *domestic* buildings except that the demolition of any building will always be vatable at 15 per cent.

The above future changes will take effect from 1 April 1989. The normal transitional rules will apply for establishing tax points in the circumstances of a change from the zero-rate to the standard rate; these are set out in the Appendix F of the VAT Guide (Notice 700 October 1987). However, in addition work done or payments received under a written contract signed *and sealed* prior to 21 June 1988 will remain eligible for zero-rating under the existing law as a special transitional relief even if the relevant tax points would otherwise be on or after 1 April 1989 (see 12.37).

With respect to the sales of freeholds and the grants of long leases the position with respect to non-domestic buildings is to be fundamentally changed with effect (subject to transitional provisions) from 1 April 1989. The supplies will either be vatable at 15 per cent or exempt. Developers and landlords are also to get the Article 13C option which is very important. The position with respect to the letting and sale of new domestic buildings is unchanged. See 12.37.

12.21.2 Value Added Tax Act 1983, Schedule 5, Group 8A—protected buildings

Item 1 zero rates the granting, by a person substantially reconstructing a protected building, of a major interest in, or in any part of, the building or its site.

Item 2 (taken with the amendments made to Item 3 of Group 8 mentioned above made by FA 1984, s 10) zero rates the supply of goods and appropriate materials made 'in the course of an approved alteration of a protected building'.

Protected building means a building which is a listed building within the meaning of the Town and Country Planning Act (TCPA) 1971.

The meaning of building when used with the word listed in Group 8A is capable of and does in this particular case have a different meaning to the word building as used in Group 8. Building when used with the word listed in Group 8A means a building as designated by TCPA 1971; building used in Group 8 has a meaning assigned to that term in the context of the VAT legislation and not the TCPA legislation.

Even if a building is substantially reconstructed within Item 1, the taxpayer will still not make a zero rated supply unless either of the two conditions set out in Note 2 to Group 8A are satisfied. These conditions are:

(*a*) that more than 60 per cent of the actual cost of the building operations is attributable to approved alterations;

(*b*) the reconstructed building incorporates no more of the original building than the external walls, together with other external features of architectural or historic interest.

It should be noted that under Group 8A, Items 2 and 3 only supplies in the course of an approved alteration are zero rated. Approved alteration means works of alteration which may not be carried out unless authorised under, or under any provision of, TCPA 1971, Part IV.

Note 6 (to Group 8A) states that alteration does not include repair or maintenance. Additionally Note 6 states that where any work consists partly of an approved alteration and partly of other work (not necessarily limited to repair or maintenance) an apportionment should be made to determine the supply which falls within Items 2 and 3.

It is also to be noted in Items 2 and 3 that a reference is only made to an approved alteration; no reference as such is made to demolition (see below).

12.21.3 Town and Country Planning Act 1971

TCPA 1971, s 54(9) provides that a listed building means 'a building which is for the time being included in a list compiled or approved by the Secretary of State'.

TCPA 1971, s 55(1) states:

> . . . if a person executes or causes to be executed any works for the demolition of a listed building or for its alteration or extension in any manner which would affect its character as a building of special architectural or historic interest, and the works are not authorised under (Part IV) of this Act, he shall be guilty of an offence.

There are contained in s 55 various provisions setting out how consent, referred to as listed building consent, is to be given for works of demolition, alteration and extension.

It is noted that this legislation draws a distinction between alteration and extension. Group 8A, Items 2 and 3 and Note 3 thereto refer only to alterations; the reference to demolition and extension in TCPA 1971 is not incorporated into VATA 1983, Schedule 5, Group 8A and the contrast can also be made with Group 8, Item 2 of VATA 1983, Schedule 5 where there is an express reference to demolition. It may be that a partial demolition is not a demolition of a building within that legislation so that partial demolition will amount to an alteration. However, nothing in practice should turn on this point.

There has been one case on the interpretation of Group 8A, Schedule 5, VATA 1983.

The taxpayer in *Barraclough* v *The Commissioners* (LON/86/699), carried out works of alteration to listed buildings plus enlargements. The enlargements required listed building consent but the other works did not. It was held that there was no substantial reconstruction but only a minor enlargement of the building and a modernisation of its interior. In order to see whether the 3/5ths test was satisfied one had to contrast the works of approved alterations with the total cost of reconstruction. The test was failed.

12.21.4 H M Customs & Excise leaflets

VAT Leaflet 708/1/85: Protected buildings (1 February 1985)
There is an indication (although it is ambiguous) that extensions, alterations and demolition may effectively fall within the term alterations for the purposes of the listed building provisions. This indication is in para 3. There is a stronger indication in para 16(*b*) (dealing with evidence) that demolition will be treated as zero rated.

VAT Leaflets 708/2/85: Construction Industry (1 November 1985)
Paragraph 4 sets out the Customs & Excise test to determine whether a new building has been constructed. The taxpayer is to ask himself:—'Am I constructing an entirely new building or am I doing something to a building which already exists?' If the answer is, (so the Customs state): 'I am converting, reconstructing, altering or enlarging an existing building', then there will be no zero rating.

The way the Customs & Excise pose the relevant questions are different from the questions which should be posed as a matter of law. It seems to the author that Group 8, Item 1 requires the taxpayer to ask:

(*a*) Am I constructing a new building?

(*b*) If I am constructing a new building does the new building result from the converting, reconstructing, altering or enlarging of an existing building? If 'Yes' then VAT is chargeable, if 'No' then the works are zero rated.

The Customs & Excise effectively combine the two questions into one; they seem to take the view that if the taxpayer is converting, reconstructing, altering or enlarging an existing building then he is not *ipso facto* constructing a new building. It does not seem that much will turn on this particular point in many cases in practice.

The Customs in para 4(*b*) of the leaflet consider that the following *inter alia* are zero rated:

(*a*) the construction of a building making use of a part or all of the foundations of an existing building, where the former building has been demolished to foundation level;

(*b*) the construction of a building making use of what remains of an existing building where this is limited to a single wall such as a front facade, or to a single wall plus all or part of the foundations, or to a single continuous facade covering two walls on a corner site;

(*c*) the building onto an existing house of another house to form two separate semi-detached houses with no inter-connecting doors;

(*d*) the building of a new house within an existing terrace of houses on the site of a house that has been totally demolished.

It seems to the author that the above examples are intended to be mutually exclusive.

Under the proposed changes (see 12.37) Item 2 of Group 8A will be amended to remove zero-rating services in the course of the approved alteration of a non-domestic protected building. Where a building or a protected building is to be used for both non-domestic and domestic purposes, contractors and sub-contractors will have to standard rate the non-domestic element and zero-rate the domestic element by means of a fair and reasonable apportionment of the total price for the whole job.

Comments were invited by the Customs on how a domestic or non-domestic building should be defined so as to comply with the terms of the European Court's judgment (see 12.35).

Note also that all demolition work will be vatable at 15 per cent. The changes will take effect from 1 April 1989. The normal transitional provisions will apply for establishing tax points in the circumstance of a change from the zero rate to the standard; these are set out in Appendix F of the VAT Guide (Notice 700, October 1987). However, in addition work done or payments received under a written contract signed *and sealed* prior to 21 June 1988 will remain eligible for zero-rating under the existing law as a special transitional relief even if the relevant tax points would otherwise be on or after 1 April 1989.

With respect to the sales of freeholds and the grants of long leases of substantially reconstructed listed buildings not used for domestic purposes the rules, subject to transitional provisions, are to be fundamentally charged from 1 April 1989. With respect to the sale of substantially reconstructed domestic buildings and the granting of long leases of the same the rules mentioned above are unchanged (see 12.37).

12.21.5 Case law on the meaning of new building

There are a number of VAT cases which provide assistance as to the meaning of some of the difficult phrases and words contained in Groups 8 and 8A of Schedule 5 (constructing a building, conversion, reconstruction, alteration or enlargement and substantially reconstructing) although over and over again the tribunals emphasise that the terms are not to have technical meanings. They are to have the meanings which an ordinary man of common sense in the street would apply to the terms when looking at the relevant buildings and the works carried out to them. Some of the cases deal with the provisions of what is now VATA 1983, s 21 (refund of tax to persons constructing new homes otherwise than in the course or furtherance of any business) but nevertheless they provide useful guidance.

Morton v *The Commissioners (CAR/77/137)*
This case indicates that the expression reconstruction means something akin to the rebuilding of something which formally existed. Thus if a taxpayer buys a totally dilapidated building with one wall and part of

another wall missing and with the roof missing and then recreates the building using the existing walls this is likely to amount to a reconstruction. The tribunal also indicated that there is a reconstruction of a building where a substantial part of that building is incorporated into the new building.

Medlam v *The Commissioners (LON/77/304)*
In this case the taxpayer owned stables and a garage and effectively built a house within the same keeping the old walls. It was held that such works amounted to the alteration and improvement of the stables and garage and not to the construction of a new building (p 5).

Owen v *The Commissioners (LON/78/345)*
In this case the taxpayer owned a stone lodge, Beehive Lodge. He renovated the same and constructed a new building alongside it. He also constructed a garage and loose-boxes which for these purposes were to be treated as included within the building resulting from the works. The total area of the final construction was 2,630 superficial square feet of which 458 square feet related to the original building. The tribunal held that because approximately two thirds of the work carried out constituted a new construction (even disregarding the garage and loose-boxes) there could not be said to have been an alteration to the original building; there was too much new construction for there to be an alteration. Perhaps a modest extension could amount to an alteration but not on that scale. The question, however, was whether there had been an enlargement. At p 8 the tribunal stated:

> We find this question much more difficult to decide, because there must come a point where the erection of a new dwelling adjacent to an existing building, so far exceeds the dimensions of the latter that it will be absurd to call the new dwelling an enlargement of the original building.

In the particular case it was held that there had been an enlargement of the original building. This is not a helpful case to the taxpayer.

Nimmo v *The Commissioners (LON/81/113)*
If a taxpayer owns a building and adds a bedroom thereto by extending into the garden then that is a good example of an enlargement. The expression *conversion tends to indicate a change of purpose* or function of the original structure (p 7). The tribunal also agreed that for there to be an *alteration there had to be an existing building or part of a building to alter* (p 8). Thus if the taxpayer buys a barn and converts this into a dwelling house that would amount to a *reconstruction or conversion of the building*.

Taylor v *The Commissioners (LON/82/111)*
In this case the taxpayer owned a building which comprised a garage and a store and he incorporated that into the construction of a new dwelling house. It was held that there was no reconstruction of an existing building because the garage was merely incorporated into the larger structure. There was no alteration to an existing building because once again the *garage was merely incorporated into the new house.* There was no conversion of the existing structure because the garage retained its use as

a garage serving the dwelling house in which it was incorporated. It was held, however, that the new dwelling was an *enlargement of the existing garage.* The test in *Owen* v *The Commissioners* was adopted. At p 14 it was stated by the tribunal:

> In that case (*Owen* v *The Commissioners*) the tribunal posed a visual test whether an ordinary member of the public would have described what had been done as an enlargement of the existing building, and the tribunal concluded that he would have come to that conclusion. Such a visual test would be inappropriate in the present case. But the same question could be asked of an ordinary member of the public on being shown a picture of the original garage and the new dwelling house incorporating the original garage. In the unanimous judgment of the members of this tribunal, although they consider that the case is fairly near the borderline, the conclusion is that the new dwelling house constitutes an enlargement of the garage as an existing building.

Childs v *The Commissioners (LON/82/330)*

In this case it was held that a 'granny' house built flush with the sides of the taxpayer's house comprised an enlargement of the taxpayer's house. This contrasted with the case of *Hill* v *The Commissioners* [1980] VATTR 134 where a semi-detached house was built abutting and immediately adjoining an existing dwelling and it was held that the new house comprised a separate building; the High Court approved of this decision in *Commissioners* v *Perry* [1983] STC 383.

Great Shellford Free Church v *The Commissioners (LON/84/405) (Note now Schedule 5, Group 8, Notes (1A)(b)*)

In this case it was held that a Church Hall built onto a Church comprised a separate building; the tribunal applied a functional test to decide the issue; because the Church and Church Hall functioned independently of each other, that indicated that there were separate buildings. On appeal the High Court approved of the functional test ([1987] STC 249) but the law was thereafter very quickly changed (after two attempts as the first statutory instrument designed to make the change was found to be void) to ensure that works like those carried out in the *Great Shellford* case would be vatable at 15 per cent (see Sched 5, Group 8, Notes (1A)(*b*) and 12.21.1 above).

St Andrews Building Co Ltd v *The Commissioners (EDN/86/12)*

The tribunal in this case set down what is probably the correct test. It stated at p 4:

> In the first place was there an *existing building prior to the commencement* of any works. Secondly, was there *still an existing building* once any projected demolition involved had been carried out, and thirdly, was the completed building to be described as a *conversion, reconstruction, alteration or enlargement of that existing building,* in the lesser of the senses discovered at step 1 or 2, all these phrases having their ordinary everyday use. Thus it seems to the tribunal that had, for example, there been an existing building prior to the start of any work but that the only part of it which remained after planned demolition was a particular doorway or a window or two, then it would have been difficult to say that there was any 'existing building' going

> forward through the whole process, so that the result could hardly have been called merely a conversion, reconstruction, alteration or enlargement of it. Equally had all or almost all of the original building remained and had there been some vast development round about into which the existing building was integrated, it would equally have been difficult to say that it *was merely the conversion, reconstruction, alteration or enlargement of that original building.*

In the particular case there was a ruinous existing building which was transformed into a modern house. The tribunal held that there were elements of conversion, reconstruction, alteration and enlargement of the existing building. The supplies were standard rated.

Wimpey Group Services Ltd v *The Commissioners (LON/85/556 and [1988] STC 1)*
In this case an industrial complex had existed for a number of years and the central bakery was demolished. It was held that there was one building so that on the rebuilding of the part which was demolished, rather than there being a construction of a new building, there had merely been a reconstruction of part of a former building. It was held that there had not been a conversion, enlargement or alteration. The tribunal so held.

The tribunal had sought to apply a functional test, ie, the complex in its old and in its new form functions as a single and integrated undertaking that is to say a large bakery. In the High Court, Mann J (*Wimpey Group Services Ltd* v *The Commissioners* [1988] STC 1) was not impressed by such an approach. He applied the objective test and said that the new building '. . . had no affinity in terms of structure or, as can be discerned from photographs, appearance with its predecessors'. Thus an entirely new building had been constructed and zero rating was appropriate.

Conversion works do not amount to the construction of a new building. In the case of *Gleed* v *The Commissioners* (LON/86/694) the taxpayer converted his existing stables and out-buildings to a dwelling-house and garage. The tribunal held that there was merely a conversion of the stables and out-buildings to a new house; there was no entirely new building. The supplies were vatable at 15%.

12.21.6 Conclusions on legislation, case law and practice

'Conversion' tends to denote the changing of the functions of a building from say a factory to an office. Reconstruction tends to indicate the situation where a building has been partially demolished or fallen into disrepair and is rebuilt or reconstituted. Alterations tend to indicate works being done to a particular building with perhaps a *degree of extension being classified also as alteration.* Enlargement means the extension of a building but an enlargement may be of such a size or nature that the reasonable man in the street may conclude that the works do not amount to an enlargement but the construction of a new building which makes use of some of the undemolished features of the former building. In determining whether there has been an enlargement or construction of a new building the taxpayer is directed by the tribunal in *Childs* v *The Commissioners* to have regard to the size, proportions and appearance of the new structure.

Substantial reconstruction appears to indicate rebuilding works of a substantial nature to the structure of a building.

12.22 'MAJOR INTEREST' AND VAT

In order to make a zero-rated supply under VATA 1983, Schedule 5, Group 8, Item 1, (and Schedule 5, Group 8A, Item 1 (listed buildings)) it is necessary for the person who constructed the building to grant a major interest in that building and anything less is not sufficient.

Under VATA 1983, s 48(1) a major interest in relation to land means a fee simple or a tenancy for a term certain exceeding 21 years.

The Customs & Excise to the author's knowledge take the view that only a formal grant of the legal lease can be a major interest but their views may have to change or may have changed on this (see *Margrie's* case below).

Thus, if a taxpayer enters into an agreement for a lease for over 21 years but never grants a formal lease, the supplies may be exempt, even though the taxpayer may have constructed the building. Nevertheless the law in this area is not clear cut and some guidance on the strict legal position can be found in *Margrie's* case now discussed.

12.22.1 Margrie Holdings Ltd v The Commissioners [1986] VATTR 213

The case of *Margrie* is important when determining the time of a land supply for VAT purposes.

It is a difficult case, and turns on the rules of conveyancing in Scots law.

It was concerned with the question of when the grant of a major interest takes place for VAT purposes.

From the author's understanding of the case the grant of a major interest can take place prior to the formal completion, ie, the execution of the transfer or the conveyance: 'title to property is by no means a controlling factor in deciding whether there has been a supply' (p 217E).

The supply may take place earlier if the purchaser is entitled to enter upon the property (ie, he enjoys possession of the property and control over the land) and possibly also he has paid the price for the land: 'the Appellant supplied a major interest in land to (the purchaser) when they took entry and paid the price on 15 May 1984' (the formal disposition was signed by all relevant parties on 15 and 18 May 1984).

12.23 GRANT OF MAJOR INTEREST

It is important if the taxpayer has constructed the buildings that he grants a major interest in the same; it is not enough simply to have constructed the buildings.

In the case of *American Real Estate (Scotland) Ltd* v *CCE* [1980] VATTR 88, X Ltd purchased land and erected a number of houses thereon. It then sold rights to occupy such houses for specified weeks each year for holiday purposes. It issued certificates to the purchasers, each granting to the holder thereof the right to occupy a particular house upon the estate for a particular week or weeks in perpetuity. The Tribunal held that the issue of such certificates did not confer upon the holder thereof any heritable right in the house concerned and accordingly there was no grant of a major interest in the house. Additionally the issue of a certificate amounted to the provision of holiday accommodation for the purposes of Schedule 6, Group 1, Item 1(*a*). The supply was therefore vatable. The tribunal held that that holiday accommodation item was not confined to short term arrangements.

It may be possible for a freeholder-builder to grant 'time-share licence' certificates for say 35 years to licensees for premiums agreeing also to sell the freehold at the end of the 35 years and divide the proceeds amongst the then licensees. The author is aware of at least one VAT office which has accepted that the entire supplies made by the freeholder-builder in this case can be zero-rated.

Note: A lease of over 21 years with an option to terminate earlier should qualify as a major interest (Notice 742 para 23 and see the stamp duty case of *Cummins Engine Co Ltd* v *IRC* [1981] STC 604).

Note: Assignments of leases which have over 21 years to run at the time of assignment are also supplies of major interests (Notice 742, para 23).

12.24 CIVIL ENGINEERING AND NEW BUILDINGS

Under the present law if X (developer) owns the freehold of Blackacre and commissions Y (builder) to construct a new factory and various roads and other civil engineering works on the site, Y's supplies will be zero-rated. When X sells the factory and its site (which would include the roads and civil engineering works) it will make a zero-rated supply because it is selling a new building with its site or the composite supply doctrine applies; there is no zero-rating as such on the sale of a civil engineering work.

The Customs give detailed guidance in VAT leaflet No 708/3/85 as to what comprises civil engineering works. They make the following initial points:

> To qualify for zero-rating as the construction of a civil engineering work, the services you supply must be of a civil engineering nature and must lead

to the creation of a new civil engineering work. It is not enough for the work done simply to be described as civil engineering. A new civil engineering work means *either* a work or structure which is entirely self-contained and wholly separate from an existing civil engineering work *or,* if it is connected to an existing one it:

(*a*) occupies its own separate area of ground, whether on or under the surface, and

(*b*) is not the reconstruction, on the same ground, of an existing civil engineering work; and

(*c*) is large enough to count as a civil engineering work in its own right, even if it depends on the existing civil engineering work to perform a useful function.

The term civil engineering as used in VATA 1983, Sched 5, Group 8, Item 2 is not defined. The Shorter Oxford Dictionary refers to a civil engineer as being one who designs and constructs works of public utility. A work may nevertheless still be a work of civil engineering even though it does not serve a public purpose, for instance, works with respect to domestic land and accommodation are not excluded from being civil engineering works just because they may serve a particular house (but note Sched 5, Group 8, Notes (2)).

Civil engineering tends to involve a significant amount of removal of earth and the construction of such works as bridges, roads, canals, railways, harbours, drainage works, gas and water works and the like. The term has a very wide meaning although it would not include the installation of plant and machinery (*GKN Birwelco Ltd* v *The Commissioners* [1983] VATTR 128).

The author feels that importance but not decisive importance should be attached to the fact that members of the civil engineering profession would say that the particular works amount to works of civil engineering (*En-tout-cas Ltd* v *The Commissioners* [1973] 1 VATTR 101, *UDF Ltd* v *The Commissioners* [1981] VATTR 199 and *GKN Birwelco Ltd* v *The Commissioners* [1983] VATTR 128). Perhaps the correct test is what conclusion would the informed ordinary man reach having heard expert evidence as to what is a work of civil engineering.

A shopping precinct comprising a number of shopping units with a covered archway is not a work of civil engineering. It is not similar to the items listed above—bridges, road, canals, railways, harbours etc. It does not have any additional function akin to that that a bridge, a road, a canal or a railway etc. A shopping precinct is more akin to a building than a work of civil engineering although it may be that some works of civil engineering amount to buildings so that there is a degree of overlap. The definitions are necessarily mutually exclusive.

Under the *proposed changes* the construction and demolition of any civil engineering works whether new or not will be vatable at 15 per cent. Thus all supplies of civil engineering works by builders will become vatable. At present the construction and demolition of new civil engineering works are zero rated. In the Parliamentary Statement (see 12.34.2) Mr Peter Lilley said:

> Public sector construction programmes will be protected by allowing, where necessary, compensating adjustments to the relevant central Government expenditure provision. Full refund of VAT on non-domestic construction will be available to health authorities and local authorities.

The sale, after 31 March 1989, of a new civil engineering work (and for that matter also an old civil engineering work) is likely to, in most cases, give rise to a vatable supply (15 per cent).

Articles 13B(*g*) and (*h*) and C and 4(3) may not be applicable and the last indent of Article 17 of the Second Directive (which brings Article 28 of the Sixth Directive into operation) will not be satisfied (because there was no 'exemptions with refund of the tax paid at the preceding stage' legislation in the UK relating to civil engineering works in force on 31 December 1975, and even if there was (see [1988] STC 456 at pp 458(*d*) and 472(*b*) the court has decided that works by the builders of civil engineering works are vatable (15 per cent) and any sales of civil engineering works have always been exempt).

It may be that if some civil engineering works are sold with a building they will comprise part of the site of the building and thus giving rise to exempt supplies if Article 13B(*g*) is appropriate. Note also the definition of 'building' in Article 4(3)(*a*).

12.25 DEVELOPMENT SCHEMES AND VAT

This section looks at a number of property development situations and the present VAT rules applicable thereto.

12.25.1 The developer (commercial development: present law)

It is critical that the real developer (the person constructing the building) is clearly identified and property transactions correctly analysed.

Example: VAT and the developer

X Ltd introduces Blackacre to Y Ltd and it is agreed that Y Ltd will develop the land and dispose of the same to a Pension Fund with X Ltd taking 30 per cent of the profit. Y Ltd's supplies would be zero-rated but X Ltd should charge Y Ltd VAT on its 30 per cent profit as it is possibly no more than an introduction fee. If it has omitted to provide for this in the agreement it will be treated as having charged a VAT inclusive figure. Y Ltd would normally be able to claim back the VAT charged. X Ltd will have 'lost' 15 per cent of its profit.

Developers may enter into the following types of situations with institutions and landowners.

(*a*) Developer (D Ltd) contracts (ie enters into binding contracts to purchase) and completes (ie has the freehold title vested in his name) the purchase of land from the vendor (V Ltd) and then contracts and completes the sale of the same to the ultimate purchaser (UP Ltd) without having carried out any development works. That would be an exempt transaction (Schedule 6, Group 1, Item 1) (see Figure 12.5 below).

Figure 12.5

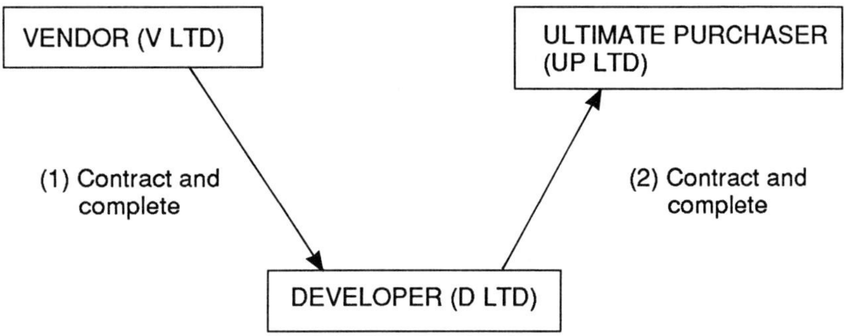

(*b*) It may happen in that case that the developer (D Ltd) of the land after having disposed of the property entirely to UP Ltd—under contract and with completion—will enter into a contract undertaking to construct a building thereon. In this event, the only way the development profit, to be obtained by D Ltd, can be zero-rated is if the same comes with Schedule 5, Group 8, Item 2. This it should normally do. Item 1 can have no application. The land sale by D Ltd will be exempt (see diagram below).

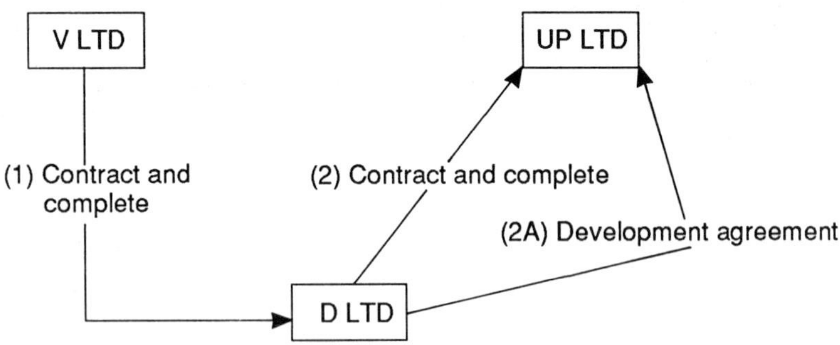

(*c*) Customs and Excise generally consider the date of 'granting' to be the date when completion takes place. D Ltd may purchase land under contract and complete the same. He may unconditionally contract to dispose of the land to UP Ltd and at the same time undertake to put a building on the same and to complete the sale only when the building is put up. In this case the 'granting' would take place after the building has been put up by D Ltd so that he would appear to come within Schedule 5, Group 8, Item 1 (see diagram below).

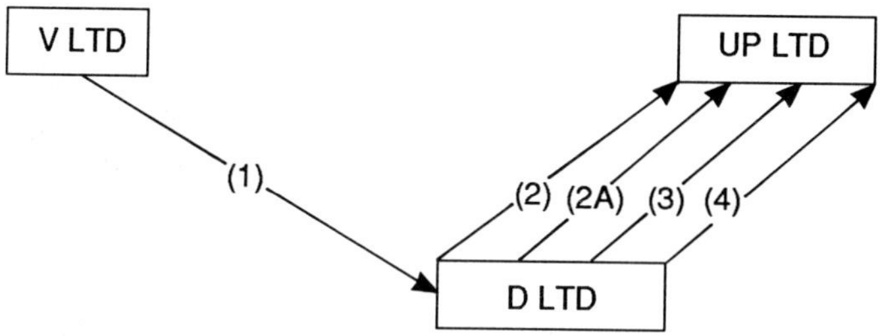

(1) Contract and complete (to purchase)

(2) Contract (to sell)

(2A) Development agreement

(3) Development completed

(4) Complete sale of freehold

(*d*) If D Ltd were to purchase the property by way of exchange of contracts and complete in the name of UP Ltd direct, after having contracted to sell to UP Ltd, the supply of the land to UP Ltd would appear to be exempt. If completion is the relevant date, however, it appears that it may be that the land never belonged to D Ltd because it never completed the purchase in its name. In this event the transaction could be ignored for VAT purposes; the alternative and possibly better interpretation, however, is that the supply is an exempt supply so affecting D Ltd's VAT recovery position. The developer's profit for putting the building up could be made to be zero-rated in the usual way (see diagram below).

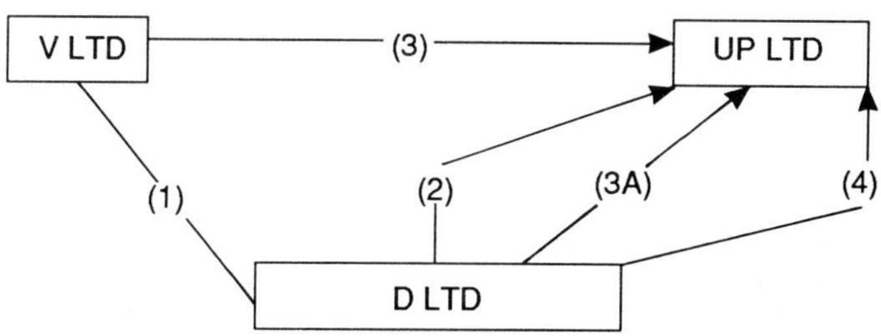

(1) Contract to purchase

(2) Contract to sell

(3) Complete (legal)

(3A) Development agreement

(4) Development completed

With respect to the proposed changes see 12.37. The above rules will still apply to the construction and sale of new domestic buildings.

12.25.2 Supplies of materials (commercial developments: present law)

The supply of materials in connection with the construction of a new building in order to be zero rated must come within VATA 1983, Schedule 5, Group 8, Item 3, ie, there must be a supply by the persons supplying the construction services and in connection with those services, of the materials.

In *The Commissioners* v *Willmott* [1987] STC 692, X contracted to build for Y but sub-contracted the actual building works to Z. X supplied Z with the materials: there was a sale of the materials by X to Z. It was held that under the main contract X was a person supplying services in the course of construction of a building and was therefore a person supplying services within Item 2. Whether the supply of materials to Z was a supply in connection with the supply of services within Item 2 was a question of fact. The supply of materials by X to Z were as a matter of fact, the supply in connection with a supply by it of services within Item 2. The reference in Item 3 to persons supplying services within Item 2 was not limited to one supplying services to the person to whom the materials in question were supplied. It followed therefore that the supply of materials by the taxpayer company (X) to Z was zero rated and to that extent the Customs' appeal was dismissed.

With respect to the proposed changes see 12.37. The above decision is still of relevance with respect to the construction and sale of new domestic buildings.

12.25.3 Is there a VAT trap on sub–sale?

The situation may arise where X Ltd owns freehold land. It agrees with Y Ltd to sell the land to Y Ltd after Y Ltd has constructed a new building thereon. Y Ltd will be the person constructing the building for the purposes of VAT.

Y Ltd then having virtually completed the works contracts to sell the land and the completed building to Z Ltd.

When the works are completed formal legal completion takes place, with X Ltd transferring the freehold to Z Ltd.

On the face of it, it will appear that no zero rating is available. X Ltd could not obtain zero rating because it was not the person constructing the building.

Y Ltd could not obtain zero rating because it did not grant the major interest; the Customs generally take the view that in order for there to be a grant of a major interest it is necessary for the formal legal title to be granted (eg a legal lease or the transfer of the formal freehold estate).

However, it seems to be quite clear from Note (1) to Group 8 of Schedule 5 that if the benefit of the grant accrues to the person constructing the building zero rating will be available (to Y Ltd). Because the Note refers to the benefit in consideration of the grant going to the person constructing the building it *seems* to be necessary (although it is unlikely the Customs will take any point in this respect) that the entire consideration paid by Z Ltd goes to Y Ltd even though Y Ltd may be under a further obligation to pay the monies or part thereof to X Ltd.

A similar type of situation can arise where X Ltd has vested the freehold estate of his land in Y Bank plc or in the name of another company with the bank or that other company being mere nominees of the land for X Ltd. When X Ltd has constructed the building on the land and disposed of the same directing the nominee to transfer the legal estate into the names of the purchaser zero rating would be available to X Ltd because of Note (1) to Group 8 of Schedule 5.

If X Ltd in the first example (instead of there being a deal under which the freehold is to be disposed of) were to agree to grant a lease to Y Ltd and Y Ltd directed that X Ltd let the formal lease to Z Ltd with Y Ltd taking a cash sum on the transfer over of the rights to Z Ltd, the Customs may argue that Note (1) is not applicable because the benefit of the consideration has not gone to Y Ltd; only part of the consideration has gone to Y Ltd with another part in the form of rents being paid to X Ltd. The Note requires that the benefit of the consideration goes to the person constructing the building. There is nothing in the Interpretation Act to say that a reference to the whole shall include a reference to part. It is a question of construction and intentment of the legislation. There is no reference in the Note to the whole *of the consideration* having to go the person constructing the building. Clearly leases are conceived of as being within the Note because they are major interests provided they are over 21 years. The author feels that there is a good case that *the relevant consideration,* which goes to the person constructing the building, is zero rated even though part may go elsewhere (to X Ltd in the example, in the form of exempt rents).

Figure 12.3 Sub-sales and sub-leases

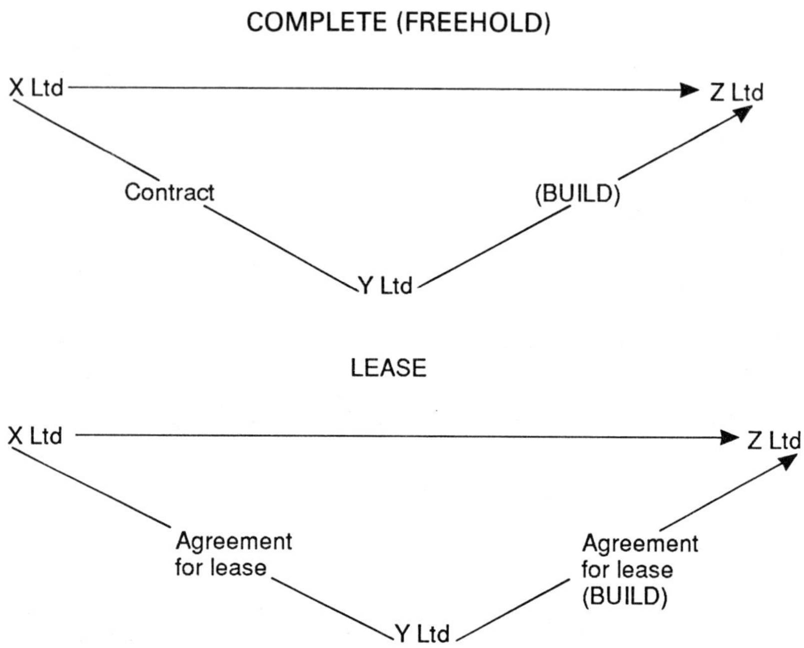

For the effects of the *proposed changes* see 12.37.

12.25.4 Falling into VAT traps

Often taxpayers fall into VAT traps because negotiations over development agreements and projects often extend over long periods with variations and amendments to documents being be made without the parties realizing that the original structure as it existed did not give rise to VAT problems but the ultimate structure does.

Example 12H: Supervisor not developer

X, a pension fund, may want to employ Y as a developer. Draft documents are prepared and gradually the pension fund feels concerned about the abilities of Y to do the job. Ultimately the situation has arrived where the pension fund feels that it should do more of the work and ends up employing the builder direct with Y the developer being more of a supervisor. It may be in this case that monies paid to Y the developer are vatable as Y is a person acting in a consultancy or supervisory capacity.

Example 12J: Contracts with 'developer' and builder

A corporation tax group of companies may negotiate with a fund to act as developer (company A in the group) and builder (company B in the group).

After many months of negotiation the documents are executed with the fund employing B the builder direct and A the developer direct instead of the fund just employing A who will in turn employ the builder. In this case A is exposed and isolated in VAT terms and would appear to be a person acting as a consultant or at least a person acting in a supervisory capacity hence making vatable supplies (see VAT Leaflet 708/2/85, 1 November 1985, paras 12 and 13).

For the effects of the proposed changes see 12.37.

12.25.5 Developer's profit

The developer's profits on the construction of a new building will generally be zero-rated.

The developer will generally be the person constructing a building. The Commissioners extend this so that it applies to a person who commissions the construction of a building, ie if supplies of construction services are made to him and he exercises some measure of control over the construction of the building.

The term 'person constructing a building' does not, however, include a person who merely grants a lease or licence to another person to enter onto his land for the purposes of constructing a building.

The VAT Tribunal in *Hulme Educational Foundation* v *Commissioners of Customs & Excise* [1978] VATTR 1979 at 189, construed the words 'a person constructing a building' as follows:

> In our opinion, the normal meaning of these words means that a person must either himself construct the building in the sense of putting brick upon brick or stone upon stone, or must himself or by an agent enter into a contract or arrangement with another under which that other puts brick upon brick or stone upon stone. In other words the construction must be physically done by the person concerned or by his servants or agents or the person concerned must himself directly enter into a contract or arrangement for another to do the physical construction works.

In *Hulme's* case, to simplify the facts, the landlord let property to a tenant with the tenant employing the builder. The builder carried out works for the tenant and not for the landlord. The VAT tribunal held that the landlord was not the person constructing the building just because it retained certain powers to approve relevant plans and specifications or to supervise actual building works. The tribunal felt that such powers are the normal precautionary powers one would expect to see retained by a freeholder when a tenant of his was arranging for the construction works to be carried out.

In the case of *Monsell Youell Development Ltd* v *CCE* [1978] VATTR 1, X Ltd acted as developer arranging for the construction of a building to be put up on the land of Y Ltd. Both companies were members of the same corporation tax group but were not members of the same VAT group because there was no group registration. The tribunal held that X

Ltd was the developer so that when Y Ltd disposed of the land that was not a zero-rated supply because Y Ltd was not the person constructing the building. The tribunal stated at p 9:

> The documentary evidence, such as the invoice in respect of building costs, the contract and special conditions, the National House Building Council agreement and the specifications all emphasise the separate functions of Y Ltd (the landowning company) and X Ltd (the construction company). The invoice is issued by X Ltd, the contract provides that Y Ltd will sell the land and X Ltd will build the house, the specification refers to the contractor (X Ltd) and the house purchaser's agreement is between the registered builder, X Ltd and the purchaser.
>
> In our view, to find that the functions performed by Y Ltd that consist basically of the purchase of land, the design of the houses to be built thereon and the provision of roads and sewers are those performed 'by a person constructing a building' would be to ignore the substance and reality of the matter, and strain the ordinary use of the English language.

The reference to the documentary evidence (the invoice etc) is very important as it is clear that such matters can have great significance in determining which taxpayer was the person constructing a building for the purposes of making zero-rated supplies for VAT.

Apart from the Tribunal decisions mentioned above, the courts have not as yet been called upon to comment on the expression 'person constructing a building'.

It is just possible, that the courts would give a very narrow meaning to the words 'person constructing a building', restricting the term to a builder as opposed to a developer who in a sense may be said to supervise the builder. In an old bankruptcy case (*Stuart* v *Sloper* 1849 3 Exch Rep 701) Rolfe B at 704 stated:

> this man . . . is not a builder unless the taking of these pieces of land and employing builders to build on them makes him a builder. Now, with all deference, if it is supposed to have been laid down by the Court of Bankruptcy that, under any circumstances, that creates a man a builder, I confess I have considerable doubt on that subject. If a man gained his entire livelihood by looking out for what would be the most convenient place near London upon which to build, and purchased the ground, and then employed builders to build upon it, although that would make him a jobber and speculator in houses. I very much doubt whether it would make him a builder. The plaintiff did not become liable under the laws as a builder, because he took these lands and built upon them; for although that might make him a speculator, and bring him within the mischief intended to be remedied by the bankrupt laws, I think it does not make him a builder, as at present advised. However, that question does not arise here, because, in this case, the jury have found that what was done was not a part of a general system. This gentleman took a lease of the land, and profitably employed that land by causing houses to be built upon it by others. It is impossible to contend that that makes him a builder, within any meaning that can be given to the bankruptcy law.

In the author's opinion it is clear, as a matter of interpretation, that a taxpayer can amount to a person constructing a building for the purposes of Schedule 5, Group 8, Item 1 even though he is not the person who actually puts brick upon brick. A gang foreman on a building site may not actually put brick upon brick yet it could hardly be denied that he is a person who is carrying out activities which comprise the construction of the building. It is equally clear if a landowner merely employs a builder to construct a building on his land and does nothing else except check up on and use the end product that the landowner would not be a person constructing a building. However, a developer who supervises the actual builder and all the other professionals involved in arranging for the building to be constructed can be said to be a 'person constructing a building' in the author's opinion, as a matter of law, if he plays such an important role with respect to the construction works that his intervention in the building process is important in determining the final outcome of the building programme. For instance, if the developer (the term developer is not a term of art) is closely involved with the works carried out by the builder (visiting the site and directing how things should be done) then the developer effectively intervenes into the building process and becomes part of that process and hence can be said to be a person constructing a building. The fact that he may be called a 'supervisor' is not disadvantageous and indeed at the end of the day may be proved to be positively advantageous because of the contrast between the wording of Items 1 and 2 of Group 5.

It may be the case therefore that if X owns land and he acts as developer to develop his own land with Y the builder then X and Y are persons constructing a building. It is sufficient that X is one of the persons constructing the building and it is not relevant that Y may also be a person constructing a building with regard to Group 8, Item 1: X can make a zero-rated supply if he grants a major interest in or an interest in any part of the building or its site.

Note: The express exclusions in Schedule 5, Group 8, Item 2 indicate that the term 'person constructing a building' has a wide meaning.

The expression 'person constructing a building' will under the proposed changes only be relevant with respect to domestic buildings (see 12.37.)

12.26 DEVELOPMENT AGREEMENTS (COMMERCIAL DEVELOPMENT: PRESENT LAW)

Development agreements may take many forms and it is vital that VAT is taken into account when drafting these.

12.26.1 Typical situation

X (Developments) Ltd (the developer) may contract to purchase land and sub-sell the same on to a Fund for, say, £1M. At the same time the developer would enter into a Development Agreement with the Fund under which the developer agrees to arrange for the construction of an office block on the site ultimately receiving, say, £3M from the Fund for those works. The developer would employ the builder and all other necessary consultants and advisers to ensure that the construction of the building is completed.

12.26.2 Sale of land

On the sub-sale of the land for £1M to the fund, the developer will be making an exempt VAT supply (VATA 1983, Sched 6, Group 1). Stamp duty may, however, be mitigated by virtue of the sub-sale relief provisions (Stamp Act 1981, ss 58(5)) and the fact that at the time of completion there will be no building on the land (see *Law Society Gazette* (1957), p 450 as amended in December 1987).

12.26.3 Option

If instead of carrying out a sub-sale of the land the developer buys the land outright from the landowner and gives the Fund an option to purchase the same when the building is completed, the disposal of the land and the building thereon would be a zero-rated supply (VATA 1983, Sched 5, Group 8, Item 3) although substantially more stamp duty may be payable (see *Law Society Gazette* (1957), p 450 as amended in December 1987).

Figure 12.4 Development situation

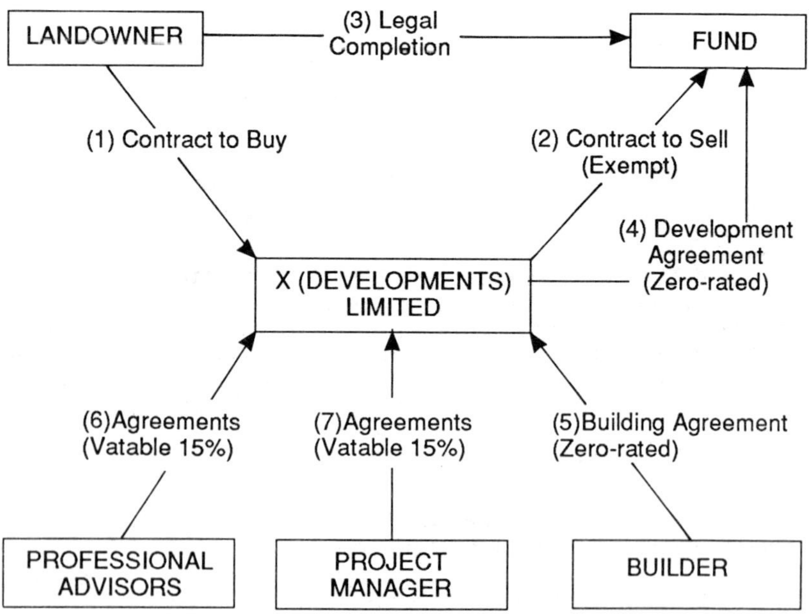

12.26.4 Construction works

The supplies by the builder to the developer will be zero-rated (VATA 1983, Sched 5, Group 8, Items 2 and 3) although supplies such as consultancy fees and legal fees will be vatable (VATA 1983, ss 1 and 2 and Sched 5, Group 8, Item 2). The supplies by the developer to the Fund in return for the £3M should be zero-rated supplies (VATA 1983, Sched 5, Group 8, Items 2 and 3 and see Customs and Excise Notice 742, para 24 and *Hulme Educational Foundation* v *Commissioners of Customs & Excise* [1978] VATTR 179 at 189).

12.26.5 If the developer agrees to find tenants

If the Development Agreement provides that the developer is to obtain an extra sum if it were to find tenants for the premises, the VAT position is unclear. Much depends on the precise form of the deal and how the documentation is worded. Customs and Excise may contend that that extra sum is a payment for what is, effectively, estate agency work and vatable under general principles (VATA 1983, ss 1 and 2(1)) although the Customs seem now to have lost interest in this point.

In the author's opinion, if the Fund and the developer simply appoint independent estate agents to find tenants and there is no obligation upon the developer to find tenants and the additional sum is a payment for construction works payable if and only if a tenant is found, the supply is zero-rated.

If the developer is under an obligation to the Fund to use its best endeavours to find tenants and, as is usual, it appoints independent agents to actually do the work on its behalf, the Customs & Excise may have a case (if they sought to argue it) that the additional sum, or part thereof, is vatable.

12.26.6 VAT planning

(*a*) The purchase of land under contract and the sub-sale of it to a Fund by a developer is an exempt supply. Developers should consider holding on to the land until the building is completed (having previously given the Fund a call option) so that a zero rated supply will be made when the building is completed and the formal legal sale takes place.

(*b*) The normal developer's profit should be a zero-rated supply.

(*c*) If the developer is additionally taking on the obligation to find tenants he must give careful consideration to the VAT position.

For the effects of the proposed changes see 12.37.

12.27 GOLDEN VAT BRICKS (COMMERCIAL BUILDING: PRESENT POSITION)

In certain cases if a taxpayer can commence a development project on his land prior to the sale of the land substantial tax savings can arise.

If a person constructing a building sells his freehold interest or grants a lease of over 21 years in or in any part of the building or its site the supply will be zero-rated (VATA 1983, Sched 5, Group 8, Item 1).

On the other hand if a taxpayer merely disposes of land which he has not developed the supply will virtually always be an exempt supply (VATA 1983, Sched 5, Group 1, Item 1).

If a developer starts the construction of a building and disposes of the same before having completed the same the disposal of the building plus its site will (in the author's opinion) comprise a zero-rated supply. It is not necessary (in the author's opinion) for the taxpayer to have completed the building for zero-rating to apply (see fig 12.5 below).

In the case of *Stapenhill Developments Ltd* (MAN/82/229) the taxpayer had dug a trench to contain the foundations of some houses but it had dug the same in the wrong place and it had abandoned the project. The taxpayer had not even commenced the construction of a building.

Figure 12.5 Golden VAT brick

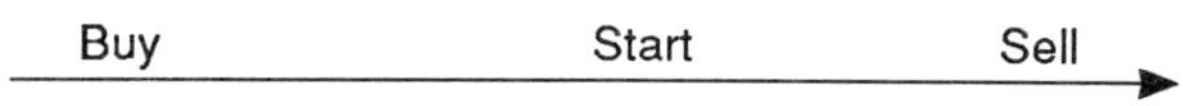

The tribunal held that to obtain zero rating it was not necessary that the taxpayer had completed the building which was to be put on the land. The Tribunal at p 16 stated: 'The operative word is *constructing* and not a *person who has constructed'.* The question is to be decided as a matter of substance and degree whether or not, on the facts of the case, what has been done on the land was sufficient to bring the work within the ambit of the expression.

The tribunal held that it was only necessary that the building 'must be seen to be under construction on the land at the time of the disposal'.

Thus if the vendor makes a *bona fide* start to the project before sale because, for instance, there is a delay in the sale but the vendor, who must be a developer or builder, wishes to start the project straight away because 'time is money', zero-rated supplies will result from the sale (see however *R* v *IRC, ex parte Harrow London Borough Council* [1981] STC 246, and the *Taxation of Land Development* (Butterworths), footnote 3 on p 257).

The works should comprise the construction of the whole or part (preferably the whole) of the foundations of the building plus some actual brick work which will comprise part of the building itself. Hence the reference to 'VAT Bricks' which bricks can in appropriate cases be worth their weight in gold especially if the developer or builder must make a zero-rated supply in order to claim back, for instance, the VAT charged on a project manager's fee, legal fees etc made to him in connection with the project and the site acquisition and sale.

The author does not feel that the trench works (where the land is held as an investment) will, in the normal course of events, result in an appropriation of the land to trading stock (see the *Hudson's Bay Co Ltd v Stevens* 5 TC 424 at 437, *C H Rand* v *Alberni Land Co Ltd* 7 TC 629 at 638, *Pilkington* v *Randall* 42 TC 663 at 672 and *The Alabama Coal, Iron, Land and Colonisation Co Ltd* v *Mylam* 11 TC 232 at 253).

The commencement of the works may in appropriate cases, bring the situation within TA 1970, s 488(2)(*c*) (now ICTA 1988, s 776(2)(*c*)) (see *Winterton* v *Edwards* [1980] STC 206 at 217d and see s 488(7) now s 776(7)).

12.27.1 Tax planning

When land is being disposed of by a builder or developer he should see whether this would give rise to an exempt VAT supply. If that is the case he should see whether it is possible to make a *bona fide* start on the construction of the project building and foundations prior to the disposal in order to convert the exempt supply into a zero-rated supply.

Any such transaction to mitigate VAT must carefully take into account the *Ramsay* doctrine (*IRC* v *Ramsay* [1981] STC 174) if the development transactions are entered into exclusively to avoid tax and there is a pre-ordained scheme comprising a number of steps which enable tax to be avoided.

For the effects of the proposed changes see 12.37.

12.28 DESIGN AND BUILD CONTRACTS—ARE THEY VATABLE? (COMMERICAL BUILDING: PRESENT LAW)

X Ltd owns Blackacre. It pays Y (Designers) Ltd £50,000 to design a building to be put on the land and it pays Z (Builders) Ltd £500,000 to construct the new building on the land. VAT will be chargeable on the £50,000 but not on the £500,000 (VATA 1983, Sched 5, Group 8, Item 2).

What is the position if Z (Builders) Ltd simply agrees to design and build the building for X Ltd for £550,000? The legal position is determined by the composite supply doctrine (as formulated by the Court of Appeal in *British Railway Board* v *CCE* [1977] STC 211 which disapproved of the test in *CCE v The Automobile Association* [1974] STC 192 and was followed and applied in *CCE* v *Scott* [1978] STC 191 and *CCE* v *Bushby* [1979] STC 8 and see *Sharman* v *CCE* [1983] STC 809 and the 'Sharman Gambit'). Very broadly the test is whether in substance the main thrust of the supply comprised the supply of construction services. If the main thrust of the supply was that of construction services then the entire supply will be zero-rated as construction services. All the supplies which necessarily follow from that supply are zero-rated as construction services. Thus, if building works are to be carried out it follows that the building must be designed. If that is the case, and the above test is applied, the entire supply by Z Ltd will be zero-rated even though part thereof related to design works.

12.28.1 Customs' practice (practice 708/2/87)

> A client may obtain the necessary design work for a building project from a contractor as part of a 'Design and Build' package deal with the contractor. Where the design, workmanship and materials are supplied by a contractor to his client under a 'Design and Build' lump sum contract without any separate identification of the part of the lump sum relating to the design element, the VAT liability of the design element will follow that of the building work. For example, where a new building project is concerned, if the building works supplied by the contractor are zero-rated the design is also zero-rated. This also applies where, within a lump sum design and build contract, the part of the lump sum for the design element is shown separately solely for internal analysis purposes by the two contracting parties. But if there is a separate supply of design or other similar professional services to a client, it is always standard-rated.

Figure 12.6 Design and build

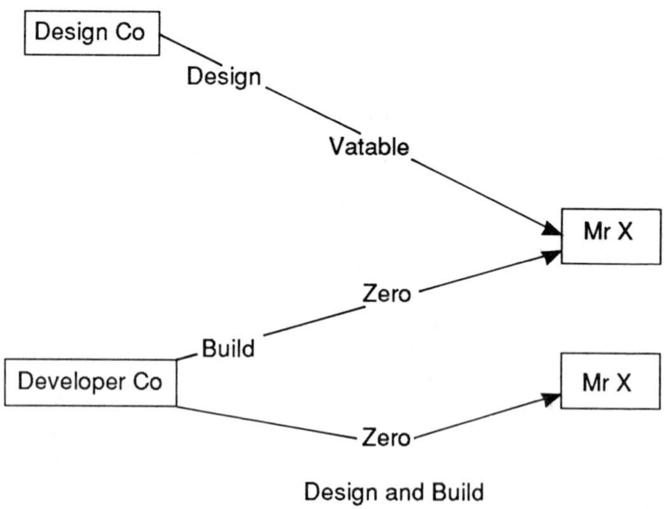

With respect to the proposed changes in the law, see 12.37.

12.29 REVENUE ATTACK ON 'INVESTOR-DEVELOPER' AND VAT

A pension fund may own a parcel of land. It may agree with D Ltd (the Developer) for D Ltd to arrange for a building to be constructed on the land and for D Ltd to take a lease. D Ltd will then grant an occupational lease. Let us say that of the £100 paid by the tenant, D Ltd has to pay £70 to the fund. Thus D Ltd takes its developer's profit in the form of a land interest. It is assumed that D Ltd decides to hold onto the land as an investment.

It appears that the Revenue argue that the value of D Ltd's land interest must come in as effectively a fee paid by the pension fund to D Ltd for carrying out development works.

The Revenue has been known to take this point even where D Ltd was given an agreement for lease by the fund at the start.

If that is the case it may be that D Ltd will have made a supply for VAT though the author is not aware of any situation where the Customs and Excise have taken a point such as this.

Figure 12.7 Investor-developer and VAT

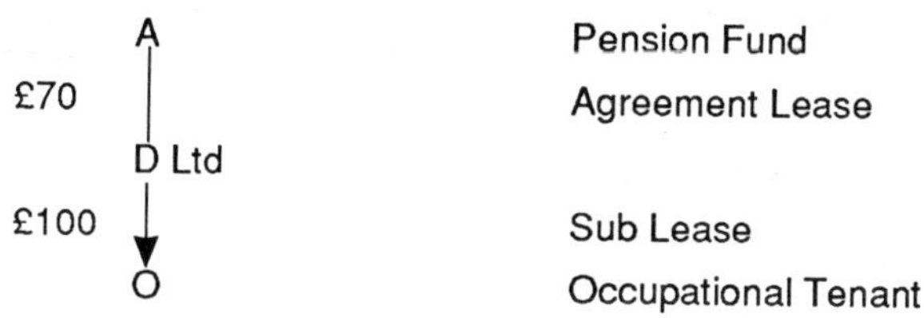

PART IV EXEMPT LAND DISPOSALS

Most land transactions at present will give rise to exempt supplies.

12.30 EXEMPT TRANSACTIONS

The principal exemption with regard to land is contained in VATA 1983, Sched 6, Group 1. The grant, assignment or surrender of any interest in or right over land or of any licence to occupy land, subject to certain exceptions, are exempt supplies.

X Ltd buys an office block and sells it making a trading profit. The supply by X Ltd will be exempt so that it may have to bear the input tax, eg on solicitor's fees and agency fees, in connection therewith (General Regulations 1985 (as amended), reg 30).

The term 'grant, assignment or surrender' would include the sale of a freehold, the grant of rights over land, the grant of leases regardless of the length of the term of the lease. It would also include the disposals of equitable interests in land such as the sale of a contract to buy the legal estate in land.

Example 12J: Sale of contract

Mr X contracts to buy Blackacre from Mr Y from £1M. Mr X sells that contract for £50,000 to Mr Z. Mr X will have made an exempt land supply within Schedule 6, Group 1.

For the future changes in the law see 12.37.

12.30.1 Surrenders are exempt

If a developer constructs a building and surrenders a lease of over 21 years can that under the present law amount to a zero rated supply?

A developer can only obtain zero rated premiums or rentals or disposal consideration if he grants a major interest.

The Customs and Excise agree that if a taxpayer assigns a major interest such as a lease with over 21 years to run (or a freehold) zero rating will be applicable.

If a taxpayer surrenders a major interest this is neither a grant nor an assignment and will give rise to an exempt supply even if the tenant constructed the building and the lease is over 21 years.

A land transaction may be structured in terms of the surrender of a land interest in order to mitigate stamp duty, ie, a surrender by operation of law is stamp duty free even if, it is submitted, the transaction is preceded by a contract under which it is anticipated that after say, four weeks, the formal surrender will take place by operation of law.

Figure 12.8 Do not surrender: good for stamp duty, bad for VAT

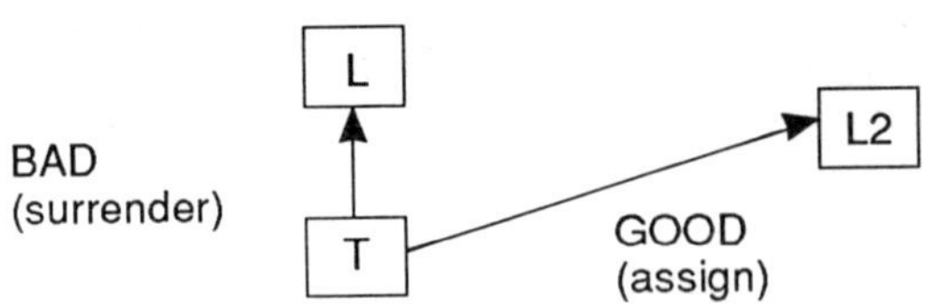

The VAT position of such a transaction must be carefully taken into account. Under the present rules a surrender will always be exempt. Under the *proposed changes* a surrender will always be vatable at 15

per cent. It is proposed that the Article 13C option will not be available. Clause F of the Consultative Document reads thus:

> *F Surrenders of interests in property*
>
> It is proposed to remove the relief for 'surrenders' from Item 1 of Group 1 of Schedule 6. If this is not done, there would be an added complication in relation to the landlord's option for taxation. Also there is no provision to relieve 'surrenders' under Article 13 of the EEC Sixth VAT Directive.

12.30.2 In normal development transactions taxpayers must watch out for exempt supplies

X Builders Ltd may buy land for £1m and then sell the same to Y Fund agreeing at the same time to construct a building thereon for Y Fund for an additional £3m. There will have been an exempt supply of £1m.

It is extremely unlikely that the taxpayer could call in aid the composite supply doctrine (see below) to overcome that exempt supply problem. The author does not feel that X will have been the person constructing the building if he has not even started work on the same at the time of the sale (the grant of the major interest).

In *Court Barton Property plc* [1985] VATTR 148, X Ltd agreed to provide holiday accommodation for the benefit of Mr Y in consideration of Mr Y buying shares in X Ltd for a premium equal to the benefit of the holiday accommodation given to Mr Y. Mr Y would pay £100 of which part was equal to the nominal capital of the shares and part was paid effectively for the use of the holiday accommodation.

X Ltd sought to argue that the monies were paid for shares and that was an exempt supply and (alternatively) under the composite supply doctrine the whole supply should be treated as exempt. The tribunal at p 158 stated:

> The mere fact that one element of the supply made for the consideration paid by the shareholder is a share in a public limited company does not, in the judgment of the tribunal, enable a curtain to be lowered so as to conceal the other element of the supply made for the same consideration, which is the right of occupancy of a specified cottage for a specified week in each year. The tribunal accordingly finds that what has been supplied for the consideration paid by the shareholder is a multiple supply consisting of a share (exempt) and holiday accommodation (standard rate) with the result that there must be an apportionment of the consideration between these two elements.

For the position under the proposed changes, see 12.37.

12.31 RELYING ON COMPOSITE SUPPLY

This doctrine may prove to be the taxpayer's saviour in many cases.

The leading case is *BRB* v *The Commissioners* [1977] STC 221, especially at 224.

From that case it is clear that the correct test is:—what did the taxpayer supply to the purchaser in consideration of the monies it received from purchaser?

It may be that in any particular case a taxpayer has supplied a number of things. One must, however, ascertain what may be called the main thrust of the supply or the main supply. Once one has ascertained that then even though there may have been other supplies made by the taxpayer which are related to the main supply those other supplies take on the same character as the main supply. To an extent of course that still begs the question as to what is the main thrust or the main supply. Guidance can be obtained on this point from the case of *The Commissioners* v *Scott* [1978] STC 191, especially at 194. If one ascertains the main supply then any other supplies which are necessary components of the main supply will take on the nature of the main supply. Thus if X undertook, for payment, to look after the horse of Y on X's land a necessary component of that supply is the supply of accommodation, the supply of food (grass) and the supply of skilled care. Such supplies could not be broken up (for VAT purposes) and they will take on the nature of the main supply. Such supplies are known as composite supplies. The court indicated that the answer was largely a matter of *first impression* and a degree of *common sense* was required.

A supply may also take on the nature of the main supply if it could be said to be an *integral part* of the main supply or an *inseparable part* of the main supply (*British Airways plc* v *The Commissioners* (1987) VATTR 120 at 126).

Additionally even though the supply may not be a necessary part of the main supply or an integral part or an inseparable part from the main supply it may nevertheless take on the nature of the main supply if it is merely *incidental* to that supply (*British Airways plc* v *The Commissioners* at 128H).

To ascertain whether particular supplies on *incidental* to, or an *integral* and *inseparable* part of, or a *necessary* component of, the main supply (so as to take on the same nature as the main supply) as well as applying *common sense* and being governed by one's *first impressions* Lord Granchester in *British Airways plc* v *The Commissioner* at 128E indicated that one must look to the *substance and reality* of the situation.

If one is unable to find that the supplies are incidental, etc to the main supply (so as to take on the character of the main supply) then the supplies must be dealt with under the VAT legislation as if they were separate supplies: exempt and vatable as the case may be (*The Commissioners* v *The Automobile Association* [1974] STC 192, *Hazelwood Caravans and Chalets Ltd* v *The Commissioners* (1985) VATTR 179 and *British Airways plc* v *The Commissioners*). Such separate supplies are called multiple supplies.

It is quite clear if a supply comprises a composite supply, as opposed to a multiple supply, that the fact that the taxpayer charges separately for items comprised within a composite supply will not cause the otherwise composite supply to be a multiple supply (*The Commissioners* v *Scott* and *British Airways plc* v *The Commissioners* at 127B).

The supply of invoices, however, in marginal cases may be significant. The supply of separate invoices may tend to indicate that the supply is capable of division and should probably be treated as a separate supply of multiple services and/or goods (see *Lylybet Dishwashers (UK) Ltd* v *The Commissioners* (LON/79/244).

The doctrine will still have relevance in appropriate cases after the proposed changes following the European Court case have been implemented.

PART V THE SIXTH DIRECTIVE AND THE IMPLICATIONS OF THE EUROPEAN COURT DECISION

This part summarises the present VAT rules with respect to land transactions as dealt with in earlier parts of this chapter. It then examines the implications of the Sixth Directive and the decision of the European Court of Justice in *Commission of the European Communities* v *United Kingdom* (Case 416/85) and what the Government and Customs have stated with respect thereto.

12.32 SUMMARY OF PRESENT VAT POSITION

Under the present VAT rules as contained in the Value Added Tax Act 1983 and the 1985 Regulations (as amended) the following should be noted:

(*a*) Generally the construction of all new buildings is zero rated and so also are the grants by the constructor of major interests in such new buildings.

(*b*) Special rules apply to listed buildings.

(*c*) There are specific headings dealing with car parking etc where VAT must be charged, otherwise land transactions will comprise exempt transactions. For example the disposal of undeveloped land would comprise an exempt transaction.

(*d*) Charges by professionals and project managers require VAT to be charged and these rules are wholly unchanged by the European Court decision.

12.33 THE SIXTH DIRECTIVE

Article 13B(*b*) of the Sixth Directive states that the leasing or letting of immovable property shall comprise an exempt supply.

However, the leasing or letting of the following immovable property is excluded from that exemption and will comprise vatable supplies chargeable at 15 per cent. These are:

(*a*) The provision of accommodation, as defined in the laws of the Member States, in the hotel sector or in sectors with a similar function, including the provision of accommodation in holiday camps or on sites developed for use as camping sites.

(*b*) The letting of premises and sites for parking vehicles.

(*c*) Lettings of permanently installed equipment and machinery.

(*d*) Hire of safes.

Member States may apply further exclusions to the scope from the exemption so that if a Member State wanted VAT to be charged on the leasing or letting of immovable property for other purposes then it can so provide (Article 13B(*b*)).

The list of the items excluded from exemption is presently contained in VATA 1983, Sched 5, Group 1, Item 1(*a*)–(*h*) (see 12.13).

Article 13B(*g*) exempts the supply of buildings or parts thereof, and of the land on which they stand, other than land as described in Article 4(3)(*a*).

Article 13B(*h*) exempts the supply of land which has not been built on other than building land as described in Article 4(3)(*b*).

Article 4(3)(*a*) refers to the supply *before first occupation* of buildings or parts of buildings and the land on which they stand. It also goes on to state, within Article 4(3)(*a*), that Member States may determine the conditions of application of this criterion to transformations of buildings and the land on which they stand. Member States may apply criteria other than 'first occupation', such as the period elapsing between the date of completion of the building and the date of first supply or the period elapsing between the date of first occupation and the date of subsequent supply, provided that these periods do not exceed five years and two years respectively. 'A building' shall be taken to mean any structure fixed to or in the ground. It is quite clear that Article 13B(*g*) effectively requires that the supply of the buildings and land described in Article 4(3)(*a*) must be vatable at the positive rate. It is not clear whether this relates to the disposal of a building before first occupation or a building which satisfies some other criteria other than first occupation as laid down by the Member States. The author is of the view that it refers to a building which is disposed of before first occupation as that is the only type of building described in Article 4(3)(*a*). Nevertheless the point is an arguable one.

Article 4(3)(*b*) refers to the supply of building land. Building land shall mean any unimproved or improved land as defined as such by the Member States.

Thus it seems clear that the effect of Article 13B(*h*) is to ensure that any disposal of building land will give rise to a vatable supply at the positive rate—15 per cent.

Article 13C states that member states may allow taxpayers a right of option for taxation in cases of:

(*a*) Letting and leasing of immovable property.

(*b*) The transactions covered in (*inter alia*) Article 13B(*g*) and (*h*).

It should be noted that the options enable a landlord, for instance, to charge VAT on the letting and leasing of immovable property whether an old or a new property. If the Member State chooses the option can be exercised with respect to rents and/or premiums.

It should also be noted that on the disposal of a building plus the land on which it stands before first occupation (or the like) VAT at 15 per cent must be charged. There is no option in that matter. The same applies to the disposal of building land: under the Directive there is no option in that matter. VAT must be charged. However, on the disposal of land other than building land or on the disposal of a building after first occupation (or the like) the UK government can give the vendor an option to charge VAT.

It is also noted that the Member State may restrict the scope of the right of the option and also fix the details of the option. Clearly the Member State could decide that the option with respect to a particular building whilst held by the particular landlord once exercised shall be irrevocable.

Article 28 sets out the critical transitional provisions which the UK Government has breached.

12.33.1 *Commission of the European Communities* v *United Kingdom* (Case 416/85)

The European Court of Justice (following closely the Opinion of Mr Advocate General Marco Damon in Case 416/85 (December 1987)) decided that the UK government was in part in breach of the provisions of the Sixth Directive and had therefore failed to fulfil its obligations under the EEC Treaty. It held that the supplies of goods and services by builders and developers in relation to the construction of industrial and commercial buildings and community and civil engineering works could not be zero rated and VAT at the positive rate had to be charged.

However, it is quite clear that supplies by private developers and builders as well as by a local authority in connection with the construction of houses, flats etc for residential purposes will be zero rated.

Although one will need to look at the final print in the legislation to be contained in the Finance Act 1989 it is possible that if a builder carries out works for residential purposes (so that no VAT is charged) and subsequently it is decided to use it for commercial purposes nevertheless the VAT will be saved. That is very likely to be the case if the property is first used for residential purposes and subsequently converted to commercial purposes: it is possible that the legislation would provide for some sort of claw-back.

12.33.2 What the Government has said

When the judgment was delivered by the European Court of Justice, Mr Peter Lilley the Economic Secretary to the Treasury made a Statement in Parliament (Hansard vol 135, No 170 col 957–995).

His statement which was made on 21 June 1988 establishes the following critical points:

- The legislation to implement the judgment will be brought before the House of Commons for approval in the 1989 Budget.
- He assured the House of Commons that no changes will take effect before the 1 April 1989. That is a critical pledge. It means that developers have time to arrange their affairs to take into account the possible implications of the decision.
- Non-domestic construction works by builders and developers will be taxed at the standard rate from 1 April 1989.
- The sale of new non-domestic buildings will be taxed at the standard rate from 1 April 1989.
- The sale of building land for non-domestic development will be taxed at the standard rate from 1 April 1989.
- All contracts entered into before 21 June 1988 for the construction of new buildings will continue to be zero rated.
- Payments made (and, presumably, received) before 1 April 1989 in connection with the construction of new buildings will be vatable at the zero rate.
- Public sector construction programmes will be protected by allowing, where necessary, compensating adjustments to the relevant central Government expenditure provision. Full refunds of VAT on non-domestic construction will be available to both health authorities and local authorities.

- Owners of non-domestic property will be given the option to charge VAT on rents (the author hopes that this is extended to premiums).

- The owners of non-domestic property will be given the option to charge VAT on the sale of used buildings. This option to charge VAT and the one above referred to with respect to rents will apply from *1 August 1989*.

- The Economic Secretary also stated that the option will apply to existing buildings as well as new buildings. The statement is a bit ambiguous. It seems that the Secretary when referring to the option means the option to charge VAT on rents, ie, the option to charge VAT on rents will be available to existing buildings as well as new buildings.

- Where the option to charge VAT on rents is exercised landlords and tenants will be able to reclaim VAT on input costs in the normal way. This means that where buildings are occupied by fully taxable businesses neither landlord nor tenant will be worse off.

- To protect tenants who are not fully taxable any VAT on rents will be phased in over two years. For charities the transitional period will be five years.

- It is hoped that the detailed provisions will be published in the draft Finance Bill which should be ready in January 1989.

- Because the Government has agreed to make the option available the 'sting' has been taken out of many potentially problematic areas.

The following examples will show how the new rules may work in practice assuming in all the examples that the new rules as suggested by the Financial Secretary are in operation and that none of the transitional provisions are relevant.

Example 12K: Fully taxable tenant

L Ltd employs a developer to construct a new building on its land. It is an office block. The builder will charge VAT. L Ltd grants a lease to T Ltd (the length of the lease is not relevant). The concept of the major interest contained in VATA 1983, Sched 5, Group 8, Item 1 is not relevant. If L Ltd exercises his option to charge VAT then it can reclaim the input tax which it bore on the charges by the developer but must charge T Ltd VAT on the rents. T Ltd if it is a fully taxable person will be able to reclaim the VAT on the rents. The tax position is therefore neutral and nobody has lost as a result of the EEC decision apart from the cashflow disadvantage.

Example 12L: An exempt tenant

L Ltd employs a developer to put up an office block on its land. It lets the same to a tenant who cannot reclaim the VAT in whole or in part—a bank or a finance company or an insurances company. If L Ltd exercised its option to charge VAT then it can reclaim the input tax charged to it but it must charge VAT on the rents and the tenant will have to bear that VAT in whole or in part. Alternatively, L Ltd may decide not to exercise the option in which case it cannot reclaim the VAT charged to it by the developer but will also not have to charge VAT on the rents.

12.34 THE EUROPEAN COURT DECISION AND THE GENERAL REGULATIONS

The general regulations were substantially amended in 1987 so that broadly input tax can only be reclaimed insofar as supplies made to the taxpayer (on which input tax was charged) are wholly used or were to be wholly used in making taxable supplies. This is the strict direct attribution method and in the author's opinion it is in keeping with the requirements of the EEC Sixth Directive (Article 17).

Taxpayers may find it difficult to apply these rules where property is let.

A developer may arrange for an office block to be built on the developer's land. As the law presently stands, if a developer subsequently grants a major interest, in the form of a lease, in the property, to a tenant he can reclaim any value added tax charged to him in connection with the development. The claim will be by virtue of reg 30(1)(*b*). It is very difficult for the Customs to clawback that relief even if the developer makes an exempt supply of the property within six years (see *Sheffield Co-operative Society* v *The Commissioners* MAN/86/396). Subsequently Regulation 34(1)(*b*) presupposes the making of an exempt supply *before* the zero rated supply is made. The Customs have been considering how to remedy such defects in the regulations and hence the proposal set out in the 'Capital Goods' consultative document (12.10).

Under the proposed changes in the law, consequent on the European Court decision, if a landowner grants a lease he should be able to reclaim any VAT charged to him if he exercises the Article 13C option. Once the option is exercised, however, it will be irrevocable. It would not be possible for a developer to exercise the option for a short period, reclaim all the VAT charged to him and then revoke the option so that he need no longer charge VAT on the rents. It may be that problems such as this can be overcome by the original landowner exercising the option, reclaiming the VAT charged to him and then transferring the property to a connected company. The connected company would not exercise the option. The problem is that any sale proceeds received by the original landowner will be vatable and if the sale is one of *goods* market value may be substituted for the sale price if the sale price is less than the market value of the property.

It seems that if the taxpayer incurs VAT on refurbishment works at present (ie, before the new rules come into operation) but nevertheless intends to exercise the option in the future when the refurbishment works have been completed, that the VAT on any inputs may be reclaimed if the property is let after, or rent first arises after, the end of July 1989. This will be because there will be an intention to make a taxable supply on the grant of the new lease consequent on the exercise of the option (see regs 30(1)(*b*) with 34(3) and 35(3) not being applicable). However, the author understands that the Customs do not accept the above conclusion and the point is arguable. In this event practitioners may want to in certain cases delay payment until after 31 July 1989.

12.35 SO WHO SUFFERS?

If a landlord grants a lease to a tenant who cannot reclaim the VAT then on the face of it the tenant will suffer. The rents will be increased by 15 per cent and these cannot be reclaimed.

A Ltd may be a landlord who has held a building for many years. If he lets the same to a tenant who cannot reclaim the VAT he will probably not exercise the option to charge VAT. The amount of input tax which he cannot reclaim as a result of that is likely to be minimal. On the other hand if B Ltd has recently constructed a building and borne VAT he will want to charge the exempt tenant rent plus VAT. It is clear that the exempt tenant will want to take a lease of A Ltd's property. To that extent B Ltd will suffer and he may have to reduce his rent plus the VAT so that it equates with the rent charged by A Ltd.

12.36 THE CUSTOMS AND EXCISE CONSULTATION PAPER (21/6/88)

On the date of the ruling by the European Court of Justice—21 June 1988—the Customs and Excise issued a Consultation Paper giving further details of the proposed changes in the value added tax legislation and inviting comments from interested parties or representative bodies.

The following are the main points which can be made with respect to the Consultation Paper:

A Services by building and civil engineering contractors and sub-contractors.

The following supplies of services and materials by builders and developers will under the proposed changes become vatable:

(*a*) services in the course of the construction of a non-domestic building;

(*b*) services in the course of the construction or demolition of any civil engineering works; and

(*c*) services in the course of the demolition of any building.

To implement those changes VATA 1983, Sched 5, Group 8, Item 2 and also Item 3 will be amended.

In addition VATA 1983, Sched 5, Group 8A, Item 2, will be amended to remove from zero rating services in the course of the approved alteration of a non-domestic protected building.

It is quite clear that the present rules with respect to the construction of new buildings and the grants of major interests will continue to apply with respect to domestic buildings.

It is also clear that the present rules with respect to approved alterations to listed buildings will apply insofar as the listed buildings are domestic buildings.

Where a building or a protected building is to be used for both non-domestic and domestic purposes contractors and sub-contractors and developers will have to standard rate the non-domestic element and zero rate the domestic element by means of a fair and reasonable apportionment of the total price for the whole job.

The Customs and Excise invited comments on how a domestic or non-domestic building should be defined so as to comply with the terms of the European Court's judgment.

The question of the definition of domestic and non-domestic buildings is not an easy one. The European Court has said that zero rating is appropriate to the housing sector. However, with regard to the commercial and industrial sector and to community and civil engineering works zero rating is not appropriate. The Court has not held, for instance, that all housing works are zero rated whilst all other buildings are vatable. Nor has it held that all commercial and industrial buildings etc are vatable at 15 per cent whilst all other buildings are capable of having zero rating applied to them.

The author feels that to comply with the Directives and the Court's decision the Government should seek to define domestic accommodation (to which zero rating can apply); all other building works should be vatable at 15 per cent or exempt unless the Government can come up with a middle category (which can be zero rated) which can satisfy the last indent of Article 17 of the Second Directive.

The above amendments which are very relevant to contractors and builders and sub-contractors will take effect from the 1 April 1989. The normal rules will apply for establishing tax points in the circumstances of a change from the zero rate to the standard rate. These rules are set out in Appendix F of the VAT Guide Notice 700 October 1987. Clearly it is possible for builders and contractors to be paid upfront (before 1 April 1989) by landowners where a new building is being constructed in order to ensure that zero rating is appropriate.

There is also an additional relief introduced. Any work done or payments received under a written contract signed and sealed prior to 21 June 1988 will remain eligible for zero rating under the existing law even if the relevant tax points would otherwise be on or after 1 April 1989.

It is extraordinary that there is a requirement that the contracts be signed and *sealed.*

Hopefully the Customs will drop the requirement that the contracts be sealed. It is not normal to seal contracts. One may have hoped that the Government would have in fact have gone further and allowed the reliefs to be available if there had been 'arrangements' not necessarily amounting to binding contracts in existence before the 21 June 1988 (see FA 1974, Sched 4, para 4, DLTA 1976, s 45(7) and *Pogson* v *Lowe* [1984] STC 117).

It is far too strict a requirement that the contracts be sealed. Perhaps the legislation will provide that if the type of contract required sealing then it must be sealed. If the contract did not require sealing then it need only be sealed.

The following example may show how the transitional provisions may work.

Example 12M: Pre–1 April 1989 payments

X Plc employs Y builders to construct a new office on its land. X Plc pays Y builders all the building costs—the cheque is cleared—prior to 1 April 1989. VAT need not be charged.

B Freehold sales and long leases of buildings by a builder or developer: freehold sales of building land

The critical Schedule 5, Group 8, Item 1 provisions are to be amended to remove from zero rating the freehold sale or grant of a lease in excess of 21 years of non-domestic buildings or their sites.

Thus under the proposed rules if X Plc, a developer, constructs a new non-domestic building and sells the same the disposal will *not* give rise to a zero rated supply.

Also Schedule 5, Group 8A, Item 1 dealing with listed buildings will be similarly amended so that the disposal of a substantially reconstructed protected building or its site by way of the sale of a freehold or the grant of a lease in excess of 21 years will not be zero rated unless the building is used for domestic purposes.

All the provisions therefore dealing with the construction of new buildings or the substantial reconstruction of listed buildings will remain good law if the buildings comprise domestic buildings.

It is proposed to remove certain disposals from Schedule 6, Group 1, Item 1. These disposals will give rise to charges to VAT at 15 per cent. The options will not be available with respect to these. These disposals are:

(*a*) The freehold (not leasehold) sale of a new non-domestic building; to strictly comply with Article 4(3)(*a*) of the Sixth Directive the author feels that this must comprise the disposal before first occupation of a building or part of a building and the land on which it stands. However, the Customs and Excise propose that a new building for this purpose would be one which is sold either prior to its completion or within a specified period from the date of its completion (it is suggested that this period might be either three or five years). The Customs therefore propose to give a wide interpretation to Article 4(3)(*a*) and Article 13B(*g*) which may well not be justified on the strict interpretation of the Directive. This is because the Directive does seem to indicate that a sale which takes place *before first occupation* of the building shall be vatable at 15 per cent. The Customs and Excise guidance simply says that VAT must be charged if it is sold either prior to completion or within a specified period from the date of its completion, presumably whether or not it is first occupied.

(*b*) Also VAT at 15 per cent must be charged on the freehold (not leasehold: such sales are exempt and no option may be available) sale of building land other than building land sold with planning permission wholly for residential development.

(*c*) The EEC Sixth Directive Article 4(3)(*b*) states that building land shall mean any unimproved or improved land defined as such by the Member States. It is hoped that some guidance will be provided in the legislation as to what building land is.

(*d*) The above rules are to take effect from 1 April 1989. The Customs say that the normal rules will apply for establishing tax points when there is a change of tax liability from, say, exemption to 15 per cent. The Customs say that the rules in Appendix F of the VAT Guide No 700 October 1987 will apply. In addition it is provided that *contracts*:

(i) for the freehold sale of buildings at present qualifying for zero rating under Item 1 of Group 8 or Group 8A; and

(ii) for the freehold sale of non-residential building land at present qualifying for exemption under Item 1 of Group 1, if already signed *and* sealed prior to 21 June 1988 but with a tax point date on or after 1 April 1989 will still qualify for zero rating and exemption respectively.

Once again it is extraordinary that the requirement should be one of signature and sealing; it is very unusual to seal a contract. Hopefully that requirement will be dropped when the final legislation comes through.

There are also transitional reliefs for leasehold transactions. Zero rating, the Paper states, may be retained for payments under long leases signed and sealed prior to 21 June 1988 only to the extent of *capital sums* received on or after 1 April 1989 and *payable under the terms of the lease.* Zero rating may not be retained for any payments of rent received on or after 1 April 1989.

It is clear that the Government is not going to allow leases granted before 21 June 1988 to give rise to zero rated rents for years into the future. However, with regard to capital sums payable under the terms of the lease it would appear that zero rating will always be available regardless of when the sums are received provided the leases are signed and sealed (there is more justification for the 'sealing' requirement in this case) prior to 21 June 1988.

The Customs invited comments on the definition of domestic or non-domestic building and on the most appropriate definition of building land.

C Option for taxation

The Consultation Paper also throws some light on the nature of the option provisions referred to in the Statement by Peter Lilley.

It is proposed that from the *1 August 1989* (not 1 April) any person making a supply in respect of any non-domestic building, eg, the sale of an office block, or of any developed land (other than building land) used for a non-domestic purpose, which would be an exempt supply under Item 1 of Group 1, Schedule 6, will be able to opt to convert that supply, and all his future supplies in respect of that particular building or land, into a taxable supply.

The main features of this option scheme will be as follows:

(*a*) The option is entirely at the discretion of the supplier; he will not be obliged to consult the recipient before deciding whether to opt although he may choose to do so in practice. The option can therefore be exercised on the sale of property and on the grant of a lease. The length of the term of the lease is not relevant.

(*b*) The option applies to both new and existing buildings and must be exercised on a building by building basis. Once exercised it cannot be varied for any future supplies (lettings or sale). The Consultation Paper and the Statement in Parliament is unclear in certain respects. It seems to the author that the provisions of the Sixth Directive do require that certain land transactions must have VAT charged on them. These are the transactions referred to in Article 13B(*g*) and (*h*) and in Article 4(3)(*a*) and (*b*). It may be that it is intended that those transactions will be vatable but there are parts of the Consultation Paper which seem to indicate that that may not entirely be the case. In particular the reference to the option being applicable to new buildings would seem to indicate that the legislation may not be complying totally with the requirements of the Sixth Directive.

(*c*) The option is to be exercised with respect to a particular building. There is much case law in this area (see *Moir* v *Williams* (1892) 1 QB 270, *Stevens* v *Gourley* (1859) 7 CBNS 99, *Brown* v *Leicester Corn* (1892) 57 JP 70 and pages 47 to 51 hereof).

There are likely to be areas of difficulty.

(*d*) Once the taxpayer has exercised an option with respect to a particular building he cannot vary that option. This is likely to give rise to arrangements where property is transferred to connected persons, so that the option position can be looked at afresh. Anti-avoidance provisions may well be incorporated into the new legislation. Maybe the building will always be subject to the exercised option whoever owns it.

(*e*) Under the new rules landlords will have to send to Custom and Excise a list of the buildings for which they are opting except where the only supplies eligible for option treatment in respect of a particular building are licences to occupy as opposed to leases/tenancies. It is not at all easy to distinguish between a licence to occupy and a tenancy (see *Taylor* v *Caldwell* (1863) 3 B&S 826; *Somma* v *Hazlehurst* [1978] 2 All ER 1011; *O'Malley* v *Seymour* (1979) 250 EG 1083 and *Street* v *Mountford* [1985] 2 All ER 289).

(*f*) A landlord will not be able to opt for taxing a lease/tenancy/licence to occupy any part of a building which is to be used as a dwelling: any supply relating to a dwelling must remain an exempt supply or in an appropriate case under Group 8 or Group 8A a zero rated supply.

(*g*) There is to be a transitional relief. In respect of existing buildings landlords will have to charge value added tax as if the consideration for each supply under the option was one half of the rent due for the period 1 August 1989 to 31 July 1990. Tax will become chargeable on the basis of the full rent due for periods from 1 August 1990 onwards. For charities the phasing-in would be over a five year period commencing on 1 August 1989 with appropriate adjustments being made to the proportions of rent chargeable with value added tax. For new buildings unoccupied by tenants or licencees at 1 August 1989, tax will become chargeable on the basis of the full rent due from the commencement of the lease or licence.

(*h*) A landlord who exercises the option to charge taxation from 1 August 1989 will be able, in respect of lettings which up until 31 March 1989 were zero rated under Item 1 of Group 8 or Item 1 of Group 8A, to disregard for partial exemption purposes the four months from April to July 1989 in which the rents became exempt. In addition a landlord who has opted for any building or land and who has to apply the transitional relief described in (*g*) above will be able to treat the input tax incurred in respect of that building or land for the years concerned as fully deductible subject to the normal rules.

(*i*) The Customs invited comments on whether the option should apply to agricultural and undeveloped land (other than building land).

D Self supply of building services

It is proposed that value added tax will be charged on businesses which do their own building works. The new provisions will be brought into effect by an Order made pursuant to VATA 1983, s 3(6).

The Consultation Paper states that this is an anti-avoidance provision designed to prevent exempt or partially exempt businesses avoiding value added tax on the salary, labour and profit element of the building process.

The old arrangements of taking builders on to the staff to become employees of the company in order to avoid value added tax may well be caught by these new anti-avoidance provisions.

E Exhibition stands

It is proposed that the current exclusion from Item 1 of Group 1, Schedule 6 will be deleted. This relates to exhibition organisers. It is felt that exhibition organisers will be able to use the option facility if they wish to tax their supplies of space and stands to exhibitors.

F Surrenders of interests in property

Surrenders of land interest are to be taken out of the specific exemption provisions in Schedule 6, Group 1, Item 1. Surrenders are also not covered and will not be covered by the zero rating provisions relating to land transactions. Thus surrenders of land interests will give rise to vatable supplies (vatable at 15 per cent).

12.36.1 Non-domestic buildings—falling between two or more stools

Under the EEC Sixth Directive all supplies in the course or furtherance of a business are vatable (at 15%) unless an exemption is available.

It should be noted that under Article 13B(*b*) generally the leasing or letting of immovable property will be exempt. It is also clear that under Article 13C the UK can give landlords the right of option to charge tax in the case of the letting and leasing of most immovable property.

The supply of buildings or parts thereof and the land on which they stand under Article 13B(*g*), unless it is the disposal before first occupation (or the like) of a new building, is exempt. Additionally, the supply of land which has not been built on, other than the supply of building land, is exempt.

Thus it seems to be the case that if land (assume it is not building land) has been built on, but there is no building as such thereon, the supply may be vatable at 15%. Thus if X has put a new structure on his land—it could be a civil engineering work—and that structure does not comprise a building (and assume the land is not building land because, for instance, it is not intended that new buildings be put thereon), then the supply will be vatable at 15% *unless* the sale falls within the last indent of Article 17 to the Second Directive which the author feels it is virtually impossible for it to do bearing in mind the European Court decision and the 31 December 1975 cut-off date in Article 28(2) of the EEC Sixth Directive. The problem may be overcome if 'building' is comprehensively defined to include a civil engineering work (see, for example, Article 4(3)(*a*)).

12.37 WHAT VAT PAYERS SHOULD DO BEFORE 1 APRIL 1989

12.37.1 Pre-21 June 1988 building contracts

All building contracts entered into before 21 June 1988 for the construction of new buildings will continue to be zero rated. Hopefully the requirement that the contract must be 'sealed' as stated in the Consultation Paper (see p 84) will not find its way into the final legislation.

12.37.2 Pre-1 April 1989 leases

There is little to be gained by granting leases early (before 1 April 1989) as the Consultation Paper states that the rents under such leases will not be zero rated if received on or after 1 April 1989. Capital sums, however, paid after 31 March 1989 will be zero rated but only if paid under the terms of the lease. There will therefore be little scope to make use of that transitional relief.

12.37.3 Early sales

Sales of new buildings and building land will give rise to vatable supplies (15 per cent) after 31 March 1989; otherwise the sale of property will only give rise to vatable supplies if the Article 13C options are exercised although in the case of the disposal of a new domestic building (or a substantially reconstructed listed domestic building) by the constructor, zero rating will apply provided the disposal comprises the grant of a major interest. It may be that if taxpayers are in the course of constructing a new building and have borne substantial amounts of input tax and the ultimate users are to be exempt persons the property should be sold (this would comprise a zero rated supply) before the 1 April 1989. This would enable the VAT on the construction works up to the date of sale to be reclaimed, but for the sale proceeds to be VAT free (there will be a zero rated supply).

12.37.4 Payments up-front

If the taxpayer anticipates letting commercial or industrial buildings to exempt tenants then he should consider ensuring that the payments are received by the builder before 1 April 1986. The supplies would therefore be zero rated.

Bank guarantee
The simplest procedure would be for the landowner–developer to employ the builder and pay him the building price securing a bank guarantee from the builder's bank.

'Fluid' account bank guarantee
If the money paid to the builder is credited to the builder's account with a bank requirement that it should never go below a particular figure (that figure would be an amount to cover the bank's guarantee at any particular moment of time) then there should be no problems under *Ramsay* or under any other provisions in the VAT legislation.

'Deposit funds' bank guarantee
If that cannot be achieved the author is of the view that if the landowner pays the builder up front and without the landowner being concerned the builder then deposits the money to back the bank guarantee given by the builder's bank to the landowner this should succeed in its object: the VAT point would be the time when the cheque is cleared by the builder to be on the safe side (see 12.2).

Builder's loan
If the builder lends the landowner the necessary monies for the work with the landowner then using those monies to pay for the building works up-front there should be no difficulties. As the building progresses the landowner will have to use his own monies or his own borrowings to repay the loan made by the builder to him. The tax point will arise when the monies (for the building works) are actually received by the builder (see 12.1.7). It may be prudent for a zero-rated VAT invoice to be issued by the builder to the landowner at the same time but that is not vital and it is arguable that a VAT invoice is not appropriate in a case such as that.

Stakeholders
Arrangements under which the monies are paid to, say, an independent stakeholder with the monies then being released as the development progresses must be avoided (see 12.2).

'Frozen monies' ('Dormers' accounts')
In *Dormers' Builders (London) Ltd* v *The Commissioners* (1988) STI 339 a bank in effect advanced monies to the client in the sum of £600,000 who paid the same over to the builder by crediting the monies to the builder's deposit account at the bank. However, the builder was prevented from requiring the transfer of any part of the £600,000 to its current account until presentation of architects' certificates showing that certain works had been completed. McNeill J held that there was no sensible alternative to the conclusion that the builder was in reality the recipient of the payment when the monies were credited to the deposit account. The monies were placed at the disposal of the builder. The credit to the deposit account (which was made before 1 June 1984) was payment received by the builder. The payment discharged the client from a liability to pay for the building works and additionally the builder had no right to sue the client for the sum so credited. This is a very borderline case and is barely distinguishable from a stakeholder's account so that such arrangements should only be used if one or other of the first four above mentioned arrangements cannot be used.

13 STAMP DUTY

13.1 INTRODUCTION

Stamp duty is a highly technical tax, administered by the Controller of Stamps under the auspices of the Commissioners of Inland Revenue. It is governed by the Stamp Act 1891 (as amended by Revenue Acts and Finance Acts), and all statutory references in this chapter, unless otherwise stated, are to that Act.

Stamp duty is an ancient levy chargeable on certain legal instruments (which are defined to include every written document—s 122(1)). For there to be a charge there must be a document (*per* Lord Esher MR in *IRC* v *Angus & Co* (1839) 23 QBD 579 and 589).

Unstamped or insufficiently stamped documents are not to be given in evidence in any Court of Civil Judicature or before any Arbitrator or Referee except in criminal proceedings or to be available for 'any purpose whatever' (s 14(4)).

The general rule is that a document is subject to stamp duty if:

(*a*) it is executed in the UK; or

(*b*) it is executed outside the UK but relates to property situated, or to any matter or thing done or to be done, in the UK.

Documents have to be stamped within certain time limits.

13.2 THE VALIDITY OF STAMP DUTY INDEMNITIES

The Stamp Act 1891, s 117 is a provision of unclear meaning. It can make certain stamp duty indemnities void. Section 117 reads thus:

> Every condition of sale framed with the view of precluding objection or requisition upon the ground of absence or insufficiency of stamp upon any instrument executed after the sixteenth day of May one thousand eight

hundred and eighty-eight (16 May 1888), and every contract, arrangement, or undertaking for assuming the liability on account of absence or insufficiency of stamp upon any such instrument or indemnify against such liability, absence, or insufficiency, shall be void.

(*a*) The section is on the face of it capable of bearing two meanings. It could mean that a taxpayer who agrees to indemnify another taxpayer with respect to stamp duty 'upon any instrument excluded after 16 May 1888' will not be able to enforce that agreement because it will be void. Alternatively the provision could have a much more restricted meaning and indeed the author feels the provision does have a much restricted meaning. Such a restricted meaning would effectively cause the section to read as follows:

> Every contract, arrangement, or undertaking for assuming the liability on account of absence or insufficiency of stamp upon any instrument executed after 16th May 1888 (being an instrument which could have been the subject of objections or requisitions at the time of a sale) or indemnifying against such liability, absence, or insufficiency, shall be void.

(*b*) In other words, the section envisages a situation where X is proposing to sell to Y. X may have documents improperly stamped or not stamped at all. The provision prevents X being able to agree with Y that Y will assume the liability for the stamp duty and not raise any objections or requisitions with respect to stamp duty or indemnify with respect to such liability.

(*c*) The following appear to be the decisive points with respect to the interpretation of the provision:
(i) The reference to *such* instrument is well capable of meaning not just an instrument executed after 16 May 1888 but an instrument which *could* have been the subject of objections and requisitions when the property is in the course of being sold; clearly one could not raise objections and requisitions with respect to the actual agreement or deed of sale. It must refer to presale documents.
(ii) Documents under which one party agrees to bear stamp duty in a particular way are common place.
(iii) The Law Society Notice Opinion no 1398 assumes that one party can agree to bear the stamp duty which would normally fall on another party.
(iv) The decision of *Abbott* v *Stratton* (1846) 91 Eq R 233, properly interpreted, and ignoring the misleading headnote, indicates that indemnities for stamp duty are valid (see also *Sergeant and Sims on Stamp Duties* 9th Edition, p 23 and 183 and 8th Edition p 13) although the position may be different with regard to indemnities to bear stamp duty penalties (the author feels that such indemnities would not be valid).
(v) The provisions of the Law of Property Act 1925, s 42 which declare certain stipulations to be void if they seek to preclude a purchaser from effectively dealing with certain *weaknesses in title all deal with earlier links in title.* Section 117 is a similar type of

provision declaring a particular stipulation (relating to stamp duty) to be void.

(vi) There is no rule in the UK stamp legislation that particular persons shall be liable to stamp documents. The list of persons in SA 1891, s 15(2)(*d*) are only for the purposes of penalties. Thus the basis of s 117 does not seem to be one under which Parliament had intended that particular persons should bear the duty as is the case with respect to the Land Commission Act 1968, s 82(2)(*c*). There is therefore *no compelling reason to hold that the provision is designed to catch the particular actual document of transfer because Parliament* wants the purchaser to bear the stamp duty as opposed to the vendor. If one goes back to the early cases which may have prompted the legislation which was first introduced in 1888, one will see from those cases (*Whiting* v *Loomes* [1881] 17 ChD 10 and *Ex p Birbeck Freehold Land* [1883] 24 ChD 119) that the Courts had difficulties with respect to situations where property was sold by X to Y but earlier links in the title of X were defective because the documents had not been properly stamped. Once again, this points to earlier links in title as being the types of transactions which s 117 is aimed at.

13.3 STAMP DUTY STRATEGY IN LAND TRANSACTIONS

Stamp duty should never be overlooked in any commercial property transaction. There are a number of heads of stamp duty but the important ones with respect to land transactions are:

(*a*) conveyance or transfer on sale duty (s 54 to s 58),

(*b*) contract duty (s 59),

(*c*) freehold exchange duty (s 73),

(*d*) duty on premiums and rents received on the grants of leases (Sched 1),

(*e*) agreements for lease duty (s 75),

(*f*) rent increases duty (s 77(5)),

(*g*) fixed duties (Sched 1).

These above seven heads can conveniently be dealt with under three major heads:

Head A Conveyance or transfer on sale duty (heads (*a*)–(*c*) above) (see page 269),
Head B Lease duty (heads (*d*)–(*f*) above) (see page 298),
Head C Fixed duty (head (*g*) above) (see page 311).

The conveyance or transfer on sale duty is 1% but the lease duty can be up to 24%.

13.4 HEAD A: CONVEYANCE OR TRANSFER ON SALE DUTY

13.4.1 Introduction

Conveyance or transfer on sale duty is charged at 1% by virtue of s 1 and the First Schedule to the SA 1891. The following provisions contain the appropriate rate and definition:

FA 1963, s 55(1)
. . . the stamp duty chargeable under the heading 'Conveyance or Transfer on Sale' in Schedule 1 to the SA 1891 shall be charged . . . at . . . the rate of £1 for every £100 or part of £100 of the consideration.

SA 1891 s 54
. . . 'conveyance on sale' includes every instrument . . . whereby any property, or any estate or interest in any property, upon the sale thereof is transferred to or vested in a purchaser, or any other person on his behalf or by his direction.

13.4.2 The six fundamental transactions and conveyance or transfer on sale duty

The charge to Conveyance or Transfer on Sale duty is now examined with respect to the following transactions:

(*A*) X contracts to sell his freehold to Y.

(*B*) X declares that he holds the freehold as nominee for Y.

(*C*) X contracts to sell his freehold to Y and Y assigns the contract.

(*D*) X contracts to sell his freehold to Y who contracts to sell it to Z with X transferring the formal title to Z direct.

(*E*) (*a*) and (*b*) above may be combined in a particular transaction.

(*F*) X may contract to sell the freehold to Y who may contract to sell it back to X.

13.5 TRANSACTION (*A*)—CONTRACTS

A contract to convey land is by definition not a conveyance; it is merely an agreement to convey and is thus stamp duty free under general principles (*IRC* v *Angus* [1889] 23 WBD 579).

It is submitted that the agreement cannot be stamped under SA 1891, s 59(1) because it will be an agreement for the sale of the legal estate in the land whereas that provision only applies to an agreement for the sale of an equitable estate or interest in the land.

13.5.1 Revenue View

The Revenue have indicated to the author that if there is a contract to sell land to, say, a company at £1m which is the then market value and 5 years later completion takes place the stamp duty will still be based on £1m even though at the time of completion the value of the land may have gone up.

13.5.2 Warning

If the parties never intend to complete the legal transfer the contract may be stampable as comprising the sale of an equitable interest in land within SA 1891, s 59 (see *West London Syndicate Ltd* v *IRC* [1898] 2 QB 507 at 520).

13.6 TRANSACTION (*B*)—DECLARATION OF TRUST

It is not possible to avoid conveyance or transfer on sale duty by a declaration of trust by a vendor in favour of a purchaser.

Example 13A: Declaration of trust

In consideration of £1m paid by the purchaser to the vendor the vendor declares that it holds Blackacre for the absolute benefit of the purchaser. £10,000 stamp duty is payable on the declaration of trust.

Duty is payable on declaration of trust

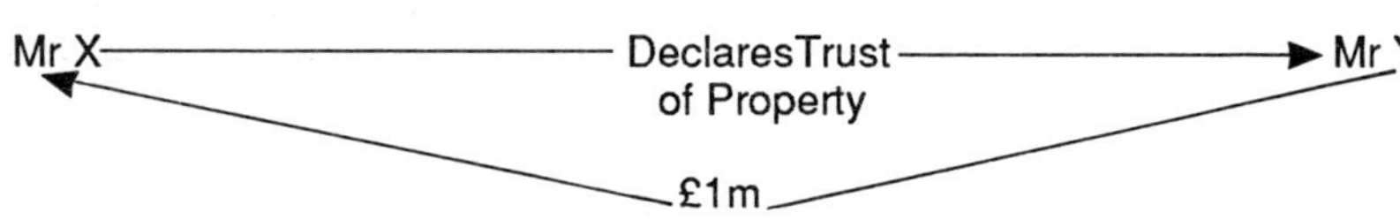

13.6.1 Chesterfield Brewery Case

In *Chesterfield Brewery co* v *IRC* QB [1899] 7 there was a declaration of trust of shares in consideration of the person making the declaration receiving consideration (other shares). Wills J at p 13 stated:

> I am satisfied that . . . the real intention of the parties was that this agreement (agreement which effectively amounted to a declaration of trust) should be the new company's only document of title and that it should not be followed by a legal transfer of the shares in the old company . . . . Under

> those circumstances the natural influence is that the parties would wish to avoid the expense of an actual transfer.
> Further, speaking for myself, I entertain no doubt that this agreement is not only a 'conveyance on sale' under s 54, but that it is also a contract for the sale of an equitable interest in property within s 59.

The reason why there is a charge is that the declaration of trust is basically a completed transaction. There is nothing more to be done. This is also the reason why option agreements over land may be stampable.

In *George Wimpey & Co Ltd* v *IRC* [1975] STC 248, M granted the taxpayer company an option to purchase the land for a consideration. It was held that an option to purchase land constituted property and that the grant of it for consideration constituted a sale thereof. This is the case whether the option was under seal or merely in the form of an agreement.

13.6.2 Note:

If the option cost is less than £30,000 a certificate of value is probably appropriate even though if exercised a substantial sum will be paid to purchase the land.

13.7 TRANSACTION (*C*)—A SALE OF AN EQUITABLE CONTRACT IS STAMPABLE

A contract to sell as equitable interest in land is stampable (SA 1891, s 59).

A contracts to buy land. He enters into an agreement to assign the same to B for £1m. That agreement is stampable under SA 1891, s 59. Section 59(1) reads thus:

> Any contract . . . for the sale of any equitable estate or interest in any property whatsoever, or for the sale of any estate or interest in any property except lands, tenements, hereditaments, or heritages, or property locally situated out of the UK, or goods, wares or merchandise, or stock or marketable securities, or any ship or vessel . . . shall be charged with [*ad valorem* stamp duty].

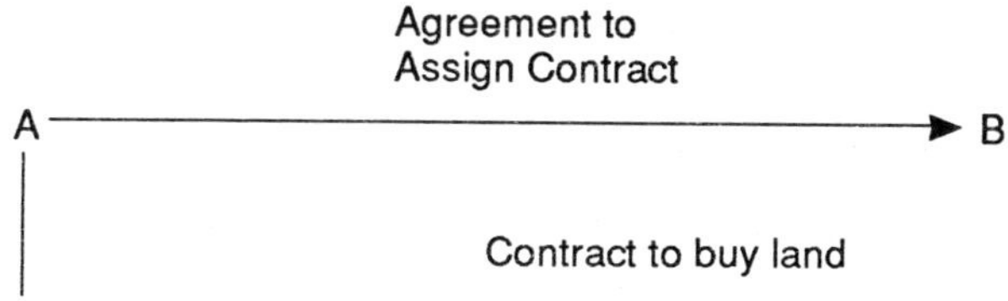

This must be distinguished from

(1) a sub-sale and

(2) a declaration of trust

One must also note the two relieving provisions in s 59(5) and (6) which in many cases will take the sting out of the section.

13.7.1 The equitable contract oversight

It may be that the failure to stamp a document within the 30 days time limit which is a contract within s 59 will not result in the s 15(2) penalties because it is not specifically listed in s 15(2)(*d*).

Note that s 75 agreements for lease or tack are included in the list of penalty documents.

13.8 TRANSACTION (*D*)—SUB-SALES

If A sells property to B, who then sells the same property to C, provided the conveyance is made direct from A to C duty is chargeable only on the price paid by C to B provided the price paid by C is the same as (or more than) the value of the property immediately before the contract of sale to him (s 58(4)).

Stamp duty can thus be saved by sub-selling property and relying on the provisions of SA 1891, s 58.

If the sub-sale relief is not available it is clear that duty on both lots of consideration will be exigible (*Fitch Lovell Ltd* v *IRC* [1962] 3 All ER 685 at p 698 and *Escoigne Properties Ltd* v *IRC* [1958] 1 All ER 406 at p 413).

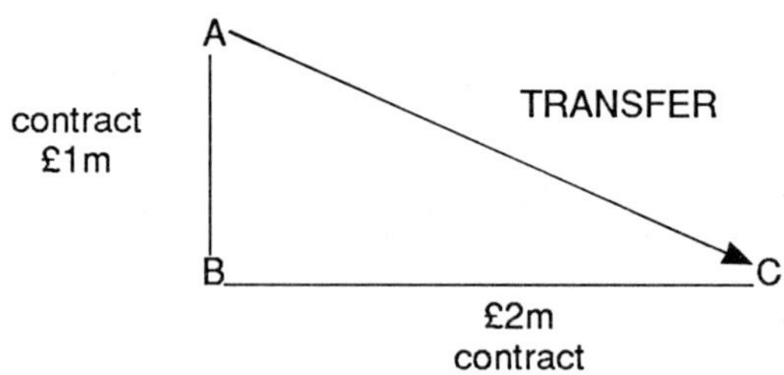

If no sub-sale relief is available duty on £3m is payable on the transfer document.

If the original purchaser only sub-sells part of the property a proper apportionment of the price paid for the land retained and the land sold on must be made (*Maples* v *IRC* [1914], 3 KB 303).

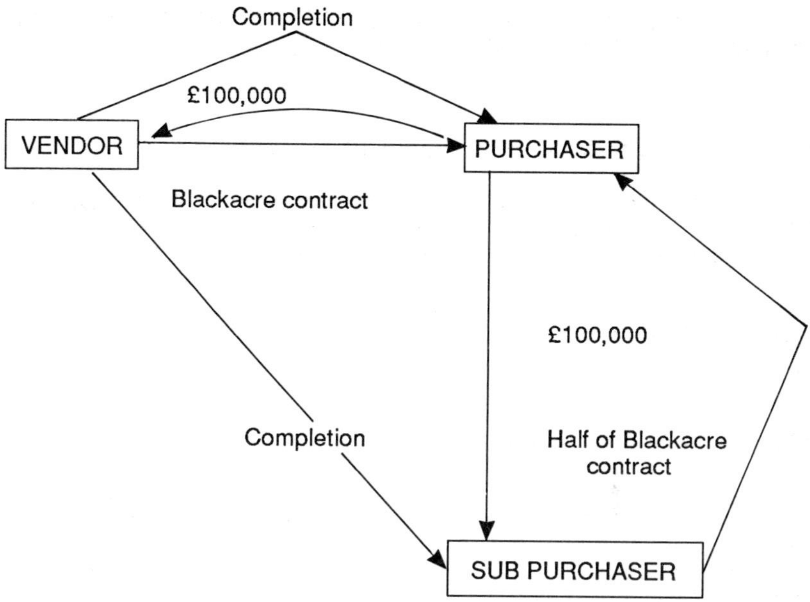

The stamp duty is £1,500, ie, 1% of £50,000 and £100,000.

(This assumes that the half of Blackacre retained by the purchaser is worth £50,000).

Planning
Always make use of this relief if feasible.

13.8.1 Sale and exchange

A sale and an exchange is unlikely to amount to a sub-sale.

X contracts to sell Cedar Cottage to Y for £1m and then Y exchanges Cedar Cottage for Greenacre with Z. Sub-sale relief is unlikely to be available and the exchange document/transfer would be stampable on £1m.

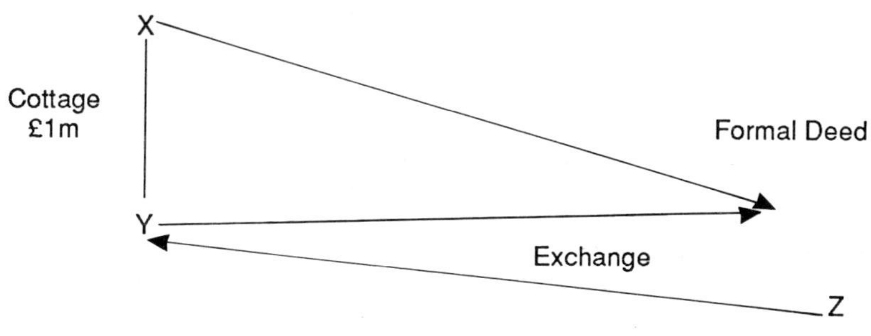

13.9 TRANSACTION (*E*)—CONTRACTS WITH A DECLARATION

It is clear that if X contracts to sell the legal estate in Blackacre to Y, that the contract is not stampable even though the equitable interest passes.

If, however, X contracts to sell the freehold in Blackacre to Y but states in the contract that X shall also be a bare trustee of the property for Y, the Stamp Office will argue that stamp duty is payable on the agreement under SA 1891, s 59, or, more simply, because the document in that case amounts to a conveyance on sale, following the case of *Chesterfield Brewery Co v IRC* [1899] 2 QB 7.

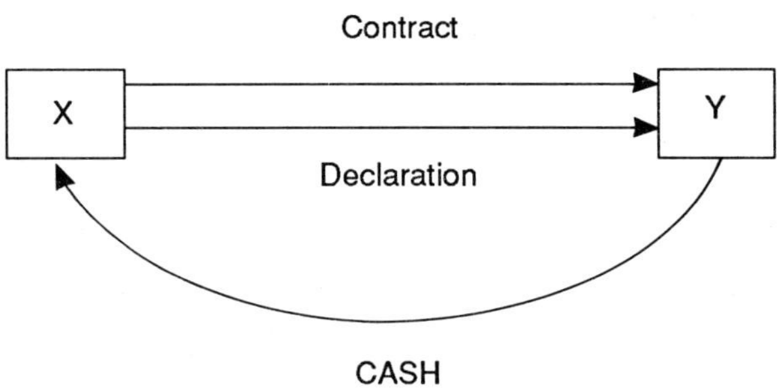

13.10 TRANSACTION (*F*)—LAND-LEND

It is difficult to see how the Stamp Office can get duty on a land-lend transaction.

A may contract to sell Greenacre to B for £50,000. B builds thereon and contracts to sell back for £100,000, the title never leaving A. It is difficult to see how the Stamp Office can get duty in those circumstances. This may be done for VAT purposes.

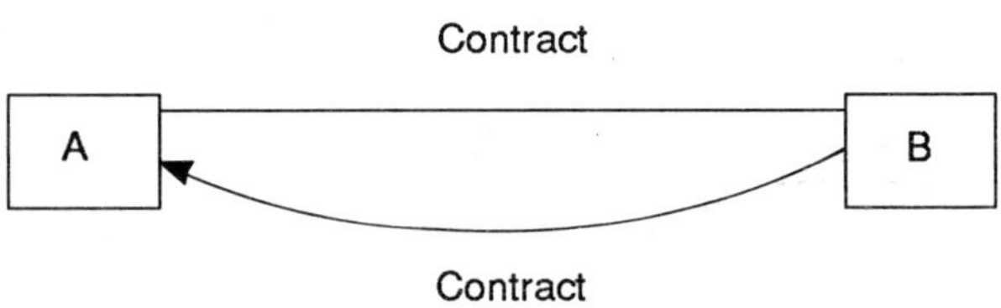

13.11 FINDING THE STAMPABLE CONSIDERATION

13.11.1 No cash, no duty

The broad maxim, which is subject to exceptions, is that if there is no cash there can be no duty.

13.11.2 Statute

The relevant head is 'conveyance or transfer on sale' duty. 'On sale' generally denotes a sale for cash. A further head of charge refers to 'the amount or value' of the consideration. The words 'or value' do not import that *ad valorem* duty is payable in respect of the consideration given in the instrument regardless of whether it is money or otherwise. These words have been inserted because for the purposes of the Stamp Act 1891 the consideration for a sale may not be only money but foreign or colonial currency (s 6), stock, including shares and units under a Unit Trust scheme (FA 1946, ss 55(1) and 54(1)), marketable and other securities (s 55) and debts and transfers made certainly or contingently for any money or stock (s 57 (see *Sergeant & Sims on Stamp Duties,* 9th Edition, p 123).

13.11.3 IRC v Littlewoods Stores

The leading case on exchange is *IRC* v *Littlewoods Stores Ltd* [1962] 2 All ER 279. In this case leasehold property was exchanged for freehold property. It was held that the deed of exchange was not liable to *ad valorem* stamp duty as a conveyance or transfer on sale because although it was not an exchange or excambion within the meaning of SA 1891, s 54 and Sched 1, it was also not a conveyance or transfer 'on sale' since sale connoted, amongst other things, a price in money paid or promised. Viscount Simmonds at p 283c stated:

> If stamp duty is to be assessed on the instrument as a conveyance or transfer on sale an extended meaning must be given to the words 'on sale'. For neither in form nor in substance is exchange a sale according to the ordinary legal terminology . . . *Prima facie,* therefore, exchange is not a conveyance on sale. There is no price in money paid or promised on one side or the other. On the contrary the consideration was expressed to be on the one side the conveyance of the fee simple, on the other side the assignment of the lease.

The Court was of the view that there had to be a price in money paid or promised in order for there to be a sale.

It should be noted that an exchange of freeholds may be stampable at 50p under SA 1891, Sched 1 and s 73. Other exchanges may come with *IRC* v *Littlewoods* as being stampable at 50p as being miscellaneous conveyances.

13.11.4 Two sales is no good

Two sales of two assets for cash is not an exchange (*Portman* v *IRC* [1965] 35 ATC 349). The exchange must be carefully carried out. If the deed of exchange is preceded by contracts selling the properties for cash duty will not be avoided.

13.11.5 Tax planning

It appears, therefore, that if, for example, a tenant assigns his leasehold interest to an assignor and this is done under exchange no *ad valorem* duty will be payable thereunder provided the exchanged property does not fall within the prohibited classes, eg, securities etc.

One could exchange the leasehold interest for another leasehold interest or another land interest or furniture, vehicles, etc.

Thus, the general principle, subject to restricted exceptions, is 'no cash, no duty'.

There is a good argument that if freehold land is exchanged for furniture or a leasehold (but not for another freehold) no stamp duty is payable on any equality money. This conclusion derives from:

(*a*) SA 1981, ss 54 and 73 and *Littlewoods Mail Order Stores Ltd* v *IRC* [1963], AC 153.

(*b*) *James Cormack and Others* v *IRC* [1924] SC 819 at p 828.

(*c*) 'The Scope for Reforming Stamp Duties' (C.D.) para 6.16.

The equality money must bear a proper relationship to the assets exchanged, the author would suggest. If X 'exchanged' a car worth £1,000 plus £99,000 equality money for £100,000 worth of leasehold (transferred to X by Y) there is unlikely to be an 'exchange'. If the figures were reversed so that the car was worth £99,000 and £1,000 of equality was paid for the leasehold, stamp duty would be avoided.

13.12 SALES AT UNDERVALUE

If land is sold at an undervalue duty is only payable on the actual consideration.

If Mr X sells freehold land worth £1m to Mr Y for £1/2m duty is only payable on £1/2m. The author does not see how the Revenue could charge duty on anything but the actual consideration passing.

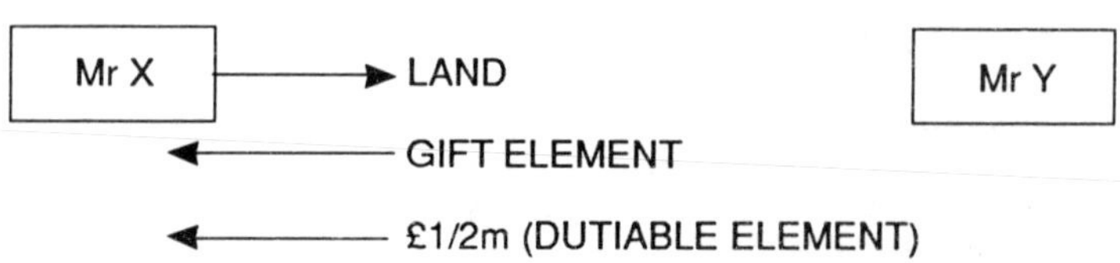

13.13 FIND THE CONSIDERATION

13.13.1 Gifts do not give rise to *ad valorem* charges

X Ltd a Jersey company may transfer shares in a UK Company or UK land to another Jersey Company in return for shares. Duty may be payable.

X Ltd may be owned by Mr X who also owns Y Ltd. If X Ltd gives UK land to Y Ltd could the increase in the value of the shares (in Y Ltd) be stampable consideration? The author has not heard of this point being taken by the Stamp Office.

13.14 SEVERANCE OF JOINT TENANCY

The partition of land held upon trust for sale where for instance A and B are joint tenants of the beneficial interest can be carried out under the Law of Property Act 1925, s 28(3), or the proviso to s 36(2) by a notice to sever. Such a notice, which must be in writing, does not require any *ad valorem* Stamp Duty.

13.15 CONVEYANCE IN CONSIDERATION OF DEBT

Where any property is conveyed to any person in consideration, wholly or in part, of any debt due to him, or subject either certainly or contingently to the payment or transfer of any money or stock, whether being or constituting a charge or encumbrance upon the property or not, the debt, money or stock is to be deemed the whole or part, as the case may be, of the consideration in respect whereof the conveyance is chargeable with *ad valorem* duty (SA 1891, s 57 which reproduces SA 1870, s 73 which was amended by SA 1853, s 10 to overcome the 'loophole' revealed by *Marquis of Chandos v IRC* (1851) 6 Exch 464).

Example 13B: Debts

This provision may be applicable if Mr X accepts property in satisfaction of a debt which is owed to him.

13.15.1 Inherent liabilities

Liabilities inherent within the property itself do not come within this provision (*Swayne* v *IRC* [1900] 1 QB 172(CA)—the Revenue cannot capitalise a rental obligation).

13.15.2 Exchanges—real or false

On apparent exchanges of land one must make sure that one does not inadvertently get caught by this provision.

13.15.3 Width

The section applies (if the transaction is one of sale) whether the purchaser is personally liable for the burden or not (*IRC* v *City of Glasgow Bank* liquidators [1881] 8 R 389) and it makes no difference that the sale is part of a family arrangement (*Marquess of Bristol* v *IRC* [1901] 2 KB 336). If a creditor takes over the property of the debtor and releases the debt the transaction is a sale chargeable under this head (*IRC* v *North British Rly Co* [1901] 4 F 27, see *Sergeant and Sims on Stamp Duties,* 9th Edition, p 137).

13.16 THE MORTGAGE GIFT TRAP

13.16.1 Some apparent gifts may be stampable

Mr X may give Mr Y Greenacre (worth £1m) subject to a mortgage which Mr Y has to discharge of £0.25m. Duty on £0.25m is chargeable by virtue of SA 1891, s 57.

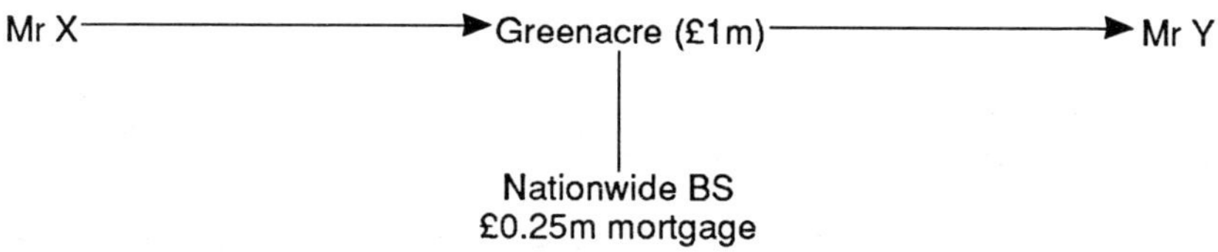

13.17 AVOID THE CONTINGENCY

13.17.1 Sales subject to a contingency should be avoided

X may sell land for £1m with the purchaser taking over possible obligations to a financial institution up to a ceiling of £10m.

The chances of that obligation being called in may be negligible.

Perhaps X could do two transactions.

(*a*) He could 'sell' the obligation to the purchaser paying the purchaser £1,000 being the value of the obligation: there should be no duty on that.

(*b*) Sell the land for £1m. The duty may thus be reduced to £10,000. The duty would otherwise have been £110,000. Note: it is assumed that FA 1900 s 10 is not applicable.

13.18 NO DOCUMENT NO DUTY

13.18.1 Purchase of freehold and surrender

Where a purchaser is proposing to take an assignment of a lease he should perhaps consider acquiring the freehold reversion on which stamp duty (perhaps a small amount) would be payable and then taking a surrender of the lease by operation of law.

13.18.2 Planning

It may also be possible for the purchaser when he cannot purchase the freehold to be granted an overriding lease on which duty (perhaps a small amount) would be payable with the tenant then surrending by operation of law. The possible application of the *Ingram* decision (see below) must be considered in this and all other stamp duty mitigation schemes.

13.19 ANTI-AVOIDANCE

Stamp duty is chargeable on documents. It had been hoped that the *Ramsay* doctrine would not apply to the duty (see the decision of *Ramsay v IRC* [1981] STC 174). Vinelott J in the Chancery Division decision of *Blendett v IRC* [1983] STC 17 at p 24b stated:

> I would add that consideration of the substantial effect of a transaction is not always appropriate in the field of stamp duty where also the presumption that the legislature intended to create a rational and coherent system of taxation is at least weaker than in other fiscal fields.

It seems clear from *Ingram* v *IRC* [1985] STC 835 that *Ramsay* does apply to stamp duty avoidance schemes.

Example 13C: Stamp duty avoidance and Ingram

X Ltd has a freehold. It grants a 999 year lease to its subsidiary SX Ltd. Z buys the freehold and takes a surrender. If this was done to avoid stamp duty *Ingram* may apply

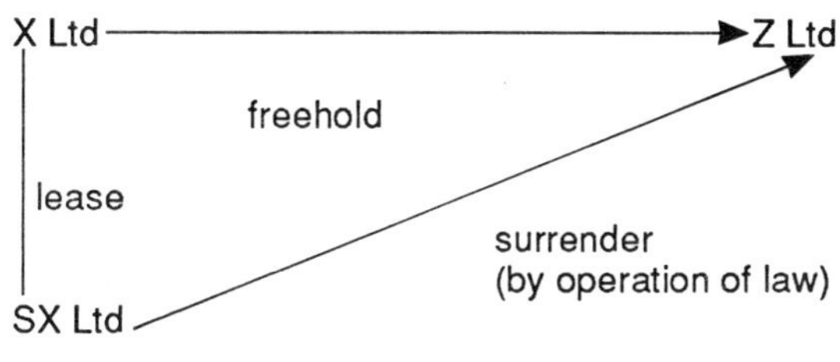

Example 13D: No tax avoidance purpose

X Ltd many years ago granted a lease to its subsidiary SX Ltd not with a view to avoiding tax. Duty in this case may be avoided if Z Ltd buys the freehold and takes a surrender. SX Ltd should not assign the lease to Z Ltd.

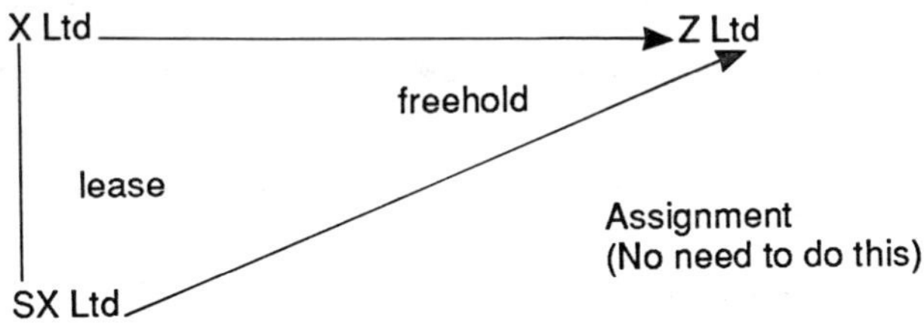

13.20 SMALL SALES RELIEF

For sales for £30,000 or under there is no duty provided the deed contains a certificate of value (FA 1963, s 55).

The relief does not apply to the sale of 'stock or marketable securities' (FA 1963, s 55(1A)). For the relief to be available the deed must contain a statement:

> certifying that the transaction effected by the instrument does not form part of a larger transaction or series of transactions in respect of which the amount or value, or aggregate amount or value, of the consideration exceeds (£30,000).

(FA 1958, s 34(4)).

13.21 REVENUE STATEMENT 12 NOVEMBER 1985

13.21.1 Sales of property below the stamp duty threshold

Note should be made of this Statement, which provides as follows:

> There is to be a change in the stamp duty rules which will help to simplify the conveyancing procedures for many home buyers (Stamp Duty (Exempt Instrument) Regulations 1985 (SI 1985 No 1688)).
>
> From 1 January 1986 home buyers or their agents will in most cases no longer need to submit conveyancing documents to the Inland Revenue where it is clear that no stamp duty is payable. Where the change in ownership has to be registered, conveyancing documents can, from the new year, be sent direct to the Land Registry.
>
> The new arrangements *will apply*:
>
> (i) to sales of commercial premises and land as well as houses; and

(ii) to assignments or surrenders of existing leases.

They will *not apply*:

(i) to any sale of property which attracts stamp duty;

(ii) to sales which do not fall to be registered with the Land Registry;

(iii) to grants of new leases (on which there is nearly always some stamp duty to pay); or

(iv) to sales of property in Scotland and Northern Ireland to which different procedures apply.

The stamp duty threshold for sales of property is £30,000.

13.22 SMALL SALES AND NON-CHARGEABLE CONSIDERATION

13.22.1 A certificate for value may be appropriate on certain exchanges

If X exchanges his freehold for Y's freehold with £30,000 worth of equality money changing hands the duty is nil if a Certificate for Value is appropriate.

13.23 NOMINEESHIP

One can generally change trustees or nominees paying only a fixed 50p duty (if anything at all).

A conveyance under which no beneficial interest passed and which is not made on a sale is not chargeable *ad valorem.*

A conveyance to a nominee is an example of such a conveyance; but if A agrees to sell the legal estate to B who thus acquires an equitable title to the land, the subsequent conveyance to B is a conveyance on sale (*Oughtred* v *IRC* [1965] 3 All ER 623, *per* Lord Denning at p 629A

> . . . every conveyance or transfer by which an agreement for sale is implemented is liable to stamp duty on the value of the consideration.

Conveyances in contemplation of sales may also be dutiable (see below).

13.24 CORY LOOPHOLE LONG SINCE CLOSED

It has not been possible since 1965 to simply transfer property into the name of a nominee as a prelude to selling the property.

In *W M Cory & Son Ltd* v *IRC* [1965] 1 All ER 917, property was transferred into the name of a purchaser in contemplation of a sale. It was held in that case that a simple transfer of the bare title into the name of the purchaser was not a transfer 'on sale' and duty in this way could be avoided.

13.24.1 Loophole closed

FA 1965, s 90(1) now provides:

> ... any instrument whereby property is conveyed or transferred to any person in contemplation of the sale of that property shall be treated for the purposes of the Stamp Act 1891 as a conveyance or transfer on sale of that property for a consideration equal to the value of that property.

13.24.2 This does not save duty

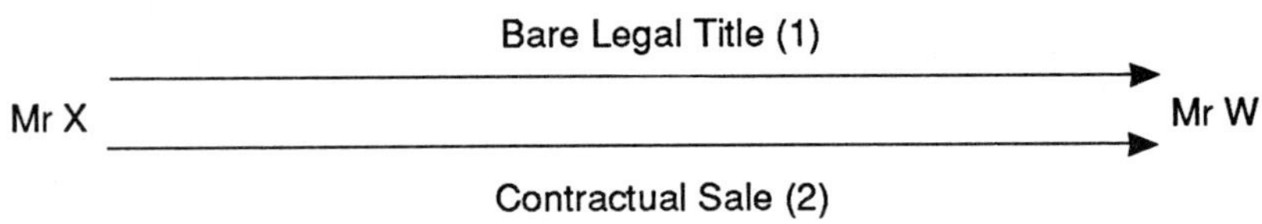

Sometimes in development schemes the parties put property into the name of a nominee for convenience. If a sale is envisaged FA 1965, s 90(1) may be in point.

13.25 INDIRECT SALES

13.25.1 Indirect conveyances on sales

In the case of *Oughtred* v *IRC* [1960] AC 206, property was held in settlement for A for life and then B absolutely. A transferred some shares to B in consideration of B orally agreeing to transfer B's reversionary interest to A, so bringing the trust to an end. The trustees were directed to transfer the assets in the trust to A and a formal transfer was entered into. It was held that although there may have been an informal non-stampable transaction with respect to the transfer of the reversionary interest that was quite irrelevant; the transfer of the assets by the trustees to A was the way in which the parties chose to complete the transaction and was thus stampable. Lord Denning stated at p 233:

> It is clear to me that, by the transfer so made by his (B's) authority, she (A) acquired his reversionary interest as effectively as if he had conveyed it direct to her (A). And that is quite enough to attract stamp duty. In my opinion, every conveyance or transfer by which an agreement for sale is implemented is liable to stamp duty on the value of the consideration. It is not necessary for the instrument of implementation to be between the

> same parties as the agreement for sale, nor for it to relate to the self same property as the agreement for sale. Suffice it that the instrument is the means by which the parties chose to implement the bargain they have made. It is then a 'conveyance or transfer on sale' of any property—which I take to mean a conveyance or transfer consequent upon the sale of the property and in implementation of it . . . . Thus, when an equitable owner of shares (registered in the name of a nominee) agrees to sell them to a purchaser, and it is implemented by a transfer by the nominee to the purchaser, the transfer is a conveyance upon sale of any property—although, of course, the parties to the agreements are different from the parties to the transfer. And when two people are equitable co-owners of shares—and one of them agrees to sell his interest to the other—and it is implemented by a transfer of the shares by the trustees (with the authority of the owner) to the other, the transfer is a conveyance upon sale of any property—although, of course, the property which is transferred is different from the property in the agreement.

Example 13E: Transfer of nominee

X is the beneficial owner of Blackacre and Blackacre is the name of Y the nominee of X. X contracts to sell the freehold in Blackacre to Z. That contract is not stampable. Y on the directions of X transfers the freehold to Z. Even though on the transfer no beneficial interest may pass (it passed on the contract) and the legal estate is not in the name of X, nevertheless *ad valorem* stamp duty is payable on the transfer because that is the way in which the agreement for sale was implemented.

Example 13F: Surrender

X has a twenty year lease of Blackacre. It surrenders that by operation of law receives cash from the landlord and also takes a new twenty-five year lease. The Stamp Duty Office may contend that on the surrender of the old lease for consideration stamp duty should be chargeable thereon because the new lease was the method of implementing the surrender. The author feels that the better argument is that that is not the case. The surrender of the old lease was an entire transaction and the new lease itself was not the method of implementing the surrender of the old lease. The surrender by operation of law was the method of implementing that conveyance on sale.

13.26 AVOID DUTY ON BUILDING COSTS AT ALL COSTS

When the taxpayer is carrying out building operations the Revenue statements set out below of 1987 and 1957 must be noted. They are based on some very difficult old case law.

13.26.1 Statutory provisions

The following two statutory provisions should be noted:

(*a*) Stamp Act 1891, s 77(2), states that a lease made for any consideration in respect whereof it is chargeable with *ad valorem* duty and in further consideration either of a covenant by the lessee to make, or of his having previously made, any substantial improvement of or any addition to the property demised to him, or of any covenant relating to the matter of the lease, is not to be charged with any duty in respect of such further consideration.

(*b*) FA 1900, s 10 states a conveyance on sale made for any consideration in respect whereof it is chargeable with *ad valorem* duty, and in further consideration of a covenant by the purchaser to make, or of his having previously made, any substantial improvement of or addition to the property conveyed to him, or of any covenant relating to the subject matter of the conveyance, is not chargeable, and should be deemed not to have been chargeable, with any duty in respect of such further consideration.

13.26.2 Inland Revenue Statement (22 December 1987)

Stamp duty: new houses

The Revenue have published today a Statement of Practice (SP 10/87, see below) setting out their view of the law on the stamp duty payable on the sale of a new house.

The Statement is being issued in respect to a number of enquiries and disputes about the correct duty to be paid where the builder and the vendor are the same person.

Notes

Stamp duty on a new house
1 The precise form of the contractual arrangements for the sale and purchase of a new house can make a big difference to the stamp duty bill. For example, someone who pays £15,000 for a plot on which a house costing £35,000 is to be built would in some cases pay no duty (because the land is below the £30,000 stamp duty threshold), whereas a buyer who pays £50,000 for the land and a completed house would pay £500 stamp duty.

Statement of practice
2 A Statement was issued in 1957 summarising the Revenue's view of the law on this matter. In brief this is that if in reality the purchaser is buying a completed house duty is payable on the total amount paid for the land and the building work, but that if there are two separate transactions (for example the purchaser makes a separate deal to build the house after buying the land) duty is payable on the price of the land only.

3 Conveyances are, however, being submitted for stamping showing a sale price which, the Revenue are advised, is less than the amount on which stamp duty is chargeable. The Statement of Practice confirms that the 1957 Statement is still regarded as a correct summary of the law.

Standard forms of contracts
4 The Revenue has written to builders (or their solicitors) to withdraw

assurances which had been given in respect of standard forms of contract which it is now felt do not constitute two separate transactions. Those assurances will however be honoured where purchasers were already committed to buy their houses.

Other conveyances outstanding
5 The Statement of Practice confirms the practice of the Inland Revenue Stamp Office in seeking duty on the full price where the terms of the statement in 1957 lead to this result. Some 400 conveyances of this kind have been held over pending the Board's advice on this point. The Stamp Office will be contacting people whose transfers have not been stamped to invite them to accept an assessment and pay the duty on the full price, or to pay the duty and appeal. The Statement of Practice does not affect in any way a taxpayer's right to appeal against the assessment.

6 However, in view of the misunderstandings which existed at the time of these purchases, the Revenue will

(*a*) not seek duty on the full amount where there is evidence that the purchaser (or the purchaser's agents) were given wrong advice by the Revenue about the effect of the *specific contracts;* and

(*b*) consider evidence that the duty would cause hardship.

Settled cases
7 Conveyances which have been stamped in the past are not affected and will not be reopened.

Submission of documents
8 Any document submitted for stamping should be accompanied by all the relevant facts and circumstances. Where the total price of the land and the completed building exceeds the stamp duty threshold and the buyer takes the view that duty is payable on some lesser amount than the total price, the conveyance should be submitted to the Stamp Office together with a copy of the agreement(s) for sale and details of any contractual arrangements not covered in the agreement(s).

13.26.3 SP10/87 (22 December 1987)

Stamp duty: conveyances and leases of building plots

Introduction

1 In 1957 the Revenue published the attached statement [see 13.24.4 below], summarising the law dealing with the stamp duty payable on conveyances and leases of building plots where, at the date of the contract, no house was built or a house was only partly built.
2 The Revenue are advised that the 1957 statement still accurately reflects the law on this subject. That statement has however sometimes

been misconstrued or misapplied. This Statement therefore restates the view the Revenue takes and subject to the proviso that ultimately each case depends on its own facts, clarifies the position in a number of respects.

General

3 The principle on which the statement is based is that the conveyance or lease is liable to *ad valorem* duty by reference to the amount of consideration fixed by and payable under the contract of sale to which that instrument gives effect. If there is a single bargain for the sale of a completed house, the aggregate consideration payable by the purchaser or lessee will provide the measure of the charge to stamp duty. If there is one contract for the sale of the land in its undeveloped state or with a partly erected house, and another (independent) contract for building work, the conveyance or lease is liable to duty by reference to the consideration payable under the former contract alone. In every case the question is whether there is one contract or two.

4 No single factor will be conclusive in answering this question, but whether one document or two is used is irrelevant. The Revenue's view is that, in general, arrangements for the sale of the land and for building work which are so interlocked that the purchaser or lessee cannot obtain vacant possession of the land until he has paid both the land price and the full building price, provide a strong indication that there is a single bargain for the sale of a completed house as a package deal.

Specific comments

5 The 1957 statement should be read as a whole, but the following points should be borne in mind in considering particular paragraphs.

Paragraph (i)

6 This paragraph covers the situation in which the parties intend to reach separate agreements for the sale of the land and the construction of the house. It applies only where—

(*a*) no building work has been started at the date of the contract for sale;

(*b*) independent contracts are made for the sale of the land and the building of the house; and

(*c*) the purchaser or lessee is entitled to a conveyance or lease in consideration only of the land price or the rent.

7 If the purchaser or lessee can only obtain a conveyance or lease for the land price or rent plus some other consideration, such as an undertaking or guarantee that he will pay the building price, condition (*c*) is not satisfied because the additional consideration is also part of the consideration for the sale.

Paragraph (ii)

8 This paragraph deals with the situation in which the parties intend to create a package deal. Since there is no entitlement to a conveyance or lease until after the building has been completed by the vendor or lessor, duty is chargeable on the total price for the land and the completed building.

Paragraph (iii)

9 This paragraph covers the rare situation in which a package deal has been varied, perhaps because one party or the other is unable to perform the original contract. Although there is no entitlement under the contract to a conveyance or lease until the building has been completed by the vendor or lessor (as in paragraph (ii)), the contract has been varied both as to the subject matter of the sale and the consideration payable. As a result of the variation the house is sold in its incomplete state at the date of the conveyance or lease for a proportion of the original aggregate purchase price. Duty is payable on that proportion, ie the revised consideration.

Paragraph (iv)

10 This paragraph was included to cover cases that would fall within (i) were it not that a house had been partly erected at the date of the contract for the sale of the land. It follows that the other conditions of paragraph (i) must be met: there must be independent contracts and an entitlement to a conveyance or lease giving the purchaser or lessee vacant possession in consideration only of the purchase price or rent of the site.

11 *Subparagraph (a)* applies in such a case if the partly erected building has been built by the vendor or lessor. The conveyance or lease is chargeable with *ad valorem* duty on the land price or rent plus the consideration for the building work at the date of the contract. If the purchaser or lessee is obliged to provide additional consideration for the completion of the building before he can obtain possession, that additional consideration forms part of the consideration, for the conveyance or lease.

12 *Subparagraph (b)* applies where the partly erected building has been built by the purchaser or lessee. In this case the value of the work done at the date of the contract for sale does not normally form part of the consideration for the conveyance of the lease, and in consequence is not normally chargeable to duty.

Paragraph (v)

13 This paragraph emphasises the need to consider all the contractual arrangements between the parties. Any amendments of a printed form of contract and any other agreements, oral or written, between the parties relevant to the arrangements between them forms part of those arrangements and therefore part of the contract.

Procedures for submitting instruments

14 Where a person accepts that a conveyance or lease of a building

plot is chargeable on the total price paid for the land and the completed building, it should be submitted for stamping in the usual way together with a covering letter giving the aggregate price and a remittance for the duty appropriate to that price.

15 Where the total price does not exceed the amount up to which the instrument is liable to nil duty (currently £30,000) and a certificate of value is included, a conveyance may be sent direct to the Land Registry in England and Wales under the Stamp Duty (Exempt Instruments) Regulations 1985 (SI 1985/1688) [see *Simon's Tax Intelligence* 1985 p 679], where appropriate, or, in Scotland, to the Keeper of the Registers of Scotland. A lease will need to be stamped in respect of the rent.

16 Where the total price for the land and the completed building exceeds the threshold for duty and the applicant takes the view that duty is payable in some lesser amount than the total price, the instrument should be submitted to the Stamp Office even if such lesser amount does not exceed the threshold and a certificate of value is included. The instrument should be accompanied by a copy of the agreement(s) for sale etc and a letter stating the amount which the applicant regards as chargeable consideration, identifying separately any amount attributable to building work. Details of any contractual arrangements not covered by the agreement(s) should be given in the covering letter.

13.26.4 The 1957 Revenue statement (Law Society Gazette 1957 page 450)

The statement (by way of preamble) is said to concern cases where at the date of contracts no house or only part of a house has been erected on the site and at the date of the conveyance/lease a house has been wholly/partly erected on the site. It provides as follows:

(i) Subject to what is said under para (iv) below, if under the contract for the sale or lease the purchaser or lessee is entitled to a conveyance or lease of the land in consideration only of the purchase price or rent of the site, the *ad valorem* duty on the conveyance or lease will be determined only by the amount of the purchase price or rent, although it may have been agreed that a house is to be built on the site at the expense of the purchaser or lessee (see Figure 13.1).

In such a case, the concurrent existence of a contract with the vendor or lessor or with any other person for the building of a house on the site will not increase the stamp duty chargeable on the conveyance or lease.

(ii) If under the contract the purchaser or lessee is not entitled to a conveyance or lease until a house has been built on the site at his expense and if the house is to be built by the vendor or lessor or by his agent or nominee the payment of the building price by the purchaser or lessee will be part of the consideration for the conveyance or lease and will be liable to *ad valorem* duty accordingly (Figure 13.2).

(iii) When the position is as in para (ii) above, and a purchaser or lessee not entitled to a conveyance or lease until a house has been erected at his expense in fact obtains a conveyance or lease when the house has been only partly erected, *ad valorem* duty is payable on the conveyance or lease on the proportionate amount of the building price attributable to the partial erection of the house as computed at the date of the conveyance or lease (see Figure 13.3).

(iv) (*a*) If, at the date of the contract, a house has been wholly or partly erected by the vendor or lessor or his agent or nominee or by a builder not employed by the purchaser or lessee, it normally forms part of the subject matter of the sale or lease and the consideration or apportioned consideration for the building (as existing at the date of the contract) is accordingly liable to *ad valorem* duty.

(*b*) If, at the date of the contract, a house has been wholly or partly erected by the purchaser or lessee or by any person on his behalf the consideration for the house wholly or partly erected will not normally form part of the consideration for the sale or lease and accordingly will not be liable to *ad valorem* duty (see Figure 13.4).

(*c*) This paragraph is subject to what is said in paras (ii) and (iii) above.

(v) The contract referred to above may be contained in more than one instrument or it may be partly written and partly verbal. It includes an contractual arrangement between the parties.

These observations explain, so far as is possible in general terms, the view of the law at present adopted by the Board, but they have not, of course, the force of law, and are promulgated merely with the object of assisting the taxpayer. The Board are not bound by them, and the circumstances of any particular case may call for special consideration.

Figure 13.1: Sale then build (statement para (i))

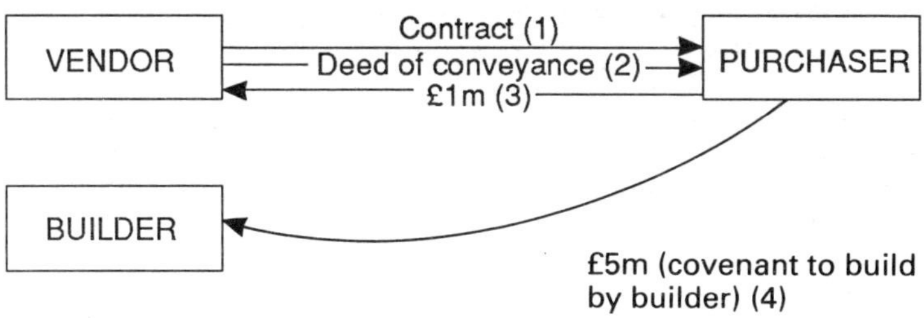

The stamp duty is 1% of £1m according to the 1957 statement. The position is unchanged according to the 1987 statement if the condition of paras 6 and 7 and the 1987 statement are in addition satisfied or the Revenue accepts one or other of the three points made at page 293 below.

Figure 13.2: Build then sale (para (ii))

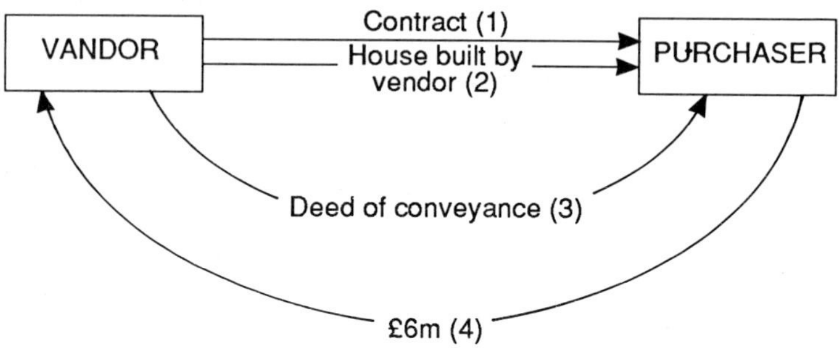

Stamp duty: £6m + 1% = £60,000

Figure 13.3: Half build, sale, complete building (para (iii))

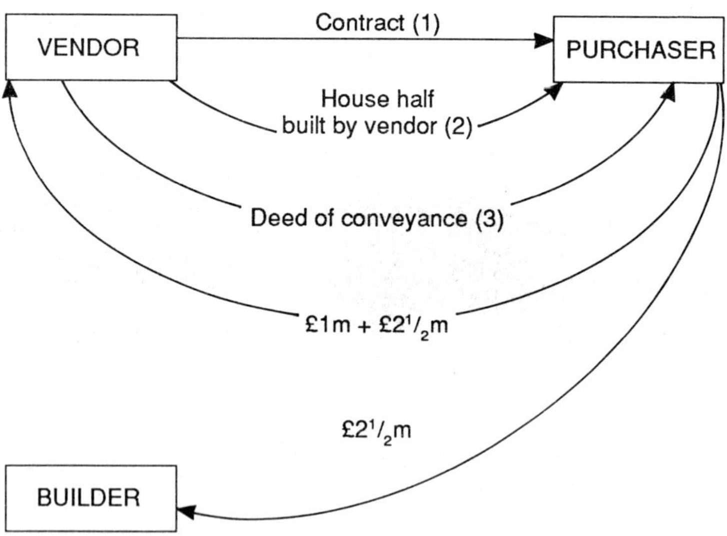

Stamp Duty: £1m + £2½m) × 1% = £35,000

Figure 13.4: Purchaser pays builder (para (iv)(b))

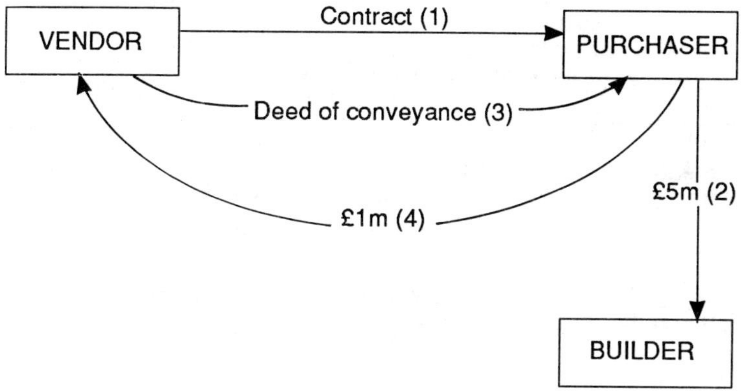

Stamp Duty: £1m + 1% = £10,000

(These figures are not part of the revenue statement and they assume the land is worth £1m and it cost £5m to put up the building.)

13.26.5 Has the new revenue statement 'changed' the law?

The new Statement of 1987 is intended to clarify the Statement issued in 1957. The results of the clarification is that what was considered to be fairly clear law for 30 years may become unclear with respect to certain building contracts.

X Plc may buy a site (ie takes the freehold site) from Y Plc for £1m. At the same time X Plc may enter into a building contract with Y Plc under which X Plc agrees to pay Y Plc £10m for a building to be constructed on the freehold site by Y Plc. What is the stamp duty position? Note that the £10m may not be taxable under general principles if it cannot be ascertained or no maximum or minimum figure is ascertainable (see *ITA* v *IRC* [1961] AC 427). It is assumed, however, that the sum can be quantified.

Clearly X Plc pays 1% stamp duty on the £1m purchase price of the freehold.

The old statement

Prior to the Revenue Statement of 22 December 1987 it had always been accepted (in the author's experience) that no stamp duty would be payable with respect to the £10m payable under the building contract.

This could be seen from a simple reading of paragraph (i) of the 1957 Statement:

> . . . if under the contract for the sale . . . the purchaser . . . is entitled to a conveyance . . . of the land in consideration only of the purchase price . . . of

> the site, the *ad valorem* duty on the conveyance . . . will be determined only by the amount of the purchase price . . . although it may have been agreed that a house is to be built on the site at the expense of the purchaser . . . . . In such a case, the concurrent existence of a contract with the Vendor . . . or with any other person for the building of a house on the site will not increase the stamp duty chargeable on the conveyance . . . .

The new statement

The Revenue Statement of the 22 December 1987, in paragraphs 4 and 7, implies that duty may not be avoided on the £10m if, inter alia, the purchaser (X Plc)

(*a*) cannot obtain vacant possession of the land when it completes (legally) the purchase of the freehold site

OR

(*b*) the purchaser can only obtain the legal conveyance on payment of the land price and the provision of some other consideration *such as an undertaking that it will pay the building price.*

Thus, in the above example if X Plc cannot obtain vacant possession when it completes the purchase of the legal estate on day one or it enters into an undertaking at the time when it completes the purchase of the legal estate that it will pay the building price, then, according to the new Revenue Statement, stamp duty may be payable not only on the £1m purchase price of the freehold, but on the £10m worth of future building cost (the total duty jumps from £10,000 to £110,000).

The old case law

This new 1987 Statement may be inconsistent with the 1957 Statement and it is inconsistent with the line of cases which originally gave birth to the 1957 correct Statement. The cases are *Kimbers & Company and Another v IRC* [1936] 1 KB 132, *M'Innes* v *IRC* [934] SC 424 and *Paul* v *IRC, Span v IRC* and *Blair* v *IRC* [1936] SC 443. One may also refer to the case of *Re Bolton's Lease* [1870] LR 5 Exch 82. It is not felt that *Ingrams* v *IRC* [1985] STC 835 affects the position.

In the three cases of *Paul, Span* and *Blair* the Court developed the 'one bargain' concept which it is anticipated the Revenue are relying on for their (possible) change of practice. The court decided that if there was one bargain for the sale of the freehold with a house thereon then the sale consideration plus the building price could be chargeable to duty. However, before there could be one bargain (i) the vendor (or his agent or nominee) had to be the builder *and* (ii) the contracts (the land and building contracts) had to be so interlocked that '. . . *if default is made on either, the other is not enforceable by either side*'. That was likely to be a rare occurrence as the Court pointed out. A purchaser will normally keep the freehold regardless of what occurs with respect to the building agreement.

FA 1900 s 10

Additionally, FA 1900 s 10 states:

> A conveyance on sale made for a consideration in respect whereof it is chargeable with *ad valorem* duty and in further consideration of a covenant by the purchaser to make . . . any substantial improvement of or addition to the property conveyed to him, or of any covenant relating to the subject matter of the conveyance, is not chargeable, and should be deemed not to have been chargeable, with any duty in respect of such further consideration.

Action

If the Stamp Office do seek to charge duty in a case such of that of X Plc and Y Plc mentioned above then they will only be doing this because they think that at the time of legal sale vacant possession within paragraph 4 of the 1987 statement was not given to X Plc because X Plc the builder is in occupation of the property by virtue of the building works or because they take the view that the *undertaking* to complete the work is part of the consideration for the purchase.

If the Revenue do seek to charge duty on the £10m the taxpayer must ask them:

(*a*) How they reconcile that with the express provision exempting the transaction from the charge to duty, contained in FA 1900 s 10.

(*b*) How they reconcile that with the decision in *Paul* v *IRC* etc where the court said that before the building costs could be brought into charge the building and land contracts had to be so interlocked that if default is made on either the other is not enforceable by either side.

(*c*) One may also ask the Revenue how they reconcile such a view with the *preamble* to the 1957 statement (the body of the statement seems to go wider than its *preamble*).

The author is of the view that the 'clarification' of the old Statement is perhaps a 'change'. Since the 'change' in practice the author has seen a number of cases going through the stamp office like that of X plc where the office have not claimed duty on the building cost. It may be that the Revenue allows the *preamble* to restruct the body of the Statement (see (c) above).

13.27 COLLECTIVE INVESTMENT SCHEMES

Taxpayers should carefully look at their property structures to ascertain whether or not they have created a collective investment scheme which amounts to a unit trust scheme defined by reference to s 75 of the Financial Services Act 1986.

On sales of units in a unit trust scheme (see FA 1946, s 57(1)) only 0.5% duty is payable and not 1%. This can be relevant if interests under property unit trust schemes are sold or exchanged. Instead of respectively a 1% charge and a nil charge, there is a ½% charge and a double charge to duty at ½%.

13.28 INTRA-GROUP TRANSFERS

13.28.1 Basic rules

Relief from stamp duty for transfers between associated companies is granted for any conveyance or transfer on sale (FA 1930, s 42 as amended by FA 1967, s 27).

The relief applies to any instrument which conveys or transfers a beneficial interest in property from one body corporate to another and for the purposes of the provision the bodies are associated if one is the beneficial owner of not less than 90% of the issued share capital of the other or a third such body is the beneficial owner of not less than 90% of the issued share capital of each of the companies (see FA 1930, s 42(2) and (3)).

The relief will not apply unless it can be shown to the satisfaction of the Revenue that the instrument in question was not executed in pursuance or in connection with an arrangement (see *IRC* v *Payne* 23 TC 610, *Escoigne Properties Ltd* v *IRC* [1958] AC 549) whereunder:

(*a*) the consideration, or any part of the consideration, for the conveyance or transfer was to be provided or received, directly or indirectly, by a person other than a body corporate which at the time of the execution of the instrument was associated with the tranferor or the transferee; or

(*b*) the said interest was previously transferred or conveyed, directly or indirectly, by such a person; or

(*c*) the transferor and the transferee ceased to be associated within the meaning of s 42 by reason of a *change in the percentage* of the issued share capital of the transferee in the beneficial ownership of the transferor or a third body corporate (see FA 1967, s 27(3)).

13.28.2 Note:

(*a*) The inter-group relief provisions are not available for the lease duty charges on rents and premiums.

(*b*) The companies do not have to be UK companies, but they must be bodies corporate.

Example 13G: Conveyance of legal estate

A Limited sells Blackacre to an associated company of which it owns more than 90% of the shares. The transfer is effected by a simple conveyance by the one company to the other. Such a conveyance is exempt from *ad valorem* stamp duty because the effect of the transfer is to transfer the beneficial interest in the property from the one company to the other. The means of achieving that transfer is by conveying the legal estate (Lord Denning in *Escoigne Properties Limited* v *IRC* [1985] AC 549 at p 566). This assumes that FA 1967, s 27(3) is not offended, ie that the sale consideration does not come from a person who is not a member of the group etc.

Example 13H: Equitable interest

A Ltd holds the legal estate as trustee for X Ltd which has the equitable interest in the property. X Ltd sells that equitable interest to its associated company Y Ltd in which it holds more than 90% of the shares. Such a transfer is exempt from stamp duty because the effect thereof is to transfer the beneficial interest from one company to another and both companies are in the stamp duty group (Lord Denning in *Escoigne Properties Limited* v *IRC* [1958] AC 549 at p 566).

13.28.3 'Non-group' consideration and transfers

It is critical that none of the consideration for the conveyance or transfer intra-group comes from a body outside the group. This can give rise to complications with regard to loans. The Revenue Practice is set out in *Sergeant and Sims on Stamp Duties,* 9th Edition, p 375 where it is stated:

> So far as loans are concerned, s 42 refers to the provision of 'the consideration, or any part of the consideration'. The completion of a purchase by a transferee company with the aid of a loan would not, it is thought, deprive the instrument of transfer of the exemption except where the lender is party to an arrangement whereunder he is to provide the consideration, or part of it albeit on loan. Where the lender is not party to any arrangement but merely puts cash into the hands of the transferee company which, without being under any obligation to do so, applies that cash in paying the purchase consideration, it would not be said that the lender had provided the consideration under an arrangement.

Example 13I: Bank loans

X Ltd sells Blackacre to Y Ltd for £1m. Y Ltd is the 100% subsidiary of X Ltd. The companies are associated. In order to finance the purchase Y Ltd borrows £1m from an unconnected bank (Z plc). The purchase is completed. If Z plc is not a party to the arrangement but merely puts cash into the hands of Y Ltd which, without being under any obligation to do so, applies that cash in buying the property it could not be said that Z plc had provided a consideration under an arrangement.

It is also to be noted that before the relief is available it must be shown to the satisfaction of the Revenue that the instrument was not executed in pursuance of or in connection with an arrangement whereunder the beneficial interest in the property was previously conveyed or transferred directly or indirectly by a person other than a company which at the time of the execution of the instrument was associated with either the transferor or the transferee.

Thus in the *Escoigne* case Mr C contracted to sell properties to company number one which sub-sold subsequently to company number two which was associated with it (ie number one had the beneficial ownership of not less than 90% of the shares of company number two). Subsequently Mr C or at least the executors of Mr C conveyed the legal estate direct to company number two. It was held that the relief was not available because the beneficial interest had previously been transferred or conveyed directly or indirectly by a person who was not a member of the group and there had been an arrangement to that effect. This was the case even though at the time of the agreement to sell to company number one the creation of company number two was not in contemplation as a sub-purchaser of the property. There was one entire arrangement. Such a conveyance would not be within the relieving words which must be confined to instruments which attract duty by reason of the transfer from one associated company to another. This attracts duty by reason of the transfer from the original vendor to the sub-purchaser.

In *IRC* v *Littlewoods Mail Order Stores Ltd* [1963] AC 135 a lease was held to operate as a conveyance or transfer of the beneficial interest in the property comprised therein from the lessor to the lessee. The lessee subsequently assigned the lease to an associated company. That assignment was held not to be entitled to relief because it was executed in pursuance of or in connection with an arrangement to which the lessor, the lessee and the transferee company were parties whereunder the beneficial interest in the property comprised in the lease was previously transferred by the lessor.

13.28.4 Bridge structures

The group relief share structure for stamp duty is not too difficult to attain as it is simply based on the amount of the issued share capital (see *Canada Safeway Ltd* v *IRC* [1972] 1 All ER 666).

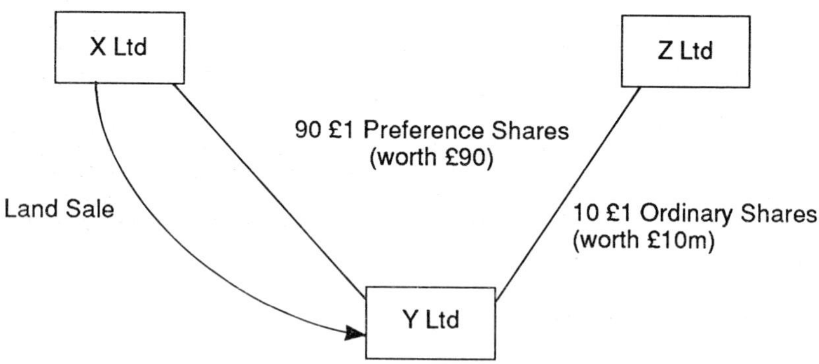

Total Share Capital of Y Ltd — 90 £1 Preference Shares; 10 £1 Ordinary Shares

Section 27 Relief available

But note that if the cash for the intra-group company sale comes from the outside the stamp duty group the relief is lost (FA 1967, s 27(3)(*a*)). Getting the share structure right is not enough.

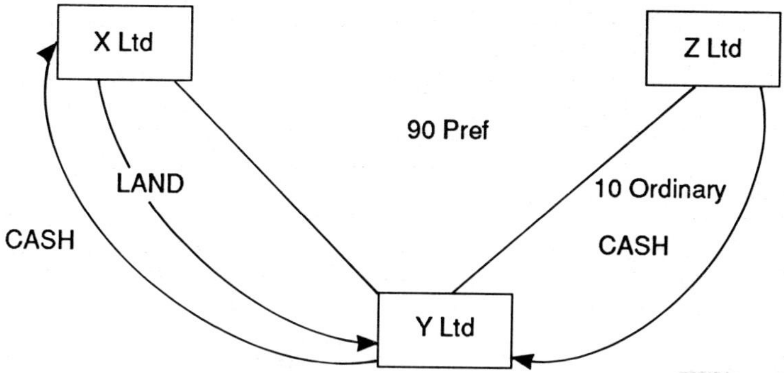

Relief is lost.

13.28.5 Inter-group transfer and then grant of lease

The position where there is an inter-group transfer and a grant of a lease by the transferee outside the group is complex.

Sargeant and Sims at p 375 state:

> The question arises then as to whether the claim for relief under s 42 is available. It is a question to which a definite answer cannot be given as it would depend on the precise circumstances in which the transaction was effected. The Commissioners of Inland Revenue would have to be satisfied that the long lease was not executed 'in pursuance of or in connection with any arrangement whereunder' any of the anti-avoidance provisions of FA 1967, s 27(3) was infringed. For example, if there was an arrangement whereunder the premium or rent payable by the 'outside' company was to be used to pay part of the intergroup consideration, the FA 1967, s 27(3)(*a*), would deprive the conveyance or transfer of s 42 relief. Where it is the intention of the transferee company to grant a long lease over the property transferred to an 'outside' company particulars of the transaction should be furnished in the statutory declaration and the information so provided would enable the Commissioners to investigate whether in their view FA 1967, s 27(3) had been infringed.

13.29 THE OVERSEAS ELEMENT

Duty may be postponed or mitigated if the relevant documents are executed overseas.

Although an instrument executed abroad may be liable to duty no penalty is payable thereon until 30 days after the document has been received in the UK (s 15(2)(*a*)). It is thus possible for a document to be left outside the UK and only brought into the UK, and therefore brought within the stamp duty regime, when it is required.

It is possible, *Ramsay* and *Ingram* permitting, in this way to dispose of equitable interests in land and legal interests in land without giving rise to any charge to stamp duty with the purchaser possibly having the legal estate vested in his name and paying only the fixed 50p duty under the 'conveyance or transfer of any kind not hereinbefore described' heading contained in Sched 1; this would require the agreement for the sale of the equitable interest in the land to be outside the UK and also any declaration of trust with regard to the legal estate to be left outside the UK.

Thus, A Ltd may agree to sell its equitable interest in Blackacre (registered land) to X Ltd for £50,000. This agreement will be executed and kept outside the UK. By a declaration of trust also executed and kept outside the UK, A Ltd would declare itself a trustee of its legal estate in the property for X Ltd. A Ltd as trustee would vest the legal estate in the property in X Ltd who is absolutely entitled thereto in equity.

The agreement for sale of the equitable interest in the property, notwithstanding s 59, should not attract stamp duty unless and until it is brought into the UK (s 15(2)(*a*)). Similarly, the declaration of trust of the legal estate of the property should not attract stamp duty unless and until it was brought into the UK (s 15(2)(*a*)). The deed of transfer vesting the legal estate in X Ltd would attract a 50p duty, being a fixed duty under the heading 'conveyance or transfer of any kind not hereinbefore described'. It is thought that HM Land Registry cannot query the transfer which is within the proprietor's (A Ltd) powers.

In the case of unregistered land the arrangements should be successful in deferring stamp duty until the property is sold. It is unlikely that the duty can be actually avoided altogether because a purchaser from X Ltd would almost certainly raise requisitions regarding the declaration of trust and the stamping thereof.

If an overseas company (X Ltd) wants to sell land (UK land) to another overseas company (Y Ltd) it may be possible for it to give the land to its (X Ltd's) overseas subsidiary (Z Ltd) and then sell Z Ltd to Y Ltd without a stamp duty charge.

13.30 HEAD B: LEASE DUTY (RENT AND PREMIUMS)

This is an important head of charge. It is imposed by s 1 of the Act which refers to the following in the First Schedule to the Act:

(2) For any definite term less than a year:

(*a*) Of any furnished dwelling-house or apartments where the rent for such term exceeds £500 duty: £1 (*b*) Of any lands, tenements, or heritable subjects except or otherwise than as aforesaid, duty: generally 1% of average rent.

(3) For any other definite term or for any indefinite term:
Of any land, tenements, or heritable subjects:
Where the consideration, or any part of the consideration moving either to the lessor or to any other person, consists of any money, stock or security:
In respect of such consideration . . . 1%
Where the consideration or any part of the consideration is any rent:
In respect of such consideration:
If the rent, whether reserved as a yearly rent or otherwise, is at a rate or average rate: [see Table 13.1].

Table 13.1

	If the term does not exceed 7 years or is indefinite	*If the term exceeds 7 years but but does exceed 35 years*	*If the term exceeds 35 years but does not exceed 100 years*	*If the term exceeds 100 years*
	£p	*£p*	*£p*	*£p*
Not exceeding £5 per annum.	Nil	0.10	0.60	1.20
Exceeding £5 and not exceeding £10.	Nil	0.20	1.20	2.40
Exceeding £10 and not exceeding £15.	Nil	0.30	1.80	3.60
Exceeding £15 and not exceeding £20.	Nil	0.40	2.40	4.80
Exceeding £20 and not exceeding £25.	Nil	0.50	3.00	6.00
Exceeding £25 and not exceeding £50.	Nil	1.00	6.00	12.00
Exceeding £50 and not exceeding £75.	Nil	1.50	9.00	18.00
Exceeding £75 and not exceeding £100.	Nil	2.00	12.00	24.00
Exceeding £100 and not exceeding £150.	Nil	3.00	18.00	36.00
Exceeding £150 and not exceeding £200.	Nil	4.00	24.00	48.00
Exceeding £200 and not exceeding £250.	Nil	5.00	30.00	60.00
Exceeding £250 and not exceeding £300.	Nil	6.00	36.00	72.00
Exceeding £300 and not exceeding £350.	Nil	7.00	42.00	84.00
Exceeding £350 and not exceeding £400.	Nil	8.00	48.00	96.00
Exceeding £400 and not exceeding £450.	Nil	9.00	54.00	108.00
Exceeding £450 and not exceeding £500.	Nil	10.00	60.00	120.00
Exceeding £500: for any full sum of £50 and also for any fractional part thereof.	0.50	1.00	6.00	12.00

13.30.1 How the rent and premium duty works

One calculates the duty by reference to the rent and the term of the lease.

The rates of rent duty are as set out above.

For an example of how the table applies in a simple case see the 'Average Rent' example under the Contingency Principle section below (see 13.30.4).

If a premium is charged the duty is 1% of the same although a certificate for value may be appropriate (see FA 1963, s 55(2)). There is no upper limit on the charge to *ad valorem* duty (FA 1963, s 55(3)).

Example 13J: Lease at premium

X grants a lease to Y for £100,000 premium. The stamp duty on the premium is £1,000.

The rent and premium duty are only concerned with grants of leases (or entry into agreements for lease). The sale or surrender of a lease for instance does not concern rent and premium duty; one looks in those cases to conveyance or transfer on sale duty.

No duty is payable on licences (*Addiscombe Garden Estates Ltd* v *Crabbe* [1958] 1 QB 513, *Street* v *Mountford* [1985] 2 All ER 289).

13.30.2 The basic features of the contingency principle

If, for example, at the time of the grant of a lease the rent cannot be ascertained it is possible that no stamp duty of an *ad valorem* nature can be properly affixed thereto.

It may be the case the rents that a tenant has to pay are ascertainable at the date of the agreement for the lease or as at the date of the lease in which case consideration must be given to the application of what is known as the contingency principle.

13.30.3 Coventry City Council Case

The facts of *Coventry City Council* v *IRC* [1979] Ch D 142 were as follows:

On 1 August 1975 Coventry City Council ('the corporation') granted a head lease of a site to the Norwich Union Life Insurance Society ('the Norwich Union'). The lease was part of a transaction to secure the development of the site and was for a term of 125 years at an annual rent of £17,500. On the same day the Norwich Union granted an underlease of the site to the corporation for 125 years less one day. By clause 4 of the underlease the corporation covenanted with the Norwich Union to erect at their own cost a building on the site. By clause 2 of the underlease the Norwich Union covenanted to reimburse the corporation for the amount they had expended on erecting the building provided that the liability of the Norwich Union, after taking into account certain additional payments, did not exceed a total sum of £1,300,000. In the underlease the rent payable by the corporation to the Norwich Union included, by clause 3(A), a yearly rent equivalent to 8.142% of the total expenditure of the Norwich Union up to but not exceeding £1,300,000 on certain specified items which included (i) the legal costs of the Norwich Union, which were quantified at £2,500, and (ii) the cost of erecting the building and, by clause 3(*d*), a rent of £17,500 per annum.

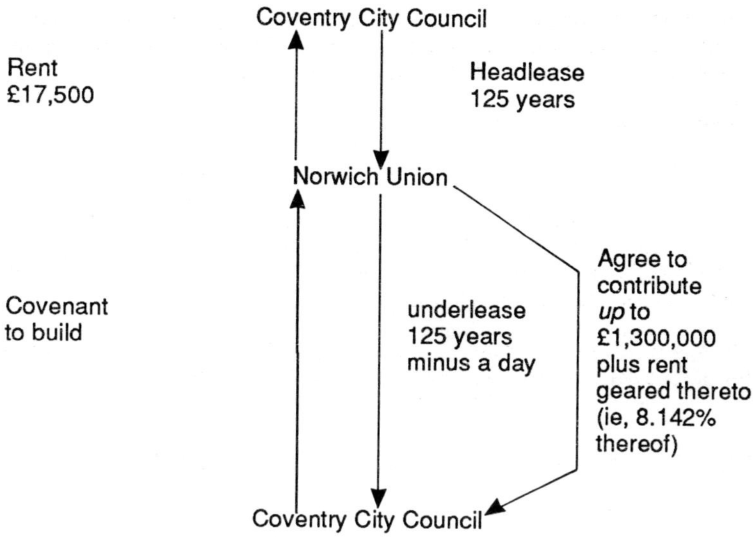

The Revenue assessed the underlease to rent duty on 8.142% of £1,300,000 and succeeded.

Brightman J in *Coventry City Council's* case stated at p 162:

> The rent ... may be viewed as a broad band extending from 8.142% of £2,500 to 8.142% of £1,300,000, that is to say, £105,846, all of which is potentially reserved by the underlease and all or a part of which will ultimately prove to be payable. If one were asked to describe the £105,846, I cannot for myself think of a more accurate description than to say that it is the maximum rent which may become payable under the terms of the underlease. It is not essentially different in this respect from the maximum annual payment on which *ad valorem* duty was held to be payable in the second *Underground Railways Case* [1916] 1 KB 306.

Thus being the maximum rent stamp duty was chargeable by reference to the same.

If one can only find a minimum rent in a lease then the stamp duty can be calculated by reference to that minimum rent. The fact that the rent may only be payable provided a number of contingencies occur is quite immaterial (see *Underground Electric Railways Company of London, Ltd* and *Glyns, Mills, Currie and Co* v *IRC* [1916] 1 KB 306).

Even though a maximum amount cannot be calculated, duty can be charged on any minimum amount which can be calculated. This is even though the minimum sum may possibly be reduced if certain contingencies occur in the future (see *Underground Electric Railways Company, of London Ltd* v *IRC* (1905) 1 KB 174).

Where there is neither a maximum nor a minimum figure available but there is a sum prima facie payable or there is a basic payment which has to be made duty can be levied on that sum.

Lord Ratcliffe in *ITA* v *IRC* [1961] AC 427 at p 433 stated:

> What is necessary is that it should be possible to ascertain from the agreement that there is some specified sum agreed upon as the subject of payment which may perhaps fairly be called the prima facie or basic payment.

Example 13K: Contingency principle

A may grant a lease to B for an amount equal to 20% of the rents which B gets from subletting to C. No *ad valorem* duty should be payable with respect thereto. However the author feels if A lets to B at an amount equal to 20% of the rents received by B from subletting up to £1m and thereafter 15% of the rent over £1m the stamp office may well have a good argument that stamp duty shall be payable by B on a rent of £200,000 (ie, 20% of the £1m contingent rent payable to B by subtenants). The author has been told of one case where the stamp office apparently did not seek to charge duty on the £200,000 rent but the risk of the stamp office applying the ITA case or the general principles implicit in the contingency principle must be appreciated.

Where the rent is to vary during the term, and the amounts are ascertainable from the outset, the average rent throughout the term forms the basis of the charge, not just the initial rent. Where, however, the initial rent is ascertainable but, after a pre-agreed period or periods, is to be reviewed in accordance with a stated formula (eg, open market rent at the date of review) the future rent is as yet unascertainable. In these circumstances only the initial rent attracts the *ad valorem* charge. The Inland Revenue have stated ((1963) *Law Society's Gazette,* pp 175–6) that their practice is to treat separately the initial rent and levy duty thereon as though the property was the subject of a separate lease for that part of the term during which it is payable. The balance of the term is then treated as another lease, with an unascertainable rent, attracting the fixed lease duty of a further £2.

Applying the above, a lease for, say 25 years with a fixed rent for only the first 5 years, with the rent to be agreed thereafter on a 5 yearly basis, with default provisions for arbitration, bears *ad valorem* duty as though it were a lease for 5 years only, ie, at 1% instead of 2%. A similar lease for a term in excess of 35 years will attract duty, not at 12% but at the considerably reduced rate of 1%. With regard to planning ideas see 13.32.

Lease duty is determined according to the rent reserved under the lease or the average rent. With the contingency principle applying it follows that average rent has to be calculated on the average of the highest ascertainable rents over the relevant period of the lease. The following examples illustrate how the duty is calculated.

13.30.4 Average rent

X Ltd grants Y Ltd a lease for 21 years. The rent in the first 7 years is £100,000 the second 7 years £200,000 and the final 7 years £300,000. The average annual rent is £100,000 × 7 + £200,000 × 7 + £300,000 × 7 = £4,200,000. One divides that figure by 21 to find the average annual rent. This is £200,000. As the term is for a period exceeding 7 years but not exceeding 35 years (ie, 21 years), the rate of duty from the table is £1 for every £50 of annual rent. That gives a duty of 2%. Thus the stamp duty payable is £4,000.

13.30.5 Rent reviews

A Ltd grants a lease to B Ltd for 21 years. The duty in the first 5 years is £100,000 subject to rent review increases every 5 years. The duty is based on a rent of £100,000. The duty is therefore 2% of £100,000 ie, £2,000.

13.30.6 Rent—the higher of two amounts

L Ltd grants T Ltd a lease at an annual rent equal to whichever is the higher of 50% of the rents which T Ltd obtains when it grants a sub-lease to ST Ltd or £100,000. The term is for 125 years. The duty is £12 for every £50 ie, 24% on the minimum rent which is £100,000. The duty is therefore £24,000.

The *ad valorem* duty is chargeable on rent which, though the amount is not specified in the lease, is immediately ascertainable (*Parry* v *Deere* [1836], 5 Ad & El 551).

13.30.7 Note:

The contingency principle applies to the lease duties (rents and premiums) and to Conveyance or Transfer on Sale duty.

13.31 DIVIDE AND CONQUER

It may be possible to sell land in two or more parcels to avoid the contingency problem.

The vendor of land may wish to sell that land to the purchaser for £2,000,000 plus an additional £3,000,000 if planning permission is obtained. Completion would take place four weeks after exchange of contract so that stamp duty would be payable on the entire consideration of £2,000,000 paid on completion and on the additional £3,000,000 under the contingency principle.

It may be possible for the parties to mitigate the duty by the vendor selling part of the land for £2,000,000 and arranging for completion to take place. The remaining part of the land would be contracted to be sold on day one (on which no stamp duty would be payable) with completion only taking place if the permission is obtained. If no permission is obtained then no duty will be payable.

As to whether this arrangement can be entered into in any particular circumstances depends on the facts of the particular case.

13.32 MITIGATING LEASE DUTY

13.32.1 Practice note option

Under the Practice Note in the *Law Society Gazette* of March 1963 the Stamp Office accept that if there is a lease for, say, 101 years with a fixed rent for 5 years and then a complete floating rent then they apply duty on the fixed rent for a 5 year term.

However, if there is a fixed ground rent throughout the term then the higher rates may apply but the average rent may be substantially reduced.

13.32.2 March 1963 Practice Note: 'Stamp Duty on Leases'

The relevant part of the Practice Note reads as follows:

> *The Basis of Assessment*
> The Board of Inland Revenue have recently given consideration to the basis of assessment of duty on leases which contain one or more of the following provisions:
>
> (*a*) . . .
> (*b*) . . .
> (*c*) a rent or rents fixed for part only of the term, the rent for the remainder of the term to be agreed subsequently.
>
> Leases of type (*c*) present great difficulty and the Board are advised that, in the absence of authority, it cannot be said with certainty how the provisions of the lease head of charge should properly be applied. In the absence of such authority and with the object of securing a consistent practice, hitherto lacking, and to bring the assessment of duty as far as possible into line with the facts, the Board have decided that such leases shall be assessed by treating separately the part of the term in respect of which the rent is known from that in respect of which it is unknown: *ad valorem* duty under 'Lease (3)' will be assessed in respect of the former part as if it were a lease at the known rate or average rate of rent for a term of that length, and fixed duty under 'Lease (4)' will be assessed in respect of the latter part.
> The practice explained above in relation to leases of type (*c*) will not affect the basis of assessment of leases where there is a rent of one description (eg a ground rent) of known amount for the whole of the term and a further rent of another description (eg, a service rent) ascertainable for

part only of the term. In such cases the basis of assessment will continue to be *ad valorem* duty under 'lease (3)' on the average ascertainable annual rent payable throughout the term and fixed duty under 'Lease (4)' on the further uncertain rent.

13.32.2 Stamp duty—'head over heels lease'

Stamp duty may be mitigated by rearranging a property transaction to create a reverse rental situation. For example a local authority may let the freehold at a peppercorn rent to a pension fund which is to obtain 80% of the occupational rents. The pension fund may let the property to the council in return for that 80% and the council in turn let the property to the occupational tenant. If the tenant pays a rent of £100, stamp duty will be payable thereon. Additionally when the pension fund lets to the council for £80, stamp duty will be payable thereon. Effectively stamp duty is therefore payable on £180.

However, if instead of carrying out the transaction in that way the council were to let to the pension fund which in turn let to the occupational tenant the position would be that the occupational tenant will pay duty based on £100 and the pension fund will only pay duty based on £20 ie, the amount it pays to the council. Thus by taking out interests in a chain or in appropriate cases inserting interests in a chain one can save duty.

Figure 13.5

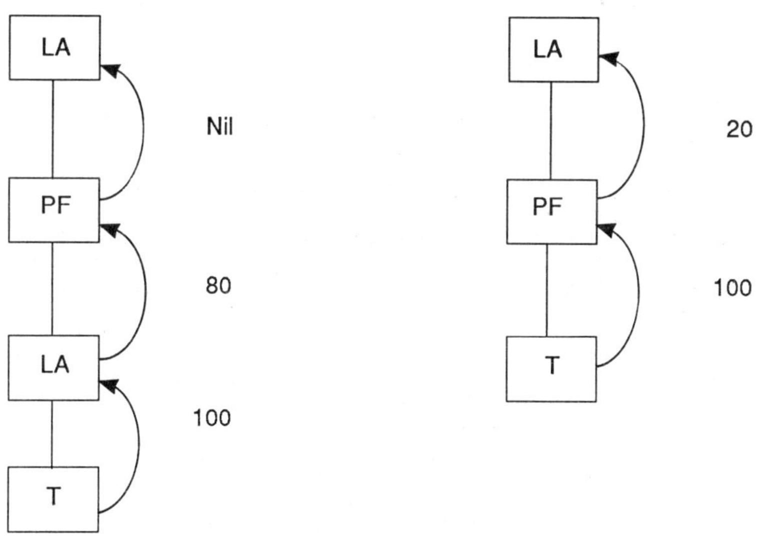

13.33 LEASE OR TACK AND REVERSIONARY LEASES

It may be possible to reduce lease duty by granting a lease for 21 years with a reversionary lease granted for a further 35 years or longer (commencing at the end of the first 21 year lease). The first lease can never be longer than 21 years. This is because a reversionary lease, to be valid, has to take effect within 21 years from the date of the instrument creating it (Law of Property Act 1925, s 149(3)).

13.33.1 Statute

The saving arises because if the term exceeds 7 years but does not exceed 35 years the duty is 2%. If the term exceeds 35 years but does not exceed 100 years the duty is 12%. If the term exceeds 100 years the duty is 24%. Sometimes the rent under the reversionary lease can be unascertainable at the date of the grants.

13.33.2 Other taxes

One must always bear in mind the consequences with regard to other taxes. In particular, the 21 year lease technically may not be a major interest for the purposes of VAT which may be relevant if the lessor constructed the building and is therefore capable of granting a zero-rated interest.

13.34 UNASCERTAINABLE RENT

Duty may be saved by having an unascertainable rent.

The following clause in a lease *may* succeed in avoiding duty:

> by way of yearly rental such amount as would equal the price of £100,000 6 3/4s Treasury Stock 1995–1998 at the beginning of the fiftieth day after the lease is granted.

13.35 VALUATION

Duty may be avoided by leaving the rent to be fixed by a formula. It *may* be that if L lets to T with the rent to be equal to the market value of the property (with principles for ascertaining laid down) as at 6 weeks hence (failing agreement there should be an arbitration) duty will be avoided. If it is to be so ascertained as to the date of the lease the Revenue may be able to wait and see.

13.36 SOME COMMON LEASEHOLD TRANSACTIONS

13.36.1 Sale and leaseback: double duty

Where land is sold with the vendor taking a leaseback at a premium or rent or a mixture of both, stamp duty is payable twice. It is paid on the cash paid for the purchase of the property and on the lease premium and rents (SA 1891, s 54 and Sched 1 (lease or track)).

Figure 13.5: Sale and leaseback

13.36.2 Planning

It may be possible to mitigate the duty by selling the property at half its market value with a leaseback at half the market rent. The landlord can then pay a duty free reverse premium to increase the rent with additional duty only being payable on the rent increase.

13.36.3 Alterations to leases

The terms of a lease may be varied so that the landlord, for instance, obtains an increased rent. He may pay the tenant a capital sum for this. It is important that the stamp duty consequences of the transactions are carefully taken into account.

Example 13L: Alteration to a lease

L may have granted T a lease for 30 years. After the expiry of 5 years the parties may agree to a variation of the lease. L pays T £100,000 so that the rents for the remainder of the term are increased. The stamp duty consequences of this are set out below.

13.36.4 Increase in rent

The mere increase in rent does not result in a surrender and regrant (*Jenkin R Lewis & Son Ltd* v *Kerman* [1971] 1 Ch 477). Thus if there is a separate deed increasing the rent, *ad valorem* duty may be payable in respect of the increase in the rent (if it is ascertainable) and only in respect of the increase in the rent (SA 1891, s 77(5), FA 1971, s 64).

If there is such an increase in rent and the landlord pays the tenant £100,000 no *ad valorem* duty, in the author's opinion, is payable on the £100,000.

If the increase in rent, however, is carried out under the terms of the lease, for example, under a rent review clause, no *ad valorem* duty is payable in respect of the increase in rent.

13.36.5 Surrender and regrant

If the effect of the alteration in the terms of the lease is that there is a surrender and regrant (for example because the term of the lease is extended or reduced (see *Savile Settled Estates* [1931], 2 Ch 210 at p 217 and *Ive's Case* [1597], 5 Co Rep 11a)) the full *ad valorem* duty is payable on the rent charged under the new lease (and not just on the increase in rent) and although no duty is payable in respect of the surrended lease (SA 1891, s 77(1)) the author is of the view that *ad valorem* duty is payable on any sums paid by the landlord to the tenant for the deemed surrender (SA 1891, s 54).

13.36.6 Payment to landlord to take back lease

Following the case of *In re Duke of Westminster's Settled Estates (no 2)* [1921] 1 Ch 585 it would seem there is no stampable sale if a tenant pays his landlord compensation to take back the tenant's lease.

13.36.7 Surrender of a lease

A surrender by a tenant to his landlord is a conveyance; if it is done in return for a consideration it is a conveyance on sale (*Doe d Phillips v Phillips* (1840) 11 AE 796). The LPA 1925, s 52(1), provides that all conveyances of land or of any interest therein are void for the purposes of conveying or creating a legal estate unless made by deed. Sub-section (2) provides however that that general rule does not apply to surrenders by operation of law, including surrenders which may, by law, be effected without writing.

If a lease is surrendered by operation of law no stamp duty is payable because there is no stampable document although if the parties do seek to record the transaction in a memorandum or receipt, the memorandum or receipt, as the case may be, may be stampable under the 'all one transaction' doctrine (*Cohen and Moore* v *IRC* [1933] 2 KB 126; *Fleetwood-Hesketh* v *IRC* [1936] 1 KB 351).

Figure 13.6: Surrender by operation of law

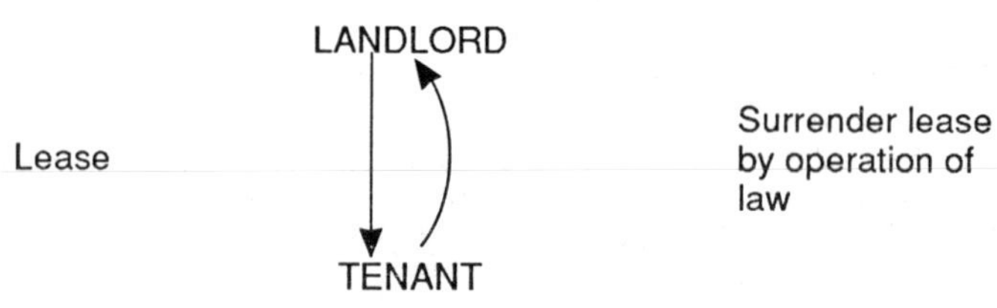

13.36.8 Planning

Whenever possible surrender by operation of law. *Note* that the surrender by operation of law may be evidenced by a *solicitor's statutory declaration*.

13.36.9 Building costs as premium

Sometimes stamp duty is payable on building costs where they are basically a premium.

It seems (following the case of *A-G* v *Brown* (1849) 3 EX 662) that consideration moving from a tenant can amount to a premium even if paid to a third party.

L may agree to let to a Developer (D). D may build and direct that the lease go direct from L to T. T will be liable for duty on what he pays L and what he pays D.

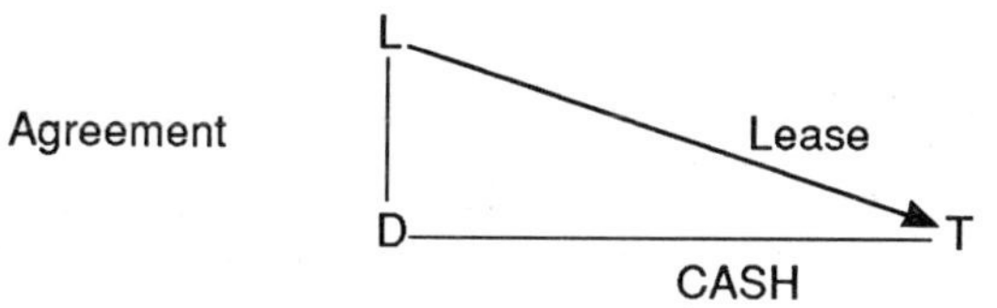

13.36.10 Planning

It may be possible to avoid the duty by T being granted a reversionary lease superior to that of D with D then surrendering his lease by operation of law in consideration of the sale price.

13.37 THE NEW DUTY ON AGREEMENTS FOR LEASE

13.37.1 Stamping an agreement for lease

It should be noted that a taxpayer is not obliged as such to stamp an agreement for a lease (see *Marx* v *Estates & General Ltd* [1976] 1 WLR 380, especially p 388) although if he does omit to stamp the same and subsequently needs to have it stamped he will suffer the penalties in SA 1891, s 15(1) and (2)(*c*). Clearly if the taxpayer feels that there are conditions precedent such that there is a strong likelihood that completion will never take place he should give some consideration as to whether he should have the document stamped. If completion does take place once again he need not produce the agreement and have it stamped. The position may arise therefore that the formal lease has to be stamped let us say that this involved £100,000 in stamp duty. Subsequently the situation arises that the tenant needs to rely on the agreement because some of the clauses still subsist or because the Inland Revenue want confirmation as to the acquisition date for capital gains tax purposes and the tenant must get the document stamped. In this case he must pay the duty and the penalties which are broadly 2 lots of £10 plus an amount equal to the amount of the duty plus interest at the rate of 5% *per annum* from the date on which the instrument was first executed up to the time when the amount of interest is equal to the unpaid duty. However, there is no provision in SA 1891, s 75 to provide relief for the earlier duty of £100,000 paid on the grant of the formal lease.

Example 13M: Agreement for lease duty

Landlord Ltd enters into an agreement to grant a lease to Tenant Ltd for a term of 90 years running from the date of the grant to the formal lease. The formal lease will be granted when the completion of the construction of the building on the land takes place. The works are to be completed within 1 year from the date of the agreement for the lease. Tenant Ltd is to pay £1m to Landlord Ltd at the date of the agreement for the lease, another £1m when the works have been completed and another £1m when the formal lease is granted. They are premiums. When the formal lease has been granted Tenant Ltd is to pay Landlord Ltd a rent of £10 per sq ft. It is provided in the agreement for the lease that the development is to comprise a construction of offices of not less than 50,000 sq ft. There is a condition precedent in the agreement for the lease that planning permission must be obtained for certain works within 3 months of the date of the agreement for the lease. What is the stamp duty on the agreement of the lease?

The position is as follows:

(*a*) The fact that the agreement is subject to a condition precedent is not (*in the author's opinion)* relevant; the contingency principle will ensure that that condition is ignored (see *Coventry City Council* v *IRC* [1978] STC 151 especially at p 156J).

(*b*) 1% lease premium duty will be payable on the £3m premium ie, £30,000.

(*c*) 12% stamp duty would be payable on the figure of £500,000 ie, £10 × 50,000 that will be £60,000.

(*d*) The total duty is therefore £60,000 + £30,000 = £90,000.

13.37.2 Planning

One may be able to mitigate the problem by

(*a*) Having put and call options or

(*b*) entering into the agreement overseas.

13.38 HEAD C: FIXED 50P DUTY

The 50p duty may still be chargeable on many documents.

If A by deed gives property to B there is a 50p charge (according to the statute) there being a 'Conveyance or Transfer of any kind not hereinbefore described' (SA 1891, Sched 1).

The document must also be adjudicated (s 82(5)).

The above is subject to regulations (s 82(9)) and these have substantially eliminated the problem (see the Stamp Duty (Exempt) Instruments Regulations, 1987); the regulations are reproduced in (1987) STI 270–272.

14 SUBCONTRACTORS IN THE CONSTRUCTION INDUSTRY

14.1 INTRODUCTION

Self-employed subcontractors will be chargeable to tax under Schedule D, Case I and no tax under general principles should be deducted at source. By virtue of the subcontractor provisions in TA 1988, ss 559–567 there may be an obligation, upon persons paying a subcontractor, to deduct tax at 27% (reduced to 25% from 31 October 1988).

There have also been a number of regulations made under the legislation. (Income tax (Subcontractors in the Construction Industry) Regulations SI 1975/1960, SI 1980/1135 and SI 1985/1351.)

The provisions apply where the subcontractor carries out works of construction, installation, repair, decoration, demolition etc. The Revenue has issued a guide to these provisions, *Construction Industry Tax Deduction Scheme*, IR 14/15.

14.2 BASIC REQUIREMENTS

14.2.1 Deduction of tax

Where a contractor enters into a contract with a subcontractor which is not a contract of employment but requires the subcontractor to carry out construction operations, the contractor must deduct tax at 25% from so much of the payment as is not shown to represent the direct cost to any other person of materials used or to be used in carrying out the construction operations to which the contract relates (TA 1988, s 559(1) and (4)). The tax must be paid over to the Revenue.

Example 14A: Deductions of income tax at source

X Ltd pays Y £10,000 for labour-only services on a building site in connection with construction operations. Y has no exemption certificate.

X Ltd pays as follows:

	£
Gross cost	10,000
Less 25% deduction	2,500
Net payment to Y	7,500

X Ltd pays the £2,500 to the Revenue and Y has a tax credit of £2,500; X Ltd will give Y a deduction certificate evidencing the deduction.

14.2.2 Subcontractor

A subcontractor is broadly a person who is under a duty to the contractor to carry out the construction operations or who is answerable to the contractor for the carrying out of the construction operations (TA 1988, s 560(1)).

14.2.3 Contractor

The contractor is broadly the person who carries on a business which includes construction operations, ie, building firms. However, the rules have been extended to non-building firms which spend a substantial amount on construction operations, ie, if a firm's average annual expenditure on construction operations in the 3 years ending with its last accounting date exceeds £250,000 or if it has not been trading for the whole of the last 3 years, its total expenditure on construction operations for the part of the period during which it was trading exceeds £750,000.

This may apply to large manufacturing concerns, departmental stores, breweries, banks, oil and insurance companies and others.

The following persons are not contractors:

(*a*) private householders with regard to work done on their own houses etc;

(*b*) a business whose activities do not include carrying out construction operations where its average annual expenditure on works on its own premises in recent years, determined as above, has not exceeded £250,000.

14.3 EXEMPTION

If the subcontractor has an exemption certificate (or in certain cases an appropriate certifying document) there is no obligation upon the contractor to deduct tax at source.

It is the Revenue who issues to the subcontractor the relevant certificate and the Revenue has power to make regulations in connection with the certificates. It also has the power to cancel certificates if, for instance, they have been obtained by false statements.

Certificates are, broadly, issued to bona fide businesses in the construction industry which, *inter alia*, have satisfactory tax histories. Contractors should always enquire with the subcontractor as to whether he has an appropriate certificate. Only if he does can all payments be made without any deduction of tax.

14.3.1 Conditions to obtain exemption

TA 1988, ss 562, 563, 564 and 565 set out the conditions which must be satisfied by individuals, partners, firms and companies before certificates will be issued.

14.4 CONSTRUCTION OPERATIONS

Construction Operations are defined in TA 1988, s 567. The following operations are construction operations:

(*a*) construction, alteration, repair, extension, demolition or dismantling of buildings and structures (whether permanent or not), including offshore installations (that is to say, installations which are maintained, or are intended to be established, for underwater exploitation or exploration to which the Mineral Workings (Offshore Installations) Act 1971 applies);

(*b*) construction, alteration, repair, extension or demolition of any works forming, or to form, part of the land, including (without prejudice to the foregoing) walls, roadworks, power-lines, aircraft runways, docks and harbours, railways, inland waterways, pipe-lines, reservoirs, water-mains, wells, sewers, industrial plant and installations for purposes of land drainage, coast protection or defence;

(*c*) installation in any building or structure of systems of heating, lighting, air-conditioning, ventilation, power supply, drainage, sanitation, water supply or fire protection;

(*d*) internal cleaning of buildings and structures, so far as carried out in the course of their construction, alteration, extension, repair or restoration;

(*e*) operations which form an integral part of, or are preparatory to, or are for rendering complete, such operations as are previously described, including site clearance, earth-moving, excavation, tunnelling and boring, laying of foundations, erection of scaffolding, site restoration, landscaping and the provision of roadways and other access works; and

(*f*) painting or decorating the internal or external surfaces of any building or structure.

The following operations are *not* construction operations:

(*a*) drilling for, or extraction of, oil or natural gas;

(*b*) extraction (whether by underground or surface working) of minerals; tunnelling or boring, or construction of underground works, for this purpose;

(*c*) manufacture of building or engineering components or equipment, materials, plant or machinery; delivery of any of these things to site;

(*d*) manufacture of components for systems of heating, lighting, air-conditioning, ventilation, power supply, drainage, sanitation, water supply or fire protection; delivery of any of these things to site;

(*e*) *the professional work of architects or surveyors, or of consultants in building, engineering, interior or exterior decoration or in the laying-out of landscape*;

(*f*) the making, installation and repair of artistic works, being sculptures, murals and other works which are wholly artistic in nature;

(*g*) signwriting and erecting, installing and repairing signboards and advertisements;

(*h*) the installation of seating, blinds and shutters; and

(*i*) the installation of security systems, including burglar alarms, closed-circuit television and public address systems.

14.5 INTERACTION WITH VAT

Where a payment by a contractor to a subcontractor is subject to VAT the amount for the purposes of the deduction scheme is the payment excluding the amount of the VAT, ie, it is not 27% of the payment plus the VAT, only 25% of the payment.

Where a payment by a contractor to a subcontractor is subject to deduction, except to the extent that the payment represents the cost of materials, the amount which may be excluded from the payment before the deduction is calculated is the VAT-exclusive cost of the materials (see IR 14/15 paras 162 and 163).

14.6 THE SUBCONTRACTOR PROVISIONS—ADVANCES, PAYMENTS AND LOANS

14.6.1 What the parties to a property development must bear in mind

Under the subcontractor provisions, a contractor is liable to deduct tax on payments to his subcontractor made under the terms of a contract relating to construction operations. An omission to deduct under these provisions can be devastating. The following points should be taken into account with respect to the subcontractor provisions.

14.6.2 Types of contractors

There are basically two types of contractors:

(*a*) any person who carries on a business which includes construction operations and

(*b*) any person carrying on a business at any time if his average annual expenditure on construction operations, generally, exceeds £250,000 a year.

The first class of persons is narrow and there has apparently been a Special Commissioners case (which is referred to in *Simon's Taxes*) which gave it a narrow meaning. Perhaps even certain 'developers' who employ builders to do everything may not be persons carrying on a business which include construction operations but that is a very rare phenomena. In *Hulme Educational Foundation* v *The Commissioners* [1978] VATTR 179, the tribunal had to decide the meaning of the term 'a person constructing a building'. This expression is not totally different from the expression used in the subcontractor provisions ie, 'a person carrying on a business which includes construction operations'. In that case at p 189 the tribunal held:

> We therefore return to the main issue. On this, in our view, the words in Item 1 of group 8 *'a person constructing a building'* should be given their normal everyday meaning. Neither party before us had suggested otherwise. In our opinion, the normal meaning of these words mean that a person must either himself construct the building in the sense of putting brick upon brick or stone upon stone, or must himself or by an agent enter into a contract or arrangement with another under which that other for him puts brick upon brick or stone upon stone. In other words, the construction must be physically done by the person concerned or by his servants or agents or the person concerned must himself *directly enter into a contract or arrangement for another to do the physical construction works*.

The words in italic above are clearly too wide as they would include a person who simply employed a builder without the employer being a 'developer' (which is not a term of art). Nevertheless, it demonstrates that one cannot restrict oneself just to the man who puts brick upon brick.

Reference should also be made to the decision of Rolfe B in *Stuart* v *Sloper* [1849] 3 Exch 700 at p 704 where it is stated thus:

> If a man gained his entire livelihood by looking out for what would be the most convenient place near London upon which to build, and purchased the ground, and then employed builders to build upon it, although that would make him a jobber and speculator in houses, I very much doubt whether it would make him a builder.

Note that a taxpayer need not deduct in so far as part of the expenditure relates to materials to be purchased by the builder.

Note also that under TA 1988, s 599(4) the amount laid out shall be treated as for the purposes of income tax or as the case may be corporation tax as not diminished by the amount which has to be paid to the Revenue under the subcontractor provisions. This could be especially important if investors, for instance, wish to obtain enterprise zone capital allowances.

Note that if the subcontractor can produce a tax exemption certificate within TA 1988 s 561 then the contractor would not have to deduct tax at source.

The provisions do not apply to contracts of employment.

The following examples illustrate how the provisions work.

Example 14B: Supermarket

X plc, a large supermarket chain, employs Y Builders to refurbish one of its supermarkets. If the £250,000 limit is exceeded then tax must be deducted at source.

Example 14C: Developer

A Ltd is a property development company. It employs B Builders to carry development works. Tax may have to be deducted at source.

Example 14D: Pension fund

X pension fund employs Y developer to construct a new building. X pension fund is a person carrying on a business within TA 1988 s 560(2)(*f*) and may have to deduct tax at source if the £250,000 limit is exceeded.

Example 14E: Purchase of building

Z Ltd buys a new building from Y builders. The subcontractor provisions do not apply as there was no contract relating to construction operations; there was simply a contract to buy the property.

Example 14F: Pension fund to finance and buy

W pension fund agrees with Y developer to pay Y developer £1m to fund the construction of a building on the land owned by Y developer, X pension fund having a contract to buy the land when completed or having an option to buy the land when completed for £1m (equal to the building monies laid out by the pension fund) plus £0.2m being equal to the value of the land.

This is an unclear area and the safest course is to ensure that there is a subcontractor's certificate. If not, the result may depend on the precise nature of the transaction. A 'substance' approach concerning plant and machinery allowances was adopted by the Revenue in *Stokes* v *Costain* unsuccessfully. In *Stokes* v *Costain* 57 TC 688, Fleming lent money to

Costain to enable Costain to carry out building works and the amount of the loan was discharged by Costain procuring the grant of a head-lease in the property to Fleming. Harman J at p 699E stated:

> The satisfaction of these loans by the transfer of an asset does not change the nature of the loans at the time they were made, and is merely a way of paying off debts . . . it is clear on the facts that the taxpayer undoubtedly bore the risk of the cost of the development had there been an overrun in the cost . . . it seems to me that the truth of this matter was that, although the financing arrangements were somewhat odd, there was a genuine incurring of the expenditure by the taxpayer, who was at risk of having to repay the loans, the advances, made from time to time by Fleming by payment of the expenses and that had any event occurred which prevented the taxpayer from procuring the grant to Fleming, eventually, of the head lease, plainly, and beyond any question the taxpayer would have been liable to repay Fleming all the monies advanced. In those circumstances, it seems to me impossible to say that the monies advanced by Fleming were in any genuine sense being paid for the work done. Those payments, at the time they were made, were undoubtedly, in my judgment loans. The loan was discharged by the procuring of the grant of the head lease.

The form of the documentation may therefore be important:

(*a*) is the funding referred to in terms of an advance payment of purchase price of the completed building?

(*b*) is the funding by way of loan? Is there simply a requirement that the developer completes the development?

(*c*) is the funding in terms of a building/development agreement with a requirement simply that the property be transferred over at the end of the day?

Note that if a fund makes a *loan* of monies to a contractor to do the works these subcontractor provisions are in point.

Note that a *project manager* may need to produce a sub-contractor certificate unless there are no construction operations because of s 567(3)(*e*). Developers will need to produce certificates in appropriate cases unless they can show that they are not providing construction operations because of, for instance, s 567(3)(*e*).

14.7 TAX PLANNING

(*a*) These provisions, because of the wide meaning of construction operations, can apply to a large number of transactions. It is important that contractors are aware of their obligations in this respect and the term 'contractor' can include companies which are not in the building industry.

(*b*) Subcontractors should apply for certificates in appropriate cases.

(*c*) The provisions do not affect the ultimate tax liability of the parties—they are merely a tax collection procedure designed to minimise tax evasion.

(*d*) Failure by a contractor to deduct tax in a situation where he should have deducted tax means that he may be made liable, out of his own pocket, for the tax he should have deducted.

(*e*) In complex land transactions these provisions should be be overlooked; it would be a shame after careful tax planning with regard to capital allowances, VAT etc, to find that a developer will lose all his profits because he overlooked the subcontractor provisions.

(*f*) It should not be assumed that subcontractors have certificates.

(*g*) There are obligations upon contractors and subcontractors to make various annual and other returns, and these obligations must be complied with.

(*h*) If all else fails and a contractor has omitted to deduct tax he may be aided by ESC B21 which reads thus:

Construction industry tax deduction scheme: failure to make deductions from uncertified sub-contractors
1 A contractor who fails to make the proper deduction from payments to sub-contractors (Section 69(4), F (No 2) A 1975 (now TA 1988 s 559(3))) remains liable to pay to the Collector of Taxes the amounts he should have withheld. The Collector has power under The Income Tax (Sub-Contractors in the Construction Industry) Regulations 1975 to waive the contractor's liability where he is satisfied that reasonable care was taken to comply with the rules of the deduction scheme and that the under-deduction or failure to deduct was due to an error made in good faith. If these conditions are not satisfied, the contractor remains liable in law for the sums he should have withheld from the sub-contractor.
2 However, under this concession the Board will not pursue the liability where they are satisfied that:

- the failure to deduct or the under-deduction was due to carelessness or neglect and was not a deliberate attempt on the part of the contractor to ignore the rules of the deduction scheme; and
- the sub-contractor has properly accounted for the whole of the gross payments for tax purposes.

15 PRIVATE RESIDENCES AND EMPLOYEES' ACCOMMODATION

PART I PRINCIPAL PRIVATE RESIDENCE

15.1 INTRODUCTION

Important tax reliefs and exemptions are available to the taxpayer in connection with his principal residence. Gains made on the disposal of the residence will normally be totally free of tax without limitation. Subject to a £30,000 limit, monies borrowed to purchase the residence will entitle the taxpayer to deduct the amount of interest from his total income for tax purposes.

There are no particular reliefs for stamp duty and Inheritance Tax.

15.2 CAPITAL GAINS TAX

15.2.1 Basic requirements for exemption

A gain made by an individual on the disposal of a dwelling-house or part of a dwelling-house which has been the taxpayer's only or main residence at any time during his period of ownership of the house may be relieved (in part or in whole) from a charge to CGT (CGTA 1979, s 101).

There is no requirement that the dwelling-house must be in the UK in order to qualify for relief.

Permitted area
Land occupied and enjoyed with the residence as its garden or grounds up to the 'permitted area' may also be exempt from CGT (CGTA 1979, s 101(1)). The 'permitted area' is an area (inclusive of the site of the dwelling-house) of 1 acre (CGTA 1979, s 101(2)).

An area larger than 1 acre may come within the permitted area and therefore be exempt from CGT on the disposal of the same if the General or Special Commissioners are satisfied that having regard to the size and character of the dwelling-house a larger area is required for the reasonable enjoyment of it as a residence (CGTA 1979, s 101(3)).

It is essential that the land enjoyed with the residence is sold not later than when the house is sold. In *Varty* v *Lynes* [1976] STC 508 the owner of a qualifying residence sold the dwelling-house together with part of the garden and grounds. The remaining part of the garden and grounds was sold on a later occasion. It was held that as this remaining part was not actually held for the occupation and enjoyment of the residence at the date of the disposal, s 101 could not apply. The Revenue have stated that they 'would not take the point established in *Varty* that the private residence exemption might be lost in respect of the garden if the taxpayer ceased to occupy the house before he sold it, unless the garden had development value' (see *IR Practices and Concessions*, Oyez Longman FRP5/B25). This covers a very narrow point and not the more usual problem area where the house and land are sold separately.

The taxpayer must take special care in this area. In *IR Booklet CGT4* at p 4, it is provided thus:

> What if I sell just part of my garden? The sale will be exempt in the same way as when the garden is sold with the house. But the same conditions must be satisfied as if you were selling the house and whole garden together.
>
> If you sell your house but keep part of your garden, a later sale of that part will not be exempt.

Dwelling-house

It is curious that the headnote of Part V of the Act, which includes s 101, refers to 'private residences'. This expression is not used in the various sections. The word used is 'dwelling-house' and this may be restricted to a house only. As a matter of practice, however, bungalows, flats and maisonettes come within the exemption.

In *Batey* v *Wakefield* [1980] STC 572, the taxpayer occupied a dwelling-house and there was a separate chalet bungalow erected in the grounds of the residence which was eventually occupied by a caretaker. Ultimately, the chalet bungalow was no longer required and was disposed of. The taxpayer contended that no CGT was payable as the word 'dwelling-house' should be construed as meaning the private residence of the taxpayer and this would include all appurtenant buildings used and occupied for the enjoyment of the primary residence. This would include garages, summer houses; and premises occupied by servants and caretakers. Browne-Wilkinson J accepted that interpretation and held that 'dwelling-house' should be given that wide meaning and therefore the gain was free of CGT. His decision was upheld in the Court of Appeal ([1981] STC 326). See also *Green* v *IRC* [1982] STC 485, TCA 146, where it was held that the wing of part of a mansion house on the facts, comprised part of the taxpayer's residence, thus entitling the taxpayer to complete exemption when he sold the manor house with its garden.

In *Williams* v *Merrylees* [1987] STC 445, Vinelott J affirmed the General Commissioners decision that a separate four-roomed lodge bungalow comprised part of a single entity with the main dwelling-house in a four acre estate. Thus the CGT exemption was available on the sale of the lodge. He held that separate buildings could be regarded as a single dwelling-house if they could be said to form an entity which could sensibly be described as a dwelling-house split up into different buildings performing different functions. In deciding whether this test was satisfied on the facts of a particular case, the commissioners had to look at all the circumstances, including the scale of the buildings and the layout.

Caravans and houseboats are not specifically mentioned in the legislation but in *Makins* v *Elson* [1977] STC 46 it was held that a caravan could amount to a 'dwelling-house' for the purposes of the relief.

15.2.2 Election

Where an individual has two or more residences in any period it is necessary to establish which one is his main residence. The individual may conclude the question by a notice in writing to the Inspector given by him within 2 years from the beginning of the period in question. He has a right to vary that notice by a further notice in writing to the Inspector as respects any period beginning not earlier than 2 years before the giving of the further notice. If such a notice is not given the question can be concluded by the Inspector, although the individual has a right of appeal to the General Commissioners or the Special Commissioners against any such determination by the Inspector (CGTA 1979, s 101(5)).

15.2.3 Husband and wife

Where a husband and wife are living together they can only have one residence or main residence and if they wish to elect that a particular residence is their main residence the notice must be given by both (CGTA 1979, s 101(6)(*a*)).

15.2.4 Job-related accommodation

Where an individual is engaged in a full-time occupation he may well be compelled to reside in a place for business purposes. Such an individual may purchase a residence for future occupation, perhaps even for eventual retirement. Even though the residence may not be occupied by the owner it may still qualify for relief if the owner resides in job-related accommodation (see CGTA 1979, s 101(8 and 8A)).

15.2.5 Different interests

Special provisions apply where the taxpayer has different interests at different times in a dwelling-house (CGTA 1979, s 101(7)).

15.2.6 Amount of relief

If the dwelling-house or part of the dwelling-house has been the individual's only or main residence throughout the period of ownership or throughout the period of ownership except for the last 24 months, no part of the gain shall be chargeable to CGT. Thus, if X has lived in Greenacres for 10 years but is out of occupation of the premises for the last 24 months or less and he disposes of the same he will not be chargeable to CGT on any of the gain (CGTA 1979, s 102(1)).

Where that absolute relief does not apply only a fraction of the gain will fall out of charge to CGT. That fraction shall be:

(*a*) the length of the part or parts of the period of ownership during which the dwelling-house or part of the dwelling-house was the individual's only or main residence but inclusive of the last 24 months of the period, divided by

(*b*) the length of the period of ownership

15.2.7 Only or main residence

In ascertaining whether the residence was the individual's only or main residence during any particular period the individual shall be deemed to be using the premises as his only or main residence in the following three cases:

(*a*) during a period of absence not exceeding 3 years (or periods of absence which together do not exceed 3 years);

(*b*) during any period of absence throughout which the individual worked in any employment or office all the duties of which were performed outside the UK; and

(*c*) during any period of absence not exceeding 4 years (or periods of absence which together do not exceed 4 years) throughout which the individual was prevented from residing in the dwelling-house or part of the dwelling-house in consequence of the situation of his place of work or in consequence of any condition imposed by his employer requiring him to reside elsewhere, being a condition reasonably imposed to secure the effective performance by the employee of his duties.

It should be noted in connection with those three deemed periods of residence:

(*a*) they are cumulative;

(*b*) they only apply if the individual has used the dwelling-house as his only or main residence for a period before and after the particular deemed periods; and

(*c*) for the purposes of the provisions 'a period of absence' means a period during which the dwelling-house or part of the dwelling-house was not the individual's only or main residence and throughout which he had no residence or main residence eligible for relief under the section. This is an important restriction on the provision and should be borne in mind.

When applying the section it should be noted that a period of ownership of a dwelling-house does not include any period before 6 April 1965.

Delay by owner-occupier in taking up residence
The Revenue issued the following statement on 29 August 1972 (SP4/1972 in *Inland Revenue Practices and Concessions*):

> Where an individual acquires land and has a house built on it, and he thereupon goes into occupation of the house as his only or main residence, then, provided that the period of ownership of the land up to the date of occupation of the house does not exceed a year, or somewhat longer if there are good reasons for exceptional delay, the Inland Revenue will regard that period as part of his period of occupation of the house as his only or main residence within the terms of [ss 101–105]. The same practice will be applied where an individual purchases an existing house and before moving into occupation as his sole or main residence he arranges for alterations or redecorations, or completes the necessary steps for disposing of his previous residence.

Periods of absence
The Revenue has issued three extra-statutory concessions (for which see *Inland Revenue Practices and Concessions*, Oyez Longman): The first one, D3, provides as follows. In determining how far an individual's gain on the disposal of his residence is exempt from CGT under CGTA 1979, ss 101–105, s 102(3) provides that, within specified limits, periods of absence are to be treated as periods of residence if, *inter alia*, the absence was a result of his employment. Where in the case of a husband and wife who are living together this condition is satisfied as regards the spouse who is not the owner of the residence, it is treated as satisfied as regards the spouse who is the owner.

The second, D4, states that in determining how far an individual's gain on the disposal of his home is exempt from CGT under CGTA 1979, ss 101–105, certain periods of absence are treated as periods of residence if he resumes residence there at some time after the absence. This condition will be treated as satisfied where after a period of absence falling within CGTA

1979, s 102(3)(*b*) (absence on duty overseas) or (*c*) (other absences due to conditions of employment) an individual is unable to resume residence in his previous home because the terms of his employment require him to work elsewhere.

In the third concession, D6, the Revenues declare that where a married couple separate or are divorced and one partner ceases to occupy the matrimonial home and subsequently as part of a financial settlement disposes of the home, or an interest in it, to the other partner the home may be regarded for the purposes of CGTA 1979, s 101 as continuing to be a residence of the transferring partner from the date his or her occupation ceases until the date of transfer, provided that it has throughout this period been the other partner's only or main residence. Thus, where a husband leaves the matrimonial home while still owning it, the usual CGT exemption or relief for a taxpayer's only or main residence would be given on the subsequent transfer to the wife, provided she has continued to live in the house and the husband has not elected that some other house should be treated for CGT purposes as his main residence for this period.

15.2.8 Business user

If a gain accrues from the disposal of a dwelling-house and part of it has been used exclusively for the purposes of a trade or business or of a profession or vocation the gain shall be apportioned so that a tax charge arises in connection with the part referable to the business user (CGTA 1979, s 103(1)).

It should be noted that this provision only applies if part of the dwelling-house has been used exclusively for the purposes of a trade etc. If there is no part exclusively so used the provision may not apply to restrict the CGT relief (there is a strong contrary argument to this which the Revenue do not appear to take based on CGTA 1979, s 103(2)).

15.2.9 Intention to make a gain

If the dwelling-house was acquired wholly or partly for the purposes of realising a gain from the disposal of it or if expenditure was incurred after the beginning of the period of ownership wholly or partly for the purposes of realising a gain from the disposal then the CGT exemption may not be available or it may be restricted (CGTA 1979, s 103(3)).

Example 15A: intention to make a gain

Mr X owns the leasehold of Blackacre which is his main residence. He buys the freehold and makes a gain by selling the freehold with vacant possession. The part of the gain referable to the purchase of the freehold estate may not qualify for the exemption although the part referable to the leasehold estate would.

15.2.10 Alteration in parts occupied

If during the period of the taxpayer's ownership of the premises he alters the parts which are occupied as his residence or he uses part of the building for trade purposes etc then the Commissioners may apportion the amount of CGT relief available as they consider to be just and reasonable in the circumstances (CGTA 1979, s 103(2)).

15.2.11 Principal private residence and settlements

The benefit of the principal private residence exemption from CGT afforded by CGTA 1979, s 101, as amended by FA 1980, s 80, is by virtue of CGTA 1979, s 104 available for gains accruing to trustees on the disposal of a residence if during the period of ownership by the trustees the house has been occupied by a beneficiary as his only or main residence. The beneficiary, however, must have been 'entitled to occupy it under the terms of the settlement'.

The relief is also given in respect of a residence occupied, by permission of the trustees of a settlement, by an individual who is entitled, under the terms of the settlement, to the whole income from the residence or from its proceeds of sale.

In *Sansom* v *Peay* 52 TC 1, beneficiaries under a discretionary trust were permitted to reside in a house owned by the trustees pursuant to the following power given to the trustees:

> power to permit any beneficiary in any dwelling-house to occupy any property or building which or the proceeds of sale of which may for the time being be subject to the trusts hereof upon such conditions as to payment of rent, rates, taxes and other expenses and outgoings and as to repairs and decorations and for such period and generally upon such terms as the trustees in their decision shall think fit.

Brightman J held that the trustees had exercised a power expressly conferred by the settlement to permit the beneficiaries into the premises and to stay there until the permission was withdrawn. Therefore, looking at the matter at the date of the disposal of the premises by the Trustees, the beneficiaries were the persons who, in the events which happened, were entitled to occupy the house. The principal private residence exemption was therefore available.

Example 15B: Private residence and settlement

X creates a trust under which the trust property is held for A for life and B absolutely. The trust property comprises a dwelling-house which A lives in pursuant to the terms of the settlement. If the trustees sell the dwelling-house then the principal private residence exemption should, if the usual conditions are satisfied, be available under the provisions of CGTA 1979.

IHT consequences

Allowing a discretionary beneficiary, however, to occupy a dwelling-house which forms part of a trust fund could have IHT consequences. The Revenue has issued a statement on this matter. This is SP 10/79 (15 August 1979) and reads as follows:

> Many wills and settlements contain a clause empowering the trustees to permit a beneficiary to occupy a dwelling-house which forms part of the trust property on such terms as they think fit. The Inland Revenue do not regard the existence of such a power as excluding any interest in possession in the property.
>
> Where there is no interest in possession in the property in question the Inland Revenue do not regard the exercise of the power as creating one if the effect is merely to allow non-exclusive occupation or to create a contractual tenancy for full consideration. The Inland Revenue also takes the view that no interest in possession arises on the creation of a lease for a term or a periodic tenancy for less than full consideration, though this will normally give rise to a charge for tax under paragraph 6(3) of Schedule 5 to the Finance Act 1975. On the other hand, if the power is drawn in terms wide enough to cover the creation of an exclusive or joint right of residence, albeit revocable, for a definite or indefinite period, and is exercised with the intention of providing a particular beneficiary with a permanent home, the Revenue will normally regard the exercise of the power as creating an interest in possession. And if the trustees in exercise of their powers grant a lease for life for less than full consideration, this will also be regarded as creating an interest in possession in view of paragraphs 1(3) and 3(6) of Schedule 5.
>
> A similar view will be taken where the power is exercised over property in which another beneficiary had an interest in possession up to the time of the exercise.

Under the new IHT code contained in IHTA 1984, para 6(3) of Sched 5, FA 1975 is basically replaced by IHTA 1984, s 65(1)(*b*) and only if an interest in possession is 'qualifying' will it be 'non-relevant' property and therefore outside the discretionary trust regime (IHTA 1984, ss 58 and 59). Paragraphs 1(3) and 3(6) of Sched 5, FA 1975 have been replaced by IHTA 1984, ss 43(3) and 50(6).

Personal representatives

The Revenue has also issued the following extra-statutory concession, D5:

> Capital Gains Tax Act 1979, section 104 extends the exemption from capital gains tax for private residences to cases where a trustee disposes of a house which has been the only or main residence of an individual entitled to occupy it under the terms of a settlement. Relief under Capital Gains Tax Act 1979, section 104 is also given where personal representatives dispose of a house which before and after the deceased's death has been used as their only or main residence by individuals who under the will or intestacy are entitled to the whole or substantially the whole of the proceeds of the house either absolutely or for life.

15.2.12 Private residences occupied by dependent relative

If an individual disposes of property which is used by a dependent relative of his as a sole residence and the individual does not charge rent or any other consideration then the CGT exemption may be available under the provisions of CGTA 1979, s 105.

'Dependent relative' for the purposes of this provision means in relation to an individual:

(*a*) any relative of his or his wife who is incapacitated by old age or infirmity from maintaining himself; or

(*b*) his or his wife's mother who, whether or not incapacitated, is either widowed, or living apart from her husband, or a single woman in consequences of dissolution or annulment of marriage.

Not more than one dwelling-house or part of a dwelling-house may qualify for relief as being the residence of a dependent relative of the claimant at any one time nor, in the case of a man and his wife living with him, as being the residence of a dependent relative of the claimant or of the claimant's husband and wife at any one time (CGTA 1979, s 105(3)).

This relief, *subject to certain savings* contained in FA 1988 s 111(2) and (3) cannot apply to disposals made after 5 April 1988 (see FA 1988 s 111).

15.2.13 Relief for owner-occupiers who let living accommodation

FA 1980, s 80 introduced a new relief from CGT for owner-occupiers who let living accommodation in their homes. The Revenue has issued a statement of practice, SP 14/80, explaining how they will apply the new relief (see *Inland Revenue Practices and Concessions*, Longman). Note that the example in para 3 of the statement is not correct.

The new relief applies where the owner disposes after 5 April 1980 of a dwelling-house which has been his only or main residence during his period of ownership but which he has wholly or partly let as residential accommodation. That part of the gain which would previously have been taxable is now exempt from CGT up to the *lower* of £20,000 and the amount of the exemption attributable to his own occupation. The amount of the gain on the let part depends on two things:

(*a*) how much has been let; and

(*b*) the length of time during which it was let.

Example 15C: Let accommodation

Mr X sells Blackacre, making a gain of £500,000, £400,000 of that gain is not a chargeable gain because of the residence exemption. £100,000 is (but for any s 80 relief) a chargeable gain because Mr X had let part of Blackacre as residential accommodation. The £100,000, however, is only a chargeable gain under FA 1980, s 80 to the extent it exceeds the lesser of £400,000 and £20,000. Thus £80,000 will be the chargeable gain.

Whether the let accommodation is part of the owner's dwelling-house or is itself a separate dwelling-house will depend on the facts of particular cases (see SP 14/80).

15.3 REDUCED RELIEF ON SALE OF PRINCIPAL PRIVATE RESIDENCE

The tax exemption available to persons on the disposal of their only or main residence (house, flat etc) under CGTA 1979, s 101 is extremely valuable. Taxpayers who have often struggled for years to mitigate tax on the sale of shares and property investments may find themselves making substantial sums on the disposals of their residences sometimes not being able to believe that the gain is wholly tax free. There are, however, tax traps to be watched out for.

15.3.1 The Additional Expenditure Restriction

CGTA 1979, s 103(3) provides that the exemption:

> shall not apply in relation to a gain so far as attributable to any expenditure which was incurred after the beginning of the period of ownership and was incurred wholly or partly for the purpose of realising a gain from the disposal.

Thus the taxpayer may have a principal residence worth £200,000. He may incur considerable expenditure in obtaining planning permission wholly or partly for the purpose of realising a gain from the disposal of his residence. If the property with the planning permission is worth £500,000 it may be argued that under this restriction £300,000 worth of gain is not protected under the residence exemption.

The author has not known the Revenue to take this point although it seems open to them to take it. It may be prudent in cases such as that for the developer who may be intending to buy the property from the taxpayer to incur all the expenditure relating to the planning permission. The section does not actually refer to who should incur the expenditure but it seems arguable that the expenditure has to be incurred by the taxpayer or his agent. This could be a difficult area if the Revenue chose to take the point in any particular case.

15.3.2 The Chose in Action Problem

If the taxpayer disposes of his principal residence to a developer for a contingent unquantifiable amount (eg, a percentage of what the developer may obtain from any subsequent development of the property) then the value of that right to receive consideration (worth say £100,000) would comprise incorporeal property (a chose in action) for the purposes of capital gains tax. That incorporeal property would comprise the disposal consideration of the house. The receipt of that right would be free from capital gains tax because it is the disposal consideration (the value of the right) of the principal residence (see *Marren* v *Ingles* [1980] STC 500 and *Marson* v *Marriage* [1980] STC 177 and 9.4.4).

The problem is that when the actual consideration is ultimately paid by the developer there is a disposal of that chose in action. If the amount ultimately paid by the developer is £250,000 then capital gains tax (subject to any available exemptions such as the annual exemption) is chargeable on the difference between £100,000 and £250,000, ie, £150,000. The principal residence exemption cannot apply to protect that gain from a charge. It is a disposal of a chose in action. It is not a disposal of the principal residence. No special capital gains tax relief is available.

15.4 OTHER CHARGES AND RELIEFS

15.4.1 Trading gains

There is no exemption from a tax charge under Case I of Schedule D (trading gains) for the principal private residence.

Thus, if the badges of trade exist the gain can be chargeable as a trading gain (see page 46).

If the dwelling-house were purchased wholly or partly for the purposes of realising a gain from the disposal of it the gain may not in the circumstances amount to a trading gain but the CGT exemption may still be lost (CGTA 1979, s 103(3)).

15.4.2 Interest relief

Interest relief is generally restricted to a loan of £30,000 per dwelling and is available where money is borrowed to purchase the only or main residence of the taxpayer (see Chapter 7).

15.4.3 Capital allowances

Capital allowances will not normally be available for expenditure on the principal private residence and the plant and machinery therein (see 8.17.1).

15.4.4 IHT

There are no particular reliefs available.

15.4.5 TA 1988, s 776

TA 1988, s 776 does not apply to a gain which accrued to an individual which by virtue of the CGT principal private residence exemption CGTA 1979, (ss 101–105) is exempt from CGT or which would be exempt but for the provision of CGTA 1979, s 103(3) (where the residence is acquired partly with a view to making a gain).

This exemption is, therefore, more favourable than the CGT exemption in that an individual's dwelling-house acquired wholly or partly for the purposes of realising a gain is exempt from charge under s 776; such a gain is not exempt from CGT.

15.4.6 VAT

If a builder carries out works to the principal private residence of the taxpayer VAT may be chargeable (VATA 1983, Sched 5, Group 8, Items 2 and 3 and Note 2(2)).

When the taxpayer buys his residence the vendor will normally be making an exempt supply or in appropriate cases a zero-rated supply.

Where a person otherwise than in the course or furtherance of a business lawfully constructs a dwelling he may be able to claim back the tax charged, on items supplied to him, for goods which are incorporated in the building or its site under VATA 1983, s 21 and VAT (Do-It-Yourself Builders) (Relief) Regulations 1975 SI 1975 No 649.

15.4.7 Stamp duty

There are no particular reliefs available.

15.5 TAX PLANNING

(*a*) The CGT private residence exemption from tax is an extremely valuable exemption. Substantial gains can be made without any question of tax being payable.

(*b*) If the taxpayer purchases a number of properties over a period to do up, live in and sell, he may be caught as a trader in land so that no exemptions will be available.

(*c*) Taxpayers should try and make use of the £30,000 loan interest relief which is available.

(*d*) The actual CGT exemption provisions are very technical and the requirements of the legislation must be carefully considered. Certain 'periods of absence' are deemed to be 'periods of residence' under s 102(3) but only if there is no other residence available for exemption and the taxpayer takes up residence before and after the 'period of absence'.

(*e*) Where an individual has two houses which may qualify for the CGT relief careful consideration must be given to the making of an election and the time limits must not be overlooked.

PART II ACCOMMODATION FOR EMPLOYEES

15.6 INTRODUCTION

This part deals briefly with the Schedule E tax position where an employer provides accommodation to employees or directors and also where the employer pays the employees' or directors' removal expenses.

It does not deal with any of the company law aspects of the transactions.

15.7 SCHEDULE E GENERALLY

Tax is chargeable under TA 1988, Sched E on emoluments from any office or employment (TA 1988 s 131(1)). 'Emoluments' include 'all salaries, fees, wages, perquisites and profits whatsoever' (TA 1988 s 131(1)).

The general rule is that a benefit provided to an employee cannot be chargeable to tax under Schedule E unless it is convertible into money. It therefore follows that if some non-convertible benefit is provided to an employee he will not, on general principles, be chargeable to tax on that benefit. Where a benefit provided to an employee can be converted into cash the charge to tax is levied on him on the resale value of the benefit and not on the cost to the employer. There are exceptions to those general principles: one is that the benefit can be assessed under the living accommodation provisions contained in TA 1988 s 145; the other is where the person receiving the benefit is a director or a higher-paid employee (TA 1988 s 153 *et seq*).

15.8 DIRECTORS AND HIGHER-PAID EMPLOYEES

TA 1988 Part V Chapter II s 153 *et seq* contains a detailed code which generally applies only to directors and higher-paid employees. Any benefits they receive are expressly made chargeable according to the cost of the benefit less so much, if any, of the benefit as is made good by the director or higher-paid employee to those providing the benefit (TA 1988 s 156(1)).

The expressions 'directors' and 'higher-paid employees' mean:

(*a*) a director of a company regardless of the level of his emoluments. However, a director is not a director for the purposes of these provisions if he is not interested in more than 5% of the company and either:
  (i) his employment is as a full-time working director; or
  (ii) the company is a non-profit-making company (meaning that it does not carry on a trade and its functions do not consist wholly or mainly in the holding of investments or other property) or it is established for charitable purposes only (TA 1988 s 167(1) and (5));

(*b*) an employee who has emoluments at the rate of £8,500 a year or more. For these purposes one takes the cash emoluments and adds in the taxable value of benefits to see whether the £8,500 limitation is exceeded. If an individual does not fall within the definition of director above he may still fall within this definition of higher-paid employee (TA 1988 s 167(1)).

15.9 ACCOMMODATION

When living accommodation is provided for an employee—whether or not a director or a higher-paid employee—he will be taxable on the value to him of the accommodation less any contributions made by the employee. The value of the accommodation is equal to the annual value ascertained under TA 1988 s 837 (see TA 1988 s 145). This will generally mean the rateable value, although the author understands that in some cases the Revenue may seek to attribute a higher and more realistic market value. Note, however, TA 1988 s 146 referred to below.

The amount of the charge might be higher if the employer has himself rented the property and pays a rent of an amount higher than the annual value.

In three cases the employee will not pay any tax on his use of company property. These are:

(*a*) where it is necessary for the proper performance of the employee's duties that he should reside in the accommodation;

(*b*) where the accommodation is provided for the better performance of the duties of his employment and his is one of the kinds of employment in the case of which it is customary for the employers to provide living accommodation for employees;

(*c*) where, there being a special threat to his security, special security arrangements are in force and he resides in the accommodation as part of those arrangements (TA 1988 s 145(4).

Exemptions (*a*) and (*b*) above may not be available to a company director in certain cases TA 1988 s 145(5).

If one of the three exemptions apply and the employee is employed as a director or a higher-paid employee then a tax charge can arise in connection with heating, lighting, repair work, cleaning etc incurred on the property by the company. The overall limit is 10% of the emoluments of the employment TA 1988 s 163(3)(*a*).

Where one of the exemptions applies, the employee is not taxable with respect to the rates payable on the premises if the employer pays the rates assessed on the premises TA 1988 s 145(4).

15.9.1 Directors' house schemes

There are schemes available under which directors or employees sell their houses to their company either with an option to purchase the same back or with an obligation to purchase the same back at a particular date—say, 5 to 7 years—in the future. These schemes can be attractive but the difficulty is to ascertain the value of the obligation or option to purchase back. That value must be added to the buy-back price properly discounted or it must be included in the price of the option. These schemes can be very useful where the director or higher-paid employee does not have sufficient funds to buy the house which he requires. They are therefore useful where no better method is available to enable the individual to purchase the house or have the right to purchase the house at today's price (plus a small premium) in the future. They are based on *Abbott* v *Philbin* [1961] AC 352. The House of Lords in *Abbott* v *Philbin* was quite clear in holding that the taxpayer could only be charged a tax when the option (in this case it was an option to buy shares) was granted and not when it was exercised. Viscount Simonds at p 118 held that there could not be one perquisite at the date of the grant and a second perquisite when the shares were taken up. Lord Radcliffe stated:

> The advantage which arose by the exercise of the option . . . was not a perquisite or profit from the office during the year of assessment: it was an advantage which accrued to the appellant as the holder of the legal right which he had obtained in an earlier year, and which he exercised as option holder against the company. The quantum of the benefit, which is the alleged taxable receipt, is not in such circumstances the profit of the service: it is a profit of his exploitation of a valuable right.

The FA 1983, s 21, (inserting a new s 33A into FA 1977 now see TA 1988 s 146) was passed to counteract the house option scheme but the provision does not entirely stop the same.

TA 1988 s 146 charges tax at the appropriate rate prescribed by the Treasury (as at the beginning of the year of assessment in question) upon the employee based on the costs of providing the accommodation which the employer incurred provided this exceeds £75,000. Note IR 'Benefits in kind: living accommodation' 18 August 1988 (1988) SI No 670).

Thus if the employer purchases a house jointly with the employer only providing £75,000 the employee will still be taxed under TA 1988 s 145 on broadly the amount of the annual value rather than at the appropriate percentage rate. In this case the employee could still enter into the option scheme or the contract purchase scheme mentioned above and obtain the tax advantages.

Example 15D: Charge under Schedule E

In 1984/85 Mr X occupies a house which his employer paid £200,000 to purchase at the beginning of that year. Mr X pays rent equal to the annual value of the property. Mr X's tax charge for 1984/85 is:

	£
Cost to employer	200,000
Less	75,000
	125,000
125,000 × 12% =	15,000

(12% was the appropriate percentage rate for 1984/85)

15.10 DIRECTORS' OVERSEAS HOLIDAY ACCOMMODATION AND THE MULTIPLE TAX CHARGE

Where an employer provides living accommodation for a director or an employee by reason of his employment then income tax charges can arise by virtue of TA 1988 s 145 and 146. These provisions can impose punishing tax charges on directors and employees.

15.10.1 The modest charge—the annual value charge

Under TA 1988 s 146 where living accommodation is provided for an employee then generally he will be charged to income tax on an amount equal to the annual value of the property. This will usually be based on the rateable value of the property ascertained under the General Rate Act 1967. That charge is generally very modest and usually gives rise to no cause for concern.

15.10.2 The not so modest charge—the percentage cost charge

Under TA 1988 s 146 and the Income Tax (Official Rate of Interest on Beneficial Loans) Order 1988, 1988/1622, if the employer acquires accommodation at a cost exceeding £75,000 then, very broadly, the director or employee pays income tax of 10.75% (if it is the relevant percent) *per annum* of the amount exceeding £75,000 without there being any relief for the above mentioned annual value charge under TA 1988 s 145.

Example 15E: Percentage of cost charge

In 1985/86 Mr X occupies a house which his employer bought for £200,000 at the beginning of that year. Mr X's tax position is:

	£
Cost to employer	200,000
LESS	75,000
	125,000
£125,000 × 12%	15,000
Add annual value (say)	2,000
Total (taxed as income)	17,000

(12% was the appropriate percentage rate for 1985/86)

15.10.3 The immodest charge—the overseas property

The fact that there is a double charge under s 145 and s 146 does not normally present too great a problem; the charge under s 145 is normally quite modest and the charge under s 146 only begins to bite when the cost of providing the accommodation exceeds £75,000.

However, the charges *per annum* become astronomical if, for instance, overseas holiday accommodation is bought for a director or employee. There is a very impressive argument that holiday accommodation is not 'living accommodation' for these purposes but let us assume it is.

In this case the Revenue cannot look to a rateable value when charging under s 145 as the General Rates Act 1967 is not applicable. The charge will be very similar to a full market rental charge. That can give rise to a hefty charge. In addition the Revenue can still make a charge under s 146 so that there is potentially a massive double income tax charge.

15.10.4 Inland Revenue letter, 7 July 1983

The only published Revenue material (which the tax editor can find) in this area is the following extract from *Moores & Rowland's Tax Guide 1986–87:*

> FA 1983, s 21 and FA 1977, s 33A (Living accommodation provided for employee) (now TA 1988 s 146).
> We shall be grateful for your comments with regard to the situation where an excessive charge to tax could arise in the case of living accommodation situated outside the United Kingdom where s 33 and 33A, FA 1977 (now respectively s 145 and 146 of TA 1988) are relevant.

FA 1977, s 33 refers to annual value being computed by reference to TA 1970, s 531 (now TA 1988 s 837). Whilst that value may very well be less than the commercial rent in the case of United Kingdom situated property it would seem that in the case of living accommodation situated outside the United Kingdom that the annual value for the purposes of the said s 33 will equal or approximate to the open market rent. Where this is the case then the additional benefit of 12% (now possibly 10.75%) of the cost of providing the accommodation in excess of £75,000 mentioned in s 146 would represent an excessive amount to be taxed. It would seem that the purpose of s 146 was to take account of the fact that the gross annual value for rating purposes of UK situated residential property is significantly less than the commercial rent and therefore in such a case the benefits falling to be assessed under the two sections together would start to approach what would be a commercial rent. However, in the situation where the living accommodation is outside the United Kingdom it would appear that the s 145 benefits represents the full commercial rent and therefore in such a case there is placed upon the taxpayer an onerous tax burden which it would not seem that Parliament had in mind.

Having regard to the foregoing we shall be grateful for your comments with regard to our understanding of the legislation. Also, would you please let us know whether or not in such a situation the Revenue Authorities are prepared to ensure that the amounts assessable under the two sections together do not exceed what would be a full commercial rent, thereby preventing what would otherwise clearly be an injustice.

Revenue reply
May I thank you for raising this particular point. I can confirm your understanding both of the purpose of the new section and of the way that on present wording it would apply in relation to living accommodation situated outside the United Kingdom.

It would greatly assist us in our consideration of the point you raise if you could give brief (if you prefer, anonymised) details of any particular cases you have in mind, indicating the cost and location of the property, the use to which it is put and the method adopted for computing the current charge under s 145 of TA 1988.

15.10.5 The multiple charge

If accommodation is made available to the director or employee throughout the year he may still be charged on the full value even though he may only use it for say four months in that year. In practice, in the author's experience, the Revenue allows apportionment but not invariably.

15.10.6 Reducing the charge

If the accommodation is made available to a number of directors and employees during the full year the Revenue attempt to apportion and amount (probably without statutory authority) amongst the directors and employees.

The author is of the view that if a director or employee is only entitled to use the accommodation for say two particular weeks in the year under the terms of his service contract then the Revenue can only charge him on an apportioned amount of the full yearly charge. Thus if he can only use it for the month of May 1988 only one twelfth of the yearly charge can be apportioned to him. Much may turn, however, on the particular facts of the case.

15.11 HOUSING SCHEMES

In *Jenning* v *Kinder* (1958) 35 TC 673 and *Hochstrasser* v *Mayes* [1960] AC 376, payments made to employees in respect of loss suffered on the sale of their houses when they were transferred from one location of business to another were held not to be taxable. The same arguments apply to reasonable removal expenses and the like (see ESC A5 and SP 1/85 ((1985 STI 27 (1987) STI 805 and (1988) STI 290). The ability to make over tax-free sums and certain loans to employees in connection with removals should not be overlooked.

15.12 TAX PLANNING

(*a*) The provision of accommodation for employees and the ability of an employer to pay removal expenses, etc in a tax-free form represent very attractive perks for employees.

(*b*) The directors' house schemes for modest size houses should not be overlooked.

(*c*) Loans made to employees to defray money applied for qualifying purposes within s 353 etc do not give rise to any Schedule E liability (TA 1988 Sched 7 paras 6 and 7). This would include loans made to an employee to buy his only or main residence up to the £30,000 limit (see Chapter 7). This assumes that the employer himself does not have to borrow (and pay interest on the loan) in order to lend to the employee.

PART III ACCOMMODATION FOR PROFESSIONALS

15.13 TAX FREE USER OF PREMISES

If a trader or professional person is allowed by his client to use premises owned by the client rent free, then if certain conditions are satisfied no tax is payable by the trader or professional person with respect to that rent free user. The position contrasts sharply with the tax liabilities which arise if an employer allows an employee or director the free use of domestic and certain other accommodation.

Messrs X, Y and Z may be a professional partnership (taxed under Case II of Schedule D) providing services to W Ltd. W Ltd may be charged reasonable fees by the partnership but may in addition allow the partners the rent free use of accommodation whether business or domestic. The question is whether the market value of that rent free user should come into the Schedule D income tax computations of Messrs X, Y and Z.

15.13.1 Tennant v Smith

The old case of *Tennant* v *Smith* 3 TC 158 held that the user of premises was not 'income' and therefore could not be taxable upon Messrs X, Y and Z provided the user could not be converted into money. Assuming therefore that Messrs X, Y and Z could not sublet the premises for a rental profit or assign the property, then the user would not amount to income. They should be given a mere revocable licence (see also the cases of *Californian Copper Syndicate (Limited and Reduced)* v *Harris* 5 TC 159, *Cordy* v *Gordon* 9 TC 304, *Daly* v *IRC* 18 TC 641 and *Gold Coast Selection Trust Ltd* v *Humphrey* 30 TC 209).

It would be helpful if the fee charged by Messrs X, Y and Z to W Ltd were reasonable in the circumstances. Also there must not be a deal that the amount of the fee is to be reduced pound for pound to compensate W Ltd for the rent it may otherwise have charged on the letting of the property (see the case of *Heaton* v *Bell* 46 TC 211).

Where the premises of W Ltd are used by Messrs X, Y and Z for the purposes of their business, then often there is little advantage to be obtained by the procedure because the partnership may otherwise have charged an appropriate fee and paid W Ltd rent, which would have ensured that there would have been no taxable benefit upon the partnership. However, if W Ltd is not resident in the United Kingdom, there may well be an advantage in allowing the premises to be used rent free, as that procedure may be saving effectively 25% tax for non-resident W Ltd.

The principle that free use of accommodation is not income is based on sound law. *Whiteman and Wheatcroft on Income Tax* (2nd edition) at 1–19 states '. . . indeed, only one general principle appears to be applicable . . . that is, that money, for tax purposes, must be money or something capable of being turned into money; a mere privilege although of value to the person who enjoys it, is not part of his income.'

15.13.2 Employees—different rules apply

The position is very different if an employee or director is allowed the use of accommodation by his employer; in that case there is an elaborate code which seeks to tax the benefit in appropriate cases (see above).

15.13.3 Tax planning

The client who provides rent free use of accommodation to traders and professionals (taxed under Schedule D) is not paying them 'income' and provided the user cannot be converted into money by the trader or professional and there is no 'fee sacrifice' arrangement, the trader or professional, as the law stands, does not pay income tax on the benefit.

PART IV IHT AND THE HOME

15.14 INTRODUCTION

15.14.1 IHT, gifts and reserving benefits

The taxpayer may want to give a house away and make a Potentially Exempt Transfer (PET). If he seeks to benefit from the gift or retain an interest therein IHT will not be saved; there will have been a Reservation of Benefit (ROB) and the property on his death is brought back into his estate for IHT purposes (FA 1986, s 102). The ROB provisions in s 102 must be avoided.

There is a ROB where *on or after 18 March 1986* an individual disposes of property by way of a *gift* and either:

(*a*) possession and enjoyment of the property is not *bona fide* assumed by the donee at or before the beginning of the relevant period; or

(*b*) at any time in the relevant period the property is not enjoyed to the entire exclusion, or virtually to the entire exclusion, of the donor and of any benefit to him by contract or otherwise.

'Relevant period' means a period ending on the date of the donor's death and beginning seven years before that date or, if it is later, on the date of the gift (s 102(1)).

If the deceased dies with property subject to a ROB, that property 'shall be treated for the purposes of inheritance tax as property to which he was beneficially entitled immediately before his death' (s 102(3)).

If Mr X gives property subject to a ROB which subsequently ceases to be subject to a ROB, Mr X at the time of the cessation, is treated as having made a PET at that time and must survive seven years from that time (s 102(4)).

Making FA 1986 s 102 manageable
It is important to break down s 102 into its fundamental parts in order to fully understand its implications.

Three limbs and associated operations

There are three limbs to s 102. First, the donee must take possession and enjoyment of the property. Secondly, the property must be enjoyed by someone to the entire exclusion or virtually to the entire exclusion of the donor. Thirdly, the donor must not have any benefits by contract or otherwise which (the author assumes) are related in some way to the gifted property or are related in some way to the enjoyment of the gifted property by the donee or other persons to the exclusion of the donor.

Thus, if Mr A gives Greenacre to his son B, who takes possession and enjoyment of the same, then the first limb is satisfied. If the father is kept off Greenacre, then the second limb is satisfied. If the son had agreed with the father that he would put monies into a separate bank account for the father or allow the father to live on the son's property (Yellowacre), then the third limb may be infringed as it related to the gifted property, or if the nexus of 'related to the gifted property' is too vague, then the associated operations provisions through FA 1986, Sched 20, para 6(1)(*c*) may be applicable causing there to be a ROB.

Benefit related to the gift

Another essential structural feature of the provision is that with regard to the second limb if the donor is allowed to enjoy the gifted property even though he pays full consideration for the same the provision is offended. The decision in *Chick* v *Commissioner of Stamp Duties* [1958] AC 435 is clear authority for that. The full consideration does not take the taxpayer out of the second limb. The taxpayer cannot claim, just because the donee has not suffered a detriment, that the second limb is not offended. The position may be different with regard to the third limb, which in that case it may be relevant in ascertaining whether a benefit by contract or otherwise has reached the donor; it may be relevant in that case to see whether the benefit derived by the donor is one that impairs or detracts from the donee's enjoyment of the gift (p 449). It is an open question. It may be necessary to have such an impairment restriction to ensure that the third limb is properly controlled in its effect. It may be that nothing much will turn on the requirement with regard to the third limb because of the associated operations provision in FA 1986, Sched 20, para 6(1)(*c*).

It should be noted that FA 1986, Sched 20, para 6 sets out a number of important heads which provide that, if full consideration is provided by the donor, the second and third limbs will not be offended, eg, if full rent is paid for the use of land (by the donor) which land was given by the donor to the donee, then the provisions will not be offended.

Carve out

The final structural feature of the ROB provisions is that the donor can carve out an interest from property which he owns and only give away that carved out interest. In this case, provided he does not benefit with respect to the carved out interest which he gave away, the provisions are not offended. The fact that the benefits from the interest he retained is not relevant. Thus, if X owns a field of ten acres and gives away six acres, the fact that he retains four acres does not mean that the provisions are offended.

Lord Reid in *Oakes* v *Commissioner of Stamp Duties in New South Wales* [1954] AC 57 at p 76 and 79 put the position as follows:

> If a donor reserves to himself a beneficial interest in property and only gives to the donees such beneficial interest as remains after his own reserved interest has been satisfied it is now well established that such reservation of a beneficial interest does not involve any benefit to the donor within the meaning of the section.
>
> ... the question is not whether the donees permitted the donor to take benefits. It is whether the donor took benefit out of that which was given. If a benefit arises by way of reservation out of interests which were given then no doubt the donees' interests are inherently insusceptible of being so possessed and enjoyed as to preclude the donor from taking that benefit, but the section applies because there is no entire exclusion of the donor or of benefit to him from the interests comprised in the gift. The contrast is between reserving a beneficial interest and only giving such interests as remain on the one hand, and on the other hand reserving power to take benefit out of, or at the expense of, interests which are given ....

Cut-off date for ROBs

The ROB cut-off date is 18 March 1986. If Mr X gifts property into trust on or after 18 March 1986, the ROB provisions are relevant. If, however, he had created the trust before 18 March 1986, the ROB provisions are not relevant even though he has retained a benefit in the gifted assets.

15.14.2 The 'cash deal' loophole and property

The cash loophole and settlement trap in FA 1986, Sched 20;, paras 2 and 3 must be borne in mind.

If A gives land to B, A must not reserve a benefit with respect thereto.

If B sells, exchanges or otherwise disposes of the land, then any property received by B is treated as the property A gave to B, and A, if he offends the ROB provisions, pays duty on the substituted property as if it were part of his estate.

These provisions apply for the purpose of ascertaining (1) the property comprised in the gift and (2) what property is brought into A's estate on his death and (3) whether the ROB provisions are offended.

This is because FA 1986, Sched 20, para 2(1) states that:

> '... the principal section (s 102) and the following provisions of this Schedule (Sched 20) shall apply as if the property, if any, received by the donee in substitution for that property had been comprised in the gift instead of that property (but in addition to any other property comprised in the gift)'.

Example 15F: Substituted property

Thus, A may give Greenacre to B. B may exchange Greenacre with C for Redroofs. If A lives in Redroofs the ROB provisions are offended, and on A's death, A is treated as if he owned Redroofs.

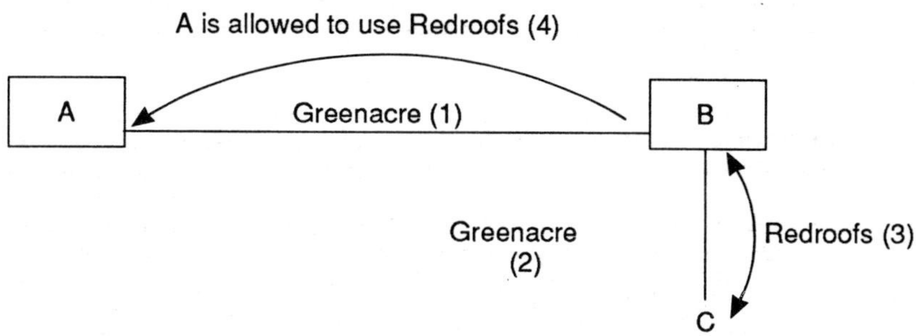

If X gives Yellowland to Y, that is a PET. If Y gives it to Z, Y is deemed to possess and enjoy the property within s 102(1)(*a*); see Sched 20, para 2(4). X must still not benefit from the property (by, for instance, going to live there or by being granted a rent free lease thereof by Z) as the ROB provisions will still be offended.

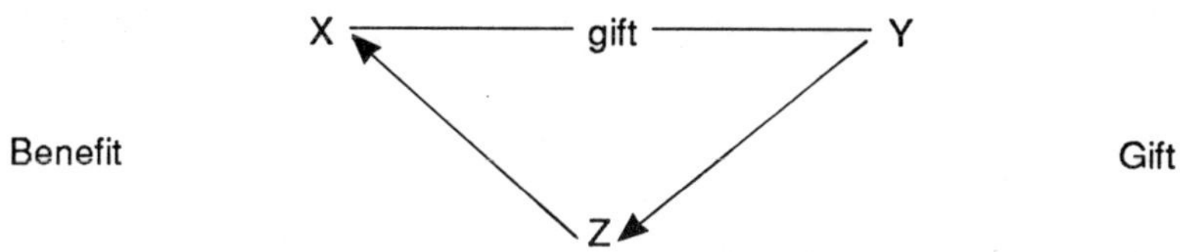

If A gives sterling (or any other currency) to B, B can do whatever he likes with it and the ROB provisions are not offended (FA 1986, Sched 20, para 2(2)(*b*)).

Thus, if A gives cash to B who subsequently uses it to buy property in which A lives rent free, the ROB provisions are not offended.

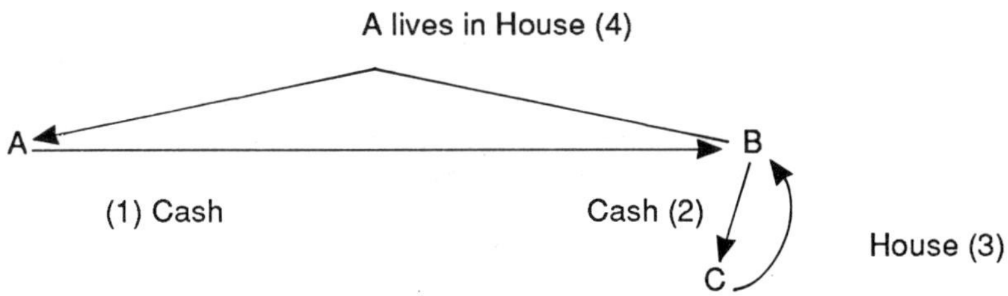

It is difficult to see how the associated operations provisions can re-characterise this deal where the original gift was of cash (see *IRC* v *Brandenburg* [1982] STC 555 at 564b).

Practitioners must also consider the application of the *Ramsay* doctrine to a plan such as this.

If X gives land to Y who then sells it to Z using the sale proceeds to buy other land it appears the ROB provisions have no application as they do not go on ad infinitum. That, however, is an arguable point.

15.14.3 Giving the home away under inheritance tax

The fundamental change made to the death duty rules under the FA 1986 which introduced a new inheritance tax, is that an individual (the donor) can give property to another individual and certain trusts and not pay any inheritance tax provided the donor survives the gift by seven years. However, the property given away will still be deemed to be that of the donor's for the purposes of inheritance tax if it is not enjoyed by the donee or others to the entire exclusion, or virtually to the entire exclusion, of the donor and of any benefit to him by contract or otherwise (FA 1986, s 102).

The following summarises the new approaches to be adopted with respect to giving away the principal residence.

Carve out
If the taxpayer can, for instance, carve an interest out of the property which is given away, then he will not have made a gift subject to a reservation. Thus, if, for instance, the donor and his spouse could retain a right to live in the property for say 20 years at a nominal rent by granting a lease out of the freehold to themselves subsequently giving the freehold to the children, then there should be no charge to inheritance tax on the gift of the freehold to the children if the donor survives the gift to the children by seven years. He will not have reserved a benefit so that there will be no charge on his death with respect to the freehold property given to the children (*Monro* v *Commissioner of Stamp Duties* [1934] AC 61, cf *Nichols* v *IRC* [1981] STC 174), but the position must be carefully considered (for a more detailed analysis of this scheme see 15.14.4 below).

Continuing to live in house
If the taxpayer gives property to his son and the taxpayer simply continues to live there, then this will give rise to problems under the new legislation because the property would not have been enjoyed by the son to the exclusion or virtually to the entire exclusion of the donor. This means that whenever the donor dies he will pay inheritance tax on the property (s 102(1)(*b*)).

Occasional visits
If the father gives property to the son and the son lives in the property with the father making occasional visits (eg for Sunday lunch) to the son, then the legislation will not be offended; provided the father survives the gift by seven years, inheritance tax will not be payable on the father's death, or indeed, when the gift was made (s 102(1)(*b*)).

Full consideration
If the father gives property to the son and subsequently (or at the same time as the gift) takes a lease from the son paying full consideration for the same in money or money's worth, then the legislation will not be offended so that there will be no inheritance tax on the making of the gift and on the death of the donor, provided the seven-year period is survived (FA 1986, Sched 20, para 6(1)(*a*), and see *Chick* v *Commissioner of Stamp Duties* [1958] AC 435 and FA 1959, s 35(2) but note the danger of TA 1988 s 34 being applicable).

Donor Falls on Hard Times
If the donor makes a gift of land to the donee and subsequently falls upon difficult times then he may, in certain circumstances, be able to move back into the house without offending these inheritance tax provisions (FA 1986, Sched 20, para 6(1)(*b*)).

Sale
If X sells the property at full value to his son, inheritance tax would not be in point. The reservation of benefit provisions would not apply because there would be no 'gift' (FA 1986, s 102).

15.14.4 House carve out scheme

The house carve out scheme under which the taxpayer carves out a leasehold interest and gives away the reversion can mitigate IHT, but the general tax consequences of the arrangement must be carefully taken into account.

Under this scheme the taxpayer would transfer the freehold of his house into the name of two nominees for himself. He would then be granted a lease for a fixed term equal to his life expectancy plus, say, 7 years. The freehold would then be given to the donee and this would be a PET. The ROB provisions would not be offended because the taxpayer has not reserved a benefit in the freehold. He simply carved out and retained the lease (see *Munro* v *The Commissioner of Stamp Duties* [1943] AC 61; *St Aubyn* v *AG* (*No 2*) [1952] AC 15).

The Revenue attitude
The Capital Taxes Office appear to accept that the principle concerning pre-existing rights (ie carve outs) established by cases like *Munro* and *St Aubyn* applies for the purposes of inheritance tax. Some people appear to have interpreted correspondence published in *The Law Society Gazette* of 10 December 1986 as meaning that the CTO have given their 'blessing' to these carve-out schemes.

In that correspondence, the CTO were asked for their view on the application of the ROB provisions where:

> D owns freehold property and grants a lease to himself and his wife for 20 years at a peppercorn. D then gives the reversionary interest in the property to his son.

The Revenue, in a very carefully worded answer, replied

> If the true construction of the transactions here is that the gift to the son is of the reversionary interest only in the property then the gift would not constitute a gift with reservation.

It is to be noted that this makes no reference to the *Nichols* case and the need for a 'prior independent transaction'. It also has to be read in conjunction with the comment at the end of the letter that:

> I would emphasise that each case be looked at in the light of its own particular facts. Too much should not be read, therefore, into general comments on the bare situations outlined in your letter which may not, in the event, be found to apply to the facts of an individual case.

'Prior independent transaction'
In *Nichols* v *IRC* [1975] STC 278, the Court of Appeal recognised the pre-existing right principle, *provided that* the pre-existing right arose by virtue of a 'prior independent transaction'. It is understood that the Revenue *may* be considering the possibility of using this qualification as a means of countering certain carve-out arrangements. See also 'Capital Taxes' 1987 No 3, 49 where the CTO refer to a 'prior independent transaction'.

Associated operations
Concern has been felt in some quarters that the carving out of the lease is itself a benefit to the donor. The author does not agree with this, because he does not see how an individual can confer a benefit on himself. The subject matter of the gift is the encumbered freehold, and the donor reserves no benefits in respect of that.

The Ramsay doctrine
The view has been expressed that, under the *Ramsay* doctrine, the Revenue will be entitled to disregard the interposition of the carved-out lease as a step inserted into a preordained series of transactions for the purpose only of avoiding tax. In the author's view this argument is misconceived, because the donor's sole purpose in carving out the lease is not the avoidance of tax. He has another purpose, namely arranging matters so that he has security of tenure.

Other tax points
The following points should be noted in connection with the scheme:

(*a*) The donees will not be entitled to any principal private residence exemption with respect to the property they receive.

(*b*) Tax charges may arise under TA 1988 s 35 if the donor disposes of the lease.

(*c*) It is preferable that the donor leaves the lease in his will to someone other than the donee otherwise the Revenue may seek to apply the associated operation rules, ie, on the donor's death he made a disposition of the unencumbered freehold by an associated operation.

16 LEASEHOLD TRANSACTIONS

16.1 INTRODUCTION

This chapter deals with the various taxation provisions to be taken into account when a lease is being granted or assigned or if a reversion is being assigned or alterations are being made to a lease or a lease is being surrendered. It also deals with the taxation position which arises on the sale and leaseback of land.

16.2 GRANT OF A LEASE

16.2.1 Rental income

This will be taxable as it arises under Schedule A (or exceptionally under Schedule D, Case VI or even more exceptionally Case I).

Rental income derived from and held as trading stock by a land dealer is still assessable under Schedule A and expenses attributable thereto would be deductible under that Schedule.

If the Schedule A income is insufficient to give relief for the expenditure the excess may be used to reduce trading profits (see the Revenue's booklet IR 27, *Notes on the Taxation of Income from Real Property*).

16.2.2 The lease premium provisions

On the grant of a lease or a sub-lease at a premium, part of the same can be deemed to be income under the provisions of TA 1988, s 34.

Where premiums are paid and part of the premium is deemed to be income in the hands of the lessor under TA 1988, s 34, the lessee may be able to obtain a deduction from his IT or CT liability for a proportionate part of the premium under the provisions of TA 1988, s 87.

16.2.3 Traders

If the person granting the lease is a land trader any premium will amount to profits taxable under Case I of Schedule D (see, however, the lease premium provisions contained in TA 1988, s 34 and 3.2.5).

16.2.4 Industrial building allowances and enterprise zone allowances

A grant of a lease will not involve the disposal of the 'relevant interest' for the purpose of industrial building allowances and enterprise zone allowances (unless an election under FA 1978, s 37 is made) thus enabling a possible balancing charge to be avoided.

16.2.5 Plant and machinery allowances

With regard to plant and machinery allowances the position is governed by FA 1971, s 46 and FA 1985 (see p 125 *et seq*).Generally, the lessor will retain the allowances unless an election is made under FA 1985, Sched 15.

16.2.6 Capital gains tax

If the taxpayer holds land as an investment the grant of a lease will give rise to a disposal for CGT (or CT) purposes although there will be no tax charge unless a premium is payable. There may also be a charge if property is let at an undervalue.

Where the payment of a premium is required under a lease of land or otherwise under the terms subject to which a lease of land is granted, there is a part disposal of the freehold or other asset out of which the lease is granted (CGTA 1979, Sched 3, para 2(1)).

In applying the part-disposal rule, the property which remains undisposed of includes the right to any rent or other payment, other than a premium payable under the lease, and those rights are valued at the time of the part disposal (CTGA 1979, Sched 3, para 2(2)).

16.2.7 Inheritance tax

Leases granted at an undervalue can give rise to charges to IHT. Leases may form part of an associated operation for IHT purposes (IHTA 1984, s 268).

16.2.8 TA 1980, s 776

On the grant of a lease for a capital sum a charge to tax under this section (Case VI of Schedule D) may arise.

16.2.9 Value added tax

The rent will be zero-rated if the letting is of a major interest in land by the person who constructed the building. The premium in that case would also be zero-rated.

Otherwise, the rents will generally be exempt unless the letting falls within one of the restricted circumstances where VAT at the standard rate is charged or it is a transaction which is disregarded for VAT purposes (eg, inter-VAT group transfers).

For the proposed changes in the VAT rules to be contained in FA 1989, see 12.37.

16.2.10 Stamp duty

On the grant of a lease, stamp duty can arise under the lease duty provisions or if a premium is obtained under the lease premium provisions (SA 1891, Sched 1).

16.3 ASSIGNMENT OF A LEASE

16.3.1 Trading

If the assignor is a trader he may be chargeable to IT or CT under Case I of Schedule D.

16.3.2 Industrial building allowances and enterprise zone allowances

The lease may be the 'relevant interest' for industrial building allowances purposes and enterprise zone allowances purposes so that a balancing charge may arise on the sale (see 8.3).

16.3.3 Plant and machinery allowances

The assignor may have obtained plant and machinery allowances and a balancing charge may occur on the disposal of the lease (see FA 1971, s 46(2) and FA 1988 Sched 15).

16.3.4 Capital gains tax

On the assignment of a lease there can be a charge to CGT or CT on chargeable gains.

16.3.5 Inheritance tax

If the lease is given away a charge to IHT may arise.

16.3.6 TA 1988, s 776

On the assignment of a lease a charge to tax can arise under this section.

16.3.7 Stamp duty

Stamp duty may be chargeable on the assignment of a lease under the heading of conveyance on transfer of sale.

16.3.8 Value added tax

If the interest being disposed of is a major interest in land and the assignor is the person who constructed the building, the transfer may be a zero-rated transfer for VAT purposes but otherwise it is likely to be an exempt transfer.

For the proposed new rules see 12.37.

16.4 ASSIGNMENT OF REVERSION

On the assignment of a freehold reversion (after the grant of a lease) the following points should be considered.

16.4.1 The lease premium provisions

In certain cases the lease premium provisions can apply where a freehold is sold with a provision that a lease be granted to the vendor or a person connected with him by the purchaser (see TA 1988, s 36).

16.4.2 Traders

Any profits (or deemed profits under *Sharkey* v *Wernher* [1956] AC 58) can be taxable under Case I of Schedule D in the case of a land trader.

16.4.3 Industrial building allowances and enterprise zone allowances

If the reversion is the 'relevant interest' a balancing charge or balancing allowance may arise.

16.4.4 Plant and machinery allowances

A balancing charge or allowance may arise.

16.4.5 Capital gains tax

The assignment of a reversion can give rise to a charge to CGT (or CT).

16.4.6 Inheritance tax

IHT can be payable on the gift of a reversion or on a sale at an undervalue.

16.4.7 TA 1988, s 776

A charge under this section may arise.

16.4.8 Value added tax

The sale of a reversion may be a zero-rated supply or an exempt supply or under the proposes changes in FA 1989 there may be a 15% charge in certain cases (see 12.37).

16.4.9 Stamp duty

A charge to stamp duty can arise

16.5 VARIATIONS AND SURRENDERS OF LEASES

16.5.1 Traders

If sums are received by landlords in connection with the variation of leases and the landlord is a trader a tax charge may arise on the sums under Case I of Schedule D.

16.5.2 Capital allowances

When leases are surrendered or varied or if there are re-grants of leases, the capital allowances position must be carefully considered (see CAA 1968, s 77 and FA 1971, Sched 8, para 15(4)).

16.5.3 Capital gains tax

Where a lease is varied there may be a part disposal for CGT purposes under CGTA 1979, s 20, if a capital sum is received, although it may be possible to rollover the charge if the monies are received as compensation for damage to the capital asset and the monies are used in restoring the asset (CGTA 1979, s 21); this is a very important relief which should not be overlooked.

The author is of the view that the surrender of a lease is a disposal for CGT purposes so that charge to CGT (or CT) can arise.

16.5.4 Inheritance tax

Gratuitous alterations to leases or surrenders of leases may result in a chargeable transfer for IHT purposes.

16.5.5 TA 1988, s 776

Capital sums received in connection with the surrender of leases or the regrant of leases or variations to leases may be chargeable to tax under Case VI of Schedule D under TA 1988, s 776. A charge to tax under that section, however, cannot apply in connection with income rental receipts, at least as far as the receiver of the receipts is concerned because of the requirement that the taxpayer must obtain a capital sum before a charge can arise (TA 1988, s 776).

16.5.6 TA 1988, s 780

The sale and leaseback provisions contained in TA 1988, s 780 (which charge capital sums to IT where a lease having not more than 50 years to run is sold and there is a leaseback for a term not exceeding 15 years) are adapted to cover situations where, by agreement with his landlord, the lessee varies the terms of his original lease (the lease not having more than 50 years to run) in such a manner that in return for a capital sum the lessee undertakes to pay, during the period ending not later than 15 years after the capital sum is paid to the lessee, a rent greater than that payable under the original lease.

If the provision applies by virtue of such a variation the lessee is treated as having surrendered the original lease for the consideration he received and as having been granted a new lease for a term not exceeding 15 years but otherwise on the terms of the original lease as so varied (see page 355).

Example 16A: Sale and leaseback to effect variation

X Ltd has a 30-year lease. The rent it pays is £500,000 per annum with 5-yearly rent reviews. The lease is varied and the tenant receives £1,000,000 from the landlord in consideration of paying an increased rental for the first 5 years of £700,000 per annum. After the first 5 years the rent will go down to £500,000 per annum. Section 780(6) is badly drafted and in this case must be read with s 780(2). It appears that in this situation that the leaseback will be deemed to be a 5-year lease so that the amount of £1,000,000 taxable as income will be:

$$£1{,}000{,}000 \times \frac{16 - 5}{15} = £733{,}333$$

16.5.7 Value added tax

Where a major interest has been granted by the person constructing the building the rents will be zero-rated. Any variation to the leases should be carried out to ensure that the interest resulting after the variation will still be a major interest. Otherwise the rents may be converted from being zero-rated to exemption.

16.5.8 Stamp duty

The surrender of a lease by operation of law does not give rise to any charge to stamp duty although if the surrender is incorporated into an instrument there could be a charge because a surrender may be a conveyance on sale (see 13.36.7). For the stamp duty position where a lease is varied, see 13.36.3.

17 SALE AND LEASEBACK—A TAX EFFICIENT OPERATION

17.1 INTRODUCTION

This chapter looks at the position where a freeholder or a leaseholder sells his interest to a purchaser and then takes a leaseback of the premises.

The aim is to enable the landowner to raise cash by way of the sale proceeds. By virtue of the leaseback he will be able to stay in occupation of the premises. He intends that the rent he will pay will be tax deductible for the purposes of his trade and even the capital sum which is received, which will normally be chargeable to capital gains tax or corporation tax on chargeable gains, may have the gain rolled over under the provisions of CGTA 1979, s 115 (replacement of business assets).

There is set out below the provisions which the taxpayer should take into account when contemplating a sale and leaseback arrangement.

Figure 17.1: Basic sale and leaseback structure

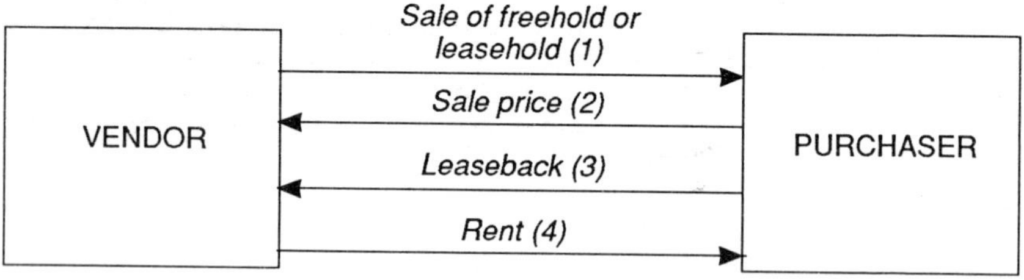

17.1.2 Income tax and corporation tax on income

Sale proceeds
If the land is trading stock the proceeds can be taxed under Schedule D, Case I. If TA 1988, s 776 applies the gain will be taxed as income under Case VI of Schedule D. If the gain is not caught by the above provision

it will normally be capital. However, there are certain provisions which deem the capital to be income.

17.1.3 TA 1988, s 780

Basic charging provisions: where a lessee under a lease having not more than fifty years to run assigns that lease (the original lease) to another person for a capital sum and the lessee is granted another lease (the new lease) of the whole or any part of the land which was subject to the original lease and the term of the new lease does not exceed fifteen years then a proportion of the consideration received by the lessee may be taxed as income and not as capital.

The proportion taxable as income: the proportion of the capital sum which is treated as income will be determined by the following formula:

$$\textit{Capital sum} \times \frac{16 - N}{15}$$

where N is the term of the new lease expressed in years or, if that term is less than a year, N is 1. The proportion which is taxable as income can be taxed as a trading receipt or as a receipt of a profession or vocation or otherwise under Case VI of Schedule D.

Deemed length of leases: it is clear that in order to avoid the provisions the leaseback should be for a period exceeding fifteen years. There are provisions in the TA 1988, s 780(2) which deem leases which apparently exceed fifteen years to be for less than fifteen years. If the total of the rents payable under the new lease in respect of any 'rental period' which falls before the fifteenth anniversary of the date on which the term of the new lease begins is greater than the total of the rents payable under the new lease in respect of a period of equal duration beginning on the date following that date the term of the new lease shall be treated as ending on that date TA 1988, s 780(2)(*a*). 'Rental period' means a period in respect of which a payment of rent falls to be made and in the case where the rental period is a quarter or a month each such period shall be treated as of equal duration (TA 1988, s 780(8)).

Example 17A: Deemed short lease

X Ltd has a fifty year lease. It sells this to *Y* Fund for £1,000,000 and takes back a twenty year lease. The rent for the first five years is fixed at £100,000 per annum. For the balance of the term it is fixed at £90,000 per annum. For the purposes of TA 1988, s 780 the lease will be deemed to be a five year lease.

Harmful clauses

If the rent is £100,000 per annum for the first five years and after five years it is to be fixed at market rent at that time with a minimum rental of, say, £50,000 per annum, it is not clear whether the Revenue must ascertain the position at the inception of the lease (there is no particular provision requiring this) or whether it must simply wait to see whether the rent is in fact fixed at a lower amount after the end of the five years. Although this seems to give rise to assessment problems and uncertainty the latter view appears to be the correct one.

If under the terms of the new lease *either the lessor or the lessee has power to determine the new lease at a time before the expiry of the term granted* or the lessee has power to vary his obligations under the lease so as to reduce the rent which he would otherwise have to pay or in any other manner beneficial to him, s 780(2)(*b*) provides that the term shall be deemed to end on the earliest date with effect from which, in the exercise of that power, the lessor or the lessee could determine the new lease or, as the case may be, the lessee could so vary his obligations. Lease documents may have to be carefully examined to eliminate harmful clauses such as these.

17.1.4 TA 1988, s 36

This section is part of what is generally known as 'the lease premium code'. TA 1988, s 34 attempts to tax part of any premiums received by a landlord on the grant of a lease as income if the lease does not exceed fifty years. Section s 36 is designed to catch the landlord who might otherwise have been tempted to structure his deal in that way, ie by granting a lease at a premium, but has been dissuaded from doing so by virtue of the fact that part of the premium will be treated as income.

Section 36 applies to the situation where the landowner receives a capital sum from selling his land but retains a right to call on the purchaser to sell it back to him. It treats the interval between the sale and the re-conveyance as if this interval were itself a lease and therefore as if the sale proceeds were a premium charged to the vendor on granting it. Additionally, a re-conveyance by way of a leaseback by the purchaser to the vendor is brought within the scope of this section (TA 1988, s 36(3)). However, the provision does not apply if the lease is *granted and begins to run within one month after the sale*. Thus, the normal sale and leaseback can easily be arranged to avoid coming within these provisions. It is important that this technical point is taken into account (see however 3.5.2).

17.1.5 Deductibility of rent

The rent may be disallowed as a deduction in computing the profits of the vendor under one or more of three heads:

(1) TA 1988, s 779
This is a very widely worded provision and deals with situations which are not just limited to sale and leaseback situations. It provides that if

land or any estate or interest in land is transferred from one person to another and:

(*a*) as a result of a lease; or

(*b*) as a result of any other transaction or a series of transactions.

the transferor becomes liable at the time of the transfer or subsequently to pay any rent under a lease of the land in question, or any part of the land, the amount of rent which is deductible for income tax or corporation tax purposes may be restricted.

TA 1988, s 779 is designed to disallow as a tax deduction any rent or other revenue payment in calculating profits insofar as it exceeds a commercial rent.

The structure of s 779
The section is divided into three parts:

(*a*) *Ambit:* the ambit provisions which determine whether a particular transaction comes within the ambit of s 779;

(*b*) *Consequence:* the consequence provisions which determine the consequences in tax terms which arise if a transaction is caught by the ambit provisions; and

(*c*) *Explanatory:* the explanatory provisions which explain various terms used in the ambit provisions and in the consequence provisions.

Ambit provisions
Section 779(1) determines the ambit of the section. It provides that (i) if land is transferred from one person to another and (ii) as a result of a lease of the land granted at that time or subsequently by the purchaser to the vendor (iii) the vendor becomes liable to pay rent under the lease, the section shall apply. It is clear that a sale and leaseback transaction will come within the ambit of s 779.

Consequence provisions
Section 779(4) sets out the consequences which arise if the taxpayer falls within the ambit of the section. It provides:

> A deduction by way of any *relevant tax relief*, being a deduction in respect of rent . . . shall not exceed the *commercial rent* for the period for which the rent . . . is made.

Explanatory provisions
Relevant Tax Relief: Section 779(13)(*b*) defines "relevant tax relief". This includes a deduction in computing the profits or gain or losses of a trade, profession or vocation. Thus in the case of a retail trader if this provision applies the trader (lessee) will not be entitled to claim the rent, or a relevant portion thereof, as a trading expense.

Commercial rent: Section 779(4) requires a comparison to be made between:

(*a*) the *rent actually payable* under the lease for the period for which the rent is paid—a one year period if the rent is payable annually; and

(*b*) the *commercial rent* for the period for which the actual rent is paid.

Section 779(8) states that 'commercial rent' shall mean:

> ... the rent which might be expected to be paid under a lease of the land negotiated in the open market *at the time when the actual lease was created*, being a lease which is of the same duration as the actual lease, which is, as respects liability for maintenance and repairs, subject to the terms and conditions of the actual lease and which provides for rent payable at uniform intervals and—
> (a) at a uniform rate, or
> (b) if the rent payable under the actual lease is rent at a progressive rate (and such that the amount of rent payable for any year is never less than the amount payable for any previous year), a rent which progresses by gradations proportionate to those provided by the actual lease.

Subsection (8) is the critical provision. It defines commercial rent. If the actual rent payable under the lease exceeds the commercial rent then the amount of the excess is not tax deductible in the year it is paid although it can be carried forwards to subsequent years and this will be relevant if in subsequent years the actual rent is less than the then commercial rent (see subsection (5)). The author's comments on subsection (8) are as follows:

(*a*) *Open market negotiation:* Commercial rent means a rent which might be expected to be paid under a lease of the land negotiated in the open market at the time when the actual lease was granted. If the type of rent formula would have been adopted by the parties *regardless of the sale and leaseback* it is felt that subsection (8) would also *by definition* mean that the rent actually charged would be the commercial rent. The provision merely states that the rent must be the type of rent which one would expect to be paid if the lease were negotiated in the open market; any formula is acceptable if that formula would have been accepted, after negotiation, in the open market.

(*b*) *Assumptions as to lease:* The above is not sufficient to cause the section to be of no relevance in the normal case. One has to assume that the lease which was created has the following features:
  (i) it is of the same duration as the actual lease; and
  (ii) it is as respects liability for maintenance and repairs subject to the terms and conditions of the actual lease; and
  (iii) it provides for the rent to be payable at uniform intervals and
    - at a uniform rate or
    - at an appropriate progressive rate.

(*c*) It is with respect to the assumptions which must be made as to the terms of the lease etc that difficulties arise.

(*d*) One is required to assume that the commercial rent is charged at a uniform rate unless subsection (8)(*b*) can apply.

(*e*) Subsection (8)(*b*) is critical. It can be interpreted in one of two ways. These ways could be termed (i) 'the time of grant approach' and (ii) 'the wait and see approach'.

The 'time of grant' approach
Subsection (8) does seem to envisage that one looks to the time when the actual lease was created to determine whether subsection (8)(*b*) applies. In a normal lease where there is a rent review clause enabling the rent to be increased the author does not see how if one looks at the position at the time of the grant of the lease one can say that the rent is a progressive rent and is chargeable at a progressive rate or that the rent progresses by gradations proportionate to those provided by the actual lease. In a normal rent review the rent may not increase. Thus on the author's interpretation of the provision if there is, for instance, a 35 year lease with rent reviews every seven years (rent upwards only) with the rent in the first seven years being, say, £100,000, subsection (8)(*b*) would not be applicable. If that provision is not applicable then subsection (8)(*a*) is applicable. If that is the case then the deemed commercial rent under subsection (8)(*a*) must be at a uniform rate. It seems to the author that in ascertaining that rate *which is to be a fixed rate throughout the 35 years* the rent in the earlier years must exceed a £100,000. Let us say at the time of the grant of the lease the valuers estimate that the rent for the first seven years will be £100,000 and for the next seven years, consequent upon a rent review, £200,000 per year and then £300,000 per year, consequent upon a rent review, for seven years and so on with £400,000 for the next seven years and £500,000 for the last seven years. If the rent is to be a uniform rent throughout it clearly could not be £100,000. It is likely to be a figure in the region of say £300,000. This means that in the first seven years there is no difficulty. The taxpayer can deduct the full £100,000 per annum which he pays. In the second seven year period when the rent review is completed and the rent is, let us say, increased to £200,000, once again there is no problem. The same in the third seven year period. However, in the fourth seven year period when the rent is reviewed to say £400,000 and in the final seven year period when the rent is reviewed to £500,000 the rent exceeds the commercial rent of £300,000. The excessed in those two years will be disallowed. The defect in the legislation is that the "credits" (for the want of a better word) in the two initial seven year periods when the amount of the commercial rent exceeded the rent actually payable cannot be carried forward to subsequent years; the legislature seems to have overlooked that point, although as mentioned earlier, there is relief if the amount of the actual rent exceeds the commercial rent; the excess can be carried *forward* (but not backwards) until such time as the actual rent is less than the commercial rent when relief in part or in whole will be available.

The 'wait and see' approach
The question therefore is whether subsection (8)(*b*) can assist the taxpayer if a wait and see approach is applied. Clearly subsection 8(*b*) would assist

the taxpayer if when the lease is granted it is specifically provided that the rent for the first period of seven years is £100,000 per annum and then for the next seven year period £200,000 per annum and the next seven year period £300,000 per annum etc, although that is an extremely rare occurrence. It is normal, however, to have a rent review clause or some other rent increase mechanism in the lease:

If subsection (8)(*b*) is applied adopting the wait and see approach then there are no difficulties with regard to the common sale and leaseback transactions where there are rent review clauses in the lease. This is because one is able to compare the actual rent charged, consequent on a review, with the increases in the deemed commercial rent which take place because of subsection (8)(*b*). The author finds it very difficult, however, to see that that is the correct approach on the wording of subsection (8) which refers to the ascertaining of the rent "at the time when the actual lease was created". It may be that the Revenue accept the wait and see approach.

Additionally, the types of cases which this legislation was passed to stop were cases where the rent for the earlier years was excessive with a view to trying to get additional tax relief; it was designed to cover situations where X disposed of the freehold for say a half a million pounds when it was only worth say a quarter of a million pounds and paid massive rents for say 5 years to the purchaser with low rents being paid thereafter. That said, of course, one must read the legislation as it stands. That background, however, indicates that the Revenue may be inclined to take a generous approach with respect to these provisions and apply a wait and see rule.

Conclusions
It seems to the author that s 779 is an anti-avoidance section designed to catch property owners who want to pay *excessive* rents (as part of a sale and leaseback transaction) and obtain extra income or corporation tax relief.

The section is a very difficult one and it is likely the Revenue are applying a wait and see approach; thus if as a result of a rent review the rent goes up the deemed commercial rent at that time is automatically adjusted upwards. If they *do apply* such an approach there should be no problem with respect to the common sale and leaseback transaction.

If the Revenue *do not apply* a wait and see rule or do not give some other form of "credit" for the earlier years there could be serious tax problems in the later years of a leaseback lease.

(2) TA 1988, s 74(a)
If the rent paid under the leaseback is excessive it may be disallowed as not having been wholly and exclusively laid out for the purposes of the trade of the lessee.

(3) TA 1988, s 74(f)
If a leasehold interest is disposed of in return for a leaseback at a higher

rent the Revenue may argue that the excess rent is not deductible as it is paid in return for the capital sum received on the sale (see *IRC* v *LSIT* [1969] 2 All ER 430) and *Littlewoods Mail Order Stores Ltd* v *McGregor* ((1969) 45 TC 526). The Revenue, however, does not appear to raise the point on leaseback situations.

Industrial building allowances and Enterprise Zones
On the sale of the property to the purchaser a balancing charge or allowance may result (CAA 1968, s 3). If there is a lease at a premium to the purchaser and a sub-lease back to the transferor, however, the allowances may be retained by the transferor as he would not have disposed of the 'relevant interest' (CAA 1968, s 11(3)).

Plant and machinery
A balancing charge or allowance may arise on the vendor on the sale of the plant and machinery to the purchaser. Note also the special sale and leaseback provisions in FA 1971 Sched 8 para 3(1)(*b*), (2)(*b*), 3(*b*) and FA 1972 s 68(3).

17.1.6 Capital gains tax and corporation tax on chargeable gains

The sale will be a disposal for capital gains tax purposes. Although not entirely clear as a matter of law it is felt that the better view is that *only a part disposal* rather than a total disposal takes place at the sale. This is provided it is a term of the sale that a leaseback takes place.

The date of the disposal of the land if completion takes place is the date of the *unconditional exchange of contracts* (CGTA 1979, s 27).

In *Sargaison* v *Roberts* ((1969) 45 TC 612) the taxpayer settled certain freehold agricultural land on trust, it being a term of the settlement that the trustees would grant him a forty year lease of the land concerned. If those transactions constituted a full disposal of the land the taxpayer would have ceased to be entitled to the agricultural building allowances for the expenditure on the land before the disposal. CAA 1968, s 68(4) gives the allowances from the date of the disposal to the new owner rather than the original one where the whole of the interest in the land in question is transferred. If, on the other hand, the settlement and the leaseback could be looked at as not representing a total disposal, as reducing but not destroying the original owner's interest in the land, then he could continue to claim his allowances, without s 68(4) disentitling him. Megarry J said:

> I think I am entitled to distinguish between the substance of the transaction and the machinery to carry it through. Processes such as that of having reservations, on the one hand, and that of a grant and regrant on the other . . . seem to me to be matters of machinery. I am encouraged to look at the realities at the expense of the technicalities. The taxpayer's interest has . . . been merely reduced from ownership of the freehold to ownership of the leasehold; the whole of his interest in the land has therefore not been transferred to another.

The normal part disposal rules will apply. If the lease is at a rack rent so that there is no value or virtually no value in what is retained the total acquisition cost can be offset against the sale proceeds. The Revenue approach appears to be to treat the disposal as a total disposal if the leaseback is at a rack rent, although the strict position depends on whether the lease has any value, as far as the tenant is concerned. Otherwise they treat it as a part disposal. If it is not a term of the transaction that a leaseback takes place there is clearly a total disposal and a subsequent separate letting back.

Where leaseback is a total disposal
X Ltd has a freehold factory worth £1,000,000 which it bought in 1983 for £250,000. It sells this to a pension fund for £1,000,000 in 1988 with a leaseback at a rack rent. The disposal proceeds will be £1,000,000 and the Revenue apparently will treat the disposal as a total disposal so that *inter alia* the total acquisition costs of the freehold (£250,000) will be offset against the proceeds of sale of £1,000,000 to ascertain the chargeable gain.

17.1.7 Value Added Tax

On the sale of the interest to the purchaser the proceeds may be zero-rated or exempt (VATA 1983, Sched 5, Group 8, Item 1 and Sched 6, Group 1, Item 1). The rents in the hands of the purchaser will be exempt (VATA 1983, Sched 5, Group 8, Item 1 not satisfied and see *PMP (1969)* v *CCE* (MAN/77/59)).

Plant and machinery which is sold and which is not part of the land and buildings may be chargeable to VAT (VATA 1983, s 2(1)).

In certain cases the Customs may be prepared to treat the sale and leaseback as a continuous transaction but individual cases must be cleared with them.

Example 17B: VAT and sale and leaseback

X Ltd has constructed a new office in Blackacre. It sells this to a pension fund in 1988 and takes back a 50-year lease. It grants a 30-year sub-lease to *Y* Ltd in 1988. The sale to the fund would be a zero-rated supply. The leaseback will be an exempt supply by the fund. The sub-lease by *X* Ltd to *Y* Ltd will give rise to zero-rated rents if the Customs agree that *X* Ltd has only made a part disposal to the fund (even though the leaseback to *X* Ltd is at a rack rent) and thus continues to own an interest in the property which it constructed in spite of the sale to the fund. Note 12.37 for the likely changes in this area in FA 1989.

17.1.8 Stamp duty

The possible stamp duty charges on a sale and leaseback must be carefully taken into account. There will be a conveyance or transfer on sale charge on the sale of the freehold and there will be lease or tack duty on the leasehold (Stamp Act 1891, Sched 1).

Example 17C: Stamp duty on sale and leaseback

X sells Blackacre to *Y* for £1m and takes a lease back for 21 years at a rent of £100,000 per annum. Conveyance on sale duty is payable on the £1m (ie, £1m × 1% = £10,000) and lease or tack duty on the £100,000 by reference to a 21-year lease period.

17.1.9 Conclusions on sale and leaseback

(*a*) There are substantial advantages to be obtained from a sale and leaseback, ie, the receipt of a capital sum plus the payment of tax-deductible rent.

(*b*) The tax provisions mentioned in this chapter must be carefully considered so that the taxpayer does not fall into any of the pitfalls which may turn an attractive tax situation into a fiscal nightmare; the capital sum may be taxed as income and the rent not tax-deductible.

18 FINANCE LEASES

18.1 INTRODUCTION

The tax courts may often ignore technical land law points and concepts in tax cases and look to the substance of transactions. Labels attached to particular transactions may also be ignored in favour of looking to the substance of what is being created.

18.2 CASE LAW

In the case of *IRC* v *Land Securities Investment Trust Ltd* 45 TC 495 a property investment company (X) had a lease of a number of properties from a charity (Y). Rent was payable to the charity each year and this was clearly deductible in calculating X's profits tax liability. The amount of the rent was £62,500 pa. X then bought the capital reversions in consideration of the payment of rent charges totalling £96,000. The question was whether the rent charges were tax deductible. Lord Donnovan delivering the judgment of the House of Lords, which found unanimously in favour of the Revenue, looked at the matter in a very simple fashion. The property company (X) purchased capital assets. Why should the payments laid out to purchase those capital assets, even though they are called rent charges, be tax deductible when the purchase price, had the properties been paid for outright, or even by instalments, would not have been tax deductible?

The judge, however, admitted that capital assets may be purchased by income payments and he reserved his position as to what the position would have been if perpetual rent charges had been the consideration in the present case.

The question was also raised as to whether the rent charge payments could be dissected into capital and interest components with relief being available for the interest components. This is because effectively the rent charges could have been looked upon as delayed capital payments for the property with interest being charged for that delay in payment by Y. The judge held in this case that the payments could not be dissected because there had been no figure agreed in advance as being the purchase price. Reference should also be made to the *Church Commissioner's* case and the case of *Littlewood Mail Order Stores Ltd* v *MacGregor* 45 TC 526. In the latter case 'rent' paid to acquire an asset was held to be capital.

18.3 FINANCE LEASES

The Land Securities case is an important one to consider when looking at finance-lease situations where, for instance, a bank acquires property and pays a builder to construct a building thereon which is subsequently let to a commercial or industrial user in an enterprise zone. Some transactions such as that may develop into a deal which more resembles a loan with interest payments rather than payments for the construction of a building and the receipt of rents. This is especially the case if the builder and the tenant are connected. If the payments to the builder are reasonable and the rents are not too out of line with market value rents then the author feels that generally with regard to transactions such as that the Revenue will not be able to upset the position relying on cases such as the Land Securities case mentioned above. Much depends on the particular facts. If, for instance, the building price is inflated with an arrangement under which the rent will equally be inflated then problems could clearly occur.

18.4 SSAP21

SSAP 21 is important as it may have a bearing on the tax treatment of particular leases. It distinguishes between finance leases and operating leases and it applies to land and buildings. In a borderline case the accountancy treatment of a lease as a finance lease under SSAP 21 may tempt the Revenue to argue that an apparent payment of rent is really a payment of interest. A rent review clause, with the reviewed rent being based on market value of the land interest, goes a long way to ensuring that a finance lease is not created (pages 342, para 140).

Practitioners and Accountants/Auditors are often required to classify particular leases according to SSAP21. The author has extracted the following nine indicia from pp 288–354 of the Accounting Standards Booklet issued by the Institute of Chartered Accountants for 1987/1988 which may assist practitioners to accomplish this unenviable task.

18.4.1 Economic substance

One should look to the economic substance of the arrangement. A finance lease may be akin to a loan (p 319, para 73). In the case of a finance lease the lessor provides finance and may expect a return calculated by reference to the finance so provided rather than by reference to the value of the land interest (p 319, para 71). Thus if the rental returns are calculated by reference to a formula incorporating references to general money rates that would indicate that there was a loan type arrangement and therefore a finance lease.

18.4.2 Three broad categories

Finance lessors fall into three broad categories. They may be companies, including banks and finance houses, which provide finance and enter into lease contracts to enable a single customer to acquire the use of an asset for the greater part of its useful life. Alternatively they may operate a business which involves renting out assets for varying periods of time probably to more than one customer. Finally they may be manufacturer or dealer lessors who use leasing as a means of marketing their products which may involve leasing a product to one customer or to several customers (p 288, para 4).

18.4.3 Rent review clause

If there are regular rent reviews, especially if the rent is reviewed by reference to property values, this is an indication (and the author would have thought a strong indication) that the lease is an operating lease; such a lease would not have the characteristics so much of a financing arrangement as of the provision of a service, namely the use of the building (p 342, para 140).

18.4.4 The 90% risks and rewards test

A Finance lease is a lease which transfers substantially all the risks and rewards of ownership of an asset to the lessee. It is presumed that such a transfer of risks and rewards occurs if at the inception of the lease the present value of the minimum lease payments including premiums amounts to substantially all (normally 90% or more) of the fair value of the leased asset (p 290, para 15).

Even if a lease meets that test the presumption that the lease is a finance lease can be rebutted if it can be clearly demonstrated that the lease in question does not transfer substantially all the risks and rewards of ownership (other than legal title) to the lessee. Correspondingly the presumption that a lease which fails to meet the conditions is not a finance lease may in exceptional circumstances be rebutted. It would seem to be implicit from para 71 on p 319 that a stream of rentals is not a reward of ownership, as far as the lessor is concerned, within the risks and rewards test. If instead of a *stream of rentals* (which indicates the existence of a finance lease) there is a *rent review clause* then the rent review clause would tend to indicate that there is an operating lease; see p 343, para 142 which indicates that a lessor may lease property to a lessee with the lease containing a rent review clause; such a rent review clause indicates that the risks and rewards are retained by the lessor. This indicates the existence of an operating lease.

When applying the risks and rewards test it is clearly necessary to ascertain what the asset is.

Although there are parts of the guidance notes which indicate that perhaps the asset is merely the building (p 342, para 140 and 141), it seems to the author that the intention is that the land and buildings would comprise the asset (see p 342, para 139 and p 343, para 142).

Thus if X bank buys freehold land, constructs a building thereon and grants a lease to Y for 10 years obtaining rental payments referable to current money market rates and at the same time, for instance, gives Y an option to buy the freehold for a nominal sum at the end of the 10 years that would clearly result in the creation of a finance lease; the risks and rewards of ownership vest in the lessee. The same result would ensue if at the end of the 10 years the building is likely to have become of no economic use and the property is within an enterprise zone and it is felt that the value of the land is negligible. It would seem to the author that in both these cases the 90% test would be satisfied and the lease would be a finance lease.

18.4.5 The 10% risks and rewards test

An alternative way of considering whether substantially all the risks and rewards are transferred to the lessee and whether or not the lease is a finance lease is to consider whether the present value of any amounts excluded from the minimum lease payments exceeds 10% of the fair value of the land and building (p 340, para 134). Thus if a bank constructs a building which has a 10 year life and grants a non-renewable lease to X for 5 years and at the end of the 5 years the building still has an economic life of 5 years to go this would show the existence of an operating lease.

18.4.6 The economic life of the asset

If the lessee obtains a lease for only a small part of the useful life of the building then there is likely to be an operating lease rather than a finance lease. An operating lease involves the lessee paying a rent for the use of an asset for a period of time which is normally substantially less than its useful economic life (p 289, para 7 and p 342, para 140).

18.4.7 Most leases of land are operating leases

Paragraph 140 on p 342 states that most leases involving land and buildings would be classified as operating leases.

18.4.8 Form of documentation

The form of the documentation may be relevant in appropriate cases (p 339, para 133).

18.4.9 Lease premiums

Nothing in the Standard precludes the recognition as a fixed asset of an amount paid in the form of a premium as consideration for a leasehold interest (p 343, para 144).

19 MORTGAGES

19.1 INTRODUCTION

Property is often mortgaged to raise money. This is a very efficient way of raising money for tax purposes because a mortgage does not involve a disposal of the land, so there will be no charge to CGT nor indeed a charge under Case I of Schedule D (trading).

For the nature of a mortgage see 1.2.7.

19.2 CAPITAL GAINS TAX

19.2.1 Creation of mortgage is not a disposal

The creation of a mortgage is not a disposal for CGT purposes so no tax charge can arise. Under CGTA 1979, s 23(1) any transfer of property to a mortgagee (lender) as security for the mortgage is ignored for CGT purposes. So also is any re-transfer of the property on redemption of the security.

19.2.2 Dealings by mortgagee

Where the mortgagee deals with the assets for the purpose of enforcing or giving effect to his security, he is deemed to be carrying out the transaction as nominee for the person who owns the property which is the subject matter of the security or charge (CGTA 1979, s 23(2)).

Example 19A: Effect of sale by mortgagee

X owns Blackacre, which is worth £100,000. He purchased it in 1983 for £50,000. He mortgages it to a building society and raises £80,000. He defaults in the mortgage payments and the building society exercises its power of sale and sells it for £100,000 on 1 June 1987, giving £20,000 to X after satisfying the

£80,000 loan. Ignoring incidental expenses and allowances etc and assuming X has used up his annual exemption, the chargeable gain is:

Sale proceeds	£100,000
Less acquisition cost	£50,000
Chargeable gain	£50,000

19.2.3 Transactions subject to mortgages

An asset shall be treated as having been acquired free of any right or interest by way of security subsisting at the time of the acquisition and as being disposed of free of any such right or interest subsisting at the time of the disposal.

Where an asset is acquired subject to any such right or interest, however, the full amount of the liability thereby assumed by the person acquiring the asset shall form part of the consideration for the acquisition and disposal in addition to any other consideration (CGTA 1979, s 23(3)).

Where an asset is disposed of and at the same time, the transferor grants a loan to the transferee, secured on the asset, the disposal consideration is the full amount payable, treating the loan agreement as a separate transaction from the sale. Repayment of the loan does not therefore affect the computation of the gain on the disposal of the asset (*Coran* v *Keighley* [1972] 48 TC 307).

19.3 OTHER CHARGES AND RELIEFS

19.3.1 Lease premium provisions

The creation of a mortgage will not be a transaction which causes a tax charge under the lease premium provisions (see Chapter 3). For these provisions although a 'lease' includes an agreement for lease it does not include a mortgage (TA 1988, s 24(1)).

19.3.2 Trading

The creation of a mortgage over land held as trading stock will not cause a realisation of the land for the purposes of computing a charge under Case I of Schedule D (see Chapter 4).

19.3.3 Interest relief

Income tax relief may be available for the interest paid under the mortgage (see Chapter 7).

Income tax relief is not available for the capital repayments made under the mortgage (see 7.2.8).

Relief is not available for a loan taken out to buy a mortgage (see 7.2.5).

19.3.4 Capital allowances

The raising of money by mortgage will not result in any balancing adjustments for the purposes of industrial building allowances, Enterprise Zone allowances or plant and machinery allowances. Also, if money is borrowed to purchase plant and machinery or to cover expenditure in constructing an industrial or Enterprise Zone building, this will not prevent the borrower obtaining allowances (*Stokes* v *Costain* [1984] STC 204 CA).

Example 19B: Effect of mortgage on capital allowances

X Ltd borrows £1,000,000 from a bank to construct an industrial building which contains plant and machinery. If the appropriate conditions are satisfied (see Chapter 8 Part 1) X Ltd will obtain the appropriate capital allowances. The fact that X Ltd borrowed the money rather than used its own funds will not be relevant.

19.3.5 Inheritance tax

If a mortgage debt is gratuitously created over the taxpayer's property IHT must be considered (see, for example FA 1986 s 103—Treatment of certain debts and incumbrances). Special provisions apply to the mortgage of reversionary interests under settlements. A 'mortgage' for IHT purposes includes a security constituted over any interest in movable property (IHTA 1984, s 272).

19.3.6 TA 1988, s 776

The mere creation of a mortgage over property should not cause any tax charge to arise under this provision although a mortgage may form part of an overall tax-avoidance scheme which could bring the section into operation.

19.3.7 Value added tax

The interest paid on the advance will arise from an exempt supply by the mortgagee (lender) (VATA 1983, Sched 6, Group 5, item 2(*a*)). Thus, no VAT is charged on the interest, on the capital repayments nor on the money lent to the mortgagor (borrower).

19.3.8 Stamp duty

The position with regard to stamp duty is dealt with in Chapter 13.

19.4 TAX PLANNING

(*a*) The creation of a mortgage is a very effective way of raising money by a property investor because it does not involve a disposal of his land and therefore a charge to CGT. The transaction is made cheaper by virtue of the fact that no stamp duty will be exigible.

(*b*) Tax relief will also normally be available on the interest payments (see Chapter 7), either under the CT provisions or because the loan is taken out for a qualifying purpose. The mere fact that property is charged by way of mortgage does not enable interest relief to be available on a loan; the monies actually borrowed must be used for a qualifying purpose (see 7.2.3).

(*c*) Because the taxpayer retains his asset the future growth in the property will accrue for his benefit.

(*d*) The raising of money by a mortgage should be compared to the raising of money by sale and leaseback; the former appears to be the most attractive method when taking into account taxation and other factors.

(*e*) Interest-free loans repayable on demand (whether on mortgage or not) do not generally give rise to any IHT consequences.

(*f*) Interest-free loans repayable on demand (whether on mortgage or not) which are 'inspired by ordinary business considerations' will not be caught by the income tax settlement provisions in TA 1988, Part XV (see *IRC* v *Levy* [1982] STC 442, TCA 142).

(*g*) Loans to participators (and their associates), whether on mortgage or not, in close companies have to be 'grossed up' under TA 1988, s 419, so taxpayers must make sure that they are not caught by that provision.

20 LAND OPTIONS

20.1 INTRODUCTION

This chapter deals with the taxation position of options over land.

An option can be useful as a tax planning instrument because for most taxes it will enable a disposal to be delayed until the option is exercised.

20.1.1 Land law position

Interest in land
An option to purchase land creates an immediate interest in land because the grantee can compel the grantor to bring into effect a binding contract to transfer the land to him (*London & South Western Railway Co* v *Gomm* (18820 20 CHD 562).

Estate contract
An option can be registered as an estate contract under Land Charges Act 1972, s 2(4)(iv). Registration will bind a purchaser of the land.

20.2 CAPITAL GAINS TAX

20.2.1 Option is an asset

An option is specifically declared to be an asset for the purposes of CGT (CGTA 1979, s 19(1)(*a*)).

20.2.2 Grant and exercise of option

The grant of an option and, in particular:

(*a*) the grant of an option where the grantor binds himself to sell what he does not own; and

(*b*) the grant of an option in the case where the grantor binds himself to buy an asset which he does not (because the option is abandoned) ultimately acquire.

is a disposal of an asset (namely the option) (CGTA 1979, s 137(1)). The grant is not treated as a part disposal.

If X holds land as an investment and gives a builder an option for a non returnable figure of £100,000 exercisable within, say, 5 years, to buy the land from X for £500,000 a charge to CGT can arise as set out below.

If the option is not exercised by the builder, X will have made a chargeable gain of £100,000, and he will have no acquisition base cost to offset against that gain. He will, however, be able to deduct legal expenses and the normal incidental costs incurred in connection with the option (*Strange* v *Openshaw (Inspector of Taxes)* [1983] STC 416).

20.2.3 Exercise of option

If the option is exercised and the land is transferred to the grantee of the option pursuant to the terms of the option, both these transactions are treated as a single transaction and accordingly:

(*a*) if the option binds the grantor to sell, the consideration for the option is part of the consideration for the sale; and

(*b*) if the option binds the grantor to buy, the consideration for the option shall be deducted from the cost of acquisition incurred by the grantor in buying in pursuance of his obligations under the option

(CTGA 1979, s 137(2)).

Example 20A: Consideration on exercise of option

X grants Y an option to buy Blackacre from him for £50,000. The price to be paid is a further £250,000 if the option is exercised. X's total consideration for CGT purposes if the option is exercised is £300,000 and that—£300,000—is also Y's acquisition cost. The legislation implies that the disposal of the land (Blackacre) takes place when the option is exercised (with legal completion—i.e. the legal estate by way of transfer or conveyance being vested in Y—following thereafter). See 9.4.4.

20.2.4 Option to grant lease

Similar rules apply where there is an option binding the grantor to grant a lease for a premium or similar types of disposals; these provisions are not restricted to simple sales and purchases (CGTA 1979, s 137(7)).

20.2.5 Abandonment

Special rules apply to situations where options are abandoned (CGTA

1979, s 137(4)) as opposed to surrendered for a consideration (see *Golding* v *Kaufman* [1985] STC 152 and *Powlson* v *Wellbeck Securities Ltd* [1986] STC 423.

20.2.6 Forfeited deposits

Special rules apply where a deposit is forfeited in connection with the acquisition of property (CGTA 1979, s 137(8)). The vendor is required to treat the forfeited deposit as if it were consideration for the grant of an option. Thus, the full sum (the forfeited deposit) will be treated as the disposal consideration without any base cost (this is because it is not a part disposal; there may be some fees and expenses which can be deductible in respect of the abortive transaction).

20.2.7 Options to acquire wasting assets for trade

The CGT rules which apply to wasting assets and the restrictions on allowable expenditure under CGTA 1979, s 38 (straight line deductions to be made from allowable expenditure for wasting assets) do not apply to an option to acquire assets exercisable by a person intending to use them, if acquired, for the purposes of a trade carried on by him (CGTA 1979, s 138(1)(*b*)).

20.2.8 Connected persons

CGTA 1979, s 62 (as amended by FA 1981, s 86) applies where a person acquires an asset and the person making the disposal is connected with him. The parties are treated as if they had carried out a transaction otherwise than by way of a bargain made at arm's length. This means, broadly that market value may be substituted for any consideration actually given (CGTA 1979, s 29A and FA 1981, s 91).

Where the asset which is transferred is an option to enter into a sale or other transaction given by the person making the disposal, a loss accruing to the person acquiring the asset shall not be an allowable loss unless it accrues on a disposal of the option at arm's length to a person who is not connected with him (CGTA 1979, s 62(4)). In certain cases an option over land may be ignored when calculating the value of a transferor's interest and this can in certain cases amount to a tax trap (CGTA 1979, s 72(5) and (6)).

20.2.9 Time of disposal and acquisition where asset is acquired under contract

If a contract is conditional and in particular if it is conditional on the exercise of an option, the time at which the disposal and acquisition takes place for CGT is the time when the condition is satisfied (CGTA 1979, s 27(2)).

20.3 OTHER CHARGES AND RELIEFS

20.3.1 Trading

Profits made from the acquisition or exercise of options may be chargeable to tax under Case 1 Schedule D if the requisite badges of trade are present.

If a taxpayer has an option to acquire property (eg to acquire the freehold premises from which he carries out his trade) and he subsequently decides to exercise the option in order to sell on the property to make a trading profit, he may only be chargeable to tax under Case 1 of Schedule D on the profit arising since he appropriated the option to trading stock. This gain may be small. The gain up to the appropriation may be of a capital nature, chargeable only to CGT (or CT on chargeable gains) (see *Bath & West Counties Property Trust Ltd* v *Thomas* (1977) 121 SJ 730; *cf Clark* v *Follett* (1973) 48 TC 677 and 3 PLB 22).

20.3.2 Inheritance tax and TA 1988 s 776

If options are granted gratuitously or are given away or sold at an undervalue there may be a transfer of value for IHT purposes. The existence of an option granted gratuitously, may be ignored for certain IHT valuation purposes (IHTA 1984, s 163(1)).

20.3.3 TA 1988, s 887

The provisions of TA 1988, s 776 can apply to any capital gains made from property deriving its value from land and this includes any option affecting the disposition of land (TA 1988, s 776(12)(*b*)(ii)). In connection with put and call options, see 11.2.3.

20.3.4 Stamp duty

Ad valorem duty may be chargeable on the grant of an option in consideration of a cash sum (SA 1894, s 54, Sched 1; it may alternatively be chargeable under s 60).

Example 20B: Options are stampable

X gives the builder an option over his (X's) land for £100,000. That option agreement is stampable *ad valorem* (1%). Duty will also be payable when the option is exercised and the property is transferred to the builder for £500,000 (on top of the £100,000 already paid for the option). In the case of that transfer the duty will be at the rate of 1% of £500,000 so that the total duty is 1% of £600,000 (see *George Wimpey & Co* v *IRC* [1979] 1 WLR 995). See also page 271.

21 LAND PARTNERSHIPS AND LAND EXCHANGES

PART I LAND PARTNERSHIPS

21.1 INTRODUCTION

This part deals with the taxation position of land partnerships and joint ventures. It is especially important that the tax consequences arising from parties being found to be partners are clearly identified. Land partnerships may be created between parties without the parties realising it. A partnership is a relationship which subsists between persons carrying on a business (not necessarily a trade) in common with a view to profit (Partnership Act 1890, s 1).

In England a partnership is not a legal entity separate from the partners (*Sadler* v *Whiteman* (1910) 1 CIP 686 (CA)).

21.2 CREATION OF A PARTNERSHIP

An agreement between the parties, whether express or implied, is the source of the partnership relationship. There must also be some consideration put into the partnership by the parties, for example, contributions of capital or labour or any act which may result in liability to third parties.

No particular formalities are necessary for the creation of a partnership, although land disposals require Law of Property Act 1925, s 40 to be satisfied or there must be a sufficient act of part performance (*Foster* v *Hale* 5 Ves 303, *Dale* v *Hamilton* 5 Ha 369 and *Chaddick* v *Skidmore* 2 De G & J 52 and see page 9 hereof).

The question whether a partnership exists is a mixed question of law and fact (Harman J in *Keith Spicer* v *Mansell* [1970] 1 WLR 333). In determining whether a partnership exists Partnership Act 1890, s 2 provides some assistance. Joint tenancy, tenancy-in-common, joint property, common property or part ownership does not of itself create a partnership as to anything so held or owned, whether the tenants or owners do or do not share any profits made by the use thereof.

The sharing of gross returns does not of itself create a partnership, whether the persons sharing such returns have or have not a joint or common right or interest in any property from which or from the use of which the returns are derived.

The receipt by a person of a share of the profits of a business is *prima facie* evidence that he is a partner in the business but receipt of such a share, or of a payment contingent on or varying with the profits of a business, does not of itself make him a partner in the business and in particular (Partnership Act 1980, s 2):

(*a*) a contract for the remuneration of a servant or agent of a person engaged in a business by a share of the profits of the business does not of itself make the servant or agent a partner in the business or liable as such;

(*b*) the advance of money by way of loan to a person engaged or about to be engaged in a business on a contract with that person that the lender shall receive a rate of interest varying with the profits, or shall receive a share of the profits arising from carrying on the business, does not of itself make the lender a partner with the person or persons carrying on the business or liable as such provided that the contract is in writing, and signed by or on behalf of all the parties thereto.

It is clear that common ownership of property alone is insufficient to establish a partnership in respect of that property even though a partnership may exist between the co-owners.

If each co-owner of property does nothing more than take his share of the gross returns obtained by the use of the common property, partnership does not result. On the other hand, if the owners convert those returns into money, bring that money into a common stock, defray from the common stock the expenses of obtaining the returns, then divide the net profits, partnership may be created in the profits although it may not be created in the property which yields the profits.

If tenants in common of a house let the same and divide the rent equally between them, they are not partners although they may pay for repairs out of the rent before dividing it (see *French* v *Styring,* 2 CB [NS] 357).

To establish a partnership in property there must be a carrying on of business in relation thereto with a view to profit such as land speculation (*Re Hulton, Hulton* v *Lister* (1890) 62 LT 200).

It is not absolutely essential that a person should contribute property in order to be a partner. If he contributes skill or labour and is entitled to share the profits and is bound to share the losses he is very likely to be a partner. In *Moor* v *Davis* Ch D [1879] 261, the defendant was to provide the necessary capital and the plaintiff was to give his knowledge and experience, as a land agent and surveyor, to the project and superintend and control the building operations to be carried out on the property. The profits and losses arising from the speculation would be shared between the parties equally. In the agreement between the parties it was stated that the same was not to be construed as a partnership. Hall VC held that the parties were in partnership. He stated at p 265:

> '. . . the agreement was that the Plaintiff should bear half of any losses there might be in respect of any of the transactions, and generally he was to receive and bear one half of the profits and losses upon the whole of the transactions. Such language is a very strong feature in favour of a partnership . . . .'

21.2.1 Joint ventures

In *George Hall & Son* v *Platt* (1954) 35 TC 440, a farmer and a farmer/merchant agreed to grow a crop on land occupied by the farmer. The farmer provided horse labour, the farmer/merchant provided seed, manure, hand labour, harvesting and selling expenses. The balance was divided equally. This was held to be a joint venture and not a partnership.

In the case of *London Financial Association* v *Kelk* (1884) 26 Ch D 107, it was held that where a Company (X) entered into an agreement with A and B for them to acquire an estate in common and for A to carry out construction works and X to raise money to acquire materials this did not make the parties partners. Each of them held their separate shares in the property and paid for their shares on separate accounts. There was not a sufficient working together or sharing of property rights to enable a partnership to be found.

In *IRC* v *Williamson* (1928) 14 TC 335, a lease of land was taken in the name of a father and three sons. It was run as a farm. The father provided all capital and ran the bank account. He sold and bought farming stock. The sons only worked on the farm receiving casual amounts from the father now and then. No proper books were kept. It was held that this was a joint family venture and not a partnership.

In *Fenston* v *Johnstone* (1940) 23 TC 29, the appellant wished to buy and develop some land but lacked the necessary finance. The land was purchased by S who found the money in accordance with an agreement which further provided that the appellant should be paid one-half of any profits. If there should be a loss the appellant was to be responsible for one-half of such loss. The agreement stated that it was not to constitute a partnership between the parties. The appellant claimed that the proper amount received by him was remuneration paid by a principal to an agent and was not a share of the profits. Wrottesley J held that there was a very strong presumption in favour of a partnership where persons have agreed to share the profits and losses and accordingly held that a partnership existed.

In *Walker West Developments* v *Emmett* (1979) 252 EG 1171, there was a building agreement between a developer and a builder. The builder sold land to the developer and the builder built according to the developer's specifications.

On the sale of the houses to the purchasers, the developer received the sale proceeds from the purchasers and after certain adjustments shared them with the builder. The builder's initial expenses were also shared but there was no provision for sharing losses. The project was advertised as a joint project between the developer and the builder. There was a clause in the agreement requiring such advertising. The Court of Appeal held that there was a partnership, and regarded as an important pointer the public advertisement of the project as a joint project.

21.2.2 The importance of labels

A statement that an agreement is not to create a partnership is certainly not conclusive of the situation. In *Weiner* v *Harris* [1910] 1 KB 285 at p 290 *Cozen-Hardy* MR stated:

> Two parties enter into a transaction and they say 'it is hereby declared that there is no partnership between us'. The Court pays no regard to that. The Court looks at the transaction and says 'is this, in point of law, really a partnership?' It is not in the least conclusive that the parties have used a term or language intended to indicate that the transaction is not that which in law it is.

The use of the word 'syndicate' does not automatically imply the existence of a partnership (*Tyser* v *The Shipowners' Syndicate (Reassured)* [1896] 1 QB 135).

21.2.3 Actions to be taken to show that there is no partnership

The following actions may be taken to try and show that there is no partnership in existence:

(*a*) The method of dividing the profits and losses must be looked at. The sharing of net profits and losses is a very strong indication that there is a partnership.

(*b*) there should be no separate notepaper referring to both parties to the transaction;

(*c*) there should be separate bank accounts;

(*d*) there should be as little sharing of debts as possible; and

(*e*) there should be no reference to the parties carrying out a 'joint project' etc in any advertisement.

21.3 CONSEQUENCES OF A PARTNERSHIP

The Partnership Act 1890, s 9 provides that every partner in a firm is liable jointly with the other partners for debts and obligations of the firm incurred whilst he is a partner.

Partners are jointly and severally liable for tortious acts (Partnership Act 1890, ss 10 and 12).

21.3.1 Joint liability for income tax

TA 1988, s 111 states that where a trade is carried on by two or more persons jointly, *income tax* in respect thereof shall be computed and stated jointly and a joint assessment shall be made in the partnership name.

21.3.2 Company

A company is chargeable to CT on profits arising to it under any partnership (TA 1988, s 8). Where a company, however, is in partnership, TA 1988, s 114(2) deems the company to be carrying on a trade separately from the trade carried on by any other partners.

Thus, a company can never, in the author's view, be liable for another company's CT on profits. This reduces the seriousness in tax terms of a particular transaction being found to be a partnership transaction where companies are concerned and corporation tax is in point.

21.3.3 Non-residents

(See 26.3.)

21.3.4 Capital gains tax (or corporation tax on chargeable gains)

The position is governed by CGTA 1979, s 60. It should be noted that when land is brought into partnership there may be a disposal for CGT purposes. Partners are connected persons for CGT purposes so that market value may be substituted on transfers between partners although this does not apply to acquisitions and disposals of partnership assets pursuant to bona fide commercial arrangements between the partners (CGTA 1979, s 63(4)).

The Revenue have issued a comprehensive statement of practice (17 January 1975) concerning the taxation of partnerships so far as CGT is concerned (see 1/1975 in *Inland Revenue Practices and Concessions,* Oyez Longman).

PART II LAND EXCHANGES

21.4 INTRODUCTION

Exchanges of rights over land can give rise to charges to taxation. Where joint projects are envisaged by taxpayers they should ensure that any joint development agreements do not cause immediate charges to tax to arise (see p 166).

21.5 CAPITAL GAINS TAX

21.5.1 Exchange of separate interests

If one parcel of land is exchanged for another parcel of land a charge to CGT may arise.

Example 21A: Effect of exchange of separate interests

A Ltd exchanges Blackacre with B Ltd for Whiteacre. A Ltd has disposed of Blackacre for a consideration equal to the value of Whiteacre and vice versa.

Rollover relief or holdover relief may be available in appropriate cases (CGTA 1979, ss 115–121 (see 9.4.8)).

21.5.2 Partition amongst co-owners

The Law of Property Act 1925, ss 34 and 35 prevent the creation of legal tenancies-in-common in property and provide instead that where such shares are intended to be created the property is held on trust for sale (the statutory trusts defined by s 35) and the rights of tenants-in-common exist in the rents and profits until sale, and in the proceeds of sale when they arise.

In *Kidson* v *Macdonald* [1974] STC 54, it was decided that property held on the statutory trusts is nominee property for the purposes of CGT, ie, no settlement is created for CGT purposes although there is a trust.

Where particular parcels of property are appropriated to co-owners (eg Mr X and Mr Y own Greenacre as tenants in common and they each take one half of the land absolutely) it can be argued that each co-owner owned an equitable share in the whole of the property and there must therefore be a disposal of the rights of the other co-owners to the person who takes the share absolutely. However, this charge to tax can be avoided if the Revenue Concession on Co-ownership applies (see p 166).

21.5.3 Surrender and regrant—the disappearing base cost

Where a landlord and tenant agree that the lease to the tenant should be varied by the tenant surrendering his lease and the landlord granting a new lease to the tenant without any sums changing hands, it may well be that CGT problems will arise.

L may have let property to T some years ago. The lease may have a substantial value and L and T may agree that T will surrender the lease to L and L would grant a new lease to T containing new terms. The lease may be a longer one and there may be different rent review provisions. Assume that no cash passes between the parties, what is the CGT position?

Under general principles, and it seems that the Revenue take that view, a charge to CGT would arise; the surrender of the old lease is a disposal and the grant of the new lease is the consideration for the disposal of the old lease.

In certain cases relief from the tax charge may be available, for instance, under CGTA 1979, s 111A or because one or other of the published concessions contained in Section D of the Revenue Booklet on concessions is applicable.

In the normal situation, however, a CGT charge will, as a matter of law, arise.

The Revenue, however, have always taken the view that there will be no charge provided no separate capital sum is received by the lessee and the new lease is in respect of the same property as the old and is in terms that differ from the old only in respect of rent and duration.

What appears to be new in the revenue approach from correspondence which the author has seen with Technical Division is the Revenue view that any base cost of the *old* lease is not to be allowable in any CGT computation when the new lease is disposed of.

The author had understood that the Revenue Practice had been to allow the base cost expenditure of the old lease as a deduction when the new lease was disposed of under the provisions of CGTA 1979, s 36 (assets derived from other assets).

Practitioners should take note of this 'disappearing base cost' practice which the Revenue appear to adopt on surrenders and regrants.

21.5.4 Exchange of rights

Rights over land may be exchanged and this can give rise to charges to CGT (see 9.4.13).

21.5.5 General rollover relief

Where a trader disposes of property from which he carried out his trade and uses the proceeds, or an amount equal to the proceeds to acquire new trade premises and he does this in the period beginning 12 months before the disposal and ending 3 years after the disposal (or such longer period as the Revenue may allow) he can postpone the charge to CGT (or in the case of companies, corporation tax on chargeable gains) (see CGTA 1979, s 115).

Example 21A: Rollover relief

X Ltd uses premises to carry out its manufacturing trade and disposes of the same for £1m. Within 3 years it purchases other trade premises for £1m. The charge to corporation tax on chargeable gains is rolled over.

The relief is also available to professions. It is restricted, however, to certain relevant assets as set out in CGTA 1979, s 118, such as land, fixed plant or machinery, etc. Special rules apply to wasting assets, ie broadly assets which have a life not exceeding 50 years (CGTA 1979, s 117(6)). Note also the special rules applicable to furnished let holiday accommodation (see FA 1984 s 50 and Sched 2 para 1 (2)(*f*)). See page 162.

21.5.6 Rollover relief on compulsory acquisition

Rollover relief will be available where a landowner disposes of land to an authority exercising or having compulsory powers and he did not take any steps by advertising or otherwise to dispose of the land, or to make his willingness to dispose of it known to the authority or others and the consideration for the disposal is applied by the landowner in acquiring other land. This relief is not restricted to landowners who use the land for the purposes of carrying out their trade. Thus, property investment companies can obtain this relief.

It had been thought that technically the relief would not be available on an exchange of land because the rollover situation above envisaged the consideration received on the disposal of the old asset being applied in the acquisition of the new asset. This could not apply on an exchange because on a strict reading of the legislation, the consideration for the disposal of the old asset was the new asset.

Revenue view
Fortunately, the Inland Revenue indicated in *Tolley's Practical Tax,* 17 November 1982, p 183 and also in correspondence with the author that they will not apply such a strict interpretation. Thus rollover relief will be available in the case of an exchange. Perhaps the Revenue is adopting the principles of tax interpretation restated by Lord Wilberforce in *W T Ramsay Ltd* v *IRC* [1981], STC 174 at 179j, ie, when applying tax legislation one must not apply too literal an interpretation to the provisions; one must look to the context of the particular words and the scheme of the relevant Act as a whole.

21.6 OTHER CHARGES AND RELIEFS

21.6.1 Trading

An exchange of property can also give rise to a trading profit.

21.6.2 Capital allowances

On an exchange of property balancing adjustments may be made for the purposes of capital allowances (see CAA 1968, s 77 and FA 1971, Sched 8, para 15(4)).

21.6.3 Inheritance tax

An exchange of property will not normally give rise to a charge to IHT unless the value of the land being acquired is less than that being disposed of and the transaction is not part of a commercial deal.

21.6.4 TA 1988, s 776

An exchange of property can also give rise to a charge under TA 1988, s 776.

21.6.5 Value added tax

VATA 1983, s 10(2) states that if the supply of any goods or services is for a consideration in money its value shall be taken to be such amount. If the supply is not in money the value of the supply shall be taken to be its open market value.

Thus, on a land exchange when land is transferred in exchange for other land, the value of the land transferred has to be taken at its market value in order to ascertain the value of the supply.

21.6.6 Stamp duty

Ad valorem stamp duty is not payable when there is an exchange (assuming no money consideration passes) of freehold land for freehold land (SA 1891, s 73) or freehold land for, say, leasehold land (SA 1891, Sched 1 (Conveyance or Transfer of any kind not hereinbefore described) and *Littlewoods Mail Order Stores Ltd* v *IRC* [1963], AC 135). This is assuming that there is a genuine exchange of interests.

Two sales
There must not effectively be two sales. In *Lord Portland* v *IRC* (1956),

35 ATC 349, the parties agreed to sell their separate parcels of land to each other under contract and subsequently incorporated this in a Deed of Exchange; it was held by Danckwerts J that there were really two sales so that two amounts of *ad valorem* duty were payable.

22 CAPITAL LOSS COMPANIES

22.1 INTRODUCTION

It may happen that a company in a group of companies has capital losses (S Ltd). Land or other assets may be transferred to S Ltd by other members of the group for onward sale by S Ltd to non-connected purchasers. The assets will usually be sold down by the relevant company in the group P Ltd at the same price as it is intended the assets will be sold out to the outside parties by S Ltd.

This chapter looks at the taxation consequences of the proposals in general terms. Particular rules may apply to particular cases. For instance, if there is a part disposal through S Ltd through the charging of a premium on the grant of a lease, TA 1988 s 34 must be taken into account, as part of that premium may be taxed as income. Also, if shares are disposed of the relevant circumstances in TA 1988 s 704 may have to be considered.

22.1.1 Basic position of tax losses

Capital losses cannot be surrendered inter-group (TA 1988, ss 402 and 403).

When a company leaves a group the tax losses will not, by virtue of leaving the group, be disallowed; this is because TA 1988, s 768 does not apply to capital losses.

A disposal of assets inter-group will result in the acquiring company taking over the original base cost of the company which disposed of the assets (TA 1970, s 273).

S Ltd must be grouped with whichever company makes the inter-group transfer. It is assumed that the company making the transfer to S Ltd will be making a transfer of a capital asset.

When the gain accrues in S Ltd the earlier capital losses which have accrued in S Ltd will be deductible from the gains under the provisions of TA 1988, s 345(1)(*a*).

22.2 TRADING

It is not felt that any difficulty should arise under Case 1 of Schedule D on the proposed transactions. This is because S Ltd will not be making a profit on the transaction (it will buy and sell the property at the same price) and is not intending to make a profit on the transaction, although it will be holding the asset for a very short period of time and may be doing a number of such transactions.

TA 1970, s 274 provides that where a member of a group acquires an asset as trading stock from another member of the group and the asset did not form part of the trading stock of any trade carried on by the other member of the group, the company acquiring it shall be treated for the purposes of corporation tax on chargeable gain as having acquired the asset otherwise than as trading stock and having then immediately appropriated it for the purposes of the trade as trading stock. In this event the asset will be deemed to have been disposed of by the company—S Ltd—so crystallising a capital gain. When the property is sold on there will be no further gain on the difference between the market value at the date of appropriation and the sale to the outside purchaser. If there is such a gain it is likely to be very small if there is a short period between the acquisition and disposal.

It may happen that a parcel of land is to be sold through two capital loss companies ie, P Ltd sells the land to S Ltd and T Ltd—its two subsidiaries—who then sell it to the outside purchaser. In this event if the Revenue were to argue that the recipient companies had received the land as trading stock there could be gains of a trading nature made in the two recipient companies because of the provisions of TA 1970, s 274 applying (transfers within a group: trading stock). The market value of the separate parcels of land, valued separately, may be worth less than the disposal proceeds. However, one may argue that the separate parcels which should be acquired as tenants-in-common, must be valued with a view to the sale in mind and that one of the owners could have compelled the other owner to sell if he refused to sell by application to the Court. It may be prudent, however, to have a provision in the documentation stating that if one of the owners wishes to sell the other owner shall be obliged to sell.

22.3 CAPITAL ALLOWANCES

There could be a balancing charge on the disposal of an industrial building or an Enterprise Zone building (see CAA 1968, Sched 7).

There could be a balancing charge on the disposal of plant and machinery (FA 1971, s 44(6)).

22.4 CAPITAL GAINS TAX

The time of disposal and acquisition of an asset for CGT purposes is deemed to be the time when the contract is made and not, if different, the time at which the asset is conveyed or transferred. If the contract is conditional the time at which the disposal and acquisition is made is the time when the condition is satisfied (CGTA 1979, s 27).

Thus, when the unconditional contracts are entered into to dispose of the asset to S Ltd, S Ltd is deemed to acquire the asset at that time. If S Ltd then contracts to dispose of the asset to an outside party, S Ltd is deemed to have disposed of the same at that time so causing a charge to CGT to arise.

The fact that, on the directions of S Ltd, another group company P Ltd vests the legal title to the land in the outside party does not affect the position with regard to CGT. Thus, an unconditional contract inter-group with a further contract disposing of the property to the outside party and with a direct completion between the outside purchaser and the transferor member of the group(P Ltd) of the legal estate is the usual way of dealing with the matter from the point of view of crystallising the capital gain in the appropriate company. Because of the deeming provisions it is not important at what price the property is transferred inter-group. It could be, and should be, the same price as that being received from the outside purchaser.

22.5 TA 1988, s 776

In order for there to be a liability to tax under s 776, three conditions must be satisfied:

(*a*) the transactions must fall within one of the three situations set out in s 776(2);

(*b*) there must be a disposal of land; and

(*c*) a gain of a capital nature must be realised.

The three situations set out in s 776(2) are:

(*a*) where land, or any property deriving its value from land, is acquired with the sole or main object of realising a gain from disposing of land; or

(*b*) where land is held as trading stock; or

(*c*) where land is developed with the sole or main object of realising a gain from disposing of the land when developed.

In order not to cause this provision to apply by virtue of the inter-group transfer it is generally felt that the best course is to ensure that no book profit will arise in S Ltd as a result of the purchase and sale by S Ltd, otherwise the Revenue may argue that the land has been acquired by S Ltd with the sole or main object of realising a gain from a disposal of the land.

It is understood that the Revenue does not normally take the point whether the land is sold at a profit or not. However, it is felt that there should be no profit on the deal in case the Revenue does take the point and also it reduces the risk that the transaction was a trading transaction.

22.6 VALUE ADDED TAX

If S Ltd is a member of the VAT group within VATA 1983, s 29, the transfer of the property inter-group is disregarded (VATA 1983, s 29).

On the sale by S Ltd to the outside party the disposal of the land will be an exempt transfer under VATA 1983,Sched 6, Group 1, unless the disposal is by the person who constructed the building and is of a major interest in the building or its site within VATA 1983, Sched 5, Group 8 (in which case the supply will be zero rated), or VAT at the positive rate of 15% is in point under any changes to be made in FA 1989.

With regard to the fixtures and fittings attached to the land these will have the same VAT rates as the land itself.

The VAT group provisions in VATA 1983, s 29, must always be carefully considered; their effect is very narrow but nevertheless the inter-group transfer should not have the effect of creating unwanted exempt supplies.

Sales of shares are exempt (VATA 1983, Sched 6, Group 5).

22.7 STAMP DUTY

As the transfer inter-group will be on sale the relevant heading with regard to the charge to stamp duty is the conveyance on sale duty heading contained in Stamp Act 1891.

'Conveyance on sale' includes every instrument and every decree or order of any Court or of any Commissioners whereby any property, or any estate or interest in any property, upon the sale thereof is transferred to or vested in a purchaser or any other person on his behalf or by his direction.

FA 1930, s 42 provides relief from conveyance on sale duty where the beneficial interest in property is transferred from one body corporate to another and the bodies in question are associated, that is to say, one is the beneficial owner of not less than 90% of the issued share capital of the other, or a third such body is the beneficial owner of not less than 90% of the issued share capital of each.

However, that exemption is subject to the provisions of FA 1967, s 27 and because it is intended that the property will be sold to an outside party very shortly after S Ltd acquires it, it is not felt that the inter-group transfer relief will be applicable.

Stamp Act 1891, s 59 provides that any contract or agreement for the sale of any equitable estate or interest in any property whatsoever shall be charged with *ad valorem* duty as if it were an actual conveyance on sale of the estate or interest. Thus, an instrument by which A transfers an equitable interest to a purchaser is liable to duty as a conveyance on sale (*Chesterfield Brewery Co* v *IRC* [1899] 2 QB 7).

If, however, A agrees to sell a legal estate in land to B, the agreement itself operates to transfer an equitable interest to B and A holds as trustee for B; but this is not a conveyance on sale, it is an agreement and not a conveyance (*IRC* v *Angus & Co* (1889) 23 QBD 579 (CA), *per* Lord Esher MR at p 591).

The parties could thus allow the matter to 'rest on contracts'. However, the parties should ensure that there is a fixed completion date otherwise the Revenue could argue that there was never any intention to transfer a legal estate and that all that occurred was the transfer of an equitable interest and no further acts were intended. One has to read with that provision the provisions of Stamp Act 1891, s 58(4):

> Where a person having contracted for the purchase of any property, but not having obtained a conveyance thereof, contracts to sell the same to any other person and the property is in consequence conveyed immediately to the sub purchaser . . . the conveyance is to be charged with *ad valorem* duty in respect of the consideration moving from the sub-purchaser.

The anti-avoidance provisions in FA 1984, s 112 must be noted but they will not usually be in point.

Thus, it is felt that if there is an inter-group contract and a further contract with the outside purchaser the inter-group contract will normally fall outside Stamp Act 1891, s 59(1) and there will only be a charge to *ad valorem* duty on the vesting of the legal title in the outside party under Stamp Act 1891, s 58(4). The outside purchasers will be liable to pay stamp duty and no stamp duty charges will fall on S Ltd or P Ltd or, indeed, any other member of that group.

It is not felt that the 'all one transaction' rule enunciated in *Cohen and Moore* v *IRC* [1933] 2 KB 126 would be extended by the Court to cover a situation such as this and nor will the Ingrams decision be relevant (see page 279).

22.8 MECHANICS

22.8.1 Nomineeship

S Ltd must not be found to be a bare trustee or nominee with regard to any property which it acquires from other members of the group otherwise the intervention of S Ltd will have no tax consequences (TA 1970, s 238(2)).

The point may be raised, therefore, that S Ltd should make some small profit on the transaction which can be recorded in its accounts in order to show that it acquired and disposed of the beneficial interest in those assets. However, it is felt that as a matter of law the beneficial interest will be passing so that it is not essential to have a profit. The profit also raises the question of the applicability of s 776 and also the question of trading.

It is also important that there is no clear contract in existence to dispose of the asset acquired by S Ltd as soon as it is acquired. Otherwise, the asset may be deemed to have been disposed of direct to the outside purchaser without having gone through S Ltd.

22.8.2 Form and substance

The purchase of a capital loss company in order to save CGT by making an intra-group transfer may be caught by the *Ramsay* doctrine (see 1.4.5). However, the using up of capital losses which arose to one member of a group of companies whilst it was a member of the group, by an intra-group transfer by another member of the group may not be caught by the doctrine. The Revenue indicated in a meeting with the accountancy bodies on 6 January 1982 in CCAB, 26 March 1982, ref TR 456, that it may well apply the doctrine to groups which have purchased a company with capital losses but may not apply it to the situation where the capital losses has been incurred whilst the relevant company with the losses was a member of the group. This approach probably reflects a correct analysis of the *Ramsay* doctrine.

The following additional statements have also been made:

> *Hansard*
> . . . nor is there any question of the Inland Revenue challenging [under *Ramsay* and *Furniss* v *Dawson*], for example, the tax treatment of straightforward transfers of assets between members of the same group of companies. (Chief Secretary to the Treasury, 10 April 1984, H.C. Deb. Cols. 254—5.)
>
> *CAEW*
> *Capital losses*
> **4** This is perhaps the most important area; it was referred to in the Ministerial statement which mentioned 'straightforward transfers of, assets between members of the same group' and there is also earlier guidance following the *Ramsay* case [*W T Ramsay Ltd* v *IRC* [1981] STC 174, HL] where it was stated at our meeting on 6 January 1982 that the decision would not generally be applied to 'the routing of assets through a company within the same Group which has allowable capital losses and had not been acquired after these had arisen'. You indicated at the meeting that this statement is still regarded as valid following *Furniss* v *Dawson.*
> **5** Although this guidance is of considerable help in a clear cut case problems can still arise. We touched upon some at our meeting. For example, a significant group might be acquired for demonstrably commercial reasons but one of the companies in that group has capital losses. We remain unclear

whether the routing of assets from a member of the acquiring group to use that loss would be attacked.

6 We indicated in our discussions that we would have preferred the *Furniss* v *Dawson* doctrine to be identified as applicable under this heading only where a company with a capital loss was acquired with that loss being its sole or main asset and with a motive of acquisition to utilise the loss in question. We believe that confirmation of this approach would do much to clarify the area of what constitutes 'straightforward transfers of assets between members of the same group'.

Revenue response: I agree that this is an important area where, in our view, the *Ramsay* principles are likely to have considerable application. Let me say at once that the Board stands by the assurance given on 6 January 1982, about straightforward transfers of assets between members of the same group. By contrast, as you are no doubt aware, inspectors have advanced *Ramsay* contentions in a number of cases where the effect of a series of transactions has been to transfer the benefit of capital losses from one group to another. Whether the 'new approach' is thought to be applicable will depend on the facts of particular cases bearing in mind, for example, the relationship between the amounts of the loss involved, the period for which the company with the loss has been within the group and on the circumstances in which the losses have arisen. On this approach it would seem unlikely that the judgment would be invoked where the losses were a relatively insubstantial element in the acquisition, as evidenced by the circumstances in which they were utilised and the commerciality of the circumstances surrounding the acquisition (1 CAEW TR 588: *Furniss* v *Dawson,* 25 September 1985, (1985) STI 568).

22.9 TAX PLANNING

(*a*) There should be an unconditional contract to dispose of the particular asset inter-group to S Ltd.

(*b*) There must be a fixed completion date.

(*c*) There should be no existing obligation to sell the asset to the outside purchaser at the time when the asset is contracted to be purchased by S Ltd.

(*d*) Completion should take place direct between the outside purchaser and the member of the group which holds the legal title to the property.

(*e*) The acquisition and sale price of the property paid and received by S Ltd should be identical.

(*f*) The companies' shareholdings should always be checked to ensure that they are grouped for relevant tax purposes.

23 DEDUCTING TAX AT SOURCE

23.1 INTRODUCTION

There are a number of occasions where transactions involving property require a purchaser or payer to deduct tax at source. It is important that these situations are clearly identified because the purchaser or payer may well be liable to the Inland Revenue for the tax he omits to deduct. Some of these provisions have been dealt with elsewhere in the book but this chapter brings the tax deduction provisions together so as to act as a check list.

23.2 DEDUCTIONS AT SOURCE—LAND

23.2.1 Rent

Rent paid directly to a person whose usual place of abode is outside the UK must be paid under deduction of tax at the basic rate (TA 1988, s 43).

Example 23A: Payment of rent

X is a tenant of property in the UK and he pays rent directly to the landlord whose usual place of abode is in Guernsey. X must deduct tax at 25% from the rent he pays the landlord (see 2.4).

23.2.2 Lease premiums

Where a premium on a lease is to be charged by a person whose usual place of abode is outside the UK and part of the premium is chargeable to income tax under the lease premium provisions contained in the TA 1988, s 34 *et seq,* tax may have to be deducted at source with respect to part of the premium (TA 1988, s 43 and Inland Revenue Booklet 1978 *Notes on the Taxation of Income from Real Property,* para 58).

Example 23B: Payment of premium

X Ltd, a Jersey company, grants a lease of, say, 30 years to Y Ltd at a premium. Y Ltd may be required to deduct tax at 25% from part of the premium (see 3.6).

23.2.3 Artificial land transactions (TA 1988, s 776)

If the Board of Inland Revenue feel that any person disposing of land may be chargeable to tax under TA 1988, s 776 and that person is not resident in the UK, it can issue a notice to the purchaser requiring him to deduct tax at the basic rate (TA 1988, s 777(9)).

There is no obligation to deduct unless there is such a notice from the Inland Revenue and the author in practice has only come across one case where such a notice has been issued.

It may be that an overseas vendor of land would wish to exchange and complete a sale at one and the same time in case a notice is issued to the purchaser after exchange of contracts but before completion (see 11.3.5).

23.2.4 Mines etc

Rental sums for the following have to be paid net after deduction of tax:

(*a*) Mines and quarries (including gravel pits, sand pits and brickfields)

(*b*) Ironworks, gasworks, saltworks, springworks, aluminium mines, waterworks and streams of water

(*c*) Canals etc

(*d*) Fisheries

(*e*) Market, fairs, tolls, bridges and ferries

(*f*) Railways (and other ways)

(*g*) Concerns of a like nature to those in (*b*) and (*e*) above

(TA 1988, ss 55 and 119).

23.2.5 Sub-contractor provisions

A contractor paying a sub-contractor for carrying out building operations etc must deduct tax at 25% from the payment (except for such part of the payment as is shown to represent the direct cost to the sub-contractor of materials) unless the sub-contractor has a current certificate entitling him to exemption. A contractor is, broadly, a person carrying on a business in the construction industry and any other person spending on average more than £250,000 per annum on construction operations (see Chapter 14).

24 CHOOSING THE LENGTH OF A LEASE

Taxation factors can be critical when deciding what length of lease a landlord should grant. In certain cases the consequences can be disastrous if the lease is even a day less than that prescribed by the relevant legislation.

24.1 THE FOUR BASIC CONSIDERATIONS

When discussing with a client the length of the term of a lease to be granted and the taxation factors to be taken into account one must:

(*a*) choose the correct term for the legal lease bearing in mind that a legal lease can only take effect from the date of the instrument.

(*b*) consider how the entering into of an agreement for lease prior to the legal lease will affect the situation;

(*c*) consider the provisions in the taxation legislation which can deem leases to be of different terms than those set out in the documents. This will often require a careful examination of the documents and the deletion of any 'offensive' provisions;

(*d*) ensure that one tax is not looked at in isolation from other taxes. The author has come across schemes which effectively mitigate stamp duty liability but result in the client not obtaining the more valuable machinery and plant allowances.

24.2 CAPITAL GAINS TAX—OVER 50 YEARS

A lease of land is not a wasting asset for CGT purposes until the time when its duration does not exceed 50 years (CGTA 1979,Sched 3, para 1(1)).

If a lease is a wasting asset then part of the acquisition cost for it year by year is gradually reduced in accordance with the table set out in Sched 3, para 1, of the CGTA 1979.

A lease for those purposes includes an agreement for lease, so that in calculating the period which is to exceed 50 years one starts, in the author's view, from the date of the unconditional agreement for lease (CGTA 1979, Sched 3, para 10(1)(*a*)).

There are special provisions in Sched 3, para 8 to deem a lease to be shorter or longer than that specified in the document.

24.3 VALUE ADDED TAX—OVER 21 YEARS

The granting by a person constructing a building of a major interest in the building or its site is a zero-rated supply.

A 'major interest' means the fee simple or a tenancy for a term certain *exceeding* 21 years.

It is unclear whether the grant takes place on the entering into of the agreement for lease or when the actual lease is granted. The Customs & Excise appear to take the view that 'granting' only takes place when the lease is formally entered into (but see 12.22.1).

24.4 LEASE PREMIUM PROVISIONS—OVER 50 YEARS

Under TA 1988, s 34, if the lease is granted at a premium and the duration of the lease does not exceed 50 years, part of the premium may be treated as income rather than as capital which it will normally be treated as in the hands of an investor. A lease for these provisions includes an agreement for lease. However, they only apply if there is a 'grant'. It may be argued that they do not apply unless a formal lease is granted (see *City Permanent Building Society* v *Miller* [1952] Ch 840).

There are special provisions contained in TA 1988, s 38 which may deem the length of the lease, for the purposes of the provision, to be different from that contained in the documents.

24.5 IHT OVER 3 YEARS AND LIFE

The length of the lease will not normally have much significance for IHT purposes.

Under the 'associated operations' provisions in IHTA 1984, s 268 the granting of a lease for full consideration in money or money's worth shall not be taken to be associated with any operation effected more than 3 years after the grant.

A lease of property for life can amount to a 'settlement' for CTT purposes unless the lease was granted for full consideration in money or money's worth (IHTA 1984 s 43 (3)).

24.6 SALE AND LEASEBACK PROVISIONS—OVER 50 OR OVER 15 YEARS

Under the sale and leaseback provisions contained in TA 1988, s 780, consideration received, *inter alia,* on a disposal of a lease having not more than 50 years to run can be treated, as to part, as if it were income, subject to income tax rather than CGT, where there is a leaseback for a term not exceeding 15 years.

24.7 INDUSTRIAL BUILDING ALLOWANCES AND ENTERPRISE ZONE ALLOWANCES—OVER 50 AND 25 YEARS

Where a landlord constructs a building and then grants a lease the duration of which exceeds 50 years and the tenant pays a premium the relevant interest for industrial building allowances purposes and Enterprise Zone allowance purposes may effectively be surrendered to the tenant so that he (the tenant) can obtain the allowances (FA 1978, s 37(1)). There are special provisions to deem the lease to be of a different length than that provided in the document in certain cases (FA 1978, s 37(4)).

The writing down allowance available for industrial buildings and structures will be written off over 25 years. Enterprise Zone allowances are 100% (initial allowances) and 25% (writing down allowances). Thus the allowances can be used up very quickly although if the used building is sold by the initial investor the purchaser (from the initial investor) will obtain allowances written off evenly over what is left of a 25 year period beginning with the date when the building was first used (CAA 1968 s 2(3)).

24.8 STAMP DUTY—7, 35 OR 100 YEARS

The lease or tack duty which is payable by reference to the rent chargeable on a lease or agreement for a lease, varies in its rates according to the length of the term. The maximum charges are as follows:

If the term does not exceed 7 years or is indefinite	1%
If the term exceeds 7 years but does not exceed 35 years	2%
If the term exceeds 35 years but does not exceed 100 years	12%
If a term exceeds 100 years	24%

25 CHOOSING A DEVELOPMENT STRUCTURE

25.1 INTRODUCTION

There are many entities available to taxpayers through which to carry out property developments.

Parties to developments may hold different interests in the same land – for example, freeholds and leaseholds. These are vertical interests. On the other hand, they may hold horizontal land interests such as beneficial tenancies in common.

A development may be carried out through a joint venture. A joint venture is not a term of art. Many joint ventures simply mean the land is owned by the joint venturers as tenants in common. Some joint ventures may amount to partnerships.

A partnership can either comprise a normal partnership, with each partner being liable for the usual debts of the partnership, or a limited partnership may be created under the Limited Partnership Act, 1907.

The parties may decide to carry out the property development through a company with each party owning shares in the company.

The company may be a public limited company or a private company.

If the company is to carry out a single development the parties may want to ensure that the trading profits made by the company are distributed to the owners of the company either by way of dividend or the repayment of debenture capital plus interest or perhaps by the repayment of a deep discount stock which may have been issued by the company.

The parties may also decide to carry out the venture through a trust. This could be an unauthorised unit trust. In this case the Collective Investment Scheme legislation provided for in the Financial Services Act 1986 must be taken into account.

One may also have a combination of the above entities, such as two companies which enter into a partnership with the majority of the profits being repaid to the debenture holders in the companies.

Finally, one may also have 'shadow' structures where the entity may be in one form but the fruits derived therefrom are based on what the position would have been if the entity had been in another form—'the Pincs membrane' (see 25.2.13).

25.2 STRUCTURES

25.2.1 Structure 1: classical structure (fund purchases land, carries out development and then lets property to tenant)

Under this structure the fund (eg a pension fund, insurance company) will purchase the property, often under subsale from the developer or the original landowner, then employ the developer to:

(*a*) carry out the works, and

(*b*) find the tenants for the completed development.

This is a well-established structure and no special income tax, corporation tax or capital gains tax problems should arise. The parties will not normally be in partnership but see Chapter 21.

If a new building is being put up the payments to the developer by the fund should presently be zero-rated for VAT purposes (see p 221). The fund should ensure in appropriate cases that the developer produces a sub-contract certificate (see p 313). The builder should also hope to produce such a certificate and in certain exceptional cases, so also must the project manager (see page 318). With respect to his agreement for lease, the tenant will have to pay rent duty (1–24%) (Stamp Act 1891 (Sched 1)) unless the rent is unascertainable at the time of the agreement for lease and the lease (see 13.30.2).

25.2.2 Structure 2: core and shell (fund purchases land, carries out the development up to core and shell stage and then lets the property to the investor (or non-trader) tenant who puts in the plant)

These are common arrangements. They are designed to ensure that the capital allowances are not lost.

The landlord will build the main structure of the building (the core and shell) and the tenant (often a bank) will do the fitting-out works, and bear

Structure 1: classical structure

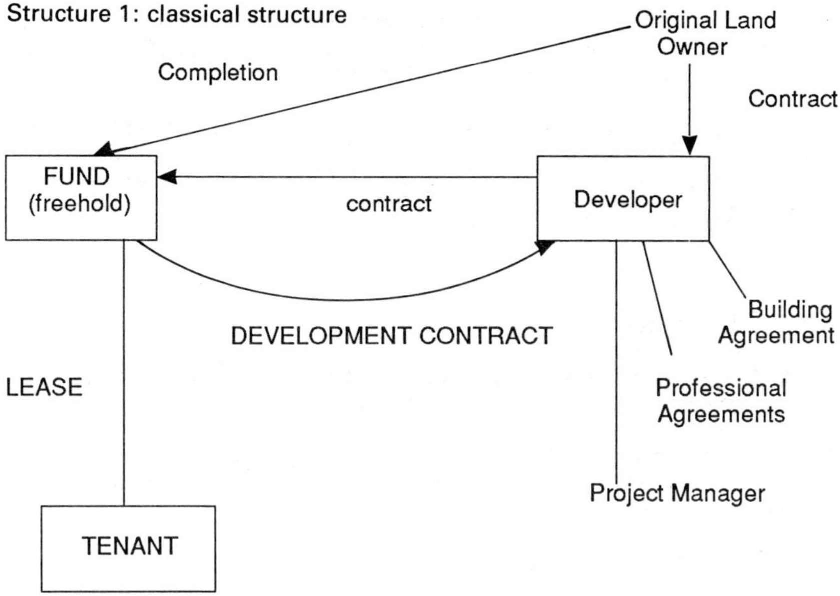

the costs of the same. Often the works will qualify for capital allowances (see p 125). The following points should be noted:

(*a*) Any contributions by the landlord towards the tenant's fitting-out expenditure would be vatable although if the landlord grants a major interest and constructed the building the VAT should be reclaimable (see 12.6).

(*b*) If the landlord cannot claim any capital allowances then the author is of the view that the contributions should be ignored when calculating the tenant's entitlement to capital allowances (see 8.17.7).

(*c*) If the tenant is not under an obligation to do the works TA 1988 s 34 (2) should not be a problem (see p 33). Even if the tenant is under an obligation to do the works it may be that in many cases no problem will arise under that provision (see p 33).

(*d*) The tenant will normally be receiving something akin to a capital sum which would not be chargeable to income tax; it would be useful in that respect if the contribution could be earmarked for capital purposes in the documentation. Case VI would be the Case the Revenue would seek to apply if they sought to tax these contributions on the tenant.

(*e*) It is not felt that any capital gains tax liability should arise with respect to the receipt.

25.2.3 Structure 3: the dangling cherry—the investor supplies a land interest to the developer who sub-lets the same and receives occupational rents—the developer keeps the intermediate interest as an investment.

The position may arise under which the landlord which has the freehold grants a lease to the developer who then carries out the various development obligations with the developer then granting a sublease to the occupational tenants. The landlord may fund the development.

This is the dangling cherry structure.

Normally there should be no tax problems with respect to this arrangement: the developer will assign or sell his interest which he holds as trading stock (see Structure 4 below). Problems can arise, however, if the developer decides to 'stay-in'. This is because the Revenue may argue that the market value of the completed building is a trading receipt of the tenant, therefore giving rise to a tax charge under Schedule D, Case 1 (see 4.4.5).

25.2.4 Structure 4: land dealing development—the landlord lets the property to a tenant—developer who wants to deal in the interest by selling the same

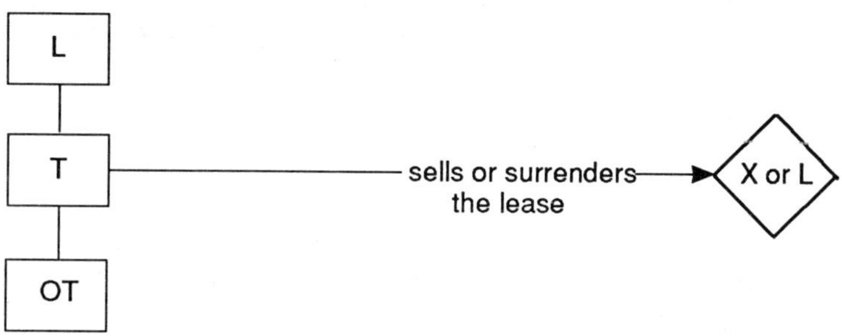

L (the freeholder) may employ T (a developer) to develop his land. L may pay T by agreeing to grant and then granting an intermediate land interest (a lease) to T when the development is completed. T may also be obliged to find an occupational tenant (OT). When this has been achieved T may surrender his lease for cash or may sell the lease. The sale proceedings arising from the surrender or sale will normally come in as trading receipts in the books of T although when completion takes place and the formal lease granted the receipt (the land interest) could be bought in then, (see also Structure 3 above).

If, instead of taking the formal lease, T directs L to grant it direct to a third party the stamp duty position should be noted (see 13.36.9).

25.2.5 Structure 5: complex assemblies—a number of landowners agree to pool their land and carry out a development

It may be that there are a number of landowners who own adjoining land and who need to effectively hand over rights over their own land to each other in order to acquire rights over the land of their neighbours. The parties could then employ a developer to develop the property with a view to letting the property and staying in as investors or alternatively disposing of the completed development as part of a property dealing transaction.

If the parties wish to stay in and hold the property as an investment then they will be concerned with the charges to capital gains tax or corporation tax on chargeable gains which may arise when land interests are swapped at inception (see 9.4.13).

If the parties wish to trade in the land then they may not be so concerned about that point although they will be concerned that their capital may have been appropriated early to trading stock.

The parties may also be concerned about the application of TA 1988, s 776.

Even if the parties decide to hold onto the property as an investment they may run into difficulties under the Collective Investment Scheme Legislation (see 25.2.10).

Also if the parties are tempted to put the property into the name of a nominee they may suffer on immediate stamp duty charge under FA 1965, s 90.

25.2.6 Structure 6: enterprise zone structures

Deals which are structured to enable investors to obtain the 100% enterprise zone allowance tend to fall into one of three patterns each of which require four conditions to be satisfied (or to be deemed to be satisfied) (see 8.12).

25.2.7 Structure 7: normal partnership

Taxpayers may enter into normal partnerships (ie, not limited partnerships) to carry out property developments.

A partnership may be an attractive vehicle through which a development can be carried out. There may be problems if the two partners own separate land interests and they put these land interests into the partnership common stock (see Chapter 21).

The VAT position must also be considered (see Chapter 12).

The partners will be liable for each other's debts etc, but not for each other's charges to corporation tax. Many joint ventures amount to partnerships but not all joint ventures are partnerships.

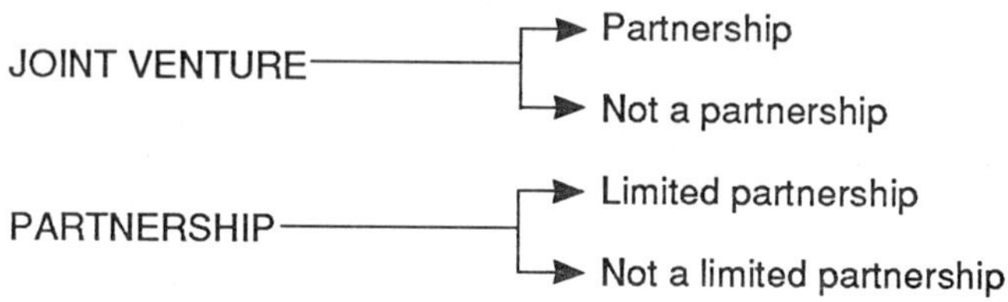

25.2.8 Structure 8: limited partnerships

The parties may decide to make use of the Limited Partnership Act 1907.

Instead of setting up a normal partnership the parties may decide to set up a limited partnership. This would supply protection to the limited partner but he must have virtually no involvement in the project.

A limited partner is, however, a partner and carries on the business with the other partners. Thus if a pension fund enters into a limited partnership with a managing partner to carry out a property deal the Revenue take the view that the profit made by the pension fund limited partner is not free of income tax. See also page 408.

25.2.9 Structure 9: public limited company

The parties may decide to carry out the deal through a public limited company.

The shares can be freely dealt with on the stock exchange. The company would pay corporation tax on its profits. When dividends are paid, advance corporation tax must be paid. Exempt shareholders such as pension funds and charities can claim back the advance corporation tax. The advance corporation tax is not a deduction from profits.

The company may seek to borrow money and obtain full tax relief against its profits for the interest which is paid on any borrowing.

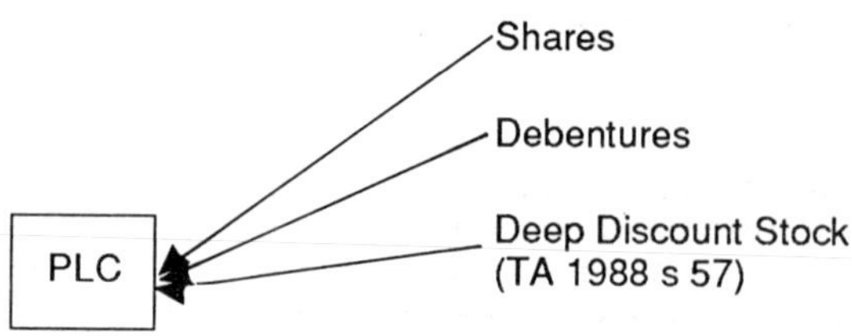

The company may also issue deep discount stock which may enable it to obtain tax deductions year by year even though nothing may be paid to the lender. The lender is also normally taxed only when the loan is repaid. Non-UK resident lenders may find deep discount stock particularly attractive as they can be paid without tax being deducted at source and the Revenue will not pursue them for the tax.

SAPCOS
The single asset property company (SAPCO) concept involves a company (a plc) buying a single property and holding it as an investment.

Investors would purchase shares in the company. In that case the company would be liable for corporation tax at up to 35% of its profits but the investors would get a tax credit of 25% when a dividend is paid. Alternatively, investors could put their monies into the company by way of deep discount stock in which case the company would be deemed to have paid interest at the appropriate amount year by year with the recipient (the lender) being charged to tax in the usual case when the deep discount stock is redeemed. Alternatively, the lender could invest their monies by way of debenture with the debenture interest being deductible either as a charge on income or as a trading expense. In certain cases the interest may be deemed to be a dividend (see 25.2.15).

The Stock Exchange requirements (see section 10 of the Stock Exchange Yellow Book) and the Financial Services Act 1986 requirements must be taken into account if a SAPCO is contemplated.

25.2.10 Structure 10: collective investment schemes

Taxpayers should carefully look at their property structures to ascertain whether or not they have created a collective investment scheme.

CGT
Under the CGTA 1979 a unit trust scheme is deemed to be a company, the rights of the unit holders are deemed to be shares in the company and in the case of an authorised unit trust the company is treated as resident and ordinarily resident in the UK.

The definition of a unit trust scheme is very wide and a new taxable entity may be created between other entities without the parties realising it. Under CGTA 1979, s 92 a unit trust scheme has the same meaning as in the Financial Services Act 1986 although the Treasury may make regulations to provide that any scheme of the description specified in the regulations shall be treated as not being a unit trust scheme for the purposes of the Act.

Income Tax
Income arising to the trust is deemed to be the income of the trustees only and only the trustees can obtain capital allowances (TA 1988, s 469). The income can in certain cases be taxed twice on the unit holders when there are deemed distributions and actual distributions.

Section 75 of the FSA 1986 reads as follows:

> (1) In this Act 'a collective investment scheme' means, subject to the provisions of this section, any *arrangements* with respect to property of any description, including money, the purpose or effect of which is to enable persons taking part in the arrangements (whether by becoming owners of the property or any part of it or otherwise) to participate in or receive profits or income arising from the acquisition, holding, management or disposal of the property or sums paid out of such profits or income.
>
> (2) The arrangements must be such that the persons who are to participate as mentioned in subsection (1) above (in this Act referred to as 'participants') *do not have day to day control over the management of the property in question,* whether or not they have the right to be consulted or to give directions; and the arrangements must also have either or both of the characteristics mentioned in subsection (3) below.
>
> (3) Those characteristics are:
> (*a*) that the contributions of the participants and the profits or income out of which payments are to be made to them are pooled;
> (*b*) that the property in question is managed as a whole by or on behalf of the operator of the scheme.
>
> (4) Where any arrangements provide for such pooling as is mentioned in paragraph (*a*) of subsection (3) above in relation to separate parts of the property in question, the arrangements shall not be regarded as constituting a single collective investment scheme unless the participants are entitled to exchange rights in one part for rights in another.
>
> (5) Arrangements are not a collective investment scheme if:
> (*a*) the property to which the arrangements relate (other than cash awaiting investment) consists of investments falling within any of paragraphs 1 to 5, 6 (so far as relating to units in authorised unit trust schemes and recognised schemes) and 10 of Schedule 1 to this Act;
> (*b*) each participant is the owner of a part of that property and entitled to withdraw it at any time; and
> (*c*) the arrangements do not have the characteristics mentioned in paragraphs (*a*) of subsection (3) above and have those mentioned in paragraph (*b*) of that subsection only because the parts of the property belonging to different participants are not bought and sold separately except where a person becomes or ceases to be a participant.
>
> (6) The following are not collective investment schemes:
> (*a*) *arrangements operated by a person otherwise than by way of business;*
> (*b*) arrangements where each of the participants carries on a business other than investment business and enters into the arrangements for commercial purposes related to that business;
> (*c*) arrangements where each of the participants is a body corporate in the same group as the operator;
> (*d*) arrangements where:
> (i) each of the participants is a bona fide employee or former employee (or the wife, husband, widow, widower, child or step-child under the age of eighteen of such an employee or former employee) of a body corporate in the same group as the operator; and

(ii) the property to which the arrangements relate consists of shares or debentures (as defined in paragraph 20(4) of Schedule 1 to this Act) in or of a member of that group;

(*e*) arrangements where the receipt of the participants' contributions constitutes the acceptance of deposits in the course of a business which is a deposit-taking business for the purposes of the Banking Act 1979 and does not constitute a transaction prescribed for the purposes of section 2 of that Act by regulations made by the Treasury;

(*f*) franchise arrangements, that is to say, arrangements under which a person earns profits or income by exploiting a right conferred by the arrangements to use a trade name or design or other intellectual property or the good-will attached to it;

(*g*) arrangements the predominant purpose of which is to enable persons participating in them to share in the use or enjoyment of a particular property or to make its use or enjoyment available gratuitously to other persons;

(*h*) arrangements under which the rights or interests of the participants are investments falling within paragraph 5 of Schedule 1 to this Act;

(*i*) arrangements the purpose of which is the provision of clearing services and which are operated by an authorised person, a recognised clearing house or a recognised investment exchange;

(*j*) contracts of insurance;

(*k*) occupational pension schemes.

(7) No body incorporated under the law of, or of any part of, the United Kingdom relating to building societies or industrial and provident societies or registered under any such law relating to friendly societies, and no other body corporate other than an open-ended investment company, shall be regarded as constituting a collective investment scheme.

(8) In this Act

'a unit trust scheme' means a collective investment scheme under which the property in question is held on trust for the participants;

'an open-ended investment company' means a collective investment scheme under which:

(*a*) the property in question belongs beneficially to, and is managed by or on behalf of, a body corporate having as its purpose the investment of its funds with the aim of spreading investment risk and giving its members the benefit of the results of the management of those funds by or on behalf of that body; and

(*b*) the rights of the participants are represented by shares or securities of that body which: 'trustee', in relation to a unit trust scheme, means the person holding the property in question on trust for the participants and in relation to a collective investment scheme constituted under the law of a country or territory outside the United Kingdom, means any person who (whether or not under a trust) is entrusted with the custody of the property in question;

'units' means the rights or interests (however described) of the participants in a collective investment scheme;

'the operator' in relation to a unit trust scheme with a separate trustee, means the manager and, in relation to an open-ended investment company, means that company.

(9) If an order under section 2 above amends the references to a collective investment scheme in Schedule 1 of this Act it may also amend the provisions of this section.

Regulations have been passed to exclude certain types of unit trust schemes from the tax effects of this legislation and these must be referred to: they relate to Enterprise Zones, Limited Partnerships and Charities.

If a number of landowners buy a building and employ an agent to run the same, there may be a collective investment scheme. If they run the property themselves then there is unlikely to be a scheme (FSA 1986, s 75(6) (*a*)). It may also be the case that, even though an agent is employed to run the property, that a simple land owning structure does not amount to an 'arrangement' within FSA 1986, s 95(1).

The reason why limited Partnerships have to be taken out of the Act by regulation is that the let out in s 75(2) would not be available. That let out should be available to most normal development partnerships.

If the property is not held on trust the adverse tax consequences mentioned above (p 405) will not apply. Thus if X Ltd owns Blackacre and it agrees to pay the profits by way of dividend and loan interest to Y and Z there can be no unit trust scheme (as there is no trust) and the provisions are not relevant.

A taxpayer may be able to set up a unit trust scheme to invest in land and buildings. The scheme would issue units to investors to raise money. In order to be able to advertise the manager of the scheme must be authorised under FSA 1986 and so also must the trustee of the scheme which must have a substantial capital backing. In addition the scheme must be an authorised unit trust scheme. The authorisation must be under FSA 1986 s 78. Authorised unit trust schemes do not pay capital gains tax or corporation tax on chargeable gains when they dispose of assets (FA 1980 s 91). If such a scheme is not authorised then there will be a double charge to capital gains tax: the trust could be charged to tax at 35% and the investors when they dispose of their units could be charged to tax at a rate as high as 40%: total tax charge 61%. However, if the unauthorised unit trust scheme invests in, say, appropriate holiday accommodation roll-over relief may be available on the disposal of such accommodation if the proceeds are used to purchase similar accommodation (this will be under CGTA 1979 s 115).

The SPUT

One approach to the unitisation of a large building is to create a single property unit trust (a SPUT).

Such an arrangement is a trust with the unit holders having interests under the trust (this compares with the interests of PINCS investors who have contractual rights and SAPCO investors who have share rights in a company or normal debenture rights or deep discount stock rights).

There are fundamental tax disadvantages with respect to this structure; there is a double incidence of charge on capital gains when the scheme is an unauthorised unit trust. Such arrangements would comprise collective investment schemes.

25.2.11 Structure 11: private company

Parties may decide to carry out the deal through a private company.

There are restrictions with respect to the public sale of shares. Any dividends paid will require advance corporation tax to be accounted for. It may be that the company could issue debentures with the interest payments comprising charges on income or trading expenses.

Where the interest varies with the success or otherwise of the development special anti-avoidance provisions must be taken into account (see 25.2.15).

Consideration may also be given to the issue of a deep discount stock by the company.

Many of the companies will be 'close companies' for the purposes of corporation tax (TA 1988, s 414).

The special apportionment provisions in TA 1988, ss 423–430 should be taken into account especially by close property investment companies.

Property trading companies
The trading income of a property trading company cannot be shortfalled (TA 1988, Sched 19, para 1 and 2(2)).

Property investment companies
If a non-trading company (TA 1988, Sched 19, para 7) has estate or trading income up to 50% thereof can be shortfalled (TA 1988, Sched 19, para 2(1)).

The defence
With respect to property investment companies the shortfall can only relate to so much of the estate or trading income as can be distributed without prejudice to the requirements of the company's business 'so far as concerned with the activities or assets giving rise to estate or trading income'.

Thus, for instance, a property investment company which carries out one or two trading transactions, on the face of it, has a limited business requirements defence against an automatic shortfall assessment of the trading income.

The defence curtailed
The defence, however, is curtailed by TA 1988, Sched 19, para 8(1). It is provided that any sum applied or available to be applied out of income in either of the following ways by a company which is not a trading company (or a member of a trading group) is deemed to be available for distribution:

(*a*) in or towards the redemption, repayment or discharge of any loan capital or debt (including any premium thereon) in respect of which any person is a loan creditor and (*b*) in or towards the acquisition of an estate or interest in land or the construction or extension of a building not being a construction or extension which constitutes an improvement or development of farm land or market garden land.

Loans, farms and market gardens
The following two points should be noted:

(*a*) A person carrying on a banking business is not treated as a loan creditor in respect of a loan made by him in the ordinary course of that business; thus a sum expended in the repayment of such a loan would reduce the company's relevant income.

(*b*) It is to be noted that the expenditure incurred on the acquisition of farm land or market garden land is not exempt from the restriction.

Example 25A: Shortfall

X Ltd is a property investment company. It carries out a land trading deal and ploughs the profit back into more trading stock (land). The company could be subject to a relevant income proportionment with respect to the land trading profit even though it used the proceeds to buy another parcel of stock.

25.2.12 Structure 12: hybrid structures—amalgamated partnership and company structures

One could have an arrangement where X and Y, both being companies, enter into a partnership with a return from the particular development being

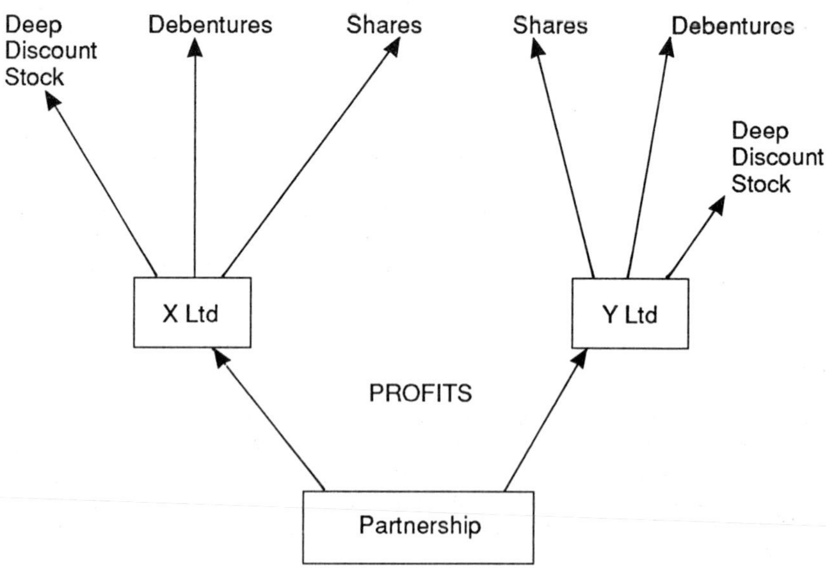

taken by the companies according to their agreed partnership shares and then distributed by the companies to shareholders of the companies as dividends or as debenture capital and interest or as repayment of deep discount stock (TA 1988, s 57). No special tax problems should arise with this fairly common structure.

25.2.13 Structure 13: PINCS—the issue of property income certificates (PINCS) is one method of unitising shares in a large single property.

In essence the problem with unitising shares in properties is that if one uses a company there is potentially a double charge to capital gains tax—35% in the company and 40% in the hands of the individual shareholders. If alternatively one uses a unit trust scheme the same double incidence of capital gains tax arises assuming of course that it is an unauthorised unit trust (CGTA 1979, ss 93 and 96).

Note that since 1987 if a company pays a dividend and the company has made a capital gain the advance corporation tax which the company must pay is available for offset against the corporation tax charge on the capital gain (FA 1972, s 85(1) as amended by F(No 2)A 1987, s 74 but now see TA 1988 s 239).

Nevertheless, there will be unrelieved corporation tax (the company pays corporation tax at 35%: the tax credit is 25%).

The PINCS approach involves the landowner ('the original landowner') granting a lease (headlease) to a paying agent at a premium. Let us say that the premium is 50% of the open market value of the property and let us say that the rent would represent the remaining 50% of the market value of the property. In order to fund the premium the paying agent would issue to the investors property certificates. The paying agent would grant an underlease to PINCS plc for 100% of the underlying rents and PINCS plc would grant a lease to the occupational tenants for the full rent.

The original landowner would own, let us say, 50% of PINCS plc. When the PINCS investors received their certificates they will also obtain shares in PINCS plc; the shares and PINCS are part and parcel of the same thing.

PINCS plc has an underlease and receives the occupational rents. It forthwith pays the rents to the agent. There is then a curious tax 'membrane'.

The Revenue apparently accept that the amounts paid to the PINCS investors by the agent under a contractual obligation is an annual payment under which tax must be deducted at source and which is effectively fully tax deductible against the 50% rents received on behalf of the PINCS investors. The remaining 50% of the rent is paid to the original landowner.

Somehow the rental income has left the corporate world without comprising a distribution.

The Revenue also apparently accept that on a disposal of the headlease by the agent there is no second level of charge to CGT or corporation tax on chargeable gains; the PINCS investors simply pay the capital gains tax on the disposal of their certificate rights.

The original owner has to be careful. If he has recently had the property constructed and then grants a lease at a premium that may comprise a trading transaction or if the original owner wishes to keep capital allowances and he has recently had the property constructed and grants a lease at a premium the Revenue may query whether the original expenditure was really capital expenditure for the purposes of allowances. One must also be careful that there are no special circumstances which would indicate that the lease would subsist for a period of less than fifty years otherwise this may raise problems under the lease premium provisions in TA 1988, s 34 or may even cause problems as to the CGT base cost (CGTA 1979, Sched 3, para 8(3)).

Figure 25.1 PINCS

Assume the property is worth £20m.

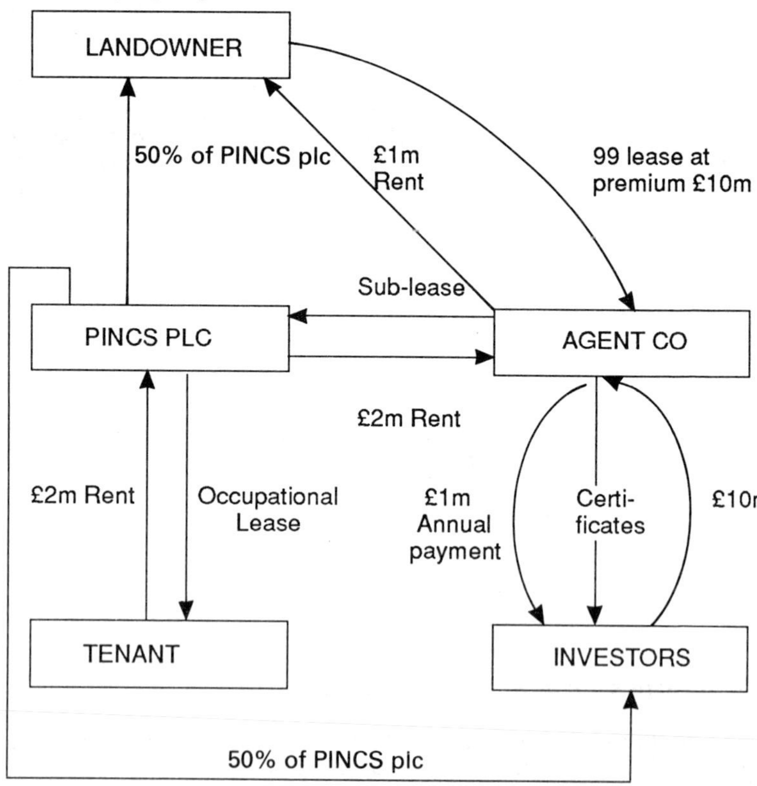

or may even cause problems as to the CGT base cost (CGTA 1979, Sched 3, para 8(3)).

Finally, the original landowner has to take a view as to the application of TA 1988, s 776.

25.2.14 Structure 14: off-balance sheet loan structures

It may be that the taxpayer wishes to create an off-balance sheet loan arrangement in order to avoid having to consolidate the accounts of a subsidiary company.

The accounts of a holding company and its subsidiary have to be consolidated under the Companies Act 1985. A company is deemed to be a subsidiary of another company if the provisions of CA 1985, s 736(1) are satisfied.

It will normally be possible to avoid consolidation but nevertheless enable the parent and subsidiary company to be grouped for the purposes of stamp duty, corporation tax on chargeable gains and group relief (income) by ensuring that the taxpayer plc (the parent company which wants to be grouped with the subsidiary for the above stamp duty and tax purposes) owns, out of a share capital of say 100 £1 shares, 96 preference shares and 2 'A' Ordinary shares with the remaining 2 'B' Ordinary shares (being of little value) being owned by some independent third party such as a bank (see TA 1988, s 832 ordinary share capital) ss 839, 402—413 and 410 and TA 1970, s 272—281 and *Irving* v *Tesco Stores (Holdings) Ltd* [1982]STC 881, FA 1930, s 42 (stamp duty) and CA 1985, s 744 and s 736: the share rights have to be carefully drafted taking into account these provisions).

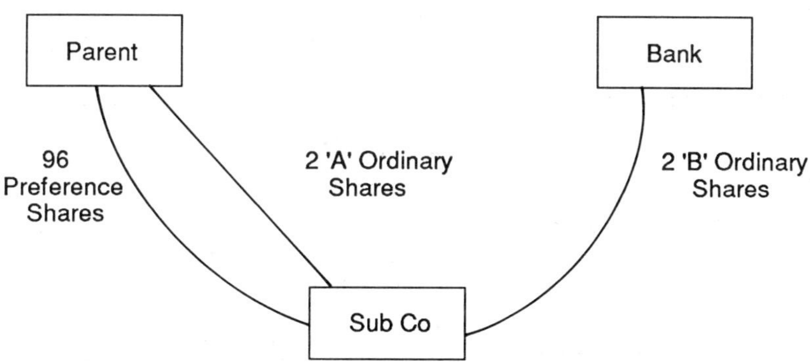

25.2.15 Structure 15: developers' dividend trap

Company property developers should beware that when monies are lent to them by individuals, overseas companies and pension funds, the interest may be deemed to be dividends which can have adverse tax consequences.

If an individual, a company not within charge to CT or trust lends money to a developer and the interest is to be at the rate of X% plus an amount equal to the net profits on the disposal of a particular development, the interest (all the interest) will be deemed to be a dividend under the provisions of TA 1988, s 209 (2) (*e*) (iii).

No tax relief
The development company, instead of obtaining tax relief for the interest in computing its profits, will in fact be deemed to be paying a dividend and this, depending on the circumstances, could give rise to adverse corporation tax problems.

The problem may be overcome by ensuring that the interest is not in any way dependent on the success of the project, in which case only if the interest exceeds a reasonable commercial return can the excess be treated as a dividend (TA 1988, s 209 (2) (*d*)).

Also, if the person lending the money is a UK company (a company within the change to corporation tax) the interest will not be deemed to be a dividend except to the extent it exceeds a reasonable commercial rate (TA 1988, s 212). However, if the lender is a UK company acting as a nominee for individuals and overseas companies and trusts, it is doubtful that the problem will be overcome.

These corporation tax problems are avoided if the 'lender' becomes a partner in the project and takes a share in the partnership rather than taking interest on the monies lent to the development company (see *Euro Hotel (Belgravia) Ltd* 51 TC 293).

Non-Recourse loans made
Modern project finance loans are sometimes made on a non-recourse basis by UK companies under which the borrower is only required to make payments of interest and repayment of principal, to the extent of the value of the project property which is disposed of. In such cases the interest would be dependent on the results of the company's business. However, even though the UK lender company may charge a very high rate of interest, the interest would not normally exceed a commercial return for the monies lent and thus should not give rise to dividends. The monies should retain their character of interest.

25.2.16 Structure 16: the Utol trap—profit shares

Companies must take note of the Utol trap. A company (Y) may own property and agree to carry out a development. If it (Y) agrees for instance with another company (X) that the net profits are to be shared 70—30 then following the *Utol* case the possibility is that the payment would comprise a distribution or dividend—a division of profits—even though the other company (X) may not own shares in the relevant company (Y).

In *Utol Ltd* v *IRC* 10 TC 517 at p 524 Macnaghten J states:

> dividend . . . is not confined to a share of profits paid to a shareholder, but includes a share of profits payable under contract.

See also *British Sugar Manufacturers Ltd* v *Harris* 21 TC 528, *Pondicherry Railway Co Ltd* v *IRC* (1931) 58 IA 239 and *Last* v *London Assurance Corporation* 2 TC 100, *Tata Hydro-Electric Agencies Ltd(Bombay)* v *Bombay & Aden Income Tax Commissioner PC* [1937] 2 All ER 291 and *Indian Radio and Cable Communications Co Ltd* v *Bombay & Aden Income Tax Commissioner PC* [1937] 3 All ER 709.

26 THE TAXATION OF NON-RESIDENTS WHO DEVELOP, INVEST AND DEAL IN UNITED KINGDOM PROPERTY

26.1 INTRODUCTION

The taxation rules which apply to non-residents who develop, invest and deal in United Kingdom property fall into three basic areas. These are:

26.1.1 Basic principles

The basic rule of income tax is thus: following *Colquhoun* v *Brooks* 2 TC 490, income is chargeable to United Kingdom taxation if it arises in the United Kingdom or the taxpayer is resident in the United Kingdom. Thus, if a non-resident individual carries out a land deal in the United Kingdom so that the profit arises in the United Kingdom that individual could be chargeable to income tax at rates as high as 40%. Similarly if a non-resident individual receives rent from land in the United Kingdom the tenant will deduct tax at 25% and the individual will be liable for further tax up to 15%. There are no published or other Revenue concessions, to the author's knowledge, in that area.

26.1.2 Special provisions for non-resident persons

There are special provisions designed to deal with the taxation of non-resident persons. For instance, a non-resident company is specifically brought within the charge to corporation tax by TA 1988, s 11 to the extent that it carries on a trade in the United Kingdom through a branch or agency.

26.1.3 Anti-avoidance provisions

There are anti-avoidance provisions. The general theme of these provisions is to ensure that a taxpayer's non-resident status does not result in United

Kingdom tax being avoided if the profits arise in the United Kingdom or if United Kingdom based persons are behind the overseas structures.

Provisions to consider
- Basic rules
- Special rules for non-residents
- Anti-avoidance

26.2 FAILED 'NON-RESIDENT' COMPANIES

In many tax planning arrangements involving a foreign element, it will be critical to establish that a company is resident outside the United Kingdom. In many cases taxpayers fail to do this and the Revenue can easily attack the situation. The guidelines set out below should be noted.

In the case of *De Beers Consolidated Mines Ltd* v *Howe* 5 TC 198 the Lord Chancellor at p 213 stated:

> a company resides for the purpose of Income Tax, where its real business is carried on. I regard that as the true rule; and the real business is carried on where the central management and control actually abides.

In that case there was a company registered in South Africa which worked diamond mines in South Africa. The directors' meetings were held in London. The meetings where real control was exercised were in London. That real control was exercised in practically all the important business areas of the company except the actual mining operations. At p 213 the Lord Chancellor stated:

> London has always controlled the negotiation of the contracts ... has determined policy in the disposal of diamonds and other assets, the working and development of mines, the application of profits and the appointment of directors. London has always controlled matters that require to be determined by the majority of all directors, which include all questions of expenditure except wages, materials and such like at the mines, and a limited sum which may be spent by the directors at Kimberley.

In *New Zealand Shipping Co Ltd* v *C H Thew* 8 TC 208, a shipping company was incorporated in New Zealand. The board of directors in London conducted all the business affairs of the company in the United Kingdom and had exclusive control of the financial and administrative business and decided all important questions of policy. Subject to those powers a separate board of directors existed in New Zealand to conduct the actual business affairs of the company in Australasia and negotiate independently important freight contracts. The general books of the company were kept in London where the accounts were made up and dividends declared. General meetings of the company were held in London and Christchurch. It was held (by the Lords) that the company was resident in the United Kingdom. The test of central management and control was adopted.

In *Union Corporation Limited* v *IRC etc* 34 TC 207 it was reaffirmed that the central management and control test was the correct one and the Court of Appeal (The Lords did not need to consider the point) found that if the central management and control was divided between, for instance, two countries then the particular company could be resident in both countries. The Court held that there had to be substantial business operations in a particular country and some part of the superior and directing authority in that country before it could be said that the company was resident in that particular country. Applying that test, of course, a company could be resident in a number of countries.

In *Bullock* v *The Unit Construction Co Ltd* 38 TC 712 a United Kingdom parent company controlled some companies trading in Africa. The overseas companies were not trading successfully and the United Kingdom company took over the control and management. After that take over all decisions on matters of major importance and many minor matters were made by the parent in the United Kingdom. The African directors never met as Boards and did not all have access to the documents and information concerning their companies. Decisions were, however, taken on the day to day running of the companies' trading activities within the general policy directions of the parent company. It was found that the companies were controlled and managed in the United Kingdom.

It was held that for the company to be resident in the United Kingdom active central management and control of the company had to be in the United Kingdom.

Merely having board meetings in the United Kingdom is not sufficient. The board meetings must be concerned with the central management and control of the company's activities. Whether they be trade and business activities or financial activities that control must be actively exercised. Overseas executive committees who merely know that the power exists in the United Kingdom without there being any exercise of the same may cause the residence of the company to reside where the executive committee resides.

26.2.1 Revenue statement

The Revenue statement on company residence of 27 July 1983 (SP6/1983) confirms, as the above tax cases indicate, that one must look to the highest level of control to determine where the central management and control of a company resides. Emphasis is laid on where the board of directors meet in the cases and the Revenue accept this. The Revenue claim that although the locations of board meetings is important it is not necessarily a conclusive factor. In para 6 of the statement it is stated:

> In some cases, for example, central management and control is exercised by a single individual. This may happen when a chairman or managing director exercises powers formally conferred by the company's Articles and the other board members are little more than cyphers, or by reason of a dominant

shareholding or for some other reason. In those cases the residence of the company is where the controlling individual exercises his powers.

Also paras 7, 8, 9 and 10 of the Revenue statement are instructive. They read as follows:

7 In general the place of directors' meetings is significant only in so far as those meetings constitute the medium through which management and control is exercised. If, for example, the directors of a company were engaged together actively in the United Kingdom in the complete running of a business which was wholly in the United Kingdom, the company would not be regarded as resident outside the United Kingdom merely because the directors held formal board meetings outside the United Kingdom. While it is possible to identify extreme situations in which central management and control plainly is, or is not, exercised by directors in formal meetings, the conclusion in any case is wholly one of fact depending on the relative weight to be given to various factors. Any attempt to lay down rigid guidelines would only be misleading.

8 Generally, however, where doubts arise about a particular company's residence status, the Revenue adopt the following approach:

(i) they first try to ascertain whether the directors of the company in fact exercise central management and control,

(ii) If so, they seek to determine where the directors exercise this central management and control (which is not necessarily where they meet),

(iii) In cases where the directors apparently do not exercise central management and control of the company, the Revenue then look to establish where and by whom it is exercised.

Parent/subsidiary relationship

9 It is particularly difficult to apply the 'central management and control' test in the situation where a subsidiary company and its parent operate in different territories. In this situation, the parent will normally influence, to a greater or lesser extent, the actions of the subsidiary. Where the influence is exerted by the parent exercising the powers which a sole or majority shareholder has in general meetings of the subsidiary, for example to appoint and dismiss members of the board of the subsidiary and to initiate or approve alterations to its financial structure, the Revenue would not seek to argue that central management and control of the subsidiary is located where the parent company is resident. However, in cases where the parent usurps the functions of the board of the subsidiary (such as in Unit Construction itself)or where that board merely rubber stamps the parent company's decisions without giving them any independent consideration of its own, the Revenue draw the conclusion that the subsidiary has the same residence for tax purposes as its parent.

10 The Revenue must recognise that there may be many cases where the company is a member of a group having its ultimate holding company in another country which will not fall readily into either of the categories referred to above. In considering whether the board of such a subsidiary company exercises central management and control of the subsidiary's business, they have regard to the degree of autonomy which those

> directors have in conducting the company's business. Matters (among others) that may be taken into account are the extent to which the directors of the subsidiary take decisions on their own authority as to investment, production, marketing and procurement without reference to the parent.

Careful note should also be taken of the provisions in FA 1988 s 66 which provide that a company which is incorporated in the UK shall be regarded for the purposes of the Taxes Act as resident in the UK even if the company is controlled and managed outside the UK. Note also that under FA 1988 ss 105–107 that if a UK resident company ceases to be resident in the UK corporation tax on chargeable gains tax can arise.

26.3 NON-RESIDENT COMPANY CARRIES OUT UNITED KINGDOM LAND TRADING TRANSACTION

What happens if a non-resident company carries out a United Kingdom trading transaction (for instance, it buys some land with a view to selling the same at a profit and sells the same within a short period)?

26.3.1 Liability

Looking at general income tax principles it is clear that it is necessary to ascertain whether the profit arose in the United Kingdom; if it arose in the United Kingdom there can be a charge to tax at the basic rate. The tax charge will be under TA 1988, s 18. This charges tax 'in respect of any trade carried on (in the United Kingdom or elsewhere)'. The charge would be only at the basic rate because the non-resident company cannot be liable to the higher rates of tax which only apply to individuals and nor can it be liable to the additional rate which only applies to certain trusts.

However, if the Revenue can show that the non-resident company carries on a trade in the United Kingdom through a branch or agency then any trading income arising directly or indirectly through or from the branch or agency will be charged to corporation tax (TA 1988, s 11). For the purposes of that provision branch or agency means 'any factorship, agency, receivership, branch or management' (TA 1988, s 834). The *Shorter Oxford Dictionary* item 7 refers to a branch as being a local or subordinate office of business which is a good working definition. It denotes the existence of some local office or place of management under the auspices of the main place of management.

26.3.2 Collection

If there are tax charges on the land profits and the non-resident does not pay the tax how can the United Kingdom tax authorities collect the tax?

TMA 1970, s 78
The Revenue could go under TMA 1970, s 78 which states that a person

not resident in the United Kingdom shall be assessable and chargeable to income tax in the name of any . . . branch or agent, whether the branch or agent has receipt of the profits or gains or not, in like manner and to the like amount as such non-resident would be assessable and charged if he were resident in the United Kingdom and in the actual receipt of such profits or gains. Note that if the non-resident is not chargeable to tax, then the agent cannot be liable under s 78 (*Greenwood* v *Smith* 8 TC 193). Also if the non-resident can be properly made liable he cannot avoid the assessment by claiming the Revenue must go for the agent (*Tischler* v *Apthorpe* 2 TC 89).

TMA 1970, s 82

There is a saving provision in TMA 1970, s 82 which states that these provisions shall not render a non-resident person chargeable in the name of a broker or in the name of an agent not being an authorised person carrying on the regular agency of the non-resident person, in respect of profits or gains arising from sales or transactions carried out through such a broker or agent. Provided that where sales or transactions are carried out on behalf of a non-resident person through a broker in the ordinary course of his business as such and the broker:

(*a*) is a person carrying on *bona fide* the business of a broker in the United Kingdom, and

(*b*) receives in respect of the business of the non-resident person which is transacted through him remuneration at a rate not less than that customary in the class of business in question.

then, notwithstanding that the broker is a person who acts regularly for the non-resident person as such a broker, the non-resident person shall not be chargeable in the name of that broker in respect of profits or gains arising from those sales or transactions. In this provision broker includes a general commission agent. In *Fleming* v *London Produce Co Ltd* (1968) 44 TC 582 at 596 stated:

> Helpful though Counsel have been, I do not find myself in a position from which I can advance with any great clarity to the task of defining or explaining the term 'general commission agent'. I feel little temptation in the process of defining each of the words separately and then adding the bits together: for such an operation is notoriously unreliable, as, indeed, the Holy Roman Empire and the Lord Privy Seal have long testified. But I do derive some assistance from the context in which the expression is used. First [s 82(1)] provides: '. . . In this subsection,"broker" includes a general commission agent.' Parliament may, of course, do anything; but in the absence of any indication to the contrary, I begin with the assumption that, when a statute provides that 'A includes B', B has a meaning which is ejusdem generis with A, or at least appears to be suitable for inclusion as an expanded form of A. Whatever the urge to brevity, I would not expect 'black' to be defined as including 'white', nor 'the United Kingdom' as including 'Europe'. Accordingly, I consider that a 'general commission agent' must have sufficient broker-like qualities to make it reasonable for Parliament to provide that 'broker' should include him. After all, brokers are essentially negotiators for commission. Second, the general trend of the proviso is to confer exemption on non-residents who

> merely employ brokers for broking in the ordinary way, even if they regularly employ the same one. The words 'ordinary course of his business', 'carrying on *bona fide* the business' and 'a rate not less than that customary in the class of business in question' seem to me to be significant: in relation to broking the proviso is redolent of ordinariness. Third, the word 'general' in the phrase 'general commission agent' itself must have some import; and in the context I think the most likely sense is that of a commission agent who holds himself out as being ready to work for clients generally, and who does not in substance confine his activities to one principal, or an insignificant number of principals. This, perhaps, is another facet of his broker-like qualities: he must be broker-like in his receipt of custom.

TMA 1970, s 79
The Revenue may also look to s 79 of that Act. This provides that a non-resident person shall be assessable and chargeable to income tax in respect of any profits or gains arising, whether directly or indirectly, through or from any branch or agency, and shall be so assessable and chargeable in the name of the branch or agent.

TMA 1970 s 85
If corporation tax is in point then TMA 1970, s 85 has to be referred to. It states that the provisions of TMA 1970 relating to income tax so far as they are applicable to tax chargeable on a company, shall apply with any necessary adaptations in relation to corporation tax chargeable on companies not resident in the United Kingdom.

A Solicitor is not normally an 'agent' of his client in a normal conveyancing transaction.

26.3.3 Conclusion on non-resident company trading in the United Kingdom

It is clear that a non-resident company trading in the United Kingdom could be liable to income tax (25%) or corporation tax (35% top rate) under general principles and that the Revenue if they could not get the tax from the non-resident would seek to apply the provisions of TMA 1970, ss 78—85 in order to collect the tax from a UK-based person.

26.4 NON-RESIDENT COMPANY CARRIES OUT A CGT TRANSACTION AND TA 1988, s 776 IS NOT IN ISSUE

It may be that the non-resident company will carry out a transaction which gives rise to a CGT gain. What liability to tax will arise?

The general rule is that a non-UK-resident and non-UK-ordinarily resident person cannot be liable to CGT unless he is/was carrying on a trade in the United Kingdom through a branch or agency in which case he shall be chargeable 'on the capital gains accruing on the disposal:

(*a*) of assets situated in the United Kingdom and used in or for the purposes of the trade at or before the time when the capital gain accrued or

(*b*) of assets situated in the United Kingdom and used or held for the purposes of the branch or agency at or before that time, or assets acquired for use by or for the purposes of the branch or agency' (CGTA 1979, s 12).

Of course once there is a branch or agency in the United Kingdom and the non-resident (a company) is trading in the United Kingdom then corporation tax on chargeable gains comes into point and TA 1988 s 11 makes the necessary adaptations. It reads thus:

> For the purposes of corporation tax the chargeable profits of a company not resident in the United Kingdom but carrying on a trade there through a branch or agency shall be . . .
>
> (*b*) such chargeable gains accruing on the disposal of assets situated in the United Kingdom as are by [section 12 of the Capital Gains Tax Act Act 1979] made chargeable to capital gains tax in the case of an individual not resident or ordinarily resident in the United Kingdom.

Branch or agency means any factorship, agency, receivership, branch or management but does not include any person within the exemptions in TMA 1970, s 82 (see CGTA 1979, s 12).

Thus if the non-resident company buys an office block in the United Kingdom from which it receives rent and subsequently disposes of that making a capital gain, subject to the application of TA 1988, s 776 there will be no charge to tax on the disposal. This is because the taxpayer is non-resident and was not carrying on a *trade* in the United Kingdom; merely holding the property in order to obtain rents does not amount to a trade; it may amount to a business but not a trade (see *Griffiths* v *Jackson* [1983] STC 184, *Gittos* v *Barclay* [1982] STC 390, *Fry* v *Salisbury* 15 TC 266, *Webb* v *Conelee* [1982] STC 913 and *Croft* v *Sywell Aerodrome* 24 TC 126: see also *The Commissioners* v *Morrisons' Academy* (1978)).

Thus the general rule is the making of capital gains by non-resident companies on the disposal of UK properties gives rise to no United Kingdom tax problems and in that respect the United Kingdom may be looked upon as a tax haven. It should be noted however:

(*a*) A trade must not be carried out from the premises. For instance, if the property is a hotel and the non-resident carries out a hotel trade then there could be problems under CGTA 1979, s 12. In this event the non-resident company may want to grant a full rack rent lease to its United Kingdom resident subsidiary which subsidiary in turn carries out the trade (see *Stanley* v *The Gramophone and Typewriter Ltd* 5 TC 358 at 374 and 376).

(*b*) Income tax (but not corporation tax) will be chargeable on the rents received by the non-resident company and the tenant under TA 1988, s 43 will seek to deduct tax at the basic rate from the payment if the

SECTION 12 PROBLEM

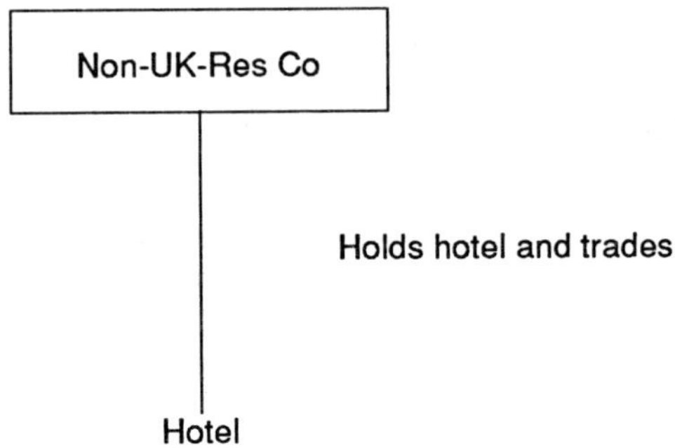

NO SECTION 12 PROBLEM

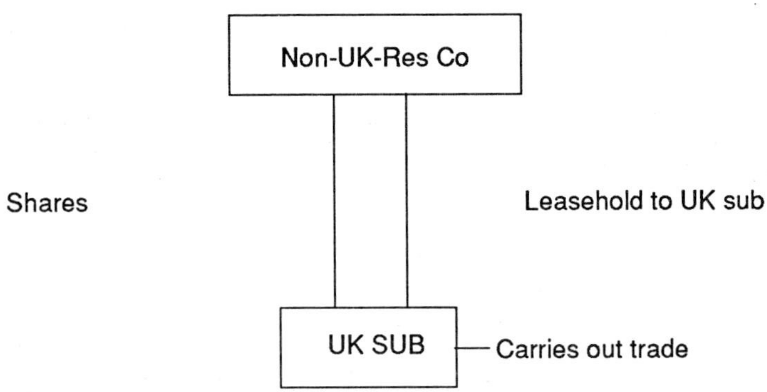

landlord's usual place of abode is outside the United Kingdom. He (the tenant) may pay the rent to the landlord's United Kingdom estate agent in which case the tenant can pay the agent gross but the agent when paying monies to the landlord whose normal place of abode is outside the United Kingdom will deduct tax. This is the case if the monies are paid into an overseas or a United Kingdom bank account of the landlord. The landlord may seek to reduce the tax charge on the income by ensuring he has a qualifying borrowing within TA 1988, s 353 *et seq.* In particular it should be noted that the provisions specifically envisage non-resident companies (which are not within the charge to corporation tax) being eligible for relief under s 353 *et seq* (see below: note the bank must carry on a *bona fide* banking business in the UK).

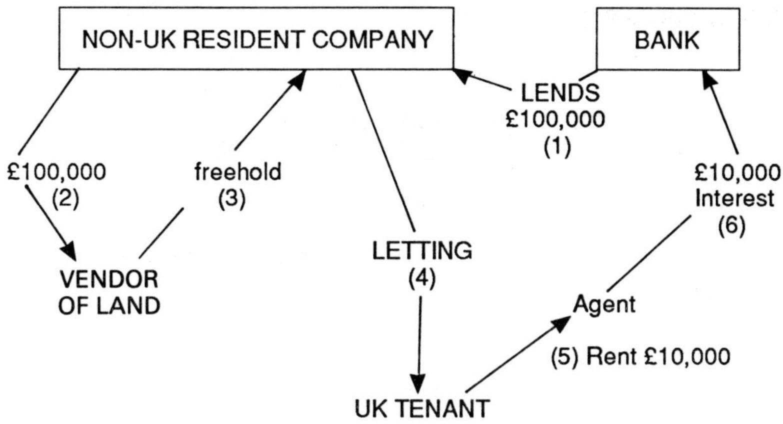

26.4.1 Appropriations—stock/capital

If a non-resident company appropriates stock to capital a tax charge can arise (income tax or corporation tax) (see 9.4.8).

If a non-resident company appropriates a capital asset to stock there should be no charge to tax unless CGTA 1979, s 12 can be made to apply (see also CGTA 1979, s 122, *Sharkey* v *Wernher* 36 TC 275 and *Pilkington* v *Randall* 42 TC 662).

As well as charges arising on appropriations to and from stock, note that charges (including charges under s 776) can also arise on land exchanges and variations of land interests (see *Californian Copper Syndicate* v *Homes* 5 TC 159, *Gold Coast Selection Trust Ltd* v *Humphrey* [1948] AC 459 and *Craddock* v *Zero* 27 TC 267)) unless in the case of CGT one or other of the Revenue concessions or reliefs are available eg under s 115 or s 111A of CGTA 1979 or under a Revenue Concession (see D16, D19, D22, D23, D25 and D26).

26.5 THE NON-RESIDENT COMPANY CARRIES OUT A CAPITAL TRANSACTION BUT TA 1988, s 776 IS IN ISSUE

When does s 776 charge capital profits (profits which do not fall to be included in any computation of income for the purposes of the Tax Act)? Section 776 charges capital profits which result from a disposal where:

(*a*) Land, or any property deriving its value from land, is acquired with the sole or main object of realising a gain from disposing of the land or

(*b*) Land is held as trading stock or

(*c*) Land is developed with the sole or main object of realising a gain from disposing of the land when developed.

The provision probably applies even if there is no element of tax avoidance (*Page* v *Lowther* [1983] STC 799 of *Yuill* v *Wilson* [1979] STC 486 at 491). Thus in order for there to be a liability to tax under s 776 three or (just possibly but very unlikely) four conditions must be satisfied.

(*a*) there may have been an element of tax avoidance; this is very unlikely following the Court of Appeal decision in *Page* v *Lowther* [1983] STC 799;

(*b*) the transactions must fall within one of the three situations set out in s776(2);

(*c*) there must be a disposal of land; and

(*d*) a gain of a capital nature must be realised.

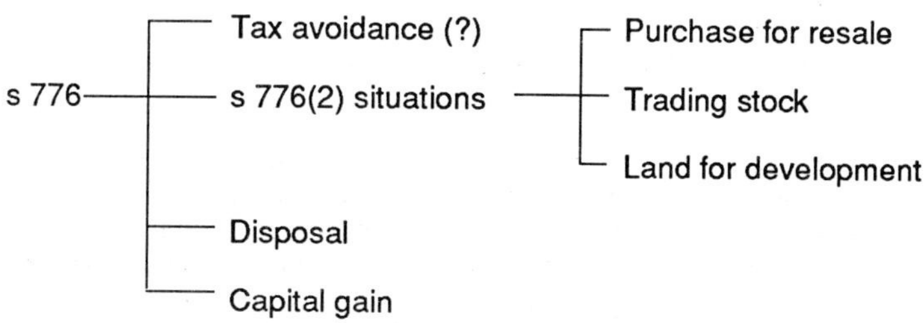

Thus, the non-resident company may buy land in the United Kingdom and sell the same within, say, a year. The land may have been bought with a view to disposing of the same at a gain but the Revenue may find it difficult to establish that the transaction was a trading transaction because, for instance, it was the only transaction which the company did. In this case the Revenue are likely to seek to apply TA 1988, s 776 to the gain.

The provision applies even though the taxpayer is not resident in the United Kingdom although it is arguable that the provision only applies to land in the United Kingdom. Note that the Revenue do have a power to direct a proposed purchaser to deduct the basic rate of tax from the sale proceeds of the land (TA 1988, s 776(9)).

Note also that this provision *as well as TA 1988, s 703* could apply on the sale of shares for a capital sum. Such a sale could result, for example, in an indirect disposal of trading stock (the trading stock being held by the company). Provided the taxpayer has not entered into any arrangements or schemes then it may be that a charge will not be exigible because of the relieving provision in TA 1988, s 776(10). However, if the property (owned by the company) is held on capital account and the Revenue, for instance, can show that the land was acquired with a view to the disposal of the same at a profit then s 776 could apply on the disposal of the shares in the foreign company.

26.6 TRADING, CAPITAL GAINS TAX AND s 776—WHICH ONE WILL THE REVENUE APPLY?

If the overseas taxpayer buys a block of flats with a view to refurbishing the same and then selling long leases of the same then it is very likely the Revenue would succeed, applying general principles, under a trading assessment.

If the overseas taxpayer—the non-resident company—buys property, obtains planning permission and then sells the same then that is very likely to, under general principles, be assessed as a trading transaction.

If the overseas taxpayer purchases property, develops the same and then sells the same then that is likely to be a trading transaction.

If the overseas taxpayer purchases the property, develops the same and then lets out the property and then finally sells the property once again that is likely to be a trading transaction.

If the overseas taxpayer purchases property, develops the same, lets the same and then holds onto the property for say four or five years that transaction is likely to amount to a capital gains transaction given rise to a tax free gain. If the Revenue, however, are able to show that the property was developed with the sole or main object of realising a gain from the disposal of the property when developed or the land was acquired the sole or main object of realising a gain from disposing of the same then s 776 may apply. Board minutes are important; 'the law is not important, all that is important is the minute'!

If the overseas taxpayer assembles a number of land interests then that is a point indicating trading; that would be relevant if the property is ultimately disposed of.

Practitioners take different views as to how long property should be held onto in order to ensure that it comprises an investment.

The author likes a five to six year period with the property being income producing for that period (see, however, 4.3.16).

26.7 IF THE NON-RESIDENT COMPANY IS CHARGEABLE TO INCOME TAX OR CORPORATION TAX UNDER GENERAL PRINCIPLES—CASE 1 OF SCHEDULE D OR UNDER TA 1988, s 776—CAN A DOUBLE TAXATION AGREEMENT HELP?

The position with regard to a Double Tax Treaty is best illustrated by taking a close look at what would happen if a Jersey income tax paying company carried out a United Kingdom land deal.

Assume that an overseas investor (someone who is neither resident nor ordinarily resident nor domiciled in the United Kingdom) wishes to use money to purchase land in the United Kingdom, carry out refurbishment and alteration works and sell the same to make a trading profit. Assume that investor capitalises a Jersey company which is liable to Jersey income tax at 20% on its profits which company then finances the development, ie, the purchase of the land and the refurbishment works. What are the income and corporation tax points to consider taking into account the double tax treaty.

26.7.1 Income and corporation tax

(*a*) The Jersey company must be controlled and managed in Jersey to be resident in Jersey. One looks to the place where actual *de facto* management and control takes place (*De Beers Consolidated Mines Ltd* v *Howe* (1906) 5 TC 198 and *Bullock* v *Unit Construction Co Ltd* (1959) 38 TC 712).

(*b*) That being the case under general principles the company could be liable to a 25% tax charge under TA 1980 s 18 (see *Rhodesia Metals Ltd* v *IRC* [1940] AC 774) or possibly under TA 1988 s 776. Alternatively, if it has a branch or agency in the United Kingdom it may be liable to corporation tax under TA 1988 s 11.

(*c*) If there are such tax liabilities then agents or managers in the United Kingdom could be liable in certain circumstances to pay the tax (TMA 1970, ss 78 and 82).

(*d*) There will be no liability to United Kingdom tax (income tax or corporation tax), however, if the profit is protected by the Double Taxation Treaty with Jersey (the Double Taxation Relief (Taxes on Income) (Jersey) Order 1952 No 1216). The profits will be protected (in the author's opinion) from United Kingdom income tax and corporation tax if the Jersey company is controlled and managed in Jersey and not in the United Kingdom and there is no permanent establishment in the United Kingdom.

Permanent establishment means a branch, management or other fixed place of business but does not include an agency unless the agent has, and habitually exercises, a general authority to negotiate and conclude contracts on behalf of such enterprise. Also a general commission agent acting in the ordinary course of his business would not amount to a permanent establishment.

(*e*) It is critical therefore that there is no permanent establishment in the United Kingdom. Some guidance as to the meaning of permanent establishment can be derived from the case of *Masri* v *Minister of*

National Revenue [1973] FC 848, a Canadian case concerned with land dealing transactions carried out by an American resident with respect to Canadian land. At p 59 it was stated by the Court:

> Here, all management and executive decisions concerning the appellant's business . . . were taken in New York; there were no employees in Canada; no office in Canada; no person resident in Canada having authority to contract or conduct business on behalf of the appellant . . . all documentation regarding the acquisition and sale of the Canadian property was executed in New York; all instructions concerning the property came from New York; the appellant . . . acted in Canada only through commission agents and brokers. Counsel for the (Revenue) sought to attach significance to the fact that in the course of the Canadian land venture, the partners used the services of two town planners, a land surveyor, two brokers, two law firms and a notary. In my view, these circumstances strengthen my conviction that the appellant cannot be said to have a permanent establishment in Canada because all of the above noted agents have one thing in common, they are independent agents, not employees, performing services on a fee for service basis.

(*f*) Thus, if the transaction is a fairly simple one under which the Jersey company would employ a builder, lawyers, agents and architects to carry out the refurbishment work then there is a very good chance that there will not be a permanent establishment in the United Kingdom. If, on the other hand, it is necessary to appoint somebody to supervise the work such as a project manager, regardless of what label may be attached to him, it may be argued that there is a place of management in the United Kingdom or even that an agent has been appointed or even a branch so that the profit would not be protected by the treaty.

26.7.2 Charge under s 776

The Revenue can give a direction to a purchaser to deduct tax at 25% if land is disposed of giving rise to monies which are not brought into a trading computation. The double tax treaty, if the taxpayer comes within its terms, should protect the Jersey company from a charge under s 776 although the 25% tax deduction may occur in the first instance so that the taxpayer may have to prove his case to effectively get his money back. The treaty *may* even protect a United Kingdom individual who may have presented the gain to the overseas company.

26.7.3 Tax planning

There clearly is some advantage in non-resident persons carrying out certain land trading transactions through countries which have favourable Double Tax Treaties with the United Kingdom. These treaties should override national law (*Padmore* v *IRC* [1987] STC 36).

Note that it is extremely difficult for a non-resident who buys and sells land in the United Kingdom to show that the gain (the trading gain) had not been made in the United Kingdom. If X buys land obtains planning permission and arranges for estate agents to find purchasers and then sells the land it is very likely to be the case that the profit has been made in the United Kingdom thus giving rise to a United Kingdom tax charge. In *Liquidator, Rhodesia Metals Limited* v *IRC* [1940] AC 774 the sole business operation of an English company was the purchase of a moveable property—mining claims—in Southern Rhodesia and their development in that territory for purposes of transfer there at a profitable price. The company never adventured any part of its capital except on those mining claims. Both the contracts of purchase and subsequent sale were made in England, and the consideration for the sale was received there. It was held that the company received the sale price from a source within the territory, namely, the mining claims which had been acquired and developed there for the very purpose of obtaining the particular receipt and that so much of it was profit which was accordingly assessable to income tax. Lord Atkin states at p 790:

> ... their Lordships find themselves dealing with a case where the sole business operation of an English company is a purchase of immovable property in South Rhodesia and its development in that territory for purposes of transfer in that territory at a profitable price. The company never adventured any part of its capital except on that or those immovables. As a hard matter of fact the only proper conclusion appears to be that the company had received the sum in question from a source within the territory, namely, the mining claims which they had acquired and developed there for the very purpose of obtaining the particular receipt.

26.8 THE ANTI-AVOIDANCE PROVISIONS

What are the anti-avoidance provisions which have to be taken into account? Reference has already been made to s 776 of the Taxes Act. Following the case of *Page* v *Lowther* [1983] STC 799 it appears that the provision applies even though the taxpayer did not enter into the particular arrangements with a view to avoiding tax.

United Kingdom based taxpayers (ie, individuals who are resident,

ANTI - AVOIDANCE

- s 776 (TA 1988)
- s 739 (TA 1988)
- s 740 (TA 1988)
- Part XV (TA 1988)
- s 775 (TA 1988)
- s 770 (TA 1988)
- s 80 *et seq* (FA 1981)
- s 15 (CGTA 1979)

ordinarily resident and domiciled in the UK—'Mr X' in the examples following) may enter into what may be termed *bounce-back arrangements* under which for instance they set up an overseas resident company with a view to carrying out, for instance, a United Kingdom trading deal with a view to benefits ultimately being provided to the United Kingdom based taxpayers. The question is how would such transactions be taxed? The examination of the tax situation will bring out the significance of the relevant anti-avoidance provisions.

26.8.1 Mr X in the United Kingdom sets up a non-resident company (he owns 100% of the shares thereof) which carries out a United Kingdom trading transaction

In this case the overseas company would be liable to income tax under general principles. Assuming there was no branch or agency in the United Kingdom there will be no charge to corporation tax. As it is a trading transaction s 776 discussed above will not be applicable. The question arises, however, as to whether the Revenue could obtain more tax than just the 25%. In this case the Revenue would be looking to TA 1988, s 739 to obtain the additional tax.

TA 1988, s 739
This provision was enacted to prevent the avoiding by individuals ordinarily resident in the United Kingdom of a liability to income tax by means of a transfer of assets by virtue or in consequence whereof either alone or in conjunction with associated operations income becomes payable to persons resident or domiciled outside the United Kingdom. Section 739 (2) provides:

'Where by virtue or in consequence of any such transfer . . . such an individual . . . has power to enjoy . . . any income of a person resident or domiciled outside the United Kingdom which, if it were income of an individual received by him in the United Kingdom, would be chargeable to income tax . . . that income shall . . . be deemed to be the income of that individual.'

Thus the Revenue would say that the setting up of the overseas company was done to avoid United Kingdom tax and that the taxpayer had the power to enjoy the income because, for instance, a dividend could be paid on the shares. That being the case the total income would be chargeable to tax under Schedule D, Case VI although relief would be given for any basic rate tax which had been paid (s 743 (1)).

The taxpayer may argue that the profit is not chargeable to tax under TA 1988, s 739 by virtue of, for instance, a relevant treaty such as the treaty with Jersey. The claim will be that the treaty protects the gain from tax. If that is the case the Revenue may argue that the section (s 776) can nevertheless still apply because the disposal proceeds of the land will give rise to a 'capital sum', for the purpose of s 776, although under general principles the profit may be a trading profit. The United Kingdom Revenue may also seek to apply TA 1988, s 739 stating that the income is deemed to be that of the individual for United Kingdom tax purposes and not that of the company. Thus the treaty will not apply to protect such an individual. Also to get the treaty relief the 20% Jersey tax must be paid. This is therefore a risky transaction.

26.8.2 The tentacles of s 739

Section 739 is far reaching.

Example 26A: Transfer of assets abroad

Mr X may set up Jersey Ltd (a Jersey incorporated and resident company) which owns United Kingdom Ltd (a UK incorporated and resident company). Jersey Ltd may not receive any income but to the extent that the income of United Kingdom Ltd could be 'shortfalled' (TA 1988, Sched 19), Mr X can be assessed under s 739. This could be relevant if United Kingdom Ltd makes a s 776 gain or receives rent.

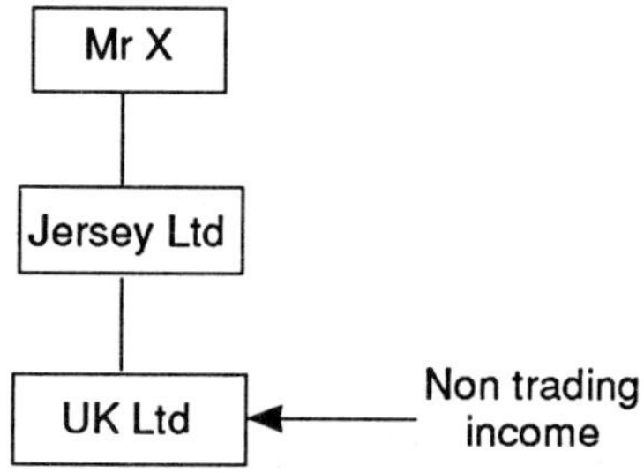

Mr X may have a United Kingdom trading company. He may set up Panama Inc (a Panamanian incorporated and resident company) which receives rent from a letting of property to the United Kingdom trading company. As well as having to consider s 770, one must consider s 739.

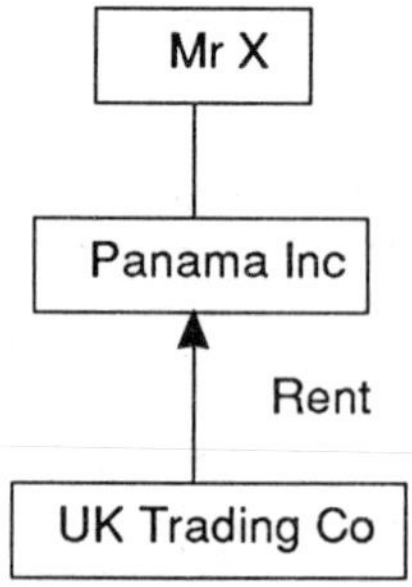

26.8.3 Transfers between non-resident companies

If Panama Inc (one) transfers land by way of gift to Panama Inc (two) (both companies being incorporated and resident in Panama) the position is:

(*a*) If the land is stock *Sharkey* v *Wernher* (1956) AC 58 may be relevant.

(*b*) CGT could not be chargeable (unless s 12 is in point) but in an appropriate case CGTA 1979, s 15 can be relevant (note also the s 16 relief).

(*c*) Section 776 should not apply as consideration has not been paid but note s 777(2)(*b*).

(*d*) Stamp duty should not be in point either because of FA 1930, s 42 (if relevant) *or* because there is a gift.

26.8.4 Mr X in the United Kingdom sets up a non-resident company which carries out a United Kingdom CGT transaction

It may be that the non-resident company will not carry out a trading transaction in the United Kingdom and not get caught by s 488 of the Taxes Act. In this case the gain will comprise a capital gain.

Under general principles the non-resident company is not chargeable to CGT. This assumes CGTA 1979, s 12 is not relevant.

However, under CGTA 1979, s 15 the gain can be apportioned to the shareholders who are resident or ordinarily resident in the United Kingdom at the time the gain accrues. There is also a requirement, if the shareholder is an individual, that he is domiciled in the United Kingdom.

Note that this 'see-through' provision contained in CGTA 11979, s 15 does not apply in relation to any amount in respect of a chargeable gain which is distributed whether by way of dividend or distribution of capital or on the dissolution of a company to persons holding shares in the company or creditors of a company within 2 years from the time when the chargeable gain accrued to the company (CGTA 1979, s 15(5)(*a*). That is an interesting relief. It should be compared with the situation if a United Kingdom company makes a capital gain and is then liquidated.

By using a non-resident company and then liquidating within 2 years one effectively avoids the double charge to CGT which is inherent in the holding of assets through the corporate structure.

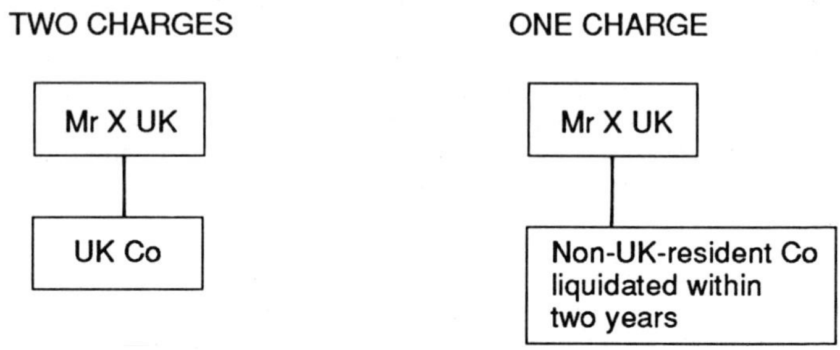

Note that a s 15 charge can be postponed or protected to an extent by having a trust holding the shares in the non-resident company or possibly under the terms of a double taxation treaty.

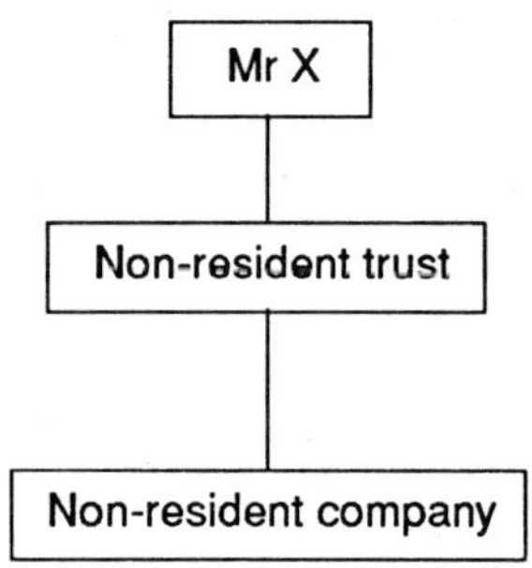

Note also that if a non-resident trust, which is within FA 1981, s 80 *et seq,* makes a loss on the sale of, say, land and the proceeds are advanced to a United Kingdom beneficiary there is a good argument following *Ritchie* v *McKay* [1984] STC 422 that the losses can be 'surrendered' to the beneficiary under CGTA 1979, s 54(2) without the restrictions in s 62(3) applying.

26.9 MULTI-LINEAL STRUCTURES

Multi-lineal structure is one where, for instance, the taxpayer sets up a discretionary trust which is not resident in the United Kingdom which trust in turn owns a foreign resident company which company in turn owns the United Kingdom property. How are these structures taxed?

Once trusts come into the picture new anti-avoidance provisions may well apply. The first one is *TA 1988, s 740.* The section has effect where:

(*a*) by virtue or in consequence of a transfer of assets, either alone or in conjunction with associated operations, income becomes payable to a person resident or domiciled outside the United Kingdom; and

(*b*) an individual ordinarily resident in the United Kingdom who is not liable to tax under s 739 of the Taxes Act (prevention of tax avoidance by transfers of assets abroad) by reference to the transfer receives a benefit provided out of assets which are available for the purpose by virtue or in consequence of the transfer or of any associated operations.

Also one must consider *TA 1988, Part XV* which applies broadly where a taxpayer sets up a settlement or other arrangement so that there is an element of bounty and the taxpayer or his spouse can benefit from the arrangement.

The tax position, if such a company made a trading gain, would be as follows:

(*a*) Under general principles the gain would be chargeable to income tax assuming the company does not have a branch or agency in the United Kingdom through which it carries on a trade. The gain may be protected by a double tax treaty although the Revenue may not apparently accept that.

(*b*) The Revenue may seek to argue that any such gain assuming that there is no treaty in existence (or the treaty does not help) is liable for the basic rate tax under general principles but can also be chargeable to tax under TA 1988, s 739 if the arrangement was set up to avoid United Kingdom tax and the settlor is ordinarily resident in the United Kingdom and he and his spouse are not excluded from all benefit under the structure. The charge to tax would arise as the income arises. If the settlor and his spouse has no connection with the United Kingdom or he and his spouse cannot benefit under the structure then the profits would only be chargeable to tax when benefits accrued to persons who are ordinarily resident in the United Kingdom. This will be under TA 1988, s 740.

(*c*) If the settlor or the spouse of the settlor are beneficiaries under the arrangement then the Revenue may seek to charge the profit as it arises under the provisions of TA 1988, Part XV.

(*d*) The fact that the settlor may not be domiciled in the United Kingdom would not as such help because the profit would have arisen in the United Kingdom.

Example 26B: TA 1988 s 740 (UK settlor)

X is resident, ordinarily resident and domiciled in the United Kingdom. He creates an overseas discretionary trust and X and his spouse are excluded from all benefit. The trust funds an overseas resident company. The overseas resident company carries out a United Kingdom land deal. Assuming there is no double taxation treaty point involved the company would be liable to basic rate tax on the profit under general principles assuming that it has no branch or agency in the United Kingdom through which the trade is carried on. The provisions of TA 1988, s 739 would not apply because the settlor and his spouse are excluded from all benefit. The provisions of TA 1988 Part XV would not apply because the settlor and his spouse are excluded from all benefit. However, if benefits are provided to beneficiaries in the United Kingdom (they are ordinarily resident in the United Kingdom) then tax charges can arise, as and when the benefits are provided, under TA 1988, s 740.

Example 26C: TA 1988 s 734

Mr Y is resident, ordinarily resident and domiciled in the United Kingdom. He sets up an overseas discretionary trust under which he is one of the beneficiaries. The trust funds an overseas resident company. The overseas resident company carries out a UK land trading transaction. Assuming that no arguments concerning double tax treaties are in point the company will be liable to basic rate tax under general principles assuming there is no branch or agency in the United Kingdom through which it trades. Part XV is unlikely to apply (see *Vestey* v *IRC* 31 TC 1 and *Chamberlain* v *IRC* 25 TC 317). However the Revenue are very likely to succeed in charging the higher rate of tax under TA 1988, s 734 as and when the profit is made.

Example 26D: TA 1988 s 740 (non–UK settlor)

Z is not resident, nor ordinarily resident and not domiciled in the United Kingdom but has children in the United Kingdom who are ordinarily resident therein. Z may, with a view to mitigating United Kingdom tax, set up an overseas trust which in turn owns an overseas company which carries out the United Kingdom land trading transaction. Although it may not be critical, assume that the settlor and his spouse are excluded from benefit under the trust. In this case, when the trading gain is made, the company would be liable for the basic rate of tax (assuming there are no arguments available with regard to double tax treaties). Any further charge to tax would only arise when benefits are provided to the United Kingdom children. This will be under TA 1988, s 740.

Note that to avoid the applications of TA 1988 s 739 the settlor and his spouse should be excluded from possible benefit under the structure. There is dicta in *Vestey* v *IRC* [1980] STC 10 that it is also necessary for persons 'associated' with the creation of the trust etc to be excluded from benefit but no guidance was provided as to what 'associated' meant.

26.9.1 CGT

If the trust makes a capital gain or its underlying company makes a capital gain then *FA 1981, s 80 et seq* may be in point. This may tax (to CGT) capital payments made by the trustees to beneficiaries who are resident or ordinarily resident and domiciled in the United Kingdom.

26.10 TAX INEFFICIENT BRACKETT STRUCTURES

Taxpayers who set up non-resident companies owned by non-resident

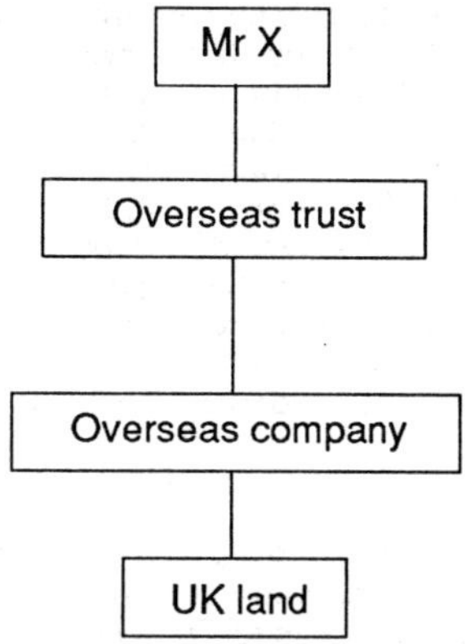

trusts to assist in United Kingdom tax mitigation schemes concerning land transactions should pay special attention to the pitfalls revealed in the case of *IRC* v *Brackett* [1986] STC 521.

In the *Brackett* case the taxpayer created an overseas trust. He excluded himself and his spouse from all benefit. The trust set up an underlying trading company.

When a client required property advice the taxpayer would mention to the client that he was employed by the Jersey company (which was in fact the case). Payments for the advice were then made to the Jersey company. All the technical advice emanated from the taxpayer who received some payments of salary.

The taxpayer also sold some of his properties which could not otherwise be sold on the market to the Jersey company and the Jersey company also repaired some of the taxpayer's properties.

The Jersey company also made some payments to discharge the taxpayer's moral obligations with regard to his married daughter.

The taxpayer was throughout resident in the United Kingdom and presumably also ordinarily resident and domiciled in the United Kingdom.

Hoffmann J in the High Court held that the structure did not result in a saving of any United Kingdom taxes on income. Practitioners who have set up structures similar to that in *Brackett* should note the following areas of United Kingdom tax risk.

26.10.1 Control and management overseas

Ensure that the overseas company is resident outside the United Kingdom.

This issue did not arise in the *Brackett* case (it was taken for granted that the company was resident outside the United Kingdom). However, it is important to bear this point in mind. The company is resident where it is controlled and managed and that must be outside the United Kingdom. Note also that, subject to transitional . . . provisions, a UK incorporated company is deemed to be resident in the UK for the purposes of the Taxes Act (see FA 1988 s 66).

26.10.2 Trading in the United Kingdom

If an overseas entity trades in the United Kingdom then it can be liable for *income tax* under general principles on its profits. If the Revenue can find a branch or agency in the United Kingdom then they may assess the branch or agency in respect of any profits or gains arising, whether directly or indirectly, through or from any branch or agency. The assessment would be under TMA 1970, s 79. Thus the rule is that if any profit is made in the United Kingdom it is chargeable to income tax; if the Revenue can find any branch or agency in the United Kingdom (directly or indirectly) through or from which the profits or gains arose then they can assess that branch or agency; if there is no branch or agency there is nobody they can assess apart from the non-resident person which may not get them very far.

If the overseas company trades through a branch or agency then any trading income arising directly or indirectly through or from the branch or agency is chargeable to *corporation* tax (and not income tax) (TA 1988, s 11). In this case under TMA 1970, s 75 if the Revenue cannot get the money from a non-resident company they can assess the branch or agent in the United Kingdom. Mr Brackett was such a branch or agent.

26.10.3 Taxes Act 1988, s 739

Hoffman J found that when the taxpayer entered into the contract of employment with the Jersey company he transferred an asset overseas. That is the basic prerequisite of s 739 applying. 'Transfer' for these purposes would include the creation of rights. The taxpayer's earning capacity was an asset. The Judge said that when one looked at the substantial effect and result of the transactions which the court was obliged to do the taxpayer was benefiting from the overseas income derived from the Jersey company's trade. One such benefit was he sold properties to the structure at a time when they could not otherwise be disposed of on acceptable terms in the open market.

26.10.4 Part XV of the Taxes Act 1988

These provisions which tax income arising in a settlement upon the settlor were not raised in the *Brackett* decision. Generally income arising in an overseas trading company owned by an overseas trust is not income arising to the settlement for the purposes of these provisions so that even though the settlor may benefit from the income arising in the company that is not the same as if he benefited from the assets held in a settlement, namely the shares (*Chamberlain* v *IRC* (1943) 25 TC 317). It seems quite right that this provision was not raised in the *Brackett* case.

26.10.5 Taxes Act 1988, s 739—sale by individual of income derived from his personal activities

This is an important provision to bear in mind if taxpayers are setting up overseas arrangements. It has effect where transactions or arrangements are effected or made to exploit the earning capacity of an individual in any occupation by putting some other person in a position to enjoy all or any part of the profits or gains or other income derived from the individual's activities in that occupation. The provision applies if one of the main objects of the transactions or arrangements was the avoidance or reduction of liability to income tax. Also it is essential that part of the arrangement is that a capital amount is obtained by a person and a capital amount is broadly an amount which does not come into any computation of income for the purposes of the Tax Acts.

The provision was relevant in the *Brackett* case because the monies paid by the clients to the Jersey company could have amounted to capital amounts—because the taxpayer claimed that they did not come into a United Kingdom computation for income tax purposes and the employment arrangement may have been part of a tax avoidance scheme to enable the income from Mr Brackett's profession to be paid overseas instead of to him. In the circumstances of the *Brackett* case the court did not have to take a final decision as to whether or not that particular section applied; this was because the overseas income was already taxable upon Mr Brackett under s 739.

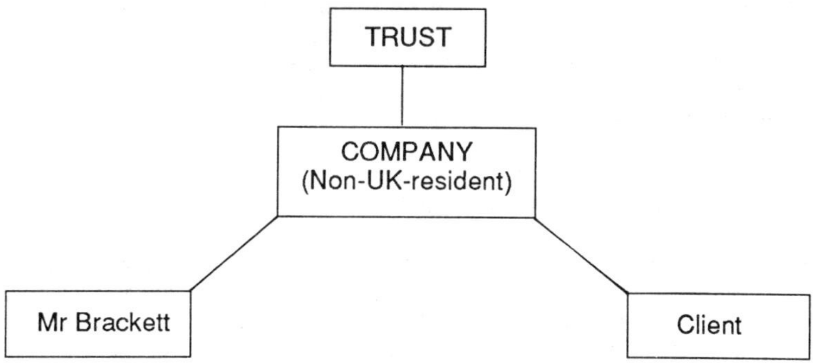

26.11 WHAT ABOUT AN ANSTALT? (MULTI-MULTI-LINEAL STRUCTURES)

Sometimes when the client comes from a civil law jurisdiction he would prefer that an anstalt controls the underlying company which company then does the land deal. The anstalt will probably be treated for United Kingdom IHT purposes as comprising a settlement. The persons entitled to the founder's rights will probably be treated as having interests in possession. If the structure was set up for the avoidance of United Kingdom tax and the settlor is ordinarily resident in the United Kingdom and can benefit under the anstalt then TA 1988, s 739 may apply. If the settlor and his spouse are, for instance, not beneficiaries then charges could arise under TA 1988, s 740 when benefits are provided to persons who are ordinarily resident (and in some cases also resident) in the United Kingdom.

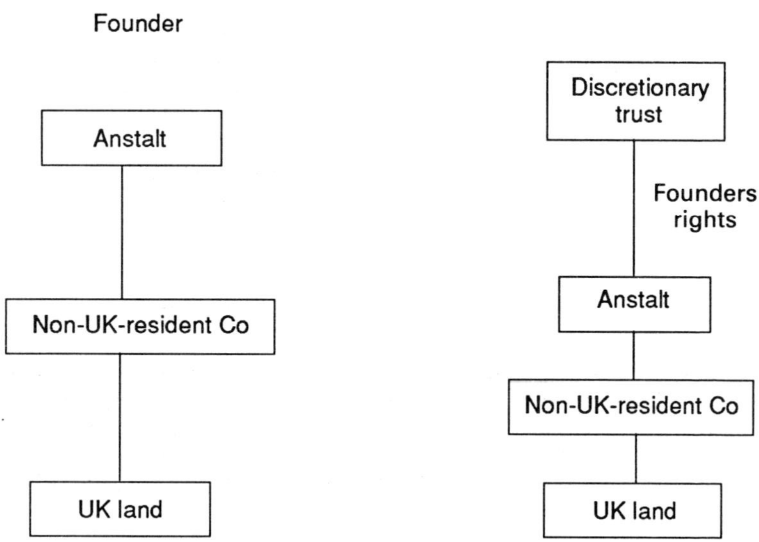

In an appropriate case it may be preferable to settle the rights of the anstalt into a discretionary trust.

26.12 MULTIPLE LINEAL STRUCTURES AND IHT

A person who is not domiciled in the United Kingdom may set up an overseas trust to hold United Kingdom land. This would not be a good IHT transaction because the trust would not be holding assets located outside the United Kingdom (IHTA 1984, s 48). The taxpayer may therefore decide to set up an overseas company which has its registered office not in the United Kingdom (place of residence is not relevant for IHT purposes: this contrasts with the income tax rules: *Eric Beach Co Ltd* v *AG* [1930] AC 161,

American Thread Co v *Joyce* 6 TC 163, *Bradbury* v *English Sewing Cotton* 8 TC 481 and ST B6.220) which will hold the United Kingdom property and therefore IHT will not be in point.

A person from a civil law jurisdiction may, for instance, set up an anstalt which holds property in the United Kingdom. This would not be an attractive transaction from the point of view of IHT and once again an underlying company should be set up. If it is desired not to set up an underlying company perhaps the founder's rights could be settled into an overseas discretionary trust and it may be that provided the settlor is not domiciled (when he carries out that transaction) in the United Kingdom it will be an IHT excluded property structure.

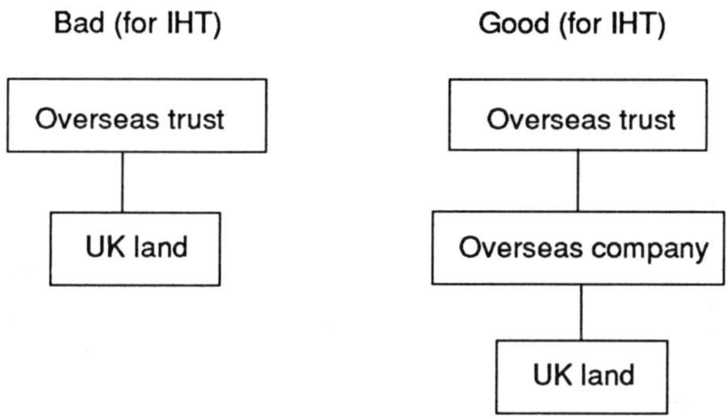

NB The Revenue issued a Consultative Paper in July 1988 entitled 'Residence in the United Kingdom' under which it is proposed that the liability to UK income tax and capital gains tax should be based on an individual's place of residence (which is to be newly defined). Ordinary residence and domicile may no longer be relevant. The provisions may come into effect on 6 April 1989.

APPENDIX 1: LAND TAX CHECK-LIST WITH EXPLANATIONS

There is set out below a check list of items with a brief explanation which advisers dealing with complex land transactions should consider:

1 Legal nature

Has the nature of the transaction been properly analysed from the general legal point of view? It is important to distinguish licences from leases. An apparent licence may in fact amount to a lease. There is no lease or tack duty (SA 1891, Sched 1) on licences.

2 Tax status

Is the entity which has made the gain entitled to any particular tax exemptions or reliefs by virtue of its special status? An exempt pension fund under TA 1988, s 590 *et seq* does not pay CGT, nor does it pay income tax on its investments. Charities are exempt from a large number of taxes.

3 Tax position of client

What is the general tax position of the taxpayer? For instance, has he got losses available from earlier years which can be carried forward against trading profits under TA 1988, s 393? Is group relief available under TA 1988, s 402?

4 Rental income

Does the transaction give rise to income profits from land which can be taxable under TA 1988 Sched A or Sched D? Can this charge be mitigated by borrowings with the interest on the borrowing being offset against the rent?

5 Schedule E

Can a tax change arise under TA 1988 Sched E, because an employer has made accommodation available to an employee?

6 Lease premium provisions

Do the lease premium provisions contained in TA 1988, s 34 *et seq* apply? Those provisions can apply where a lease of a duration not exceeding 50 years is granted at a premium, where a lease granted at an undervalue is assigned (TA 1988, s 35) or where land is disposed of with a right to obtain a reconveyance of the land (TA 1988, s 36). In certain cases where the landlord has to pay under the lease premium provisions a tenant can obtain a measure of tax relief under TA 1988, s 37, and more especially under s 87 (deductions where premiums etc are taxable).

7 Taxable gains

Has a land trading gain been made thus giving rise to a profit which can be chargeable as an income profit? To ascertain whether a transaction is a trading transaction it is necessary to examine the cases dealing with the badges of trade (see Chapter 4).

8 Allowable expenditure

Does any expenditure on the land amount to revenue expenditure which can be offset against trading profits? Does the expenditure amount to repair and maintenance which may be deductible under Sched D, Case 1? Alternatively, is it expenditure of a capital nature for which relief may not be available? (See Chapter 5).

9 Interest relief

Is tax relief available for any interest payments? A company may obtain relief for interest because it may amount to a trading expense or a charge on income. An individual may obtain relief because the interest may amount to a trading expense or because he satisfies the conditions of TA 1988, s 353 *et seq* (see Chapter 7).

10 Capital allowances

Can capital allowances be claimed in connection with industrial buildings (CAA 1968), plant and machinery (FA 1971, Pt III, Ch 1), mines and minerals (CAA 1968) and agricultural land and buildings? Additionally, can allowances be claimed under the provisions for dwelling-houses on assured tenancies contained in FA 1982 s 76 Sched 12 or under the Enterprise Zone provisions (FA 1980 s 94 and Sched 13). Will the transaction give rise to a balancing charge (ie recapture of the allowances)? (See Chapter 8).

11 Capital gains tax (or corporation tax on chargeable gains)

Will a charge to CGT or CT on chargeable gains arise under the provisions of CGTA 1979? Alternatively, will losses occur? Is the disposal to be made in a particular tax year? A disposal usually takes place when unconditional contracts are entered into; are the contracts unconditional?(see Chapter 9).

12 Inheritance tax

Have there been any gratuitous transfers by individuals, trusts or close companies which may give rise to a charge to IHT under IHTA 1984?

13 Case VI of Schedule D (general)

Can a charge to tax arise under the provisions of Case VI of Schedule D? For instance a one-off commission paid to an individual or company for introducing a land deal may be caught by that provision (see Chapter 10).

14 TA 1988, s 776

Does s 776 of the TA 1988 apply to the transaction? That provision could apply provided the transaction falls within one of the three situations set out in s 776(2), there is a disposal of land and a gain of capital nature is realised from the disposal of land (see Chapter 11).

15 Value Added Tax

Can a charge to VAT arise? For instance, a project manager's fee may be chargeable to VAT. On a particular transaction, even if there is no actual charge to VAT at 15%, is it clear that the transaction is an exempt transaction or is it a zero-rated transaction? (See Chapter 12).

16 Stamp duty

Will a charge to stamp duty arise? The most important headings would be the conveyance or transfer on sale duty, and the lease or tack duty contained in SA 1891, Sched 1 (see Chapter 13).

17 The sub-contractor provisions

Will the sub-contractor provisions apply? These provisions can require tax at 25% to be deducted from payments made to sub-contractors. The governing legislation is TA 1988 s 559 *et seq* (see Chapter 14).

18 The sale and leaseback provisions

These are certain provisions designed specifically to deal with sale and leasebacks although the wording of the actual provisions is much wider. These provisions should be considered especially in connection with the alteration of leases or where a sale and leaseback transaction is proposed (see Chapter 17).

19 Land partnership

Does the transaction give rise to a land partnership and if so what are the consequences of the same? It is important when people are joining together to carry out a transaction that they clearly ascertain so far as possible whether a land partnership has been created or will be created and what the consequences of this will be (see Chapter 21).

20 Appropriation to stock

Has capital land been appropriated to trading stock or has land been taken out of trading stock and been appropriated to capital account? If this is the case, and such an appropriation may be implied in any particular circumstances, what are the tax consequences? (See 9.4.8).

21 Exchange of land

Have there been any exchanges of interests in land between the parties giving rise to disposals of land? Have there been any exchanges of rights over land by virtue of partnership or joint venture agreements being entered into? (See Chapter 21).

22 Exemptions

Are there any special exemptions available for instance for transfers between groups of companies, transfers of the principal private residence in the case of CGT or transfers between spouses?

23 *Ramsay* doctrine

Have the transactions been caught by the Ramsay doctrine (*IRC* v *Ramsay* [1982], STC 174]? Under that doctrine the Courts will look at the substance of transactions to counteract tax avoidance schemes (see 1.4.5).

24 Inter-action

Do the various taxes which apply to the transaction properly interact to ensure that there is no double taxation?

25 Deduction at source

Must tax be deducted at source from any of the payments? (See Chapter 23).

26 Tax mitigation

Are there any tax mitigation arrangements which can be entered into?

27 Liability for another's tax

Can the taxpayer be liable for another taxpayer's tax if the person initially liable for the tax does not pay it? For example, under CGTA 1979, s 56 (gifts: recovery from donee) a donee can be liable for the donor's CGT if he does not pay the same within certain time limits.

28 Conveyancing mechanics

In a complex transaction can the conveyancing mechanics of the transaction be ignored under the doctrine of *Sargaison* v *Roberts*? Under this doctrine the Courts may look to the substance of land transactions to ascertain precisely what has occurred in order to tax the situation in a proper way. The doctrine can be applied whether or not the taxpayer has entered into the transaction to avoid tax (see 1.4.2).

29 Double tax treaty

Can the particularly profits or gains be protected under the terms of a double tax treaty with a foreign country?

There are also treaties which cover IHT (see, for instance, USA Convention 19 October 1978 (SI 1979, No 1454) and these should be referred to. One should also check to see that the terms of any double tax treaty are valid and that they do not exceed the authority of the governing UK legislation, ie the provision in the taxes legislation which permits the treaty to override 'national' tax law. One may have to see whether foreign taxes may be chargeable on a particular transaction and examine the same in the context of the double tax treaty.

30 EEC Directives

These may be relevant especially in the case of VAT. The directive will override apparent 'national' law.

31 Avoiding the recovery of tax

Is the transaction one which avoids the recovery of tax and therefore potentially amounts to the unlawful evasion of tax? See *IRC* v *Stype Investments (Jersey) Ltd* [1982] STC 625 CA. If so, it cannot be carried out.

32 Enterprise Zones

Is the property in an Enterprise Zone? If so, do any special tax reliefs apply? (See FA 1980, s 74).

33 Revenue 'see through' doctrine

Can the Revenue apply this approach to a particular transaction? If so, have the clients been warned?

34 Future changes

Are there any proposed changes in the law which may affect the decision to carry out the transaction? (See page 441 and of course the changes to be made to the VAT legislation discussed in Chapter 12).

INDEX